Self report - problems with
pg 76 ⌐

denial - p. 356

MEASUREMENT STRATEGIES IN HEALTH PSYCHOLOGY

MEASUREMENT STRATEGIES IN HEALTH PSYCHOLOGY

Edited by
PAUL KAROLY

A Wiley-Interscience Publication
JOHN WILEY & SONS
New York / Chichester / Brisbane / Toronto / Singapore

Library of Congress Cataloging in Publication Data:

Main entry under title:

Measurement strategies in health psychology.

(Wiley series on health psychology/behavioral
medicine)
"A Wiley-Interscience publication."
Includes index.
1. Sick—Psychology. 2. Psychological tests.
I. Karoly, Paul. II. Series. [DNLM: 1. Psychological
Tests. 2. Psychology, Medical. BF 176 M484]

R726.5.M38   1985   616'.001'9   84-27153
ISBN 0-471-89395-1

Printed in the United States of America

10 9 8 7 6 5 4 3 2 1

For

Len, Debbie, Richard, and David

(the Kalifornia Karolys)

Contributors

John T. Cacioppo, Ph.D., Associate Professor, Department of Psychology, The University of Iowa, Iowa City, Iowa

Patricia A. Cluss, M.S., Doctoral Candidate, Department of Psychology, University of Pittsburgh, Pittsburgh, Pennsylvania

Leonard H. Epstein, Ph.D., Associate Professor of Psychology, Western Psychiatric Institute and Clinic, University of Pittsburgh, Pittsburgh, Pennsylvania

Erik E. Filsinger, Ph.D., Professor, Department of Human Development and Family Studies, College of Home Economics, University of Alabama, Tuscaloosa, Alabama

Catherine J. Green, Ph.D., Associate Professor, Psychological Services Center, Department of Psychology, University of Miami, Coral Gables, Florida

Robert T. Guenther, M.A., Doctoral Candidate, Department of Psychology, Arizona State University, Tempe, Arizona

Robert M. Kaplan, Ph.D., Professor and Director, Center for Behavioral Medicine, Department of Psychology, San Diego State University, San Diego, California

Paul Karoly, Ph.D., Professor and Director of Clinical Training, Department of Psychology, Arizona State University, Tempe, Arizona

Robert D. Kerns, Ph.D., Director of Counseling and Health Psychology, Psychology Department, West Haven Veterans Administration Medical Center, West Haven, Connecticut

Suzanne C. Ouellette Kobasa, Ph.D., Associate Professor, Department of Psychology, The Graduate School, City University of New York, New York, New York

Howard Leventhal, Ph.D., Professor, Department of Psychology, University of Wisconsin, Madison, Wisconsin

Beverly Marshall-Goodell, Ph.D., Assistant Professor, Department of Psychology, University of Iowa, Iowa City, Iowa

Rudolf H. Moos, Ph.D., Professor, Department of Psychiatry; Director, Social Ecology Laboratory, Stanford University School of Medicine, Stanford, California

David R. Nerenz, Ph.D., Psychologist, William S. Middleton Memorial Veterans Hospital; Assistant Professor, Department of Psychology, University of Wisconsin, Madison, Wisconsin

Lawrence A. Palinkas, Ph.D., Research Associate, Department of the Navy, Naval Health Research Center, San Diego, California

Richard E. Petty, Ph.D., Associate Professor, Department of Psychology, University of Missouri, Columbia, Missouri

Carol W. Runyan, Ph.D., Research Assistant Professor, Department of Social and Administrative Medicine, University of North Carolina School of Medicine, Chapel Hill, North Carolina

Irwin N. Sandler, Ph.D., Associate Professor, Department of Psychology, Arizona State University, Tempe, Arizona

Dennis C. Turk, Ph.D., Associate Professor, Department of Psychology, Yale University, New Haven, Connecticut

Stephen G. West, Ph.D., Associate Professor, Department of Psychology, Arizona State University, Tempe, Arizona

Richard A. Winett, Ph.D., Associate Professor, Department of Psychology, Virginia Polytechnic Institute and State University, Blacksburg, Virginia

Series Preface

This series is addressed to clinicians and scientists who are interested in human behavior relevant to the promotion and maintenance of health and the prevention and treatment of illness. *Health psychology* and *Behavioral medicine* are terms that refer to both the scientific investigation and interdisciplinary integration of behavioral and biomedical knowledge and technology to prevention, diagnosis, treatment, and rehabilitation.

The major and purposely somewhat general areas of both health psychology and behavioral medicine which will receive greatest emphasis in this series are: theoretical issues of bio-psycho-social function, diagnosis, treatment, and maintenance; issues of organizational impact on human performance and an individual's impact on organizational functioning; development and implementation of technology for understanding, enhancing, or remediating human behavior and its impact on health and function; and clinical considerations with children and adults, alone, in groups, or in families that contribute to the scientific and practical/clinical knowledge of those charged with the care of patients.

The series encompasses considerations as intellectually broad as psychology and as numerous as the multitude of areas of evaluation, treatment, prevention, and maintenance that make up the field of medicine. It is the aim of the series to provide a vehicle which will focus attention on both the breadth and the interrelated nature of the sciences and practices making up health psychology and behavioral medicine.

THOMAS J. BOLL

The University of Alabama in Birmingham
Birmingham, Alabama

Preface

Opinions on the health psychology/behavioral medicine "explosion" are varied, with the majority view no doubt one of cautious optimism. New journals, professional societies, textbooks, and clinical training programs attest to the vigor with which a renewed liaison between psychology and medicine is being sought. However, not everyone is sanguine. Neal Miller has warned of potential pitfalls awaiting the fledgling field, not the least hazardous of which is the tendency to promise more than can currently be delivered. Or, as Stanley Rachman notes, the field has "done wonders for psychologists, but not quite as well for patients." Clearly, the domain of health psychology has evolved in a relatively brief span of time; and, like the child who is taller than his or her peers, the new field may be receiving undue attention, misplaced confidence, and unfair challenges.

Because the interface of psychology (and other behavioral sciences) and biomedicine is yet in its formative stages, it is extremely important that its products be nurtured in an open, yet safe environment; in an atmosphere with real, if permeable boundaries. Perhaps the key boundary-defining question is, "What does psychology currently have to offer medicine?" In all likelihood the answer would *not* be its strong theoretical foundations or a proven set of interventions capable of remediating or preventing the psychosocial antecedents or consequences of illness. Instead, it would appear that *our most valuable asset involves the theory and technology of measurement (assessment at both the basic and applied levels) and an appreciation for model building and theory construction. In this regard, all branches of psychology are relevant.* It is with this fundamental orientation in mind that the present volume was undertaken.

Several specific goals guided the design of this book. The editor's first concern was with providing students (in psychology, medicine, nursing, social work, sociology, and other "allied health sciences") an up-to-date compendium of both the molar and multifaceted approaches to health assessment and the most common molecular (or focused) modes of measurement. To provide maximum conceptual leverage to the student, the volume is organized according to the *how* and *why* of assessment rather than by clinical targets. No single theoretical framework or "popular" disease state was given special consideration. On the other hand, some *purposeful omissions* have been made. In the section on "specialized methods" there is no chapter-length coverage of behavioral observation methods, clinical interviewing techniques, intellectual assessment, or neuropsychological testing. Paradoxically perhaps, their omission is an indicator of their importance. These four areas have played such a key role in the emergence of the field of clinical health psychology that book-length treatments of each are now readily available.

Part I of this volume contains a chapter by the editor in which the current status of measurement in health psychology is critically reviewed. The dominant paradigms of traditional personality and strict behavioral assessment are taken to task for sometimes artificially constraining investigatory efforts and for sometimes being stretched beyond their interpretive limits. Thus, although the *logic* of assessment is empirical, the *character* of assessment is very often parochial. The chapter also addresses the growing body of procedures that, when used in an integrative and systematic fashion, "permits psychologists and other behavioral scientists to bring their full analytic skills to bear on the all-important objective of validating a biopsychosocial model of health and disease." This body of procedures is covered in depth in the remaining chapters of this volume. Chapter 1 also addresses directions or "possibilities" for health assessment.

In Part II, assessment procedures that are built squarely upon the biopsychosocial perspective are described and illustrated. Epidemiologic methods, naturalistic and quasi-experimental designs, prospective and longitudinal methods, ecobehavioral approaches, and quality-of-life assessment are considered in depth by a talented and insightful group of young, active scientists. Breadth in terms of assessment targets, methods, and rationale is the hallmark of "molar" approaches. The cynical dictum that there must be an inverse relationship between the importance of the research question and the tightness ("goodness") of the design may well be losing its incisiveness. Old dichotomies—such as *outcome*−*process*, *health*−*illness*, *physical*−*mental*, and even *cause*−*effect*—are likewise beginning to erode in the current ecumenical atmosphere in research and evaluation.

Part III of the text is devoted to a presentation of methods with specialized functions, including psychophysiological recording, psychodiagnostic methods, cognitive-behavioral procedures, and cluster analytic methods for empirical classification. Although perhaps more focal than the approaches discussed in Part II, the four topics included in Part III, nonetheless, have general appeal and applicability. When used in concert with each other and some of the more "established" techniques (like the interview, direct observation, or the laboratory analog experiment), these strategies hold considerable promise.

Finally, in Part IV a number of specialized targets of assessment in health psychology are considered by a group of innovative investigators. A decade hence these topics may no longer be at the forefront of the field. However, currently, the concepts of medical noncompliance, life events, social support networks, chronic pain, and illness schemas are among the most discussed in the literature. The final chapter delves into the policy implications of the assessment enterprise. It is fitting that the volume close on the important, but neglected, question of the public health uses to which health assessment data are (or can be) applied.

I am most indebted to the contributors, whose efforts on behalf of this volume and its themes reach beyond the words on the printed page. Gratitude is also extended to the editors and production staff of John Wiley & Sons. Finally, to my most efficient and patient secretary, Mrs. LaVaun Habegger, a special note of thanks is herewith tended.

PAUL KAROLY

Tempe, Arizona
March 1985

Contents

MEASUREMENT STRATEGIES IN HEALTH PSYCHOLOGY

PART

INTRODUCTION

1

The Logic and Character of Assessment in Health Psychology: Perspectives and Possibilities

PAUL KAROLY

Modern medicine is changing, and the social and behavioral sciences are involved, with varying degrees of commitment, certainty, and flair, in the contemporary "health revolution." As individuals and government agencies bemoan the $200 billion cost of health care, and as chronic illnesses take center stage (along with the importance of "stress" and life-style patterning in their time course and etiology), the sovereignty of technologically oriented biomedicine is gradually weakening. In place of "imperialistic" medicine a new world view is emerging, one that focuses upon

3

comprehensiveness of care, decentralization, patients' rights and responsibilities, and preventive interventions. Further, it is now taken as axiomatic
(by most medical and nonmedical health authorities) that illness and disease
in modern industralized societies are not rigidly bounded biological events
resulting solely from the action of specific microorganisms and requiring
specific biomedical treatments. Rather, as one prominent cardiologist put it,
we now confront "diseases of choice rather than chance" (Eliot & Breo, 1984,
p. 224). Similarly, it is assumed that health can be best defined as the
confluence of propitious physical, social, psychological, and ecological factors (rather than defined, subtractively, as the "absence of illness").

In this context, psychologists and other social scientists face unique
opportunities and challenges (Miller, 1981; Weiss, 1982). The emerging
discipline of health psychology offers a potentially valuable platform from
which to operate, in the service of a systems-oriented, "biopsychosocial"
model of health and illness (cf. Engel, 1977). As defined by Matarazzo
(1980), health psychology refers to

> the aggregate of the specific educational, scientific, and professional contribu-
> tions of the discipline of psychology to the promotion and maintenance of
> health, the prevention and treatment of illness, and the identification of
> etiologic and diagnostic correlates of health, illness, and related dysfunc-
> tion . . . (p. 815).

And, as recently suggested,

> to the analysis and improvement of the health care system and health policy
> formation (cf. Matarazzo & Carmody, 1983).

In arguing for the legitimacy of a place for psychology and allied sciences
in health care, health promotion, illness prevention, and systems design,
advocates have had to face the historical failures of the Freudian-inspired
psychosomatic tradition (cf. Alexander, 1950; Rees, 1983) as well as the folly
of attempting to build a foundation for an interdisciplinary undertaking
upon a broad-based critique of modern medicine's structural weaknesses
and economic disappointments. Confronted with a formidable "credibility"
problem, psychologists in the mid- and late 1970s chose to ally themselves
with neither the psychiatric branch of medicine (perhaps the shakiest limb
on that tree) nor the holistic health movement, but rather, with the scientific
aspirations of modern medical practitioners who seek the "ideals" of precise
and objective assessment as well as empirical validation of treatment
modalities (cf. Norton, 1982).

The concepts and procedures associated with the learning-theory tradition, particularly the operant and classical conditioning and modeling perspectives, proved especially timely and quite compatible with the molecular, external control-oriented medical world view (cf. Melamed & Siegel,

1980; Pomerleau & Brady, 1979). Methods such as biofeedback, relaxation training, differential reinforcement, behavioral rehearsal, and the like helped to build a sturdy technological bridge to medicine. In addition, the behavioral assessment enterprise offered a powerful tool for the quantification of functional relationships in "high risk" problems (such as obesity, cigarette smoking, alcoholism, drug addiction), in the thorny domain of medical noncompliance, in chronic pain, and in the province of brain-behavior relationships (Prokop & Bradley, 1981). The potential for functional analysis within the individual case (the so-called $N = 1$ experiment; cf. Chassan, 1979; Hersen & Barlow, 1976) was a further zone of conceptual overlap between biomedicine and behavioral psychology. Behavioral assessment had the additional virtue of apparent simplicity; for, according to Keefe and Blumenthal (1982), five "basic principles" could be derived from learning theory and applied to the problems of health assessment. These principles can be stated as follows:

1. Symptoms should be defined in observable, objective, and measurable terms rather than in vague, mentalistic terms.

2. Interactions between observable behaviors and physical/social events should be assessed.

3. Assessments should have clear-cut treatment implications.

4. Assessments should be repeated over time.

5. Treatment techniques should be introduced systematically to allow treatment efficacy to be unambiguously assessed.

It would appear as though the needs and directions of health psychology with respect to diagnostic measurement, intervention, and programmatic evaluation are compelling and obvious. There can be no doubt, for example, that psychology's sophistication in research methodology and evaluation is a major asset in the 1980s—perhaps its strongest suit. Continued deployment of functional analytic models in the areas of pain and stress, medical noncompliance, patient-therapy matching, risk factor modification, and the like is strongly advocated. The integration of covert processes and cognitive activities (attitudes, beliefs, expectancies, etc.) into the aforementioned enterprises is likewise a "healthy" direction. Yet, however self-evident the preceding list of needs may appear, it will not suffice (at this stage in the development of the field), owing to its *atheoretical* nature. If health psychology is to survive as a discipline, it must do what old-style "psychosomatic medicine" failed to do—build a solid pathway from theory and research to clinical application and interventive technology (Agras, 1982).

It is here asserted that what psychology has done to date to gain its current level of visibility and respectability as a "health profession" (i.e., applying powerful behavior analytic methods and potent behavior change procedures to the problems set forth by medicine) probably cannot serve as a model for the future development of psychology as a recognized health discipline. More is needed because: (1) the technological "achievements" thus far noted have not been fully validated by controlled investigations with long-term follow-ups; (2) those apparently successful applications, being medically motivated, can easily be co-opted by medicine; (3) those procedures proving to be minimally effective will cast serious doubt on the viability of the psychology-medicine liaison, and (4) the infrequent use of a broad-based conceptual model forces the field to take its direction from outside itself, thus limiting its potential for integrated growth and development (cf. Miller, 1981; Schwartz, 1982).

It may well be possible to employ the biopsychosocial perspective to provide the reference for the framing of guiding questions in health psychology, such as: what to study, why, and by what means; and how to intervene and demonstrate interventive effectiveness. Since this volume is concerned with measurement, I shall address myself mainly to the assessment implications of the so-called "multicategory, multicause, multieffect" models of health and illness that have been proposed under the banner of *systems* theory (Engel, 1977; Leventhal, 1983; Schwartz, 1979, 1982). In doing so, I shall attempt to illustrate the wisdom of the following assertions.

Health psychology will be judged (by both MDs and PhDs), in the years ahead, by how well it addresses important medical topics and issues.

The success of health psychology will be proportional to its willingness and ability to transcend the medical world view in pursuit of a liaison with medicine.

The success of health psychology will also require modifications of the traditional behavioral-science approaches to human problems.

The modes and models of evaluation (research, diagnosis, measurement) in the study of health and illness must be more integrated, dynamic, and process-oriented than has been the case thus far. Subareas within psychology—cognitive science, engineering psychology, developmental, social, physiological, personality, and so on—can provide the means for achieving a unified paradigm, capable of addressing the key questions that lie at the interface of psychology and medicine.

However, prior to a consideration of potential directions for the domain of assessment in health psychology, I shall present a brief overview of current perspectives. Painting with broad strokes, I shall try to provide the reader with a structural map of the terrain, leaving the many details to the chapters that follow in this volume.

TARGETS, SOURCES, AND PURPOSES OF ASSESSMENT IN HEALTH PSYCHOLOGY/BEHAVIORAL MEDICINE

We begin with the assumption that two analytic traditions have been brought to bear on the measurement of individual or group health status—

the tradition of general psychology (the so-called health psychology approach) and that one associated with the experimental analysis of behavior (the perspective of behavioral medicine). Both domains converge in their acknowledgement of the importance of assessment, while adhering to distinct models of measurement (Karoly, 1982).

The present exegesis will be aided by referring to Table 1.1, in which the major contemporary targets, data sources, and purposes of assessment are summarized. To simplify somewhat, we can assert that behaviorally oriented clinicians and researchers have generally sought to assess states of bodily response to controlled stimulation, individual illness patterns, or daily health habits by means of direct observational or physiological methods for the design and evaluation of treatment or rehabilitative pro-

TABLE 1.1.   TARGETS, SOURCES, AND PURPOSES OF ASSESSMENT IN HEALTH PSYCHOLOGY

I. *Targets of assessment*
    State(s) of illness (individual; group)
    State(s) of health (individual; group) and well-being
    Daily health habits and functional effectiveness levels
    Psychological processes in illness (cognitive, behavioral, social, affective)
    Processes of natural recovery from illness (time-bound; longitudinal)
    Responses to controlled laboratory inductions (stress tests)
    Rehabilitative processes (time-bound; longitudinal)
    Prevention and health promotion: life-style process and outcome
    Socioeconomic conditions affecting health (e.g., poverty, overcrowding, etc.)
    Ecological hazards to health
    Health care utilization/compliance

II. *Sources of knowledge*
    Self-report (e.g., health history; diary recording)
    Psychometric tests
    Key informant reports
    Structured interviews
    Physical examination
    Invasive/noninvasive physiochemical analyses
    Telemetric monitoring
    Archival records
    Epidemiologic surveys
    Direct observational procedures

III. *Purposes of assessment*
    Classification/diagnosis/prediction
    Treatment/rehabilitation
    Prevention/health promotion
    Health maintenance (care)
    Policy planning
    Research
    Teaching

grams.[1] By contrast, health psychologists have mainly attempted to employ clinical interviews and questionnaires that predict or explain individual and group states of illness or daily health habits in order to sharpen diagnostic methods and, less often, to assist in the design of interventions. Given their respective measurement traditions, both camps have acted in a reasonable and logical manner. Next, I shall illustrate how behavioral and psychometric methods of investigation can be adequately matched to uni-dimensional targets and purposes, how they can sometimes be ill-suited for the questions addressed, and how a multimethod approach can extend the range of both.

Consider, for example, the work of Traughber et al. (1983) on the development of a cost-efficient procedure for the assessment of nutrient consumption in extended care facilities for the elderly. These behaviorally oriented investigators reasoned that any empirical analysis of diet management (an important concern in risk factor control, as well as in health maintenance) would require a valid and reliable system for the assessment of food and nutrient intake. They also argued that recall or self-monitoring methods would not be useful with elderly, institutionalized populations and that individual food-weighing procedures are invariably time-consuming and costly. These authors, thus, developed the Consumption Monitoring System (CMS), involving a Nutrient Assay component and a Nutrient Intake Weekly Summary section, to be used by nonprofessional staff.

Developed over a 3-year period and utilized by more than 60 nurse aides, the CMS requires an estimate of patient food consumption (the percentage of a preplanned meal that has been eaten). The caloric value and nutritional content of the foods, having been predetermined, can then be counted for each meal, summarized for an entire day, and then transferred to a weekly summary sheet. The only other requirement of this system is that menus be preplanned to permit prior determination of the nutrients contained in each portion. The CMS developers report that the total time required to monitor a single patient's food intake over the course of a week is 1 to 1½ hours. According to Traughber et al. (1983), the CMS can be used reliably by aides after brief training and practice sessions, while the validity of the system (calculated by comparing aides' estimates to the criterion of actual food weighing procedures) is also generally acceptable. Since the CMS manual allows for the conversion of nutrient assays into percent of the Recommended Dietary Allowances (RDAs) of each food, the procedure can be used in a "deficiency detection" analysis, and hence, as an outcome measure, should a diet counseling or behavioral management of malnutrition program be instituted.

---

[1]Bradley and Prokop (1982) have noted that the major "traditional psychological tests" employed by behaviorists have included the Wechsler intelligence scales, the Halstead-Reitan neuropsychological battery, and personality assessment instruments such as the MMPI, the Rotter I-E scale, measures of mood, and various life events schedules.

The psychophysiological responses of various patients tested under stressful real-life or laboratory conditions can also be assessed and linked empirically to health risk outcomes or to patterns of recovery under varied forms of intervention. For example, Blanchard et al. (1983) administered a battery of psychophysiological measures (including heart rate to assess overall arousal, skin conductance to assess peripheral sympathetic activity, fingertip temperature as an index of peripheral vascular activity, and forehead EMG to assess tension in the facial muscles) to a group of 93 chronic headache patients. Data were collected under several conditions, including self-relaxation and a set of stress inductions consisting of mental arithmetic, stressful imagery, and immersion of the hand in ice water. The authors' goal was to assess the degree to which the various indexes would predict the outcome (success or failure) of relaxation and biofeedback training programs with various groups of clients (e.g., migraine sufferers, those with tension headache, and a combined group).

Although the outcomes of this experiment are complex, and there is good reason to doubt the statistical reliability of regression analyses that rely upon a rather small ratio of subjects to predictors, the findings are nonetheless intriguing. Patient characteristics, assessed physiologically, do seem to correlate somewhat with the outcome of various treatment modalities. Thus, the practice of matching patients to treatment (or restricting certain treatments to high likelihood responders) becomes a clinical possibility.

Blanchard et al. (1983) also discuss the comparative value of psychological versus physiological predictors of treatment outcome, making use of data collected in a previous experiment (Blanchard et al., 1982). This comparison, in the eyes of the authors, tended to demonstrate the relative advantage or superiority of physiological versus psychological factors. Blanchard et al. (1983) quite wisely suggest that "this advantage should be interpreted cautiously . . .," but nonetheless leave the reader with the sense that one set of assessment targets and data sources (the more operational or "objective" set) is probably superior to the other (the subjective, paper-and-pencil set). For our present purposes, we can read the Blanchard et al. (1982, 1983) findings differently—in both *fact* and *spirit*.

In fact, the study utilizing psychological predictors had a much better subject-to-variable ratio (6 predictors and 86 subjects versus 12 predictors for 93 subjects), meaning that the multiple R in the 1982 (psychological variables) study is probably more *stable* (likely to exhibit less shrinkage) despite its being somewhat smaller. A more telling fact than this, of course, is the authors' failure to report the *adjusted* R^2s in either of the two experiments. Therefore, not only are physiological predictors probably not better than psychological ones (according to the preceeding analyses), but *neither* are especially predictive when examined on an absolute basis.

This brings us to the *spirit* issue. Although just illustrated by reference to a behaviorally oriented study, the following assertion holds as much for research using "traditional" personality assessments: *Contemporary invest-*

igators often design experiments and interpret data in a manner consistent with preexisting beliefs, expectations, or "biases." To my mind, the only antedote to such a situation is for psychologists and other health professionals to be *more broadly based conceptually and more flexible methodologically.* Thus, although the logic of assessment is currently "experimental" in nature, the character of contemporary work remains both parochial and atheoretical.

The strengths and limits of the *psychometric* approach to measurement can be illustrated in a manner congruent with that of the previous discussion. That is, traditional personality assessment instruments can be applied appropriately to health psychology issues that seem to call for an "intrapsychic" analysis, just as the need for a cost-effective measure of nutrient consumption was fittingly handled by the CMS of Traughber et al. (1983). On the other hand, the measurement and prediction of complex biopsychosocial processes (like coping and response to treatment) do not often yield ready solutions when approached parochially (no matter how "objective" the measures appear to be).

For example, because the subjective experiences associated with various illnesses, including symptom perceptions, illness-related anxiety, and depression, might be closely tied to important factors such as help-seeking, medical compliance, and rehabilitation potential, it is reasonable to seek to construct psychometrically reliable and standardized procedures for the assessment of the stable psychological components of specific diseases. A good example of such an undertaking is the multidimensional psychological analysis of the symptoms of chronic bronchitis and emphysema reported by Kinsman et al. (1983). After interviewing 29 patients with chronic airway limitations, the authors derived a list of 89 symptoms and experiences. The list was presented to 146 chronic bronchitis and emphysema patients who rated each item on a 1 to 5 scale of occurrence frequency. All patients had satisfied the American Thoracic Society standards for classifying their disease. The data were then subjected to key cluster analyses that produced a Bronchitis-Emphysema Symptom Checklist (BESC), measuring 10 empirically derived discrete symptom categories, plus an eleventh category to cover the classic symptom of dyspnea. The BESC can be used to examine the structure of symptom experience in diverse groups of patients and, potentially, to assist in the design of interventions that address the unique illness-coping styles of individuals with chronic bronchitis and emphysema. The work of Kinsman et al. (1983) nicely illustrates the strengths of a psychometric approach to the direct measurement of illness-relevant personal reactions.

Consider now a study succinctly titled "The MMPI and Chronic Pain," in which Strassberg et al. (1981) sought to explore the use of the Minnesota Multiphasic Personality Inventory (MMPI) in predicting long-term (20-month) outcomes of "psychiatric" versus "anesthesiologic" treatments of pain patients. Until recently, the MMPI has largely been used in clinical descriptive studies or to provide the base for a differential diagnosis of "organic" versus "functional" pain. Strassberg et al., noting the limitations of prior research, directed their efforts at forecasting therapeutic outcomes—clearly a more practical goal than that characterizing much of the literature involving the psychometric assessment of chronic pain.

To accomplish their goals, the investigators identified two groups—one ($n = 67$) assigned to such anesthesiologic treatments as nerve blocks, acupuncture, or transcutaneous electrical nerve stimulation, and the second ($n = 45$) group receiving brief psychotherapy, hypnosis, relaxation, and medication adjustment. Two stepwise multiple regression analyses were conducted, using MMPI subscales as predictors and two posttreatment self-report indexes (medical outcome and subjective outcome) as criterion variables. The authors report that subjective outcome could be predicted by several clinical scales (*Hy, Mf,* and *Pa*) for patients in the anesthesiologic treatments, whereas only one scale *(Mf)* predicted subjective outcomes for psychiatrically treated patients. Interestingly, no MMPI scales were predictive of medical outcome in the anesthesiologic group, but again masculinity-femininity *(Mf)* was a predictor for the psychotherapy group (along with the *K* and *Hs* scales). The adjusted R^2 for the latter regression was .40. The authors concluded that the MMPI has considerable merit as a predictor of long-term treatment for chronic pain.

There is no doubt that the MMPI has been used and will continue to find extensive application in medical psychology contexts. But what kinds of information (knowledge) are we, in fact, gleaning from traditional personality inventories, be they empirically derived or content-specific? Do the varied inventories, from the MMPI to the 16 PF, currently finding application with medical patients, delineate mind-body relationships, provide an interpretive background for relating psychosocial characteristics to treatment outcome or planning, or supply sufficient information to assist in the design of preventive interventions? As Green asks (in her chapter in this volume), does the clinical analysis capture the "dynamic flow" of the interrelationships among person, context, and behavior? The present position, not surprisingly, is to question the clinical utility of measurement based upon, or indexed by, the "average response" of a heterogeneous group of people to test items of questionable personal significance and of questionable predictive significance to health status. Note that the present position is neither a repudiation of individual differences nor of paper-and-pencil (or interview) methods. Rather, the view here espoused assumes that individuals possess unique and characteristic ways of viewing (perceiving and thinking about) their world and themselves and "sets of temporally stable prototypic behaviors" (Mischel & Peake, 1982) with which they adapt to both constant and changing circumstances. Assessment methods should mirror these characteristics.

Traditional "personality measures" are typically static, consistency-seeking, group-centered, and universalistic in orientation, reducing the person to a score or score profile in such a manner as to transform vital biographical patterning and cohesion to a numerical regularity reminiscent of a chemical equation (only with far less precision and accuracy). At their best, however, traditional personality measures could be shown to be reliable, predictive (usually of other "summary" scores), and often theory-derived or theory-relevant. Unfortunately, the strengths of the psychometric approach are not widely in evidence in many health psychology applications.

Let us return, therefore, to the MMPI study just described. The assignment of patients to the two forms of treatment would appear to be a fundamental diagnostic and treatment decision, necessarily related to the potential for replication of the reported findings. Nonetheless, the authors indicate simply that the decision "was based primarily on the recommendation of the referring physician" (Strassberg et al., 1981, p. 221). The clinical outcomes of the study were based upon an 11-item self-report instrument, administered either by phone or in person, for which factor scores were reported, but with no information provided about reliability. Similarly, in much of the literature using the MMPI or other measures to predict "medical outcomes," the reliability of the diagnoses is either not reported or moderate in value (cf. Watson & Kendall, 1983).

Questions of validity are even more difficult to settle. First, the MMPI, which is designed to assess psychopathology, may not be the most appropriate instrument for use with medical populations. A common justification for its use with chronic pain patients is the frequent finding of elevations for such individuals on the so-called "neurotic triad" of the MMPI (the hypochondriasis, depression, and hysteria subscales). However, it cannot be determined whether these or other scale elevations are the antecedents of poor treatment outcome or poor hospital adjustment or the consequences of illness and prior treatment regimens. In the Strassberg et al. (1981) experiment, we are given to assume the clinical relevance of the MMPI on the basis of the nominal distinction between the treatment modalities—one being *medical* (anesthesiologic) and the other *psychiatric*. However, this reviewer is hard pressed to justify labeling one clinical intervention as "psychiatric" because the treatment consisted of "a program of brief psychotherapy, monitoring of pain levels, adjustment of medication, hypnosis, and relaxation training" (p. 222).

Further, the conceptual implications of various MMPI-derived measures are often difficult to discern. Nothing is said, in the paper, about what set of personal characteristics (traits or "styles") would predispose individuals to respond differentially to physical versus psychological interventions across medical and subjective indexes of outcome. The "most consistent" finding, of a positive relationship between pretreatment scores on masculinity-femininity and outcome, could not be attributed to gender (as sex was partialed out of the regression equations). The authors, examining possible "correlates" of *Mf* performance, were led to the conjecture that education (and psychological mindedness) might be the critical mediator(s) of treatment success. Unfortunately, even if we had an a priori theoretical rationale to link MMPI subscale scores with health status outcomes, it would be a difficult undertaking. As Watson and Kendall (1983) point out,

> The clinical scales were constructed from items differentiating a relevant clinical group from normals; thus, the logic of their development means they are for the most part quite heterogeneous in their content and internal structure. . . . Relative to the homogeneous content scales (such as factor or cluster scales) . . . the heterogeneous MMPI clinical scales are undesirable for use in predictive analyses (either as a predictor or as a criterion) or correlational research because of their low internal consistency reliability coefficients (p. 60).

It is not necessary to dwell upon either the potential deficiencies of one psychometric device or behavioral measure as used in health research or the misapplication of data-analytic procedures (e.g., regression analysis). The general theme thus far has been that, in health psychology, *what* is assessed, *how*, and *why* are frequently being defined in comparatively narrow terms, without much regard for theory or ecological validity. Although sometimes the singularity of focus is appropriate to the problem being addressed, often the assessment approach is stretched beyond its interpretive range. Multi-determined health outcomes are being sought or predicted by either uni-dimensional behavioral methods (often requiring an inordinate degree of situational control) or broad-band psychometric approaches (often lacking precision and focus). And too often what has been demonstrated "empirically" has been in the service of preconception. Yet, the structural map that I promised to draw of the health psychology terrain need not be centered entirely upon the craters and deserts. Thoughtful assessment programs have begun to yield promising findings, and investigators have been able to draw inferences of an explanatory nature based upon an appreciation of the complexities of health-assessment targets, data sources, and purposes.

Bradley et al. (1981) have evaluated the use of the MMPI in predictive studies with chronic pain patients and, although noting many methodological difficulties, also point to several well-designed studies in the area and a need for investigators to

> develop actuarial diagnostic procedures for pain patients and then conduct controlled, prospective studies of responses to specific treatments by MMPI profile subgroup members with pain of the same etiology (p. 101).

It should be possible then to transcend the weaknesses associated with the psychometric tradition (while retaining the important emphases upon reliability and validity) through a recognition that not all patients with the same clinical label are alike, that empirical methods can be used to organize predictors in nonintuitive ways, and that causal mechanisms can be discerned via well-controlled prospective (rather than retrospective) analyses.

Most importantly, it is also possible to employ psychometric tests especially devised and validated for use with medical populations or health outcomes.

Similarly, not all behaviorally oriented studies need be focused on narrowly defined targets or molecular predictors assessed under nonrepresentative conditions. A good illustration is a study reported by Lowe and Fisher (1983). These investigators were interested in the emotional (stress-related) antecedents of a major health risk factor—obesity. If obesity, which has been statistically linked to heart disease, can be regulated via the control of affective arousal, then a major step will have been taken toward the prevention of this country's number one source of mortality. Even though a number of theories posit a relationship between emotion and eating (Bruch, 1973; Schachter & Rodin, 1974; Slochower, 1976), the exact nature of the relationship remains both complex and unclear. Starting with an epidemiologic reality and a set of findings suggestive of emotion-triggered eating in the obese, Lowe and Fisher (1983) set out to assess the relationship between measures of food intake (self-monitoring records, calories consumed, and actual weight), mood (self-assessment records, mood adjective checklists), emotional reactivity (total number of self-reported negative emotions and emotional intensity prior to meals), and emotional eating (calories consumed subsequent to negative or positive emotions) in a group of normal weight and obese undergraduate women in their natural environments. Although they did not do so, these investigators might have also monitored their subjects' arousal via portable psychophysiological recording devices, to add yet another index of emotionality. Similarly, observer ratings of subjects' eating styles might have been included as well. Nevertheless, Lowe and Fisher's correlational analyses revealed that the obese/normal differences often found in laboratory studies are "partly generalizable" to emotion-based eating patterns in the natural environment. The relationship was stronger during snack eating than during meal consumption (possibly because the presence of other people at meals served to reduce emotional distress or to inhibit overeating).

Clearly, no assessment device or research design is without flaws or limitations. My task has not been to pick out the "good" and "bad" ones. Rather, I have sought to underscore the view that, within the general rubrics of the *traditional personality assessment* model and the *strict behavioral assessment* model, the what, how, and why of measurement have sometimes been well matched, sometimes artificially constrained, and sometimes the methods used did not fully address the complexities of the assessment targets. However, I have also pointed to efforts to broaden both the conceptual and procedural horizons of assessment in health psychology. It is now time to do more than point to contemporary instances of flexibility in design and operationalization. Therefore, I shall next briefly outline what I believe to be the key methods of assessment that, when used in a systematic and integrated fashion, may well yield the kinds of data capable of truly advancing the discipline of health psychology in the decades ahead. Readers will not be surprised that they constitute the topics covered in the remaining chapters of this volume. Following this, I shall speculate about possible avenues of approach to assessment that deserve special attention.

PERSPECTIVES ON ASSESSMENT IN HEALTH AND ILLNESS

An examination of Table 1.1, and the belief that it represents an accurate picture of the important and potential targets, sources, and justifications for assessment, leads to the inevitable conclusions that psychologists must widen their field of vision as regards what to study and alter the way they procedurally "slice the measurement pie"—from taking vertical slices to (piggishly) cutting horizontally. The procedures I have termed *molar* tend to be those that address broad health-relevant questions using methods that bear no true allegiance to particular conceptual schools. Of course, no single investigation can include all possible health outcomes and data resources, nor can it address all possible investigatory questions. However, it is encouraging to note that *a body of assessment strategies currently exists that permits psychologists and other behavioral scientists to bring their full analytic skills to bear on the all-important objective of validating a biopsychosocial model of health and disease.* Despite the fact that no genuinely integrative (systems-based) model of assessment and intervention is yet available, the field of health psychology is best served by those who are ecumenical in orientation and who permit their questions to dictate their methods rather than the reverse.

Recently, Schwartz (1982) has acknowledged Leigh and Reiser's (1980) *Patient Evaluation Grid* (PEG) approach to assessment as a workable (interim) integrative device. In it, the dimensions of biological, personal, and environmental information are crossed with current states, recent events, and background (formative) experiences to provide a diagnostic or treatment-oriented blueprint for the screening of patients. Such a blueprint is compatible with the dimensions of Table 1.1 and helps to provide yet another illustration of the essential multidimensionality of the evaluational task confronting us.

Epidemiology

A starting point for validating the biopsychosocial perspective in health and illness is the accumulation of reliable data on the distribution of disease in relevant populations. Epidemiologic methods are particularly useful in the quantitative assessment of general health/illness patterns in the natural environment. By carefully evaluating the different disease rates across groups, places, and times, the epidemiologist (like the good detective) employs logic and common sense to zero in upon causal relationships (Lewis & Craft, 1982). Behavioral or psychosocial epidemiology specifically seeks to demonstrate "that a change in behavior produces a change in morbidity or mortality" (Sexton, 1979, p. 17). The power of such demonstrations represents the single most important force for legitimating social-behavioral science in the eyes of physicians and public health professionals. A primer of psychosocial epidemiology is provided by Palinkas (in Chapter 2 of this volume).

Health Status Assessment

According to Kasl (1983),

> The most fundamental and persistent problem to the biopsychosocial methodologist is the need to have an adequate assessment of health status (at the initial point from which the disease is examined) and an analytical schema, which controls for the effect of initial status on later outcome, thereby allowing for a relatively convincing demonstration of the role of psychosocial factors (p. 699).

Clearly, measures of health outcome are the bricks for the epidemiologic edifice. The formal, quantitative analysis of health outcomes has existed for only about 20 years, varying in accordance with whether the focus is on health or illness, whether the data are laboratory-based, archival, or impressionistic, whether the focus is on individuals or populations, whether the range of outcomes is narrow or broad, and the purpose for which the data are collected (Sechrest & Cohen, 1979). In his chapter in the present volume, Kaplan reviews current methods for describing the impact of disease upon well-being and functional effectiveness. He compares the psychometric approach to the decision theoretic model, with special emphasis upon the derivation (from the latter) of the "quality-adjusted life-year"—a sophisticated and promising direction for quality-of-life measurement.

Both our Table 1.1 and the PEG model acknowledge the role of social, cultural, institutional, and familial forces shaping individual and group health status. Thus, another important assessment avenue is afforded by the so-called *ecobehavioral* perspective. Margolis et al. (1983) have, for example, suggested how the link between the type A behavior pattern and coronary heart disease might be further clarified by an approach that "incorporates numerous levels of human experience"—a multilayered ecological model. These authors point to four Western institutional characteristics that the sociological literature implies might promote the type A pattern: reward systems for aggressive competition, numerous role demands, limited predictability of outcomes, and time demands. Thus, one of their ecological propositions is: "The prevalence of Type A behavior will vary by the nature of the reward systems within an institution" (p. 253).

I have found it helpful to categorize the "independent variables" potentially driving the myriad assessment targets in terms of a three-tiered orbit of influence, including contextual, person-centered, and medical-professional forces. Table 1.2, which lists these varied sources of impact upon health and

TABLE 1.2.   INTERDEPENDENT STRANDS OF INFLUENCE ON HEALTH/ILLNESS OUTCOMES

Strand 1:   Sociocultural-institutional-contextual influences

  A. Family of origin (e.g., beliefs about illness and the sick role; coping models; life goals; support systems).
  B. School (e.g., knowledge of biology, anatomy, hygiene; vocational aspirations).
  C. Religion (e.g., value systems; belief in an afterlife).
  D. Media (e.g., attitudes toward medical profession; life-style information involving diets and exercise, sexual behavior, etc.).
  E. Vocational setting (e.g., job stress; career aspirations; models for illness-promoting or health-promoting life-styles; health insurance).
  F. Marriage/intimate relatonships (e.g., relationship stresses; support systems; life-style aspirations).
  G. Peer group (e.g., models and/or supports for health promoting or illness promoting life-styles such as drug-taking behavior, cigarette smoking, etc.).
  H. The ecology (pollutants in air, water, etc.).
  I. Government (e.g., public health laws; regulation of food and drug preparation and sales; health insurance; hospitals; support for medical research; social programs, etc.).
  J. The economy (e.g., cost of living; inflation; etc.).

Strand 2:   Intrapersonal-experiential influences

  K. Acute illness/injury experience
  L. Chronic illness experiences
  M. Daily health practices (habits)
  N. Inherited disorders
  O. Hospitalization experiences
  P. Person variables (including knowledge, values, skills, and cognitive styles)

Strand 3: Medicine and allied health professions

  Q. Family doctors and their technology
  R. Dentists and their technology
  S. Hospitals: Their technologies and bureaucracies
  T. Contemporary models of health care and preventative training
  U. Research in medicine, dentistry, and allied health professions

---

illness status (called *strands of influence*), should assist the assessor in identifying potential measurement directions. Winett's discussion (also in this volume) provides yet another antedote to the traditional "paradigm of the contextless individual." Both the conceptual and practical aspects of eco-behavioral assessment are presented in Winett's chapter.

Rounding out the discussion of molar assessment models, in Part II of this volume, there are presentations focusing upon approaches that, although more familiar to contemporary clinical researchers than the preceding ones, are probably no better understood. Whether psychometrically or behaviorally oriented, many first-generation health psychology investigators have been reared on manipulative research designs. In his presentation on *naturalistic and quasi experimental methods,* West (this volume) offers health psychologists a thorough introduction to field experiments and to selected quasi-experimental methods with particular relevance to the analysis of such processes as coping and stress mediation. Similar health issues are approachable from the perspective of *longitudinal and prospective designs,* the subject of the chapter by Suzanne Kobasa. Professor Kobasa considers the methodological and theoretical relevance of longitudinal and prospective methods for health psychology research. Comparing these with the more frequently employed single observation and retrospective approaches, Professor Kobasa identifies both the questions they promise to answer and the new problems or research challenges they introduce. This chapter presents a variety of longitudinal and prospective techniques and relates them to a number of health psychology topics, ranging from patients' perceptions of their illness and its treatment to the early life precursors of adult health. Stress and stress-resistance, however, are singled out as research topics for which these methods have special relevance. Neither of the two molar approaches discussed by West and Kobasa are infallible. But they do provide a larger net to cast than does the traditional controlled experiment.

Parts III and IV of the present volume provide an overview of specialized methods and special targets of assessment. Although a strong case can be made organizing a review of assessment strategies around the unique characteristics of medical disorders and populations (e.g., neurological assessment, methods for studying sexual dysfunctions, assessment strategies in geriatric patients, etc.), we continue to adhere to a broad-based didactic orientation, even when the topics become both "special" and "specialized."

Considering that the term *behavioral medicine* was originally coined to refer to a technique of psychophysiological intervention—biofeedback—it is fitting that our initial foray into specialized methods be directed at the assessment of central and peripheral nervous system activity. Although *psychophysiological recording of internal bodily function* was popular in the mid-1960s as a step in the conditioning of autonomically mediated responses, today's health psychologists are interested in a wider field of application—including assessment and treatment of cardiac functioning, hypertension, various sexual disorders, vascular and muscular headache, general tension, cerebral dysfunction, respiratory (airway) disorders, gastrointestinal problems, and many other areas (cf. Fischer-Williams et al., 1981; Katkin & Goldband, 1980; Keefe & Blumenthal, 1982). Cacioppo et al. (Chapter 7) review psychophysiological methods by partitioning their chapter into three "increasingly abstract levels of analysis," involving the physical, social, and inferential contexts of measurement. This exceedingly useful chapter structure should be of enormous assistance to would-be physiological assessors. It will certainly discourage those who thought such assessment would simply be a matter of "plugging in the machine and hooking up the subject."

Psychodiagnostic questionnaires have never lost their appeal in the clinical assessment enterprise. They are, alongside interview procedures (only briefly reviewed in the present volume), the most popular mode of personal measurement. Fortunately for health psychology, an emerging trend is the design and validation of instruments for use with various medical populations. Green (Chapter 8) reviews research-oriented instruments, those designed for individual assessment, and broader scale "personality" inventories, including the recent Millon Behavioral Health Inventory (MBHI).

Cognitive-behavioral methods are considered next. Stimulated by the "cognitive revolution" in general psychology and by the emergent social learning model (e.g., Bandura, 1977; Meichenbaum, 1977; Mischel, 1973), in personality-clinical psychology, the cognitive-behavioral psychologist has sought to integrate an information-processing perspective with a learning theory view of adaptation. Operationalizations of such a hybrid conceptualization have been neither easy nor without their share of critical reaction. Measurement procedures have tended to be multidimensional, making use of observational, self-report, interview, physiological, and innovative methods for the recording and analysis of thoughts and feelings and their relationship to clinical outcomes (including health status). Turk and Kerns (Chapter 9) deal with issues, methods, and directions for cognitive-behavioral modes in health psychology.

The final chapter in Part III deals with a promising but, as yet, rarely used set of analytic procedures for classifying, typing, grouping, or clustering entities (disease states, styles of coping used by individuals, stress reactions, social perceptions, etc.) on the basis of their similarities—so-called *numerical taxonomy* or *taxometric methods*. A well-defined and empirically constructed classificatory system is a fundamental organizing principle for any scientific field. Filsinger and Karoly (Chapter 10) argue that, given its relative infancy, health psychology would be well served if it started out with better descriptive systems during its "formative" years. They provide a brief, but detailed, overview of the basics of numerical taxonomy (particularly cluster analytic) procedures.

Readers will no doubt feel that several other specialized assessment methods relevant to health psychology deserve consideration. At least four important assessment procedures currently in use come to mind: *direct observation methods, interviewing procedures, intellectual assessment*, and *neuropsychological assessment methods*. Because the current volume is not a *handbook*, and primarily because the aforementioned approaches are adequately covered in a variety of easily available texts and treatises, they were omitted. Their impact upon contemporary measurement is nonetheless acknowledged. Readers are referred to the handbook by Hersen et al. (1983) for introductory material on each of these procedures, as well as for an interesting discussion of medical disorders that present as psychological problems (Chapter 23, by Ganguli).

The final section in this volume deals with "special targets" of assessment. These targets represent currently popular directions, due either to their perceived relevance or their hoped-for relevance to health-related outcomes. Cluss and Epstein discuss the measurement of *medical compliance,* a topic that falls well within the acknowledged expertise of social scientists, but one with a controversial history (cf. Haynes et al., 1979). Rudolf Moos's discussion of *social network resources* and their evaluation is also consistent with a biopsychosocial perspective. His review covers the accomplishments of contemporary investigators (including his own pioneering studies) and the needs facing those who would clarify the mechanisms involved in stress mediation. Karoly's consideration of *pain assessment* provides both a conceptual and practical analysis of current and needed directions in the measurement of the single most common and psychologically saturated symptom in the field of medicine. It focuses particularly on *chronic pain* and the unique issues it raises for the assessor-clinician. Leventhal and Nerenz delve into the subjective aspects of illness, factors purportedly involved in the processes at the interface of bodily activation and mental representation, so-called *illness cognitions. Stressful life events* and their assessment are the subject of Sandler and Guenther's analysis. Viewing the life events methodology as being at a critical crossroads, these authors discuss current models and instruments and point to needed modifications. The final chapter in this volume addresses the *public policy aspects of assessment*—the all too often neglected question of how our data are applied—ostensibly for the betterment of the public's health. Runyan's policy analysis perspective provides a *values-oriented* framework for conceptualizing the products of health psychology assessment.

The second half of this chapter will be devoted to a consideration of issues or topics not yet widely addressed by the body of assessment strategies heretofore discussed. Although they are topics of clinical and research interest to me (particularly self-regulatory models in health), their inclusion in this review is based upon their general appropriateness and promise.

DIRECTIONS FOR THE FUTURE: SOME ADDITIONAL HEALTH ASSESSMENT DOMAINS AND RESOURCES

The Study of Clinical Reasoning Processes in Health Psychology

At the bottom of the list of assessment purposes (Table 1.1) are *research* and *teaching.* They are located at the undermost point because relatively little research is currently being done on the assessment process per se, and even less on the processes of transmitting and acquiring relevant health assessment skills. Moving these purposes (or metapurposes) ahead would require a wider acceptance of the important practical and intellectual roles played by clinical information processing. The key questions, as Elstein and Bordage (1979) put it, concern "how clinical decisions are made and how they ought to be made" (p. 333). The process of clinical reasoning has not gone unstudied in general medicine, psychiatry, and clinical psychology; and the time is ripe for health psychological applications due, as Rachman (1983) notes, to the "expansion of the scope of clinical psychology from its psychiatric base to include the full range of medical subjects and services" (p. 320).

One obvious question that arises at the outset is whether the information processing of the health psychologist differs in any meaningful way from that of the consulting psychiatrist, the physician, the nurse, or the hospital-based clinical psychologist working with medical patients. In one sense this is an empirical question; and one can expect to see application of the familiar methods of decision theory, computer simulation, or Bayesian analysis to its resolution. On the other hand, the question has conceptual implication—for if the health psychologist is taking a genuinely transactional or biopsycho-social approach to assessment, there ought to be clear divergences from the linear, "germ-theory" stance associated with traditional biomedical analysis. At base, the biopsychosocial decision maker should cast a wider net in the search for relevant diagnostic, prognostic, and treatment-oriented informa-tion relative to the "purely" medical or psychiatric judge or clinician. Similarly, the multidimensionalist should use a unique weighting system in arriving at clinical judgments. Whether the biopsychosocial assessor has *too much* to do (and would be better off using simple additive models) is as yet unknown.

A principle considered basic to the analysis of all clinical reasoning has been termed *bounded rationality* (Elstein & Bordage, 1979). The term implies inherent limits to human information-processing capabilities. Selective at-tention (or limited attention span) and limited short- and long-term memory storage are two often cited examples of our bounded rationality. The number, type, complexity, and organization of our constructs certainly represent another source of cognitive restriction. Here again, one wonders if the "mind-body-context" rationale associated with transactional or systems theory would not provide increased degrees of freedom to the contempo-rary health psychologist.

Rachman (1983) cites irrationality as another fundamental tenent of clinical reasoning. This principle assumes that "people are indeed fallible and prone to make particular kinds of errors of reasoning" (Rachman, 1983, p. 324). Thanks to the work of Kahneman and Tversky (1973, 1979), Nisbett and Ross (1980), Fischoff (1983), and others, there is a growing list of decisional or judgmental errors that people (including trained scientists) are prone toward making in situations of uncertainty. Because of the urgency associ-ated with medical decision making, clinicians might be prone to adopt a more conservative attitude in framing their choices. However, it is equally plausible to assume that the added importance of the decisions serves only to heighten arousal, thus magnifying the tendency to focus upon recent events, vivid events, or factors that appear "representative" (but are not). If, as Rachman (1983) suggests, clinicians will be spending less time in formal testing (thanks to automation), then there may indeed be excellent opportu-nities for us to examine empirically our assessment skills and proclivities.

Assessment of Cognitive Processes/Structures: The "What" Versus the "How" of Illness Cognition

The bulk of what is currently being done in the name of health promotion and attitude change, medical compliance, and rehabilitation is *content-oriented*. That is, physicians, psychologists, nurses, and other health professionals are seeking to teach their intractable or high-risk patients *to think different thoughts* about themselves, their bodies, their illness, their relationships with the medical system, and the like. The essence of the plan for cognitive alteration is the substitution of new ideas for old ones. Although this scheme seems reasonable, it has one major drawback—it usually does not work.

The complete documentation of the preceding assertions would take us far afield. The domain of compliance/adherence to medical care recommendations, however, can serve as an excellent illustrative vehicle. First, few would doubt that the most active conceptual efforts have focused upon modeling the ingredients in health-related actions, beliefs, intentions, and motivations (e.g., Becker & Maiman, 1975; Hochbaum, 1958; Kirscht & Rosenstock, 1979; and others). Recently, Cummings et al. (1980) brought 14 separate models of health behavior together, identified a set of 109 variables emphasized by these models, and had a panel of expert judges sort the variables into categories. A Smallest Space Analysis procedure (a form of nonmetric multidimensional scaling) was used to analyze association among the variables, yielding the following six factors: (1) accessibility to health care services; (2) attitudes toward health care (e.g., beliefs about quality of care of potential benefits of treatment); (3) perception of disease threat (beliefs about symptoms and their consequences); (4) knowledge about disease; (5) social network characteristics, and (6) demographic factors (social status, income, and education). Factors 1, 5, and 6 are situational dimensions (not likely to be affected by psychological interventions), and the remaining factors focus upon beliefs, attitudes, and knowledge—that is, upon *what people think* about health and illness. There is little evidence of a concern for *how people think* about these critical issues.

That content-specific, information-oriented change programs do not significantly improve adherence or health-promoting activities on the part of patients (particularly over extended periods) is amply documented (cf. DiMatteo & DiNicola, 1982; Haynes et al. 1979; Stuart, 1982). In general, attempts to alter individuals' behavior patterns and the structure of their social support networks appear more effective than seeking to change the content of their ideas. Still, over the long haul, externally managed interventions do not often yield persistent life-style modifications (cf. Karoly & Kanfer, 1982; Karoly & Steffen, 1980). Perhaps it is time to change gears.

A focus on the "how" of thinking (e.g., structural organization, dialectical modes, problem-solving processes, self-instructional strategies, etc.) is certainly not new to general psychology, personality, or clinical work (e.g.,

Beck, 1976; Ellis, 1962; Guidano & Liotti, 1983; Kelly, 1955; Kreitler & Kreitler, 1976; Meichenbaum, 1977; Merluzzi et al. 1981; Neisser, 1976; Royce & Powell, 1983). However, it has been slow in impacting upon health psychology. To date only a few have ventured into the never-never land of cognitive process and/or structure. Jones and his colleagues (1981) have examined the meaning structure of physical symptoms. Fabrega (1977) has examined cognitive organization of illness episodes. And, most notably, Howard Leventhal and his colleagues (1980) have explored commonsense representations of illness dangers and have related patients' cognitive schemes to their efforts at symptom self-regulation (cf. Leventhal, Meyer, & Nerenz, 1980). His latest work and suggestions for assessing the content and organization of illness cognitions are detailed in Chapter 14 of the present volume.

It is my belief that efforts at appraising cognitive organization and/or stylistic aspects of information processing can ultimately be put to good use in understanding some of the neglected targets of health assessment (such as the self-regulation of daily health habits, the temporal processes involved in coping with illness, and natural rehabilitative sequences) as well as in illuminating the much studied thorny problems, such as noncompliance and risk factor modification.

My students and I are presently involved in a series of studies aimed at assessing and exploring the functional significance of the layperson's (the healthy as well as sick layperson's) *philosophy of knowledge* vis-à-vis health and illness. The guiding assumption underlying this work is that an individual's epistemology (stable ways of obtaining knowledge) represents a general or superordinate cognitive organizing principle, one with implications for understanding a person's bounded rationality as well as irrationality, and hence, for predicting what, how much, and how well he or she will learn in the future. Although this approach can be seen as just another attempt to examine *what people believe* (with respect to evaluating the sources of knowledge), it is also an attempt to specify the processes (albeit inferentially) through which beliefs come about and are altered over time.

Our work on health epistemologies draws upon the concepts and procedures of Joseph Royce and his associates at the Center for Advanced Study in Theoretical Psychology (University of Alberta, Canada). Over the years, Royce has evolved a model detailing three valid "epistemic styles"—rationalism (deductive knowing), empiricism (inductive knowing), and metaphorism (analogical knowing)—and a psychometric procedure (the Psycho-Epistemological Profile) for their assessment (cf. Royce, 1975; Royce et al., 1978; Royce & Powell, 1983). Our assessment device, the Health Epistemologies and Learning Orientation Record (the HEALOR) diverges from Royce's in that we postulate four ways of knowing: empirical, rational, intuitive, and authoritarian. Although Royce has come to reject intuition and authoritarianism as being *invalid* ways of obtaining knowledge (they rest on themselves and nothing more), we have included them for that very reason. We acknowledge and wish to tap the irrational nature of thinking about health and illness as well as the more workable styles. We also postulate (but have not yet demonstrated with data) that, with respect to thinking about health and illness: (1) the rational approach is relatively unpopular, (2) physicians prefer the patients in active treatment to adopt an authoritarian stance, and (3) long-term adherence to sound health-promoting practices requires a commitment to both empirical and rational thinking (a composite style we call "interactionist"). Some items from a preliminary version of the HEALOR are reproduced in Table 1.3. At present we have no plans to develop illness-specific HEALORs. However, because we are *empiricists,* the data may eventually lead us to just such an approach. Of course, recognizing a possible need for such an approach also makes us *rationalists.*

Delineating and Assessing the Content and Process Dimension of Self-Regulation and of Self-Regulatory Dysfunction in Health and Illness

Among the most common assertions in the health psychology literature (and one that offers a major justification for psychological applications in medicine) is that contemporary illnesses and their expression are often the

TABLE 1.3. SAMPLE ITEMS FROM THE HEALOR—FORM 1

1. My daily health habits are the result of:
    _____ a. My best intuitions about what's good for me.
    _____ b. Advice from my parents, teachers, and/or doctors.
    _____ c. Years of experimenting and discovering what keeps me feeling fit.
    _____ d. My knowledge of how the human body works, what it needs, why it malfunctions, and so on.
2. The "meaning" of any physical illness I may contract will depend primarily upon:
    _____ a. The physician's diagnosis of the ailment.
    _____ b. The immediate reaction of my senses to the particular illness.
    _____ c. My expectations of how the illness will impact on my current activities and plans.
    _____ d. The exact relationship between the cause(s), the symptom(s), and the treatment(s) of the disorder.
3. Most of what I know about *preventing* illness comes from:
    _____ a. Direct experience with various preventive tactics.
    _____ b. Talks with my doctor.
    _____ c. Listening to and trusting the messages of my body.
    _____ d. My understanding of what *causes* illness.

result of "personal life-style choices." Using this reasoning the Surgeon General's Report (1979) asserts,

> It is the controllability of many risks—and, often, the significance of controlling even a few—that lies at the heart of disease prevention and health promotion (p. 13).

Because many factors relating to the onset, course, psychomaintenance, and amelioration of disease, as well as its prevention, are believed to be largely under the individual's control, self-managed interventive models are increasingly suggested as cost-effective, psychologically based prescriptions for health (Fisher et al., 1982; Mahoney & Arnkoff, 1979; Marlatt & Parks, 1982; Thoresen & Kirmil-Gray, in press). Indeed, with the possible exception of socioeconomic and ecological "hazards," all other fundamental health targets (outlined in Table 1.1) can be, at least partially, mediated by individual decisions, behavioral enactments, and plans (the two exceptions are seen as requiring coordinated social efforts).

How well have the requisite self-management activities been specified? How thoroughly have they been operationalized and assessed? To what extent has research demonstrated a causal link between the effective self-management of thought, action, and/or emotion on the one hand and biophysiologic responsivity on the other? In general, the tangible evidence in support of the cost effectiveness of a self-managed life-style modification approach or a self-administered treatment approach to the alleviation of prevention of disease is meager (cf. the special issue of the *Journal of Consulting and Clinical Psychology*, 1982, Vol. 50; especially reviews by Lichtenstein, Brownell, Blanchard, & Andrasik; Keefe; Creer; and Epstein & Cluss). Among the needs in the domain of self-management and health are the following: (1) better specification of the components of effective self-management *in general* and with respect to the amelioration of *particular* disease complexes; (2) improved methods of determining how, from a process perspective, self-management components are systematically integrated both in the context of training (acquisition) and in the context of daily health application; (3) concepts and measurement procedures that address the myriad factors operating to inhibit, counteract, delay, or reorient self-care acts and intentions, and (4) a better appreciation of the role of self-regulatory processes and dysfunctions in the *etiology* or *early onset* of illness or disability. Let us briefly examine each of these issues in order.

Measurement dimensions are dictated by theoretical commitments, and arguably the most heuristically valuable model of self-management is associated with the control theory or systems view (Carver & Scheier, 1981; Miller et al., 1960; Powers, 1973; Toates, 1975; von Bertalanffy, 1968; Wiener, 1948). The basic concepts and assumptions of control theory, summarized in Table 1.4, provide a useful set of guidelines for the would-be assessor.

TABLE 1.4.   KEY CONCEPTS AND ASSUMPTIONS OF CONTROL THEORY

1. Goal-directedness of behavior is assumed.
2. Goals are represented (explicitly or implicitly) by individuals as standards of comparison and as means (plans, programs, scripts) for achieving a match between current status and desired reference levels.
3. Adequate self-regulation of goals requires an *openness to feedback* about the consequences of one's output (behavior).
4. Short- and long-range goals, compatible and incompatible goals, concrete and abstract goals are organized within the individual in a *hierarchical* fashion.
5. Control systems operate in real time and in accordance with the vicissitudes of memory.
6. Affect (emotion) can be an imput, output, or mediating mechanism in the control process.
7. Control systems in human behavior can operate at various levels of automaticity.
8. Control systems, even self-regulating systems, do *not* operate in a vacuum. Social and nonsocial cues and contingencies affect system functioning.
9. Standards, goals, or reference levels *change* as a result either of internally or externally mediated *reorganization processes*.
10. Control systems are subject to various forms of disruption, the two most important forms being "disregulation" and "misregulation."

The concept of a *standard* (reference level, set point, goal, evaluative criterion, comparison level, etc.) lies at the heart of a control theory approach to human behavior. Standards are typically indexed by asking people to specify their objectives, desires, plans, or intentions. Standards are typically differentiated on the basis of their level of abstractness-concreteness and ease versus difficulty of attainment. Recent theorizing examines the organization of standards, usually assuming a hierarchical structure (Carver & Scheier, 1981; Powers, 1973).

Assessment of standards is usually achieved via short-term direct observation or an outcome-specific self-report. This can be problematic for several reasons. Not all standards refer to objectifiable goals. People possess standards not only for what *outcomes* they wish to attain, but also for how they wish to *feel* along the way and for how they would like to *perceive themselves* and have *others perceive them*. When Powers (1973) and his followers wisely counsel us to examine primarily "what variables people are seeking to control," we tend to believe that we can do so by either asking people or observing them. Unfortunately, self-reports will fail when individuals are *unware* of all the elements of their current motivational system or when the elements are in conflict. Short-term direct observation can tell us *only* what outcomes a person *is* currently achieving but not necessarily what is being sought after consistently. Therefore, a more complete and effective approach to assessment of standards would, in all likelihood, include an analysis of peoples' *outcome standards* (goals and values), *performance-outcome standards* (what people expect or prefer to do in order to obtain their goals), *performance-affect standards* (how people want to feel as they pursue goals), *performance-self-perception standards* (how people want to see themselves as they pursue their goals), and their *performance-social perception standards* (how people want to look to others during the course of goal-directed behavior). Similarly, the assessment should take place across different settings and over a meaningful period of time, long enough to permit an accounting of *outcome variability*. That is, one can detect successful self-regulation in others most readily by noting which outcomes are occurring with the least amount of variation across diverse contexts (Powers, 1973).[2]

A final point about standards or reference levels needs to be made. Successful goal attainment over extended periods suggests that the individual is in possession of a set of skills or habit patterns that function in the service of his or her standards. Over the years, theorists have proposed a number of self-regulating skills, including: self-monitoring (observation of one's behavior and its outcomes), self-directed verbalization, standard setting, planning, anticipating the future, problem solving, self-reinforcement (tangible and symbolic), self-criticism, emotional modulation (coping skills), responsivity to feedback, and others (cf. Karoly & Kanfer, 1982). The general clinical consensus appears to be that self-management training involves (1) encouraging the decision to self-regulate, (2) selecting and/or teaching the appropriate standard(s), and (3) encouraging or teaching the requisite supportive skills (as listed). Likewise, assessment in self-management might be said to require measurement of motives and expectancies (e.g., health locus of control), measurement of performance standards (e.g., typical self-help behaviors, activity levels), and measurement of the supportive repertoire (e.g., symptom monitoring, medication planning, anxiety management, and the like). The previous discussion suggested that standards need to be studied in more detail and more carefully. At this juncture, I would like to suggest further that the establishment of appropriate reference levels and the skills that enable the individual to control behavioral variability are by

---

[2]It is important not to confuse this definition of stable self-regulation with the notion of inflexibility, rigidity, or lack of discriminatory ability. The control theory assertion is that outcomes (consequences, the reactions of others) are held within a certain range, *not* the behaviors that elicit these outcomes. In fact, the control model predicts that the skilled self-regulator does whatever is necessary behaviorally to bring about the desired state of affairs (or perception). If a person is controlling being liked by others, he or she may be passive with acquaintance *A* and dominant with acquaintance *B*, provided that these emitted patterns yield the same outcome (*A* likes passive people; *B* likes dominant people). Powers (1973) also suggests that an assessor can test any hypothesis about what a client is "controlling for" by introducing a probe "disturbance" into the system. Each probe influence should elicit an opposite (stabilizing) reaction from the person.

themselves insufficient to guarantee long-term success at self-management. I believe that there are at least eight facets of self-directedness (discernible in diverse clinical and research literatures) that together may form the necessary and sufficient elements of self-guidance. These are listed in Table 1.5. The health psychology assessor should seek, in the years ahead, to find

TABLE 1.5.   EIGHT FACETS OF SELF-MANAGEMENT: AN ELEMENTAL (COMPONENT) MODEL

1. Skills (requisite abilities)
      e.g., self-monitoring, realistic goal-setting (across diverse types of standards), self-instructional skills, self-reward, self-criticism, problem solving, planning, emotional control.
2. Knowledge base/functional awareness
      e.g., knowledge of the temporal conflict associated with current behavior; knowledge of the expectancies of others (society); knowledge of environmental controlling variables; *metaknowledge* about all eight facets of self-management.
3. Motivational readiness/current concerns
      e.g., salience of self-control or self-regulatory cues; priming of goal state(s); cognitive ecology unblocked; alignment of values favorable to execution of controlling or regulating routines; rewards available for self-managed patterns; attentional focus directed at long-term goals; feelings of *mastery* engendered.
4. Effectiveness appraisals
      e.g., self-efficacy; expectations of long-term payoff; perceptions of self as a self-manager; attributional patterns for success (past-present)and failure (past-present).
5. Integrated behavioral routines (or programs)
      e.g., motor programs; instrumental acts capable of linking intention to outcome via complex chaining of components; action programs for *what to do, where to do it, how to do it, how to stop, how to resume.*
6. Values
      e.g., outcome preferences; social responsibility, self-sufficiency, honesty and the like as higher-order programs; faith in and preferences for one's own evaluative judgment.
7. Social supports
      e.g., facilitative environments; encouragement for self-change; models of self-regulation/self-control; cultural trends; social facilitation or social comparison.
8. Biophysical dispositions
      e.g., temperament factors (low threshold arousability and sensation-seeking tendencies versus high threshold arousability and emotional control) and physiological states (e.g., physical dependency, sympathetic arousal versus good health, adequate nutrition, etc.).

Source: See Karoly, 1977, 1981 for a fuller discussion of the meaning of varied self-management elements.

adequate and cost-effective methods for gauging elements 2 through 8, as well as those listed under "Skills."

A second major issue in the domain of human self-direction is the need to determine whether and how well various self-management components are employed and coordinated in the real world (versus the clinical training setting) and whether there is a functional relationship between their use and important outcomes (particularly, for our present purposes, measures of health status). Thus, there is a need not only for a component model, but for a process model as well—and for an effective set of measurement procedures to gauge the unfolding of cognition-affect-behavior sequences.

Perhaps the most thorough process model of self-regulation is that of Kanfer and Hagerman (1981). The model postulates a series of five motivational sequences, including: (1) uncertainty, conflict, or failure-produced self-monitoring (e.g., an asthmatic child detects that he cannot achieve his base rate of airflow into a portable peak flow meter); (2) situational categorization as to the potential sources of dominant control (e.g., the asthmatic child can find no physical or external reason for the reading, so he looks at his own activity over the past hour); (3) criterion selection and performance evaluation (e.g., the asthmatic child views the poor peak flow reading as important to his long-range goal of achieving better health, and hence, accesses a standard relating to how much physical exertion he should demonstrate); (4) causal attribution (e.g., the asthmatic child attributes the failure to keep the peak flow reading within a certain "safe" range to his recent physical activity, a soft ball game); and (5) self-reward or self-criticism (e.g., the asthmatic child, believing that his behavior has led to the substandard reading, that the degree of the discrepancy between the actual and desired readings is high, and that he really can change in the future, administers a covert self-punishing response in the form of a self-rebuke). From here, according to Kanfer and Hagerman (1981), the individual would move into a *problem-solving sequence*, provided the self-criticism was not so severe as to provoke discouragement or anger.

As the reader can see, the process model makes use of most of the components outlined in Table 1.5, including the skill, attributional, and motivational elements. The process model assumes the knowledge base built on previous experience, as well as on preexisting values and biological (genetic) differences. The model implies that, over time, the process becomes somewhat automated and that a supportive environment contributes to its consolidation. I illustrated the model by reference to childhood asthma, primarily because a national effort has been underway to develop self-management programs for youngsters with chronic respiratory disorders (Creer, 1979, 1982; Creer & Leung, 1981). However, the model, or similar ones, are applicable across a broad range of medical problems, provided behavior variability has been empirically related to morbidity or mortality and that individual choice and control can be consistently mobilized in the ongoing management of behavioral variability.

Of course, the major challenge facing assessors is the design of truly informative procedures to measure the actual employment of model-based components according to hypothesized sequences and to determine whether medical outcomes are significantly influenced by factors attributable to self-management versus other possible explanatory elements (maturation, disease fluctuations, medication, social setting changes, or some combination of these). To my mind, not only will answers to these basic measurement questions require the use of traditional controlled experiments, interviews, and direct observational assessment methods, but also the deployment of practically all the additional techniques discussed in the present volume, from diaries and specific questionnaires to cognitive-behavioral assessments of self-statements and environmental perceptions, laboratory simulations of self-management tasks, physiological assessments of arousal, and the like. No singular approach to such a complex process can do more than scratch the surface (and, often, in a misleading way).

It is also important to note that when health self-regulation fails, the unsuccessful outcome can be attributed to *inadequate assessment* of patients' needs and competencies, to *inadequate training* of self-management components (or failure to monitor learning), or to *inadequate conceptualization* of the nature or role of self-management in the health-related disorder. Or, it is possible for all to be well in these three domains, but for disruptive elements to have inadvertently entered the clinical picture. Fortunately, the problems of relapse (e.g., Marlatt & Parks, 1982), inadequate learning and lack of generalization (e.g., Karoly & Steffen, 1980), and contributors to self-regulatory disruption (e.g., Kirschenbaum & Tomarken, 1982) have begun to be addressed. There is much to be done in each of these areas, particularly in translating or modifying them for various health applications. The reader is urged to consult the cited references to gain a fuller understanding of complexities involved. For present purposes, it is sufficient to point out that assessment is vital across all phases of the clinical (treatment) enterprise. To date, we know comparatively little about whether and why self-management succeeds or fails because investigators and practitioners have tolerated gaps in data collection. Perhaps the strong tradition of precision in medical assessment will have a salutary effect on health psychology assessors.

Finally, we have suggested that a control theory or self-regulatory model might be useful in articulating the etiologic aspects of certain diseases; for not only do individuals self-regulate *symptoms*, they also self-regulate many of the hypothesized *antecedents* to illness. Because health protection and promotion are often self-mediated acts, the control model has obvious preventive implications as well. For a discussion of the potential role of self-regulation in general health promotion/illness prevention, the reader is referred to Leventhal and Hirschman (1982), Leventhal and Nerenz (1983), and Leventhal, Nerenz, and Straus (1980). Next, I shall briefly outline a self-regulatory approach to a specific illness, *coronary heart disease*, by showing how a general systems (control) perspective integrates a number of findings associated with the type A (coronary-prone) behavior pattern. Assessment implications will, of course, be highlighted.

SELF-REGULATORY DYSFUNCTION, TYPE A, AND HEART DISEASE

The constellation of personal characteristics and behavioral manifestations that constitutes the construct known as the type A behavior pattern (TABP) has been studied primarily as a descriptive risk factor in coronary heart disease (cf. Friedman & Rosenman, 1974; Jenkins et al., 1974; Rosenman et al., 1975). Verification of the predictive ability of the TABP, which includes competitiveness, a sense of time urgency, free-floating hostility, achievement striving, and an intense and rapid pace of speech and behavior, has generally overshadowed the search for underlying mechanisms that may serve to establish and/or maintain the pattern as well as for the specific processes through which the pattern is transduced into physiological changes leading to heart disease. However, perhaps because of the broad acceptance of TABP as an important risk factor, investigators have recently begun to emphasize the need to probe more deeply into its psychological in addition to its purely epidemiologic significance (cf., Matthews, 1982; Price, 1982).

Price (1982) and Matthews (1982) have recently presented excellent analyses of the inadequacies of the *implicit trait* conceptualization that Friedman and Rosenman (1974) inadvertently introduced into the behavioral literature, despite the attempt to incorporate situational triggers into their definition. Among the problems with the original formulation are: (1) its tacit allegiance to a disease model; (2) its presentation of TABP as a global and unitary construct that serves to prevent the explication of its obviously multidimensional properties; (3) the extent to which the formulation overlooks individual differences; (4) the extent to which the so-called "action-emotion complex" fails to capture the interdependent relationship among thoughts, feelings, behaviors, and environments; (5) the lack of clarity as to the meaning of type B patterns (which, rather than possessing predictive properties of their own, are merely the absence of type A characteristics); (6) the degree to which the TABP approach focuses on negatively valued patterns, locking investigators into a limited "pathogenic" model rather than a broader, potentially more predictive adaptational perspective; and (7) the restrictive consequences of labeling the TABP as "coronary-prone," thereby limiting investigatory efforts to the search for linkages to heart disease exclusively.

Whether we take the position that the descriptive work on the type A pattern provides a strong and definitive beginning for a fuller conceptual understanding of the antecedents of coronary heart disease (CHD) or that the descriptive work is intrinsically limited, we are nonetheless faced with a need to provide a theoretical superstructure for an essentially atheoretical enterprise. Although I believe that any effort to conceptualize the TABP is a needed step, I expect that a control systems view can provide the most comprehensive understanding. Interestingly, both Matthews and Price take an *implict* control theory perspective in their recent reformulations.

For example, Matthews (1982) described and evaluated extant efforts to "identify the psychological dimensions underlying the established behavioral characteristics of Type A persons" (p. 305). One model, put forward by Scherwitz et al. (1978), introduced the concept of *self-involvement* as a potential mediator of type A speech characteristics and autonomic reactions. Essentially, it is argued that type A's are acutely atuned to the consequences of their behavior, while also possessing excessively stringent standards of performance. A second model, perhaps the most well known in the field, is Glass's *uncontrollability* theory. According to this view (Glass, 1977), type A persons are *chronically attempting to maintain control* over aspects of their environment that they perceive as potentially dangerous, harmful, or uncontrollable. Glass's experimental work typically involves the exposure of type As and Bs to uncontrollable noise with the expectation, derived from Seligman's learned helplessness theory (Seligman, 1975), that A's will work very hard and vigorously to overcome the perceived stress until the point at which the lack of control is seen as inevitable. At this recognition, the A's are expected to "give up" and become "helpless." Particularly noteworthy in Glass's writings is the attempt to address the question of how a style of personal functioning is linked to cardiovascular pathogenesis. An increase in sympathetic nervous system activity and elevated catecholamine levels during chronic attempts to cope with stress are among the hypothesized physiological mediators. Finally, Matthews herself offers a model of the TABP that attributes the origins of the syndrome to "a combination of a strong value in productivity and ambiguous standards for evaluating that productivity" (Matthews, 1982, p. 311).

In commenting upon the uncontrollability, self-involvement, and ambiguous standards hypotheses, Matthews (1982) notes that "all share a concern with the ways in which Type As evaluate themselves" (p. 312). In addition, all the approaches identify in the type A person what Matthews calls a special sensitivity to "psychological stimuli"—which can perhaps be more meaningfully interpreted to mean a concern with the consequences of performance (output) across diverse settings. Clearly, control theory offers a preexisting framework within which to encompass these concepts of the TABP, a framework that also captures the implicit assumption in much of the recent research that the psychological and not the overt action characteristics of the type A represent the central or mediational core. Type A's are dysfunctional in control theory terms because of the nature of their standards (or reference levels) and the ways in which these reference levels are accessed via self-attentional processes (cf. Carver & Scheier, 1981).

Price (1982) has presented a cognitive social learning model of TABP. She selected a cognitive social learning perspective because of its test ability, its relevance to therapy, and its emphasis upon information processing, learning, individual differences, and controlling conditions (both antecendents and consequences). To these factors, Price has added the physiological parameter that is not usually discussed within the cognitive social learning rationale.

For our purposes, perhaps the most important dimension is what Price (1982) refers to as the "core" of the TABP—personal beliefs and fears. She argues that the speech and motor characteristics noted by Friedman and Rosenman (1974) are inadequate by themselves to account for the increased risk of CHD.

> That is, no physiological mechanism could reasonably be thought to link observed speech characteristics (e.g., explosive intonation) or motor mechanisms (e.g., excessive gesturing) to heart disease (p. 64).

Price likens the TABP to an iceberg, with the tip represented by the overt characteristics derived from a structured interview and the foundation consisting of three basic beliefs and their attendant fears: (1) the belief that an individual must constantly prove him or herself, (2) the belief that no universal moral principle exists, and (3) the belief that all resources are scarce. The first is considered by Price to be the "essence" of the TABP. This essential core may be viewed as a *set of related standards,* existing at high levels within the structural hierarchy [at what Powers (1973) would call the "principle" or "program" levels].

Previous conceptualizations of the psychological substrates of the TABP provide the pieces of the puzzle, whereas the control systems approach would appear to offer a broader and more structural model of behavioral regulation—a model that recognizes the role of motivation, individual differences, behavior, information flow, feedback, setting effects, and a host of other important parameters that, if considered by other theorists, have rarely been considered together. This breadth is the source of control theory's appeal as a guide to assessment and clinical practice.

Basically, I suggest that the specific mechanisms discussed by Matthews (1982)—self-involvement, ambiguous standards, uncontrollability—as well as the social learning type A iceberg model of Price are readily interpretable as aspects of self-regulatory failure or as dysfunctions in the hierarchical control process.

We can begin at the top of the hierarchy of standards at the level of principle control. It is this standard that specifies the reference values to the next lower level that controls the level below it, and so on down the hierarchy. Type A individuals would appear to have no trouble specifying desired goals or end states—all of which are organized around the notion of winning, being best, making it to the top, and so on. Indeed, one way of characterizing type A's is that their principles (or "metascripts") are too well defined, too firmly in place to allow them the freedom to regulate change or to notice that the system is paying a price for its rigid organization. We can hypothesize, therefore, that the type A's would have to learn to dampen their awareness of the lower levels of feedback (which occur on a moment-to-moment basis) and that potentially inform them of how well they are regulating the many sensations, relationships, and programs not closely tied to the predominant goal or metascript. This would explain the single-mindedness of the type A, and because the self-directed attention is accessing the highest level standard exclusively, it would explain why type A's interpret most environmental events as relevant to their achievement-oriented pursuits. If one's perception was that almost every event was pertinent to the pursuit of excellence, only certain standards and programs would ever be exercised. Decisions, expectancies, and actions would tend to take on an automatic coloration.

Thus, the type A person is not the kind of patient who fails to regulate (disregulation), but rather, is prone to *misregulation,* a process that Carver and Scheier (1982) describe as occurring when "the person either is utilizing irrelevant perceptual input or is using a standard that is inappropriate to effective self-regulation at higher levels of control" (p. 111). The TABP may be a rare form of misregulation to the extent that it is the superordinate principle level that is responsible for undercutting effective functioning at the lower levels.

Have I said anything new? Or have I merely rebottled some old wine? If there is anything new in the proposed control dysfunction model, it can be succinctly stated as follows: It is not the content of the type A person's standards, beliefs, or action programs that are basically at fault, but the structural relationship among elements in the evaluational system. Similarly, the assessment implications of the preceding formulation focus squarely upon the need to measure the level, content, and structure of an individual's short-term, midrange, and long-term standards; the situational factors that evoke these standards; and the nature of the system dysfunction(s) that allows an individual to suffer physiological deterioration and/or damage in the service of chronically unattainable reference levels. It is quite likely also that the TABP emerges in an extended, temporal sequence: At first the bodily antecedents of heart disease, such as elevated blood pressure, are intrinsically undetectable; then, after a time, the individual may actively work to suppress internal feedback (fatigue, anxiety, tension, etc.) and external input (criticism from others); and, eventually perhaps, the type A person may come to monitor selectively both the internal and external indicators of hyperarousal as validating evidence of his or her pursuit of (lethal) standards of behavioral excellence. Assessment of the TABP should, therefore, be *intensive* (i.e., based upon external or self-observational data collected over extended periods) and *centered upon styles of information processing and organization.*

There are many empirical questions that can be addressed from a self-regulatory framework on TABP, provided we do not fix the assessment enterprise too firmly in any one measurement mode (self-report, observational, attitudinal, and the like). For example, the kind of "miscalibration of standards" just described can be examined by asking type A or type B individuals to self-monitor daily "progress" toward goal achievement, to attribute causes of perceived success or failure, to note short- and long-term expectancies, and periodically to report on their moods. Knowledgeable informants could track the A and B individuals over the same time intervals and settings, making note of their behavioral enactments, apparent emotions, and their interpersonal consequences. Such an analysis might reveal how stable (e.g., rigid) the perceptual patterns are, the degree of affective distortion, the role of expectancies in the maintenance of maladaptive behavior, and the range of the actor's behavioral repertoire and its flexibility under changing environmental circumstances. Methods of cognitive-behavioral intervention could, then, be tailored to suit the particular pattern of regulatory dysfunction identified by the multimethod, multitarget, and multisetting assessment.

Intensive, Single-subject, Structural Methods in Health Psychology: Approaching the "Transduction" Question Idiographically

Previous discussions have underscored the utility of the view that we must seek to transcend the assessment of what people do, think, or feel, and even of how people act, think, or feel at single points in time, if we are going to relate psychological and physiochemical processes in a more dynamic fashion. In health psychology to date, investigators have frequently sought to answer "why" questions with "what" methodologies. That is, the health psychologist has been unduly influenced by the traditions of psychosomatic medicine, trait psychology, simple S-R analysis, and group statistics. Data derived from procedures designed to detect differences or similarities among collections of people (a perfectly reasonable undertaking when testing classificatory systems or clinical hypotheses based upon experience with individual clients) will not suffice in the search for the organizing principles guiding individual reaction patterns vis-à-vis disease states, antecedents of illness, or rehabilitative processes.

An important clinical goal can be said to be the examination of so-called *transduction processes*, that is, those mechanisms by which alterations in nervous system activity (either permanent or temporary) are brought about by the psychological (perceptual, cognitive, emotional, or behavioral) reactions to encountered situations. These processes are undoubtedly influenced by situation-specific factors (such as the timing and intensity of environmental demands), by body-specific factors (such as the state of short-term and ongoing physiological patterns), short-term *psychological factors* (such as attentional focus and feelings of social affiliation), and relatively "stable" habits (such as overlearned action patterns, self-appraisals, and coping styles) (cf. Depue et al., 1979; Horowitz, 1982; Weiner, 1977). No matter how descriptive they may be, scores on a single administration of a standardized instrument are not likely to capture the emergent quality or the unfolding of these various parameters. In addition, we should bear in mind that factors that provoke illness or its antecedents are likely to be distinct from those that predispose, maintain, ameliorate, or potentially prevent disease—and that do so gradually over time and across settings.

At this early stage in the development of health psychology, it is imperative that testable hypotheses about biopsychosocial transduction be derived from, among other things, in-depth analysis of the regularities in individual life histories. Wholesale repudiation of idiographic techniques can only stifle the emergence of a viable clinical health psychology. Uncritical reliance upon group designs also restricts the potential data producers to those investigators with strong institutional support (in terms of money, access to large populations, basic research priorities, etc.)—that is, university and medical school-based clinical researchers. Clinicians in private practice, often assigned the role of ill-equipped consumers of experimental research, are in fact in an excellent position to collect basic data about transduction (cf. Hayes, 1983). Scientifically valid tools applied directly in the "clinical environment" can only add to the total empirical effort in health psychology. When we consider how many of the assessment purposes and targets listed in Table 1.1 are currently being explored, we can hardly fault even fledgling attempts to employ intensive designs in health psychology.

Single-case experimental designs have traditionally been associated with behavioral models of assessment, focusing exclusively upon observable (externally verifiable) targets and requiring systematic control over the introduction and withdrawal of manageable independent variables (treatments) after the establishment of a stable baseline of performance (cf. Hersen & Barlow, 1976). Such a perspective on idiographic measurement is needlessly restrictive (as was discussed in the early sections of this chapter). In recent years, investigators in the single-subject camp have attempted to expand the range of applicability of their general procedures by arguing that a strict molecular focus and emphasis upon immediate environmental control are not necessary or inherent assumptions of their assessment framework. Consider the following statements.

> A behavioral model emphasizes sound empirical procedures and when valid research procedures support genetic, physiological, or cognitive determinants, the role of these factors must be acknowledged (S. Haynes, 1978, p. 20).

> Even though the case study is not experimental research, under several circumstances it can lead to knowledge about treatment effects for a given client that approximates the information achieved in experimentation (Kazdin, 1981, p. 183).

> good clinical practice seems often to be a type of single subject experimentation in that the logic of the two enterprises is so similar. . . . [P]racticing clini-

cians . . . need only (a) take systematic repeated measurements, (b) specify their own treatments, (c) recognize the design strategies they are already using, and (d) at times use existing design elements deliberately to improve clinical decision making (Hayes, 1981, p. 194).

Health psychologists and physicians working with various medical clients and research-oriented professionals schooled in either traditional group design methods or the strict behavioral approach to assessment would be well advised to consider the advantages of a liberalized behavioral framework (cf. also Kanfer & Saslow, 1969; Lazarus, 1976). A list of some of the requirements for ruling out threats to internal and external validity in "liberalized" single-case experimental approaches is presented in Table 1.6.

Their potential explanatory power and practical applicability notwithstanding, the body of procedures associated with single-case experimentation are by themselves probably insufficient to the task of explicating fully the nature of mind-body-context relationships in health and disease. Some clinician control over so-called "independent variables" (or treatment conditions) is still required, despite the broadening of the base for permissible "dependent" measures (Hayes, 1981, 1983; Kazdin, 1981). Fortunately, the search for scientifically acceptable methods of assessment in naturalistic contexts is a continuing enterprise. Rather than having to restrict him- or herself to a single "proven" method, the assessor is offered a choice of

TABLE 1.6.   SOME CHARACTERISTICS OF INTENSIVE SINGLE-CASE, EXPERIMENTAL ANALYSES THAT HELP MAXIMIZE INTERNAL AND EXTERNAL VALIDITY

1. Repeated or continuous measurements of multiple variables.
2. Availability of multiple assessment sources (e.g., self-report, observer recording, biochemical assays).
3. Knowledge of the patient's illness history and the "normal" course of the disease (including possibility of remissions).
4. Assessment of patient's outcome expectancies.
5. Assessment of patient's causal hypotheses/illness models.
6. Use of placebo treatments (and other motivational probes).
7. Repetition of treatment(s) with patients of different backgrounds (but with the same diagnosis).
8. Assessment of symptoms and outcomes across distinct settings (work, home, hospital, etc.).
9. Assessment of the indirect effects of symptoms or of treatment intervention.
10. Assessment of the effects of treatment modalities by the use of specific single-case design elements (e.g., simultaneous treatment, multiple baseline across patients, alternating treatments, etc.).
11. Clear and detailed specification of patient-clinician exchanges over time.

measurement options, each suited to a particular purpose. As W. M. Runyan (1982) notes,

> Single case experimental designs seem relatively more effective for assessing the effects of therapeutic interventions, for recording behavior baselines in the current time period, and for measuring changes in quantifiable aspects of behavior and functioning. On the other hand, traditional or naturalistic case studies seem relatively effective for interpreting the origins and historical course of disorders; for providing a context for understanding the meaning of specific acts, statements, or feelings; for providing a sketch of the entire life history as a background for understanding current problems . . . (p. 147).

In many areas of health psychology, we are not ready to try to rule out plausible rival hypotheses, by either randomization or including certain design features (Table 1.6) that might help increase the strength of our causal inferences. To some, this state of affairs would simply reduce any analytic efforts to a "prescientific" status. However, contemporary philosophers of science recognize that not all science conforms to the hypothetico-deductive strategy and that not all scientific "laws" need be linear and causal in nature. For example, Cummins (1983) has distinguished between two very different explanatory strategies—the *casual subsumption* approach, associated with *transition theories*, and the *analytic* approach, associated with *property theories*. Transition theories are concerned with *what* happens in a system and *when*, seeking to pinpoint the occurrence of state changes as a function of some disturbing event(s). Property theories, on the other hand, are not concerned with the clockwork aspects of the universe. Instead, they focus upon understanding the properties of a system. The characteristic analytic question underlying property theories is: "What is it for system S to have property P?" Cummins (1983) suggests,

> Many of the most pressing and puzzling scientific questions are questions about properties, not about changes. We know a lot about what causes pain, but there is no very good theory of how pain is instantiated (p. 15).

Indeed, such questions as the instantiation of pain in one individual or the development of coronary heart disease in another are the very questions that health psychologists have not been able to address satisfactorily through the use of traditional cause-effect reasoning (either in group designs or via single-case experiments).

An examination of the possible avenues for operationalizing an analytic assessment of the organizational properties of biopsychosocial systems is beyond the scope of this chapter. An excellent review of modern idiographic methods can be found in W. M. Runyan (1982, 1983), and a provocative proposal for assessing the patterned organization of psychological and behavioral variables within the individual can be found in Epstein (1983). I shall illustrate the potential of a property theory approach by reference to the recent work of Palys and Little (1983).

Stress and stress-related disease impact upon the individual by providing both tangible and subjectively experienced obstacles to the pursuit of goal-directed behavior. Assessing the structural properties of goal systems in a way that captures and preserves the unique, personal meanings of motivational operations while still being capable of producing more generalizable (nomothetic) laws was the objective behind Palys and Little's *Personal Projects Matrix* (PPM) methodology. The procedure involves first introducing the concept of a *personal project* (an interrelated sequence of activities intended to achieve a personal goal. The project may be concrete or abstract, short or long term, done alone or with others) and then asking respondents to list up to 10 activities currently being pursued. Thus, the "items" of the PPM are personally meaningful and (presumably) ecologically valid. Next, a series of questions is asked about each of the listed projects. Project dimensions can be elucidated in terms of their subjective importance, time involvement, social involvement, perceived control, difficulty level, enjoyment level, and so on, and in terms of relationships among the dimensions (such as the discrepancy between a project's short-term importance and its visibility or the discrepancy between a project's long-run importance and its visibility within the participant's daily activities). In addition, a "cross-impact matrix" can be obtained by asking subjects to compare each project with every other one and indicate the degree of conflict or mutual facilitation. Both comparative (normative) data and ipsative indexes can be obtained via the PPM (Palys & Little, 1983). As the authors' note,

> the PPM is a flexible methodology whose particular form will be influenced by the interest and concerns of the investigator (Palys & Little, 1983, p. 1223).

Given the interests and concerns of health psychologists, the potential of the PPM approach—particularly for clarifying the instantiation of diseases or negative health outcomes within persons—would appear to be quite good (assuming the data are reasonably reliable and predictively valid at the level of the individual). Palys and Little (1983) report on the utility of their system for predicting well-being and life satisfaction among nonpatient samples.

My students and I are currently exploring the PPM as a method of examining the self-regulatory approach to the type A behavior pattern (discussed in the previous section of this chapter). Among the questions we are asking are: What is the nature of the relationship between personal project goals and standards for goal attainment among type As and Bs? Do As and Bs differ in the structure of their short- versus long-term projects? What do the cross-impact matrices of As look like versus those of Bs? The reader can no doubt develop related experimental questions on the basis of previous discussions.

A FINAL STATEMENT

A great deal of territory has been covered in this chapter. In discussing both the current state of health psychology assessment and potential new directions, I have sought to emphasize the opportunities for innovative contributions as well as the limitations imposed by narrow theoretical models and unidimensional measurement approaches.

The biopsychosocial perspective on illness, health maintenance, rehabilitation, risk reduction, and prevention has yet to be tried and tested in any systematic fashion. If there is to be a viable alternative to the mind-body separation that characterizes the contemporary health services professions, then basic conceptual bridges, between and within disciplines, must be erected upon firm foundations. It has been asserted that modern psychology possesses a broad armamentarium of assessment methods and theory-building procedures that can serve to provide the necessary scaffolding for this enterprise. Our greatest "enemies" at this stage are self-limiting preconceptions about both what constitutes "good science" and who may be permitted to participate in its pursuit.

References

Agras, W. S. (1982). Behavioral medicine in the 1980s: Nonrandom connections. *Journal of Consulting and Clinical Psychology, 50*, 797–803.

Alexander, F. (1950). *Psychosomatic medicine: Its principles and applications.* New York: Norton.

Bandura, A. (1977). *Social learning theory.* Englewood Cliffs, NJ: Prentice-Hall.

Beck, A. T. (1976). *Cognitive therapy and the emotional disorders.* New York: International Universities Press.

Becker, M. H., & Maiman, L. A. (1975). Socio-behavioral determinants of compliance with health and medical care recommendations. *Medical Care, 13* 10–24.

Blanchard, E. B. (Ed.). (1982). Special Issue: Behavioral Medicine. *Journal of Consulting and Clinical Psychology, 50* (Whole No. 6).

Blanchard, E. B., Andrasik, F., Arena, J. G., Neff, D. R., Saunders, N. L., Jurish, S. E., Teders, S. J., & Rodichok, L. D. (1983). Psychophysiological responses as predictors of response to behavioral treatment of chronic headache. *Behavior Therapy, 14*, 357–374.

Blanchard, E. B., Andrasik, F., Neff, D. F., Arena, J. G., Ahles, T.A., Jurish, S. E., Pallmeyer, T. P., Saunders, N. L., Teders, S. J., Barron, K. D., & Rodichok, L. D. (1982). Biofeedback and relaxation training with three kinds of headache: Treatment effects and their prediction. *Journal of Consulting and Clinical Psychology, 50*, 562–575.

Bradley, L. A., & Prokop, C. K. (1982). Research methods in contemporary medical psychology. In P. C. Kendall & J. N. Butcher (Eds.), *Handbook of research methods in clinical psychology.* New York: Wiley.

Bradley, L. A., Prokop, C. K., Gentry, W. D., Van der Heide, L. H., & Prieto, E. J. (1981).

Assessment of chronic pain. In C. K. Prokop & L. A. Bradley (Eds.), *Medical psychology: Contributions to behavioral medicine.* New York: Academic Press.

Bruch, H. (1973). *Eating disorders.* New York: Basic Books.

Carver, C. S., & Scheier, M. F. (1981). *Attention and self-regulation: A control-theory approach to human behavior.* New York: Springer-Verlag.

Carver, C. S., & Scheier, M. F. (1982). An information-processing perspective on self-management. In P. Karoly & F. H. Kanfer (Eds.), *Self-management and behavior change: From theory to practice.* New York: Pergamon Press.

Chassan, J. B. (1979). *Research design in clinical psychology and psychiatry* (2nd ed.). New York: Irvington Publishers.

Creer, T. L. (1979). *Asthma therapy.* New York: Springer.

Creer, T. L. (1982). Asthma. *Journal of Consulting and Clinical Psychology, 50,* 912–921.

Creer, T. L., & Leung, P. (1981). The development and evaluation of a self-management program for children with asthma. In *Self-management educational programs for childhood asthma.* Bethesda, Md.: National Institute of Allergic and Infectious Diseases.

Cummings, K. M., Becker, M. H., & Maile, M. C. (1980). Bringing the models together: An empirical approach to combining variables used to explain health actions. *Journal of Behavioral Medicine, 3,* 123–145.

Cummins, R. (1983). *The nature of psychological explanation.* Cambridge, Mass.: MIT Press.

Depue, R. A., Monroe, S. M., & Shackman, S. L. (1979). The psychobiology of human disease: Implications for conceptualizing the depressive disorders. In R. A. Depue (Ed.), *The psychobiology of the depressive disorders.* New York: Academic Press.

DiMatteo, M. R., & DiNicola, D. D. (1982). *Achieving patient compliance.* New York: Pergamon Press.

Eliot, R. S., & Breo, D. L. (1984). *Is it worth dying for?* Toronto: Bantam Books.

Ellis, A. (1962). *Reason and emotion in psychotherapy.* New York: Lyle Stuart.

Elstein, A. S., & Bordage, G. (1979). Psychology of clinical reasoning. In G. Stone, F. Cohen, & N. E. Adler (Eds.), *Health psychology.* San Francisco: Jossey-Bass.

Engel, G. L. (1977). The need for a new medical model: A challenge for biomedicine. *Science, 196,* 129–136.

Epstein, S. (1983). A research paradigm for the study of personality and emotions. In M. M. Page (Ed.), *Personality—Current theory and research: 1982. Nebraska Symposium on Motivation.* Lincoln, Neb.: University of Nebraska Press.

Fabrega, H. (1977). Group differences in the structure of illness. *Culture, Medicine, and Psychiatry, 1,* 379–384.

Fischer-Williams, M., Nigl, A. J., & Sovine, D. L. (1981). *A textbook of biological feedback.* New York: Human Sciences Press.

Fischoff, B. (1983). Predicting frames. *Journal of Experimental Psychology: Learning, Memory, and Cognition, 9,* 103–116.

Fisher, E. B., Levenkron, J. C., Lowe, M., Loro, A. D., & Green, L. (1982). Self-initiated self-control in risk reduction. In R. B. Stuart (Ed.), *Adherence, compliance, and generalization in behavioral medicine.* New York: Brunner/Mazel.

Friedman, M., & Rosenman, R. H. (1974). *Type A behavior and your heart.* New York: Knopf.

Ganguli, R. (1983). Medical assessment. In M. Hersen, A. E. Kazdin, & A. S. Bellack (Eds.), *The clinical psychology handbook.* New York: Pergamon Press.

Glass, D. C. (1977). *Behavior patterns, stress, and coronary disease.* Hillsdale, NJ: Erlbaum.

Guidano, V. F., & Liotti, G. (1983). *Cognitive processes and emotional disorders.* New York: Guilford Press.

Hayes, S. C. (1981). Single case experimental design and empirical clinical practice. *Journal of Consulting and Clinical Psychology, 49,* 193–211.

Hayes, S. C. (1983). The role of the individual case in the production and consumption of clinical knowledge. In M. Hersen, A. E. Kazdin, & A. S. Bellack (Eds.), *The clinical psychology handbook.* New York: Pergamon Press.

Haynes, R. B., Taylor, D. W., & Sackett, D. L. (1979). *Compliance in health care.* Baltimore: Johns Hopkins University Press.

Haynes, S. N. (1978). *Principles of behavioral assessment.* New York: Gardner Press.

Hersen, M., & Barlow, D. H. (1976). *Single case experimental designs: Strategies for studying behavior change.* New York: Pergamon Press.

Hersen, M., Kazdin, A. E., & Bellack, A. S. (Eds.). (1983). *The clinical psychology handbook.* New York: Pergamon Press.

Hochbaum, G. M. (1958). *Public participation in medical screening progams: A sociopsychological study.* Washington, DC: U.S. Government Printing Office.

Horowitz, M. J. (1982). Psychological processes induced by illness, injury, and loss. In T. Millon, C. Green, & R. Meagher (Eds.), *Handbook of clinical health psychology.* New York: Plenum Press.

Jenkins, C. D., Rosenman, R. H., & Zyzanski, S. J. (1974). Prediction of clinical coronary heart disease by a test for the coronary-prone behavior pattern. *New England Journal of Medicine, 290,* 1271–1275.

Jones, R. A., Wiese, H. J., Moore, R. W. & Haley, J. V. (1981). On the perceived meaning of symptoms. *Medical Care, 19,* 710–717.

Kahneman, D., & Tversky, A. (1973). On the psychology of prediction. *Psychological Review, 80,* 237–251.

Kahenman, D., & Tversky, A. (1979). Prospect theory. *Econometrica, 47,* 263–292.

Kanfer, F. H., & Hagerman, S. (1981). The role of self-regulation. In L. P. Rehm (Ed.), *Behavior therapy for depression; Present status and future directions.* New York: Academic Press.

Kanfer, F. H., & Saslow, G. (1969). Behavioral diagnosis. In C. M. Franks (Ed.), *Behavior therapy: Appraisal and status.* New York: McGraw-Hill.

Karoly, P. (1977). Behavioral self-management in children: Concepts, methods, issues, and directions, In M. Hersen, R. M. Eisler, & P. M. Miller (Eds.), *Progress in behavior modification* (Vol. 5). New York: Academic Press.

Karoly, P. (1981). Self-management problems in children. In E. J. Mash & L. G. Terdal (Eds.), *Behavioral assessment of childhood disorders.* New York: Guilford Press.

Karoly, P. (1982). Cognitive assessment in behavioral medicine. *Clinical Psychology Review, 2,* 421–434.

Karoly, P., & Kanfer, F. H. (Eds.). (1982). *Self-management and behavior change: From theory to practice.* New York: Pergamon Press.

Karoly, P., & Steffen, J. J. (Eds.). (1980). *Improving the long-term effects of psychotherapy.* New York: Gardner Press.

Kasl, S. V. (1983). Social and psychological factors affecting the course of disease: An epidemiological perspective. In D. Mechanic (Ed.), *Handbook of health, health care, and the health professions.* New York: Free Press.

Katkin, E. S., & Goldband, S. (1980). Biofeedback. In F. H. Kanfer & A. P. Goldstein (Eds.), *Helping people change.* New York: Pergamon Press.

Kazdin, A. E. (1981). Drawing valid inferences from case studies. *Journal of Consulting and Clinical Psychology, 49,* 183–192.

Keefe, F. J., & Blumenthal, J. A. (Eds.). (1982). *Assessment strategies in behavioral medicine.* New York: Grune & Stratton.

Seligman, M. E. P. (1975). *Helplessness: On depression, development, and death*. San Francisco: Freeman.

Sexton, M. M. (1979). Behavioral epidemiology. In O. F. Pomerleau & J. P. Brady (Eds.), *Behavioral medicine: Theory and practice*. Baltimore; Williams & Wilkins.

Slochower, J. (1976). Emotional labelling an overeating in obese and normal weight individuals. *Psychosomatic Medicine, 38*, 131–139.

Strassberg, D. S., Reimherr, F., Ward, M., Russell, S., & Cole, A. (1981). The MMPI and chronic pain. *Journal of Consulting and Clinical Psychology, 49*, 220–226.

Stuart, R. B. (Ed.). (1982). *Adherence, compliance, and generalization in behavioral medicine*. New York: Brunner/Mazel.

Thoresen, C., & Kirmil-Gray, K. (In press). The psychology of self-managed change and the treatment of childhood asthma. *Journal of Allergy and Clinical Immunology*.

Toates, F. (1975). *Control theory in biology and experimental psychology*. London: Hutchinson Educational.

Traughber, B., Erwin, K. E., Risley, T. R., & Schnelle, J. F. (1983). Behavioral nutrition: An evaluation of a simple system for measuring food and nutrient consumption. *Behavioral Assessment, 5*, 263–280.

U.S. Department of Health, Education, and Welfare (1979). Healthy people: The Surgeon General's report on health promotion and disease prevention. Washington, DC: DHEW (PHS) Publication No. 79-55071.

von Bertalanffy, L. (1968). *General systems theory*. New York: Braziller.

Watson, D., & Kendall, P.C. (1983). Methodological issues in research on coping with chronic disease. In T. G. Burish & L. A. Bradley (Eds.), *Coping with chronic disease. Research and applications*. New York: Academic Press.

Weiner, H. (1977). *Psychobiology and human disease*. New York: Elsevier.

Weiss, S. (1982). Health psychology: The time is now. *Health Psychology, 1*, 81–91.

Wiener, N. (1948). *Cybernetics*. Cambridge, Mass.: MIT Press.

PART II

MOLAR APPROACHES TO ASSESSMENT

2

Techniques of Psychosocial Epidemiology

LAWRENCE A. PALINKAS

Epidemiology is concerned with the origin and spread of disease in human populations. In its infancy, epidemiology was primarily concerned with infectious diseases; later, chronic disease became a focus for intensive research. As new information is obtained about the relationships among the physiological, social, and environmental aspects of disease, the methods employed by epidemiologists are revised and broadened. One example of this refining process is the emergence of a distinct subfield of *psychosocial epidemiology*. Psychosocial epidemiology displays a certain measure of continuity with other areas of epidemiologic research in its approach to disease and the methodology employed. It diverges from other epidemiologic studies in its selective focus on psychosocial components of disease and greater reliance on psychometric methods. Psychosocial epidemiology has often been identified with an interest in the problem of stress, which serves to link the psychological, social, environmental, and physiological components of health.

This chapter is intended to summarize the techniques employed in psychosocial epidemiology. The summary is divided into three major sections: research design, data, and data analysis. Many of these techniques will be discussed in greater detail elsewhere in the volume; the objective here is to provide a context for their use and to demonstrate the ways these techniques are based on the particular focus of investigation. In the course of this presentation, the strengths and limitations of these techniques will be examined and evaluated.

Epidemiologic Foundations

A brief overview of the epidemiologic foundation of these concepts and methods is necessary before detailing the concepts and methods employed in psychosocial epidemiology. Epidemiology can best be defined as "the study of the distribution of a disease or a physiological condition in human populations and of the factors that influence this distribution" (Lilienfeld, 1978, p. 87). Although epidemiology utilizes qualitative, clinical data, the emphasis is on quantitative data and analyses. According to Lilienfeld and Lilienfeld (1980), the epidemiologist uses a two-stage sequence of reasoning. The first stage involves the determination of a statistical association between a characteristic and a disease. The second stage is the derivation of biological inferences from such a pattern of statistical inferences.

The distribution of a disease in a particular population may be influenced by one or more of three sets of variables: *agent, host,* and *environment.* The agents of disease include etiological factors, including nutritive elements such as vitamins or minerals, chemical agents such as poisons or allergens, or physical agents such as ionizing radiation and noise. A second set of variables pertain to the disease hosts, the individual or individuals experiencing the disease episode. These include genetic factors; demographic characteristics such as age, sex, and race; social factors such as education and income; cultural factors such as ethnic group and religion; behavioral factors such as stress-coping strategies; health-impairing habits and lifestyles; and personality factors such as ego defense mechanisms and self-esteem. The third set of variables comprise the environment in which a disease episode occurs. This includes the physical environment (geology, climate), biological environment (flora, fauna), and social environment (social networks, residence, occupation). These three sets of variables together form the "epidemiologic triad" of agent, host, and environment; and their interrelations are the primary focus of investigation.

Psychosocial Epidemiology and the Stress Concept

Although psychosocial epidemiology is usually identified with a grouping of studies employing particular screening scales or survey methods, this subdiscipline can actually be said to embody a range of epidemiologic studies on a biological-social-psychological continuum. Thus, certain aspects of traditional biomedical epidemiology and of psychiatric epidemiology can be considered part of psychosocial epidemiology. What distinguishes the psychosocial from the biomedical and psychiatric forms of epidemiology is a focus incorporating all three components (biological-social-psychological) and their interrelations. As such it shares certain techniques with the other two branches of epidemiology and employs certain techniques that are unique. Similarly, elements of psychosocial epidemiology can be found in the other two branches.

A distinguishing characteristic of psychosocial epidemiology is the emphasis on the role of stress in the distribution and spread of disease. Although several definitions of stress exist, perhaps the best known is the one provided by Selye (1956) who defined it as a nonspecific response of the body to any demand. Since the pioneering work of Cannon (1929) and Selye (1956), several models have been developed that highlight the importance of physiological and psychological manifestations of stress in the etiology and outcome of disease. The basis of these models is the notion that environmental factors may act to create a physical or psychological strain on the host, be it an individual or a social group. These environmental factors may be present or anticipated, physical, psychological, or sociocultural. These stressors serve to stimulate both the pituitary-adrenal axis (Selye, 1956) and the sympathetic-adrenal medullary system (Cannon, 1929), producing increased levels of catecholamines and corticosteriods. Although this stimulation is viewed as an adaptive response, sustained levels of stress can result in the weakening of the immunologic system and excessive strain on the body in general, leading in turn to increased susceptibility to both infectious and chronic diseases. Despite the need for further elaboration of existing models, the notion of stress is an important one in psychosocial epidemiology, tying together all three components of illness: social, psychological, and physiological.

RESEARCH DESIGN

Several considerations are involved in the selection of a particular research design in a psychosocial epidemiologic study. For the sake of convenience, these considerations can be grouped into the categories of objectives and resources. Before undertaking a study, we should have a clear sense of what needs to be done. This involves specification of issues underlying the phenomena to be investigated, data needs and data limitations, hypotheses to be tested, and methods available for data analysis. Once a decision has been made as to what has to be done and/or what is desirable in investigating the phenomena of interest, these decisions must be evaluated in terms of what can be done given the available resources. The characteristics of available resources pose both opportunities and limitations to an epidemiologic study. Before deciding what type of study design to employ in investigating a specific disease or stress response and set of characteristics, we must ascertain the nature of the resources involved in both obtaining information on the phenomena under investigation and analyzing the data. Availability of time, money, and personnel are always important considerations; insufficient quantities of any of these will limit the options available for data gathering and analysis. The type of data available also plays an important role in the selection of a particular study design.

There are several different study designs that can be used in psychosocial epidemiology, and distinguishing among them on the basis of their objectives and methods can be difficult at best. The use of the same label to refer to different types of study, or different labels to refer to the same type of study, often leads to confusion as to the design being implemented (cf. Feinstein, 1979). Thus, we will begin with an attempt to summarize the criteria used to classify epidemiologic studies.

Observational and Experimental Studies

At the broadest level, epidemiologic studies can be grouped into two major categories: *observational* and *experimental*, distinguished on the basis of the degree of control exercised by the researcher. Observational studies are those in which the phenomena under investigation are not amenable to control by the researcher. The researcher cannot specify the conditions under which a particular disease pattern occurs but must observe the event in its natural context. Experimental studies, on the other hand, are subject to direct intervention by the researcher. Variables can be manipulated and controlled, thus reducing the possibility of spurious relationships and confounding factors. Performance studies of stress in which subjects are exposed to similar experiences to determine their biochemical reactions to the experimental induction are examples of such studies. When subjects can be randomly allocated into exposed and nonexposed groups, this study is known as a *clinical trial* (Lilienfeld & Lilienfeld, 1980). In a clinical trial, the focus of investigation is upon the individual. When random allocation is not possible, the experimental study is known as a *community trial*. Studying the effects of changes in treatment policy among military personnel diagnosed as alcoholics is an example of a community trial. The policy is subject to manipulation by the investigators, but random allocation of military personnel into cases and controls is not possible, nor can all extraneous variables be controlled. Moreover, the focus of the study is the group as a whole (i.e., military personnel), not individuals within the group.

Descriptive and Analytic Studies

Because of the difficulty of conducting well-controlled epidemiologic experiments on human populations on the one hand and the availability of observations of past or ongoing events on the other, observational studies are more common, and the variables under study are indirectly controlled through the use of quantitative methods of data analysis. There are two major categories of observational study: *descriptive* and *analytic*. The objective of a descriptive study is to describe the phenomena under investigation through the use of standardized rates of morbidity or mortality, the amount of variability in sets of observations among groups of individuals, and relationships among dependent, independent, and intervening variables of interest. Such studies utilize rates of incidence, prevalence, or mortality in describing the pattern of disease in a population on the basis of time, place, and population characteristics such as age, sex, and race.

Analytic studies are typically conducted to *explain* the observed pattern of disease occurrence. Their purpose is to determine whether or not an association is present between a certain characteristic or combination of characteristics and the disease or level of stress in a group of afflicted individuals. Whenever possible, the causal relationship between independent and dependent variables is also examined. In these studies, comparisons are made between a group of persons who have the disease under investigation and a control group that does not. There is a great deal of overlap between descriptive and analytic studies, but the latter is usually more focused and concerned with the testing of specific hypotheses.

Both descriptive and analytic studies can be further subdivided on the basis of causal and time perspectives. Cross-sectional and retrospective studies focus on the dependent variable, proceeding from effect to cause. These studies are often referred to as case control studies, although, as Lilienfeld and Lilienfeld (1980) observe, the case control perspective is also utilized in prospective studies. Prospective or cohort studies focus on the independent variables, proceeding from cause to effect. All three types of study design involve comparisons among individuals who experience a disease episode and those who do not with respect to one or more characteristics or exposures. The model for these comparisons, represented in its simplist form, is a 2 × 2 table such as Table 2.1

Cross-sectional and Retrospective Studies.   The object of cross-sectional and retrospective studies is to determine whether or not a relationship exists between a particular trait or set of traits and a specific illness or disease. Subjects are selected on the basis of presence or absence of the disease under investigation and then compared on the basis of one or more characteristics. Subjects with the disease are referred to as cases, whereas those who do not have the disease serve as controls. If a higher proportion of individuals with the characteristic is found among the cases than among the controls, an association between the disease and the characteristic is indicated.

Cross-sectional and retrospective studies are distinguished from one another on the basis of time. In the cross-sectional study, the characteristic or attribute being compared is present in both cases and controls at the time

TABLE 2.1.   FRAMEWORK FOR AN EPIDEMIOLOGIC STUDY

| | | Retrospective Cross-Sectional Effects | | |
| | | Number of Individuals | | |
	Characteristic	With Disease (Cases)	Without Disease (Controls)	Total
Prospective (Cohort) Causes	With	a	b	$a + b + = N_1$
	Without	c	d	$c + d = N_2$
	Total	$a + c$ M_1	$b + d$ M_2	$a + b + c + d = N$

Source: Lilienfeld & Lilienfeld, 1980. Copyright 1980, Oxford University Press.

of the investigation. These studies are also known as "prevalence" studies. The study of suicidal behavior in basic military trainees by Gaines and Richmond (1980) provides an example of a cross-sectional study. Sixty basic trainees were selected for the study, 30 of whom had been brought to the attention of authorities for having made a suicidal gesture, and 30 non-suicidal trainees who served as a control group. Both cases and controls were evaluated on the same day and each subject was independently administered a questionnaire to obtain information on characteristics such as birth order, parents' ages, education, occupation, marital status, and so on. Perceptions of pretraining and basic training experiences were obtained and each subject was administered the Wechsler Adult Intelligence Scale (WAIS) and the Minnesota Multiphasic Personality Inventory (MMPI), using the standard administrative procedures.

Another example of a case control study is provided by Harburg et al. (1978) in their examination of the relationships among skin color, ethnicity, stress, and blood pressure in Detroit. Census areas in Detroit were ranked for their stress scores on the basis of their instability (measured in terms of levels of crime, marital breakup, and so on) and socioeconomic status. Four areas were selected for detailed study: (1) high stress, population predominately black; (2) high stress, population predominately white; (3) low stress, population predominately black; and (4) low stress, population predominately white. A random sample of 1000 adults was drawn from each area of persons of the predominant race in the census division, 25 to 60 years old, married and living with spouse, and having relatives in the Detroit area. Each subject was interviewed by a nurse who took three blood pressure readings and rated skin color on a 4-point scale. Both the dependent variable (blood pressure) and independent variables (race, skin color, residence, and the like) were present in the sample at the time of the study. Results showed that darker skin color, for black males especially, was related to higher blood pressure, independent of control variables such as age, weight, height, smoking history, educational level, and family income.

In a retrospective study, the object is to determine whether the characteristic was present in the past. The investigator looks backward in time for exposure. Most studies of stressful life events are representative of this approach. In a study of life events and disease by Antonovsky and Kats (1967), a case sample of patients with multiple sclerosis was matched with a control sample on the basis of sex, age, and region of birth. The two groups were compared on the basis of "life crises," defined as events associated with physical trauma and changes in environment, primary interpersonal relations, and status. The events were then operationalized to create a "crisis score" to indicate the intensity of the crises.

In the setup of a case control design, several considerations must be taken into account. The first and most important is the determination of where the cases and controls will be obtained. Both may be drawn from the community at large. In a study of depression, for instance, all diagnosed cases in a community, using hospital admissions, clinic visits, or physicians records as a source of data, could serve as cases, whereas the controls would consist of a sample of nondepressed individuals from the general population in a community. A second approach would be to select a sample of the general population and divide those diagnosed as being clinically depressed (on the basis of clinical examinations or the administration of a screening scale such as the CES-D) to comprise the cases and those evaluated as not depressed serving as the controls. A third option is to select a specific population, such as the patients at a particular hospital or group of hospitals, diagnosed as being clinically depressed, and compare them with a group of patients with other diagnoses. The former group would serve as the cases, whereas the latter would comprise the controls in the study.

Another consideration in a case control design involves taking into account known or suspected factors believed to be related to the disease under investigation. The idea behind random sampling in epidemiologic studies is to control, in part, for extraneous variables that could possibly influence the distribution of the disease but that cannot be anticipated ahead of time. Adjustment procedures can also be implemented to account for potential bias. Cases and controls can be compared for each level of extraneous factor such as age, sex, socioeconomic status, social supports, and so on. Cases and controls can also be matched with one another, either as a group or as individuals. A group match would stratify both the case group and the control group into levels, such as age groups. For example, the cases can be stratified into 10-year age groups, 20 to 29 , 30 to 39, 40 to 49, and so on. The control group can be similarly stratified and samples of controls randomly selected from each stratum to provide the same number of controls as cases. If the number of characteristics to be examined and controlled for is not too large, individual matching may be performed, resulting in pairs of cases and controls possessing the same characteristic or limited set of characteristics (e.g., black males, black females, white males, white females).

Several procedures are available to determine how large the sample should be for a particular study. As Schlesselman (1982, p. 144) notes, a study should be large enough to avoid both type I—claiming an association when one does not exist—and type II—claiming no association when one does exist—statistical errors. The number of subjects to be selected for a case control study depends on the specification of four values: (1) the relative frequency of exposure among controls in the target population, (2) a hypothesized relative risk associated with exposure that would have sufficient biological or public health importance to warrant its detection, (3) the desired level of significance, and (4) the desired study power. Schlesselman (1982) provides a formula that incorporates these four values in the determination of a satisfactory sample size.

There are several advantages to using a cross-sectional or retrospective design when conducting an epidemiologic study. Such designs are well suited to the study of rare diseases or those with long latency. They are relatively quick to organize and carry out. Compared with the time and effort of a cohort study, they are relatively inexpensive and require comparatively few subjects. Within certain limits, they have the advantage of utilizing existing records and do not involve any undue risk to the subjects. Finally, a cross-sectional or retrospective design allows for the study of multiple potential causes of a disease (Schlesselman, 1982).

On the other hand, there are several disadvantages to the case control format of cross-sectional and retrospective designs. Retrospective studies, for example, rely on recall or records for information on past exposure, and validation of this information is difficult if not, at times, impossible (Schlesselman, 1982, p. 18). As will be noted when specific types of data are examined subsequently, the great potential for incomplete data and confounding factors in psychosocial studies severely restrict the use of these designs. Even though the case control procedure in these designs allows for an examination of multiple independent variables, the control of these variables is likely to be incomplete. Finally, relative to the cohort design, cross-sectional and retrospective designs are inadequate as predictors of a disease or stress event. Such a design can only give estimates of relative risk and not a direct estimate of probability because, by looking at a particular segment of cases, those present at the time of the investigation, we cannot ascertain the disease episodes among cases not present. To utilize the characteristic under study in an effort to *predict* the likelihood of experiencing the disease or stress event, we find that the inference must assume the form: "Given the existence of a charactertistic (e.g., race, sex, life event), what is the probability that an individual will experience a particular event (e.g., psychological distress, depression, hypertension, ulcers)?" Answers to this question can only be obtained from prospective evidence (cf. Hirschfeld & Cross, 1982, p. 42).

Prospective Studies.   The prospective or cohort study begins with a specified population believed to be free of the stress, disease, or diseases under investigation. The population is divided into groups on the basis of one or more characteristics that may affect the risk of experiencing the stress or disease over time. The researcher looks forward in time for exposure, and analysis proceeds from cause to effect. In this approach, also known as a follow-up study, the population may be followed for several years to determine which members experience the disease event and if a particular pattern emerges with respect to one or more characteristics. The population is divided into subgroups according to the presence or absence of one or more characteristics (or the degree to which the characteristic is present or absent) initially. The subgroups are then compared with respect to the subsequent incidence of disease over a specified follow-up period. A higher incidence of disease in a subgroup possessing a particular characteristic indicates an association between the disease and the characteristic. This method provides the most direct measurement of the risk of disease development, hence, is preferred by epidemiologists.

There are two types of prospective study: *concurrent* and *nonconcurrent*. Concurrent studies begin with a presently existing cohort which is followed for an extended period of time into the future. Residents of a particular city, students attending a particular college, and all enlisted personnel in the U.S. Navy, who are to be observed and followed for the next 10 years, would be examples of such a study. A nonconcurrent study selects a cohort as it existed at some point in the past (students who graduated from a college in 1970; residents of a city from 1950 to 1955; recruits who entered the Navy in 1973) and follows them for a designated period of time, often to the present.

An example of a concurrent, prospective psychosocial study is the 1965 Human Population Laboratory Survey of a random sample of adults in Alameda County, California (Berkman & Syme, 1979). A stratified sample of Alameda County housing units was selected and visited by an enumerator who gathered demographic data on all household members of all ages. The cohort was subdivided on the basis of several characteristics, including age, race, sex, socioeconomic status, and social networks. Mortality data were then collected for a 9-year period, from 1965 to 1974, when a follow-up survey was conducted. Death certificates from those belonging to the 1965 cohort were obtained using the computer matching files of the California Death Registry or other state registries when the cohort member had moved out of the area. Through extensive follow-up, all but 4 percent of the original cohort had been located. Those lost to follow-up were not found to differ significantly from those accounted for on any of the health measures recorded in the original survey, thus reducing the possibility of a spurious relationship in survivorship. The mortality experience of particular subgroups were then compared to see if any association existed between one or more characteristics, such as social networks, and mortality risk.

Prospective studies have also been employed in studies of disease and life events. In a study by Grant et al. (1982), a cohort consisting of psychiatric outpatients from a Veterans Administration Mental Health Clinic and non-patients recruited from a university community was selected and observed over a 3-year period. At the beginning of the study, all subjects were interviewed and demographic, biographic, event, and symptoms data were obtained. For the next 3 years, each member of the cohort was sent a copy of the Holmes and Rahe Schedule of Recent Experiences (SRE) and a Symptom Checklist (SCL) every 2 months. Subjects indicated on the SRE which events occurred to them in the previous 2 months and rated all the items on the scale on a 7-point desirability scale as to whether or not the events had occurred. Thus, for every 2-month interval, it was possible to compute an event score measured by life change units (LCUs). Symptom data were obtained from a 69-item SCL of bodily, cognitive, affective, and behavioral symptoms.

The procedure for conducting a prospective study is relatively straightforward. The cohort selected can be a sample from a general population group such as a community or a specific group such as the employees of a certain corporation or members of a particular occupation. A cohort may also be selected on the basis of a known exposure to a particular etiologic factor such as individuals who have experienced a divorce or death of spouse or who work in a stressful occupation. In the latter example, an unexposed cohort should also be selected in order to evaluate the experience of the exposed cohort.

Although selection of a cohort may be a relatively simple procedure, the follow-up phase of a perspective study is much more difficult, requiring considerable resources. According to Friedman (1980), the length of the follow-up period depends primarily on the number of disease cases needed to provide reliable, statistically significant answers to the specific questions under study. This estimate requires a knowledge of the size of the cohort and an estimate of the incidence rate of the disease episode being examined. This will allow for the estimation of the number of new episodes occurring in a 1-year period. For example, if there are 8000 members in the cohort, and the incidence rate for the disease episode is 1 percent per year, about 80 new cases of the disease episode may be expected during each year of follow-up. If 1600 cases are needed to provide answers with a certain degree of reliability, then the study may be expected to last about 20 years (cf. Friedman, 1980, p. 124).

The prospective design is usually regarded as conceptually and methodologically more rigorous and accurate than the cross-sectional and retrospective designs. In principle, the prospective design provides a complete description of experience subsequent to exposure, including rates of progression, staging of disease, and natural history (Schlesselman, 1982, p. 18). Second, the design allows for the study of multiple potential effects of a given exposure, thereby obtaining information on benefits as well as on risks associated with specified characteristics. Third, the procedure permits flexibility in choosing variables to be systematically recorded. Previously unsuspected variables displaying a strong association with the disease under investigation are more likely to be detected in the course of the study than if the focus is on a predefined set of variables. Fourth, the cohort method permits thorough quality control in the measurement of study variables (Schlesselman, 1982). It does so, in part, by reducing the possibility of bias in obtaining information from cohort members.

There are certain disadvantages to using the cohort method, however. Compared to the case control design, the cohort study takes longer to conduct with a potentially long duration of follow-up. Because of the length of time involved, the possibility of confounding factors emerges since current practices or exposures to the study variables may change, making the research results irrelevant. One can reduce the length of the follow-up period by increasing the size of the cohort, but this alternative may involve considerable additional expense. Even with a longer follow-up period and smaller cohort, prospective studies involve more time, money, and personnel than do cross-sectional and retrospective studies. The potential for improved quality control also increases the potential expense of the project. For studies of rare diseases, a cohort design requires the use of a large number of subjects, also adding to the increased expense. Finally, maintaining follow-up on the cohort can be difficult, as many subjects change residence or drop out entirely from a study.

DATA FOR PSYCHOSOCIAL STUDIES

Rates and Scales

As noted previously, psychosocial epidemiology is characterized by its use of psychometric data in conjunction with the clinical data typically employed in other epidemiologic studies. These two sets of data are distinguished by their source and forms of measurement. Clinical data usually comprise a nominal set of episodes of disease morbidity or mortality. They are usually obtained from hospital records, physical examinations, or death registries but may also be obtained through the administration of various screening scales in which an arbitrary cutoff point is used to distinguish between cases and noncases (or controls). These episodes are commonly expressed in terms of rates.

A rate is a statement of probability of the phenomenon measured per unit of population per unit of time. In epidemiology, this statement of probability involves three different items of information: (1) the number of persons experiencing the episode of disease morbidity or mortality, expressed as the numerator; (2) the population at risk from which the sample of cases are drawn, expressed as the denominator; and (3) a specification of the time interval. Thus, a mortality rate attributed to alcoholism of 41.4 per 100,000 Alaskan Natives in 1970 reflects a probability of alchohol-related deaths in a specific population for a designated year and is based on the number of Alaskan Native deaths from alcoholism in 1970 divided by the Alaskan

Native population in that year. Although the actual Alaskan Native population in 1970 was much smaller than 100,000, the use of this number (or a smaller factor of 10) serves to standardize the rate, allowing comparisons across different groups to be made.

The psychometric data utilized in psychosocial epidemiologic studies comprise a set of information on both dependent and independent variables. Levels of stress, for example, are often represented in psychometric data. These data are usually obtained through one or more scales measuring life events, psychological distress, mental disorders, psychophysiological symptoms, or personality characteristics. Several scales have been developed to discriminate between patients with varied psychiatric diagnoses and nonpatients for use in epidemiologic research in the general population. These scales are very similar in content and tend to correlate with each other. However, they usually provide only a general measure of psychological distress which is analogous to measures of temperature in physical medicine (Dohrenwend et al., 1980, p. 1229). Other, more specific, scales are applied to diagnose specific forms of psychopathology.

One of the earliest and most widely used objective measures in psychosocial studies was a 22-item screening instrument, developed in connection with the Midtown Manhattan study, to provide an approximation of the degree of psychiatric impairment in community surveys (Langner, 1962). The scale does not classify individuals according to type of psychiatric disorder but provides a rough indication of where people lie on a continuum of impairment in functioning due to common types of psychiatric symptoms. A similar although less widely used measure is the Health Opinion Survey used in the Stirling County study (Macmillan, 1957). Both measures have as their core a portion of the items from the Psychosomatic Scale of the Neuropsychiatric Screening Adjunct (NSA), devised as an aid to Selective Service screening during World War II (Dohrenwend & Dohrenwend, 1982, p. 1272) and the Minnesota Multiphasic Personality Inventory (MMPI).

Dependent Variables

The major dependent variables in psychosocial epidemiology are illness and stress, although stress can also be viewed as an independent or intervening variable as well. Illness episodes can be expressed in the form of rates or in terms of psychiatric scales, whereas levels of stress are usually measured in terms of life events, patterns of behavior, psychophysiological symptoms, or biochemical indicators. The examination of medical data relating to the pattern and distribution of physical and mental illness is a critical part of psychosocial epidemiology. Not all studies examine the same types of data, however; and there is much overlap between the data examined in some studies that may be referred to as psychosocial and data examined in other types of epidemiologic investigations. This section will briefly examine three types of dependent variables: mortality, morbidity, and stress.

Mortality. Although mortality statistics are usually examined in other types of epidemiologic studies, they have played an important role in psychosocial studies as well. Several studies, for instance, have examined the effect of different forms of social support on the health status by selecting a cohort, distinguishing members of the cohort on the basis of specified psychosocial variables, and then following the cohort over a period of time (e.g., Berkman & Syme, 1979; House et al., 1982; Wingard, 1982). Death certificates obtained from a state death registry provide data on the number and causes of death for cohort members throughout the time period. Death certificates and registries can also be employed for studies of potential social factors affecting survival rates for particular diseases such as cancer (Dayal & Chiu, 1982) or coronary heart disease (Chandra et al., 1983).

Obtaining the data on mortality is only the first step in their use in an epidemiologic study. To quantify the data, we express the number of deaths in a population in terms of a rate. A mortality or death rate requires the following information: (1) the number of deaths in the exposed or affected population during a certain time period, which comprises the numerator; (2) the total population exposed to the risk of death, comprising the denominator; and (3) a specified period of time, usually a 1-year interval. Expressed formally, the annual death rate is as follows.

$$\text{Annual death rate (ADR) from all causes (per 1000 population)} = \frac{\text{total number of deaths occurring in a 1-year period}}{\text{number of persons in the population at midyear}} \times 1000$$

The units of time and population may be selected by the investigator to suit his or her own purpose, but they must be specified. Death rates can also be made specific for a variety of characteristics, such as age, cause of death, marital status, race, and occupation. Age-specific rates are perhaps the most common form of specific rate, given the high association between age and mortality. Thus, a suicide rate of 19.2 per 100,000 among 18 to 24 year olds in the United States in 1977 would be calculated as follows.

$$\text{ADR from suicide for persons aged 18 to 24 (per 100,000 population)} = \frac{\text{number of suicides of persons 18 to 24 during 1977}}{\text{number of 18 to 24 year olds in the United States as of July 1, 1977}} \times 100,000$$

Another type of rate frequently used in the "case fatality rate" is

$$\text{Case fatality rate } (\%) = \frac{\begin{array}{c}\text{number of individuals}\\\text{dying during a specified}\\\text{period of time after}\\\text{onset or diagnosis of disease}\end{array}}{\begin{array}{c}\text{number of individuals with}\\\text{the specified disease}\end{array}} \times 100$$

This rate represents the risk of dying during a definite period of time for individuals diagnosed as having a particular disease. As with the death rate, the period of time during which the deaths occur should be indicated. Case fatality rates can also be made specific for age, sex, severity of disease, or any other factors of clinical and epidemiologic importance.

Morbidity.   Morbidity statistics for both physical and mental disorders are more commonly utilized in psychosocial epidemiologic studies. Because of its association with stress and the relative ease in obtaining the data by investigators, blood pressure levels are commonly utilized in psychosocial studies (Harburg et al. 1978; Hypertension Detection and Follow-up Program Cooperative Group, 1977; Keil et al., 1977; Reed et al., 1982). Usually, three readings are taken at any one point in time by someone trained in the standard blood pressure technique and a mean average used as the reading for each subject. Blood pressure readings can be taken independently or in conjunction with a physical examination.

Physical examinations are another source of data for psychosocial investigations. Several studies have relied upon regularly scheduled medical exams by physicians in studies of coronary heart disease (Haynes & Feinleib, 1980; Marmot & Syme, 1976; Reed et al., 1982), ulcers (Cobb & Rose, 1973), cancer (Fox, 1978), and so on. These examinations may be comprehensive, including a complete biochemistry and EEG workup, or they may be specific to the disease itself, the former method being preferred because of the potential for numerous confounding factors.

Although many if not most studies involve physical examinations by study investigators, morbidity data can also be obtained from hospital records. Dayal and Chiu (1982), for instance, employed a tumor registry from a university hospital in their study of racial differences in survival for prostatic cancer.

Interview surveys are also employed to obtain morbidity data. These questionnaires usually contain details of past medical history, smoking history, physical activity, and dietary habits. Several of these interview surveys such as the Health Interview Survey (HIS) and the National Ambulatory Medical Care Survey (NAMCS) have been employed in nationwide studies; others have been used on smaller samples. An example of such a survey is the Seriousness of Illness Survey (Wyler et al., 1968), a self-report checklist of 126 commonly recognized physical and mental symptoms and diseases. This instrument includes a general severity weight for each disorder, reflecting prognosis, duration, threat to life, degree of disability, and degree of discomfort. This instrument has served as a useful tool in several stress and illness studies (e.g., Dohrenwend & Dohrenwend, 1982; Kobasa et al., 1981). Other survey instruments are specific to particular disorders, such as the London School of Hygiene Cardiovascular Questionnaire used by Marmot and Syme (1976) in their study of coronary heart disease and acculturation among Japanese-Americans.

As with physical disorders, much of the epidemiologic research on psychiatric illness has relied on data obtained from screening scales, records of hospital admissions, or clinical evaluations by study investigators. Screening scales are perhaps most frequently used in such studies. Several protocols have been developed to assess psychopathology in general such as the Minnesota Multiphasic Personality Inventory, the Hopkins Symptom Checklist, and the Present State Examination (PSE), whereas others are designed for specific forms of psychopathology such as schizophrenia (SADS-RDC scale), or depression (CES-D scale).

Another source of data on psychiatric illnesses has been derived from hospital records. In his review of studies of mental disorder and social class, Fried (1969) notes that records of psychiatric hospitalization are most often used as data, with rates usually based on the number of patients in a demographic category as the numerator and census calculations of the population at risk in these categories as the denominator.

Clinical assessments are also used frequently in the determination or psychiatric disorder. Vaillant (1976), for example, using data collected in a follow-up study of college males, went through autobiographical responses to biennial questionnaires, interviews, summaries, psychological tests, and protocols, and recorded each person's behavior in a time of crisis in the form of a vignette. Vignettes were then grouped into clusters on the basis of the type of defense mechanism employed by each study subject. The assessments of defense mechanisms were then verified in a blind evaluation by two other judges. The judges independently rated each of 50 cases, labeling vignettes according to a glossary of 18 defenses.

As with instances of mortality, the quantification of events of illness or disease takes the form of rates. There are two major types of morbidity rate: *incidence* and *prevalence*. The incidence rate of a disease is the number of new cases of the disease occurring within a specified population during a specified time period.

$$\text{Incidence rate per } 1000 = \frac{\begin{array}{l}\text{number of new cases of a}\\\text{disease occurring in a}\\\text{population during a}\\\text{specified period of time}\end{array}}{\begin{array}{l}\text{number of persons exposed}\\\text{to risk of developing the}\\\text{disease during that}\\\text{period of time}\end{array}} \times 1000$$

In order to establish the true incidence of any disease, one has to meet three basic conditions (Lemkau & Crocetti, 1958). First, the identification of the disease or illness under study should be objective and reliable. Second, all cases should be accounted for, by either recording every case that occurs in the study population or knowing the ratio of unknown to known cases. Third, the population from which the cases are drawn should be clearly defined and carefully enumerated. Although many studies are content to rely upon decenniel census statistics in calculating the population at risk, more accurate means of enumeration are available and should be used whenever possible.

   In studies where a cohort is being followed and observed over a period of time, it is often more useful to employ person-years of observation as denominators in the computation of rates. This is particularly true in studies where subjects enter and leave for varying periods of time. Moreover, the age distribution of the groups under observation will change over the course of the follow-up period, as will morbidity and mortality rates. The use of person-years makes it possible to express in one figure the period when a varying number of persons is exposed to the risk of a disease episode. Incidence rates using person-years as the denominator would take the form represented in Table 2.2. Both the number of individuals in the cohort and the duration of observation of each person are taken into account. "For example, five persons who remain under observation for twenty years contribute one hundred person-years, as would one hundred persons observed for one year" (Lilienfeld & Lilienfeld, 1980, p. 245).

TABLE 2.2.   CALCULATION OF PERSON-YEAR INCIDENCE FOR DISEASE EVENTS BY CHARACTERISTIC OR EXPOSURE IN A FOLLOW-UP STUDY

Characteristic or Exposure Groups	Number of Individuals	Person-years	Number of Events	Person-year Incidence Rate (per 1000)
A	500	1600	5	3.1
B	500	2400	7	2.9
Total	1000	4000	12	3.0

Prevalence rates measure the number of cases present at, or during, a specified period of time. The prevalence rate equals the incidence rate times the average duration of the disease. For example, if the average duration of hypertension is 3 years and its incidence rate is 15 per 1000, the prevalence rate would be 45 per 1000.

$$\text{Prevalence rate per } 1000 = \frac{\begin{array}{l}\text{number of cases of disease}\\\text{present in the population}\\\text{at a specified time}\end{array}}{\begin{array}{l}\text{number of persons in the}\\\text{population at that}\\\text{specified time}\end{array}} \times 1000$$

The two types of prevalence rates used in epidemiologic studies are *point prevalence* and *period prevalance*. Point prevalence refers to the number of cases present at a specified moment in time, such as the date the sample is drawn and the information is obtained; period prevalence refers to the number of cases that occur across a specified period of time, for example, a year. Period prevalence consists of the point prevalence at the beginning of the specified time interval plus all new cases that occur during the interval.

The use of and differences between prevalance and incidence rates can be demonstrated using data obtained in the Honolulu Heart Program study of coronary heart disease and acculturation among men of Japanese descent (Reed et al., 1982). A sample of 4653 men of Japanese ancestry was observed over a 7-year period from August 1, 1971 to January 1, 1979. The total number of cases of coronary heart disease (defined as a clinically diagnosed episode of myocardial infarction or angina) observed throughout the period was 482. Of this figure, 264 cases were recorded at the beginning of the study, August 1, 1971. The point prevalence of coronary heart disease among the subjects, therefore, was

$$\text{Point prevalence (per 1000 as of August 1, 1971)} = \frac{264}{4653} \times 1000 = 57$$

The incidence rate was calculated by taking all subjects free of the disease at the beginning of the study (4653 − 264 = 4389) and observing 218 new cases of coronary heart disease among this group throughout the 7-year period. The incidence of coronary heart disease among this sample of Japanese men, therefore, was

$$\text{Incidence rate (per 1000, 1971 to 1977)} = \frac{218}{4389} \times 1000 = 50$$

The period prevalence rate would be calculated by taking the total number of cases of coronary heart disease observed throughout the entire period and the total population at risk. The prevalence of coronary heart disease for the 7-year period, therefore, would be

$$\text{Period prevalence (per 1000,} = \frac{482}{4653} \times 1000 = 103.6$$
$$\text{1971 to 1977}$$

Both incidence and prevalence rates can be made specific for age, sex, and/or any other social or psychological characteristics.

Of the two types of rates, incidence rates are preferred in psychosocial epidemiology because they provide a true index of the risk of disease for specific populations. However, both are faced with certain types of disadvantages. Incidence rates, for example, are affected by numbers, types, and availability of services. As will be discussed in greater detail subsequently, the variability in these services for different segments of a population can bias the statistical analyses. On the other hand, prevalence rates tend to overweight problems of long-term duration and underweight those of short-term duration.

Stress.   Because stress is defined in terms of nonspecific tendencies, it cannot be measured directly, but rather, must be assessed in terms of human response. Baum et al. (1982) have grouped the measures of human response used in psychosocial studies into four broad categories: self-report, performance, psychophysiologic, and biochemical. Self-report measures involve the use of questionnaires and scales to obtain information on experiences, perceptions, and evaluations. Performance measures record gross behavioral changes in response to activities believed to be stressful. Psychophysiological measures assess organ or system function in the body, such as cardiovascular or electrodermal response, muscle tension, and respiration. Biochemical measures of stress (e.g., catecholamine and corticosteroid secretion) examine levels of activity in the endocrine system (Baum et al. 1982, p. 219).

Several scales exist that index the experience of stress based on data obtained from interviews or questionnaires. Many of the scales that screen for psychological impairment have already been discussed. These scales usually ask subjects to list psychological or somatic experiences of distress and to evaluate their intensity. In a study by Turner (1981), for instance, psychological well-being was measured through use of the Brief Symptom Inventory (BSI) scale, composed of 53 items, each item being rated on a 5-point distress scale. The BSI is scored in terms of nine primary symptom dimensions: somatization, obsessive-compulsive, interpersonal sensitivity, depression, anxiety, hostility, phobic anxiety, paranoid ideation, and psychoticism. Other self-report scales of stress include the General Health

Questionnaire used by Andrews et al. (1978) and a perceived strain index developed by Pearlin and Schooler (1978), consisting of a series of Lickert-type items encompassing financial, marital, and work-related sources of strain.

One of the most common measures of stress, however, is the number and types of life events preceding an illness event. Life events are treated here, however, as independent or intervening variables for three reasons. First, life events are presumed to occur prior to a stressful response although the causal relationship may occur in the opposite direction as well. Second, the same life events do not necessarily produce the same response in all individuals. Third, different individuals may give similar responses to entirely different events. More will be said about the relationship between life events and stress later.

Performance measures of stress rely on such indices as loss of coordination, fatigue (Appley & Trumbull 1967), increased reaction time (Frankenhaeuser, 1975), and problem solving (Glass & Singer, 1972). These measures involve exposure to a stressful task or situation and comparison of response between exposed and nonexposed subjects. A number of tasks have been identified for this purpose and measures have been developed to assess the stress experience. One such measure has been provided by Glass and Singer's (1972) research on noise and urban stress. Subjects exposed to stressful conditions generally perform more poorly on proofreading tasks requiring great concentration than do subjects exposed to less aversive conditions (Cohen, 1980; Glass & Singer, 1972). This *differential performance* seems to reflect a cost of coping with the stressful condition (Baum et al., 1982, p. 223).

Psychophysiological measures of stress are concerned with degrees of arousal or activation associated with the sympathetic nervous system (SNS) (Baum et al. 1982, p. 223). Blood pressure, respiration rate, heart rate, muscle tension, and galvanic skin response have been used in numerous studies as indices of stress.

Two major biochemical indicators serve as reliable measures of stress in psychosocial studies, urinary and plasma adrenal corticosteriod levels, and urinary and plasma catecholamine levels. Each represents the response of a different endocrine system that reacts to different perceptions of the body and to different enviromental factors. Several excellent reviews of research on the hypothalamic-pituitary-adrenal cortex axis and sympathetic-adrenal medullary axis (Baum et al., 1982; Brown, 1981; Henry, 1982; Mason, 1968a, 1975) document extensively the evidence of pyschosocial influences on activity in these systems. Corticosteriods are secreted by the adrenal cortex and serve many important functions, including regulation of body electrolytes and water, carbohydrate metabolism, protein and fat metabolism, and ability to tolerate stressors. The 17-hydroxycorticosteroids (17-OCHS), primarily cortisol, have been repeatedly demonstrated to be reliable indicators of stress. Numerous studies have found increased levels of 17-OCHS in urine and blood samples of subjects under stressful situations (Baum et al., 1982; Mason, 1975).

Catecholamines such as epinephrine and norepinephrine are released by the adrenal medulla under situations of stress and produce numerous physiological reactions, including increased cardiac output and blood pressure, increased minute volume of respiration, glycogenolysis, and mobilization of free fatty acids, stimulation of the pituitary to release ACTH, diversion of blood flow from the digestive system to the skeletal muscles, and central nervous system effects such as desensitization to pain and increased alertness (Brown, 1981, p. 77). Increased levels of catecholamines in urine or blood samples serve as reliable indicators of stress and have also been used in numerous studies.

Independent Variables

Sociodemographic Characteristics. Whether we are attempting to understand the etiology of stress or particular stress-related disorders, one or more independent variables must be taken into consideration and controlled. Demographic characteristics such as age, sex, residence, race, ethnicity, marital status, and socioeconomic status (SES) have been the subject of several different psychosocial epidemiologic studies. Most of these variables are straightforward and are relatively easy to operationalize. Others present greater difficulties. Socioeconomic status, for instance, has been operationalized in several different ways, making comparison between studies difficult. Education, income, occupation, and census tract of residence have all been used, independently or in combinations, as indices of socioeconomic status. Several scales of SES exist, including the Duncan Socioeconomic Index, the Green Manual, and the Hollingshead Two-factor Index of Social Position. Usually a two-factor index of social position, measured by education and occupation, is employed in epidemiologic studies. As McQueen and Siegrist (1982) observe, this index is used "because it is a 'quick and dirty' approximation of class which appears to satisfy many epidemiologists and is regarded as easy to interpret" (p. 353).

In studies of race, skin color has been used to examine within-group differences in health (IIarburg et al. 1978; Keil et al. 1977). The ethnic group is usually obtained from self-reports of study subjects. Other indices of ethnic group status used in epidemiologic investigations have been race, surname, language spoken, and birthplace of self, parents, and grandparents (Hayes-Bautista, 1983).

Life Events. As noted previously, life events are usually regarded as indicators of the degree of stress experienced by a particular individual or by groups of individuals. Thus, although the stress itself can be said to be a response to one or more events, the events themselves are used as an index of the degree of stress. Among the earliest and most widely used measures of stress based on the concept of life events are the Schedule of Recent Experiences (SRE) and the Social Readjustment Rating Scale (SRRS) developed by Holmes and Rahe (1967). The SRE is a list of 43 life events found to involve some sort of adjustment for most people. The scale measures the intensity and length of time necessary to accommodate to a life event, regardless of the desirability of the event. The SRRS gives different weights to each life event. Subjects are asked to rate a series of predefined events on the basis of personal experience. Marriage is given an arbitrary value of 500 and other events are scaled relative to this life event. The amount of life change is derived from the multiplication of the weight for each event by the frequency of its occurrence for the subject during the time period under study. This product is expressed as Life Change Units (LCU). Pearson product-moment correlations were used by Holmes and Rahe to determine that a universal agreement between groups and among individuals about the significance of life events under study transcends differences in age, sex, marital status, education, social class, generation American, religion, and race. Several epidemiologic studies have been conducted employing the scales developed by Holmes and Rahe.

In addition to the Schedule of Recent Experience and the Social Readjustment Rating Scale, other scales have been devised to measure the effect of life events on psychological distress and illness. In a study of Antonovsky and Kats (1967), a measure of life events was obtained by eliciting responses to 30 questions, classified into one of four subject areas: physical trauma (e.g., illness, operation, beating); change in general environment (e.g., move from village to town, migration, internment in camp); changes affecting primary interpersonal relations (e.g., marriage, death of parents); and changes in status (e.g., type of work, employment). Within each of these areas, five levels of crisis intensity were distinguished. Patients and controls were compared on the basis of six predefined scores.

1. A total crisis score (TCS) representing the number of crisis points of an individual, irrespective of crisis area, age, or number of crisis.
2. A sub-TCS within each of the four crisis areas.
3. A serious crisis score representing the number of crises scored as 4 or 5 (NSC).
4. A sub-NSC within each of the four crisis areas.
5. A crisis score for 2, 5, and 10 years before the "age at onset" and from birth until age 15.
6. A "crisis concentration" score, defined as 15 crisis points within a 5-year period.

Using this procedure, Antonovsky and Kats found that patients differed significantly from controls with respect to total crisis score, serious crisis scores, total and serious crisis scores in the areas of environmental change and interpersonal relations, and cumulative crisis scores in 2, 5, and 10 years onset.

Although scales such as these measure life events strictly in terms of the number of events, other scales measuring the quality of events have been developed. Dohrenwend (1973), for instance, developed an index of the undesirability of events experienced to test the hypothesis that the type of life event was more salient in the experience of distress than was the number of events. In this index, all events reported by the respondents were scored as culturally defined losses or gains according to the following schema: A loss was defined as an event of change generally considered to be undesirable and scored as +1; a gain was defined as an event or change generally considered to be desirable and scored as −1; and ambiguous events or changes were those whose desirability was subject to debate, scored as 0. The events were coded by two coders working independently and each individual's score was the algebraic sum of all the events he or she reported.

Related to this issue of relative importance of different life events is the fact that efforts have been made to weight life events. As noted earlier, Holmes and Rahe (1967) used life change units (LCU) to weight the amount of adjustment required by each life change. This measure was obtained by asking a standardization sample how much disruption in behavioral patterns would result from each event. An alternate procedure has been to have individuals indicate the level of idiosyncratic disruption the event caused them. Some researchers (e.g., Byrne & Whyte, 1980; Sarason et al., 1978) have argued convincingly for idiosyncratic weighting, since an event may have a different impact on one person relative to another (Newcomb et al. 1981, p. 401). However, others (Dohrenwend, 1980; Kessler, 1979) have argued that weighting confounds relationships between life events and illness.

One index that incorporates the notion of a life event and social status is level of acculturation. In their study of coronary heart disease among Japanese and Japanese-Americans, Marmot and Syme (1976) developed an Ethnic Identity Scale, a questionnaire that included three indices of acculturation; (1) culture of upbringing, (2) cultural assimilation, and (3) social assimilation. Culture of upbringing combines information on the number of years spent in Japan, the age the respondent left parents home, whether the respondent ever lived on a farm, where schooling took place (Japan or United States), years spent in Japanese language school, religion while growing up, friends while growing up, and wife's cultural background (if married). Cultural assimilation combines information on ability to read Japanese and frequency of speaking Japanese to wife, children, and friends. Social assimilation is indicated by ethnicity of prefession and ethnicity of coworkers.

Alienation is another phenomenon that incorporates elements of life events and status. In a study conducted by Seeman and Anderson (1983), the concept of alienation was operationalized, using a series of different scales that measured items such as powerlessness, degree of social integration, job satisfaction, occupational striving, and career mobility. Powerlessness is often measured in psychosocial studies by variations of the Locus of Control Scale developed by Rotter et al. (1962). In general, alienation scales consist of a series of questions designed to elicit a measure of operationally defined concepts. They represent questions from larger item pools that are subjected to a factor analysis in order to identity questions associated with specific component concepts. These questions then form a smaller scale, designed specifically to measure the construct desired. Factor loadings also indicate the extent to which a question is salient to the construct being measured.

Social Support.   One of the most heavily studied issues in the field of psychosocial epidemiology has been the impact of social supports on health and well-being. Berkman and Syme (1979) examined four sources of social contact: (1) marriage, (2) contacts with close friends and relatives, (3) church membership, and (4) formal and informal group associations. From this information, a Social Network Index was constructed, scoring subjects on a scale from I (fewest social connections) to IV (most connections). In a similar study conducted by House et al. (1982), the measures of social relationships and activities were obtained from self-administered questions in four major categories: (1) intimate social relationships (being married or single, visiting friends and relatives, going on pleasure drives and picnics); (2) formal organizational involvements outside of work (going to church or meetings of voluntary associations); (3) active and relatively social leisure (going to classes or lectures, movies, plays, fairs, museums, etc.); and (4) passive and relatively solitary leisure (watching television, listening to the radio, reading).

Other methods of obtaining data on social support networks have been employed in psychosocial epidemiologic studies. Turner (1981) employed a story identification technique developed by Kaplan (1977) composed of seven vignettes. The Sense of Support Scale developed by Panagis and Adler (cf. Aneshensel & Stone, 1982) consists of a series of Lickert-type items encompassing two types of support: socioemotional support (e.g., thoughtfulness, understanding) and instrumental help (e.g., assistance with work or with problems). Respondents are asked how often during a specified period of time someone has provided them with the listed types of support. Response categories range from 1 ("not at all") to 4 ("very often").

Personality.   Finally, measures have been developed that assess the coping style of an individual to determine its effect on the experience of psychological distress. One such measure, developed by Vaillant (1976) and used in other studies (Andrews et al., 1978) consists of questions designed to measure the maturity of the habitually used coping style. Respondents are presented with two situations with six responses listed for each situation, each situation to be rated as "like" or "not like" me. A coping style score is calculated by giving a score of +1 for each "like me" response on the items characterizing mature ego defense mechanisms and a score of −1 for each "like me" response on the items characterizing immature defenses, and then summing these scores (Andrews et al., 1978, p. 309).

Other measures have been developed that examine specific components of ego strength. Pearlin and Schooler (1978), for example, examined three personality characteristics used by individuals to help them cope with threats posed by events and objects in their environment: self-esteem, self-denigration, and mastery. Data on these variables were obtained from a series of questions on an interview schedule administered to their subjects. Responses to the questions were factor analyzed and scored to provide a measure of psychological coping resources. Kobasa et al. (1981) employed six different scales to measure the degree of "hardiness" in subjects: the alienation from self and alienation from work scales of the Alienation Test (Maddi et al., 1979); a security scale of the California Life Goals Evaluation Schedule (Hahn, 1966); a cognitive structure scale of the Personality Research Form (Jackson, 1974); the external locus of control scale (Rotter et al., 1962), and the powerlessness scale of the Alienation Test (Maddi et al., 1979).

Limitations of Data

Among the major tasks involved in a psychosocial epidemiologic study are the recognition and handling of the limitations of the data. Validity and reliability of analyses can be compromised by the nature of the disease or stress episodes themselves, the methods used to obtain the data, the spurious relationships resulting from false or defective data, and the indirect associations resulting from undetected confounding variables. This section will examine these problems and suggest methods for handling them. Methods for handling possible spurious relationships and indirect associations will also be discussed in the section on data analysis.

Problems of Definition. Many of the data limitations in psychosocial studies are associated with the nature and definition of mental illness, the sources of data, the measures of stress and life events, and the operationalization of independent variables. Perhaps the most basic problem with the data on disease episodes used in psychosocial studies is the lack of a precise definition of the disorder itself. This is a common problem in psychiatric epidemiology where changes in diagnostic policy and nomenclature can result in alteration of rates for various mental disorders. Dohrenwend and Dohrenwend (1982), for example, point to changes in nomenclature as being partially responsible for the increase in the rates of psychiatric disorders since World War II. Cross-cultural epidemiologic studies are especially subject to this limitation because the episodes can vary in content even thought the form of psychiatric disorders is essentially constant throughout the world (Kiev, 1972).

This problem is not limited to psychiatric disorders, however. Comparisons of studies of hypertension, for example, are often hindered by the fact that different criteria are employed in defining a "case" of hypertension. As McQueen and Celentano (1982) note, some studies have used blood pressure levels of 140/90 mm Hg as their cutting point for defining hypertension, whereas other studies have used levels as high as 160/95 mm Hg. Alcoholism is similarly beset with problems of definition. Differences can exist when frequency of drinking (number of drinks per unit of time) is used as a criterion for case definition and when amount consumed (measured in terms of amount purchased, blood alcohol levels, and so on) is used. The inconsistencies of these definitions lead to underenumeration or overenumeration of the disease episodes.

Inconsistency of case definition is due to other factors as well. Different diagnoses for similar phenomena may result because of the subjective nature of the diagnostic process for some disorders. Adebimpe (1981), for instance, notes four possible sources of misdiagnosis in clinical examinations of black patients: the social and cultural distance between patient and clinician, stereotypes of black psychopathology, false-positive symptoms, and biased diagnostic instruments. A similar problem of misdiagnosis emerges with respect to social class. Mischler and Scotch (1963) point to evidence suggesting that lower-class patients are often given diagnoses for more severe illnesses than their middle-class counterparts, even though the symptoms are similar. Hospitals and clinics catering to middle- and upper-class patients may also underdiagnose particular disorders, such as schizophrenia, because of the social stigma involved. Even when patient and clinician come from similar cultural or social backgrounds, the subjective nature of data collected by clinical impression can be a constant source of error.

To minimize the problems associated with episode definition, therefore, we need separate perspectives. The first perspective is that of the investigator. Agreement among investigators as to what constitutes a *case* of a particular disease should be sought. The definition of a case should have two specifications (Schlesselman, 1982): the establishment of objective criteria for the diagnosis of the study disease and a statement of eligibility criteria for the selection of individuals to participate in the study. The second perspective is that of the subjects. Objective and subjective criteria as to case definition may differ because of differences in perception and evaluation of symptoms (Kleinman et al., 1978). Hence, explanations for symptom occurrence and an account of its subjective significance should be obtained from study subjects.

It is suggested that, whenever possible, multimethod strategies of case identification and diagnosis be employed in psychosocial studies. Dohrenwend and Dohrenwend (1982) outline how such a procedure would work:

> For example, a self-report interview like the Psychiatric Epidemiology Research Interview (PERI), based on a psychometric approach to measuring dimensions of psychopathology, could be used economically to screen samples from the general population. Such screening would yield subsamples of individuals with various types of severe symptomatology. Individuals screened by high scores on the screening scales could then be followed up in a second stage of the research and interviewed by experienced clinicians with diagnostic instruments like the Schedule for Affective Disorder and Schizophrenia (SADS) or the Present State Examination (PSE) to provide rates for particular types of disorders. Such a two-stage procedure could capitalize on the ability of a psychometric instrument to provide reliable measurement over the full range of important dimensions of symptoms of psychopathology and on the abilities of a clinical examination to provide reliable diagnoses of individuals in groups where the types of symptomatology involved are not rare (pp. 1275–1276).

Moreover, these combinations of screening scales and clinical exams help establish validity of data.

Source of Data.   Another set of limitations of data on disease episodes is associated with the source of information. The number of cases of disease episodes are usually taken from records of hospital admissions and diagnostic instruments. The use of these instruments in general epidemiologic studies is hindered by the fact that they have been developed on psychiatric patients or specific groups that cannot be regarded as typical of the general population. The methodological "net" used to detect cases of psychiatic disorder, therefore, may be too fine, detecting only a certain type of case under investigation.

Second, the use of records of hospital admissions will bias the number of cases in several respects. With respect to psychiatric disorders in particular, individuals recorded as hospital admissions may not be representative of those who have experienced the disease episode under investigation. For example, Mischler and Scotch (1963) note that hospital admissions for schizophrenia are representative only of those cases that do not recover quickly. Use of these admissions, therefore, would produce distorted rates of both incidence and prevalence. Hospital admissions for other severe psychiatric disorders represent only those cases that are treated by clinicians. According to Fried (1969), ambiguities are built into the total situation in which the individual comes to psychiatric notice and is diagnosed. A common assumption is that severe disorders will come to the attention of clinicians and will inevitably be hospitalized. Unfortunately, this view is based on several unproven assumptions, including the views that psychoses are persistent and that community tolerance operates only within a narrow range, forcing the patient to seek treatment within the modern health care system.

The problem of using only treated cases in calculating rates of disease episodes pertains for all types of disease. An estimated 70 to 90 percent of all self-recognized episodes of sickness in general are believed to be managed outside the formal health care sector, usually employing popular or "folk" health care practices (Kleinman et al., 1978). These disease episodes go unrecorded, resulting in rates that are underenumerated.

Whatever the nature of the disease episode, however, comparison among exposed and nonexposed groups or cases and controls is difficult because of differences in numbers, types, and availability of services. Knowledge of, preference for, and access to health care and medical facilities are known to vary by age, sex, ethnic group, and socioeconomic status. Individuals with certain disorders may prefer not to seek professional medical care while others are restricted in the care available by virtue of lack of sufficient financial resources or distance from medical facilities. Thus, comparison of morbidity rates among different social groups may bias findings, particularly when the data are derived from a narrow range of sources such as state hospitals. Mischler and Scotch (1963) note that the use of state hospital admissions as the sole source of data for computing morbidity rates in different social groups might bias findings because other treatment resources such as private hospitals, clinics, and outpatient facilities are used disproportionately by different social groups. Morbidity rates based on state hospital admissions would reflect only those patients unable to use other health care resources, and hence, would be incomplete, overrepresenting certain social groups and underrepresenting others. This is particularly true for groups distinguished on the basis of socioeconomic status. Individuals in the higher-class groups are relatively more likely to have had their illness detected early, and, if hospitalized, to have been released after a short period of treatment. A higher proportion of their admissions would then be readmissions. This factor would also tend to reduce the apparent incidence in higher-class groups, since incidence rates are based on first admissions.

Because assessment of health risks are often obtained by using hospital admissions, a spurious association could be obtained between various diseases and such psychosocial factors as psychological coping resources, socioeconomic status, race, and ethnicity if the groups under study do not share the same probability of hospital admission with or without the disease (Berkson, 1946). This spurious association, also known as "Berksonian bias," has been demonstrated to exist for the numerous characteristics such as those listed earlier. Berksonian bias can indicate an association between a characteristic and morbidity where none exists, or it can have the reverse effect in that differences in hospital admission rates may conceal an association between the characteristic and a specific disease in a study, even though one actually exists.

Finally, the level of record-keeping efficiency varies from hospital to hospital, producing statistics that do not accurately reflect the prevalence or incidence of disease in a particular hospital or in a particular community.

Bias in the counting of disease episodes can come from the researcher as well as from the source. Nonclinical observations of disease episodes in the general population are subject to potential bias resulting from knowledge of the hypothesis or hypotheses being tested. According to McQueen and Seigrist (1982), this is particularly true in cases that are considered to be only slightly deviant, as in studies of alcohol use. An investigator eager to find a relationship between alcohol abuse and suicide, for example, may be biased in his perception of problem drinking and find instances of alcohol abuse more frequently among cases than among controls, even though the degree of drinking is similar in both groups. Such bias can be reduced, however, by utilizing two or more individuals to evaluate characteristics such as problem drinking, personality variables or measures of psychological distress. Quantitative techniques such as a Pearson product-moment correlation can then be employed to assess the degree of reliability in the judgments of the investigators/raters.

Measures of Stress.   As described previously, there are four general types of measures used in studies of stress: self-report, performance, psychophysiological and biochemical indicators. Each of these types possess a particular range of limitations. The type of measurement most frequently criticized in the literature is the self-report. The most common problem associated with self-report measures of stress is that of response bias. Some populations will say yes or no to questions regardless of content (Kennedy, 1973; Dohrenwend & Dohrenwend, 1969). "Certain types of bias seem particularly likely to occur when psychiatric symptoms form the subject of the interview because such symptoms are by definition subjective and because psychiatric conditions, particularly if they result in institutionalization, still carry a social stigma" (Vernon et al., 1982, p. 483). This problem occurs, for example, when collecting data on alcohol intake, where, as Celentano and McQueen (1978) note, survey respondents will generally underreport their consumption. In other instances, responses tend to be overdetermined. A positive response to specific questions in the measurement of personality in general and psychopathology in particular can be given by different individuals for different reasons, some of which have less to do with the presence of the characteristic being measured than with extraneous factors such as differences in how the individuals understand the meaning of words such as *depressed* or *anxious* (Dohrenwend & Dohrenwend, 1982). As a result, self-report scales may have the effect of measuring different things for different groups. The Center for Epidemiologic Studies—Depression (CES-D) scale, for instance, has been shown to produce different responses in men and women, leading to the conclusion that the scale may not be measuring the same phenomenon among the two groups (Clark et al., 1981). Response tendencies have also been shown to vary systematically across factors such as age, gender, ethnicity, and socioeconomic status. If the objective of a scale is to compare subgroups in order to study etiologic factors, it must be constructed so as to measure this phenomenon similarly in all groups (Vernon & Roberts, 1982).

Response bias can result from several additional factors. One is the differential ability of individuals to evaluate their own symptoms. Many measures tap conscious experience, but it is the experience of illness and not disease; and "illness is shaped by cultural factors governing perception, labeling, explanation, and valuation of the discomforting experience" (Kleinman et al., 1978, p. 252). Self-reports of seemingly obvious indications of changes in physiological or behavioral states will be subject to considerable individual and cultural variation.

Another factor contributing to response bias is the problem of selective recall. Monroe (1982) found that as much as 60 percent of life events recalled by subjects in a retrospective procedure may be underreported for even the most recent 4-month retrospective period. Additionally, particular types of events (desirable events) may be relatively more susceptible to such reporting distortion.

An additional factor contributing to response bias is the mediation of self-reports by the coping style of the individual. Use of particular psychological defense mechanisms in an effort to cope with stress such as denial or repression can result in distorted answers to questionnaires (Baum et al., 1982).

Two separate options are available to minimize the problem of overdetermined responses to interview questions. The first, advocated by Wing et al. (1974) is to employ cross-examination in the clinical interview. A second option, advocated by Dohrenwend and Dohrenwend (1982), is to sum conceptually related items to form scale scores. Consistency among the responses of a series of questions would indicate the scale's reliability in measuring stress or illness despite the error in responses to any particular question. Mathematical procedures such as Cronbach's alpha or Spearman's r can be used to estimate the degree of internal consistency reliability achieved with such a scale. A scale may be viewed as "reliable" in a subsample if it has a value of Cronbach's alpha of 0.50 or better.

Performance measures, a second method for assessing stress, are limited in three respects. First, there is the difficulty in differentiating between stressed and nonstressed subjects. Both groups may exhibit similar responses for entirely different reasons. Second, the stress observed is context-specific, limiting the range of conclusions that may be drawn. The artificial nature of the stressful context must, therefore, be taken into account when attempting to generalize results to the wider population. Third, the gross nature of the indices leaves open questions as to the precise nature of the mechanisms involved. Stress-induced behavioral changes reflect coping activity (Lazarus, 1966) and are strongly influenced by the context in which stress occurs and the individual's previous experience, value system, personality, and knowledge (Brown, 1981).

Physiological measures of stress are usually regarded as being highly reliable. They, depend, however, on the accuracy of the equipment and skill of the investigator in using the equipment. In certain situations, as in the event of a naturally occurring stressor involving trauma or severe loss, use of such instruments may be impractical, creating additional stress for the subject. Even in less severe circumstances, blood pressure, heart rate, and muscle tension can all the affected by factors other than general stress conditions (e.g., activity, altitude, diet, genetic factors, smoking) that need to be controlled.

Biochemical measures are usually regarded as being the most reliable indicator of stress and the easiest to obtain. Yet, even these measures are limited in certain aspects. Interpretation of corticosteroid and catecholamine levels is not always straightforward (Baum et al., 1982). For instance, in using 17-OCHS levels as a measure of adrenal cortical response to stress, one must always take into account large individual differences in coping styles and exposure to certain stressors (e.g., Mason, 1975).

A similar problem occurs with respect to the use of catecholamine levels as indices of stress. Increases in catecholamine levels are not necessarily related to stress but may be caused by the ingestion of coffee, tobacco, or alcohol (Henry, 1982). Catecholamine levels can very depending on the type of sample drawn. Plasma samples, for example, are more problematic than urine samples because fluctuations in plasma catecholamine levels are rapid and extremely sensitive to movement. On the other hand, epinephrine and norepinephrine excretion in urine samples display a circadian pattern, and hence, levels will depend upon the time of day during which the sample is drawn. (Baum et al., 1982).

Thus, although biochemical marks of stress have certain advantages over self-report scales and performance measures, they should be used in conjunction with psychological protocols. It is relatively easy to gather the required samples for bioassay (e.g., urine) and, combined with self-report measures, these would provide a better understanding of stress response.

Operationalizing Independent Variables.   The fourth set of limitations to the data in psychosocial studies concerns the problems involved in operationalizing independent and intervening variables. These problems are conceptual as well as methodological in nature. Life events are particularly representative of these problems. One concern in the measurement of life events and their use as predictors or indices of stress has been the issue of quality versus the quantity of stressful events. Life events have been the focus of considerable debate regarding the relative importance of the number of events versus the type of events. The Holmes-Rahe scale is based on the notion that change itself, whether positively or negatively valued, is the critical factor in the development of stress, whereas other studies (e.g., Brown & Birley, 1968; Johnson & Sarason, 1978) have placed greater emphasis on the quality of events. The available evidence appears to suggest that change rather than undesirability is the characteristic of life events that should be measured for the more accurate assessment of their stressfulness (Dohrenwend, 1973; Selye, 1956). However, this evidence itself is potentially constrained by the scales designed to test the hypothesis. Other evidence, relying on qualitative data (Kleinman, 1980), lead to the opposite conclusion. Although there may be no resolution to this debate (when using existing scales and techniques), we should keep in mind the theoretical foundation on which any particular scale was developed.

A second problem in the use of life events has been weak correlations between events and other measures of stress. In studies of depression, for instance, correlation coefficients obtained between life events and depression range between .09 and .30, indicating that life events account for only 1 to 9 percent of the variance in depressive disorders. Such figures clearly appear to cast doubt on the predictive significance of specific life events in depression (Hirschfeld & Cross 1982, p. 42). Similar weak correlations have been reported in prospective studies of life events and other symptoms of stress (e.g., Grant et al., 1982; Myers et al., 1971).

A third major problem in the use of life event scales is the difficulty of establishing a causal sequence. According to Susser (1981), some scales combine events, many of which do not occur prior to the manifestations under study. From any one such event, like divorce, the task of separating a stress reaction to an event from self and social selection for exposure to that event has proved difficult. A divorce, rather than precipitating the onset of disease, may itself be the indirect product of that disease as individuals become divorced and remain unmarried because they are ill. Cases may be predisposed to certain events and if such a predisposition is viewed as a latent manifestation of the dependent variable and left uncontrolled, it is not amenable to firm causal inference.

In addressing these problems, at a mininum, the investigor should ascertain two aspects of life events. First, the meaning of the event should be provided by the subject and not a priori by the investigator. Second, the context in which an event occurs should be provided. This includes the social support network of the subject, preceding and succeeding events, financial resources, social status, and so on.

Another independent variable possessing certain limitations is that of social status. Frequently, simplicity and lack of uniformity in the operationalization of status tends to confound the relationships between status and disease episodes as well as make comparison difficult, if not impossible, between studies relying upon different definitions of status. "Many epidemiologic studies treat social variables as if they were biological variables and simplify them to the point where their meaning is questionable" (McQueen & Siegrist, 1982, p. 353). The operationalization of social class or socioeconomic status (SES) is a significant problem in psychosocial studies. As noted previously, certain studies rely upon two indices, usually education and income, as measures of socioeconomic status. Other studies rely upon single indices such as census tract or occupation. As Kessler (1982) noted in his study of indices of SES, each index has a particular effect on stress, independently influencing emotional functioning. Furthermore, these indicators vary in importance with other social characteristics such as sex and labor force status.

The operationalization of racial and ethnic group categories presents another set of problems that must be dealt with in psychosocial studies. Race and ethnicity are often used interchangeably, but the two are not isomorphic. Different ethnic groups can belong to one racial category; Navaho and Sioux constitute two separate ethnic groups but one racial group. Conversely, the same ethnic group can include individuals belonging to different racial groups, as in the case of black and Caucasian Puerto Ricans. Where possible, ethnic groups are to be preferred when looking at behavioral factors. Use of race such as blacks of nonwhites can mask important differences. A high rate of alcohol abuse among nonwhites in Alaska, for example, might disguise the fact that such abuse is much lower for blacks, Chinese, and Vietnamese in Alaska than it is for Eskimos, Aleuts, and Athapaskans. Because of the variable nature of definitions of ethnic group status, self-designations are to be preferred over the use of other characteristics such as physical features, language, surname, and birthplace.

Social support is another independent variable in psychosocial studies possessing certain limitations. According to Thoits (1982), most studies suffer from inadequate conceptualization and operationalization of social support. The direct effect of life events upon social support is often confounded, either theoretically or operationally, with the interactive (buffering) effect of events with support. As in the case of life events, there is also the problem of evaluating the quantity versus quality of support and the problem of determining whether social support is an independent or a dependent variable.

When attempting to operationalize social support, we need to take into account several considerations. First, amount of support, types of support (e.g., socioemotional and instrumental), and sources of available support (e.g., spouse, friends, kin, coworkers) are all important dimensions, and measures should be employed that tap each of these dimensions. Second, a distinction should be made between measures of social support structure and function. As Thoits (1982) asserts, the structure of the social support network may have a powerful influence on the flow of supportive resources to an individual. The *structural* properties of the social support system relative to the total social support network can be measured by using indicators such as size, density, accessibility, kinship-reliance, frequency of contact, and stability. The *functional* properties of the system can also be operationalized to measure the perceived amount and adequacy of socioemotional and instrumental aid received from various support system members.

DATA ANALYSIS

With each type of research design in psychosocial epidemiology, there are numerous techniques of data analysis that may be employed to control the effects of different variables, test hypotheses, and account for associations between disease or stress episodes and one or more subject characteristics. Some of these techniques, such as the calculation of relative risk, may be utilized in several types of studies, whereas other techniques, such as the use of logistic regression models, are specifically suited to particular research designs. Whatever the research design, however, it is always recommended that data analysis proceed from the simple to the complex. All too often , sophisticated techniques are used when simple ones provide a much clearer picture of the phenomena under investigation. The first step in any study should always be the description of the phenomena under investigation. It is here that rates may be employed. The search for associations is the second step, using methods such as proportions, ratios, and correlation coefficients. Multivariate analyses is the third step and should be employed to control for extraneous variables and assess their role in any causal relationship.

Measures of Association

Relative Risk.   The most common measure of association in epidemiologic studies is "relative risk," which reflects the incidence of disease among a group possessing a characteristic relative to another group not having the characteristic. It is a *ratio of two incidence rates* and indicates the likelihood that a member of a specified population will acquire and/or succumb to a disease if he possesses the characteristic under study. Thus, a study that determines that the relative risk of schizophrenia among black enlisted personnel in the U.S. Navy is 2.5 is stating that the risk for having an episode of schizophrenia (usually a first admission to a hospital and diagnosis) is 2.5 times greater for blacks than for Navy enlisted personnel belonging to other racial groups.

The model for the calculation of relative risk is a 2 × 2 table in which the number of cases and controls are compared with respect to the presence or absence of a particular characteristic (see Table 2.1). The cross products are then multiplied and divided, producing the following equation.

$$RR = \frac{ad}{bc}$$

This equation is known as an *odds ratio* and provides an approximation of relative risk. It assumes that (1) the cases and controls have been selected at random and are representative of the larger population, and (2) the frequency of disease in a population is relatively small. If $RR > 1$, a positive association between the disease and the characteristic is said to exist; if $RR < 1$, there is a negative association; and if $RR = 1$, no association exists. An example of estimating relative risk from an odds ratio in a 2×2 table is found in Table 2.3.

As a rule, relative risk can be exactly determined only from a prospective study. In retrospective and cross-sectional studies, the odds ratio can serve as an approximation of relative risk. If the frequency of disease in a population is large or the approximation of RR proves to be inadequate, that is, in cases where there are multiple categories of groups—different subgroups by age and occupation—under study, a more accurate estimate developed by Mantel and Haenszel (1959) may be employed. The *revised relative risk* is calculated as follows.

$$RR_{MH} = \frac{\Sigma\ ad/N}{\Sigma\ bc/N}$$

In addition, Mantel and Haenszel have calculated summary relative risk equations for separate subcategories of exposure. The rationale for these equations is that "over-all relative risk estimates are averages and as averages may conceal substantial variation in the magnitudes of the relative risk among subgroups" (p. 740). However, a summary estimate may also be obtained by dividing the subcategories of exposure into a series of 2×2 tables if the exposure can be placed on a gradient.

Age-adjustment procedures are also important when calculating relative risk. One such procedure is to calculate relative risks for each age group in the population and then compare the age-specific risks with the overall crude risk. Table 2.4 provides an example of this procedure.

A second age-adjustment procedure is the *matching case method* in which a

TABLE 2.3.   POINT PREVALENCE RATES OF MAJOR AND MINOR DEPRESSION BY MARITAL STATUS, NEW HAVEN STUDY, 1967–1976

Currently Married	Cases	Controls	Total
No	14	122	136
Yes	21	354	375

$$RR = \frac{14 \times 354}{21 \times 122} = 1.9$$

Source: Weissman and Myers, 1978. Copyright 1978, American Medical Association.

TABLE 2.4.   AGE- AND SEX-SPECIFIC MORTALITY RATES AND RELATIVE RISKS FOR MEN AND WOMEN AGED 30 TO 69 YEARS, ALAMEDA COUNTY, CA, 1965–1974

Age	Number of Respondents		Number of Deaths		Death Rate[a]		Relative Risk
	Men	*Women*	*Men*	*Women*	*Men*	*Women*	*Men*
30–39	673	728	16	16	2.4	2.2	1.1
40–49	729	807	36	32	4.9	4.0	1.2
50–59	501	574	68	45	13.6	7.8	1.7
60–69	326	387	91	67	27.9	17.3	1.6
Total	2229	2496	211	160	9.5	6.4	1.5[b]

Source: Berkman and Syme, 1979. Copyright 1979, American Journal of Epidemiology.
[a]Percent died or deaths per 100 population.
[b]$p \leq 0.001$.

sample of N diseased individuals is drawn and the characteristics of each individual noted with respect to the control factors. Subsequently, a sample is taken of N individuals without the disease, with each individual matched on the control factors to one of the diseased individuals. In applying such a procedure, we find that the 2×2 table takes on a different form from that shown in Table 2.1. The cell in Table 2.5 in the upper left-hand corner contains r number of pairs in which both cases and controls possess the characteristic of interest. The marginal totals (a, b, c, d) represent the entries in the cells in Table 2.1 and the total for the entire table is $\frac{1}{2}N$ pairs, where N represents the total number of paired individuals. The calculation of the relative risk for this table would be

$$RR = \frac{s}{t} \quad \text{(provided } t \neq 0)$$

A test of whether or not the observed difference between ad and bc is due to sampling variation is provided by a chi-square test for 2×2 tables. Mantel and Haenszel have developed a chi-square formula specifically for testing the significance of a relative risk association. When testing for significance in a matched pairs example such as in Table 2.5 the McNemar test is employed, where

$$\chi^2 = \frac{(\,|\,t - s\,| - 1)}{t + s} \quad \text{with 1 df}$$

In establishing confidence limits for the test of significance, we compute confidence limits of the logarithm (to the base e) of a corrected relative risk,

TABLE 2.5.   MODEL OF CALCULATION OF RELATIVE RISK
FOR MATCHED CASES CONTROLS WITH AND WITHOUT
CHARACTERISTIC

| | Controls | | |
	With Characteristic	Without Characteristic	Total
Cases			
With Characteristic	r	s	a^a
Without Characteristic	t	u	c^a
Total	b^a	d^a	

[a] a, b, c, and d are the entries in the cells of Table 2.1.
Source: Lilienfeld & Lilienfeld, 1980. Copyright 1980, Oxford University
Press.

and then reconvert the logarithmic confidence levels to the original scale.
The addition of 0.5 to the numbers a, b, c, and d corrects for a bias that
can occur with small numbers of observations. Using the *log relative risk*
rather than the relative risk itself simplifies calculations of standard errors
necessary for computing confidence intervals.

Chi-square Tests.   The chi square has two basic uses in psychosocial
epidemiologic research: testing the null hypothesis and determining the
significance level of an association. One of the most basic methods of
assessing risk is to compare the observed rates for a specific sample, with the
expected rates based on the total population. Take, for instance, the annual
incidence rates for hypertension among air traffic controllers and second
class airmen as reported by Cobb and Rose (1973); see Table 2.6.

Here the expected rates are calculated on the basis of multiplying age-
specific rates for second class airmen by the relevant air traffic controller
population and summing across age groups. Statistical significance can then
be examined by the chi-square test, assuming that the expected values
represent population estimates (Cobb & Rose, 1973). Using the standard
chi-square formula for observed and expected frequencies, we find that the
calculation would be as follows.

$$\chi^2 = \frac{(O - E)^2}{E} = \frac{(28.0 - 5.1)}{5.6} = 103.0$$

A common fallacy in employing the chi-square test is to use the chi-square
value itself as a measure of the degree or strength of an association between
a disease episode and a particular characteristic. Even though chi square is

TABLE 2.6.   ANNUAL INCIDENCE RATES
PER 1000 MEN FOR HYPERTENSION

Age Group Year	Air Traffic Controllers	Second Class Airmen
20–24	—	—
25–29	2	1
30–34	2	1
35–39	10	1
40–44	6	—
45–49	11	4
50+	15	4

		Age	
		<40	40+
Observed (O)	28.0	16.0	12.0
Expected (E)	5.1	2.4	2.7
O/E	5.6	6.6	4.4

$\chi^2 = 103.0$ $p < .0001$

Source: Cobb and Rose, 1973. Copyright 1973,
American Medical Association.

excellent as a measure of the significance of an association, it does not indicate the degree or strength of association because it is a function of both the properties of the various cells and the total number of subjects studied. The chi square may indicate, for example, that a relative risk of 1.25 is highly significant in a study involving 2 million subjects but insignificant in a study of 2000 subjects. The degree of association present is really only a function of the cell proportion, which explains why relative risk and odds ratios are used as measures of the strength of association.

Correlation Coefficients.   There are, however, measures based on the chi-square test that provide a measure of the degree of association between an illness and a specific characteristic. One such measure is the phi coefficient. The phi coefficient of ϕ gives a numerical value, ranging from 0 to +1 for a relationship between two variables. It is calculated by using the following formula.

$$\phi = \frac{(ad - bc)}{\sqrt{(a + b)(a + c)(b + c)(b + d)}} = \frac{(ad - bc)}{\sqrt{N_1 N_2 M_1 M_2}} = \sqrt{\frac{\chi^2}{N}}$$

The phi coefficient is similar to a Pearson product-moment correlation coefficient, where the covariance (C_{xy}) of the characteristic or exposure (x)

and the disease *(y)* is divided by the square root of the product of two variances (V_x and V_y). This equation takes the form

$$r = \frac{C_{xy}}{\sqrt{V_x V_y}}$$

Both the phi coefficient and the product-moment correlation coefficient reflect the extent to which each variable is able to predict the other. ϕ^2 is the proportion of the variance in each variable explained by the other (Morgenstern, 1982).

Another measure is Pearson's contingency coefficient, where

$$c = \sqrt{\frac{\chi^2}{\chi^2 + N}}$$

Lifetime Risk.   Lifetime risk is a concept developed by Thompson and Weissman (1981) for use in cohort psychiatric epidemiologic studies. It refers to the risk for onset of a particular disorder between birth and some particular age *t*. When a single birth cohort followed from birth to age t is considered, lifetime risk to age *t* (LTR*t*) is the proportion of the cohort that would have had onset of a particular disorder by age *t* if all members of the cohort lived to age *t* or to onset of the disorder, whichever occurred first. Expressed formally, LTR*t* is measured in terms of *f(x)* which is the rate at which onset of the disorder occurs among living unaffected individuals at exactly age *x*. This can be expressed in the equation

$$f(x) = \lim_{\Delta x \to 0} \left[\frac{\Pr\{\text{onset of the disorder between } x \text{ and } x + \Delta x, \text{ given that the person is living and unaffected at age } x\}}{\Delta x} \right]$$

Thompson and Weissman also provide two alternative measures of risk for onset of a disorder between ages 0 and *t*. One is the proportion of survivors affected at age *t* (PSA*t*), referred to as "lifetime prevalence." It denotes the proportion of a cohort that, as of age *t*, has ever had the disorder. The second alternative measure is the proportion of the cohort that is affected as of age *t* (PCA*t*), based on all members of the cohort, regardless of whether they are still alive at age *t*.

Attributable Risk.   Attributable risk is frequently used in epidemiology and measures the maximum proportion of a disease attributable to a specific characteristic or etiologic factor. The measure was initially defined in terms of lung cancer and smoking as the maximum proportion of lung cancer attributable to cigarette smoking in a specified population (Levin, 1953). It is expressed as

$$AR = \frac{b(RR - 1)}{b(RR - 1) + 1}$$

where *RR* equals the relative risk of lung cancer among cigarette smokers as compared to nonsmokers, and *b* equals the proportion of the total population classified as cigarette smokers. This equation is also known as the *etiologic fraction* when expressed as a percentage. The equation reflects two sets of comparisons: (1) smokers and nonsmokers and (2) lung cancer attributed to cigarette smoking and lung cancer related to other causes. Since only a proportion of the total population is being examined, $RR - 1$ is employed in the calculation of attributable risk.

Table 2.7 shows the attributable risk, as a function of relative risk *(RR)* of different exposures or characteristics and the proportion of exposed individuals *(b)* in the target population. This table indicates the proportion of cases of a disease that are attributable to a specific characteristic (or exposure) and that would be eliminated if the characteristic or exposure were removed. The actual number of cases of disease eliminated would depend on the size of the population and the incidence rate of the disease (Schlesselman, 1982, p. 44). For example, if 50 percent of a population were exposed to a particular characteristic that increased the risk of disease only fivefold, $b = 0.5$ and

TABLE 2.7.   ATTRIBUTABLE RISKS AS A PROPORTION OF THE RELATIVE RISK *(RR)* AND THE POPULATION EXPOSED *(b)*

Proportion of Population with Characteristic or Exposed	Relative Risk[a]				
	1.5	2	4	5	10
.01	.005	.01	.02	.04	.08
.05	.02	.05	.13	.17	.31
.10	.05	.09	.23	.29	.47
.25	.11	.20	.43	.50	.69
.50	.20	.33	.60	.67	.82
.75	.27	.43	.69	.75	.87
.90	.31	.47	.73	.78	.89
.95	.32	.49	.74	.79	.90

[a]When multiplied by 100, these figures become etiologic fractions.

$RR = 5$, then 67 percent of the cases would be expected to be eliminated upon removal of the factor.

Prospective Methods and Risk Assessment

As noted earlier, prospective or cohort designs are preferred in epidemiology because they are less subject to problems of response bias and data collection and provide a true measure of relative risk of exposure to various characteristics or events. Typically, such studies begin with the selection of a cohort and following the cohort from time t_0 to the end of the study period t_n. However, not all members of the cohort participate or can be observed for the same length of time. In a study of mortality, members of the cohort may die before the end of the follow-up period. In any prospective study, cohort members may drop out or decide to withdraw from participation for any number of reasons that may or may not be related to the study itself. Similarly, individuals may enter the study and join the cohort at some time after the study begins and be observed until the end of the follow-up period. In both cases, these individuals may be observed for part but not all of the follow-up. A rate of disease or stress episode analysis based solely on those individuals observed throughout the entire follow-up period would be an accurate reflection of the risk for only a particular segment of that cohort rather than for the entire cohort. The rate, therefore, would be biased by variations in the ability and willingness of cohort members to participate throughout the entire follow-up period.

In order to provide an accurate assessment of risk for the entire cohort in a prospective study, several procedures are available. As previously discussed, person-years rather than the number of individuals was used to calculate incidence rates. Another technique commonly employed in prospective studies is the use of a *life table* to compute the rate of morbidity or mortality across a specified number of time intervals throughout the follow-up period. Both these techniques ensure that the information provided by cohort members who do not participate during the entire follow-up period is used in the assessment of risk for particular disease or stress episodes.

Life tables are also of use in estimating the probability of surviving a particular disease episode, such as a heart attack or diagnosis of cancer. This is often known as a *survival rate*. This calculation must regard time as a potential extraneous variable. Adjustment for time can be effected through estimations of survival and based on the life table or maximum likelihood estimates or through time-series techniques, such as Fourier analysis. As we discuss next, these methods are particularly useful in psychosocial epidemiologic studies of life events and stress.

Life Tables.   The life table is an important methodological device used in the calculation and adjustment of rates. Life tables are usually employed in studies of mortality as well as in morbidity and stress episode studies. The life table organizes data on disease or stress episodes, provides direct estimates of the probability of developing or dying from a disease for a given time period, and allows for relative risks to be computed as the ratio of these probabilities.

There are three types of life tables: current, cohort, and follow-up. The current life table uses mortality rates observed at a given time, such as a census year. The cohort life table follows a population born in the same year over time, applying mortality rates appropriate to that cohort at each age interval. The follow-up table is used to determine rates of survival during periods of observation when individuals may withdraw from the study, either because of death, change of residence, or lack of willingness to participate. Construction of a life table for a specific follow-up period does not require that the entire cohort be observed for that entire period. The table includes information on those who withdraw before the termination of a study as well as on those who enter at some point after the initiation of the study. In both instances, the information can be used in the calculation of rates.

Table 2.8 provides a sample of a follow-up life table. This table organizes the observations of mortality from cancer of the kidney conducted by Cutler and Ederer (1958) between 1946 and 1951. Of the 126 patients for whom information was recorded, only 9 where present at the beginning of the study. Nevertheless, the table incorporates the experience of all patients for varying lengths of time.

> *Column 1:* Interval (x to $x + 1$).   This column gives the time elapsed from the date of diagnosis in intervals of 1 year. For example, a patient who was diagnosed January 20, 1946 and died October 5, 1948, died during the third year after diagnosis or in interval 2−3.
>
> *Column 2:* Interval midpoint ($x/2$). This figure is of use when calculating the average strength of the population for the interval.
>
> *Column 3:* Interval width (h). Occasionally, life tables include intervals that differ in length of time. Interval width is important for standardizing survival rates that will be evident when we discuss them subsequently.
>
> *Column 4:* Alive at beginning of interval (1_x). The first line in this column represents the number of patients in the cohort.
>
> *Column 5:* Number of terminal events (d_x). The number who died during the interval.
>
> *Column 6:* Lost to follow-up during interval (u_x). This column includes patients whose survival status as of the end of the study was unknown. The length of observation for each patient lost to follow-up is the time elapsed between the date of entry and the date last known to be alive. It is assumed that subsequent to the date of last contact, the survival experience of lost cases is similar to that of cases continuing to be observed.

TABLE 2.8.   FOLLOW-UP LIFE TABLE AND CALCULATIONS OF SURVIVAL FUNCTIONS
DIAGNOSED 1946–1951 AND FOLLOWED UP)

(1) Interval (Years After Diagnosis) x to $x + 1$	(2) Interval Midpoint m_x	(3) Interval Width h_x	(4) Number Observed at Beginning of Interval (Number Alive) 1_x	(5) Number of Events (Died During Interval) d_x	(6) Lost to Follow-up During Interval u_x	(7) Withdrawn Alive During Interval w_x
0–1	.5	1	126	47	4	15
1–2	1.5	1	60	5	6	11
2–3	2.5	1	38	2	—	15
3–4	3.5	1	21	2	2	7
4–5	4.5	1	10	—	—	6
5–6	5.5	1	4	—	—	4

Source: Cutler and Ederer, 1958. Copyright 1958, Permagon Press, Inc.

Column 7: Withdrawn alive during interval (w_x). This includes the number of patients known to have been alive at the close of the study.

Column 8: Number exposed to risk of dying $(1_x')$. This column represents the number of individuals exposed to risk in the interval, computed as the number entering the interval minus ½ of those withdrawn.

$$1_x' = 1_x - \frac{(u_x + w_x)}{2}$$

Column 9: Proportion dying during the interval (q_x). This is also referred to as the probability of dying during the interval.

$$q_x = \frac{d_x}{1_x'}$$

This figure can be expressed as a percentage if multiplied by 100. In a study of mortality, this is known as the death rate, whereas in a study of morbidity, it could be viewed as an incidence rate. By comparing these rates for each interval between two or more groups, we may obtain an assessment of relative risk.

Column 10: Proportion surviving the interval (p_x). This can be referred to as the probability of surviving the interval or the survival rate. It is

(126 MALE CONNECTICUT RESIDENTS WITH LOCALIZED KIDNEY CANCER

(8) Number Exposed to Risk of Event lx'	(9) Proportion Dying (Incidence or Mortality Rate) q_x	(10) Proportion Surviving (Probability of Event not Occurring) p_x	(11) Cumulative Proportion Surviving Through End of Interval P_x	(12) Probability Density Function $f(x)$	(13) Hazard Function λ_x
116.5	.40	.60	.60	.24	.50
51.5	.10	.90	.54	.05	.10
30.5	.07	.93	.50	.03	.07
16.5	.12	.88	.44	.05	.13
7.0	.00	1.00	.44	—	.00
—	—				

obtained by subtracting the proportion dying during the interval from unity.

$$p_x = 1 - q_x$$

This proportion may also be expressed as a percentage by multiplying by 100.

Survival Analysis.   Survival analysis estimates the time interval between two events, a starting event and a terminal event. It is most commonly used to characterize the survival time of patients with severe illnesses and to study the effects of different treatments on the survival rate of such patients. In this case, the starting event would be either the time of diagnosis of disease or entry into the study if the two events differ. The terminal event would be either the patient's death or the end of the follow-up period. Groups of patients can then be compared on the basis of one or more characteristics or treatment regimens to determine if their survival rates, measured on a curve, differ significantly.

Survival analysis, along with life tables, have already been used in psychosocial studies with great success, and they have the potential for being utilized in research on stressful life events. The methods can be applied to most areas of research where starting and terminal events may be defined and where the interval of time between these events is of interest. In a prospective study of life events and stress, therefore, the life event under investigation, say, loss of job or divorce, may be taken as the starting event and the resulting stress in a cohort, defined in terms of hospitalization, death, or a specific psychological or biochemical measure, may be taken as the terminal event.

There are several methods available for estimating survival in a population. The two most common procedures are based on the life table and a maximum likelihood estimate. From the preceding life table model, a number of functions characterizing the distribution of survival times in a cohort can be estimated. Three of the most common ones are the *survivorship function*, *hazard function*, and *probability density function*.

The survivorship function F(t), also known as the *cumulative survival rate*, represents the probability of all cases surviving to the end of each interval. The hazard function is the probability per unit of time that an individual who has survived to the beginning of an interval will die in that interval. The hazard function is the same as an age-specific death rate. The probability density function is the probability per unit time of dying within a given interval.

To demonstrate how these functions are derived from a life table, let us return to the data contained in Table 2.8. Columns 11, 12, and 13 contain the estimates of the survivorship function, probability density function, and hazard function, respectively.

Column 11 represents the cumulative proportion of individuals surviving from diagnosis through the end of the interval (P_x). This cumulative survival rate at the end of each interval is obtained by multiplying the probabilities of survival up through the present interval.

Column 12 contains the estimate of the probability density function $f(x)$. This function is computed as follows.

$$f(x) = \frac{P_x - P_{x+1}}{h_x} = \frac{P_x q_x}{h_x}$$

Column 13 contains the hazard rate (λ) which is computed as the number of deaths or episodes of the disease under investigation in the interval, divided by the average number of survivors (or those not experiencing the episode) at the midpoint of the interval.

$$\lambda_x = \frac{2(1 - p_x)}{h_x(1 + p_x)} = \frac{2q_x}{h_x(1 + p_x)}$$

The rates obtained from these functions can be graphed in the form of curves that can be used to describe the experience of mortality from a particular disease occurring in a population. The life table procedure may also be modified for use in studies of morbidity as well, yielding similar survival rates (e.g., Chan et al., 1982). In either case, these rates can be employed in comparing the morbidity or mortality experience in two or more populations. The procedure has been employed in studies comparing survival rates for prostatic carcinoma by race and socioeconomic status (Dayal & Chiu, 1982) and for myocardial infarction by marital status (Chandra et al., 1983). In the latter study, use of the life table to calculate survival rates among married and unmarried men yielded the data shown in Figure 2.1.

To determine whether these survival curves for married and unmarried men are significantly different, a log rank test is performed. Also known as the Mantel-Haenszel procedure for comparing the survival experience of two or more groups, this test involves a comparison between a group of the observed number of events (deaths or disease episodes) with a group of the expected number of events (Peto et al., 1976). The comparison yields a chi-square statistic that indicates level of significance. One of the advantages of this procedure is that through stratification it allows the comparisons to be adjusted for the distribution of other factors. This becomes particularly important when examining the relations among variables of interest. Thus, in Dayal and Chiu's (1982) study of prostatic cancer, it is possible to compare the survival experience of the two races, adjusting for the distribution of factors like age, stage, histologic grade, and SES, and thereby conclude whether or not a particular factor "explained" the racial difference in prostate cancer survival. Using the life table to calculate survival functions

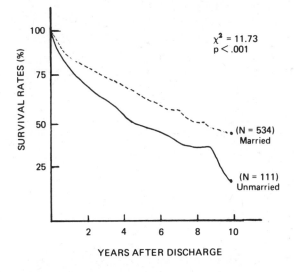

FIGURE 2.1. , Survival rates of male patients with myocardial infarction discharged alive, by marital status, Baltimore SMSA, 1966–1967 and 1971. (From Chandra et al., 1983.)

requires grouping the data and is appropriate only when the sample size is fairly large (Gehan, 1969). A second procedure for estimating survival functions, the maximum likelihood procedure, is appropriate for small or large samples and grouped or ungrouped data. The procedure is explained in detail elsewhere (Kaplan & Meier, 1958).

Fourier Analysis. In a prospective study by Grant et al. (1982), Fourier analysis was used to examine possible associations between life events and psychiatic symptoms. Fourier analysis is a standard statistical technique in which time series are reduced to their sinusoidal (periodic) components. In this study, the time series were symptoms and events measured in 2-month intervals. Through the related statistical technique of spectral analysis, the relative strengths of these components are described as a function of frequency. The study of spectral relationships between two time series has been termed "cross-spectral analysis." The strength of the relationship of the two series at a given frequency is expressed as coherency (of that frequency). The sampling distribution of the squared coherency (which is somewhat analogous to R^2 of the regression analysis) was used to compute attained significance levels (P values) for the coherencies observed in study subjects (Grant et al., 1982, p. 599).

The following graph (Figure 2.2) summarizes the results of a Fourier analysis of life events and psychiatric symptoms for a sample of the study poulation characterized as being coherent and in phase. The solid line represents changes in events, measured by LCU scores, whereas the broken line represents fluctuations in symptoms, measured by Symptom Checklist (SCL) scores. Here the series is coherent at higher frequency ranges (every 4 months) and the coherency squared of this frequency is 0.668, well above a defined criterion level of 0.35. The phase is 0.94, which shows that the two series are almost perfectly synchronized. [A phase of 1.0 or 0.0 at a given frequency indicates that the two series are perfectly synchronized at that frequency. A phase of 0.5 means that one series lags behind the other by half that cycle length (Grant et al., 1982, p. 599).]

Although time-series analysis appears to hold promise as a technique for the organization and analysis of prospective data, it should be pointed out that even in this study, life events and symptoms were "coherent and in-phase" for only one third of the cohort members, leading Grant and his associates to conclude that there was no significant correlation between life events and symptoms of psychiatric distress. However, this may be more a factor of the scale used to measure the variables than the Fourier analysis itself.

Adjustment and Controlling for Confounding Variables

Even though the object of a psychosocial study may be to examine the relationship between a disease or stress episode and one particular character-

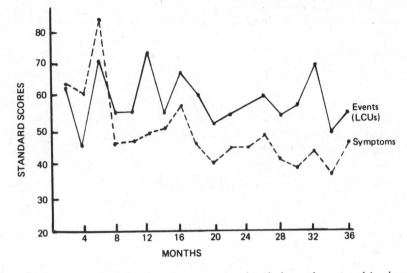

FIGURE 2.2.   Life event and symptoms time series classified as coherent and in-phase by Fourier analysis. (From Grant et al., 1982.)

istic or form of exposure, inevitably there will be other characteristics or types of exposure that need to be accounted for. These extraneous variables potentially confound the association, wholly or partially accounting for the apparent effect of the characteristic or exposure under investigation, or masking an underlying true association. The confounding variable must satisfy both of two conditions: (1) it is a risk factor for the study disease and (2) it is associated with the study exposure but is not a consequence of exposure (Schlesselman, 1982, p. 58). One of the best examples is the confounding effect of cigarette smoking with respect to an association between alcohol consumption and heart disease. Although an apparent association may be detected between alcohol consumption and heart disease, this association exists because many individuals identified as heavy drinkers are also cigarette smokers, and the "real" association is between smoking and heart disease.

Several techniques are available to control for extraneous variables that are potential confounders. In this section, three specific techniques are presented: *specification, age adjustment,* and multivariate methods.

Specification.   The most elementary technique use to control for possible confounding variables is specification. The importance of specification has already been discussed and there is no need for further elaboration. By using specific rates for subgroups of subjects, we may exercise control of extraneous factors (at a rudimentary level) in the assessment of risk. Age and sex, because of their relationships with many forms of disease and stress, are the most common variables for which specific rates are determined. Race is another common variable, although less so than age and sex.

Age Adjustment.   Typically, adjustment procedures are applied in controlling for differences in age between groups because of the high association between age and the risk for particular disease episodes, particularly mortality. These procedures are limited in certain respects. The age-adjusted rate cannot provide an accurate description of a population, for it is only to be used as a summary of age-specific rates. The age-adjusted rates can also hide important differences between groups if the age-specific rates vary in different ways across the age groups selected. For example, a summary comparison of age-adjusted rates for depression among blacks and Caucasians in the United States may disguise the fact that the rates are higher for young blacks (age 15 to 24) than for young Caucasians, but are higher for older Caucasians (age 65 and above) than for older blacks. This difference could be hidden by standardization.

Despite this limitation, the arguments for age adjustment are considerable. Fleiss (1981) provides three major reasons in favor of age adjustment. First, a single summary index for a population is more easily compared with other summary indices than are entire schedules of specific rates. Second, if some age groups are comprised of small numbers of subjects, the age-specific rates for these groups may be too imprecise and unreliable for use in detailed comparisons. Third, for small populations, or for some groups of special interest, specific rates may not exist. Summary statistics allow for the inclusion of these subgroups in the overall assessment of risk in the absence of specific rates.

There are two major methods of age adjustment, *direct* and *indirect*. The direct method involves the application of the age-specific morbidity or mortality rates from the samples being compared to the number in the same age groups of a so-called "standard population." For studies involving groups in the United States, the standard population is usually the population of the United States as determined in a decennial census. This procedure gives the number of episodes that can be expected in the standard population if the age-specific rates from the observed groups have prevailed in the standard population. As an example, take the data on mortality from the Alameda County study found in Table 2.9. By multiplying the mortality rates for males and females with the respective age categories of the total population of the United States in 1970, an estimate of the expected number of deaths in the total population can be obtained. The total number of expected deaths are then divided by the total standard population to obtain the age-adjusted rate. For both males and females, the age-adjusted rate is slightly higher than the crude rate.

The indirect method of age adjustment is more commonly used in epidemiologic studies because of the often small size and lack of specific rates for study populations. It is preferable to the direct method when there are small

TABLE 2.9.   AGE-ADJUSTED DEATH RATES FOR MEN AND WOMEN
OF ALAMEDA COUNTY, CA, 1965–1974, USING THE DIRECT METHOD OF
AGE-ADJUSTMENT

Age	Death Rate (per 100) Men (1)	Death Rate (per 100) Women (2)	Standard Population 1970 U.S. Census Men and Women (3)	Expected Number of Cases Men (1) × (3)	Expected Number of Cases Women (2) × (3)
30–39	2.4	2.2	22,537,287	540,894.9	495,820.3
40–49	4.9	4.0	24,096,893	1,180,747.8	963,875.7
50–59	13.6	7.8	21,077,046	2,866,478.3	1,644,009.6
60–69	27.9	17.3	15,608,409	4,354,746.1	2,700,254.8
Total death rate (crude)	9.5	6.4			
Total population			83,319,635		
Total expected number of deaths				8,942,867.1	5,803,960.4
Age-adjusted death rate (per 100)				10.7	7.0

Source: Age-specific rates derived from Berkman and Syme, 1979.

numbers in particular age groups. "Rates used in direct adjustment would be based on these small numbers and would thus be subject to substantial sampling variation. With indirect adjustment, the rates are more stable since they are based on a large standard population" (Friedman, 1980, p. 183).

To apply the indirect method, we need four things: (1) a crude rate ($r_{observed}$) for the study population, (2) a distribution across the selected age groups for that population ($p_1, \ldots, p_i$), (3) a schedule of specific rates for the standard population ($r_{s1}, \ldots, r_{si}$), and (4) the crude rate for the standard population ($r_{standard}$) (Fleiss, 1981, pp. 240–241). The first step in the procedure is to calculate an expected overall rate for the study population by applying the schedule of specific rates for the standard population. This takes the form of the equation

$$r_{expected} = \Sigma r_s p$$

The indirect-adjusted rate is then

$$r_{adjusted} = \frac{\theta \, r_{observed}}{r_{expected}}$$

that is, the crude rate for the standard population (r_s) multiplied by the ratio of the actual crude rate for the study population ($r_{observed}$) to the crude rate ($r_{expected}$) that would exist if the study population were subject to the standard population's schedule of rates (Fleiss, 1981).

One of the most common forms of indirect adjustment is the *standardized mortality ratio*. It is defined as the number of deaths, either total or cause-specific, in a given population expressed as a percentage of the number of deaths that would have been expected in that population if the age- and sex-specific rates in the standard population were applicable. The statistic is calculated by using the formula

$$\text{Standardized Mortality Ratio (SMR) (\%)} = \frac{\text{observed number of deaths per year}}{\text{expected number of deaths per year}} \times 100$$

The expected number of deaths per year of a particular population is calculated by using the equation

$$N = \Sigma \, pr$$

where p is the number of subjects belonging to a particular age group and r is the age-specific death rate in the standard population. The sum of these calculations, N, equals the total expected number of deaths per year. This figure is then compared with the observed number of deaths for the population under study.

An example of the use of the SMR is found in Table 2.10. Among male Alaskan Natives in the 25 to 34 age category, the standardized mortality ratio is 529, meaning that the experience of mortality for that age group is 529 percent of the mortality experience of males in the United States and over four times greater than the mortality experience of non-native males in Alaska.

The standardized mortality ratio is widely used in epidemiology and is often used as an estimate of relative risk. However, the size of the SMR is not always equal to the size of the relative risk, and the discrepancy depends on the age of the population under study (cf. Gaffey, 1976). Thus, a group exposed to a specific hazard may possess a constant relative risk with respect to age but the SMR may increase with age. The SMR, therefore, will produce a biased estimate of relative risk and its bias will be different with each age group. Symons and Taulbee (1981), however, argue that the standardized mortality ratio may be a useful approximation of relative risk when three conditions are met: (1) the age-specific rates in the standard population for the cause of interest are larger than 1 per 100 per year; (2) the age intervals are not too broad, with shorter intervals being necessary when mortality rates are small; and (3) the age range for the analysis is restricted, neither beginning at too early an age nor extending too far into the older ages (55+).

TABLE 2.10. STANDARDIZED MORTALITY RATIOS FOR NATIVE AND NON-NATIVE MALES ALASKA, 1974

| | Alaska Male Population | | U.S. Mortality Rate for Males (per 1000) | Number of Deaths | | | | Standardized Mortality Ratio[a] | |
| | | | | Observed | | Expected | | | |
Age	Native	Non-Native		Native	Non-Native	Native	Non-Native	Native	Non-Native
Under 5	3,570	13,049	25.06	32	63	89	327	35	19
5–14	8,413	28,469	.52	15	19	4	15	375	127
15–24	4,956	31,943	1.92	41	82	10	61	410	134
25–34	3,216	23,323	2.17	37	66	7	51	529	129
35–44	2,696	18,565	4.10	31	81	11	76	282	107
45–54	1,880	12,988	9.68	30	88	18	126	167	70
55–64	1,319	6,619	22.89	32	131	30	152	107	86
65–74	715	1,960	165.56	22	107	118	324	19	33
75+	460	761		33	90	76	126	43	71
Total	26,955	137,677		273	727	363	1,258	75	58

Source: Population figures and number of deaths obtained from Kelso, 1977.
[a]Ratios are multiplied by 100.

Multivariate Methods.   As the number of variables increase, so does the problem of controlling for potential confounding. Analysis based on cross classification of variables becomes unwieldy and impractical. The alternative is to employ more sophisticated quantitative methods, including analysis of variance and coveriance, bivariate and multivariate regression models, and discriminant analysis. It would be impractical to go into detail here on the applications of each of these models in psychosocial epidemiology. We therefore limit ourselves to a general discussion of multivariate methods and provide an overview of one particular model used widely in epidemiology, *multiple logistic regression.*

Multiple regression is frequently employed in psychosocial studies for three different purposes. First, it provides a description of the linear dependence of a disease or form of stress on a set of characteristics or exposure of a particular population. In a study of coronary heart disease, for example, regression models describe the contribution of several characteristics of an individual, including age, sex, socioeconomic status, diet, blood pressure, cholesterol, weight, and so on, to the risk of experiencing a CHD event such as angina or myocardial infarction. Using this description, we can make predictions as to the risk of disease for an individual with a specific set of values for each characteristic (e.g., a 35-year-old male, with a high school education, earning $15,000 a year, etc.).

Second, regression models are used to control for potential confounding factors in order to evaluate the contribution of a specific variable or set of variables. In the Honolulu Heart Study of acculturation and coronary heart disease, for example, several covariables are controlled using a logistic model to isolate the independent effect of each form of acculturation.

Third, regression is used to find structural relations among sets of variables and to provide causal explanations for these relationships. In their study of coping and stress, for example, Pearlin et al. (1981), employed a path model to indicate the direction and strength of association between disruptive job events and changes in economic strain, mastery, self-esteem, and depression, with life events at the beginning of the path and depression at the end. Such a technique indicates the role of other factors as intervening or mediating variables as well as provides a measure of the degree of presumed causal connection between independent and dependent variables.

A thorough explanation of the principles that underly regression can be found in most statistics textbooks. However, a brief outline of these principles is necessary to clarify the discussion to follow. Regression is used to quantify the relationship between two or more variables when the value of one variable is affected by changes in the values of other variables. The affected variable is the dependent (y) variable and the others, which are used as predictors, are independent (x) variables. When there is an orderly relationship between the dependent and independent variables, information about the x value contains some information about the y value. This orderly relationship is called a *correlation*. If the relationship is linear, such that y is a linear function of x, the relationship may be expressed as a regression equation and the straight line that is the graph of this equation is called the regression line of y on x. In a simple linear regression with only one independent variable, the probability or expected value of the dependent variable (y) is expressed as

$$p(y) = \beta_0 + \beta_i x$$

where β_0 and β_i are the coefficients (parameters), β_0 the intercept, and β_i the slope of the regression. The y intercept represents the predicted value of y when $x = 0$. The slope of the regression line β_i indicates the magnitude of the change in y for a unit change in x. A model of multiple linear regression involving k independent variables is written as

$$p(y) = \beta_0 + \beta_1 x_1 + \beta_2 x_2 + \cdots + \beta_k x_k$$

where $x_1, x_2, \ldots, x_k$ are the independent variables and $\beta_1, \beta_2, \ldots, \beta_k$ are their regression coefficients.

When the dependent and independent variables are linearly related, the relationship between them can be expressed by a single number called the correlation coefficient (r). With a perfect correlation such that all possible values of both the dependent and independent variables fall on a straight line, the slope will be $+1.0$ or -1.0, the y intercept will equal 0, and the correlation coefficient will equal $+1.0$ or -1.0, depending on whether the relationship is positive or negative. When the correlation is less than perfect, the points will show some degree of scatter around the regression line. As the amount of scatter increases, the value of r decreases. The *regression line* is that line around which the amount of scatter is smallest. The amount of scatter is most often defined in terms of the sum of squares of the vertical deviations of the points from the line. The regression line of y on x, therefore, is defined as that straight line from which the sum of the squared deviation $\Sigma (y - y')^2$ is smallest.

In order to compute the least-squares line, we must compute β_0 and β_i using the formulas

$$\beta_i = \frac{N\Sigma xy - (\Sigma x)(\Sigma y)}{N\Sigma x^2 - (\Sigma x)^2}$$

$$\beta_0 = \frac{\Sigma y - \beta_i \Sigma x}{N}$$

As noted earlier, regression models provide a means of controlling for possible confounding independent variables. A partial regression coefficient, say, β_1, in a multiple regression model such as the one represented by the equation

$$p(y) = \beta_0 + \beta_1 x_1 + \beta_2 x_2 + \cdots + \beta_k x_k$$

stands for the expected change in y with a change in one unit of x_1 when x_2 to x_k are held constant or otherwise controlled. Alternatively, β_1 can be seen as the expected difference in y between two groups that are different on x_1 by one unit but are the same on x_2 through x_k. Likewise, β_2 stands for the expected change in y with a unit change in x_2 when x_1 through x_k are held constant, and so on. Moreover, the combined effects of regression coefficients are additive. For example, if we were to change one unit on both x_1 and x_2, the expected change in y would be $(\beta_1 + \beta_2)$. This expected change can also be expressed as the expected difference in y between two groups which are different by one unit on both x_1 and x_2.

The relationship between the regression coefficient β and the correlation coefficient r is expressed in terms of the equation

$$\beta = r \frac{(S_y)}{(S_x)}$$

where Sy is the standard deviation of y and Sx is the standard deviation of x. When x and y are standardized for unit variance (i.e., the standard deviations of both x and $y = 1$), then $\beta = r$. The standardized regression coefficients are referred to as beta weights. When two or more independent variables are measured in different units (such as body weight in pounds and blood pressure in Hg), standardized coefficients provide a useful way of assessing the relative effect of each independent variable on the dependent variable.

The significance of β can be tested by either examining the confidence interval or evaluating the F ratio obtained from the equation

$$F = \frac{\Sigma(y' - y)/1}{\Sigma(y - y')/N - 2)}$$

Several bivariate and multivariate procedures have been employed in psychosocial epidemiology for the purposes of describing, controlling for confounding variables, and determining causality. The selection of a procedure depends largely on the types of questions asked in a study and the nature of the data available. Thus, data from interval scales such as blood pressure measurements or psychiatric screening scale scores may rely upon least-squares regression to obtain partial correlations. Data in the form of rates might employ a binary regression analysis using percentage deviations from overall rates (Roberts & Lee, 1980). Stepwise regression techniques have been employed on variables such as coping resources to assess the affect of each variable on stress by observing the reduction in the regression of stress on other factors such as role strain as each independent variable is added into the equation (Pearlin & Schooler, 1978).

One of the most commonly used procedures in epidemiology, however, is *multiple logistic analysis.* This technique was developed and applied to data from the Framingham Study in an effort to identify the independent contribution of several factors to the overall risk of disease. It is more appropriate than the least-squares models for analyses involving the presence or absence of disease and mortality, and its regression line assumes the form of a dose-response curve rather than a straight line. In a logistic model, a dichotomized dependent variable is predicted by one or more independent variables. One of the reasons for its wide use in epidemiology is that it provides an estimate of the relative risk of a disease associated with each variable independent of all other variables studied. Although the model is formulated in terms of prospective studies, it may also be applied to data from cross-sectional and retrospective studies.

A complete descripton of the logistic model and its application in epidemiology is found in Schlesselman (1982). Briefly, the model specifies that the probability of disease or stress response depends on a set of independent variables such that

$$p(y) = p(d = 1 \mid x) = \frac{1}{\{1 + \exp \mid -(\beta_0 + \beta_1 x_1 + \cdots + \beta_k x_k) \mid \}}$$

where d denotes either the presence ($d = 1$) or absence ($d = 0$) of the disease or stress event, and x denotes a set of k variables, $x = (x_1, x_2, \ldots, x_k)$ which may represent any potential risk factor or confounding variable, functions of them, or interactions of interest. The βs, or regression coefficients, are parameters representing the effects of the independent variables (characteristics or exposures) on the probability of disease or stress response. These parameters are usually derived from discriminant analysis or maximum likelihood estimation, the latter being the preferred procedure because it does not depend on any a priori assumption of multivariate normality (Schlesselman, 1982).

The logistic parameters can also be interpreted in terms of odds ratios. Using the model assumptions stated previously, we find that the risk of a disease or stress event among individuals wth a particular set of characteristics or exposures with the value $x = (x_1, x_2, \ldots, x_k)$ is

$$RR = \frac{p_x}{q_x} = \exp(\beta_0 + \beta_1 x_1 + \cdots + \beta_k x_k)$$

where

$$q_x = 1 - p_x = p(d = 0 \mid x)$$

This equation provides an approximation for the risk of disease among individuals with a specific set of values for each characteristic relative to individuals with different values for the same characteristics. An odds ratio per unit change in the level of any one characteristic, x_i is exp β_i.

The logistic model is often expressed directly in terms of *logits*, $\ln(p_x/q_x)$. Thus,

$$\ln RR = \ln \frac{p_x}{q_x} = (\beta_0 + \beta_1 x_1 + \cdots + \beta_k x_k)$$

This is comparable in form to the multiple linear regression model previously described. Expressed in terms of logits, a unit change in the variable x_i changes the logit of risk ($\ln p_x/q_x$) by the amount β_i.

Finally, the relative importance of characteristics or exposures may be compared in terms of standardized coefficients. As in the case of linear regression, the standardized coefficient may be expressed as a multiple of the standard deviation of x such that

$$\beta_i' = (Sx_i)$$

Each standardized coefficient measures the change in the logit of risk resulting from a change of one standard deviation in the variable x_i (Schlesselman, 1982).

Table 2.11 contains the standardized logistic coefficients from prevalence data in the study of acculturation and coronary heart disease among Japanese men in Hawaii from 1971 to 1977 (Reed et al., 1982). The effect of each variable (index of acculturation) and covariable (age, systolic blood pressure, serum cholesterol, etc.) included in the risk function is interpreted in terms of its regression coefficient, β, which represents the effect of the variable adjusted for the effects of the other variables. Here it can be seen that the total acculturation score is significantly associated with total coronary heart disease (CHD) as well as with myocardial infarction and angina in particular, independent of the covariables. The negative correlation indicates that respondents with a greater number of traditional Japanese responses on the acculturation scales have a lower prevalence of coronary heart disease. With the exception of current social assimilation, which was associated with total CHD, none of the separate measures of acculturation were significantly associated with total or specific CHD prevalence. The use of standardized coefficients also allows for a comparison of the relative importance of each of the independent variables. Thus, age and systolic blood pressure are of

TABLE 2.11.   STANDARDIZED LOGISTIC COEFFICIENTS RELATING
ACCULTURATION SCORES AND SELECTED COVARIABLES TO CORONARY
HEART DISEASE (CHD) PREVALENCE AMONG MEN OF JAPANESE
ANCESTRY, HONOLULU HEART PROGRAM, 1971–1979

Scores	Total CHD	Myocardial Infarction	Angina
Culture of upbringing	−0.08622	−0.01907	−0.15644
Current cultural assimilation	−0.09974	−0.04109	−0.15659
Current social assimilation	−0.19436[b]	−0.18058	−0.18232
Total acculturation	−0.46745[b]	−0.70480[a]	−0.67075[a]
Covariables			
Age	0.23305[b]	0.13838	0.33389[c]
Systolic blood pressure	0.21867[c]	0.25565[b]	0.11182
Serum cholesterol	0.18533[b]	0.19074[a]	0.17142
Alcohol (ounces/month)	−0.50466[c]	−0.70018[c]	−0.20460
Complex carbohydrate (g/24 hr)	−0.22961	−0.00940	−0.23972
Serum uric acid	0.12972	0.22529[a]	0.03894
Serum glucose	0.10806	0.07756	0.13328
Forced vital capacity	−0.13196	−0.29020[b]	0.11367
Physical activity index	−0.15514[a]	−0.05848	−0.24166[a]
Cigarettes/day	0.04331	0.17335	−0.10199
Body mass index	0.08428	−0.15261	0.18531
Socioeconomic status	−0.10724	−0.01103	−0.12523

Source: Reed et al., 1982. Copyright 1982, American Journal of Epidemiology.
[a] $0.05 \geqslant p > 0.01$
[b] $0.01 \geqslant p > 0.001$
[c] $p \leqslant 0.001$

equal importance in predicting the prevalence of total coronary heart disease episodes among men of Japanese ancestry in Hawaii, both covariables having standardized coefficients approximately equal to .3.

Associations and Causality

Although epidemiologic methods have been applied with great success in detecting associations between disease or stress episodes and a host of psychosocial variables, the problem of verifying causal relations in psychosocial epidemiology has been much more complex. The literature is replete with examples of correlations and speculations about causality. Often, associations have been taken as evidence for causal relations. In other studies, statements about causal relations are limited by the failure to control for all potential confounding variables. As noted previously, multivariate methods are often employed to estimate the strength and direction of associations between dependent and independent variables. Despite the efficacy of these methods, however, several considerations must be kept in mind when examining the causal relations between a disease or stress episode and characteristics or exposures. Schlesselman (1982) lists six specific observational criteria for determining causation in an epidemiologic investigation: (1) temporal sequence, (2) consistency, (3) strength of association, (4) biological gradient, (5) specificity of effect, and (6) collateral evidence and biological plausibility.

Temporal sequence is particularly important with respect to life events and social research. Although it is generally assumed that life events lead to psychological distress, they may also be a consequence of distress. The causal association between migration and psychological distress is an example of this issue. Even though research has shown migrants to have higher levels of mental disorder than do nonmigrants, cross-sectional or retrospective studies are of little use in determining whether the disorder is due to the immigration process or whether the disorder itself precipitated the migration (self-selection). To demonstrate a causal relation between life events and distress, we must show that life events occur prior to the onset of the disorder. In their study of psychological impairment and life events, Andrews et al. (1978), attempted to control for this temporal sequence by studying the cause of life events among cases and controls and by dating events at monthly intervals, making it possible to examine the correlation between symptom score and life events in specific time periods.

The consistency of an association under different conditions of study increases the likelihood of a causal relation between a disorder and a characteristic or exposure. Demonstrating an association between loss of spouse and myocardial infarction among men from different occupations, belonging to different racial and socioeconomic status groups, and living in different geographic areas (urban vs. rural) gives added weight to a hypothesized causal relationship between the characteristic and the disease.

The strength of an association as indicated by relative risk or by correlation coefficients also aids in the confirmation of a causal relationship. The larger the relative risk or correlation coefficient, the less likely the association is spurious.

The existence of a biological gradient is often used in biomedical studies to indicate a causal association. This gradient, often represented as a dose-response curve, makes a causal interpretation more plausible. In psychosocial studies, such a gradient typically involves biochemical markers or screening scale scores as dependent variables and interval scale measures of exposure.

A causal association may also be indicated by determining the specificity of the effect of one or more independent variables. A characteristic or exposure is considered to be specific to a disease or stress response if the introduction of the former is followed by the occurrence of the latter, and if the removal of the former is followed by the absence of the latter. In psychosocial studies, however, specificity is difficult to achieve and its usefulness is limited by the complex interrelations of typical characteristics of interest and the disease or stress response where multiple causes and effects are usually the rule.

Finally, the ability to marshal collateral evidence aids in the determination of a causal relation between variables. Arguments for the existence of causal relationships between certain psychosocial characteristics, such as crowding and competition, and stress responses, such as hypertension, for example, have used data from animal studies and experimental studies on humans as well as observational studies of population samples (Henry & Cassel, 1969). Although the collateral data may have been collected with different objectives in mind, they may provide important clues as to the strength and direction of associations between variables.

Although each of these conditions alone is often insufficient to establish causality in associations between independent and dependent variables, in combinations they increase the level of confidence with which statements of causality are made.

QUALITATIVE TECHNIQUES IN PSYCHOSOCIAL EPIDEMIOLOGY

Throughout this chapter we have been concerned primarily with quantitative techniques as they are employed in psychosocial epidemiology. However, it would be difficult to overemphasize the importance of qualitative techniques as well. Qualitative techniques such as participant observation, informal interviews, and taxonomic and thematic analyses can be of critical use in all aspects of psychosocial epidemiology. This last section will briefly touch upon the necessity for a qualitative perspective in three specific stages of a psychosocial study: study design, data collection, and data analysis.

Study Design

Qualitative techniques are often employed in the initial stages of an epidemiologic investigation to "scope out" the problem at hand and to identify at a broad level the relevant study parameters. Informal interviews and observation of study populations can be used to identify the issues involved in understanding a particular disease or stress response, potential problems in data collection, potential confounding variables unrecognized in previous research, and characteristics specific to the study population—that is, how it is like or unlike the general population and other groups in similar studies.

Qualitative techniques are also employed at the initial stages of a psychosocial study to develop measures of variables of interest. In Pearlin and Schooler's (1978) study of coping and emotional stress, for example, measures of life strains and coping responses were developed from a thematic analysis of answers obtained from unstructured, open-ended interviews. This information was then subjected to a factor analysis which identified certain constructs such as self-esteem or self-denigration and the questions most salient to measuring the construct.

Data Collection

The value of qualitative methods at this stage is determined by the type of data gathered and the methods used to collect them. Given the relationships among the social, psychological, and physiological components of stress and illness, an understanding of the problem usually requires at least some level of qualitative information for two reasons. First, behavior, including illness behavior and stress responses, is guided, at least in part, by numerous cultural meanings. In fact, as Kleinman (1980) observes, illness can be looked upon as a system of meaning, where perception, evaluation, and treatment of particular symptoms will be largely influenced by the cultural pattern adhered to by the individual. Second, illness occurs in a variety of social and environmental contexts, some of which are associated with the illness itself, others of which are not. Although quantitative methods can serve to identify certain features of the context in which a disease or stress episode occurs, a complete description often requires qualitative data as well.

An understanding of both the context in which a disease or stress episode occurs and the meaning the event has for an individual is crucial for a number of reasons. First, both context and meaning influence the presentation and severity of symptoms and styles of coping with disease or stress. As noted previously, coping is strongly influenced by several factors such as previous experience, cultural values, and personality, some that are largely unquantifiable, others that are better understood through qualitative techniques such as life histories and clinical evaluations. Second, the context and meaning of a particular disease or stress response will determine the extent to which quantitative techniques are valid and reliable in the data collection stage. At several points in this chapter, we noted the potential problems that can occur with certain types of data. Rates of incidence can be distorted by patient preference for treatment outside the normal health care system, by both the response bias due to coping strategies such as denial or over-reporting and the quality of interaction between researcher and subject. In each instance, qualitative information can be invaluable in recognizing the limitations of certain types of data and selecting quantitative techniques best suited to handle these limitations.

Data Analysis

Finally, qualitative techniques are useful in the data analysis stage of an epidemiologic study. Although an association, and perhaps a causal relationship, can be demonstrated using an array of quantitative techniques, each researcher must address the questions of whether the conclusions make sense and are realistic. The observational criteria for determining causality help to provide answers to these questions. Qualitative data can be employed as collateral evidence in establishing the validity and reliability of results based on quantitative analyses. If a similar conclusion can be reached with a different perspective, the validity and reliability of the conclusion is strengthened.

References

Adebimpe, V. B. (1981). Overview: White norms and psychiatric diagnosis of Black patients. *American Journal of Psychiatry, 138,* 279–285.

Andrews, G., Tennant, C., Hewson, D., & Vaillant, G. (1978). Life event stress, social support, coping style, and risk of psychological impairment. *Journal of Nervous and Mental Disease, 166,* 307–316.

Aneshensel, C. S., & Stone, J. D. (1982). Stress and depression: A test of the buffering model of social support. *Archives of General Psychiatry, 39,* 1392–1396.

Antonovsky, A., & Kats, R. (1967). The life crisis history as a tool in epidemiologic research. *Journal of Health and Social Behavior, 8,* 15–21.

Appley, M., & Trumbull, R. (1967). On the concept of psychological stress. In M. Appley & R. Trumbull (Eds.), *Psychological stress* (pp. 1–13). New York: Appleton-Century-Crofts.

Baum, A., Grunberg, N. E., & Singer, J. E. (1982). The use of psychological and neuroendocrinological measurements in the study of stress. *Health Psychology, 1,* 217–236.

Berkman, L. F., & Syme, S. L. (1979). Social networks, host resistance, and mortality: A nine-year follow-up study of Alameda County residents. *American Journal of Epidemiology, 109,* 186–204.

Berkson, J. (1946). Limitations in the application of fourfold table analysis to hospital data. *Biometrics, 2,* 47–53.

Berkson, J., & Gage, R. P. (1950). Calculation of survival rates for cancer. *Proceedings of the Staff Meetings of the Mayo Clinic, 25,* 270–286.

Brown, D. E. (1981). General stress in anthropological fieldwork. *American Anthropologist, 83,* 74–92.

Brown, G. W., & Birley, J. L. (1968). Crisis and life changes and the onset of schizophrenia. *Journal of Health and Social Behavior, 9,* 203–214.

Byrne, D. G., & Whyte, H. M. (1980). Life events and myocardial infarction revisited: The role of measurements of individual impact. *Psychosomatic Medicine, 42,* 1–10.

Cannon, W. B. (1929). *Bodily changes in pain, hunger, fear, and rage: An account of recent researches into the function of emotional excitement.* New York: Appleton-Century-Crofts.

Celentano, D. D., & McQueen, D. V. (1978). Comparison of alcoholism prevalence rates obtained by survey and indirect estimators. *Journal of Studies on Alcohol, 39,* 420–434.

Chan, L. S., Powars, D., & Weiss, J. (1982). A modified life table method to study congenital genetic disorders: An application in sickle cell anemia. *Journal of Chronic Diseases, 35,* 401–409.

Chandra, V., Szklo, M., Goldberg, R., & Tonascia, J. (1983). The impact of marital status on survival after an acute myocardial infarction: A population-based study. *American Journal of Epidemiology, 117,* 320–325.

Clark, V. A., Aneshensel, C. S., Fredrichs, R. R., et al. (1981). Analysis of effects of sex and age in response to items on the CES-D scale. *Psychiatry Research, 5,* 171–181.

Cobb, S., & Rose, R. M. (1973). Hypertension, peptic ulcer, and diabetes in air traffic controllers. *Journal of the American Medical Association, 224,* 489–492.

Cohen, S. (1980). Aftereffects of stress on human performance and social behavior: A review of research and theory. *Psychological Bulletin, 87,* 82–108.

Cutler, S. J., & Ederer, F. (1958). Maximum utilization of the life table method in analyzing survival. *Journal of Chronic Diseases, 8,* 699–712.

Dayal, H., & Chiu, C. (1982). Factors associated with racial differences in survival for prostatic carcinoma. *Journal of Chronic Diseases, 35,* 553–560.

Dohrenwend, B. S. (1973). Life events as stressors: A methodological inquiry. *Journal of Health and Social Behavior, 14,* 167–175.

Dohrenwend, B. S. (1980). The conflict between statistical and theoretical significance. *Journal of Health and Social Behavior, 41,* 291–293.

Dohrenwend, B. P. & Dohrenwend, B. S. (1969). *Social status and psychological distress: A causal inquiry.* New York: Wiley.

Dohrenwend, B. P., & Dohrenwend, B. S. (1982). Perspectives on the past and future of psychiatric epidemiology. *American Journal of Public Health, 72,* 1271–1279.

Dohrenwend, B. P., Shrout, P. E., Egri, G., & Mendelsohn, F. S. (1980). Nonspecific psychological distress and other dimensions of psychopathology. *Archives of General Psychiatry, 37,* 1229–1236.

Feinstein, A. R. (1979). Methodological problems and standards in case-control research. *Journal of Chronic Diseases, 18,* 35–41.

Fleiss, J. L. (1981). *Statistical methods for rates and proportions* (2nd ed.). New York: Wiley.

Fox, B. H. (1978). Premorbid psychological factors as related to cancer incidence. *Journal of Behavioral Medicine, 1,* 45–133.

Frankenhaeuser, M. (1975). Sympathetic-adrenomedullary activity, behavior and the psychosocial environment. In P. H. Venables & M. J. Christie (Eds.), *Research in psychophysiology,* pp. 71–94. New York: Wiley.

Fried, M. (1969). Social differences in mental health. In J. Kosa, A. Antonovsky, & I. Zola (Eds.), *Poverty and health: A sociological analysis,* pp. 113–167. Cambridge, Mass: Harvard University Press.

Friedman, G. D. (1980). *Primer of epidemiology* (2nd ed.). New York: McGraw-Hill.

Gaffey, W. R. (1976). A critique of the standardized mortality ratio. *Journal of Occupational Medicine, 18,* 157–160.

Gaines, T., & Richmond, L. H. (1980). Assessing suicidal behavior in basic military trainees. *Military Medicine, 145,* 263–266.

Gehan, E. A. (1969). Estimating survival functions from the life table. *Journal of Chronic Diseases, 21,* 629–644.

Glass, D. C., & Singer, J. E. (1972). *Urban stress: Experiments in noise and social stressors.* New York: Academic Press.

Grant, I., Yager, J., Sweetwood, H. L., & Olshen, R. (1982). Life events and symptoms: Fourier analysis of time series from a three-year prospective inquiry. *Archives of General Psychiatry, 39,* 598–605.

Hahn, M. E. (1966). California Life Goals Evaluation Schedule. Palo Alto: Western Psychological Services.

Harburg, E., Gleibermann, L., Roeper, P., Schork, M. A., & Schull, W. J. (1978). Skin color, ethnicity, and blood pressure I: Detroit blacks. *American Journal of Public Health, 68,* 1177–1183.

Hayes-Bautista, D. E. (1983). On comparing studies of different Raza populations, *American Journal of Public Health, 73,* 274–276.

Haynes, S. G., & Feinleib, M. (1980). Women, work and coronary heart disease: Prospective findings from the Framingham Heart Study. *American Journal of Public Health, 70,* 133–141.

Henry, J. P. (1982). The relation of social to biological processes in disease. *Social Science and Medicine, 16,* 369–380.

Henry, J. P., & Cassel, J. C. (1969) Psychosocial factors in essential hypertension. *American Journal of Epidemiology, 90,* 171–200.

Hirschfeld, R., & Cross, C. K. (1982). Epidemiology of affective disorders: Psychosocial risk factors. *Archives of General Psychiatry. 39,* 35–46.

Holmes, T. H., & Rahe, R. H. (1967). The social readjustment rating scale. *Journal of Psychosomatic Medicine, 11,* 213–218.

House, J. S., Robbins, C., & Metzner, H. (1982). The association of social relationships and activities with mortality: Prospective evidence from the Tecumseh community health study. *American Journal of Epidemiology, 116,* 123–140.

Hypertension Detection and Follow-up Program Cooperative Group (1977). Race, education and prevalence of hypertension. *American Journal of Epidemiology, 106,* 351–361.

Jackson, D. N. (1974). *Personality Research Form Manual.* Goshen, NY: Research Psychologists' Press.

Johnson, J. H., & Sarason, I. G. (1978). Life stress, depression and anxiety: Internal-external control as a moderator variable. *Journal of Psychosomatic Research, 22,* 205–208.

Kaplan, A. (1977). Social support: The construct and its measurement. Unpublished BA thesis, Department of Psychology, Brown University, Providence, RI.

Kaplan, E. L. & Meier, P. (1958). Nonparametric estimation from incomplete observations. *Journal of the American Statistical Association, 53,* 457–481.

Keil, J. E., Tyroler, H. A., Sandifer, S. H., & Boyle, E. (1977). Hypertension: Effects of social class and racial admixture. *American Journal of Public Health, 67,* 634–639.

Kelso, D. (1977). *Working papers: Descriptive analysis of the impact of alcoholism and alcohol abuse in Alaska, 1975. vol. IV.* Juneau: State Office of Alcoholism, Department of Health and Social Services, State of Alaska.

Kennedy, J. G. (1973). Cultural psychiatry, In J. Honigman (Ed.), *Handbook of social and cultural Anthropology,* (pp. 1119–1198). Chicago: Rand MacNally.

Kessler, R. C. (1979). A strategy for studying differential vulnerability to the psychological consequences of stress. *Journal of Health and Social Behavior, 20,* 100–108.

Kessler, R. C. (1982). A disaggregation of the relationship between socioeconomic status and psychological distress. *American Sociological Review, 47,* 752–764.

Kiev. A. (1972). *Transcultural psychiatry.* New York: Free Press.

Kleinman, A. (1980). *Patients and healers in the context of culture: An exploration of the borderland between anthropology, medicine, and psychiatry.* Berkeley: University of California Press.

Kleinman, A., Eisenberg, L., & Good, B. (1978). Culture, illness, and care: Clinical lessons from anthropologic and cross-cultural research. *Annals of Internal Medicine, 88,* 251–258.

Kobasa, S. C., Maddi, S. R., & Courington, S. (1981). Personality and constitution as mediators in the stress-illness relationship. *Journal of Health and Social Behavior, 22,* 368–378.

Langner, T. S. (1962). A twenty-two item screening score of psychiatric symptoms indicating impairment. *Journal of Health and Human Behavior, 3,* 269–276.

Lazarus, R. (1966). *Psychological stress and the coping process.* New York: McGraw-Hill.

Lemkau, P. Y., & Crocetti, G. M. (1958). Vital statistics of schizophrenia. In L. Belak (Ed.) *Schizophrenia: A review of the syndrome* (pp. 64–81). New York: Logos Press.

Levin, M. L. (1953). The occurrence of lung cancer in man. *Acta Unio International Contra Cancrum, 9,* 531–541.

Lilienfeld, A. M., & Lilienfeld, D. E. (1980). *Foundations of epidemiology* (2nd ed.). New York: Oxford University Press.

Lilienfeld, D. E. (1978). Definitions of epidemiology. *American Journal of Epidemiology, 107,* 87–90.

Macmillan, A. M. (1957). The health opinion survey: Technique for estimating prevalence of psychoneurotic and related types of disorders in communities. *Psychological Reports, 3,* 325–329.

Maddi, S. R., Kobasa, S. C., & Hoover, M. (1979). An alienation test. *Journal of Humanistic Psychology, 19,* 73–76.

Mantel, N., & Haenszel, W. (1959). Statistical aspects of the analysis of data from retrospective studies of disease. *Journal of the National Cancer Institute, 22,* 719–746.

Marmot, M. G., & Syme, S. L. (1976). Acculturation and coronary heart disease in Japanese-Americans. *American Journal of Epidemiology, 104,* 225–247.

Mason, J. W. (1968a). A review of psychoendocrine research on the pituitary-adrenal cortical system. *Psychosomatic Medicine, 30,* 576–607.

Mason, J. W. (1968b). A review of psychoendocrine research on the sympathetic-adrenal medullary system. *Psychosomatic Medicine, 30,* 631–653.

Mason, J. W. (1975). A historical review of the stress field. *Journal of Human Stress, 1,* 22–36.

McQueen, D. V., & Celentano, D. D. (1982). Social factors in the etiology of multiple outcomes: The case of blood pressure and alcohol consumption patterns. *Social Science and Medicine, 16,* 397–418.

McQueen, D. V., Siegrist, J. (1982). Social factors in the etiology of chronic disease: An overview. *Social Science and Medicine, 16,* 353–367.

Mischler, E. G., & Scotch, N. A. (1963). Sociocultural factors in the epidemiology of schizophrenia: A review. *Psychiatry,* 315–351.

Monroe, S. M. (1982). Assessment of life events: Retrospective vs. concurrent strategies. *Archives of General Psychiatry, 39,* 606–610.

Morgenstern, H. (1982). Uses of ecological analysis in epidemiologic research. *American Journal of Public Health, 72,* 1336–1344.

Myers, J. K., Lindenthal, J. J., & Pepper, M. P. (1971). Life events and psychiatric impairment. *Journal of Nervous and Mental Diseases, 152,* 149–157.

Newcomb, M. D., Huba, G. J., & Bentler, P. M. (1981). A multidimensional assessment of stressful life events among adolescents: Derivation and correlates. *Journal of Health and Social Behavior, 22,* 400–415.

Pearlin, L. I., Lieberman, M. A., Menaghan, E. G., & Mullan, J. T. (1981). The stress process. *Journal of Health and Social Behavior, 22,* 337–356.

Pearlin, L. I., & Schooler, C. (1978). The structure of coping. *Journal of Health and Social Behavior, 19,* 2–21.

Peto, R., Pike, M. C., Armitage, P., Breslow, N. E., Cox, D. R., Howard, S. V., Mantel, N., McPherson, K., Peto, J., & Smith, P. G. (1977). Design and analysis of randomized clinical trials requiring prolonged observation of each patient: Analysis and examples. *British Journal of Cancer, 35,* 1–37.

Rahe, R. H., McKean, J. D., & Arthur, R. J. (1967). A longitudinal study of life-change and illness patterns. *Journal of Psychosomatic Research, 10,* 355–366.

Reed. D., McGee, D., Cohen, J., Yano, K., Syme, S. L., & Feinleib, M. (1982) Acculturation and coronary heart disease among Japanese men in Hawaii. *American Journal of Epidemiology, 115,* 894–905.

Roberts, R. E., & Lee, E. S. (1980). The health of Mexican Americans; evidence from the Human Population Laboratory studies. *American Journal of Public Health, 70,* 375–384.

Rotter, J. B., Seeman, M., & Liverant, S. (1962). Internal vs. external locus of control of rein-forcement: A major variable in behavior theory. In N. F. Washburne (Ed.), *Decisions, values and groups*, pp. 473–516. London: Pergamon Press.

Sarason, I. G., Johnson, J. H., & Siegel, J. M. (1978). Assessing the impact of life changes: Development of the Life Experiences Survey. *Journal of Consulting and Clinical Psychology, 46*, 932–946.

Schlesselman, J. J. (1982). *Case-control studies: Design, conduct, analysis*. New York: Oxford University Press.

Seeman, M., & Anderson, C. S. (1983). Alienation and alcohol: The role of work, mastery, and community in drinking behavior. *American Sociological Review, 48*, 60–77.

Selye, H. (1956). *The stress of life*. New York: McGraw-Hill.

Susser, M. (1981). The epidemiology of life stress. *Psychological Medicine, 11*, 1–8.

Symons, M. J., & Taulbee, J. D. (1981). Practical considerations for approximating relative risk by the standardized mortality ratio. *Journal of Occupational Medicine, 23*, 413–416.

Thoits, P. A. (1982). Conceptual, methodological, and theoretical problems in studying social support as a buffer against life stress. *Journal of Health and Social Behavior, 23*, 145–159.

Thompson, W. D., & Weissman, M. M. (1981). Quantifying lifetime risk of psychiatric disorder. *Journal of Psychiatric Research, 16*, 113–126.

Turner, R. J. (1981). Social support as a contingency in psychological well-being. *Journal of Health and Social Behavior, 22*, 357–367.

Vaillant, G. E. (1976). Natural history of male psychological health: V. The relation of choice of ego mechanisms of defense to adult adjustment. *Archives of General Psychiatry, 33*, 535–545.

Vernon, S. W., & Roberts, R. E. (1982). Use of the SADS-RDC in a tri-ethnic community survey. *Archives of General Psychiatry, 39*, 47–52.

Vernon, S. W., Roberts, R. E., & Lee, E. S. (1982). Response tendencies, ethnicity, and depres-sion scores. *American Journal of Epidemiology, 116*, 482–495.

Weissman, M. M. & Myers, J. K. (1978). Affective disorders in a U.S. urban community. *Archives of General Psychiatry, 35*, 1304–1311.

Wing, J. K., Cooper, J. E., & Sartorious, N. (1974). *The measurement and classification of psychiatric symptoms*. New York: Cambridge University Press.

Wingard, D. L. (1982). The sex differential in mortality rates: Demographic and behavioral factors. *American Journal of Epidemiology, 115*, 205–216.

Wyler, A. R., Masuda, M., & Holmes, T. H. (1968). Seriousness of illness rating scale. *Journal of Psychosomatic Research, 11*, 363–375.

3

Quality-of-Life Measurement

ROBERT M. KAPLAN

Health is our most desired and sought after state of being. In attempting to determine the most valued end states of existence, Rokeach (1973) had to remove health from the list of selections because subjects unanimously valued health more than any other state. Including health as a choice reduced the chances of finding individual differences in values. Because health is so highly valued, a significant proportion of our energies and resources are devoted to achieving it. Health practices account for a very significant portion of the variance of daily behavior. We diet, exercise, and use a wide variety of products in order to achieve health. When health fails, services from an expensive and complex health care system are sought.

Despite the centrality of health in our daily lives, the concept itself is not well defined. Different definitions of health emphasize mortality, daily functioning, and symptomatic complaints (Brook et al., 1979). Yet, regard-

Supported by Grant K04-00809 from the National Heart Lung & Blood Institute of the National Institutes of Health.

less of many alternative conceptualizations of health, an emerging consensus suggests that the goals of health care should be twofold; (1) to increase the duration of life and (2) to improve the quality of life (Kaplan, 1985; McDermott, 1981; Nelson et al., 1983). In this chapter, I will review strategies for measuring health and its impact upon quality of life.

In the present context, the term *quality of life* will be used to describe the impact of disease and disability upon daily functioning. Quality of life as used here is limited to "health-related" problems. Other uses of the term, quality of life are more general. For example, in social indicators research, quality of life refers to all circumstances of living, including housing, recreation, work, environmental conditions, and the like (Campbell et al., 1976; Wingo & Evans, 1978). This chapter limits the focus to the effects of health status upon quality of life. Some authors use the term health status to describe the impact of diseases or disabilities upon functioning. In this chapter, the terms health status and quality of life are assumed to be equivalent and therefore are used interchangeably. It will be argued that health status and quality of life should be the focal point of health psychology.

Health—The Missing Element in the Conceptualization of Health Psychology

A missing element in the conceptualization of health psychology is the definition of health and health status. The definition of health is, however, rarely discussed in health psychology literature. Yet, there is an extensive literature on health status with contributions representing medicine, sociology, public health, economics, policy science, statistics, and many other disciplines (Berg, 1973). The National Center for Health Statistics has even established a Clearing House on Health Status Indexes that provides regular publications on new developments in the field.

Health status is a reasonable focal point of clinical health interventions, since all participants in the health care system have as their goal extending the duration and improving the quality of life. Variables often studied by health psychologists are only important in relation to health status. For example, stress is important because it may affect health. Similarly, lack of exercise, cigarette smoking, high sodium diets, and red meat consumption have been shown to be risk factors for poor health outcomes. Yet, these risk factors should not be confused with the outcomes. They are only important because they bear probabilistic relationships to outcome. Risk factors do not tell the "whole story," however. Heart disease, for example, is far from perfectly predicted from known risk factors. This is illustrated rather dramatically in the Pooling Project—a major effort that pooled results from the six best known prospective studies on prediction of heart disease. Within a defined 10-year period, only about 10 percent of men with two or more risk factors develop coronary heart disease. Ninety percent of men with two or more risk factors did not develop problems and more than 58 percent of those who developed heart disase had only one risk factor or did not have any of the known risk factors (Inter-Society Commission, 1970). Risk factors provide some probabilistic information but account of a limited proportion of the variance in predicting health outcomes.

In a similar vein, a study that focuses on coping stategies is of little value unless we know that these strategies mediate health. Yet, few investigations make any attempt to link measured variables to health outcomes. Those that do tend to use rather primitive conceptualizations of health status (Delongis et al., 1982). Baum et al. (1982) review psychological, behavioral, and physiological measures of the stress response without even mentioning standard measures of health status.

Many different indicators have been used as general health outcome measures. However, the most suitable are those capable of combining mortality and morbidity. Morbidity (illness) might be best assessed through its effects upon the quality of life (Kaplan, 1985). Measures should combine different types of morbidity (Sullivan, 1966) so that both benefits and consequences of treatment can be simultaneously assessed. As Mosteller noted in his presidential address to the American Association for the Advancement of Science (1981), death rates (mortality) are too crude to measure the efficacy of surgery because many surgical benefits are aimed at improved quality of life. Surgery also poses risks to lowered quality of life in addition to death. Fortunately, several measures have been proposed to provide comprehensive summaries of the impact of treatment upon mortality, morbidity, and the quality of life.

Once health status is defined, we can progress to examining its mediators. Mediators of health status include cognitive and social variables such as knowledge, coping, and social support (Sarason et al., 1983), environmental factors such as pollution, noise, exposure (Cohen et al., 1980), and the state of the immune system (Biondi, 1985). In addition, disease states may also be conceptualized as mediators of health status. Diseases are important because they affect the quality of life and mortality. Cancer is a concern because it affects the current quality of life or the probability that quality of life will be affected or that premature death will occur sometime in the future. If cancer had no effect upon quality or duration of life, it would be of little concern.

There may be considerable variability in the way the same disease affects function or quality of life. For many chronic diseases, there is no medical or surgical cure. The major function of health care is to improve or maintain functioning (often through alleviating symptoms). A remedy for a disease would be of little value if remediating the disease did not improve the quality of life or change the probability that quality of life would be affected sometime in the future.

In the following sections, methods for measuring health and the quality of life will be presented. Most contemporary strategies grew our of concern about the inadequacies of traditional approaches to health assessment.

Before reviewing quality-of-life measures used in health studies, we will consider some of the problems with traditional approaches.

TRADITIONAL APPROACHES TO HEALTH MEASUREMENT

Mortality Assessment

Mortality remains the major outcome measure in many studies in health care and epidemiology. Typically, mortality is expressed in a unit of time. time interval. In order for mortality data to be meaningful, they must be expressed in the form of a rate that is the proportion of deaths from a particular cause occurring within some defined time interval (usually per year). Usually mortality rates are expressed as age-specific mortality. This means that the number of deaths in a particular age group is divided by the total number of persons in that same age group. A related statistic is the case fatality rate that is the proportion of persons who die of a particular disease divided by the total number with the disease (including those who die and those who live).

Mortality rates are very important health statistics. In fact, they form the core of most current epidemiologic research (see also Palinkas, in this volume). A death outcome is usually referred to as "hard" data because it is an event verifiable by a public record. In addition, there is usually little disagreement that death has occurred. However, there is considerable debate about the reliability of classification for the *cause* of death (NIH, 1979).

Infant Mortality

Another important health status indicator is infant mortality. *Infant mortality* is defined as death of infants under 1 year of age per 1000 live births. Infant mortality is considered an important public health statistic because it is believed to be associated with quality of pre- and postnatal health care, environmental exposures, and proper maternal care. Since the turn of the century, there has been a substantial increase in life expectancy. Yet, there has been little change in life expectancy for those who have already celebrated their first birthday. The life expectancy statistic averages in infant deaths. The increase in life expectancy is largely caused by decreases in infant mortality (McKinley & McKinley, 1977).

Despite the many advantages of both mortality rates, there are also some obvious limitations. Mortality rates consider only the dead and ignore the living. Many important health care services can be expected to have little or no impact upon mortality rates. For example, cataract removal is one of the most common surgeries in the United States. An estimated 500,000 are performed each year (Jaffe, 1981) and, in most cases, the procedure is uncontroversial. Yet, cataract removal has little or no impact on mortality or infant mortality rates. An outcome measure that focused only on mortality might miss the value of this surgery, which proves to have benefits in as many as 95 percent of the cases. Those unable to use mortality rates to assess the effect of interventions such as cataract surgery have turned instead to morbidity indicators.

Morbidity Rates

Morbidity is typically expressed for a specific condition and reported in terms of a prevalence or incidence rate. For example, the *prevalence* of heart disease is the number of people with the disease divided by the number of people in the general population who are the same age and sex. The *incidence rate* is a measure of the rate at which new cases are occurring. It reflects the number of persons developing a problem divided by the total number at risk and is expressed per unit of time. For example, the incidence rate for chicken pox among first graders was 10 percent per day at the height of the chicken pox epidemic (Friedman, 1980).

Morbidity is also expressed in terms of its effect on function or role performance. For example, morbidity rates are sometimes reported as work days missed due to illness or disability.

There are many major problems with the use of morbidity rates as measures of health. First, serious problems exist with the reliability of classifying illnesses (Stewart et al., 1979). Second, morbidity rates do not reflect the very different impacts that the same diseases and illnesses can have upon individuals. For example, two individuals diagnosed with heart disease may be affected in very different ways. In one case, the effect may be devastating, whereas, in the other, it may be relatively minor. Morbidity rates often do not accurately represent these differences. Finally, morbidity rates ignore mortality. A truly comprehensive health status measure should combine morbidity and mortality data.

Criteria for Evaluating Quality of Life Measures

The growing recognition that the mission of health care is to extend the duration of life and improve the quality of life clarified the need for a reliable and valid method for assessing health status (Goldsmith, 1972).

Criteria for evaluating health outcome measures have been offered by several reviewers (Chen & Bush, 1976; Goldsmith, 1972; Kane & Kane 1982; Miller, 1973; Ware et al., 1981). The review by Ware and colleagues (1981) provides a "shoppers guide" for health status measures. Evaluation of the measures must begin with their rationale. Some of the uses of general health status and quality of life measurement include: (1) to measure the effects of health care interventions, (2) to evaluate the quality of care, (3) to estimate the needs of a population, (4) to improve clinical decisions, and (5) to study the causes and consequences of health status (Ware et al., 1981). Another review by Balinsky and Berger (1975) suggested that health measures should include mortality, morbidity, and combined mortality/morbidity indexes. Different reviewers have proposed many different definitions of health and many different criteria for the development of health measures. However, most reviewers agree on certain points. For example, there is a consensus that the measure must have a clear conceptual base, as well as a clearly stated purpose. Reviewers also agree that measures should be comprehensive and have clear instructions for administration and scoring. Further, all agree that measures should have adequate evidence for reliability and validity.

Although these points seem obvious and straightforward, establishing the reliability and validity of a general quality-of-life measure can sometimes be very difficult. For example, quality of life and health status cannot be considered ''traits' as conceptualized by personality theorists. Therefore, psychometric methods of reliability assessment may not be directly applicable. An intelligence test is expected to have a high test-retest reliability because the underlying trait of intelligence is assumed to be the same at each administration of the test. However, a low test-retest correlation for a health status measure may mean that either the measure is unreliable or there has been a change in underlying health status. Assessment of validity is also difficult because the construct *health* is not clearly and objectively defined. Therefore, criterion validity studies are not usually appropriate. Criterion validity assumes that there is an accepted criterion against which to validate the measure. Thus, developers of measures must follow a strategy of construct validation (Kaplan et al., 1976). Over the last decade, the documentation of validity and reliability of health status and quality of life measures has greatly improved. However, there are still many measures for which no psychometric data are available and others for which reliability data are unimpressive.

Another issue in the evaluation of quality-of-life measures is how they deal with transition among health states over the course of time. Very different health states can have exactly the same impact upon functon at a particular point in time. For example, a limitation in walking can result from a sore muscle or a central nervous system tumor. The reason the tumor is of greater concern is that is can be expected to produce the limitation chronically and might produce other disruptions in functioning. The sore muscle will likely improve within a few days. Many health status measures miss this distinction because they make no attempt to consider transitions among health states over time.

Approaches to Quality-of-Life Measurement

There are two distinctly different measurement traditions reflected in different health outcome measures. First, there is the psychometric tradition. Measures developed using this approach typically identify items believed to reflect *health* for a test of health status. A large pool of items representing all the different ways diseases and disabilities might affect daily functioning is created. Then, the items are administered to a large sample of subjects and the results subjected to factor analysis. The result is typically a series of subscales, from which a "profile" can be created that shows individual scores on a series of dimensions.

The alternative approach is rooted in decision theory. In this tradition, an investigator typically picks one dimension, such as quality of life, and obtains preferences for various cases. For example, judges might be asked to evaluate how a series of different health conditions impact upon the quality of life. These valuations or preferences are then used in a decision model that is appropriate for program evaluation or policy analysis. An important feature of this approach is that is requires that health be scaled on a single dimension. This is required in order to express the value of very different alternatives in the same unit. For example, there are different types of health care programs that have different objectives. Yet, the goal of the programs may be the same—to improve the quality of life or to extend the duration of life. By expressing the benefits of the different programs in the same quality-of-life units, we can compare interventions with different specific objectives. Health status, or quality-of-life measures following both the psychometric and decision theory traditions, will be reviewed in the following sections.

PSYCHOMETRIC APPROACHES TO QUALITY-OF-LIFE ASSESSMENT

Sickness Impact Profile

The Sickness Impact Profile (SIP) is one of the best known and widely used quality-of-life measures. It is a general measure applicable to any disease or disability group, which is also designed for use with the variety of demographic and cultural subgroups.

The initial work on the SIP began 1972 as a collaborative effort between Marilyn Bergner, a sociologist, and Betty Gilson, a physician. The first phase involved collection of statements describing the effect of sickness upon behavioral function. An original pool of 788 statements was sorted into different categories. Three hundred twelve (312) items were retained and tested in a variety fo different studies. Finally, this pool of items was reduced to 136 (Bergner et al. 1981).

SIP items are divided into 12 categories. They are further clustered into three groups: independent categories, physical, and psychosocial. Table 3.1 shows the dimensions of the SIP, the categories, and some example items. For example, category A or ambulation is in the physical cluster and includes items such as "I walk shorter distances or stop to rest often" and "I do not walk at all." these items reflect the impact of disease or disability upon the behavioral function of walking.

TABLE 3.1.   SICKNESS IMPACT PROFILE CATEGORIES AND SELECTED ITEMS

Dimension	Category	Items Describing Behavior Related to:	Selected Items
Independent categories	SR	Sleep and rest	I sit during much of the day I sleep or nap during the day
	E	Eating	I am eating no food at all, nutrition is taken through tubes or intravenous fluids I am eating special or different food
	W	Work	I am not working at all I often act irritable toward my work associates
	HM	Home management	I am not doing any of the maintenance or repair work around the house that I usually do I am not doing heavy work around the house
	RP	Recreation and pastimes	I am going out for entertainment less I am not doing any of my usual physical recreation or activities
I. Physical	A	Ambulation	I walk shorter distances or stop to rest often I do not walk at all
	M	Mobility	I stay within one room I stay away from home only for brief periods of time
	BCM	Body care and movement	I do not bathe myself at all, but am bathed by someone else I am very clumsy in body movements
II. Psychosocial	SI	Social interaction	I am doing fewer social activities with groups of people I isolate myself as much as I can from the rest of the family
	AB	Alertness behavior	I have difficulty reasoning and solving problems, for example, making plans, making decisions, learning new things I sometimes behave as if I were confused or disoriented in place or time, for example, where I am, who is around, directions, what day it is
	EB	Emotional behavior	I laugh or cry suddenly I act irritable and impatient with myself, for example, talk badly about myself, swear at myself, blame myself for things that happen
	C	Communication	I am having trouble writing or typing I do not speak clearly when I am under stress

Source: Bergner et al., 1981. By permission of Lippincott/Harper & Row.

In the early phases of the SIP project, scale values for SIP items were obtained from ratings by 25 judges. The judgments are made on a 15-point scale of dysfunction, ranging from minimally dysfunctional to maximally dysfunctional. Judgments were then used to obtain scale values for the items (Carter et al., 1976). A respondent taking the SIP endorses or does not endorse each of the 136 items. The overall SIP percent score is obtained by separating the items endorsed by the respondent, summing their scale values and dividing by the sum of all scale values for all items on the SIP. Then, this proportion is multiplied by 100. Similarly, scores are obtained for each category. Percent scores for each category can be plotted on a graphic display that looks similar to an MMPI (Minnesota Multiphasic Personality Inventory) profile (Bergner et al., 1976).

The SIP boasts an impressive record of validity and reliability. Reliability from the early studies was evaluated by using several methods, and the coefficients were typically very substantial. A series of other studies provided substantial empirical evidence for the validity of the SIP. For example, it was shown that the SIP is significantly correlated with a variety of self-assessment measures of dysfunction. In addition, the SIP correlates with clinical ratings of sickness and clinical ratings of dysfunction. In each of the studies, the SIP appears to be a stronger measure than those against which it was compared because it has substantially higher reliability. In fact, the reliability of some of the clinical ratings was as low as .41.

In a series of clinical studies, the SIP was used to evaluate improvements following treatment for three patient groups: hip replacement, hyperthyroid, and arthritis. An example of a profile for the hip replacement patients is shown in Figure 3.1. The SIP was administered prior to the surgery and then repeated three times after surgery. The patients described in this figure were highly dysfunctional for physical items (dimension I) and less dysfunctional for the psychosocial dimension (dimension II) prior to

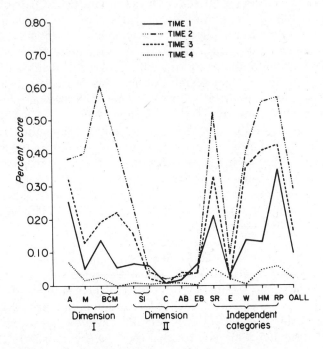

FIGURE 3.1.   Elevation of SIP category scores for total hip replacement patients at four follow-up points. (From Bergner et al., 1981, p. 800. By permission of Lippincott/Harper & Row.)

surgery (time 1). They were also more dysfunctional for the independent categories. Over the course of follow-ups, there was gradual improvement for the physical and the independent categories.

Among the many general quality-of-life measures that are available, the SIP has the most extensive record of validity and reliability. It has now been used in studies involving a wide array of patients and become the method of choice for most investigators. The difficulties with the SIP are that it neither integrates morbidity and mortality data nor easily translates into units that can be used in policy analysis. This latter point will be discussed in the section on decision theory. Although the length of the SIP has been greatly reduced, it is still somewhat cumbersome and time-consuming.

In summary, the SIP is an important measure that has undergone systematic methodological refinements. It can provide validated profiles that describe individual changes in specific categories. Although less well suited for studies in policy analysis, it still remains one of the most important measures in the field.

The McMaster Health Index Questionnaire

A similar approach has been developed by Larry Chambers and colleagues at McMaster University. The measure this group has developed is known as the McMaster Health Index Questionnaire (MHIQ). In developing their questionnaire, a multidisciplanary group of specialists in internal medicine, family medicine, psychiatry, epidemiology, statistics, and social science reviewed existing health status questionnaires. Their goal was to develop an instrument that conforms with the World Health Organization definition of health as "not merely the absence of disease or infirmity" (WHO, 1948). Similar to the SIP, the MHIQ has separate scales for physical function, emotional function, and social function.

Some of the items on the MHIQ were taken from other scales. For example, some of the physical health items were taken from the Katz Index of Activities of Daily Living Scale (Katz et al., 1970, see next section). The emotional function items were adapted or taken varbatim from a variety of sources including the Social Readjustment Rating Scale (Holmes & Rahe, 1967). This resulted in an original questionnaire with 172 items.

After validation testing, the pool of items was reduced to 59. The criteria for selection of the final items included association with observed functional changes before and after patients entered the hospital and correlation with ratings by family physicians. Later studies validated the MHIQ against a variety of other quality-of-life measures such as the Lee Index of Functional Capacity, the Spitzer Quality of Life Index, and the Bradburn Psychological Well-being Scale. The MHIQ is a self-administered questionnaire, and validity studies have demonstrated that these self-reports correlate significantly with ratings by external observers. In one study, it was demonstrated that the physical function portion of the index changes in response to therapies designed to affect physical function. For example, the physical function portion of the MHIQ improved in response to physiotherapy (Chambers et al., 1982).

One of the concerns with the MHIQ is that it has adequate but not impressive reliability. In one study of patients in a physiotherapy clinic, the MHIQ was administered twice within a 1-week period. The physiotherapists reported that functional status should not change over the short interval in this patient population. Using test-retest assessment, the interclass correlation coefficients were .53, .70, and .48 for the physical, emotional, and social function portions of the MHIQ, respectively. Another study evaluated the internal consistency of the MHIQ as assessed by KR-20 coefficients (see Kaplan & Saccuzzo, 1982). For the physical, emotional, and social function indices, the coefficients were .76, .67, and .51, respectively. Although these levels of reliability may be acceptable for group comparisons for large clinical trials, they are less than optimal. Low reliability, causing attenuation in correlations between variables, may reduce the chances of detecting important relationships. Unfortunately, many pedictors of quality of life are also measured with substantial error. For instance, some measures of social support also have reliabilities of around .50.

An example may help clarify the consequences of low reliability. Suppose that the reliability of a social support measure was .50 and we wish to show its association with the physical health portion of the MHIQ which also has a reliability of approximately .50. Further, suppose that the true correlation between these two constructs is .50. Because of attenuation due to measurement error, the observed correlation would be .25. For a sample size of 50, this would not be statistically significant. In other words, many problems in health psychology require detection of moderate relationships with moderate sample sizes. For instruments with reliabilities in the .50 range, there will be attenuation in correlations and the detection of important relationships may be missed.

The Index of Activities of Daily Living

The Index of Activities of Daily Living (ADL) is one of the oldest, widely used, and most important measures of quality of life, for Sidney Katz (1963) and his colleagues were among the very first to appreciate the importance of measuring levels of function.

The ADL is most significantly useful in studies of the elderly and those confined to long-term care institutions. It includes scales that describe six functions: bathing, dressing, toileting, transfer, continence and feeding. For each category, a judgment is made as to whether the person is independent or dependent. For the category of bathing, people are judged to be independent if they need assistance only in bathing a single part of the body or can bathe themselves. They are judged to be dependent if they need assistance in bathing more than one part of the body. Definitions of independence and dependence for the six components of the ADL are shown in Table 3.2. Once dependence or independence is ascertained in each of the six categories, an overall grade is assigned. The grades are also supplied in Table. 3.2. For example, to receive a grade of A, a person must be independent in all six categories. The B grade is assigned to those who are independent in all but one of these functions. The bottom grade, G, is assigned to those that are dependent in all six functions.

To ADL has been used in a large number of studies, and its validity and reliability are well established. For example, the ADL is significantly correlated with physical measures such as range of motion and mental measures, including the Raven Progressive Matrix Test and a mental orientation exam. It has also been demonstrated that those with higher grades on the ADL have a higher probability of longer-term survival (Katz et al., 1970). The index is also able to predict a long-term course of stroke and hip fracture as well as adaptations in terms of house confinement and mobility (Katz, et al., 1963).

The major limitation of the ADL Scale is that it does not make distinctions toward the well end of the quality-of-life continuum. General surveys have demonstrated that as many as 80 percent of the noninstitutionalized population do not have any limitations in functioning (Stewart et al., 1979). The ADL Scale would give exactly the same score to all of these (80 percent) individuals. However, as many as 50 percent of those interviewed in population surveys experience at least one symptom on any given day (Kaplan et al., 1976). Other measures are necessary in order to distinguish between those individuals who are toward the healthy end of the functioning continuum. In summary, the ADL Scale is an important and widely used measure of quality of life for the elderly and those confined to institutions. It has less value for studies involving the general population.

Karnofsky Performance Status

It is often the case in quality-of-life assessment that general measures are tailored for use with a specific disease category. For example, a measure will be designed to assess the effect of arthritis upon the quality of life. In cancer research, however, a different trend seems to have occurred. One general quality-of-life measure known as the Karnofsky Performance Status (KPS) has found widespread use in cancer research but has not been used for populations other than cancer patients. The term *quality of life* first appeared as a heading in the *Index Medicus* in 1977. Grieco and Long (1984) reviewed the 45 studies listed in the Index that used quality-of-life measures. Among those cited in *Index Medicus*, the Karnofsky Performance Status was used in about 18 percent of the studies. However, because of the diversity of outcome measures used in the studies, the KPS was actually used more often than any other technique. Yet, all studies using the KPS involved cancer patients.

TABLE 3.2. DEFINITIONS AND GRADES FOR THE KATZ INDEX OF ACTIVITIES OF DAILY LIVING

Index of Independence in
Activities of Daily Living

The index of independence in activities of daily living is based on an evaluation of the functional independence or dependence of patients in bathing, dressing, going to the toilet, transferring, continence, and feeding. Specific definitions of functional independence and dependence appear below the index.

A   Independent in feeding, continence, transferring, going to toilet, and bathing.
B   Independent in all but one of these functions.
C   Independent in all but bathing and one additional function.
D   Independent in all but bathing, dressing, and one additional function.
E   Independent in all but bathing, dressing, going to toilet, and one additional function.
F   Independent in all but bathing, dressing, going to toilet, transferring, and one additional function.
G   Dependent in all six functions.
Other   Dependent in at least two functions, but not classifiable as C, D, E, or F.

Independence means without supervision, direction, or active personal assistance, except as specifically noted below. This is based on actual status and not on ability. A patient who refuses to perform a function is considered as not preforming the function, even though he is deemed able.

Bathing (sponge, shower or tub)
Independent: assistance only in bathing a single part (as back or disabled extremity) or bathes self completely
Dependent: assistance in bathing more than one part of body; assistance in getting in or out of tub or does not bathe self

Dressing
Independent: gets clothes from closets and drawers; puts on clothes, outer garments, braces; manages fasteners; act of tying shoes is excluded
Dependent: does not dress self or remains partly undressed

Going to toilet
Independent: gets to toilet; gets on and off toilet; arranges clothes, cleans organs of excretion; (may manage own bedpan used at night only and may or may not be using mechanical supports)
Dependent: uses bedpan or commode or receives assistance in getting to and using toilet

Transfer
Independent; moves in and out of bed independently and moves in and out of chair independently (may or may not be using mechanical supports)
Dependent: assistance in moving in or out of bed and/or chair; does not perform one or more transfers

Continence
Independent: urination and defecation entirely self-controlled
Dependent: partial or total incontinence in urination or defecation partial or total control by enemas, catheters, or regulated use of urinals and/or bedpans

Feeding
Independent: gets food from plate or its equivalent into mouth; (precutting of meat and preparation of food, as buttering bread, are excluded from evaluation).
Dependent: assistance in act of feeding (see above); does not eat at all or parental feeding.

Source: S. Katz. A. B. Ford et al., (1963). Studies of illness in the Aged. The Index of ADL: A Standardized Measure of Biological and Psychosocial Function. *Journal of the American Medical Association, 185,* 94 ff.

The KPS is a simple rating form that requires a physician, an observer, or even the patient to assign a percentage score. The scores range from 0 for dead to 100 for normal with no complaints and no evidence of disease. Each 10-point interval is labeled with a descripton. For example, 90 percent is associated with "ability to carry out normal activity, with minor signs or symptoms of disease." Fifty percent is labeled "requires considerable assistance and frequent medical care."

Among the advantages of the KPS is the fact that it is easy to use and attempts to relate disease or disability to daily functioning. However, it has several deficiencies. First, it has apparently never been published and guidelines for its use are not available. Use of the KPS requires subjective judgments and there are not adequate data suggesting that these judgments can be made reliably. For example, Hutchinson et al. (1979) found interrater agreement to be only 29 to 34 percent. Yates et al. (1980) reported more positive results, with a correlation of .69 between nurses' and social workers' ratings of cancer patients. Even this higher estimate, however, is below what would be acceptable for research or for clinical practice. Despite its poor reliability, the KPS has been shown to be correlated with survival in lung cancer (Hyde et al., 1973; Stanley, 1980).

Recently, Grieco and Long (1984) revised the KPS in an attempt to improve its psychometric profile. They attempted to make the assessment more objective by using behaviorally oriented procedures. The revised procedure includes three components: (1) a structured interview, (2) a review of the medical chart, and (3) a supplemental interview with persons closely associated with the patient. Using trained observers, they were able to boost the interrater reliability to .96 and to demonstrate the validity of the KPS by showing its correlation with other established quality-of-life scales and its ability to discriminate between different patient groups.

In summary, the KPS is an interesting approach that has found widespread use in cancer research. It has the advantages of brevity and ease of administration. In a carefully controlled study, adequate reliability was obtained. However, the scores on the KPS are somewhat arbitrary and it is not clear how the KPS deals with transition among health states over the course of time. Another difficulty with the system is that it depends most often on clinical judgment of functional status. Nelson et al. (1983) have shown that there are serious discrepancies between the functional status as reported by patients and that reported by their doctors. Physicians tend to miss much of the dysfunction and may systematically underestimate the impact of illness upon the quality of life. The work of Grieco and Long is very important and may lead to substantial improvements in the KPS.

Disease Specific Quality-of-Life Measures—The AIMS

Most health-related quality-of-life measures are designed for use with any disease. However, some investigators feel that is is necessary to develop quality-of-life measures for specific diseases. Most advocates of quality-of-life measurement suggest that general measures be used in combination with disease-specific measures. For example, the RAND Corporation has produced a series of booklets describing the conceptualization and measurement of physiological health. Each booklet describes the problems in conceptualization and measurement of a specific condition—such as anemia, acne, or vision impairment. These approaches combine assessment of general function with indicators that are very specific for a particular disease or disability. Another approach is to use general quality-of-life measures and include some additional items relevant to a particular disease process. Nowhere is there a better example of this interplay than in research on rheumatoid arthritis.

Investigators studying new treatments for arthritis have been developing a whole series of quality-of-life measures that apply only to arthritis patients. The *Journal of Rheumatology* published a special issue on quality-of-life assesment in arthritis in 1982. Most of the scales are adaptations of Activities of Daily Living (Katz et al., 1970) or other functional status measures (Kaplan et al., 1976). However, the scales typically include a series of items that are very specific to the impact of arthritis upon daily functioning.

One example of a quality-of-life measure specific for arthritis is the Arthritis Impact Measurement Scale (AIMS). The AIMS is a health index designed at the Multi-purpose Arthritis Center at Boston University. It is intended to measure physical health and social well-being for patients with rheumatoid arthritis (Meenan et al., 1982). The AIMS has scales for mobility, physical activity, social activity, and activities of daily living and symptoms. In effect, it is an adaptation of a general health index developed by Bush and colleagues (see Kaplan et al., 1976), with a series of items designed to tap more specifically the effect of arthritis upon functioning and the quality of life. The resultant scale includes 67 items, with questions about functioning, health perceptions, comorbidity, and demographics (Meenan, 1982).

The psychometric properties of the AIMS were evaluated in a study involving 625 patients with rheumatoid disease. Alpha reliabilities were usually found to be acceptable ($> .7$) for the various subscales and the mean test-retest correlation was .87. In order to assess validity, the investigators correlated AIMS scores with physician ratings of health status, and these correlations were found to be highly significant. In addition, AIMS subscores were found to have convergent and discriminant validity when correlated with specific measures used in rheumatology research. For example, the physical activity portion of the AIMS correlated more highly with walking time than with grip strength. A dexterity scale of the AIMS was significantly correlated with grip strength but did not correlate significantly with walking time.

In summary, the AIMS is one of several well-documented quality-of-life measures used exclusively for arthritis research. Although there are certainly some advantages in using disease-specific measures, there continues to be some debate about their necessity (Liang et al., 1982). The advantage of disease-specific measures is that they are more precise in their description of the impact of a particular disease upon quality of life. However, in many cases it has not been established that the specific measures give signficant incremental information beyond what is provided by a general approach. Further, as will be discussed later, the exclusive use of a disease-specific measure excludes the possibility of comparing programs that are directed at different disease groups.

Summary of Psychometric Approaches

A number of investigators have used the principles of test construction to develop health status quality-of-life measures. Several of the best known measures have been reviewed in this section. The two most widely used techniques have been the Sickness Impact Profile and the Index of Activities of Daily Living. Each of these measures has a well-documented record of validity and reliability. In addition, each has been used in a variety of clinical research studies.

Despite the many advantages associated with the measures developed in the psychometric tradition, they are not suited for all purposes. One of the problems is that they typically are not designed to integrate morbidity and mortality data. A second problem is that they usually do not represent transitions among health states over the course of time. Finally, they do not map health onto a single dimension so that programs with different specific objectives can be compared. As a result of these problems, measures developed in the psychometric tradition may not be optimal for some evaluation research and policy studies. Measurement methods developed in the decision theory tradition may be better suited for studies directed toward comparison of different policy alternatives.

THE DECISION THEORY APPROACH

Health care costs have been escalating at an exponential pace. Without containment, health care costs may spiral relentlessly upward until they ruin the entire economy. It may no longer be enough to evaluate a health care program simply in terms of its efficacy. In other words, the observation that a treatment works better than a placebo or other control may not be sufficient justification for financing it. Resources to finance health care interventions are limited and administrators may soon be faced with selecting between competing health care alternatives. Their goal must be to *prioritize alternatives* in order to use the available resources to produce the greatest benefits.

There are many different approaches to the evaluation of health program benefits. For many years, the field was dominated by economists who used the "human capital approach." Human capital approaches assign dollar values to the lifetime expected earnings. A health program that keeps someone in the work force produces benefits because that person will continue earning money, will pay taxes, buy products, and help the economy. According to human capital assessment, health treatments are justifiable if they produce these economic benefits for society (Mushkin, 1962). A serious problem with the human capital approach is that it is highly discriminatory. Programs that help the rich are evaluated more favorably because the wealthy will use their health to earn more money. In the late 1960s, health policy models were developed in order to avoid some of the discriminatory biases apparent in the human capital approach. These methods attempted to determine the benefits of health programs by estimating their effects upon quality and duration of life (Fanshel & Bush, 1970). In contrast to human capital approaches, they expressed the benefits of health programs in nonmonetary units.

A number of different decision models are used in health services research. However, since space is limited, this discussion will focus on a representative model being developed in San Diego. Excellent reviews of the alternative models and methods for valuing health are available elsewhere (see Kane & Kane, 1982). Before reviewing the health decision model, we need to make the distinction between some commonly used terms. There is a major distinction between cost-benefit analysis and cost-effectiveness analysis. Both types of analysis are used to weight positive and negative alternatives in order to reach a rational decision about the utilization of resources. The methods differ in the unit they use to express the efficacy of a program or a treatment. In *cost-benefits* analysis, both the health outcome and the costs of the program are expressed in monetary units. In *cost-effectiveness* analysis, the health outcomes of a program are expressed in nonmonetary units. The most popular approaches to cost-effectiveness analysis express outcomes in terms of life-years or quality-adjusted life-years. We previously introduced a distinction between cost-effectiveness and cost-utility (Kaplan & Bush, 1982). *Cost-utility* is a special case of cost effectiveness that takes expressed preference for health states into consideration. Although we prefer the cost-utility terminology, the distinction is subtle and the terms cost-effectiveness and cost-utility are used interchangeably. Within the last decade, the growth of published cost-benefit and cost-effectiveness studies has been exponential. Recent trends suggest that cost-effectiveness analysis is emerging as the preferred method (Warner & Hutton, 1980).

Well-Years or Quality-Adjusted Life-Years

Our approach is to express the benefits of medical care, behavioral intervention, or preventive programs in terms of *well-years*. Others have chosen to describe the same outcome as quality-adjusted life-years (Weinstein &

Stason, 1977). Well-years integrate mortality and morbidity to express health status in terms of equivalents of well-years of life. If a man dies of heart disease at age 50 and we would have expected him to live to age 75, it might be concluded that the disease cost him to lose 25 life-years. If 100 men died at age 50 (and also had life expectancy of 75 years), we might conclude that 2500 (100 men × 25 years) life-years had been lost.

Yet, death is not the only outcome of concern in heart disease. Many adults suffer myocardial infarctions leaving them somewhat disabled over a long period of time. Although they are still alive, the quality of their lives has diminished. The general health decision model permits various degrees of disability to be compared to one another. A disease that reduces the quality of life by one half will take away 0.5 well-years over the course of 1 year. If it affects two people, it will take away 1.0 well-year (equal to 2 × 0.5) over a 1-year period. A medical treatment that improves the quality of life by 0.2 for each of five individuals will result in the production of 1 well-year if the benefit is maintained over a 1-year period. Using this system, we can express the benefits of the various programs by showing how many equivalents of well-years of life they produce.

Not all programs have equivalent costs. In periods of scarce resources, it is necessary to find the most efficient uses of limited funds. Decision models provide a framework within which to make policy decisions that require selection between competing alternatives. In medical research, program or treatment effectiveness is often measured using a single indicator. In chronic lung disease, for example, those indicators may be pulmonary function, ventilatory capacity, pulmonary hypertension, and so on. These measures are essential for monitoring the course of a specific disease. Yet, disease-specific indicators cannot permit comparisons across different treatments with different specific goals. For instance, it would be difficult to evaluate the relative value of programs for lung versus diabetic patients when the benefits are measured in terms of pulmonary function and plasma glucose, respectively. Further, specific indicators may allow side effects of treatments to be overlooked (Jette, 1980; Mosteller, 1981). Steriod drugs can modify many symptoms for lung patients, but may also be associated with decreased immunity and increased susceptability to many other problems in the long run. A measure focusing only on ventilatory capacity may miss the overall impact of the treatment on function and symptoms. That overall assessment requires a comprehensive measure of health status (Kaplan & Bush, 1982).

Components of a Health Decision Model

The health decision model grew out of substantive theory in economics, psychology, medicine, and public health. These theoretical linkages have been presented in several previous papers (Bush et al., 1973; Chen et al., 1975;

Fanshel & Bush, 1970). Building a health decision model requires at least five distinct steps. The practical side of these steps follows.

Step 1: Defining a Function Status Classification.   During the early phases of the Health Policy Project, Bush and a group of colleagues reviewed multiple sources to determine all the ways that diseases and disabilities can impact function. They organized items from multiple sources into three scales that represent different dimensions of daily functioning: mobility, physical activity, and social activity (Bush, 1983). Levels of these scales are shown in Table 3.3. The reader is cautioned that Table 3.3 is not the scale, but only a listing of labels representing the scale steps. Standardized questionnaires have been developed to classify individuals into one step on each of the three scales. The reliabiity and validity of these instruments is discussed elsewhere (Anderson et al., 1983).

Unique combinations of steps from the three scales are referred to as well-states (Patrick et al., 1973a, 1973b). Thus, for any particular point in time, an individual can be classified into a well-state that is a unique combination of the steps from the three scales.

In some of our previous work, we have referred to unique combinations of the three scales (the well-states) as function levels, and 43 such levels have

TABLE 3.3.   DIMENSIONS AND STEPS FOR FUNCTION LEVELS IN THE QUALITY OF WELL-BEING SCALE

Mobility	Physical Activity	Social Activity
Drove car and used bus or train without help (5)	Walked without physical problems (4)	Did work, school, or housework and other activities (5)
Did not drive, or had help to use bus or train (4)	Walked with physical limitations (3)	Did work, school, or housework but other activities limited (4)
In house (3)	Moved own wheelchair without help (2)	
In hospital (2)	In bed or chair (1)	Limited in amount or kind of work, school, or housework (3)
In special care unit (1)		Performed self-care but not work, school, or housework (2)
		Had help with self-care (1)

Source: Kaplan and Bush, 1982.

been observed to date (Kaplan et al., 1976). Several investigators have used this function status classification (or a modified version of it) as an outcome measure for health program evaluation (cf., Reynolds et al., 1974; Stewart et al., 1978).

However, classification of well-states alone is insufficient as a health outcome measure. As many as 80 percent of those interviewed in population surveys are not dysfunctional. The development of a truly comprehensive health status indicator requires several more steps.

Step 2: Classifying Symptoms and Problems.   There are many reasons that a person may not be functioning at the optimum level. Subjective complaints are an important component of a general health measure because they relate dysfunction to a specific problem. Thus, in addition to classifying people into function levels, an exhaustive list of symptoms and problems has been generated. Included in our list are 35 complexes of symptoms and problems representing all possible symptomatic complaints that might inhibit function. A few examples of these symptoms and problems are shown in Table 3.4.

TABLE 3.4.   TEN SAMPLE SYMPTOM OR PROBLEM COMPLEXES AND ADJUSTMENTS (W_i) FOR LEVEL OF WELL-BEING SCORES

Complex Number	Symptom or Problem Complex	Adjustment
C 1	Any trouble seeing—includes wearing glasses or contact lenses	0.0190
C 9	Pain in chest, stomach, side, back, or hips	−0.0382
C 11	Cough, wheezing, or shortness of breath	−0.0075
C 13	Fever or chills with aching all over and vomiting or diarrhea	−0.0722
C 15	Painful, burning or frequent urination	−0.0327
C 19	Pain, stiffness, numbness, or discomfort or neck, hands, feet, arms, legs, ankles, or several joints together	−0.0344
C 23	Two legs deformed (crooked), paralyzed (unable to move), or broken—includes wearing artificial limbs or braces	−0.0881
C 32	Loss of consciousness such as seizures (fits), fainting, or coma (out cold or knocked out)	−0.1507
C 33	Taking medication or staying on a prescribed diet for health reasons	0.1124
C 35	No symptom or problem	0.2567

Source: Adapted from Kaplan et al., 1976.

Step 3: Weights for the Quality of Well-being.   Combinations of well-states and symptom/problem complexes might describe different levels of wellness. An example of a level of wellness for a particular day might be

In house (mobility 3)
In bed or chair (physical activity 1)
Performed self-care but not work, school, or housework (social activity 2)
Cough, wheezing, or shortness of breath (symptom/problem 11)

Interview instruments are available to place individuals into defined levels of wellness.

As we noted earlier, the health decision model requires that the impact of health conditions upon the quality of life be evaluated. This indicates that the desirability of health situations must be evaluated on a continuum from death to completely well. An evaluation such as this is a matter of judgment or preference, and thus levels of wellness (or well-state-symptom/problem combinations) are scaled so as to represent precise degrees of relative importance.

However, assigning numbers to these levels of wellness is a matter of preference, value, or utility (Kaplan, 1982). Human value studies have been conducted to place the observable well-states onto a preference continuum with the anchor 0 for death and 1.0 for completely well. In several studies, random samples of citizens from a metropolitan community evaluated the desirability of over 400 case descriptions. Using these ratings, investigators have developed a model of preference structure that assigns weights to each well-state scale step and symptom/problem complex (Kaplan et al., 1976; Patrick et al., 1973). Cross-validation studies have shown that the model can be used to assign weights to all possible states of functioning with a high degree of accuracy (R^2 = 96). In fact, the model can accurately forecast ratings of the same case by different judges at a different point in time with an R^2 of .94 (Kaplan et al., 1978).

The preferences are used as weights or weighting factors for well-states. In addition, there is an adjustment for the most undesirable symptom or problem. The resultant preference weighted state is called a quality-of-well-being score. The preference for the well-state described earlier has been measured as .5715 (Kaplan et al., 1976), and adjustment for the symptom or problem was $-.0075$. Therefore, the quality-of-well-being score is .5640. In previous publications, this has also been referred to as the index of well-being.

Typically, the quality-of-well-being score is calculated from data on six consecutive days, and the mean quality-of-well-being score across these days is used to enhance reliability. For each day, the score for a group can be stated symbolically as

$$Q = \frac{1}{N} \sum_{s=1}^{S} Q_s N_s \qquad (1)$$

where N is the total number of persons in the population, N_s is the number of persons at each well-state, Q_s is the social preference (quality) score for each well-state $s = 1, 2, 3, . . ., S$, and S is the total number of well-states.

Thus, the quality-of-well-being score is simply an average of the relative desirability scores assigned to a group of persons for a particular day or a defined interval of time.

Several studies attest to the reliability (Bush et al., 1983; Kaplan et al., 1978) and validity (Kaplan et al., 1976) of the quality-or-well-being scale. For example, convergent evidence for validity is given by significant positive correlations with self-rated health and negative correlations, with age, number of chronic illnesses, symptoms, and physician visits. However, none of these other indicators were able to make the fine discrimination between health states that characterize the quality-of-well-being score.

Step 4: The Well-life Expectancy.   Quality of well-being is only one of the two major components of the health decision model. The other component requires consideration of transitions among the levels over time (Bush et al., 1971).

Consider two persons in the state described earlier; one because he had the flu, and the other because he had chronic obstructive pulmonary disease (COPD). The person with the flu may be acutely ill today but may be in a more desirable state of functioning within a few days. The COPD patient, however, may continue at a low level of functioning.

A health status measure would be incomplete if it included only the current state. To be comprehensive, it must include the expected transitions to other states of wellness over the course of time. A cigarette smoker may be functioning well at present, but in comparison to a nonsmoker, he or she may have a higher probability than a nonsmoker of transition to poorer functioning or to death in the future. Cancer would not be a concern if the disease did not affect current functioning or the probability that functioning would be limited at some point in the future.

The General Health Policy model considers the lifetime expected utility or well-life expectancy. The well-life expectancy is the product of the quality-of-well-being score times the expected duration of stay in each well-state for a standard life period. The expected duration of the stay in each state is determined by transition rates (Berry & Bush, 1978). The well-life expectancy is expressed as

$$E = \sum_{s=1}^{S} Q_s Y_s$$

where E is the well- (quality-adjusted)-life expectancy for a cohort or population in well-years, Y_s is the expected duration in each well-state, s computed from transition probability $s = 1, . . ., j$, Q_s is the quality-of-well-being score or social preference weight associated with each well-state, and S is the total number of well-states in a given analysis.

The well-life expectancy gives the current life expectancy adjusted for diminished well-being associated with dysfunctional states and the duration of stay in each state. The average diminished well-being is expressed by the preference scores [see equation (1)]. Using this system, we can simultaneously consider mortality, morbidity, and the social desirability of function states. When the proper steps have been followed, the model quantifies the health output of a treatment in terms of the equivalents of years of life that it produces or saves. Thus, a *well-year* can be defined conceptually as the equivalent of a year of completely well life, or a year of life free of dysfunction, symptoms, and health-related problems.

An example computation of the weighted life expectancy is shown in Table 3.5. Suppose that a group of individuals were in a well-state for 65.2 years, in a state of nonbed disability for 4.5 years, and in a state of bed disability for 1.9 years before their death at the average age of 71.6 calendar years. In order to make adjustments for the diminished quality of life they suffered in the disability states, we multiply the duration of stay in each state by the preference associated with the state. Thus, the 4.5 years of nonbed disability become 2.7 equivalents of well-years when we adjust for the preferences associated with inhabiting that state. Overall, the well-life expectancy for this group is 68.5 years. In other words, disability has reduced the quality of their lives by an estimated 3.1 years.

Step 5: Estimating the Cost-Effectiveness Ratio. The San Diego Health Policy group has shown in a variety of publications how the concept of a well-life expectancy can be used to evaluate the effectiveness of programs and health interventions. The output of a program has been described in a

TABLE 3.5.   ILLUSTRATIVE COMPUTATION OF
THE WEIGHTED LIFE EXPECTANCY

State	s	Y_s	Q_s	Q_sY_s
Well	A	65.2	1.00	65.2
Nonbed disability	B	4.5	0.59	2.7
Bed disability	C	1.9	0.34	0.6
Total		71.6		68.5

Current life expectancy = $\sum_{s=1}^{S} Y_s = 71.6$ calendar-years

Weighted life expectancy = $\sum_{s=1}^{S} Q_sY_s = 68.5$ well-years

Source: Kaplan and Bush, 1982.

variety of publications as quality-adjusted life-years (Bush et al., 1973), Well-years, equivalents of well-years, or discounted well-years (Kaplan et al., 1976, 1979; Patrick et al., 1973a; 1973b). Weinstein (1983) calls the same output quality-adjusted life-years (QALYS) and this has recently been adopted by the Congressional Office of Technology Assessment (1979). It is worth noting that the quality-adjusted life-years terminology was originally introduced by Bush et al. in 1973 but was later abandoned because it has surplus meaning. The term *wellness* or *well-years* implies a more direct linkage to health conditions. Whatever the term, the index shows the output of a program in years of life adjusted by the quality of life that has been lost because of diseases or disability.

By comparing experimental and control groups using a health policy model, we can estimate the output of a program in terms of the well-years it produces. Dividing the cost of the program by the well-years it yields gives the cost-effectiveness ratio.

It is possible to compare very different types of programs by using this system. The theoretical (expected utility) basis for this system is given in a variety of publications (Bush et al., 1973; Fanshel & Bush, 1970; Kaplan et al., 1976, 1978, 1979). Overviews with examples are provided by Kaplan (1982) and Kaplan & Bush (1982).

Example.   Since what has been described is a complex system, it may be worthwhile to review the steps for classifying a single person. The first step is to place him or her into a well-state. This is accomplished by using a standardized questionnaire to place the individual into one step in each of the scales shown in Table 3.3. Let us suppose that the person was in the house, walked with physical limitations, and was limited in the amount or kind of work he or she performed. The next step is to determine (using the same questionnaire) the symptom or problem that best explains this dysfunction. Let us suppose that it was back pain (relevant to symptom C-9 in Table 3.4). These two bits of information, the well-state and the symptom, define the level of wellness.

Next, a preference for the level is obtained from tables published by Kaplan et al. (1976). These tables show that on a 0 to 1.0 scale this well-state was rated as .5552. There is an adjustment of −.0382 for the particular problem experienced. So, the quality of well-being score is .5170 (.5552 − .0382 = .5170). In other words, members of the community regard this level of wellness as about 52 percent of the way between death and optimum function. Now suppose that the person is frequently reevaluated over the course of 1 year and is found to stay in exactly the same state. We can say that the person has lost .4830 well-years, or for each year in this state of dysfunction the equivalent of nearly on half a year of life is lost. Two years in this state is equivalent to losing 1 year of life (without using a discount function). Finally, suppose that behavior therapy can improve the quality-of-well-being score to .7670. The improvement is .25 units. For each four persons receiving similar benefits from the therapy, 1 well-year is generated ($4 \times .25 = 1$). Dividing the cost of the therapy by this well-year benefit gives a cost-effectiveness ratio. The cost-effectiveness figure can be evaluated in relation to similar figures obtained in evaluations of different therapies (i.e., surgery) or of different types of programs, such as behavioral programs to reduce incontinence in the elderly.

Alternative Decision Theory Approaches

There is considerable variation in the application of health decision models. Conceptually, each of these approaches is very similar. However, the methods differ in how the actual data are obtained. Investigators differ in how they obtain information on well-states and how they measure values.

Many policy analysts actually do not measure well-states directly. Instead, they estimate what the benefits of the program might be from reviews of the literature. For example, Weinstein and Stason (1983) performed a policy analysis on the benefits of coronary bypass surgery. They determined the benefits in terms of years of life added and improvements in function. These benefits were estimated from a review of the world's literature on the surgical technique. They neither performed a study themselves nor developed a specific scheme for classifying well-states. Most policy analysts do not actually observe the well-states directly. It is more common to estimate them from either clinical judgment or other forms of review and analysis. To date, there have been relatively few studies that combine the direct observation of well-states with policy analysis (Atkins et al., 1984; Toevs et al., 1984).

Minor variations in methods used to obtain well-states can have a substantial impact upon the data and the results of the analysis. For example, inadequate caution in the interview procedure can falsely inflate the number of people observed to be completely well. It has been argued that interviewers should probe actual performance of activities for classification of well-states rather than ask about hypothetical capacity to perform these activities. Employing these procedures significantly reduces the number of people observed to be completely well and increases the power of the analysis (Anderson et al., 1983).

The most debted aspect of decision analysis is the method used to obtain values (Kane & Kane, 1982). One of the requirements for scaling quality of well-being is that the values should be measured on an interval scale of measurement. A scale has the interval property if equal differences at different points on the scale have the same meaning. For example, the difference between 0.8 and 0.9 must be equivalent in meaning to the difference between 0.2 and 0.3. Aggregating partial dysfunction into well-year units rests on the axiomatic properties of a linear response scale. In order to add cases that represent different degrees of dysfunction, we need to have a scale where differences at different levels of the response scale are equal.

Our group has argued that a simple category rating scale can be used to obtain interval level values (Blishke et al., 1975) and has provided evidence from a variety of different types of studies to support this assertion (Bush et al., 1983; Kaplan, 1982; Kaplan et al., 1979; Kaplan & Ernst, 1983). However, there is still some debate on this point. Veit and Ware (1982) assert that more traditonal psychophysical methods are required to obtain meaningful values. Torrance (1982) has proposed a multiattribute utility theory method for obtaining the scale values. Economicsts have taken a different approach, arguing that values should be determined by the economic willingness to pay. Subjects are presented with hypothetical choices and asked what proportion of their income they would be willing to pay in order to avoid these circumstances. Determination of values is based on a set of axiomatic principles that are well founded in economic theory (Thompson et al., 1982). It is worth noting that the most widely cited approach to policy analysis does not measure values at all. Weinstein and Stason (1976) arbitrarily assign values to different well-states. They then simulate their policy analysis using a variety of different levels of value in an attempt to determine the impact of value variations upon the analysis.

In summary, decision-theory-based approaches have become popular for policy analysis. Conceptually, there is agreement that quality of life should be integrated with mortality data to obtain quality-adjusted life-years. However, different investigators use various methods to obtain their data. The major differences are in the method used to obtain valuations of health states. Investigators also differ in whether or not they actually measure well-states.

APPLICATIONS OF QUALITY-OF-LIFE MEASURES

Quality-of-life measures are beginning to find widespread use in clinical trials, epidemiologic studies, and in policy analysis.

Clinical Trials

The best way to evaluate a new medical therapy is through a controlled clinical trial in which patients are randomly assigned to treatment or control groups. The objective of most medical interventions is to extend the duration of life and improve the quality of life. However, new medical therapies are often associated with some risk. There have been several clinical trials in which health outcomes were actually poorer in the treated group. If the outcome measure in a clinical trial is very restricted, such as a specific blood chemistry measure, side effects of treatments that affect different systems may be missed. Thus, in addition to specific measures, general quality-of-life measures are also important to include.

Another issue in clinical trials is the definition of an end point. Traditionally, clinical trials only counted the dead. However, many modern treatments can be expected to have relatively little impact upon mortality. In fact, benefits of some surgeries are best reflected in improved quality of life.

Quality-of-life measurement is beginning to gain a foothold in major clinical trials. For example, the SIP has been used in a variety of major clinical trials including the Nocturnal Oxygen Therapy Trial (NOTT). Weinstein and Stason (1983) have shown that the efficacy of coronary artery bypass surgery is difficult to demonstrate when evaluated in terms of mortality alone. However, combining mortality with quality-of-life improvements yields data that strongly support coronary bypass surgery for patients with multiple occluded arteries. Sugarbaker et al. (1982) used quality-of-life assessment to evaluate alternative therapies in a clinical trial of extremity sarcoma. One group of patients had limbs amputated and were given chemotherapy. The other group received limb-sparing surgery plus radiation therapy. It was expected that limb-sparing surgery would produce the greatest quality-of-life benefits. However, when actual observations were made, limb-sparing surgery did not have clear advantages over amputation in terms of quality of life.

Epidemiologic Studies

Outcomes in epidemiologic studies have almost always been measured in terms of mortality. However, many preventive programs are aimed at improving quality of life in addition to extending life's duration. Kaplan (1985) reviewed quality-of-life assessment relevant to epidemiologic studies. It was shown that quality-of-life assessment may have substantial benefits for evaluating the impact of environmental variations upon health status. Combining quality-of-life assessment with policy analysis provides useful information for the expected benefits of preventive intervention. For example, some primary prevention programs are not found to be highly cost effective when subjected to this sort of analysis.

Policy Analysis

Quality-of-life data from clinical trials and from epidemiologic studies can be used in policy analysis. Within the last few years, the number of such analyses reported in the literature has grown considerably. For example, Weinstein (1982) used epidemiologic data to evaluate various priorities in cancer prevention. Consider two different approaches to cancer prevention. One approach attempts to reduce cancer mortality by spending money on carcinogen bioassays that will identify toxic chemicals in the workplace. Then, programs can be developed to reduce environmental exposures that cause cancer. A very different approach to cancer prevention involves the use of dietary supplements such as beta-carotene, a close relative of vitamin A. Growing evidence suggests that dietary intake of beta-carotene may reduce the incidence of cancer mortality. Using data from epidemiologic studies, Weinstein concluded that the wisest use of public resources is to create programs designed to increase beta-carotene consumption. The pay-off for continued vigilence of industrial chemicals was considerably less.

In another recent application of policy analysis, Riddiough et al., (1983) estimated the value of an influenza vaccination program. In recent years, the number of individuals inoculated against the flu has declined. Currently, only about 10 percent of the general population recieves flu vaccinations. Yet, nearly 16,000 excess deaths and 15 million workdays are lost each year due to the flu.

A major factor affecting declining acceptance of the flu vaccine has been concern about safety. Following the 1976 to 1977 National Infuenza Immuni-zation Program against the swine influenza virus, there were several re-ported cases of a partial form of paralysis known as Guillain-Barré syn-drome. Although these cases were very few, they received considerable public attention on popular television programs such as "60 Minutes." After carefully analyzing the expected benefits of a flu vaccination program in terms of quality of life, mortality, and increased productivity, Riddiough et al. concluded that the cost-effectiveness of a vaccination program was relatively low (i.e., good). Even for the aged, the program would cost less than $2000 to produce a quality-adjusted life-year, and for the high-risk aged it would cost abot $4000. These calculations include all the costs of paying for medical benefits for those who live longer because the vaccine prevented an earlier death. They also take into consideration any risks associated with side effects of the vaccine.

A final example of the use of quality-of-life assessment comes from a behavioral intervention clinical trial. Atkins et al. (1984) performed a study evaluating the effects of behavioral interventions for patients with chronic obstructive pulmonary disease (COPD). Substantial medical evidence sug-gests that nothing can be done to cure damaged lungs associated with diseases such as emphysema. However, regular exercise can improve oxy-gen delivery and have a variety of other benefits. Yet, exercise is painful for COPD patients and adherence rates to exercise programs tend to be low. Patients in the Atkins et al. study were randomly assigned to behavioral intervention strategies designed to increase their compliance with exercise or to control groups. Then, they were followed up on regular intervals for 18 months. Those randomly assigned to the behavioral interventions showed significant improvements in the quality-of-life relative to those assigned to control groups. Using these data, experimenter's calculated well-years or quality-adjusted life-years, and it was demonstrated that the cost to produce a well-year was approximately $23,000. This cost-effectiveness ratio com-pares quite favorably with other health care interventions. In other words, the cost-effectiveness of the behavioral intervention program was shown to be less than or equal to many widely accepted medical treatments.

SUMMARY

All participants in the health care system have common goals. These goals include the extension of the duration of life and the improvement in the quality of life. Quality-of-life measurement is relatively new to health care and medical research. Nevertheless, there are a growing number of measurement methods with documented records of validity and reliability.

Different approaches to quality-of-life assessment follow different theoretical traditions. Some of the methods are rooted in psychometric theory and methods of test construction. These include the Sickness Impact Profile, the Index of Activities of Daily Living, the McMaster Health Index Questionnaire, the Arthritis Impact Measurement Scale, and many others. Decision theory provides the basis for other methods of quality-of-life assessment. The goal of these methods is specifically to calculate a well-year or a quality-adjusted life-year that can be used in policy analysis.

Since different participants in the health care system have common goals, it is possible to evaluate alternative interventions in health care by using these same outcomes. Quality-of-life assessment may permit the direct comparison of medical, behavioral, preventive, and environmental programs. Evidence is beginning to accumulate that behavioral intervention programs do produce quality-of-life benefits. Further, some of these programs produce benefits at a cost comparable to the most effective medical interventions.

References

Anderson, J P., Bush, J. W., & Berry, C. C. (1983). Methods of classifying function for quality of life measurement: Quantitative evidence from comparative studies. Unpublished manuscript. San Diego: University of California.

Atkins, C. J., Kaplan, R. M., Timms, R. M., Reinsch, S., & Lofback, K. (1984). Behavioral programs for exercise compliance in chronic obstructive pulmonary disease. *Journal of Consulting and Clinical Psychology, 52,* 591–603.

Balinsky, W., & Berger, R. (1975). A review of the research on general health status indexes. *Medical Care, 13,* 283–293.

Baum, A., Grunberg, N. E., & Singer, J. E. (1982). The use of psychological and neuroendocrinological measurements in the study of stress. *Health Psychology, 1,* 217–236.

Berg, R. (Ed.). (1973). *Health Status Indexes.* Chicago: Hospital Research and Educational Trust.

Bergner, M., Bobbitt, R. A., Carter, W. B., & Gilson, B. S. (1981). The Sickness Impact Profile; development and final revision of a health status measure. *Medical Care, 19,* 787–806.

Bergner, M., Bobbitt, R. A., & Pollard, W. E. (1976). Sickness Impact Profile: Validation of a health status measure. *Medical Care, 14,* 57–61.

Berry, C. C., & Bush, J. W. (1978). Estimating prognoses for a Dynamic Health Index, the weighted life expectancy, using the multiple logistic with survey and mortality data. In *Proceedings of the American Statistical Association, Social Statistics Section* (pp. 716–721).

Biondi, M. (1985). Psychosomatic illness. In R. M. Kaplan & M. H. Criqui (Eds.), *Behavioral epidemiology and disease prevention.* New York: Plenum.

Blischke, W. R., Bush, J. W., & Kaplan, R. M. (1975). A successive intervals analysis of social preference measures for a health status index. *Health Services Research, 10,* 181–198.

Brook, R. H., Ware, J. E., Davies-Avery, A. et al. (1979). Conceptualization and measurment of health for adults in the health insurance studies: Overview. *Medical Care,* supplement monograph, July 1979.

Bush, J. W. (1983). Quality of well-being scale: Function Status Profile and Symptom/Problem Complex Questionnaire. San Diego: Health Policy Project, University of California.

Bush, J. W., Chen, M., & Patrick, D. L. (1973). Cost-effectiveness using a health status index: Analysis of the New York State PKU screening program. In R. Berg, (Ed.), *Health Status Index* (pp. 172–208). Chicago: Hospital Research and Educational Trust.

Bush, J W., Chen, M., & Zaremba, J. (1971). Estimating health program outcomes using a Markov equilibrium analysis of disease development. *American Journal of Public Health, 61,* 2362–2375.

Bush, J. W., Kaplan, R. M., & Blischke, W. R., (1983) Additive utility independence in a multiattribute quality of life scale for the general health policy model. Paper submitted for publication.

Campbell, A., Converse, P. E., & Rodgers, W. L. (1976). *The Quality of American life: Perception, evaluations, and satisfaction.* New York: Russell-Sage.

Carter, W. B., Bobbitt, R. A., Bergner, M., & Gilson, B. S. (1976). The validation of an internal scaling; the sickness impact profile. *Health Services Research, 11,* 516.

Chambers, L. W., Macdonald, L. A., Tugwell, P., Buchanan, W. W., & Kraag, G. (1982). The McMaster Health Index Questionnaire as a measure of quality of life for patients with rheumatoid disease. *Journal of Rheumatology, 9,* 780–784.

Chen, M., & Bush, J. W. (1976). Maximizing health system output with political and administrative constraints using mathematical programming. *Inquiry, 13,* 215–227.

Chen, M. M., Bush, J. W., & Patrick, D. L. (1975). Social indicators for health planning and policy analysis. *Policy Sciences, 6,* 71–89.

Cohen, S., Evans, G. W., Krantz, D. S., & Stokols, D. (1980). Physiological motivational and cognitive effects of aircraft noise on children: Moving from laboratory to the field. *American Psychologist, 35,* 321–343.

DeLongis, A., Coyne, J. C., Dakof, G., Folkman, S., & Lazarus, R. (1982). Relationship of daily hassles, uplifts, and major life events to health status. *Health Psychology, 1982, 1(2),* 119–136.

Fanshel, S., & Bush, J. W. (1970). A health status index and its applications to health-services outcomes, *Operations Research, 18,* 1021–1066.

Friedman, H. (1980). *A primer of epidemiology.* New York: McGraw-Hill.

Goldsmith, S. B. (1972). The status of health status indicators. *Health Services Reports, 87,* 212–220.

Grieco, A., & Long, C. J. (1984). Investigation of the Karnofsky Performance Status as a measure of quality of life. *Health Psychology* (in press).

Holmes, T. H., & Rahe, R. H. (1967). A social readjustment rating scale. *Journal of Psychosomatic Research, 11,* 213–218.

Hutchinson, T. A., Boyd, N. F., Feinstein, A. R. et al (1979). Scientific problems in clinical scales as demonstrated in the Karnofsky Index of Performance Status. *Journal of Chronic Diseases. 32,* 661–666.

Hyde, L., Wolf, J., McCracken, S., & Yesner, R. (1973). Natural course of inoperable lung cancer. *Chest, 64,* 309–312.

Inter-Society Commission for Heart Disease Resources (1970). Primary prevention of artherosclerotic diseases. *Circulation, 42,* A55–A95.

Jaffe, N. (1981). *Cataract surgery and its complications* (3rd ed.). St. Louis: Mosby.

Jette, A. M. (1980). Health status indicators: Their utility in chronic disease evaluation research. *Journal of Chronic Disease, 33,* 567—579.

Kane, R. L., & Kane, R. A. (1982). *Values and Long-term Care.* Lexington, Mass: Lexington Books.

Kaplan, R. M. (1982). Human Preference Measurement for health decisions and the evaluation of long-term care. In R. L. Kane & R. A. Kane (Eds.), *Values and long-term care* (pp. 157—188). Lexington, Mass: Lexington Books.

Kaplan, R. M. (1985). Quantification of health outcomes for policy studies in behavioral epidemiology. In R. M. Kaplan & M. H. Criqui (Eds.), *Behavioral Epidemiology and Disease Prevention.* New York: Plenum.

Kaplan, R. M., & Bush, J. W. (1982). Health-related quality of life measurement for evaluation research and policy analysis. *Health Psychology, 1,* 61—80.

Kaplan, R. M., Bush, J. W., & Berry, C. C. (1976). Health status: Types of validity for an index of well-being. *Health Services Research, 11,* 478—507.

Kaplan, R. M., Bush, J. W., & Berry, C. C. (1978). The reliability, stability, and generalizability of a health status index. *American Statistical Association, Proceedings of the Social Statistics Section* (pp. 704—709).

Kaplan, R. M., Bush, J. W., & Berry, C. C. (1979). Health Status index: Category rating versus magnitude estimation for measuring levels of well-being. *Medical Care, 5,* 501—523.

Kaplan, R. M., & Ernst, J. A., (1983). Do category scales produce biased preference weights for a health index? *Medical Care, 21,* 193—207.

Kaplan, R. M., & Saccuzzo, D. S. (1982). *Psychological testing; prinicples applications and issues.* Monterey: Brooks/Cole.

Katz, S. T., Downs, H., Cash, H., & Grotz, R. (1970). Progress in the development of the index of ADL. *The Gerontologist, 10,* 20—30.

Katz, S. T., Ford, A. B., Moskowitz, R. W., Jackson, B. A., & Jaffee, M. W. (1963). Studies of illness in the aged; the index of ADL. *Journal of the American Association. 185,* 914—919.

Liang, M. H., Cullen, K., & Larson, M. (1982). In search of a more perfect mousetrap (health status or a quality of life instrument). *Journal of Rheumatology, 9,* 775—779.

McDermott, W. (1981). Absence of indicators of the influence of its physician care on a society. *American Journal of Medicine, 70,* 833—843.

McKinley, J. B., & McKinley, S. M. (1977). The questionable contribution of medical measures to the decline of mortality in the United States in the twentieth century. *Milbank Memorial Fund Quarterly/Health and Society, 55,* 405—428.

Meenan, R. F. (1982). AIMS approach to health status measurement; conceptual background and measurement properties. *Journal of Rheumatology, 9,* 785—788.

Meenan, R. F., Gertman, P. M., & Mason, J. H. (1982). The arthritis impact measurement scales; further investigation of a health status measure. *Arthritis and Rheumatology, 25,*1048—1053.

Miller, J. E. (1973). Guidelines for selecting a health status index; Suggested criteria. In R. L. Berg (Ed.), *Health status indexes* (pp. 243—247). Chicago; Hospital Research and Educational Trust.

Mosteller, F. (1981). Innovation and evaluation. *Science, 211,* 881—886.

Mushkin, S. (1962). Health as an investment. *Journal of Political Economy, 70,* 129.

National Institutes of Health (1979). *Epidemiology of respiratory diseases task force report,* Washington DC: U.S. Government Printing Office.

Nelson, E., Conger, B., Douglass, et al. (1983). Functional health status levels of primary care patients. *Journal of the American Medical Assn. 249,* 3331—3338.

Office of Technology Assessment, U.S. Congress (1979). A review of selected federal vaccine and immunication policies: Bases on case studies of pneumococcal vaccine. Washington, DC: U.S. Government Printing Office.

Patrick, D. L., Bush, J. W., & Chen, M. (1973a). Toward an operational definition of health. *Journal of Health and Social Behavior, 14,* 6−23.

Patrick, D.L., Bush, J. W., & Chen, M. (1973b). Methods for measuring levels of well-being for a health status index. *Health Services Research, 8,* 228−245.

Reynolds, W. J., Rushing, W. A., & Miles, D. L. (1974). The validation of a function status index. *Journal of Health and Social Behavior, 15,* 271−288.

Riddiough, M. A., Sisk, J. E., & Bell, J. C. (1983). Influenza vaccination: Cost effectiveness and Public policy. *Journal of the American Medical Associaton, 249,* 9189−9195.

Rokeach, M. (1973). *The nature of human values,* New York: Free Press/Macmillan.

Sarason, I. G., Levine, H. M., Basham, R. B., & Sarason, D. R. (1983). Asessing social support; the social support questionnaire. *Journal of Personality and Social Psychology, 44,* 127−139.

Stanley, K. E. (1980). Prognostic factors for survival in patients with inoperable lung cancer. *Journal of the National Cancer Institute, 65,* 25−32.

Stewart, A. L., Ware, J. E., Brook, R. H., & Davies-Avery, A. (1978). *Conceptualization and measurement of health for adults:* Vol. 2 *Physical health in terms of functioning.* Santa Monica: Rand Corp.

Sugarbaker, P. H., Barofsky, I., Rosenberg, F. A., & Gianola, F. J. (1982). Quality of life assessment of patients in extremity sarcoma clinical trials. *Surgery, 91,* 17−23.

Sullivan, D. F. (1966). *Conceptual problems in developing an index of health,* Washington, DC.: National Center for Health Statistics.

Thompson, M. S., Read, J. L., & Liang, M. (1982). Willingness-to-pay concepts for societal decisons in health. In R. L. Kane & R. S. Kane (Eds.), *Values and long-term care* (pp. 103−125). Lexington, Mass.: Lexington Books.

Toevs, C. D., Kaplan, R. M., & Atkins, C. J. (1984). The costs and effects of behavioral programs in chronic obstructive pulmonary disease. *Medical Care*

Torrance, G. W. (1982). Multiattributes utility theory as a method for measuring social preferences for health states in long-term care (pp. 127−156). In R. L. Kane & R. A. Kane (Eds.), *Values and long-term care,* Lexington, Mass.: Lexington Books.

Veit, C. T., & Ware, J. E. (1982). Measuring health and health-care outcomes: Issues and recommendations. In R. L. Kane & R. A. Kane (Eds.), *Values and long-term care* (pp. 233−259). Lexington, Mass.: Lexington Books.

Ware, J. E., Brook, R. H., Davies, A. R., & Lohr, K. N. (1981). Choosing measures for health status for individuals in general populations. Santa Monica: Rand Corporation.

Warner, K. E., & Hutton, R. C. (1980). Cost-benefit and cost-effectiveness analysis in health care. *Medical Care, 18,* 1069−1084.

Weinstein, M. C. (1983). Cost-effective priorities for cancer prevention. *Science, 221*(4605), 17−23.

Weinstein, M. C., & Stason, W. B. (1976). *Hypertension: A policy perspective.* Cambridge, Mass.: Harvard University Press.

Weinstein, M. C. & Stason, W. B. (1983). *Cost-effectiveness of coronary artery bypass surgery.* Harvard University: Center for Analysis of Health Practice.

Wingo, L., & Evans, A. (1978). *Public economics and the quality of life.* Baltimore: John Hopkins University Press.

World Health Organization (1948). *Constitution of the World Health Organization,* In Basic documents, WHO, Geneva.

Yates, J. W., Chalmer, B., & McKegney, F. P. (1980). Evaluations of patients with advanced cancer using the Karnofsky Performance Status. *Cancer, 45,* 2220−2224.

4

Ecobehavioral Assessment in Health Life-styles: Concepts and Methods

RICHARD A. WINETT

There is a danger in the development of the emerging field of health psychology that it will closely follow prevailing psychological paradigms and become no more than the psychology of individual health behavior without regard to social, economic, environmental, or political context. This is especially true given the field's growth during a time of political conservatism and a corresponding retrenchment within psychology to the paradigm of the "contextless individual" (Sarason, 1981). The 1960s and early 1970s were seemingly a time of burial for intrapsychic paradigms with the funeral called for and attended by the behaviorists. However, despite much early promise (e.g., Bandura, 1969) and some exciting forays into extensions of the paradigm (Rogers-Warren & Warren, 1977), the burial of the intrapsychic paradigm was actually never completed, the funeral was premature, and the true message of the behavioral paradigm was apparently never understood, or today, discarded. The "true message" of the behavioral paradigm was not that we should narrowly focus on individual behavior and contingencies at the individual level of analysis but that behavior must be understood and analyzed within interrelationships to broader environmental influences and constraints (Krasner & Ullman, 1973).

This broader perspective has been momentarily derailed by the course of recent political and economic events that have influenced psychology a great deal and misdirected and returned it to its safer and more exclusive focus on the individual (Sarason, 1981). However, because health psychology is emerging at this particular point in time, it runs the danger of only becoming *a health psychology of the detached individual!*

This chapter's purpose is to help restore some balance to the scene. Although the major objective is to describe an ecobehavioral assessment perspective, assessment and intervention strategies presumably are derived from particular paradigms. Just as it makes little sense for the behavior therapist to interpret projective test results in assessment, it makes equally little sense for the ecobehaviorist to rely on narrowly conceived health behavior assessments. Thus, the first need is to articulate and flesh out an ecobehavioral paradigm for health behavior with assessment approaches following from that perspective.

AN ECOBEHAVIORAL PARADIGM

Behavioral paradigms need to delineate explicitly influences and constraints on behavior. The deceptively simple question asked in this chapter is, "Where do healthy and unhealthy life styles come from?" The ecobehavioral paradigm does not neglect or discard what is within the person. It is assumed that any environmental influence is mediated by a range of interactive, intraindividual genetic, biological, cognitive, and behavioral skill variables. However, the focus of concern for the ecobehavioral paradigm is the broader environmental influences and health behaviors of large population segments. In this way, the paradigm is similar to public health perspectives (Iscoe, 1982) and medical sociology (Mechanic, 1978) and follows other ecological health models (e.g., Catalano, 1979), as well as more general, ecological positions (e.g., Bronfenbrenner, 1979).

The purpose of this section is not to review comprehensively every potential environmental influence on health (an impossible task), but rather, to review more briefly a number of different kinds of environmental influences on health in order to illustrate this perspective and to provide a basis for ecobehavioral assessment methods. The discussion begins with an influence familiar to most psychologists, the interpersonal environment, but then moves toward larger influences, perhaps, more relevant to population-based health concerns.

THE INTERPERSONAL ENVIRONMENT

There is some evidence that the nature of a person's interactions with family, relatives, friends, and coworkers can have health protective, and possibly health promotional, benefits (Gottlieb, 1981). Recent work has gone beyond initial epidemiologic studies that showed a relationship between social isolation and illness and social support and health (e.g., Cassel, 1974). For example, a long-term follow-up of participants in the Alameda County study showed that social "connectedness" (i.e., being married, belonging to a church; Berkman & Syme, 1979) was an independent risk factor and health protector. More recent work has been concerned with delineating aspects of social support that may "buffer" stress (Cohen, 1983). Critical aspects of social support may include the perception that it is available and, indeed, the provision of the availability of nontangible (e.g., empathy, advise) support. Although this notion has wide intuitive appeal, suggests exciting preventive programs, and has resulted in an avalanche of papers and studies, the consensus is that this concept remains somewhat conjectural, and that person, interaction, and network aspects of social support are exceedingly complex (Heller & Swindle, 1983). For example, whether help is sought and then received by a person probably depends on the person's level of social skill, past history of help seeking and reciprocity, the nature of the problem, the skills and information of the helper, the timing and place of the help seeking, the nature of a person's social network, and the position of the help seeker and helpee in that network (Cohen, 1983; Heller & Swindle, 1983).

However, although acknowledging the faddish aspect and inherent complexity of social support research, what seems most important and revealing is that social connectiveness (or lack thereof) seems to crop up as an influential variable in a range of research (Felner et al., 1983; Gottlieb, 1981). If future research continues to provide evidence for the relationship of social support to health-related behaviors, then both individual and population-based assessments need to examine this variable further. This will be even more true if future research shows that social networks can be developed or modified for health promotion or restorative purposes, a research direction that has already begun (Hirsch, 1980, 1981; Wellman, 1981).

THE INFORMATIONAL ENVIRONMENT

Information that is available to citizens in a variety of forms can have a marked impact on health behaviors. For example, regulatory reform has had as one objective the freer distribution of information on foods, cigarettes, medicine, and availability and price of medical services so that consumers can make better informed choices in their health practices (Pertschuk, 1982). Recent attempts to roll back information disclosure laws by portraying them as invasive and paternalistic or harmful to business must be met by the evidence that consumers appear to appreciate and increasingly use available information in health choice. In some instances (advertising), readily available information has created a more competitive health sector, so that certain services have become less expensive and available to more people (Pertschuk, 1982). Further, it must be noted that the provision of free and easily accessible information is at the heart of democratic systems and free-market economics. The role of information in health care economics will be returned to in a later section; but here the focus will be on the broader informational context, particularly the television media.

The advent of television assuredly influenced health behaviors in terms of changing family and other social interaction patterns, and not surprisingly, changing aspects of sleep (Comstock, 1980). But most attention has been focused on the more direct effects of the medium and its message on health behaviors. However, the content and form of television can only be understood from the perspective of its major mission which, in the United States, is to deliver the largest possible audience to advertisers (Cantor, 1980). Thus, television programming is the vehicle to maintain viewership of advertiser's products, with the eventual goal of increased consumption of products. Therefore, cartoons can deliver children to advertisers, and violent shows can also deliver adult population segments. The arguments concerning health and the media involve (1) the nature of the specific program content (e.g., violence) and its effects on behavior (e.g., aggression; Leibert et al., 1982); (2) the nature of the products typically advertised during particular programs geared to particular population segments (e.g., heavily sugared cereal; a succession of beer commercials); and (3) the more pervasive and, perhaps, insidious picture provided of health and well-being (i.e., consume more), the frequent depictions of nonhealthy and unsafe behaviors (e.g., reckless driving), and a view that health problems are individually based, probably cannot be prevented, but usually, even when serious, are easily fixed (e.g., recall "Marcus Welby").

A medium virtually controlled by advertisers' dollars makes arguments about not tampering with the "free market" of the medium a bit ludicrous, and recent years have seen attempts, some successful, to modify program content, for example, with regard to violence (Liebert et al., 1982), or eliminate certain products from advertisement such as cigarettes (although some claim cigarette companies have actually monetarily gained from this ban; Pertschuk, 1982). Recent years have also seen a burgeoning of interest in the development of prohealth, media-based programs and communication campaigns (Maccoby & Solomon, 1981); and, indeed, even a 24-hour a day cable TV health network has been started. There is continued debate about the effectiveness of such programs in directly influencing targeted health practices (Lau et al., 1980; Wallack, 1981); but these efforts are seen as, at least in one small way, trying to balance the availability of correct health information. One caveat is that many of these programs may only focus on the personal aspects of health behavior, and thus, continue the distorted picture of individual "causality" and "blame" for health risk. The second caveat is that, in this country, for health programs to have wide impact, they must be supportable through advertising, a situation suggesting that programs depicting the social, economic, and environmental, much less media-based causes of ill-health, may not be commercially viable.

On the person level, this brief overview of media influences suggests careful assessment of current beliefs and information about health practices. On a population level, we are alerted to the fact that the media can reflect and maintain distorted health information and beliefs. On the other hand, the promise is that the media can become a major vehicle for health promotion and health care.

THE ECOLOGY OF CITIES

It is also impossible to assess and modify health behaviors and practices without regard to the organization and ecology of our population centers. The large cities as a place of work can be seen as a result and perhaps remnant of the earlier industrialization that required the centralization of mass operations and people (Catalano, 1979). The advent of the automobile, a determined highway policy, a rising middle class, and a federal policy to make the American dream of home ownership an inexpensive reality created the suburbs (and, later "exurbs") and the "commuting society." These arrangements have had profound effects on health behaviors in some obvious, and not so obvious, ways.

Many writers have documented the plight and numerous problems of the poverty stricken population segment left and contained in the central cities. Substandard housing, crowding, unavailable services, inadequate access to health care, and prevailing despair and powerlessness result in health statistics comparable to some of the poorest developing countries. These same conditions result in levels of crime, violence, and addiction, at times, compatible with a war zone (Catalano, 1979). These points are meant to be neither an exposé or a way to arouse guilt. Rather, they serve to remind us that, in our ecological analyses of the interplays of individual characterstics and behaviors, and environments and health outcomes, for some population segments our focus must be fixed strongly on the environment. Against the overwhelming barriers to good health ennumerated earlier, it makes little sense to explain poor health outcomes as a result of individual deficits or lack of responsibility (Rappaport, 1977). As long as the environmental conditions remain, the health statistics will remain the same.

Although this first focus has been on the entrapment and poverty of one segment of our society as a long-term result of urbanization (which is not to say that some similar conditions do not exist in some rural areas), the centralization of work and the creation of suburbs have had effects on health practices of the broad middle class. One effect has been detachment and lack of connectedness, as many communities have simply become bedroom communities where people sleep and engage in some leisure and consumption in between commuting and working. Suburban communities are also characterized by age and income segregation and, for some, social isolation (Dolce, 1976). Perhaps, a larger effect for those commuting substantial distances to work is to create a level of stress and time commitment that is ironically at odds with the historical movement to humanize work itself and reduce the hours of labor (Nollen, 1982).

In this analysis, it is essential to understand how much work and its schedule determines the ebb and flow of peoples' lives and, indeed, the daily life of cities (Robinson, 1977). It is the schedule of work that dictates when people will arise, when they will eat, when they will socialize, and when they will sleep. It is the schedule of work that determines when and where there will be massive traffic jams and unacceptable air quality. It is the schedule of work and living and commuting patterns that determine the availability of time and constraints on engaging in some health-related behaviors. For example, in one of the author's studies on alternative work patterns conducted in Washington, DC, which is not an extremely large city, it was found that the average time spent at the worksite was 8½ hours per day; however, 2½ hours per day were spent on the average in commuting and related activities, meaning that about 11 hours per day were used on the average in work-related activities (Winett et al., 1982). Recent studies have documented the stressful aspects of commuting each day (Stokols et al., 1978). But, in addition (and the main point here), is the fact that the sheer amount of time involved in work places constraints and costs on engaging in other behaviors.

For example, in an examination of some very fine-grain, time-allocation data collected from detailed time-activity logs from participants in the alternative work schedules project, it was noted that, on the average, this young ($\bar{x} = 33$ years), middle-class sample of people who were parents of younger children, minimally ($\bar{x} = 10$ minutes per day) engaged in one key health behavior, that is, exercise. Our eventual interpretation of this finding was not within the current health psychology paradigm of individual deficit and responsibility. Rather, it was noted that the time devoted to commuting, work, the family, and sleeping and eating did not leave much extra time. Time became a scarce resource and precious commodity. To devote an hour a day to exercise had some very high costs and constraints attached to this resource expenditure. Some proposed solutions to this problem can be seen in recent worksite health programs (e.g., being able to exercise at the worksite during lunch hour; Wilbur, 1981); in employers' permitting lower work hours (e.g., 6 hours per day) during life-cycle periods requiring considerable family time (Lamb & Sagi, 1983); and in efforts to decentralize work settings and make them contiguous with living centers, particularly as the nature of work has changed in our society (Nollen, 1982).

The arrangement of our urban areas and the time involved in working are only two examples of how the ecology of our society forms and constrains health-related practices. The examples are used not because they are the best, or are more inclusive of other factors, but because they are familiar and serve to remind us that health assessments and intervention strategies must focus on the environment as well as on the individual.

ECONOMIC INFLUENCES

The previous section has noted some of the health-related outcomes of poverty, but in this section, the purpose is to examine more broadly economic influences on health care practices in terms of economic policy and health care economics. The recent, pervasive, and purposely planned deep recession (Piven & Cloward, 1982) has had one favorable outcome in the behavioral sciences; it has resulted in some important research connecting changes in the economic environment to health practices and outcomes and has thrust the behavioral sciences into a major policy debate of the day. For example, Catalano and Dooley (1983) have greatly refined the earlier epidemiologic techniques of Brenner (1973), who demonstrated a relationship between economic downturn and aggregate measures of poor health outcome by more carefully assessing economic change, intervening mechanisms, and individual health outcomes. One conclusion of a study, actually conducted during a relatively good economic period (late 1970s), was that for the middle class, economic downturn did result in job and financial difficulties, which in turn increased the probability of ill-health incidence and health risk. Thus, their work provides the linkages missing in some earlier research.

Liem and Ramsay (1982) noted that considerable economic and social welfare policy has been developed based on the notion that there exists a certain underlying, but benign, level of unemployment. Given this perspective, the true social and psychological costs of unemployment have never been calculated, much less been a part of economic policy. In their research, the authors document that for for some groups, unemployment seems to result in clinical (mental health) symptomotology that may have large long-term person, family, and community costs. They also point out that in the United States, where health care benefits are attached to employment, the loss of employment automatically imperils the person and his or her family.

Thus, both the work by Catalano and Dooley and Liem and Ramsay, whose perspectives and outcomes are supported by other investigators (see Felner et al., 1983), of necessity, forces prime emphasis in ecobehavioral assessment and intervention to economic policy.

However, it is equally important to assess the role of economic variables within the health care system itself. Most recent attention has been directed to health care cost containment as data indicate that health care costs continue to increase at a rate much greater than inflation and that health costs now amount to about 10 percent of our GNP (Matarazzo, 1983). Of primary concern has been the fee for the service system that prevails in the United States and offers no incentive for providers to focus on preventive health measures or to supply the least expensive services (Navarro, 1976). Over the years, a number of alternative health models have been proposed (Roy, 1978), including the expansion of health maintenance organizations (HMOs) and other prepayment plans. In HMOs, the primary incentive can be to keep people well, since a fixed prepayment is all the money available to provide a complete range of services to the enrollee. Presumably, if the person is kept well, through more attention to preventive services, the costs to the HMO decrease. Although there are still many questions about HMOs (e.g., the possibilities of excluding from a plan too many people with expensive preconditions or even promoting underutilization of services), and some continued political opposition, burgeoning health costs have made the HMO concept more attractive. Interest in the fee structure and provision of health care service also serve to remind us that economic forces, some fairly easy to identify, and indeed, capable of being conceptualized within reinforcement terms, can have a profound effect on aggregate and individual health care practices. Such is also the case with the debate about health care insurance.

Most health care costs are now paid through third-party mechanisms, that is, health benefits/insurance and entitlement programs (Medicare and Medicaid). Although for most Americans this has resulted in the minimization of the financial hardships of long-term illness or other catastrophic event, an important outcome, it has also resulted in a situation where neither patients nor providers have any incentive to contain health costs. Thus, the true and escalating health insurance costs are both delayed in time and distant in place and saliency, meaning that such costs are often not seen as directly resulting from current practices and have minimal effects on provider or patient cost containment behaviors. Indeed, they have had the apparent effect of increasing costs. Various proposals have been put forth to change this situation, principally through empirically testing the effects of plans that require differential payments by health care consumers of portions of their fees for service utilization and health care outcomes (Newhouse et al., 1981). Other proposals call for more emphasis on a free-market approach in health care by allowing different health plans to compete more openly with each other. Finally, another approach involves more government regulation by the specification of acceptable fees for particular services; such an approach has apparently been successful in containing costs in experiments conducted by some states (*New York Times*, 1983a). However, the health insurance issue has yet another major question that links economics and behavior.

"Health insurance" is an interesting misnomer since health policies generally only pertain to illness, disability, or death. Although the value of preventive approaches has been documented (Matarazzo, 1983), they generally are not paid for by health insurance. There are historical and economic reasons for this system (e.g., see Navarro, 1976), but the main result for consumer and provider has been gross overemphasis on expensive diagnosis, treatment, and rehabilitation, and a neglect of prevention. In the search for understanding why people are not healthier or why simply preventive practices are not more widely engaged in, one must come face to face with health care economics. It simply is unlikely that people will act counter to economic contingencies. The attractive part about HMOs is that their organization of services recognizes this fact and seeks to change contingencies to foster health and well-being.

OTHER ENVIRONMENTAL CONSIDERATIONS

At the outset, it was stated that the function of the introductory sections was not to delineate every possible environmental factor related to health, which was seen as an impossible task, but to highlight some areas that make us question the prevailing paradigm in health psychology, that, for the most part, views health behaviors *out of context*. Concepts and data showing the interplay of health behaviors with interpersonal networks, the media and information environment, the organization of work and cities, and economic factors and contingencies were chosen because they represent different aspects and levels of analysis, and because (and, frankly) I have some knowledge in the areas chosen. The rather direct connection in each area of behavior and context was apparent. In this section, I will note a few current concerns, in less detail, hopefully to broaden the perspective already developed, but without any claim as to the exhaustiveness of the exposition.

Regulation

As mentioned previously, one of the major debates in governmental policy in recent years has been the role, enforcement, and effectiveness of governmental regulation. Most of these regulations have been promulgated with a prime consideration being health outcomes and costs. Two examples are the policies concerning regulation and enforcement of toxic waste procedures and debates about the clean air act. Although exact knowledge about dosage levels and exposure needed to increase health risk significantly (particularly at more typical levels) are not always clear, there seems less debate about effects given more extreme and long-term exposure to certain toxins. Indeed, recent and apparent politically motivated attempts to roll back such regulations in the guise of increasing industrial productivity (e.g., see Pertschuk, 1982) have been countered by framing the regulations within a public health perspective (*New York Times*, 1983b). Further, there does appear to be ample evidence that inappropriate toxic waste disposal has current and long-term radiating effects on health through the seepage of toxic wastes into our ground water supply (Ashworth, 1982).

Other regulations developed over the years by the Federal Trade Commission and other agencies have had as their goal increasing available, truthful information to consumers. For example, detailed labeling of the contents of foods and medicines are aimed at protecting the public, and through increased information flows, making the marketplace more competitive, with a possible reduction of costs to consumers (Engel & Blackwell, 1982).

It has been suggested that just as fluoridation and vaccination programs have had large-scale effects on health, now as in the past, current environmental and consumer regulations are needed to foster health on a population basis. Health psychologists typically are not directed toward analyzing and promoting such approaches to health care change, but the argument here is that they are of obvious, integral, but neglected concerns. For example, although smoking prevention (Evans et al., 1981) and smoking cessation programs (McAlister, 1981), and programs to change dietary habits (Maccoby & Solomon, 1981) are valuable and becoming more effective, their ultimate effect on actual health outcomes will be minimized in places where simply breathing the air may be equivalent to smoking a pack of cigarettes per day, or where knowledge about the choice of foods is limited by restricted information flows and other policies.

Nature of Work

Considerable interest through the years has focused on the nature of work and health outcomes. One connection with the brief prior section on regulation are the various health and safety regulations that are also under recent attack. Whatever is the eventual outcome of the debates concerning the degree of regulation needed, it is apparent that specifiable work conditions (e.g., work involving asbestos) greatly increases health risks. In conjunction with other health risks (e.g., smoking), certain working conditions dramatically multiply the chance of disability and early death (Matarazzo, 1983). These connections have been made through the years, but it remains to be seen as to how much health psychology work will focus on occupational health and safety.

Besides the more extreme examples of increased health risk from particular kinds of work, recent interest has also focused on the stress and strain caused more generally by work, with such stress seen as a precursor or concomitant of detrimental health behaviors (e.g., alcoholism and drug abuse) or other stress-related diseases (e.g., a range of psychophysiological problems). In this case, we are not only addressing high-stress occupations, such as air traffic controllers, but the more pervasive day-to-day stress caused by increased automation and alienation resulting from the processes and products of work. One possible interesting and very valuable secondary outcome of changes toward more participatory management practices to increase productivity may be a decrease in alienation and stress, and hence a decrease in job-related health problems.

Although work schedules as a determinant of health behavior have been discussed previously, more recent research has focused on the health costs of extreme work schedules, that is, shift work. Shift work may actually increase since the large capital investment needed for the new technology industries virtually demands some round-the-clock operations. Recent data also indicate that shift work is most prevalent in a population segment already under considerable stress, that is, dual-earner families with young children (Presser & Cain, 1983). The interactions of shift work with family patterns and health costs remains unclear.

What recent research has made clearer is that shift work can radically interfere with an individual's circadian rhythm, creating a host of predictable sleep, mood, eating, and interpersonal problems (Czeisler et al., 1982). An important ecological health psychology intervention has involved changes in shift rotations in light of biological principles so as to reduce aversive health outcomes of shift work (Czeisler et al., 1982).

Again regulations on health and safety and shift work draws us heavily into the world of work as important ground to analyze antecedents of ill-health and potential protective interventions.

Safety

Safety in terms of regulation has been alluded to in the prior section, but here the focus will be on one set of safety practices that have enormous potential individual cost and tremendous documented societal costs. The practices involve safety restraint in automobiles. Not wearing a seat belt or improper (or no) child restraint is a major health risk. Recent attempts to increase safety restraint use have included psychologically based incentives intervention, for example, to increase seat belt usage (Geller et al. 1982) and the passage of laws (of different scope and contingencies) to promote increased use of appropriate child restraints and fines for nonuse (Seekins et al., 1983). The psychological and legal approaches are very important but should not distract us from one of the original impetuses for the consumer movement—the effects of automobile design on safety (i.e., Ralph Nadar's first issue). That is, some aspects of current design can be further modified in ways to reduce the injury and death toll of accidents.

The goal of the entire first section of this chapter was to show that environmental factors must have a prominent place in the assessment of health behaviors and their eventual modification. This section has also alluded to the political nature of environmental factors and the purpose of this next, but briefer section, is to discuss further the political context of health behaviors.

POLITICAL-IDEOLOGICAL CONTEXT

The preceding sections make the case for health-related behaviors and practices being the product of a range of environmental influences from interpersonal networks to payment mechanisms for health care to the arrangement of work in our society. Throughout this background section, there were also some allusions to the political nature of these environmental influences. For example, radically different views of the role of government regulation in health and safety are likely to result in quite different outcomes. In this section, some aspects of the overarching political context will be developed further.

In some respects, an ecological position that is concerned with interdependencies is at odds with some political positions. For example, an extreme laissez-faire position tends to depict individuals as free to choose various paths of self-interest, relatively unencumbered (Friedman & Friedman, 1979). Presumably, everyone acting in self-interest will result in the greatest collective good, that is, the "invisible hand" notion of Adam Smith. Particular kinds of regulation and other government interventions are seen as undermining the workings of a free-market economy. The ecological position stresses constraints on behavior and interdependencies of actions that may, or may not, be for the collective good. Thus, the laissez-faire position seems to contradict emerging conceptions of human behavior and the workings of society. The word "emerging" was purposely used in the prior sentence to reflect the fact that the dominant American psychological paradigm has been the paradigm of the contextless individual (Sarason, 1981). It is important to see that this paradigm, not surprisingly, closely parallels a number of tenets of laissez-faire capatalism, for example, an individual free to choose. American psychology is seen as following the country's political traditions, and also as being used as an instrument of policy, for instance, in determining how and what to focus on in health programs.

Recent swings to this more conservative position *have* resulted in some deregulation (with presumably some health consequences) with the rationale of "freeing" people, that is, "getting government off the backs of people." The apparent large-scale support for certain regulations such as clean air measures suggests that a large segment of the population may not share the conservative position on this issue and sees the close relationship between environment and health.

Perhaps, an even more basic ideological battle concerns the issue of "rights" versus "duty and responsibility" in health care. This issue is also intertwined with political beliefs and conceptions of human behavior, but also has come to the forefront because of the continuous escalation of health care costs in the face of decreased resources to fund health care. An extreme rights position sees access to good health care as a basic entitlement of a citizen regardless of cost. An extreme "duty and responsibility" position sees health in large measure as being related to individual initiative and choice, and thus, has some compatibility with some conservative ideology.

One simplistic connection that has been made is between the relationship of health risk behaviors, "life-style," and morbidity. The greatest causes of morbidity today are seen in behaviors such as smoking, drinking, over eating, or poor dietary practices; disease, therefore, is potentially preventable (Matarazzo, 1983). These behaviors are largely seen as a product of individual choice (Fuchs, 1975). Government can supply information and education to promote prevention and better health choices, but in the end, the ultimate responsibility for health belongs to the individual.

Obviously, there is much truth to this position. People can and do make health choices, but this chapter has emphasized that they are choices made under environmental influence and constraint. In addition, the "responsibility and duty" perspective can and has been used as a rationale for deregulation in health and safety and for defunding of health case.

Perhaps, one of the greatest tasks in this decade is to strike a *balance* between the rights and the duty position. It becomes clear that society cannot continue to pay for more and more health care or have every aspect of life regulated. It also is clear that, even within constraints, people can and do make relatively free choices that greatly influence their health. At the same time, there seem to be certain basics in health care and environmental protection that should be the entitlement of citizens and certain health choices that are not really choices at all. This section was not meant to reduce the tension between these positions, much less solve the issue. The section was meant to show how overarching, idealogical concerns shape analyses of health behaviors.

ASSESSING HEALTH BEHAVIORS WITHIN AN ECOBEHAVIORAL FRAMEWORK

Brief Example

Although an ecological perspective makes good conceptual sense, the movement of this position into the everyday concerns of assessment and intervention can be quite intimidating for most behavioral scientists. This is not only because an ecological perspective means interactions and complexity, but, in particular, and as argued in this chapter, because it points toward analysis and intervention in larger-scale systems. This is unfamiliar turf to many behavioral scientists, especially psychologists. With some recent exceptions (e.g., Maccoby & Solomon, 1981), it is probably true that the likelihood of psychologists routinely becoming involved in macrolevel interventions is not great. Although it is apparent that there is not one solution to the dichotomy between theory and belief on the one hand and reality on the other, there seems to be a number of reasonable compromises when the issues of *levels* and *types* of assessment and intervention are addressed.

Problems can be conceptualized at different levels, that is, individual, small group, small setting, organization, institutional, community (Rappaport, 1977), and one key for psychologists in the future may be to raise their level of analysis one notch, particularly to develop strategies at the intersection of individual/group and group/setting/organizational levels. This need not mean that the behavioral scientist believes that the *entirety* of the cause and solution to the problem rests at that level of analysis or intervention, as has been noted before (Rappaport, 1977). Rather, it may represent what is feasible and practical at the time. In addition, assessments and interventions at lower levels can be made with knowledge of higher-order influences and constraints, with perhaps, some interventions empowering people to help make changes in larger systems (Felner et al., 1983).

Assessment from an ecobehavioral perspective, thus, is concerned with individual behavior within the environmental context. This approach will first be illustrated by one major health problem, smoking, particularly the onset of smoking in young adolescents. It is assumed that this is such a serious problem and so pervasive that the eventual intervention approach will be at least the small group setting level or mass-aggregate level, that is, not the individual level. But, as in traditional behavioral assessment, we can start at the individual level and tap cognitive, affective, and behavioral aspects of this problem.

Cognitive aspects include beliefs, attitudes, and information about smoking, for example, health risk now and in the future, addictive qualities, prevalence of smoking, smoking by celebrities. There are a number of available scales that tap these dimensions (see Evans et al., 1981). Affective aspects can focus on the meaning of smoking (e.g., in a peer group) and affective uses of smoking such as in anxiety reduction. Behavioral dimensions can focus on the topography of smoking (amount, nicotine and tar level, depth of inhalation), individual skills in acquiring or refusing cigarettes, and individual skills and resources to engage in behaviors incompatible with smoking. This information can also be gleaned from available questionnaires, as well as from focus groups and the like. In addition, physiological measures (thyocynate; CO level) that reflect actual smoking level can be obtained at a relatively low cost (Lando, 1975). Data on predisposing factors (i.e., parental smoking) can also be obtained. Although these data can be very rich, useful, and necessary to obtain, they are hardly a sufficient basis for understanding the problem or for intervening.

A *complete ecosystem assessment* is necessary, and such an approach can also provide some important evaluation data beyond the individual level. Of critical importance for this problem is the timing and place of onset (i.e., with the peer group at typically 10 to 12 years old); reactions of self and others to the first smoking experiences; sources of cigarettes (e.g., particular vending machines or stores); responses of older youth and adults in the community to smoking by young adolescents; school, religious organizations, and recreational center policies on smoking; enforcement of laws concerning purchase of cigarettes by minors in the community; and availability of antismoking material in stores. All these suggested areas of assessment concern the settings and organizations in the community that are related to teenage smoking. It is undoubtedly true that existing media that glamorizes smoking are, in part, responsible for teenage smoking, as is certainly the continued policy of tobacco subsidies. Those areas need to be addressed but seem out of range of most behavioral scientists. Here the focus is more on the organizational and community levels.

Although such analyses have been done before and resulted in school-based, media-assisted interventions focused on teaching children the dangers of smoking and how to refuse cigarettes, with primary assessment and evaluation at the individual level (Evans et al., 1981), the argument here is that assessment and intervention need not follow that path. For example, it is conceivable that a major emphasis can be at the legal level, with enforcement of laws concerning selling cigarettes to minors being the centerpiece. Dependent measures to evaluate this approach could include the number of fines to proprietors selling cigarettes to minors and observations of adolescents' use of vending machines. Or, efforts to preclude smoking on school grounds can be assessed by regular counts of cigarette butts on or near school grounds and in other areas frequented by youth.

Quite obviously, the intervention and evaluation measures need to follow the pivotal information found in the ecoassessment. However, when this information is gleaned, one other important aspect needs to be considered— a social marketing approach (Solomon, 1981). Here through surveys, focus groups, and other techniques, it is discerned what programs and media and modalities of delivery are seen as most appropriate and acceptable to the target population and to involved organizations and community settings. For example, it may be clear that if access to cigarettes was markedly curtailed through law enforcement, then teenage smoking may be greatly reduced. However, the police may have no way of enforcing the laws, and store owners, parents, other citizens, and youth may be hostile to this "solution." In this case, the legal approach seems doomed to failure. All these groups may favor an educational and skill-training strategy, which the ecoassessment may suggest is only part of the problem; yet, it is this approach that may be the only one that is acceptable at the time.

FOCUSED EXAMPLES

Exercise

Even though engaging in regular aerobic exercise may not be *the* health panacea promised by a range of individuals in the 1970s, regular exercise can be the focus of individual, community, and national efforts promoting health and well-being. This is because engagement in regular aerobic exercise seems to have *some* protective function in terms of initial occurrence and recurrence of heart disease (cardiac events), *may* slow down some aspects of aging, can help to stabilize body weight and body composition, is linked in general to lower levels of risk factors (e.g., HDL), and may reduce stress and everyday tension (see Cooper, 1982 for a review of these points). Perhaps, an even greater hope of further promotion of exercise is that for a variety of reasons, doing regular exercise becomes incompatible with some health-detrimental behaviors, such as smoking. In addition, it is now apparent that some minimal (2 hours per week), but consistent, and serious commitment to regular aerobic exercise is the only thing needed to glean virtually all health benefits (Cooper, 1982).

Given the great popularity of exercise, and the tremendous availability of all manner of information about and products concerned with exercise, at first glance it may seem difficult to understand why more people are *not* exercising on a regular basis in a way that is healthful. Indeed, given the seemingly supportive environment, the tendency may be to focus more on individual factors as the cause of nonexercise practices. However, if the "seemingly supportive context" is examined in more detail from the eco-behavioral perspective outlined in the introduction, then reasons for non-exercise become clearer, as do possible interventive programs.

Various forms of exercise are accepted, and indeed, "trendy" in middle and upper classes, but this seems less true in the lower classes (Cooper, 1982). If we examine different levels of influence, the reasons become clearer. Activities that are not practiced, modeled, and valued by peer groups are not likely to be emulated. Running, jogging, swimming, and other aerobic exercise activities are less practiced by lower and lower middle-class citizens for a number of reasons that are consistent with an eco-behavioral framework. By virtue of educational attainment and available resources, many poor have less access to correct health information; studies consistently show a lower level of health knowledge in poorer people (Grossman, 1972). However, there is some indication that even segments of middle-class and wealthier people may not have accurate, specific knowledge about correct exercise habits (Willard et al., 1982). Engagement in exercise also implies some investment and real hope for the future, if one of the goals of exercise is to assure a healthier future. To the extent that one's future is uncertain or does not appear promising, delaying gratification or putting "miles in the bank" simply (and rationally) may make very little sense.

As has been noted previously, excercising requires resources: access to place, availability of time, and some money. Many urban environments did not provide good access to places to exercise. City streets contain many dangers and obstacles to the exercises. Getting from one urban setting to another to exercise means having the time and money to make this change possible. Again, environmental constraints can markedly hamper poorer people, but as already suggested by the data on work hours and commuting, similar obstacles may exist for a range of people. This analysis indicates that for many people, engagement in exercise has some very high costs.

If we also reexamine the health care system, as noted, there are few, if any, incentives for practitioners and medical organizations to emphasize prevention. There also may be less willingness to step outside the tradition of medical interventions and prescribe involved, long-term changes in life-style as opposed to drugs. For example, there is reasonably good evidence that for most people, permanent weight loss will not be accomplished with drugs and dieting, but can be accomplished with dieting and a good exercise program (Wood, 1983). In fact, it seems that the *only* approach to *permanent* weight loss that works is a program of regular exercise (Wood, 1983). In addition, insomnia seems to be made *worse* by various and frequently prescribed drugs, but regular exercise may help some types of insomnia (Cooper, 1982).

Thus, this brief analysis indicates that the environment for exercise may not be so supportive as a superficial assessment may at first suggest. An ecobehavioral assessment can ascertain individual, group, setting, organizational, and overall community barriers to exercise as well as those factors positively influencing exercise.

At the *individual level*, simple surveys, interviews, and focus groups can be used to gather data on (1) present and past exercise practices; (2) places, times, and mode of exercise; (3) knowledge of exercise principles; (4) perceived obstacles to exercising; and (5) preferred times, places, modalities, and costs of exercising if not presently exercising.

Such a detailed survey is found in Appendix A. The instrument was developed and used on a university campus for planning and marketing a range of health-related programs (Willard et al., 1982), and obviously such an instrument can be tailored to any situation and given to a representative sample of individuals. Note also that this type of instrument can be used to help identify and match population segments and programs, for example, middle-aged women who prefer to exercise with other women in continuous groups that afford comfort and interaction, such as aerobic dancing. Thus, systems of natural social support can be used to increase adherence to an exercise program (King & Frederiksen, 1983). In addition, such a survey can start to identify the group, setting, and organizational and institutional barriers to exercising. For example, on this campus, staff (as opposed to faculty) had *in*flexible work hours, precluding participation in most scheduled programs. Staff also tended not to live in the community (given housing costs and generally lower salaries), but to commute to work, presenting other time and physical barriers.

Thus, such a survey purposely pointed toward the larger environment, as opposed to more emphasis on individual characteristics. As noted earlier, peer and work groups can exert great influence on individual behavior, and more detailed assessment can focus on particular groups not disposed to exercise. The emphasis can be on beliefs and mores, but again, careful attention can also be given to real and perceived barriers. Change programs can then be built on existing interests and pursuits (e.g., fun runs prior to softball games).

Assessments at the *individual and group* level should not just include paper-and-pencil measures. We have sadly found (as many before us have too) that self-reports on paper-and-pencil measures can be distorted (e.g., on willingness to pay a fee for a program). There is no substitute for face-to-face observation, situational measures, and pilot studies.

In exercise, and for other health practices, it is important to assess current knowledge, availability, and access to relevant media, as well as frequency and nature of media accounts of the targeted behaviors. Certainly, one aspect of a planned intervention can be to increase knowledge through a marked increase in mass media material (e.g., Maccoby & Solomon, 1981). This seems to be a necessary part of any approach, but not, for all the reasons already noted, a sufficient approach.

A *community setting analysis* can include (1) a delineation of where people currently exercise, that is, frequency, number, characteristics of people; (2) temporal characteristics of the settings and gaps in scheduling, that is, after work programs; and (3) accessibility and safety of the settings. Where possible, measures should be simple and observational. Note that each area of assessment suggests an intervention that can be evaluated using the same measures. For example, placing lights on a jogging trail and having some police surveillance to improve actual and perceived safety should have (if the change is publicized) effects on the use of the trail at designated times.

For purposes of this analysis, the community level means the aggregate of organizations, work settings, health care facilities, private providers, media, and recreational settings and facilities. Sampling across these domains can provide another basis for ascertaining what areas and population segments have few barriers to exercise and what areas and populations have large obstacles. For example, it would make little sense in a community-based assessment and intervention effort to focus only on professional staff in high technology business.

An *analysis of organizations* can focus on aspects such as (1) employee and management attitudes toward exercise and current practices, (2) flexibility of work schedules, (3) places to change and dress, (4) the potential and willingness to modify work settings for health and exercise programs, and (5) the potential costs and benefits to an organization of instituting exercise and well-being programs given current performance, attendance, turnover, health, and disability figures. Note that, again, the last point suggests an excellent, though ambitious, set of measures to use to assess the current status of an organization and the effects of an organizational change aimed at exercise and health habits (see Wilbur, 1981).

This overall approach also implies an interaction between levels of analysis assessment and intervention points. For example, just as supplying considerable information on exercise to the public will result in little behavior change if environmental barriers remain, removing environmental barriers (e.g., work hours, safer trails) will have little impact on health outcome given improper information and minimal self-directed or group-level motivational strategies. This point underscores the idea that assessment and intervention need to be multileveled.

Stress and Work

In recent years, there has been a burgeoning literature on stress and health. Stress from a variety of potential sources is seen as an antecedent of a range of health-related problems (Matarazzo, 1983). Therefore, stress reduction and stress management approaches seem to be of high priority for preventive health programs. However, from an ecobehavioral perspective, it appears that one shortcoming of a good deal of the applied stress management work is the lack of multilevel assessments of sources of stress and the absence of such an analysis for the development of appropriate interventions. Coupled with these problems is the apparent failure, in some instances, to apply two social marketing concepts, that is, market segmentation and assessment of delivery channels appropriate to a particular market segment.

The ecobehavioral approach will be illustrated with the stress-related problems of dual-earner families with young children. Dual-earner families now represent a large percentage of households in our country. For example, about 60 percent of mothers with school-aged children work outside the home, and 43 percent of families with children under 6 years have a mother working outside the home (Johnson, 1980). In this example, dual-earner families are being differentiated from dual-career families (Aldous, 1982). Dual-earner families represent the much greater proportion of dual-worker families. Workers from such families are seen as occupying "jobs" as opposed to career tracks, with pay being modest and work conditions (e.g., hours) being relatively inflexible. Recent research further substantiates this point by indicating that, perhaps, 30 percent of dual-earner families may have one parent who is on a rotating shift (Presser & Cain, 1983). The monetary and job situation is seen as potentially providing more stress for some dual-career families since dual-earners may have fewer resources to adjust (e.g., flexible hours) or be less able to buy their way out of their stressful circumstances (e.g., hire a full-time baby-sitter).

The major source of stress is seen as developing from the nature of work (time and effort) in our society and its incompatibility with families at a particular life cycle (i.e., when children are young), yet living at a time when two incomes are required for economic sustenance. As noted previously, when time needed for commuting is added to work time, the sheer amount of time left for other activities, such as time for spouse, children, or oneself, is limited. Additional problems of dual-earner families can include (1) inadequate child care facilities or arrangements; (2) services not available at appropriate times (e.g., doctor's offices closed at night), or not extending to more reasonable hours (e.g., schools that close at 3 P.M., resulting in unattended children, that is, the "latch-key syndrome"); (3) loss of contact with interpersonal and social support networks given time constraints; and (4) tensions concerning role definitions, since it is still not the norm in our society for men to be greatly involved in child care and home responsibilities. Given this situation, women from dual-earner homes often assume *both* the role of worker and home and child manager, creating for many a "role-overload," (i.e., the "superwoman") and a high level of stress (King et al., 1983).

This brief overview of the problems of dual-earner families has focused on the time and role problems of the worker/parents. These problems, though, are likely also to have effects at work (i.e., perhaps, lower levels of productivity), in the community (e.g., less time to participate in organizations), and at home (e.g., perhaps, less quality time available for children). This overview also suggests further assessment and analyses are needed at various levels.

1. *Individual Level.*   Except for popular literature, there are few reports on the coping strategies used by dual-earner families with young children who are without large stocks of resources. Specifically, what are the particular times, settings, circumstances (e.g., breakfast, getting off to work and getting children to school, or a child care situation) or conflicts (e.g., between work and home responsibilities, role behaviors) that are consistently sources of stress in dual-earner families? What are the range of strategies used by such families to cope with these predictable problems (i.e., a problem by coping style typology)? To this date, except for some valuable but general descriptive work (Aldous, 1982), these types of analyses have not been done.

2. *Information/Media Influences.*   With some exceptions, such as popular magazines and a few television programs (e.g., "Cagney & Lacey"), it appears that information, advice, and role models for adapting to dual-earner situations are not available. Popular information that is available often emphasizes the "superwoman" model, a seemingly nonobtainable and undesirable role model (King et al., 1983). There appears to be minimal literature and media examples of new roles for men (Lamb & Sagi, 1983). However, one important strategy prior to any program planning involves the assessment of information, beliefs, and attitudes concerning role behaviors. For example, some women may still feel that all home and child tasks are their responsibility; considerable anxiety and guilt may be attached to sharing some tasks with their spouse. Men also may feel threatened by

starting to become more involved in home and child care given lack of knowledge (e.g., cooking) and perceived peer group pressure. Programs and strategies need to be designed in light of such assessment information.

An important assessment, both locally and nationally, can be made of various information sources, but particularly within the social marketing perspective of information sources used by dual-earner families with young children. At one level, there can be attempts to increase usable information, with evaluation focusing on the effectiveness of such attempts (e.g., number of newspaper articles "pre" and "post" on the issues). Still another level of this evaluation can focus on the actual impact of new information on reported stress and the behaviors of the target audience.

3. *Group Level.*   The literature on dual-earner families hints at a loss of social connectedness as a result of involvement in multiple roles, perhaps a phenomenon more true for women who assume the dual burdens of work and home and child care (Aldous, 1982). This situation may or may not be true, but suggests the assessment of social networks of more typical dual-earner families. For example, the number and quality of social interactions can be assessed as well as the nature of a network (e.g., multidimensionality of network members as friends and coworkers; see Hirsch, 1980). Such assessments may be revealing in terms of the relationship to stress of network interactions. If such relationships are revealed and appear to be true of many dual-earner families, then intervention strategies can focus on changing the nature of social networks by teaching *simple* network access and personal reciprocity social skills, possibly through media sources.

4. *Organization.*   Recent projects have attempted to ascertain how flexible work schedules could reduce the time and stress problems of dual-earner families (Bohen & Viveros-Long, 1981; Winett et al. 1982). Overall, these studies show some minimal but positive impacts. However, compared to other countries, flexitime in the United States tends to be limited in terms of the organizations that have it and the diversity of options available to workers. In the studies cited earlier, flexitime systems were minimal and it was not surprising that beneficial outcomes were also minimal.

Other approaches have called for greater work options such as reduced hours (30-hour weeks) during times when workers' children are young (Lamb & Sagi, 1983). Note that this option means some loss in income and possible loss in benefits, seniority, and promotion.

What seems needed here, but is apparently missing, is an ecobehavioral assessment entailing a delineation of problems of dual-earner families as perceived by them, realistic work options, and what approaches are preferred by the target population. When this has been done either in a more formal or post hoc (but behavioral) way, there have been some surprises. That is, one group of dual-earner women, primarily in secretarial positions, did *not* want flexitime or some aspects of flexiplace (doing some work at home; King et al., 1983).

In another project, men and women from dual-earner families over-whelmingly, when given the option, started work early (7:30 A.M.) rather than using true flexitime, even though this meant arising at 5:45 A.M. each workday. Such hours did seem to allow more time for the family in the evening and did seem to reduce reported stress. Once again, these data show the importance of combining ecobehavioral and social marketing perspectives. A description of the time and self-reported stress measures used in the alternative work-hours project is found in Appendix B.

5. *Community.*   Several sources of difficulty have been identified at the community/institutional level. Services, schools, and child care facilities often do not have hours of operation that reflect the schedules of dual-earner parents. One suggested approach can involve a community assessment of such hours, parental preference for hours, and the effects on the service systems and parents of changes resulting from the expansion of hours. Obviously, client flow and revenue must cover the expanded service and the effects on parents must be documented (i.e., does it lead to less stress, better time management, more perceived control, and less time off from work?).

A major chunk of time can be gained each day if one or both parents worked close to home. Obviously, in a tight economy, many workers simply would not have this option. However, media sources can show the benefits of working close to home (e.g., more time, no need for a second car). Community development plans that primarily focus on economic and land-use facets of growth can see the attraction of certain businesses and indus-tries as direct quality-of-life, health promotion efforts. For example, a busi-ness concern located in an exurban area, besides providing employment, may save people 2 to 3 hours per day of commuting time.

Other larger businesses, particularly with the advent of telecommunica-tion systems, can think of expansion of their operations in terms of satellite facilities located in diverse settings. In addition to certain tax advantages, these satellite facilities can be located in smaller communities where, pre-viously, workers commuted to major population centers; thus, the satellite facilities can save workers precious time and energy.

I am not aware of specific studies that have addressed these issues, particularly with regard to family impacts. The most basic notion here is that assessments that focus on organization and community structures and planned changes at these levels may help to reduce stress and facilitate family life.

SUMMARY

This chapter has presented a perspective on assessment and interven-tion, and is not a prescription. The basic framework is ecological with an emphasis on examining multiple sources of behavior influence at the group, organizational, and community levels. The diverse examples used, teenage smoking, exercise behaviors, and problems of dual-earner families, show that higher-order factors have a profound effect on these health behaviors as they are enacted in the everyday lives of individuals. The exposition of system influences and constraints was not intended to create a paralysis in thought or action for psychologists and other behavioral scientists who are more comfortable working at the individual or small group level, and perhaps, now overwhelmed by the enormity of the task at hand. Rather, some concrete examples were provided where it appeared quite possible that assessment and intervention at a level "a notch or two higher" than usual could have important impacts. If the nature of an ecological world is interactive, then one hope of programs at strategic but reachable and manageable levels is that they will have radiating effects up and down the systems of behavior influence.

APPENDIX A

The following is an example of a health fitness survey that considers some ecological factors.

HEALTH FITNESS SURVEY OF VIRGINIA TECH FACULTY & STAFF

1. Your age - _____

2. Sex - ___ Female   ___ Male

3. Height - _____ ft. _____ in.

4. Weight - _____

5. Do you consider your weight:

   ___ much too light   ___ too light   ___ ok
   ___ too heavy   ___ much too heavy

6. Your job

   ___ Faculty   ___ Staff
   (Please fill in your job title and/or rank, no
   need to indicate department
   _____.)

7. How much physical labor is involved in your job?

   ___ none at all   ___ light   ___ moderate
   ___ heavy

8. Do you feel like you are under stress (either at your job and/or home)?

   ___ minimally stressful
   ___ moderately stressful
   ___ very stressful
   ___ not at all

9. Do you currently smoke?

   ___ no   ___ cigar/pipe
   ___ 1-10 cigarettes per day   ___ 11-20 per day
   ___ 20-30 per day   ___ 30-40 per day
   ___ more than 40 per day

10. Please answer yes/no to the following conditions:

    a. Has your doctor told you that you have:
       Yes   No
       ___   ___   high blood pressure?
       ___   ___   high blood cholesterol?
       ___   ___   juvenile diabetes?
       ___   ___   adult onset diabetes?
       ___   ___   had a heart attack?
       ___   ___   heart disease (angina, valvular (heart disease, etc.)?

    b. Also,
       Yes   No
       ___   ___   Do you lead a sedentary life?
       ___   ___   Is there a history of heart disease in your family?
       ___   ___   Is there a history of diabetes in your family?

11. Please check off the following activity(s) which you do **ESPECIALLY** for exercise and fitness and indicate the frequency of each.

<u>Activity</u>   <u>Frequency</u>

___ walking   ___ 1-2 per week   ___ 3-4 per week   ___ 5 or more per week
___ jogging/running   ___ 1-2 per week   ___ 3-4 per week   ___ 5 or more per week
___ swimming   ___ 1-2 per week   ___ 3-4 per week   ___ 5 or more per week
___ calisthenics   ___ 1-2 per week   ___ 3-4 per week   ___ 5 or more per week
___ aerobic dance   ___ 1-2 per week   ___ 3-4 per week   ___ 5 or more per week
___ dancing   ___ 1-2 per week   ___ 3-4 per week   ___ 5 or more per week
___ basketball   ___ 1-2 per week   ___ 3-4 per week   ___ 5 or more per week
___ volleyball   ___ 1-2 per week   ___ 3-4 per week   ___ 5 or more per week
___ racket sport   ___ 1-2 per week   ___ 3-4 per week   ___ 5 or more per week
___ weight training   ___ 1-2 per week   ___ 3-4 per week   ___ 5 or more per week
___ Other, please list:
_____   ___ 1-2 per week   ___ 3-4 per week   ___ 5 or more per week

12. What is the average length of time for your exercise session (<u>only</u> includes time you actually <u>do</u> exercise)?

___ less than 10 minutes   ___ 10-20 minutes
___ 21-30 minutes   ___ 31-40 minutes
___ 41-50 minutes   ___ 51-60 minutes
___ more than one hour
___ not applicable (N/A)

13. How would you describe the <u>degree of effort</u> in your <u>usual</u> exercise session?

___ very easy   ___ easy   ___ moderate
___ vigorous   ___ exhaustive   ___ N/A

14. When do you usually exercise?

___ early morning   ___ morning   ___ noon
___ early afternoon   ___ late afternoon
___ evening   ___ no specific time   ___ N/A

15. <u>Where</u> do you <u>usually</u> exercise (may check more than one)?

___ home or around home
___ campus or around campus
___ War Memorial Gym
___ Recreation Center
___ Free University
___ Other Facility (please note
_____)
___ N/A

16. Which statement best describes your exercise behavior as a <u>young adult</u> (less than 35 years)? Please answer even if you are younger than 35 years old.

___ no exercise or sports
___ infrequent exercise or sports
___ moderately frequent exercise or sports
___ frequent exercise and sports
___ very frequent exercise or sports

17. People have various reasons for not exercising REGULARLY (at least 3 times per week). Please indicate whether or not one or more of the following reasons apply to you.

___ Check here if you <u>do</u> exercise regularly -- go on to number 18.

Yes No
___ ___ no real interest or motivation
___ ___ not enough time in my day or week
___ ___ interested, but can't seem to maintain
___ ___ embarrassment
___ ___ don't really understand how to exercise properly
___ ___ my job requires a lot of physical activity - too tired to exercise regularly
___ ___ dislike the physical discomfort of exercise (sweating, etc.)
___ ___ poor health

Yes No
___ ___ shower facilities are not available at place of work
___ ___ the gym is too far away
___ ___ the gym/pool is not open when I could go and when I want to exercise
___ ___ my co-workers are not supportive
___ ___ my supervisor is not supportive
___ ___ my doctor told me that exercise is not necessary for me
___ ___ my spouse does not exercise
___ ___ my friends do not exercise
___ ___ other, please list, _____
_____

18. People who exercise REGULARLY (3 or more times per week) do so for various reasons. Please indicate whether or not one or more of the following reasons apply to you.

___ Check here if you do <u>not</u> exercise regularly -- go on to number 19.

Yes No
___ ___ interested and motivated
___ ___ part of my daily or/or weekly routine
___ ___ makes me feel good about myself
___ ___ understand how to exercise properly
___ ___ my job requires little or no physical activity - need to "let off steam"
___ ___ enjoy the physical feelings associated with exercise
___ ___ for my health

Yes No
___ ___ shower facilities are available at place of work
___ ___ the gym is close by
___ ___ the gym/pool is open when I could go and when I want to exercise
___ ___ my co-workers are supportive
___ ___ my supervisor is supportive
___ ___ my doctor has told me to exercise
___ ___ my spouse exercises
___ ___ my friends exercises
___ ___ other, please list, _____
_____

170

In this section we want to find out the type of exercise program(s) you would like available on campus.

19. I would like an exercise group to focus on (you may check more than one):

___ walking   ___ basketball
___ jogging/running ___ volleyball
___ swimming   ___ racket sports
___ cycling   ___ weight training
___ dancing   ___ none of these
___ aerobic dance   ___ other, please list
                     _____

20. I would like only fitness <u>instruction</u> or <u>information</u> that I can use on my own rather than be part of a group exercise program.

___ No ___ Yes

21. I would like to exercise in a regular <u>exercise group</u> at War Memorial Gym.

___ No ___ Yes

22. I would prefer a fitness program that is

___ indoors ___ out-of-doors ___ neither

23. I would prefer a health-fitness program that met

___ year-round   ___ academic year only
___ fall/spring quarters only
___ none of these

24. With regard to <u>nutrition/weight control</u>, I would prefer

___ nothing   ___ information only
___ a formal program

25. With regard to <u>smoking control/ cessation</u>, I would prefer

___ nothing   ___ information only
___ a formal program

26. With regard to stress management, I would prefer

___ nothing   ___ information only
___ a formal program

27. I would like an opportunity for an on-campus health-fitness screening (including blood pressure, blood analysis, EKG, body fat analysis, treadmill test)

___ No ___ Yes

28. I would be willing to have a detailed physical exam done by my family doctor before enrolling in a regular health-fitness screening and exercise program.

___ No ___ Yes

29. I would like an individualized program of exercise based on my health-fitness screening.

___ No ___ Yes

30. I would be willing to pay for an exercise group.

___ don't want to   ___ will not pay fee
___ $2-3 per week   ___ $4-5 per week
___ $6-10 per week

31. I would be willing to <u>pay</u> for health-fitness screening.

___ don't want to   ___ will not pay fee
___ $0-15   ___ $16-30 ___ $31-45
___ $46-60 ___ $61-75 ___ $76-90
___ $91-$105

32. My first and second best times for attending a regular exercise program would be

	Best	Second Best
___ don't want to		
6-7 a.m.	___	___
noon	___	___
4-5 p.m.	___	___
5-6 p.m.	___	___
6-7 p.m.	___	___
7-8 p.m.	___	___

APPENDIX B

1. A sample time-activity log used to record exact allocations of time, interactions, place of activities, and qualitative rating of activities (page 172).

2. A survey used in a repetitive form to assess work and nonwork life relationships, reported stress, and perceived changes attributable to a flexitime program (pages 173–178).

SAMPLE: Keep as an Example.

Code Number _____24680_____   Yesterday's ___Tues__ _5_ , _23_
                                             Day   Date

TIME-ACTIVITY LOG

What You Did Yesterday

Instructions: Please fill in your activities for yesterday by placing the activity within the proper time period (left). Note the primary activity first, and then note any other activity (secondary) taking place at the same time. For each new primary activity, please rate your enjoyment of the activity on the 1-5 scale on the right, where 5 = Enjoyed a Great Deal, and 1 = Disliked a Great Deal.

Please also note two additional items on the back of this page concernning how you commuted to work and home, and the time the thermostat was raised or lowered on your heating or air conditioning (or your unit turned on or off).

Yesterday I started work at _____8:15_____ AM and ended work at _____4:45_____ PM.

TIME	WHAT DID YOU DO?	TIME BEGUN	TIME ENDED	WHERE WAS THIS?	WITH WHOM?	DO ANYTHING ELSE?	Dislike		ok		Enjoy
5 AM	AWAKE	5:45		Home	wife	NO	1	②	3	4	5
6 AM	Dress; Help wife Get kids Ready	6:00	7:00	Home	wife, son, daughter	Listen to RADIO	1	2	③	4	5
7 AM	Breakfast Leave for work	7:00 7:30	7:30	Home CAR	wife, kids son	Radio, paper Drop son at school	1	2	③	4	5
8 AM	Arrive work Review Fiscal	8:15	8:15	metro. USPS	secretary	Read paper	1	2	③	4	5
9 AM	Report;				assistants	MADE phone cALLs	1	2	3	④	5
10 AM	Prepare memos						1	2	3	④	5
11 AM	on MANpower Estimates		12:00			Read mail	1	2	3	④	5
NOON	Lunch	12:00	1:00	Cafeteria at USPS	co-workers	NO	1	2	3	④	5
1 PM	Work on Summary of Fiscal Statement	1:00					1	2	③	4	5
2 PM			3:00	USPS	Alone	Phone calls	1	2	③	4	5
3 PM	meet with Budget office	3:00	4:00	USPS	STAFF	NO	1	②	3	4	5
4 PM	Review Material	4:00	4:45	USPS	Alone	NO	1	2	③	4	5
5 PM	Commute Home	5:00	6:00	metro + CAR	Alone	Talked to others	1	②	3	4	5
6 PM	DINNER + cleAn-up	6:15	7:00	Home	wife, kids	Talked about DAY	1	2	③	4	5
8 PM	Reviewed sons Homework	7:00	8:00	Home	Son	NO	1	②	3	4	5
9 PM	wrote Letters	8:00	9:00	Home	Alone	Radio	1	2	3	④	5
10 PM	Put kids to Bed & Watch TV	9:00	10:00	Home	wife, kids	Horsed Around	1	2	3	④	5
11 PM	Relax & TALK	10:00	11:00	Home	wife	Had a drink	1	2	3	④	5
MNite	Went to Bed	11:00		Home	wife	WATched TV News	1	2	3	④	5
1 AM							1	2	3	4	5

PLEASE NAME FRIENDS,
CO-WORKERS, OR
FAMILY MEMBERS

PLEASE NAME FRIENDS,
CO-WORKERS, OR
FAMILY MEMBERS

HOW ENJOYABLE WAS
THE ACTIVITY?

Date I Completed the Form: _____5/24_____

Code Number: _____

Survey of the Relationships Between Work and Nonwork Life

Instructions: This is a brief survey about how your work situation may make different aspects of your social and family life "difficult" or "easy." For each of the items, first rate on the 7-point scale how your work situation may make that part of your social or family life difficult or easy. *If you rate an item as "somewhat difficult" (5), "difficult" (6), or "very difficult" (7), then rate the degree of stress you feel or perceive in fulfilling that particular function or engaging in those behaviors.*

Please also note 5 fill-in questions that follow the items you rated. These questions concern situations, resources, and relationships that help or hinder the coordination of your work and nonwork life, and recent changes in your life.

Scale

Very Easy	Easy	Somewhat Easy	Neutral	Somewhat Difficult	Difficult	Very Difficult
1	2	3	4	5	6	7

Minimally Stressful	Somewhat Stressful	Moderately Stressful	Stressful	Very Stressful	Extremely Stressful	Almost or Sometimes Incapacitating
1	2	3	4	5	6	7

1. The time I start to work makes getting my child (children) to school or a child care setting _____ .

Very Easy			Neutral			Very Difficult
1	2	3	4	5	6	7

Minimally Stressful			Stressful			Incapacitating
1	2	3	4	5	6	7

2. If my child (children) should become ill during the day, my work situation makes it _____ to be sure the child is receiving care.

Very Easy			Neutral			Very Difficult
1	2	3	4	5	6	7

Minimally Stressful			Stressful			Incapacitating
1	2	3	4	5	6	7

3. The time I *leave* work makes it _____ to spend afternoon time with my child.

Very Easy			Neutral			Very Difficult
1	2	3	4	5	6	7

Minimally Stressful			Stressful			Incapacitating
1	2	3	4	5	6	7

4. Because of my work hours, breakfast time with my child (children) is _____ .

Very Easy			Neutral			Very Difficult
1	2	3	4	5	6	7

Minimally Stressful			Stressful			Incapacitating
1	2	3	4	5	6	7

5. My work hours make picking up my child (children) after school or from a child care setting ——.

Very Easy | | | Neutral | | | Very Difficult
1 | 2 | 3 | 4 | 5 | 6 | 7

Minimally Stressful | | | Stressful | | | Incapacitating
1 | 2 | 3 | 4 | 5 | 6 | 7

6. Because of my work hours, it is —— to spend time with my spouse/partner during the work week.

Very Easy | | | Neutral | | | Very Difficult
1 | 2 | 3 | 4 | 5 | 6 | 7

Minimally Stressful | | | Stressful | | | Incapacitating
1 | 2 | 3 | 4 | 5 | 6 | 7

7. My work hours are such that it is —— to see friends during the work week.

Very Easy | | | Neutral | | | Very Difficult
1 | 2 | 3 | 4 | 5 | 6 | 7

Minimally Stressful | | | Stressful | | | Incapacitating
1 | 2 | 3 | 4 | 5 | 6 | 7

8. My work hours are such that it is —— to share lunchtime or a coffee break with friends at work.

Very Easy | | | Neutral | | | Very Difficult
1 | 2 | 3 | 4 | 5 | 6 | 7

Minimally Stressful | | | Stressful | | | Incapacitating
1 | 2 | 3 | 4 | 5 | 6 | 7

9. Because of my work hours, commuting to and from work is _____.

Very Easy			Neutral			Very Difficult
1	2	3	4	5	6	7

10. The hours I work make having dinner with my spouse/partner and/or child (children) _____ during the work week.

Minimally Stressful			Stressful			Incapacitating
1	2	3	4	5	6	7

11. The hours I work make spending time in the evening with my child (children) _____.

Very Easy			Neutral			Very Difficult
1	2	3	4	5	6	7

12. The hours I work make pursuing additional educational (formal and informal) opportunities _____.

Minimally Stressful			Stressful			Incapacitating
1	2	3	4	5	6	7

13. The hours I work make engaging in recreational pursuits and hobbies _____.

Very Easy			Neutral			Very Difficult
1	2	3	4	5	6	7

Minimally Stressful			Stressful			Incapacitating
1	2	3	4	5	6	7

14. The hours I work make completion of shopping and household chores _____.

Very Easy			Neutral			Very Difficult
1	2	3	4	5	6	7

Minimally Stressful			Stressful			Incapacitating
1	2	3	4	5	6	7

15. The hours I work make it _____ to have relaxing evenings during the work week.

Very Easy			Neutral			Very Difficult
1	2	3	4	5	6	7

Minimally Stressful			Stressful			Incapacitating
1	2	3	4	5	6	7

16. The most *difficult* aspect(s) of coordinating my work and nonwork life is (are):

_____

_____

_____

17. Are there any community resources or facilities that you feel are *helpful* in coordinating your work and nonwork life? By community resources or facilities, we mean *anything* from stores, agencies, transportation, schools, child care centers, etc. Please detail.

_____

_____

18. Are there aspects of relationships you have with other people that you feel are *helpful* in coordinating your work and nonwork life? If yes, please explain.

_____

_____

19. What hours does your spouse/partner work now? _____

20. Since the last time you completed this survey has there been any change in:

   Your job responsibilities? Yes [ ] No [ ] If yes, please explain: _____

   Your child care arrangements? Yes [ ] No [ ] If yes, please explain: _____

   Your transportation? Yes [ ] No [ ] If yes, please explain: _____

   Your recreational activities? Yes [ ] No [ ] If yes, please explain: _____

   Other: _____

Thank you for completing this survey!

References

Aldous, J. (Ed.). (1982). *Two paychecks: Life in dual-earner families*. Beverly Hills: Sage.

Ashworth, W. (1982). *Nor any drop to drink*. New York: Summit Books.

Bandura, A. (1969). *Principles of behavior modification*. New York: Holt, Rinehart & Winston.

Berkman, L. F., & Syme, S. L. (1979). Social networks, host resistance and mortality: A nine-year follow-up study of Alameda County residents. *American Journal of Epidemiology, 109*, 186–204.

Bohen, H., & Viveros-Long, A. (1981). *Balancing jobs and family life. Do flexible work schedules help?* Philadelphia: Temple University Press.

Brenner, M. H. (1973). *Mental illness and the economy*. Cambridge, Mass: Harvard University Press.

Bronfenbrenner, U. (1979). *The ecology of human development*. Cambridge, Mass.: Harvard University Press.

Cantor, M. G. (1980). *Prime-time television: Content and control*. Beverly Hills: Sage.

Cassel, J. (1974). Psychosocial processes and "stress": Theoretical formulations. *International Journal of Health Services, 4*, 471–482.

Catalano, R. A. (1979). *Health, behavior, and community*. Elmsford, NY: Pergamon Press.

Catalano, R., & Dooley, D. (1983). The health effects of economic instability: A test of the economic stress hypothesis. *Journal of Health and Social Behavior, 24*, 46–60.

Cohen, S. (1983). Social support, stress, and the buffering hypothesis: A theoretical analysis. In A. Baum, J. E. Singer, & S. E. Taylor (Eds.), *Handbook of psychology and health* (Vol. 4). Hillsdale, NJ: Erlbaum.

Comstock, G. (1980). *Television in America*. Beverly Hills: Sage.

Cooper, K. H. (1982). *The aerobics program for total well-being*. New York: M. Evans.

Czeisler, C. A., Moore-Ede, M. C., & Coleman, R. M. (1982). Rotating shift work schedules that disrupt sleep are improved by applying circardian principles. *Science. 217*, 460–463.

Detsky, A. S. (1978). *The economic foundation of national health policy*. Cambridge, Mass.: Bollinger.

Dolce, P. C. (Ed.). (1976). *Suburbia: The American dream and dilemma*. New York: Anchor Books.

Engel, J. F., & Blackwell, R. D. (1982). *Consumer behavior* (4th ed.). Hinsdale, Ill.: Dryden Press.

Evans, R. I., Rozelle, R. M., Maxwell, S. E., Raines, B. E., Dill, C. A., Guthrie, T. J., Henderson, A. H., & Hill, P. C. (1981). Social modeling films to deter smoking in adolescents: Results of a three-year field investigation. *Journal of Applied Psychology, 66*, 399–414.

Felner, R. D., Jason, L. A., Moritsuger, J., & Farber, S. S. (Eds.). (1983). *Preventive psychology: Theory, research, and practice*. Elmsford, NY: Pergamon Press.

Frederiksen, L. W., & King. A. C. (1981). *Marketing principles and the behavior modifier*. Paper presented at the annual meeting of the Association for Advancement of Behavior Therapy, Toronto, November.

Friedman, M., & Friedman, R. (1979). *Free to choose: A personal statement*. New York: Harcourt Brace Jovanovich.

Fuchs, V. R. (1975). *Who shall live?: Health, economics, and social choice*. New York: Basic Books.

Geller, E. S., Paterson, L., & Talbott, E. (1982). A behavioral analysis of incentive prompts for motivating seat belt usage. *Behavior Analysis, 15*, 403–415.

Gottlieb, B. H. (Ed.). (1981). *Social networks and social support*. Beverly Hills: Sage.

Grossman, M. (1972). *The demand for health: A theoretical and empirical investigation*. New York: Columbia University Press.

Heller, K., & Swindle, R. W. (1983). Social networks, perceived social support and coping with stress. In R. D. Felner et al. (Eds.), *Preventive psychology: Theory, research, and practice.* Elmsford, NY: Pergamon Press.

Hirsch, B. J. (1980). Natural support systems and coping with major life changes. *American Journal of Community Psychology, 8,* 159–172.

Hirsch, B. J. (1981). Social networks and the coping process creating personal communities. In B. H. Gottlieb (Ed.), *Social networks and social support.* Beverly Hills: Sage.

Iscoe, I. (1982). Toward a viable community health psychology: Caveats from the experiences of the community mental health movement. *American Psychologist, 37,* 961–965.

Johnson, B. (1980). Marital and family characteristics of workers: March 1979. *Monthly Labor Review,* April, 48–52.

Kanter, R. M. (1977). *Work and family in the United States: A critical review and agenda for research and policy.* New York: Russell-Sage.

King, A. C., & Frederiksen, L. W. (1983). *The application of marketing principles to behavioral interventions.* Unpublished manuscript, Department of Psychology, Virginia Polytechnic Institute and State University, Blacksburg, Va.

King, A. C., Winett, R. A., & Lovett, S. B. (1983). *The effects of support and instruction on home and work behaviors in women from dual-earner families: A secondary prevention program for stress.* Unpublished manuscript. Department of Psychology, Virginia Polytechnic Institute and State University, Blacksburg, Va.

Krasner, L., & Ullman, L. P. (1973). *Personality and behavior influences.* New York: Holt, Rinehart, and Winston.

Lamb, M. E., & Sagi, A. (Eds.). (1983). *Fatherhood and family policy.* Hillsdale, NJ: Erlbaum.

Lando, H. A. (1975). A comparison of excessive and rapid smoking in the modification of chronic smoking behavior. *Journal of Consulting and Clinical Psychology, 43,* 350–355.

Lau, R., Kane, R., Berry, S., Ware, J., & Roy, D. (1980. Channeling health: A review of evaluations of televised health campaigns. *Health Education Quarterly, 7,* 56–89.

Liebert, R. M., Sprafken, I. N., & Davidson, E. S. (1982). *The early window: Effects of television on children and youth* (2nd ed.). Elmsford, NY: Pergamon Press.

Liem, R., & Ramsay, P. (1982). Health and social costs of unemployment: Research and policy considerations. *American Psychologist, 37,* 1116–1123.

Maccoby, N., & Solomon, D. S. (1981). Heart disease prevention: Community studies. In R. E. Rice & W. J. Paisley (Eds.), *Public communication campaigns.* Beverly Hills: Sage.

Matarazzo, J. D. (1983). *Behavioral immunogens and pathogens in health and illness.* Master Lecture, delivered at the annual meeting of the American Psychological Association. Anaheim, Calif.

McAlister, A. (1981). Antismoking campaigns: Progress in developing effective communications. In R. E. Rice & W. J. Paisley (Eds.), *Public communication campaigns.* Beverly Hills, Sage.

Mechanic, D. (1978). *Medical sociology* (2nd ed.). New York: Free Press.

Navarro, V. (1976). *Medicine under capitalism.* New York: Prodist.

Newhouse, J. P. et al. (1981). Some interim results from a controlled trial of cost sharing in health insurance. *New England Journal of Medicine, 305,* 1501–1507.

New York Times. (1983a). Editorial, March 6.

New York Times. (1983b). "The price of cleaning up toxic wastes." March 13 (Business Section, p. 2).

Nollen, S. D. (1982). *New work schedules in practice: Managing time in a changing society.* New York: Van Nostrand Reinhold.

Pertschuk, M. (1982). *Revolt against regulation: The rise and pause of the consumer movement.* Berkeley: University of California Press.

Piven, F. F., & Cloward, R. A. (1982). *The new class war.* New York: Pantheon Books.

Presser, H. B., & Cain, V. S. (1983). Shift work among dual-earner couples with children. *Science, 219,* 876–879.

Rappaport, J. (1977). *Community psychology: Values, research, action.* New York: Holt, Rinehart and Winston.

Robinson, J. P. (1977). *How Americans use time: A social-psychological analysis of everyday behavior.* New York: Praeger.

Rogers-Warren, A., & Warren, S. F. (1977). *Ecological perspectives in behavior analysis.* Baltimore: University Park Press.

Roy, W. R. (1978). *Effects of the payment mechanism on the health care delivery system.* Washington, DC: U.S. Department of Health, Education, and Welfare.

Sarason, S. B. (1981). *Psychology misdirected.* New York: Free Press.

Seekins, T., Fawcett, S. B. et al. (1983). Interstate evaluation of child restraint laws. Study in progress. Lawrence, Kan. University of Kansas.

Solomon, D. S. (1981). A social marketing perspective on campaigns. In R. E. Rice & W. J. Paisley (Eds.), *Public communication campaigns.* Beverly Hills, Sage.

Stokols, D., Novaco, R. W., Stokols, J., & Campbell, J. (1978). Traffice congestion, type A behavior, and stress. *Journal of Applied Psychology, 63,* 467–480.

Wallack, L. M. (1981). Mass media campaigns: The odds against finding behavior change. *Health Education Quarterly, 8,* 209–260.

Wellman, B. (1981). Applying network analysis to the study of support. In B. H. Gottlieb (Ed.), *Social networks and social support.* Beverly Hills: Sage.

Wilbur, C. (1981). *Johnson and Johnson's "Live for Life Program."* Paper presented at the annual meeting of the Association for Advancement of Behavioral Therapy. New York: November.

Willard, B. J., Scanlon, G., Herbert, W. G., & Winett, R. A. (1982). *A needs assessment instrument for health promotion programs.* Paper presented at the Annual Southeastern Sports Medicine Association, Blacksburg, Va. January.

Winett, R. A., Neale, M. S., & Williams, K. P. (1982). The effects of flexible work schedules on urban families with young children: Quasi-experimental, ecological studies. *American Journal of Community Psychology, 10,* 49–54.

Wood, P. (1983). *The California Diet.* Mountain View, Calif. Anderson World Publications.

5

Beyond the Laboratory Experiment: Experimental and Quasi-experimental Designs for Interventions in Naturalistic Settings

STEPHEN G. WEST

The rise of health psychology and other new areas of applied psychology has led to a number of exciting developments. For the methodologist, foremost among these developments is an ongoing reexamination of a

A portion of the writing of this chapter was supported by NIMH grants 1P50MH39246-01 and 1R03MH39235-01.

number of our fundamental beliefs about the relationship between basic and applied research. Beliefs that had in earlier times achieved the status of near-universal truisms have more recently been found to have only a limited range of applicability. This realization, in turn, has resulted in some important developments in the conceptualization and methodology of applied research.

As background for the discussion of some of these new developments, it is useful to review some of the unwritten, widely shared beliefs of the 1960s and to trace briefly their fate over the intervening years.

Belief 1: The health and welfare problems of the poor and the elderly could be alleviated by funding relatively simple programs that addressed these problems.

Although well intended, the "Great Society" programs of the 1960s failed to fulfill their promise. Evaluation researchers (e.g., Cook et al., in press; Sechrest et al., 1979) have repeatedly documented the difficulty of demonstrating positive effects of social interventions in many areas. Indeed, the "no effect" conclusion has become the hallmark of treatment evaluations in many applied domains. This has led to a greater appreciation of the difficulty of designing and implementing programs that are effective in alleviating problems that may have developed over long periods of time and that have numerous possible causes (e.g., smoking and obesity; see Coates et al., 1981). It has also led to a new emphasis on the use of designs that maximize statistical power, and on implementing treatments in their strongest possible form to allow new interventions to receive the fairest possible test (Sechrest et al., 1979).

Belief 2: Research on basic psychological processes holds the ultimate key to the understanding of applied issues. The knowledge gained from this research can (someday) be immediately applied to help eliminate social problems.

Theories and empirical findings from basic research often provide an important, simplified starting perspective from which to begin to understand the complexity of applied problems. Basic research can often assist in the design of interventions that have few existing counterpoints in the real world. But, basic research may often tell us more about possible human behavior under idealized circumstances than about how humans behave in actual settings of interest (see Henschel, 1980). The issue here is whether the findings of basic research, typically conducted in the laboratory or in other highly restricted settings, can be generalized to a specific applied problem. Unfortunately, analyses of generalizability and external validity have become increasingly complex and multidimensional (see the discussion of these topics later, and Cronbach, 1982). These considerations have led to increased emphasis on testing our findings in naturalistic settings to help establish the boundary conditions and range of applicability of our basic theories and empirical findings (Sloan & West, in preparation).

Belief 3: The laboratory analog experiment provides the best means of investigating nearly all psychological questions of interest.

The laboratory experiment often provides an excellent means of maximizing control over the phenomenon of interest as well as the validity of causal inferences. At the same time, the laboratory experiment may serve as a poor model for many applied research problems in health psychology. Health psychologists often investigate questions in which the problem, the population, the setting, and the outcome measures of ultimate interest are precisely specified. Given this specificity, the frequent inability of laboratory experiments to match precisely each of these parameters can maximize problems of external validity. Many problems of interest are difficult to investigate in the laboratory since they involve highly stressful procedures, interactions with significant others, and/or processes that may be extended in time. The ease of implementing treatments and ruling out certain threats to validity that is so characteristic of the laboratory experiment has left us ill-prepared to address the difficulties of applied research in real-world settings. Treatments are not always implemented as planned, random assignment of subjects to conditions is often not possible and, if attempted, very often fails, and subjects can disappear or even die before follow-up measures are taken. The increased appreciation of these problems is beginning to lead to a reexamination of the advantages and disadvantages and the range of applicability of the laboratory experiment and other designs in addressing applied questions.

The purpose of this chapter is to introduce some of the newer research designs and the newer analyses of more traditional research designs that are applicable in the health psychology area. The chapter will begin with a review of the basic concepts of *control* and *validity*. Then, four designs will be described in turn: social experiments, regression discontinuity designs, interrupted time-series designs, and nonequivalent control group designs. The assumptions, strengths, weaknesses, and range of applicability of each design will be discussed. Finally, the chapter will conclude with a brief discussion of some implications of validity and design issues for basic and applied research.

MODELS OF CONTROL

The term "control" is often invoked with near-reverence by psychologists as being the key to good research. Indeed, it is. Yet, many investigators have failed to realize that psychology has imported three distinct models of control from other areas of science (see Cook, 1983; Cook & Campbell, 1979). Each of these models has a different history and different assumptions, and has proven useful in the domain of its home science. However, the appropriateness of each of these models for the study of psychological phenomena has rarely been considered. Further, the particular hybrid of these models that is employed in laboratory experiments in psychology has only rarely received scrutiny (Cook et al., 1980).

The first approach comes from the physical sciences and involves isolation of the phenomena of interest from factors that have been empirically shown to or may theoretically influence the outcome of the investigation. Test tubes are sterilized to prevent other substances from affecting chemical reactions, lead shielding is employed to prevent external radiation from affecting studies of sensitive materials, and vacuum chambers are utilized to prevent atmospheric influences on particle motion. Such procedures are particularly worthwhile when the specific objects under study are inert, do not spontaneously change over time, and are relatively uniform. These conditions are rarely met in psychology, so that physical isolation in closed systems is normally not a sufficient method of control.

The second approach comes from agriculture and involves the random assignment of units to treatment conditions. Unlike physical scientists, agricultural researchers have been interested in studying their phenomena of interest under relatively naturalistic, open conditions. They have not been so much interested in showing that a new planting technique would improve crop yields when such variables as rain, wind, soil conditions, and amount of sunshine were precisely controlled. Rather, they were more interested in showing that a particular treatment had its effect *despite* normal variation of these and other potentially relevant factors. It was the insight of Sir Ronald Fisher (1925) that randomization would guarantee that the groups would be *initially equated* within known limits of sampling error on all possible extraneous factors that provides the foundation of modern agricultural research. This approach is most useful when it may be plausibly assumed that the experimental units are relatively passive recipients of treatment, so that they can also be considered to be *equated at the end* of the experiment. With corn plants, this appears to be a relatively safe assumption. However, human subjects in real-world settings sometimes agitate to have their treatment changed, migrate to other fields in search of better treatment conditions, or give up or try harder because of their knowledge that others are receiving a different treatment. Thus, in some areas of psychological research, randomization alone may not be sufficient to assure the equivalence of treatment and comparison groups at the completion of the experiment in the absence of any real effects of treatment.

The third approach to control has developed primarily in those social sciences such as economics, political science, and sociology where manipulation of treatment conditions is often not possible. Instead, these researchers have taken the tack of attempting to eliminate statistically the influence of important extraneous factors that may causally influence the phenomena of interest. For example, epidemiologic studies of the effects of diet on the develoment of coronary artery disease normally attempt to remove statistically the effects of known risk factors such as age, gender, and cigarette smoking. This approach provides exact control for the effects of extraneous variables when it may be assumed that (1) all important extraneous variables have been identified, (2) they are measured with perfect reliability, (3) the functional relationship (e.g., linear or quadratic) between the extraneous and outcome variable is known, and (4) all interactions among extraneous variables in producing the outcome variable have been identified. However, these conditions are not normally met in psychology, so that this method of control almost always involves some degree of uncertainty regarding the success of the statistical adjustments in removing the influence of extraneous causal factors on the outcome variable.

Given the problems of each of the methods of control in dealing with psychological phenomena, psychologists have traditionally utilized the laboratory experiment which is a hybrid of the first two approaches to control. In certain basic research areas (e.g., human learning), the isolation and closed system model of the physical sciences has been adopted in a very literal sense and combined with the open system, randomization model of agriculture. Soundproofed cubicles isolate the subject from all extraneous sounds and nonsense syllables preclude prior experience with the stimulus materials. Randomization ensures that the subjects in each group are initially comparable on all potential individual difference factors such as IQ, motivation, and anxiety. Since experiments are typically of relatively short duration and subjects are unaware of the existence of other conditions, problems of subject attrition and contamination from other conditions are minimized. However, this hybrid model reflects a tension between the divergent goals of its closed system, physical science parents and its open system, agricultural parents. It assumes that all contextual factors that occur in more naturalistic settings are simply random or systematic errors, so that eliminating such errors would provide the clearest understanding of the phenomenon under investigation. To the extent that these contextual factors alter the effects of the treatment (i.e., a context × treatment interaction occurs), generalization to the applied situation of interest may be problematic.

This hybrid model is sometimes taken one step further in social psychology, personality research, and some areas of health psychology. Extraneous factors cannot simply be removed by isolation since the context-based meaning of the situation would be greatly altered. Instead, isolation is utilized in a more metaphorical sense in which the experimenter creates a simplified model or analog of the general situation of interest. This approach has sometimes been described in terms of a dramaturgical metaphor in which the experimenter "sets the stage" for the treatment and hired accomplices follow a "script" that prescribes their verbal and physical interactions with the subject (Aronson et al., in press). In a sense then, subjects become involved in a simple, stylized play with trained actors in which the responses of the subjects serve as the dependent measures. It is assumed that the simplified analog contains all the important causal elements that are present in the applied situation of interest and does not contain additional causal elements. Since the plausibility of these assumptions is not typically investigated, the results of this approach to research will be of unknown robustness and generalilty (Cook et al., 1980).[1]

VALIDITY

Cook and Campbell (1976, 1979) have recently revised Campbell and Stanley's (1966) classic analysis of validity issues in research. Perhaps reflecting the increased experience with large-scale social experiments and quasi-experiments in the social and behavioral sciences, Cook and Campbell have proposed a refinement of the classification of the types of validity and identified several new threats to each type of validity. This section reviews Cook and Campbell's current analysis of validity, noting in particular some of the issues arising from the divergent validity priorities of basic and applied researchers.

Statistical Conclusion Validity

The first type of validity, statistical conclusion validity, refers to the ability of the researcher to detect accurately the relationship among variables. Two general threats should normally be examined with regard to statistical conclusion validity: (1) violations of the assumptions of the statistical tests and (2) the ability of the design to detect a relationship if, in fact, one does exist.

Violations of Assumptions.   The issue of violations of the assumptions of statistical tests may arise in two ways. First, each statistical test includes a set of assumptions. For example, analysis of variance assumes normality and equal variances in each treatment group. Among the assumptions of latent structure analysis is multivariate normality (Bentler, 1980). Violations of assumptions will have different effects, depending on the specific test and the nature of the violation. Simple analysis of variance with no repeated measures and relatively equivalent sample sizes is robust to nearly all violations, meaning that the probability of the type I error remains at .05 or less. Unfortunately, however, violations of the assumptions of analysis of variance may lead to reductions in the ability of the test to detect true differences among treatment groups, a fact that has often been overlooked by researchers (Levine & Dunlap, 1982, 1983). In the case of latent structure analysis,

---

[1]Another issue concerns the degree to which subjects enact unique roles in the laboratory setting. For example, Orne (1962) has argued that subjects attempt to please the experimenter and Rosenberg (1969) has noted that subjects may act in a socially desirable manner to appear "normal." Such problems can, in some cases, preclude generalizations to nonlaboratory settings.

violations of the multivariate normality assumption can lead to the far more severe consequence of serious misestimation of the relationships among variables (Bentler, 1983). The extent of the violation of each assumption can in may cases be assessed by inspection of appropriate plots of the data or statistical tests; and, if necessary, transformations of the data or alternative statistical procedures (involving less stringent assumptions) may be used.

Second, the researcher needs to consider carefully the possibility that the data are not independent. This problem may arise in longitudinal and other designs in which measures are collected on the same subject(s) at repeated times. It also arises in designs in which treatment is delivered in a group setting, such as school-based smoking prevention programs and group weight-control programs, even if outcome measures are taken from each subject separately. Although the effects of violations of the independence assumption are only beginning to be investigated (Kenny & Judd, 1983), major violations may lead to serious misestimation of treatment effects, even in such normally robust procedures as analysis of variance (Winer, 1971). If the nature of the possible violation can be specified, statistical tests that assess the extent of the problem can sometimes be performed (e.g., Anderson & Ager, 1978) or the statistical models may be respecified to allow for the possibility of correlated errors (Judd & Kenny, 1981; Kessler & Greenberg, 1981; Rogosa, 1980).

Power-related Issues.   The second class of threats to statistical conclusion validity relate to power, the ability of the design to detect the relationship among variables when, in fact, one does exist. These issues have traditionally been treated as being, at best, of only minor importance by laboratory researchers, since the costs of type II errors in this kind of research are normally quite low. Since undergraduate subjects and graduate researchers are cheap and plentiful, experiments that are less than optimal can easily be redesigned and additional subjects can be run. In contrast, research in many applied contexts involves much higher costs: Many populations of interest involve patients with low incidence illnesses (e.g., multiple sclerosis), access to the population is often difficult and time-limited, subjects frequently must be paid, and interventions must be delivered by paid professionals. The higher costs of applied research often mean that investigators may get only one chance to test their hypotheses or newly developed treatment programs, since the continuation or further funding of the project may be contingent on promising initial results. Under these conditions, the costs of type II errors can become substantial, making it imperative that the investigator implement the strongest possible form of the treatment and utilize the most powerful available design (Sechrest et al., 1979).

How can the investigator maximize the ability of the design to detect treatment effects? Most of the answers involve basic, but often neglected, principles of research.

1. **Use Reliable Measures.**   Many researchers trained in personality or social psychology have failed to appreciate the importance of reliable measures, often using one-item scales or measures of unknown reliability. Unreliablility leads to underestimates of treatment effects. Appropriate aggregation over stimuli, situations, occasions, judges, or measures can often provide another method of enhancing reliability (Epstein, 1983).

2. **Monitor Treatment Implementation.**   In many applied settings, the treatment is not delivered by the experimenter, but, rather, by other personnel such as doctors or nurses. Under these conditions, it is important to monitor treatment quality and to provide corrective feedback to the intervenor when necessary to maximize the reliability of the treatment implementation (Cook et al., in press; Sechrest et al., 1979). Extraneous factors that affect treatment quality can also sometimes be measured and their effects removed through statistical analyses.

3. **Maximize Subject Uniformity.**   The use of heterogeneous subject populations normally tends to increase error variance. Selection of more homogeneous subject samples reduces error variance, although at a poential cost in terms of external validity. Statistical analyses utilizing pretest measures that correlate with the criterion variable can also help reduce error variance in some designs.

4. **Increase N.**   Researchers trained in laboratory research often have woefully optimistic notions about the sizes of effects that can be detected with relatively small samples. All too frequently their tests have at best low to moderate power under the highly controlled conditions that prevail in the laboratory (see Cohen, 1962); in less controlled field settings, similar low N tests have little chance of detecting even large effects. Researchers should attempt to estimate the power of their tests (see Cohen, 1977) when planning their research and make arrangements to obtain a sufficient sample size to provide a fair test of their hypotheses. Sample sizes should also be kept as equal as possible across treatment groups to maximize power.

Internal Validity

Once a difference has been established between the treatment and comparison groups on the dependent measure, the issue arises as to how plausibly the effect may be attributed to the treatment. At this point, laboratory researchers normally blithely move on to issues of construct validity (see next section), secure in their assumptions that randomization could be successfully maintained throughout the experiment and that no contamination of treatments or subjects by other factors has occurred. In contrast, for the applied researcher, developing procedures that will maximize internal validity is the single most important priority in designing research.

Cook and Campbell (1979) have developed an extensive list of *potential* threats to internal validity. These are factors that may prevent the researcher from unambiguously attributing any observed effects to the treatment. The task of the applied researcher is to identify and enumerate those threats that are plausible given the specific design and area under investigation; not all threats are plausible in all designs. Then the researcher can develop additional procedures that help rule out as many of the plausible threats as possible. A partial list of threats is briefly presented here, following the organization developed by Cook and Fitzgerald (in press). Additional threats will be discussed later in the chapter in the section on social experiments.

Threats Arising from the Participants' Growth and Experience. Two threats arise from processes that may occur with the passage of time between the pretest and posttest. These are *maturation* and *history*.

1. **Maturation.**   A number of growth and decay processes occur during the life cycle without any treatment intervention. Children become physically stronger, show improvement in a variety of abilities, and become more knowledgeable about current good health practices. The elderly sometimes show just the opposite pattern.

2. **History.**   This threat arises when an event that is not part of the treatment occurs between the pretest and posttest, and it is plausible that this event could have caused the observed effect. An investigator studying the possible effects of making the environment more predictable on the health of nursing home residents could not be certain as to the effects of this treatment if a change in medication occurred at the same time.

Threats Associated with the Measurement Process.   Two threats, *testing* and *instrumentation*, arise from the measurement process itself.

3. **Testing.**   Testing subjects may affect their responses on later measurements. Teenagers who are asked about their smoking may reduce their consumption of cigarettes, patients given a health information test may remember which items were correct from a previous testing, and newly diagnosed diabetics given a checklist of diabetic symptoms may monitor those symptoms more carefully in the future.

4. **Instrumentation.**   Changes in measuring instruments can give the appearance of an effect even when none exists. Problems in this area range from the obvious, such as the difficulties of comparing scores on different instruments used at pretest and posttest, to a variety of more subtle issues, such as shifts in the reliability of observers from pretest to posttest.

Threats Associated with Sampling Design. Two threats arise from the method by which subjects are selected to be in the investigation. The first applies in designs with pretests and posttests; the second involves the comparison of a treatment with a control group.

5. **Statistical Regression.** When subjects are selected on the basis of pretest scores and less than a perfectly reliable measure is used, posttest scores will tend to regress to the mean of the population from which the sample was drawn. A group of healthy children selected because they miss an average of only 2 days of school in a year will tend to miss more days of school on the average during the following year. This problem is most severe when groups are selected that are extreme on the initial measure.

6. **Selection.** This threat refers to the comparability of the treatment and control groups prior to the delivery of any treatment. Subjects who volunteer for a new medical treatment may be more educated, less healthy, and greater risk takers than subjects who volunteer to receive the conventional medical treatment. To the extent that these or other preexisting group differences are associated with the specific health outcomes under investigation, the researcher will be uncertain as to the effects of the treatment.

Interactions with Selection. Any of the first five threats (1 to 5) can interact with selection to produce possible spurious effects. These threats arise primarily in designs that have nonrandomized treatment and control groups as well as a pretest and posttest. For example, comparisons of the effectiveness of two different protocols for the treatment of myocardial infarction using two different hospitals may be compromised if one hospital has greater staff turnover in its cardiac unit than the other (selection × history) or if one hospital serves a younger patient population than the other, leading to more complete recoveries in the younger group (selection × maturation).

Reducing Threats to Internal Validity. If one or more of the threats to internal validity discussed earlier (or the threats that will be discussed later in the chapter) are plausible, then any observed outcomes cannot be confidently attributed to the treatment. In such cases, researchers must, if at all possible, take additional steps to strengthen the internal validity of the design. Such steps normally utilize concepts from either the agricultural, physical sciences, or social sciences approaches to control. Five general strategies for minimizing the preceding threats to internal validity are presented now, listed in their typical order of preference.

1. **Random Assignment to Treatment Groups.** All the threats previously discussed are rendered implausible if subjects can be randomly

assigned successfully to treatment and control groups. Because of this strength of the randomized experiment, laboratory researchers have never had to concern themselves with attempting to identify the threats to internal validity that are plausible in their designs. But, this strength that is so characteristic of the laboratory experiment has left many researchers ill-prepared to address the difficulties of real-world research. As will be seen, social experiments conducted in real-world settings are subject to other threats to internal validity that are *not* ruled out by randomization.

2. **Other Design Improvements.** It is often possible to strengthen greatly a design by making relatively small changes to address a specific, identified threat to internal validity. For example, history can often be minimized as a threat by delivering the treatment and taking the pretest and posttest measures at nonoverlapping times in different replications. Maturation can often be ruled out by including additional pretest measures that establish the nature of any developmental trend.

3. **Measurement and Statistical Adjustment.**   Specific threats that can be identified and accurately measured can sometimes be eliminated by statistical adjustment. If it is known that age of patient is the primary difference in the populations being treated by two cardiac care units, statistical adjustments may be made that reduce the potential effect of this selection threat on the outcome measures. Note that this procedure adjusts only for the specific variable of patient age and not for other unmeasured or unknown threats, such as prior medical history of the patient.

4. **Pattern of Current Results.**   Although a threat may be plausible given the specific design that was used, it may not be plausible in the context of the specific pattern of results that were actually obtained. Statistical regression would be implausible if a group of previously unhealthy children became substantially healthier than the school average following treatment. A program focusing exclusively on the prevention of coronary artery disease would be substantially stronger in internal validity if participants showed changes in only those health-related behaviors included in the program, but not in the other health-related behaviors that were not addressed by the program.

5. **Previous Research and Theory.**   In cases where previous research has consistently ruled out specific threats to internal validity, they are less likely to be plausible in the current research. Glass et al. (1981) cite a review of the literature that found that adult stutterers do not change their speech behavior over time in the absence of treatment. This consistent finding helps minimize such threats as maturation and statistical regression as plausible explanations of the successful outcome of a treatment program. However, if a different patient

population such as child stutterers were used in an investigation, maturation and statistical regression could once again become plausible threats to internal validity. Such observations suggest that the researcher must be extremely cautious when invoking previous research or theory as a means of ruling out threats to internal validity.

Construct Validity

Successfully establishing internal validity allows the researcher to conclude that "something" about the treatment caused the observed pattern of effects. But exactly what that something is and exactly what the observed pattern of effects means have not yet been addressed. Herein lies the issue of construct validity.

In discussing construct validity, we find it useful to distinguish between two levels of the independent and dependent variables (West & Wicklund, 1980). The first is the *conceptual* (theoretical) level wherein researchers postulate the general theoretical constructs of interest and hypothesize causal relationships among them. An increase in the amount of perceived control over one's outcomes (independent variable) is expected to cause improvements in physical health (dependent variable). Faster emergency medical care (independent variable) is hypothesized to lead to a decrease in the risk of mortality and morbidity from major trauma (dependent variables). Each of these theoretical independent and dependent variables is an abstract construct that must also be specified on a second level, the *operational* level. For example, manipulations of perceived control over one's outcomes have included being able to choose the times a visitor will come (Schultz, 1976), being able to make a variety of choices about mundane aspects of one's daily life (Langer & Rodin, 1976), and giving subjects a button that they believe will terminate a noxious noise (Glass & Singer, 1972). In a parallel manner, diverse measures of physical health have been utilized. Among these are the number of doctor visits, number of sick days, nurse ratings of patient health status, and self-reports of physical symptoms. The relationships between the operational and conceptual levels of the independent and dependent variables for this example are depicted in Figure 5.1.

Issues of construct validity arise in that manipulations are potentially fallible operationalizations of the conceptual independent variable, and dependent measures are potentially fallible indicators of the conceptual dependent variable. In each case, researchers must be aware of the possibility that they have manipulated or measured something in addition to or instead of the intended theoretical construct. In our example, the manipulation of the patient's ability to make choices about her daily life may not lead to a sense of perceived control, but, rather, may lead to an increase in her ability to elicit caretaking behavior by the medical staff. Nurse ratings of the physical health of the patient may also reflect other variables such as how much the nurse likes the patient. In such cases, the theoretical interpretation

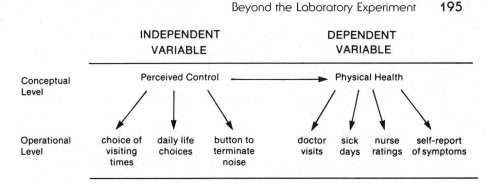

FIGURE 5.1.   Conceptual and operational levels of the independent and dependent variables.

of the results of the investigation is potentially ambiguous. That is, although the researchers may definitely conclude that the manipulation caused the results (internal validity), the conceptual basis for the results may be equivocal, since several plausible alternative explanations of the results may exist.

Strengthening Construct Validity.   A number of alternative methods of strengthening the construct validity of research that focus on different aspects of the problem have been suggested.

1.   The construct validity of the conceptual independent variable may often be established through the use of checks on the manipulation and checks for confounding. Asking subjects directly about how much control they feel they have over their outcomes or measuring the amount of time it takes paramedics to arrive at the scene of accidents in a new emergency care system provide direct checks on the success of these manipulations. In addition, checking that other potential confounding factors have not changed, such as the amount or quality of care received by the patients, decreases the plausibility of these specific alternative explanations of the results.

2.   A conceptually similar process may be used to help establish the construct validity of the conceptual dependent measure. Following the logic outlined by Campbell and Fiske (1959), potential indicators of the same conceptual dependent measure should show substantial correlation (convergent validity), whereas they should be uncorrelated with indicators of other constructs (discriminant validity). Nurse ratings of physical health should correlate with a number of sick days and number of doctor visits, but not with conceptually unrelated measures such as the nurse's liking of the patient.

3.   Aronson et al. (in press) have proposed a process that they term *conceptual replication* in which the same hypothesis is tested in multi-

ple experiments. In each experiment, the operations are changed in an attempt to rule out plausible alternative explanations. To the extent that the pattern of results remains unchanged despite changes in the manipulations and the dependent measures, the construct validity of both the independent and dependent variables is strengthened. This method is a particularly useful technique since other "random irrelevancies" (Campbell, 1968) such as the particular subjects used, the experimenter, the treatment staff, the time when the investigation is conducted, and the setting are also likely to be altered, ruling out these factors as being potentially critical components of the treatment.

4.   Perhaps the most sophisticated method of establishing the construct validity of theoretical variables within a single investigation is through the use of a structural equation approach (Alwin, 1974; Kenny, 1979; see Judd et al., in press, for an illustration). Basically, this approach involves developing a construct model that identifies (1) the specific measures that are indicators of each construct and (2) the nature of the relationship between each of the conceptual constructs. When multiple indicators of each construct are included, the data may be used to test the adequacy of the construct model.

Emphases of Applied and Basic Researchers.   Applied researchers often have more limited goals with respect to construct validity than do basic researchers. Although basic researchers are interested in pinning down the exact theoretical explanation of their results, applied researchers are often primarily interested in being sure that irrelevant factors associated with the treatment (e.g., the specific staff person who is delivering the treatment) are not causing the results. Identifying components of complex treatments that lessen the effectiveness of the treatment package or that are costly and have no effect on the outcome may sometimes also be important to applied researchers. However, identifying the specific theoretical relationships between each of the components of the treatment and a wide range of potentially relevant outcome variables is likely to be of less interest to the applied than to the basic researcher.

External Validity

Closely linked to the issue of construct validity is the issue of external validity. In construct validity, the focus is on the meaning and generality of the theoretical constructs represented by the specific manipulations and measures. In external validity, the emphasis shifts to the generality of the causal relationship between the theoretical independent and dependent variables. Researchers normally wish to reach causal conclusions that extend beyond the specific group of subjects, the specific setting, and the specific time in history that characterized their investigation. The greater the degree to which the basic findings remain unchanged despite variation in subjects, settings, and times, the greater the external validity of the causal relationship.

There are in reality two different types of external validity questions about which a researcher may be concerned (Cook & Campbell, 1979). The first, which most often characterizes basic research, is the extent to which the causal relationship may be generalized *across* different subject populations, different settings, and different times. From the perspective of the theory being tested, these factors are all irrelevant background characteristics that ideally should not affect the causal relationship. Of course, theories may include specific subject variables, setting variables, or less characteristically, time variables, as part of the central theoretical constructs. The theory of type A coronary-prone behavior includes type A and type B persons and settings with and without deadlines as central constructs (Glass, 1977; Matthews, 1982). Nonetheless, according to the theory, the basic findings should generalize across other subject variables (e.g., college students vs. business-people), other setting variables (e.g., school vs. work environment), and other time variables (e.g., experiment conducted in 1975 vs. experiment conducted in 1985) that are not specified as part of the theory. Whenever a subject, setting, or time variable is identified that alters the nature of the causal relationship, a potential boundary condition that limits the domain of application may be established.

The second type of external validity question, which more often characterizes applied research, is the extent to which a causal relationship may be generalized *to* a specific population, a specific setting, and less frequently, a specific time. Researchers who are attempting to improve the speed of recovery of open heart surgery patients through psychological preparation (Aiken & Henricks, 1971) have a specific target population (heart surgery patients) and setting (hospitals) to which they wish to immediately generalize. Schultz (1976) wished to generalize to a specific population (the elderly) and a specific setting (nursing homes) in his studies of perceived control and health. In each case, a more limited and well-defined target population of subjects and settings was identified.[2]

The major issue in external validity is the possibility that some unknown population, setting, or time variable may interact with the treatment to modify the results. Figure 5.2 depicts three sets of hypothetical results of the effects of an educationally focused preparation program on speed of recovery from major surgery. Figure 5.2*a* depicts a situation in which highly anxious patients recover more slowly when they are given educational preparation, whereas low anxious patients recover more rapidly when they are given educational preparation for surgery. Such a result would indicate

---

[2]Schultz's research, in fact, combined applied and theoretical interests. In addition to his interest in developing interventions to improve the lives of the elderly, he has been interested in a variety of theoretcial issues associated with responses to loss of control and predictability.

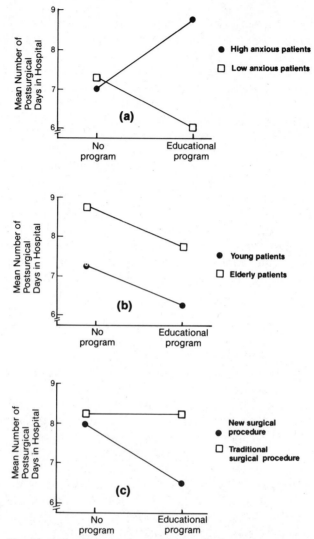

FIGURE 5.2. Hypothetical outcomes of an educationally focused preparation program on speed of recovery from major surgery. (*a*) Illustration of a population × treatment interaction. The benefits of the educationally focused preparation program are limited to low anxious patients. (*b*) Illustration of a main effect of population. Both young and old patients benefit equally from the program. (*c*) Illustration of a setting × treatment interaction. The benefits of the educationally focused preparation program are limited to patients undergoing the new surgical procedure.

that psychological preparation for surgery should be limited to (i.e., not generalized beyond) low anxious patients. Figure 5.2b illustrates a situation in which elderly patients recover more slowly from surgery than do young patients. But, note that both groups benefit equally from the educational preparation. This illustrates that *main effects* of population, setting, or time variables do not limit researchers' ability to generalize their findings. Finally, in Figure 5.2c, subjects who are assigned to receive new, experimental type of surgery benefit from educational preparation. However, subjects who are assigned to receive the traditional surgery for the same medical problem do not benefit from educational preparation for surgery. This illustrates a treatment × setting interaction, in which the benefits of educational preparation are limited to the experimental surgery treatment.

In thinking about problems of external validity, we should consider how the specific group of subjects, the specific setting, and the specific time in history that characterize an investigation are typically selected.

Subjects.   Subjects are normally selected on the basis of convenience. Psychologists located in psychology departments normally utilize the local introductory psychology students, and psychologists located in medical centers normally utilize the available population of patients who are seeking care. Each of these populations has a specific set of associated characteristics that may differ. Replications of the experiment by different investigators will often be associated with the use of relatively heterogenous samples of subjects. Examination of the effectiveness of treatments both within and across investigations as a function of subject characteristics can often help detect findings of limited generality (see Chapter 14 by Leventhal et al., in this volume).

For example, Schachter (1971) primarily used overweight college women from upper-class backgrounds in his studies of obesity. Later failures by other investigators to replicate his early findings with other subject populations have suggested that his findings may be limited to dieting individuals who happened to be heavily represented in Schachter's particular college student population (see Woody & Costanzo, 1981). In a similar manner, medical center populations often show considerable variability in age, income, medical history, medical knowledge, and a variety of other variables. To the extent that such subject characteristics interact with treatments, generalization of findings across subject populations or to other subject populations may be limited.

Settings.   In basic research, an artificial setting is created in the laboratory (Aronson et al., in press) or a specific setting is created or selected in the field (Ellsworth, 1977). In either case, the setting is designed or selected to provide a good representation of the theoretical independent variable, permit measurement of the theoretical dependent variable, and minimize the influence of other extraneous variables. Such a procedure has much to recommend it in terms of construct validity and statistical conclusion validity. However, it may lead to problems of external validity if the treatment interacts with other setting characteristics. A doctor who prescribes a treatment regimen in a highly authoritarian manner may have less compliant patients than a doctor who prescribes the regimen in a less authoritarian manner. If, however, the patient's degree of compliance could potentially be monitored at any time, it is not unlikely that the more authoritarian manner at prescription would produce the higher degree of compliance. This example illustrates a treatment × setting interaction that would limit generalization of any recommendations concerning the physician's manner in prescribing treatment regimens.

Setting × treatment interactions represent an often overlooked, but potentially very severe problem of external validity. Basic researchers often create or select the settings for their investigations on a highly intuitive, creative basis (see Aronson et al., in press; Ellsworth, 1977). Their deliberations focus on how the chances of obtaining the predicted effect of the treatment can be maximized and how potential alternative explanations can be minimized. Only rarely are they concerned with the robustness of the treatment effect across diverse settings or even across changes in background characteristics present within the same setting. When an important treatment effect is found, all background setting characteristics tend to become frozen at their current levels as the investigator rushes to establish a "research paradigm." Other researchers then adopt the same paradigm to maximize their chances of obtaining statistically significant results and to increase the comparability of their findings with those of the previous literature. This particular tradition of basic research is especially likely to lead to findings of unknown generality. Given the extreme homogeneity of the experimental settings, treatment × setting interactions which limit generalization are unlikely to be detected. Similar problems arise in applied research when the research has been exclusively conducted in one setting (e.g., compliance with practices recommended in hospital-based occupational therapy) and the researcher wishes to generalize to another setting (e.g., compliance with practices recommended in media-based health promotion programs).

Time.   All research is conducted in the context of a historical background. Normally historical factors are given little consideration and the research is conducted at whatever time it is possible or convenient. However, factors correlated with time can sometimes have profound effects on treatments. The effectiveness of a 5000-unit dose of penicillin in comparison to a 5000-unit dose of another antibacterial agent has certainly changed from 1955 to 1985 as bacteria have become more resistant to commonly used antibiotics. The effectiveness of supportive therapy for AIDS victims relative to no treatment may show an increase from 1983 to 1985 as the possibility of finding a cure improves. In both these cases, a treatment × time interaction would limit generalization of the results to a particular point in time. Since time is constantly varying, replications of the experiment at different points in time provide a basis for detecting treatments whose effectiveness is limited to a particular historical period.

Increasing External Validity.   A number of different approaches may be taken to increase the external validity of an investigation. The specific steps to be taken depend in part on whether the investigator wishes to generalize *to* a specific subject population, setting, and time, or whether the investigator wishes to generalize *across* populations of subjects, settings, and times. They also depend on a number of practical issues, notably cost and subject and setting availability.

1.   In applied research, the investigator often wishes to generalize *to* a specific target population of subjects and settings. In the Aiken and Henricks (1971) study on psychological preparation for surgery, the researchers wished to generalize to a population of heart surgery patients (subjects) and hospitals (settings). In such cases, the researcher should sample as representatively as possible from the target population of subjects and settings. Some degree of statistical conclusion and construct validity that could be achieved in more controlled, laboratory settings *may* have to be sacrificed to maximize the degree of external validity, which is critical in this case.

2.   Cook and Campbell (1979) outline three *methods of sampling* to maximize external validity. These are presented in their order of preference.

   First, when a population can be defined and resources permit, subjects and settings should be selected randomly from the population. However, it is most often the case that we cannot define the population in a precise manner (e.g., what is the population of all health care settings?) and we do not have sufficient resources in any event to select subjects or settings randomly from the population. It is often possible to select subjects randomly on a more limited scale, for example, from the population of all drug overdose patients seen in the emergency room of a large urban hospital.

   Second, the investigator can follow a strategy of deliberate sampling for heterogeneity. In this method, the investigator identifies easily discernible variables that could potentially interact with the treatment. A convenience sample is selected in such a manner to assure that a wide range of variation is present on each of the variables. A study of the effectiveness of a stress reduction program for hypertensives might make special attempts to sample various ethnic groups, various ages, and people in high- and low-stress occupations. To the extent that the treatment effects hold despite the variation in each of the subject (or setting) variables, the external validity of the finding is enhanced.

Third, using the technique of selecting impressionistic modal instances, the investigator may select one or more convenience samples that seem representative of the typical case. A study of psychological preparation for dental work might seek convenience samples of patients who are being treated for cavities and patients who are having oral surgery. These two procedures may represent the two most common classes of stressful dental procedures. The impressionistic modal instances technique is most useful when only very limited generalization is required.

3. As previously discussed, replications of the investigation can often enhance external validity. To the degree that heterogeneity of subjects, settings, and times is achieved across the various studies and the basic findings still hold, the investigator's ability to generalize the findings on each of these dimensions is enhanced.

4. Within each investigation, more molecular analyses that attempt to detect possible interactions of the treatment with subject variables and with setting variables may be conducted. Those variables that appear to limit generalization may be identified as tentative boundary conditions for the effect. Note, however, that conducting a large number of these analyses increases the likelihood that some interactions will be detected by chance, so that replication is needed to avoid unnecessarily limiting the generality of a robust treatment effect. Such analyses can also sometimes be conducted using meta-analytic techniques (Glass et al., 1981; Mabe & West, 1982; Mumford, et al., 1982) on the entire set of available investigations.

Priorities Among Validity Types

In designing research, investigators must sometimes make difficult trade-offs between types of validity. As one example, should the researcher rigidly standardize the treatment protocol, use only one intervenor, and use a homogeneous group of subjects to maximize statistical conclusion validity? Or, should the researcher allow some variation in the protocol, use a number of different intervenors, and use a heterogeneous group of subjects to maximize external validity? The priority that the investigator assigns to each type of validity will determine the nature of the trade-offs that are made.

As has been indicated earlier, basic and applied researchers often have different goals for their research, which leads to some important differences in the priorities that these groups place on the different validity types. Basic researchers, with their traditional emphasis on theory-testing laboratory experiments, would typically rank internal validity highest, followed by construct validity, statistical conclusion validity, and, finally, external validity (Cook & Campbell, 1979). Further, considerably more attention is usually given to the construct validity of the independent than of the dependent variable. It is common to find basic researchers expending enormous effort constructing investigations so that the exact meaning of the theoretical independent variable can be pinned down and possible alternative explanations of the results can be ruled out. It is far less common to see similar efforts being directed at establishing the construct validity of the dependent variable, with investigators often relying on one or two simplistically constructed measures to establish their effect (cf. Aronson et al., in press; Leventhal et al., this volume). Thus, the construct validity of the theoretical dependent variable appears to rank below statistical conclusion validity for many basic researchers.

Applied researchers, with their traditional emphasis on developing interventions to relieve specific health problems, have a different set of priorities. These investigators would normally rank internal validity highest, followed by external validity, construct validity of the dependent variable, statistical conclusion validity, and construct validity of the independent variable (Cook & Campbell, 1979). With their focus on generalizing *to* specific health-related problems, applied researchers are also sometimes willing to give up small amounts of internal validity in order to achieve a large gain in external validity. Basic researchers are normally unwilling to make any compromises in their research design that would at all weaken either internal validity or the construct validity of the independent variable.

Health psychology and other new areas of applied psychology present a unique challenge to the basic researcher, since the populations and settings to which the findings should generalize are often clearly specified. As Cook and Campbell (1979, p. 85) note,

> when targets of generalization are specified in guiding research questions, cognizance has to be taken of this in designing an experiment, and instances should be chosen that at least belong in the class to which generalization is desired.

This means that basic researchers will sometimes need to move from the familiar and well-controlled confines of the laboratory to actual health settings and populations in the real world and to become aware of the full range of validity types in research.

SOME NATURALISTIC RESEARCH DESIGNS

When researchers in health psychology take seriously the importance of being able to generalize their results to specific medical populations and settings, they often consider a shift in their research strategy. Instead of conducting highly controlled laboratory experiments with college sophomores, they begin exploring the possibility of conducting research directly in the health settings and with the medical populations of interest. Immediately, a host of new problems appear. Random assignment to treat-ment groups may be prohibited by the medical staff or may be impossible for ethical or practical reasons. Even if it can be implemented, randomization may not guarantee that all threats to internal validity have been ruled out. Medical personnel may fail to deliver treatments or deliver additional medi-cal treatments that are not called for in the treatment protocol. And patients and their families may demand additional or alternative treatments.

At this point, too many investigators forsake external validity, retreating to the safety of the laboratory where they can conduct their extremely careful experiments. Others remain in the field, forsaking internal validity by con-ducting "throw it against the wall and see what happens" correlational studies. Between these two extremes an exciting middle ground has devel-oped during the last 20 years as researchers have sought to develop experi-mental and quasi-experimental designs that seek to maximize internal validity within the constraints imposed by real-world research settings. Four of these designs are discussed in this section of the chapter.

SOCIAL EXPERIMENTS

In social experiments, the researcher identifies or develops one or more new treatment programs that can be implemented in an actual field setting. For example, a hospital may be interested in evaluating the effectiveness of two new programs to prepare patients for surgery, one focusing on in-forming the patients about the nature of the surgical procedures that they will experience, the other focusing on reducing the patients' levels of anxiety about the impending surgical procedures. In addition, the hospital would like to know whether either of these special surgical preparation programs offers any benefit beyond that provided by standard presurgical nursing care. To answer these questions, the researcher uses a design, termed the *social experiment*, in which patients are randomly assigned to one of the three treatments as soon as they are scheduled for surgery.

Social experiments enjoy a well-deserved reputation as being the method of choice for maintaining high levels of internal validity. Indeed, successful randomization immediately renders implausible all the standard threats to internal validity that were previously discussed. However, like all methods, the experiment, with its underlying randomization model of control, is based on several assumptions that must be met to ensure maximal interpre-tability of the results. Among these assumptions is that random assignment to treatment groups and the independence of the experimental units are maintained throughout the experiment. Although these assumptions are normally tenable in agricultural research and within the confines of the laboratory experiment in psychology, violations of these assumptions can and often do occur in experiments investigating important social programs in naturalistic contexts. These violations of assumptions give rise to several new possible threats to internal validity that, of course, are *not* eliminated by randomization and that must be actively considered in designing research (Cook & Campbell, 1979; Cook & Fitzgerald, in press).

New Threats to Internal Validity

Differential Mortality.   When research is conducted in real-world settings and over extended periods of time, some of the subjects will fail to complete the experiment. Subjects may die, move to a distant city, become disillusioned with the treatment program, or be unavailable for the final measures for innumerable other reasons. Whenever subjects are lost, questions may be raised about the success of randomization in equating the groups at the *end* of the experiment in the absence of a treatment effect. The most problematic issue is differential mortality in which different proportions of subjects are lost, subjects drop out for different reasons, or different types of subjects drop out in the treatment as compared to the control group. If more type A patients drop out of a heart disease prevention program (and cannot be remeasured) than from an untreated control group, any beneficial effects of the treatment cannot be unambiguously attributed to the program.

Treatment Contamination.   In designing experiments, differential treatment of control and treatment groups is always intended. Such intentions are normally easy to realize in laboratory experiments where treatment and control subjects can be isolated, subjects can be sworn to secrecy regarding the treatments they have just experienced, and subjects do not seek out the "best" possible treatment. However, in social experiments involving programs of real value several problems can arise that lead to some "treatment" of untreated control groups. Direct contamination may occur as in a pain control experiment in which participants in the program may discuss information, relaxation techniques, and medications with control subjects. Control subjects may then adopt versions of some of these treatment procedures or agitate to have certain medications included as part of their program. Or, treatment diffusion may occur as when rehabilitation therapists begin including all or part of the experimental therapy in their work with control subjects. Or, compensation may occur as when nurses believe that the experimental group is receiving superior treatment and they attempt to restore equity by giving the control group participants an unusually high level of attention. In each case, serious misestimation of the effects of treatment may result.

Atypical Reactions of Control Subjects.   The knowledge of subjects that they are participating in an experiment sometimes leads to atypical reactions. Control subjects who become aware of the "superior" treatment of the experimental subjects will sometimes work unusually hard in an attempt to outperform their "rivals." Alternatively, control subjects may simply give up when they learn that another group is receiving a superior treatment. One common form of this latter problem occurs in delayed treatment designs in which control group participants are promised treatment at a later time. In this case, subjects will often stop searching for alternative sources of help and will sometimes cease normal preventive activities, secure in the knowledge that they will later receive treatment. However, such atypical behaviors are likely to lead to more negative outcomes than would be found in the absence of promised treatment.

Strengthening Social Experiments

In response to these new threats to internal validity and an increase in the difficulty of detecting treatment effects, a number of methodological strategies have evolved over the past 20 years that can help strengthen the validity of social experiments. Among the more generally applicable strategies are the following.

Pretest Measurement.   Although not typically emphasized in standard sources on laboratory experimentation (e.g., Aronson et al., in press), pretest measurement of subjects is absolutely critical in social experiments for two reasons. First, the power of the statistical tests can often be substantially increased if subject variables that are likely to be correlated with the outcome measures can be measured prior to treatment. A test of a health improvement program should include pretest measures of variables such as current health status, cigarette smoking, alcohol consumption, weight, age, and gender. Variance associated with these variables can then be removed from the outcome measures through analysis of covariance or other statistical adjustment techniques (see Huitema, 1980), thereby raising the power of the tests. Second, if substantial attrition occurs from the experiment, the pretest measures will be useful in investigating the likely effects of subject mortality. Subjects may be compared on pretest measures to identify variables on which treatment and control group members who do not complete the experiment differ (see subsequent discussion on attrition). If necessary, statistical adjustments can then be made in outcome analyses to explore possible effects of attrition on the results of the experiment.

Treatment Monitoring.   In laboratory research it is normally assumed that careful training of the experimenter and pilot testing assures that the treatment is delivered correctly. In social experiments in which the treatment under investigation or ancilliary treatments are often delivered by health care professionals, such an assumption cannot be made. Instead, it is necessary to monitor carefully all treatments that are given. This practice helps enable the researcher to identify and document a number of forms of treatment contamination when they occur as well as failures to follow the experimental treatment protocol. Corrective feedback may then be provided to personnel to minimize treatment contamination and maximize compliance with the treatment protocol. Careful documentation of all treatments received can also provide a basis for process analyses (Cook et al., in press; Posavac & Carey, 1985; Sechrest et al., 1979) that probe the relationship between measures of the amount and quality of treatment and outcome measures.

Isolating Control and Treatment Groups.   As in laboratory research, subject contamination and atypical subject reactions can often be minimized if subjects in the treatment and control groups can be isolated from each other. Large-scale tests of smoking prevention programs (e.g., Johnson, 1980) have often assigned whole schools rather than individual classrooms to treatment and control conditions in an attempt to minimize this problem. Temporal isolation may also be used, as when all patients admitted for each of a series of nonoverlapping treatment cycles are randomly assigned to treatment or control groups. Although these procedures are normally effective in minimizing problems of internal validity, this may come at some cost in statistical conclusion validity since the larger group (e.g., school, treatment cycle) may be the appropriate unit of analysis (see Judd & Kenny, 1981; Kenny & Judd, 1983) and geographically or temporally distant groups may be less similar than more proximal groups.

Attrition.   Attrition can often be minimized by preexperimental planning and careful attention to this issue throughout the experiment. Securing the addresses and telephone numbers of subjects, their employer or school, and their close friends and relatives at the beginning of the experiment will greatly assist tracking dropouts. Keeping in touch with *both* control and treatment subjects and providing incentives for continued participation also help minimize subject loss. A number of specialized techniques now exist for tracing subjects such as the periodic mailing of address-verification postcards which result in notification by the U.S. Postal Service if a change of address card has been filed.

Even given the most careful procedures, attrition still typically does occur. Consequently, a multistep statistical procedure has been developed that can help detect possible biases introduced by differential mortality (Cook & Campbell, 1979).

1.   The first step is to test the percentage of subjects who drop out in the treatment and control groups to see if these values differ. If they do, subject mortality may be interpreted as a treatment effect, as when one treatment is more attractive or more effective than the other so that the former group of subjects are more likely to remain in treatment. However the interpretation of all other outcome variables becomes more problematic (see e.g., Sackett & Gent, 1979).

2.   The second step is to compare subjects on pretest measures. Following a procedure originally developed by Jurs and Glass (1971), subjects' scores on each of the pretest measures are entered into a series

of 2 × 2 analyses of variance. One factor in this analysis is whether the subject was originally assigned to the treatment or control group. The second is whether the subject completed or did not complete the experiment. Of most concern in this analysis are treatment group × mortality interactions which suggest that different types of subjects are dropping out of the treatment and control groups.

3. When data are available, for example, from exit interviews, on subjects' reasons for dropping out of the experiment, these reasons should be compared for treatment and control subjects. If subjects drop out of one treatment group because of unpleasant side effects of the treatment and the other treatment group because they fail to see a logical rationale for its use, the interpretation of the outcome of the experiment is likely to be biased.

The use of this multistep procedure permits the researcher to detect a wide range of types of differential mortality that may occur in social experiments. The researchers may then investigate the influence of statistical adjustments that correct for the detected types of differential mortality on their results.

Conclusion

Conducting social experiments in naturalistic settings gives rise to a number of problems not normally faced by the laboratory experimenter. However, reasonable solutions to these problems exist that help the researcher maintain relatively high levels of internal and statistical conclusion validity. At the same time, conducting research with the population and in the setting of ultimate interest leads to an enormous increase in the external validity of the results. Although quasi-experimental designs exist that permit reasonable causal inferences, the randomized experiment is the design of choice and should be used whenever possible. As Cook and Fitzgerald (in press, p. 320 of preprint) note,

> *The principal reason for choosing to conduct randomized experiments over other types of research is that they are less imperfect for making causal inference in as far as they usually rule out rival explanations better than other methods.* (italics in original)

REGRESSION DISCONTINUITY DESIGN

Researchers often confront situations in which they cannot conduct randomized experiments. One common case in which this occurs is when legal or administrative prohibitions exist against randomization. The rationale for this position is that treatment should be given solely on the basis of need or merit and should not be given on a chance basis. According to this position, denying the best possible treatment to especially needy or meritorious individuals is unethical. Although strong logical (Cook & Campbell, 1979; Tukey, 1977) and empirical (Gilbert et al., 1977) arguments can and often should be raised against this position, the rarely utilized regression discontinuity design exists as an excellent fall-back option if persuasive arguments for experimentation fail.

The regression discontinuity design takes seriously administrative pronouncements about the necessity of assigning subjects to treatment on the basis of need or merit. In this design, subjects are assigned to treatment specifically on the basis of a quantitative measure of need or merit. Patients could be assigned to dietary treatment for hypertension on the basis of having a systolic blood pressure reading of 145 or higher. College students could be assigned to receive special commendation (Dean's List) on the basis of achieving at least a 3.5 grade point average during the previous semester. In each case, subjects are assigned to treatment conditions using a known rule based on their pretest scores. Measures taken following treatment constitute the dependent variables.

Let us consider the hypertension treatment example in more detail to illustrate this design. Suppose a clinic tests 300 patients for possible inclusion in a special dietary program for hypertension. The clinic makes an a priori decision to assign patients to the treatment on the basis of need which is defined as a systolic blood pressure reading of at least 145 mm. All 125 patients who have readings of 145 mm or higher are assigned to the dietary program; the remaining 175 patients are not given any treatment, since they are within the normal range of blood pressure readings. In addition, 25 patients who have systolic readings higher than 170 mm are put on antihypertensive medication in addition to the dietary program. The systolic blood pressure of all 300 patients is remeasured 3 months after the initial blood pressure screening. Data from this hypothetical investigation are plotted in Figure 5.3.

Figure 5.3 indicates that there is a substantial correlation between the blood pressure readings taken at the initial screening and the 3-month follow-up. But, note in these hypothetical results sizable discontinuities occur at the cutting points for treatment assignment. Approximately a 10-mm drop in the follow-up systolic blood pressure reading occurs at the point of the initial reading of 145 mm, which corresponds to assignment to dietary treatment. The second 15 mm corresponds to an initial reading of 170 mm and assignment to the combined medication and dietary treatment. These two discontinuities in the regression line are potentially interpretable as treatment effects in this design.

Statistically, these effects would be evaluated through tests of the terms in the following regression equation.

$$Y = b_o + b_1X + b_2Z_1 + b_3Z_2 + e \qquad (1)$$

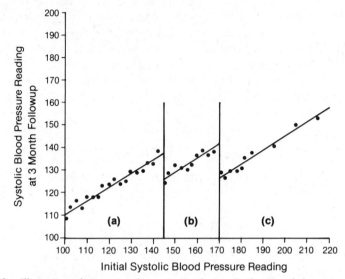

FIGURE 5.3. Illustration of regression discontinuity design: Evaluation of a hypertension treatment program. Subjects in *(a)* receive no treatment, *(b)* receive dietary treatment, *(c)* receive dietary treatment and medication.

In this equation, Y is the outcome variable, systolic blood pressure at follow-up, and X is the pretest variable, systolic blood pressure at the initial screening. Z_1 is a dummy variable that has a value of 0 if no dietary treatment is received and 1 if dietary treatment is received. Z_2 is a dummy variable that takes on a value of 0 if no medication is received and 1 if medication is received. Each of the b's is a coefficient estimated by regression programs available in any of the standard statistical packages. Of most importance, is the fact that the test of b_2 reveals whether the dietary program had a significant effect on systolic blood pressure at follow-up and the test of b_3 shows whether the medication program had any effect on systolic blood pressure at follow-up over and above that of the dietary program. The coefficients b_0 and b_1 provide estimates of the intercept and slope, respectively, of the regression line.[3] Readers desiring a more detailed presentation of the statistical procedures should consult Cohen and Cohen (1983) or Pedhazur (1982) for a general discussion of regression analysis and Judd and Kenny (1981, Chapter 5) and Trochim (1984, Chapter 5) for more thorough discussions of the analysis of the regression discontinuity design.

[3]Normally in the analysis of the regression discontinuity design, the value of X is rescaled so that it has a value of 0 at the cut point. In this case, b_0 is the estimate of the value of the outcome variable at the cut point in the absence of treatment rather than an arbitrary value. Similar rescaling procedures are utilized in time-series analysis for the same reason.

Two Important Statistical Assumptions

Underlying the use of the regression discontinuity design there are two important statistical assumptions: that (1) the functional form of the relationship between the pretest and outcome variables is correctly specified and (2) parallel regression lines may be fit to both the treatment and no treatment groups (i.e., no treatment × pretest interaction). Both assumptions should always be carefully examined and, if necessary, the regression model should be respecified.

Functional Form.   Normally in psychology researchers do not have a strong a priori theoretical or empirical basis for specifying the exact form of the relationship between two variables. Consequently, researchers typically follow the dictates of simplicity and assume that a linear model provides an adequate description of the functional form of the relationship between the two variables. Unfortunately, it is less typical for researchers then to examine the adequacy of the fit between the assumed linear model and the actual data. In the analysis of the regression discontinuity design, this often neglected step in statistical analysis is critical in order to avoid serious misestimation of treatment effects and to minimize some threats to validity.

Two simple probes of the functional form of the relationship are normally undertaken. First, a scatterplot of the relationship between the pretest and the outcome measure is carefully inspected for any systematic pattern of outliers that might indicate that the form of the relationship was misspecified. Of most importance is any systematic pattern of deviation of data points from the regression line in the vicinity of the cut point. Such a pattern would suggest that the treatment effect had been incorrectly estimated. Second, higher-degree polynomial terms (X^2, X^3, X^4) can be added to the regression equation and tested for significance. Only those terms that attain statistical significance would then be retained in the final model. Both probes of functional form are most effective with large samples. Cohen and Cohen (1983), Daniel and Wood (1980), and Mosteller and Tukey (1977) discuss strategies for probing functional form and methods of transforming variables to achieve linear form in greater detail.

Parallel Regression Lines.   Researchers normally make the initial assumption that the regression lines will be parallel in the no treatment and treatment groups. Once again, this assumption should be checked through the careful examination of scatterplots of the relationship between the pretest and outcome measures. Investigators may also test this assumption by including treatment × pretest measure interaction variables in the regression equation. In the blood pressure example discussed earlier, XZ_1 and XZ_2 terms could be added to the regression equation to probe possible changes in the slope of the regression lines in the two treatment conditions.

These checks are most effective in detecting deviations from parallel slopes when large sample sizes are used and the cut point(s) are not too extreme. Figure 5.4 depicts a set of hypothetical results for the blood pressure example in which the regression lines are not parallel.

When significant changes in slope are detected, researchers need to be cautious in their interpretation of the results. Indeed, in the absence of a discontinuity between the two regression lines (a treatment main effect), differences in slope are not usually interpretable as an effect of treatment. In such cases, the most parsimonious interpretation is that the relationship between the pretest and outcome measures is nonlinear when their full range of variation is considered. In cases where there is a substantial discontinuity at the cut point where the treatment is implemented, however, such an alternative interpretation becomes considerably less plausible.

Validity Issues

Internal Validity.   Like the randomized experiment, the regression discontinuity design utilizes a known rule for assigning subjects to treatment conditions. Thus, this design is very strong in terms of ruling out the standard threats to internal validity presented earlier in this chapter. The primary threat to be considered in this design is that of a selection × maturation interaction. In this threat, subjects above the cut point would be

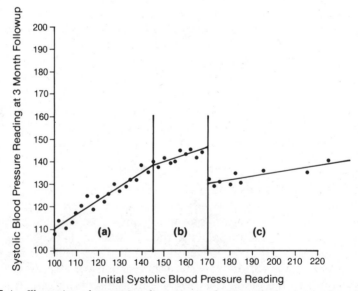

FIGURE 5.4.   Illustration of regression discontinuity design with changes in slope. Subjects in (a) receive no treatment, (b) receive dietary treatment, (c) receive dietary treatment and medication.

maturing at a faster (or slower) rate than subjects below the cut point. For example, students who are placed on the Dean's List may be growing faster academically than students with lower GPAs so that they would have shown the same subsequent gains in their GPAs whether or not they were given the special recognition associated with this honor. The existence of a strong treatment effect combined with careful examination of the statistical assumptions of the design help make this threat less plausible. More definitive evidence regarding this threat can be provided by a replication of the study using a different set of cut points (e.g., subjects are assigned to dietary treatment if they have an initial systolic blood pressure reading of at least 135 mm instead of 145 mm).

Statistical Conclusion Validity. The regression discontinuity design will typically be of substantially lower power than a randomized experiment. The degree to which power is reduced depends on the pretest-posttest correlation and the extremity of the cut points. The higher the pretest-posttest correlation, the lower the ability of the design to detect actual treatment effects. The more extreme the cut points and hence the less equal the size of the treatment and control groups, the lower the power of the test. Researchers need to plan large N studies using this technique to allow for reasonable tests of the statistical assumptions underlying the analysis and to provide a fair test of the effectiveness of the treatments.

External Validity. Regression discontinuity designs are high in external validity in the sense that they are almost always utilized with the populations and in the settings of ultimate interest. However, the confounding of the pretest score and the rule for assigning subjects to treatments in this design can limit generalization. No subject having an initial systolic blood pressure reading of less than 145 mm was assigned to treatment, limiting generalization of the positive effects of treatment to subjects having initial scores around this value. However, note that practitioners would be primarily interested in knowing the effects of the treatment on patients with elevated blood pressure readings, so that this limitation is unlikely to be a serious practical concern.

Fuzzy Assignment Rules

A major issue that may arise in the use of regression discontinuity design is that individuals having scores just below the cut points may be assigned by practitioners to treatment. For example, some subjects having initial systolic blood pressure readings of only 140 mm may be assigned to the dietary program because the physician believes they will benefit from it. Thus, assignment to treatment should be carefully monitored by the researchers to minimize this problem; subjects who are incorrectly assigned should be dropped from this analysis. Examination of the frequency distribution of initial scores can also provide a check on whether subjects are being given systematically high (or low) scores near the cut point so that they receive the more desirable treatment. Finally, delaying announcement of the cut points until after the initial testing can also help minimize this problem.

Note that this problem of "cheating" in assignment of subjects to treatment groups is not unqiue to the regression discontinuity design. Similar care must be exercised in social experiments to make sure that treatment or administrative personnel do not tamper with the random assignment of subjects to treatment groups (See Boruch et al., 1978). Indeed, careful monitoring and checking of the assignment of subjects to treatments is one of the most important aspects of field research.

Conclusion

The regression discontinuity design provides an excellent approach when subjects are assigned to conditions on the basis of a quantitative measure of need or merit. It is very high in internal validity, has reasonable external validity for many applications, but is normally considerably lower in power than the randomized experiment. The example discussed earlier provides only an introduction to the basic design. More complex versions with multiple pretest measures, multiple outcome measures, and nonidentical pretest and outcome measures can also be implemented (see Judd & Kenny, 1981; Trochim, 1984).

INTERRUPTED TIME SERIES

Another situation in which randomized experiments often cannot be implemented occurs when changes in policy are introduced. The federal government begins subsidizing the major share of the costs of dialysis for all kidney patients, a city changes from a centralized to a decentralized emergency medical care (rescue) system, or a hospital begins including presurgical psychological counseling for all major surgery patients. If relevant outcome measures have been collected, researchers may employ an interrupted time-series design to investigate the effects of such changes in policy. Like the regression discontinuity design, the interrupted time-series design provides a strong quasi-experimental alternative when randomized experiments are infeasible, particularly if additional design features can be added to help rule out threats to internal validity.

Figure 5.5 illustrates the basic interrupted time-series design using the hypothetical example of an evaluation of a presurgical psychological counseling program. Imagine that complete data for the years 1978 to 1983 are available from a large university hospital on the number of hours between the completion of major surgery and discharge from the hospital. These data

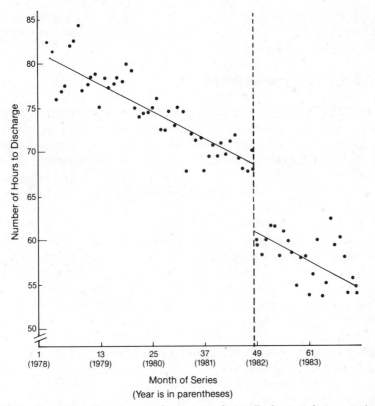

FIGURE 5.5.   Illustration of an interrupted time-series design: Evaluation of presurgical psychological counseling program.

are aggregated and presented as mean values for each month. At the beginning of January 1982, this hospital introduced a treatment program in which trained nurses provide presurgical psychological counseling for all major surgery patients. As can be detected in the data presented in Figure 5.5, the time to discharge has shown a slow decline over the years and there is a tendency for the time to discharge to be higher during the summer months. Of most importance, following the introduction of the psychological counseling program (January 1982), there is approximately an 8-hour decrease in the time to discharge for major surgery patients. Given appropriate statistical analyses and attention to threats to internal validity, this result is potentially interpretable as an effect of the treatment program.

The reader may have detected a strong similarity between the interrupted time-series design and the regression discontinuity design presented in the previous section. Note, however, there is one major difference: In the interrupted time-series analysis design, subjects were assigned to treatment groups on the basis of the time at which they enter treatment rather than on the basis of their pretest scores. As will be seen later, this change leads to a number of complications in statistical analysis and to a different set of potential threats to internal validity.

Statistical Analyses: A Brief Overview

At first glance, the analysis of an interrupted time series would seem to parallel exactly the analysis in the regression discontinuity design. To test the effect of the psychological counseling program on time to discharge from the hospital, we would use the following regression equation.

$$Y = b_0 + b_1T + b_2Z + e \qquad (2)$$

In this equation, Y is the time from the completion of surgery to discharge, T is the month of the series in which January 1978 represents month 1 and December 1983 represents month 72, and Z is a dummy variable that has a value of 0 prior to and 1 following implementation of the psychological counseling program. Once again, the b's are regression coefficients, with b_0 estimating the intercept of the regression line, b_1 estimating the slope of the regression line, and b_2 estimating the treatment effect. This equation dupli- cates equation 1 (p. 209) for the regression discontinuity design, except that only one treatment effect is being estimated and month of the series (T) has been substituted for pretest score (X). This latter change introduces a major complication: Whenever measurements are made over time, there is a strong possibility of serial dependency in the data. Data from adjacent months may be more similiar than data from months that are more removed in time or data collected during the first summer may be more highly related to data collected during other summers than to data collected during the other seasons. In such cases, the normal assumption of uncorrelated error terms in multiple regression is violated, resulting in potential misestimation of treatment effects (Hibbs, 1974).

The problem of time-series analysis is to identify the nature of the serial dependency and transform the data to remove it so that unbiased tests of treatment effects can be performed. This is accomplished by first identify- ing any trends or seasonal patterns in the data and removing them. In our example, there is a linear decrease in the time to discharge over the period of the study and a pattern in which values are high during the summer months. The data must be transformed to remove such trend and seasonal components before the analysis can proceed. Then, the correla- tion between adjacent data points (autocorrelation) is examined to identify the nature of the remaining serial dependency. When the type of the re- maining serial dependency has been identified, a transformation can be applied that will remove this problem from the data. Since the error terms in the data will now be uncorrelated, the effects of treatment can at last be correctly estimated.

The primary task in the statistical analysis of time-series data is to identify the nature of the serial dependency. Several techniques that rely heavily on graphical displays of specialized statistics have been developed to assist the analyst in this task. Good introductions to two of the more commonly used techniques are provided by McCleary and Hay (1980) for the Box-Jenkins ARIMA approach, Gottman (1981) for spectral analysis, and Hepworth et al. (in preparation) for a comparative treatment.

Threats to Internal Validity

The strength of the basic time-series design lies in its ability to rule out most threats associated with maturation, regression, and other influences of a cyclical nature. Typically more problematic are the three threats to internal validity illustrated here.

1. **History.**   New surgical or anesthetic techniques may also be implemented in the hospital, or major insurance carriers may decrease the amount of reimbursement for postsurgical hospital stays, thus possibly accounting for the decrease in recovery time.
2. **Selection.**   The patient population of the hospital may shift so that a larger proportion of younger and healthier patients are being served. These patients would be expected to recover more quickly from surgery.
3. **Instrumentation.**   The hospital may change its record-keeping procedures, reclassifying the surgical procedures that are considered to be "major." Less severe cases that could be expected to recover more quickly from surgery would now be included in the data.

In evaluating the plausibility of each of these threats, we must keep in mind an important point: Only changes that occur at *about the same point in time* as the implementation of the treatment can lead to effects that could be spuriously attributed to the treatment. If a change in anesthetic techniques occurred during month 6 of the series, it is extremely unlikely that this change would cause an abrupt decrease in postsurgical hospital stays beginning in month 49 of the series when presurgical psychological counseling is implemented. Therefore, researchers using simple time-series designs should focus on identifying other changes that coincide with treatment implementation, evaluating the plausibility with which such changes may have caused the observed outcome.

Design Improvements: Strengthening Internal Validity

Certain threats to internal validity can often be ruled out by the addition of one or more of the following design features to the simple time-series design.

No Treatment Control Series.   Comparable time-series data for the same period may be available from another unit that did not implement the treatment. Data on the length of hospital stays following major surgery may be available from another university hospital that did not implement a presurgical counseling program during the 1978 to 1983 period. If the analysis of the control series did not reveal a comparable decrease in postsurgical hospital stays in early 1981, the observed decrease in the treatment series could be more confidently attributed to the psychological counseling program. The addition of the control series rules out the threat of history, although the threat of selection × history (local history) may still be problematic, depending on the degree of comparability of the two hospitals.

Other Control Series.   Sometimes other dependent measures or other breakdowns of the data may be indentified that help serve as a control for the interruption series. Towards this end, the present data could be broken down into scheduled surgery cases that receive counseling and emergency cases that are unconscious and hence cannot receive counseling prior to surgery. Demonstrating that the effects differed in the control and treatment series at the point of intervention would further strengthen the internal validity of the design.

Switching Replications.   Perhaps the most elegant design addition is to identify a comparable series in which the same treatment is implemented at a different point in time. Cook (1983) investigated the effects of price reductions on participation rates in school lunch programs in New York State. In his examination of the monthly data for a multiyear period, he discovered that some schools lowered their prices during one month whereas other schools lowered their prices during another month of the same school year. Similar increases in participation rates occurred at the point of the implementation of price reductions in each set of schools. Based on the strong time-series design and clear-cut results, Cook was able to attribute the observed effects in participation rates to the treatment with a degree of confidence approaching that obtained through the use of a randomized experiment.

Formal and Informal Publicity

Special problems can arise in time-series designs because of the effects of formal and informal, word-of-mouth publicity of the treatment program. Publication of a laudatory newspaper article on the psychological counseling program may lead to a marked shift in the patient population being served. Such problems are particularly likely to be troublesome when the program offered is very attractive or few restrictions are placed on program participation. Thus, a private hospital that introduced a popular new program would very likely experience an influx of new patients; however, a school district that lowered the price of its lunches would be unlikely to experience an inmigration of new students. This special problem of publicity-induced selection will often be a potential threat in health-related research, since patients are normally free to select from among treatment programs. This means that careful monitoring of program-related publicity, new patients' reasons for selecting the program, and patient characteristics that are likely to be related to outcome measures will be necessary to evaluate the plausibility of this threat. In some cases, statistical adjustments may also be undertaken to probe the effects of bias introduced by publicity-induced selection.

Publicity may also impact the effectiveness of some programs in a second way. With certain programs, subjects' perceptions of the policy may be more important than the actual policy in determining the behavioral outcome. Publicity about plans to implement a "911" emergency system can lead to an increase in calls to this telephone number *prior* to implementation of the system. Later, as publicity declines over time, calls to this number may fall off as people's awareness of the system diminishes. In such cases, monitoring program publicity and periodically surveying the population's awareness of the program can be useful in interpreting program effects (Legge & Webb, 1982).

Statistical Conclusion Validity

Problems of statistical conclusion validity in time-series analysis arise primarily from two sources. The first is the issue of whether the underlying model of serial dependency has been correctly identified. Correct identification of the model is facilitated by using multiple diagnostic tools that assist in the identification of the nature of the serial dependency and by checking the transformed data to be sure this problem has been eliminated (Hepworth et al., in preparation). If more than one acceptable model of serial dependency can be identified, tests of the intervention effects should be performed with each model to provide assurance that treatment effects are not dependent on the fortuitous selection of a certain model of serial dependency. The degree of success of the various techniques for diagnosing the underlying model is also dependent on the length of the series. Most authors (e.g., Glass et al., 1975) recommend a minimum of 50 observations to provide stable estimates of the parameter values in models of serial dependency.

A second issue in time-series analysis is power. Researchers are often asked to analyze time-series data shortly after a treatment has been implemented. As in the regression discontinuity design, the ability of the analysis to detect treatment effects is greatest when the intervention occurs in the middle rather than at the end of the series. The power of time-series designs may sometimes be increased if multiple, highly comparable series are available by adjusting each point in the intervention series by the corresponding point in the control series (see e.g., Cook, 1983).

Interpretation of Treatment Effects

Time-series analyses normally attempt to detect changes in the level of the series and in the slope of the series following each intervention. Indeed, the effects of several interventions may be examined in the same series if they are sufficiently separated in time. Both changes in level and changes in slope are potentially interpretable as treatment effects if they occur immediately following the intervention point. Changes that occur at a later point in the series are more equivocal unless strong a priori theoretical or empirical arguments can be made for a delayed treatment effect. Interpretation of a decrease in birthrates beginning 9 months following the implementation of a large-scale family planning program as a treatment effect would be fully justified to the extent the normal threats to internal validity in time-series designs could be ruled out. The use of empirical evidence concerning the actual course of implementation of the treatment program can also lead to more precise models for testing the effects of the treatment. A psychological counseling program would more likely be phased in over a period of months as the nursing staff is trained in counseling techniques rather than abruptly instituted as was implied in the example. Correct specification of treatment implementation can substantially increase the power of time-series analysis to detect treatment effects.

Conclusion

Time-series designs present an excellent alternative to randomized experiments when new programs are implemented. The basic time-series design can often achieve reasonable levels of internal validity; the inclusion of additional design features further strengthens the internal validity of the design. The major practical difficulty with the design is that high-quality archival data or data collected by the experimenter must be available for a large number of time periods both pre- and postintervention to provide optimal estimates of treatment effects. This difficulty can be overcome in health care settings in many cases since patient health status must be frequently or continuously monitored and high-quality records may already exist or be instituted. Although our discussion has focused on the analysis of aggregate data, these same techniques may also be applied to single subject data (Hersen & Barlow, 1976; Horne et al., 1982).

NONEQUIVALENT CONTROL GROUP DESIGN

The most intuitively obvious and hence most utilized alternative to the randomized experiment is the nonequivalent control group design. Here a group is identified or recruited and is given a treatment. A school system institutes a health promotion program or a hospital solicits presurgical patients to participate in a psychological counseling program. Then an appropriate control group which is similar to the treatment group is identified. Another school system that does not have a health promotion program is found, or presurgical patients who choose not to have counseling or who are in another hospital without access to a counseling program are located. Measures of important outcome-related variables are taken prior to and following treatment so that the degree of improvement in the treatment group may be easily compared with the degree of improvement in the control group.[4] Or, so it seems. Unfortunately, despite their apparent simplicilty and ease of implementation, nonequivalent control group designs raise a variety of difficult statistical and interpretational issues. Indeed, many of the major methodological battles in the applied literature over the past several years have been fought over the "true" effectiveness of treatments evaluated using just this type of design (e.g., Head Start: Barnow, 1973; Bentler & Woodward, 1978; Cicarelli et al., 1969; Magidson, 1977).

At issue in the design are the often forgotten assumptions that the treatment and control groups must be equivalent in terms of important background characteristics and be growing at the same rate prior to treatment. Although these assumptions will frequently be plausible when subjects have been randomly assigned to treatment groups, this is not the case in the nonequivalent control group design. Instead, subjects are assigned to treatment and control groups on the basis of rules that are unknown to the researcher and often can only be guessed at. Ruling out the possibility that the groups may differ in these important ways prior to treatment is the central task faced by the researcher who employs this design.

General Strategies for Statistically Equating Groups

Since subjects are not assigned to treatment groups in the nonequivalent control group according to any known rule, researchers must use whatever information and intuition they have available in their attempts to statistically equate the groups. Two different general strategies may be used in this quest (Reichardt et al., in press).

1. **Causal Model of the Posttest.** Researchers may attempt to identify variables related to the primary outcome variables and measure them during the pretest. If latency of recovery from surgery were the primary dependent variable, researchers following the first strategy

---

[4]The results of other designs that do not include both a pretest and posttest and treatment and comparison groups (termed preexperimental by Campbell and Stanley, 1963) are not normally interpretable.

would measure variables such as health status, age, and level of anxiety prior to treatment.

2. **Causal Model of the Pretest.**   Alternatively, researchers may attempt to model the factors that determine treatment group assignment. Following this strategy, researchers would identify and measure factors that were likely to be associated with selection of the control or treatment hospital for surgery. Such factors might include income, area of residence, and patient perceptions of the quality of surgical care at each hospital.

Both strategies will lead to accurate estimates of treatment effects when the stringent assumptions of the adjustment procedure are met. These include identification of all important variables, perfect reliability of each of the pretest measures, correct specification of the functional form of the relationship between pretest and outcome measures, and no group × pretest interactions. The plausibility of the last three assumptions can be probed through examination of reliability estimates for the pretest measures and plots depicting the relationship between pretest and outcome measures. The detection of omitted variables depends primarily on knowledge of the rules or process(es) through which subjects were assigned to treatment and control groups. In the usual case where the assignment rules are unknown, all methods of estimating treatment effects are associated with a high degree of uncertainty. Normally, uncertainty will be least when operationally identical pretests and outcome measures are employed, time intervals are relatively short, and the measures are assessing relatively stable dispositions or behaviors (Reichardt et al., in press).

Statistical Adjustments: An Overview

When identical pretest and outcome measures are available, the first three statistical analyses described here are normally performed. Each of these analyses has a somewhat different bias. It is hoped that the results of the three analyses will converge, giving the researcher a high degree of confidence, although not certainty (Bryk & Weisberg, 1977), that the treatment effect has been correctly estimated.

1. **Analysis of Covariance.**   Simple analysis of covariance adjusts the estimate of the treatment effect for the measured pretest scores. No adjustment, of course, is made for variables that are not included in the analysis. Pretest scores will almost certainly be less than perfectly reliable, resulting in some bias in the estimate of the treatment effect. When one covariate is used, too little adjustment is made for initial differences between the treatment groups; with multiple covariates, underadjustment is also the most likely outcome, although overadjustment may also occur in some cases (Reichardt, 1979).

2.   "True Score" Analysis of Covariance.   In this procedure, an attempt is made to adjust the treatment effect based on an estimate of what the pretest scores would have been if they were measured without error (true scores). With a single covariate, a relatively simple procedure, Porter's true score analysis of covariance (see Huitema, 1980, Chapter 14), can be used to make the appropriate adjustments. The major issue in the use of this procedure is the choice of an appropriate estimate of reliability with which to correct pretest scores. The test-retest correlation for a relatively brief time interval will often provide a good estimate of this value, but other measures may be preferred in some situations (Campbell & Boruch, 1975; Linn & Werts, 1973). Hence, following the recommendations of Cook and Reichardt (1976) and Judd and Kenny (1981), it is useful to perform these analyses using a range of reliability values so as to bracket the true effect of treatment.

3.   Standardized Gain Score Analysis.   Kenny (1975) has developed an approach to the analysis of nonequivalent control group designs that is applicable when the unknown rules for assignment to treatment and control groups may be presumed to be stable over time. In this approach, pretest and posttest scores are first standardized so that the within group pretest and posttest variances are equated. Then the mean gain in the treatment group is compared with the mean gain in the control group to provide an estimate of the treatment effect (see Huitema, 1980, Chapter 15; Kenny, 1975). This approach can provide particularly good estimates of treatment effects when it may be assumed that the treatment and control groups are growing at the same rates.

4.   Other Approaches.   A variety of new, highly sophisticated approaches to the analysis of the nonequivalent control group design have been developed during the past several years. Each of these approaches provides excellent estimates of treatment effects when the assumptions underlying its use are met. However, the success with which violations of assumptions can be identified in practice and the effect of such violations on the treatment estimates is not fully known at present.

   Among the more interesting of the new developments are (1) structural equation analyses (Magidson, 1977; Magidson & Sörbom, 1980; Sörbom, 1978) in which multiple indicators are used to develop a causal model of the pretest or posttest, (2) models that use multiple pretests (Algina & Swaminathan, 1979; Marmor & Marmor, 1978; Simonton, 1977) or surrogate demographic and other background variables to estimate growth rates (Byrk et al., 1980), and (3) econometric models that attempt to estimate treatment group assignments as a function of pretest scores (Barnow et al., 1980; Trochim & Spiegelman, 1980).

In conclusion, each of the statistical adjustment procedures will produce unbiased estimates of treatment effects when its assumptions are met. Unfortunately, the assumptions will often not be fully met in practice and the extent of the violations cannot always be estimated. Hence, the strategy has evolved of conducting several different analyses that make different assumptions about underlying selection and growth processes in the hopes that they will converge on the same result, giving us some degree of confidence that the treatment effect has been correctly estimated. New, more sophisticated analyses also hold considerable promise of providing better estimates of treatment effects under some conditions. Unfortunately, when analyses yield equivocal results, researchers cannot reach any conclusion about the effects of treatment. As Huitema (1980, p. 350) notes: "The consequence of not being able to specify the selection model is not being able to state which, if any, of the analyses yield the appropriate solution."

Threats to Internal Validity

The nonequivalent control group design rules out many of the standard threats to internal validity such as history and maturation. This design does not rule out, however, threats arising from interactions with selection, of which four are the most problematic. These are illustrated using the example of a multiweek treatment program to reduce cigarette smoking.

1. **Selection × Maturation.** Suppose a group of smokers succeeds in reducing their cigarette consumption five cigarettes per week for 3 weeks prior to treatment, whereas a second group continues to smoke a constant number of cigarettes each week. If the first group were then recruited to participate in a smoking reduction program (with the second group serving as a control group), considerable ambiguity would surround the interpretation of any further decreases in cigarette consumption in the treatment group.
2. **Selection × History.** Subjects may inadvertently be selected for the treatment group whose family and friends put them under considerable pressure to stop smoking. In contrast, subjects in the control group have associates who are much more tolerant of their smoking.
3. **Selection × Regression.** Subjects may be selected for the treatment group that has been temporarily smoking an unusually large number of cigarettes, whereas control subjects may have been smoking their normal number of cigarettes each week. With the passage of time, the treatment group may be expected to return to its usual level of smoking even without treatment.
4. **Selection × Instrumentation.** Following the beginning of treatment, smokers in the treatment group may begin smoking a smaller num-

ber of cigarettes clear down to the filter, so that their actual tar and nicotine intake does not change. Control subjects may not show a similar change in their smoking habits. Note that this threat may arise in a wide variety of different forms in this design. The factor structure and the reliability of the scale may differ between treatment and control groups. Or, the interval properties of the scale itself may differ between groups, as when one of the group means is near the end of the scale making further change hard to detect (ceiling effect).

Strengthening the Nonequivalent Control Group Design

Multiple Control Groups.   Since it is virtually impossible to identify a control group that is comparable to the treatment group on all factors that could affect the outcome of the study, it is often useful to identify several, "imperfect" control groups to allow multiple tests of the treatment effect. Roos et al (1978) compared the pre- and postoperation health of tonsillectomy patients with (1) a nonoperated control group matched on age and medical diagnosis (respiratory illness with tonsillar tissue involvement) and (2) a control group of siblings who in each case were within 5 years of the tonsillectomy patient's age. Each control group has its strengths and weaknesses; however, obtaining similar estimates of the effects of treatment across each of the comparisons helps minimize the plausibility of a number of alternative explanations of the results.

Nonequivalent Dependent Variables.   Adding additional dependent variables that are conceptually related to the primary dependent measures but that should be unaffected by treatment can also help strengthen the interpretation of nonequivalent control group studies. Roos et al. (1978) examined both the number of health insurance claims made by their subjects for respiratory illness that would be expected to decrease following tonsillectomy and for other, nonrespiratory illnesses that would not be expected to decrease following tonsillectomy. To the extent that this pattern is obtained, the interpretation of the results as a treatment effect is strengthened.

Multiple Pretests.   The nonequivalent control group design can also be improved by including several pretest measurements prior to treatment. Thus, a "short" time-series design is employed to reduce the likelihood that differential regression or differential growth rates in the treatment and control groups is occurring. As we saw in our discussion of statistical adjustments, the threat of selection × maturation or differential growth can often be a major problem in the interpretation of the results of studies using the nonequivalent control group design. To the extent that an empirical basis is available for estimating growth rates in the treatment and control groups, appropriate statistical adjustments can be made to minimize the plausbility of the selection × maturation threat (e.g., Algina & Swaminathan, 1979).

Plausibility of Threats to Internal Validity: Outcome Patterns

Cook and Campbell (1979) have noted that the four major threats to internal validity in the nonequivalent control groups design may be more or less plausible depending on the specific area of research and the pattern of results that are obtained. For example, they note that the threat of selection × maturation normally involves different *rates* of growth in the treatment and control groups; cases in which one group is growing and the other is not, or in which the two groups are growing in opposite directions, are far less common. Applying this reasoning to Figure 5.6, we can see that selection × regression is likely to be a threat to internal validity in outcomes *B* and *E* but is less likely to be a threat in outcomes *A*, *C*, and *D*.

Figure 5.6 provides an excellent *guideline* for identifying the likely threats to internal validity that are associated with each outcome pattern. The crossover interaction pattern depicted in outcome *D*, for example, makes three of the four threats to validitiy unlikely, so that selection × history is the primary threat that must be examined. If examination of careful documentation of other possible influences on the treatment and control groups throughout the study failed to identify plausible historical influences that differed in the two groups, the researcher could tentatively conclude that a treatment effect had been demonstrated.

Conclusion

The basic nonequivalent control group design provides the least satisfactory alternative to the randomized experiment of the designs we have examined. Despite their apparent simplicity, nonequivalent control group designs are "very weak, easily misinterpreted, and difficult to analyze" (Huitema, 1980, p. 352). The internal validity of nonequivalent control group designs can be strengthened by including additional pretest measures, so that growth trends may be estimated; multiple control groups; and nonequivalent dependent measures. In some cases, pertinent data may be collected so that reasonable models of the group assignment processes may be developed. The use of multiple statistical adjustment procedures that converge on the same estimate of the treatment effect can produce additional confidence in the results. Finally, strong treatment effects coupled with consideration of the plausibility of the remaining threats to internal validity can often overcome a number of the limitations of this design.

SOME FINAL THOUGHTS

The approach to research presented in this chapter may seem puzzling to many traditional laboratory experimenters. These researchers are accus-

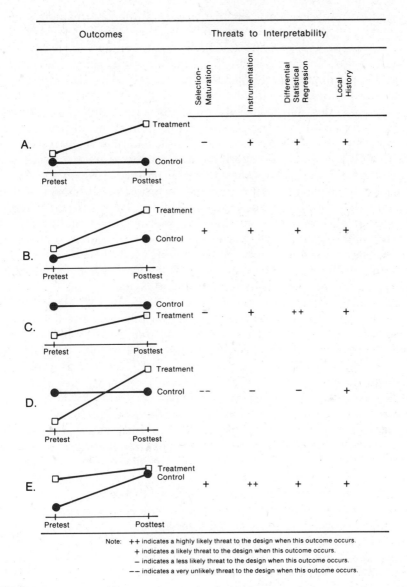

Note: ++ indicates a highly likely threat to the design when this outcome occurs.
       + indicates a likely threat to the design when this outcome occurs.
       − indicates a less likely threat to the design when this outcome occurs.
       −− indicates a very unlikely threat to the design when this outcome occurs.

FIGURE 5.6.   Interpretable outcomes associated with the nonequivalent control group design with pretest and posttest.

tomed to being able to rule out definitively all threats to internal validity and to establish precisely the conceptual meaning of the independent variable. They are used to constructing the best possible control group and conducting the one correct analysis of the data. They are used to simplifying and modifying the situation and developing highly sensitive measures so that even the most subtle effects can be detected. In short, they prefer to construct simple designs that are easy to analyze and that are unambiguously interpretable. Such designs are unexcelled for theory-testing research.

Applied researchers, in contrast, work in a more complex and less certain world. Even the strongest design, the social experiment, may not definitively rule out all threats to internal validity since problems such as differential mortality and treatment contamination are always possible in real-world settings. Weaker designs, such as the nonequivalent control group design, may not even rule out all the standard threats to internal validity. Consequently, applied researchers must carefully articulate all plausible threats to internal validity and develop specific procedures to probe the possibility that a certain threat was responsible for an observed treatment effect. Among the available procedures are the inclusion of additional design features (e.g., multiple control groups), additional measurements (e.g., time-series data), and additional statistical analysis to rule out identified threats to internal validity. The use of these procedures can in some cases produce designs that closely approach the internal validity of the laboratory experiment; in other cases, threats to internal validity may remain even after the investigators' best efforts have been undertaken.

Because of the complexity and uncertainty associated with applied research, it is important for researchers to acknowledge publicly the known limitations of the findings and to make both the data and detailed accounts of the design and procedures available for analysis by others (Cook, 1983; Sechrest et al., 1979). Public criticism of research provides an important mechanism through which possible threats to internal validity and their probable effects on the findings can be articulated. Additional studies having different strengths and weaknesses can then be conducted to help triangulate the true effect. Although considerable uncertainty may be associated with the findings of any one study, a consistent finding in a research literature can provide considerable confidence in the robustness of the effect.

In contrast to its strength in answering basic theoretical questions, the laboratory experiment is often a very poor means of investigating applied issues. Health psychologists often confront applied research questions in which the patient population, the medical setting, and the outcome measures of interest are precisely specified. In such cases, the importance of external validity and the construct validity of the dependent variable is greatly increased. The simplified setting and dependent measures used by laboratory experimenters now become potential liabilities in estimating treatment effects. Differences between the laboratory and applied setting may interact with the treatment. Or, different patterns of results may be obtained on the dependent measures utilized by the laboratory researcher and those of interest to health professionals. The result, in each case, is that the treatment effect may be seriously misestimated.

The experimental and quasi-experimental designs discussed in this chapter provide a range of methods for testing the effects of interventions in health settings and with medical populations of interest. Social experiments typically provide the strongest test of an intervention in terms of both internal and statistical conclusion validity. However, other designs, notably the regression discontinuity design and the interrupted time-series design with switching replications, can sometimes approach the internal validity of randomized experiments, particularly if they are strengthened through the use of some of the techniques described in this chapter. The choice of a particular design will depend on a variety of practical issues, and perhaps, more importantly, on the specific question that the researcher wishes to answer.

ACKNOWLEDGMENTS

The author thanks Leona Aiken, Joe Hepworth, Stefan Hormuth, Anne Maass, and Lee Sechrest for their comments on earlier versions of this chapter.

References

Aiken, L. H., & Henricks, T. F. (1971). Systematic relaxation as a nursing intervention technique with open heart surgery patients. *Nursing Research, 20,* 212–217.

Algina, J., & Swaminathan, H. (1979). Alternatives to Simonton's analysis of the interrupted and multiple group time series designs. *Psychological Bulletin, 86,* 919–926.

Alwin, D. F. (1974). Approaches to the interpretation of relationships in the multi-trait, multi-method matrix. In H. L. Costner (Ed.), *Sociological Methodology, 1973–1974.* San Francisco: Jossey-Bass.

Anderson, L. R., & Ager, J. W. (1978). Analysis of variance in small group research. *Personality and Social Psychology Bulletin, 4,* 341–345.

Aronson, E., Brewer, M. B., & Carlsmith, J. M. (in press). Experimentation in social psychology. In G. Lindzey & E. Aronson (Eds.), *Handbook of social psychology,* (3rd ed.). Reading, MA: Addison-Wesley.

Barnow, B. S. (1973). The effects of Head Start and socioeconomic status on cognitive development of disadvantaged students. Doctoral dissertation, Univerity of Wisconsin. *Dissertation Abstracts,* 1974, *34,* 6191A.

Barnow, L. S., Cain, G. G., & Goldberger, A. S. (1980). Issues in the analysis of selection bias. In E. S. Stromsdorfer & G. Farkas (Eds.), *Evaluation studies review annual* (Vol. 5). Beverly Hills, CA: Sage.

Bentler, P. M. (1980). Multivariate analysis with latent variables: Causal modeling. *Annual Review of Psychology, 31,* 419–456.

Bentler, P. M. (1983). Some contributions to efficient statistics in structural models: Specification and estimation of moment structures. *Psychometrica, 48,* 493–517.

Bentler, P. M., & Woodward, J. A. (1978). A Head Start re-evaluation: Positive effects are not yet demonstrable. *Evaluation Quarterly, 2,* 493–510.

Boruch, R. F., McSweeny, A. J., & Soderstrom, E. J. (1978). Randomized field experiments for program planning, development, and evaluation. *Evaluation Quarterly, 2,* 655–695.

Bryk, A. S., Strenio, J. F., & Weisberg, H. I. (1980). A method for estimating treatment effects when individuals are growing. *Journal of Educational Statistics, 5,* 5–34.

Bryk, A. S., & Weisberg, H. I. (1977). Use of the nonequivalent control group design when subjects are growing. *Psychological Bulletin, 85,* 950–962.

Campbell, D. T. (1968). Prospective: Artifact and control. In R. Rosenthal and R. Rosnow (Eds.), *Artifact in behavioral research.* New York: Academic Press.

Campbell, D. T., & Boruch, R. F. (1975). Making the case for randomized assignment to treatments by considering the alternatives: Six ways in which quasi-experimental evaluations tend to underestimate effects. In C. A. Bennett & A. A. Lumsdaine (Eds.), *Evaluation and experience: Some critical issues in assessing social programs.* New York: Academic Press.

Campbell, D. T., & Fiske, D. W. (1959). Convergent and discriminant validation by the multitrait-multimethod matrix. *Psychological Bulletin, 56,* 81–105.

Campbell, D. T., & Stanley, J. C. (1966). *Experimental and quasi-experimental designs for research.* Chicago: Rand McNally.

Cicarelli, V. G., Cooper, W. H., & Granger, R. L. (1969). *The impact of Head Start: An evaluation of the effects of Head Start on children's cognitive and affective development.* Athens, Ohio: Ohio University and Westinghouse Learning Corporation.

Coates, T. J., Perry, C., Killen, J., & Slinkard, L. A. (1981). Primary prevention of cardiovascular diseases in children and adolescents. In C. K. Prokop & L. A. Bradley, (Eds.), *Medical psychology.* New York: Academic Press.

Cohen, J. (1962). The statistical power of abnormal-social psychological research: A review. *Journal of Abnormal and Social Psychology, 65,* 145–153.

Cohen, J. (1977). *Statistical power analysis for the behavioral sciences* (Rev. ed.). New York: Academic Press.

Cohen, J., & Cohen, P. (1983). *Applied multiple regression/correlation analysis for the behavioral sciences* (2nd ed.). Hillsdale, NJ: Erlbaum.

Cook, T. D. (1983). Quasi-experimentation: Its ontology, epistemology, and methodology. In G. Morgan (Ed.), *Beyond method: Strategies for social research.* Beverly Hills, CA: Sage.

Cook, T. D. & Campbell, D. T. (1976). The design and conduct of quasi-experiments and true experiments in field settings. In M. Dunnette (Ed.), *Handbook of industrial and organizational psychology.* Skokie, IL: Rand McNally.

Cook, T. D., & Campbell, D. T. (1979). *Quasi-experimentation: Design and analysis issues for field settings.* Boston: Houghton Mifflin.

Cook, T. D., Dintzer, L., & Mark, M. M. (1980). The causal analysis of concomitant time series. In L. Bickman (Ed.), *Personality and social psychology annual.* (Vol. 1.). Beverly Hills, CA: Sage.

Cook, T. D., & Fitzgerald, N. M. (In press). Evaluation design. In L. S. Aiken (Ed.), *Prevention evaluation research monograph. II Outcome evaluation.* Washington, DC: National Institute on Drug Abuse.

Cook, T. D., Leviton, L. C., & Shadish, W. J., Jr. (In press). Program evaluation. In G. Lindzey & E. Aronson (Eds.), *Handbook of social psychology* (3rd ed.). Reading, MA: Addison-Wesley.

Cook, T. D., & Reichardt, C. S. (1976). Statistical analysis of data from the nonequivalent control group design: A guide to some current literature. *Evaluation, 3,* 136–138.

Cronbach, L. J. (1982). *Designing evaluations of educational and social programs.* San Francisco: Jossey-Bass.

Daniel, C., & Wood, F. S. (1980). *Fitting equations to data* (2nd ed.). New York: Wiley.

Ellsworth, P. (1977). From abstract ideas to concrete instances: Some guidelines for choosing natural research settings. *American Psychologist, 32,* 604–616.

Epstein, S. (1983). Aggregation and beyond: Some basic issues in the prediciton of behavior. *Journal of Personality, 51,* 360–392.

Fisher, R. A. (1925). *Statistical methods for research workers* (1st ed.). London: Oliver & Boyd.

Gilbert, J. P., McPeek, B., & Mosteller, F. (1977). Statistics and ethics in surgery and anesthesia. *Science, 198,* 684–689.

Glass, D. C. (1977). Stress, behavior patterns and coronary disease. *American Scientist, 65,* 177–186.

Glass, D. C. & Singer, J. E. (1972). *Urban stress: Experients on noise and social stressors.* New York: Academic Press.

Glass, G. V., McGaw, B., & Smith, M. L. (1981). *Meta-analysis in social research.* Beverly Hills, CA: Sage.

Glass, C. G., Willson, V. L., & Gottman, J. M. (1975). *Design and analysis of time series experiments.* Boulder, CO: Colorado Associated University Press.

Gottman, J. M. (1981). *Time series analysis for the behavioral sciences.* New York: Cambridge University Press.

Henschel. T. (1980). The purposes of laboratory experimentation. *Journal of Experimental Social Psychology, 16,* 466–478.

Hepworth, J. T., West, S. G., & Woodfield, T. J. (1984). *Times series analysis in the behavioral sciences: Box-Jenkins ARIMA modeling and beyond.*Unpublished manuscript, Arizona State University, Tempe, AZ.

Hersen, M., & Barlow, D. H. (1976). *Single case experimental designs—Strategies for studying behavior change.* New York: Pergamon.

Hibbs, D. A., Jr. (1974). Problems of statistical estimation and causal inference in time-series regression models. In H. L. Costner (Ed.), *Sociological methodology 1973–1974.* San Francisco: Jossey-Bass.

Horne, G. P., Yang, M. C. K., & Ware, W. B. (1982). Time series analysis for single subject designs. *Psychological Bulletin, 91,* 178–189.

Huitema, B. E. (1980). *The analysis of covariance and alternatives.* New York: Wiley.

Johnson, C. A. (1980). *Prevention of multi-substance abuse in youth.* Unpublished manuscript, University of Southern California, Los Angeles.

Judd, C. M., Jessor, R., & Donovan, J. E. (In press). Structural equation models and personality research: Stability, discriminant validity, and the prediction of behavior. *Journal of Personality.*

Judd, C. M., & Kenny, D. A. (1981). *Estimating the effects of social interventions.* New York: Cambridge University Press.

Jurs, S. G., & Glass, G. V. (1971). The effect of experimental mortality on the internal and external validity of the randomized comparative experiment. *Journal of Experimental Education, 40,* 62–66.

Kenny, D. A. (1975). A quasi-experimental approach to assessing treatment effects in the nonequivalent control group design. *Psychological Bulletin, 82,* 345–362.

Kenny, D. A. (1979). *Correlation and causality.* New York: Wiley-Interscience.

Kenny, D. A. & Judd, C. M. (1983). *Nonindependence of observations in social research.* Manuscript submitted for publication, University of Connecticut, Storrs, CT.

Kessler, R. C., & Greenberg, D. F. (1981). *Linear panel analysis: Models of quantitative change.* New York: Academic Press.

Langer, E. J., & Rodin, J. (1976). The effects of choice and enhanced personal responsibility for the aged: A field experiment in an institutional setting. *Journal of Personality and Social Psychology, 34,* 191–198.

Legge, J. S., & Webb, L. (1982). "Publicity" as a problem in the internal validity of time series quasi-experiments. *Policy Studies Review, 2,* 293–299.

Levine, D. W., & Dunlap, W. P. (1982). Power of the *F* test with skewed data: Should one transform or not? *Psychological Bulletin, 92,* 272–280.

Levine, D. W., & Dunlap, W. P. (1983). Data transformation, power, and skew: A rejoinder to Games. *Psychological Bulletin, 93,* 596–599.

Linn, R. L., & Werts, C. E. (1973). Errors of inference due to errors of movement. *Educational and Psychological Measurement, 33,* 531–545.

Mabe, P. A. III, & West, S. G. (1982). Validity of self-evaluations of ability: A review and meta-analysis. *Journal of Applied Psychology, 67,* 280–296.

Magidson, J. (1977). Toward a causal modeling approach for adjusting for preexisting differences in the nonequivalent group situation: A general alternative to ANOCOVA. *Evaluation Quarterly, 1,* 399–420.

Magidson, J., & Sörbom, D. (1980). *Adjusting for confounding factors in quasi-experiments: Another reanalysis of the Westinghouse Head Start evaluation.* Presented at the American Statistical Association meetings, Houston, TX.

Marmor, G. S., & Marmor, S. (1978). Comment on Simonton's "cross-sectional time-series experiments: Some suggested statistical analyses." *Psychological Bulletin, 85,* 1102–1103.

Matthews, K. A. (1982). Psychological perspectives on the type A behavior pattern. *Psychological Bulletin, 91,* 293–323.

McCleary, R., & Hay, R. A. (1980). *Applied time series analysis.* Beverly Hills, CA: Sage.

Mosteller, F. & Tukey, J. W. (1977). *Data analysis and regression.* Reading, MA: Addison-Wesley.

Mumford, E., Schlesinger, H. J., & Glass, G. V. (1982). The effects of psychological intervention on recovery from surgery and heart attacks: An analysis of the literature. *American Journal of Public Health, 72,* 141–151.

Orne, M. (1962). On the social psychology of the psychological experiment. *American Psychologist, 17,* 776–783.

Pedhazur (1982). *Multiple regression in behavioral research.* New York: Holt, Rinehart & Winston.

Posavac, E. L., & Carey, R. G. (1985). *Program evaluation: Methods and case studies.* (2nd ed.). Englewood Cliffs, NJ: Prentice-Hall.

Reichardt, C. S. (1979). The statistical analysis of data from nonequivalent control group designs. In T. D. Cook & D. T. Campbell, *Quasi-experimentation.* Boston: Houghton Mifflin.

Reichardt, C. S., Minton, B. A., & Schellenger, J. D. (In press). The analysis of covariance (ANCOVA) and the assessment of treatment effects. In L. S. Aiken (Ed.), *Prevention evaluation research monograph: II. Outcome evaluation.* Washington, DC: National Institute on Drug Abuse.

Rogosa, D. (1980). Comparison of some models for analyzing longitudinal panel data. *Journal of Economics and Business, 32,* 136–151.

Roos, L. L., Jr., Roos, N. P., & Henteleff (1978). Assessing the impact of tonsillectomies. *Medical Care, 16,* 502–518.

Rosenberg, M. J. (1969). The conditions and consequences of evaluation apprehension. In R. Rosenthal & R. L. Rosnow (Eds.), *Artifact in behavioral research.* New York: Academic Press.

Sackett, D. L., & Gent, M. (1979). Controversy in counting and attributing events in clinical trials. *New England Journal of Medicine, 301,* 1410–1412.

Schachter, S. (1971). *Emotion, obesity, and crime.* New York: Academic Press.

Schultz, R. (1976). Effects of control and predictability on the physical and psychological well-being of the institutionalized aged. *Journal of Personality and Social Psychology, 33,* 563–573.

Sechrest, L., West, S. G., Phillips, M. A., Redner, R., & Yeaton, W. (1979). Some neglected problems in evaluation research: Strength and integrity of treatments. In L. Sechrest et al (Eds.), *Evaluation studies review annual* (Vol. 4). Beverly Hills, CA: Sage.

Simonton, D. K. (1977). Cross-sectional time-series experiments: Some suggested statistical analyses. *Psychological Bulletin, 84,* 489–502.

Sloan, M. M., & West, S. G. (1984). *Some relationships between theory and applied research: The case of learned helplessness.* Manuscript in preparation, Arizona State University.

Sörbom, D. (1978). An alternative to the methodology for analysis of covariance. *Psychometrika, 43,* 381–396.

Trochim, W. M. K. (1984). *Research design for program evaluation: The regression discontinuity approach.* Beverly Hills, CA: Sage.

Trochim, W. M. K., & Spiegelman, C. (1980). *The relative assignment variable approach to selection bias in pretest-posttest group designs.* Paper presented at the American Statistical Association meetings, Houston, TX.

Tukey, J. (1977). Some thoughts on clinical trials, especially problems of multiplicity. *Science, 198,* 679–684.

West, S. G., & Wicklund, R. A. (1980). *A primer of social psychological theories.* Monterey, CA: Brooks/Cole.

Winer, B. J. (1971). *Statistical principles in experimental design.* (2nd ed). New York: McGraw-Hill.

Woody, E. Z., & Costanzo, P. R. (1981). The socialization of obesity-prone behavior. In S. S. Brehm, S. M. Kassin, & F. X. Gibbons (Eds)., *Developmental social psychology.* New York: Oxford University Press.

6

Longitudinal and Prospective Methods in Health Psychology

SUZANNE C. OUELLETTE KOBASA

Early in any health psychology project, the investigator faces decisions about what subjects to assess; how long to continue the project; how frequently to collect data, and at what specific points in time; and what variables to measure at each of the data collection times. For many researchers, the options offerd by *prospective longitudinal* methods appear very attractive. Consider the following possible choices for the health psychologist interested in the etiological importance of a psychological variable for cancer of the uterine cervix: healthy women from the normal population, sampled to ensure the enrollment of a substantial number of subjects high in the hypothesized psychological risk factor (e.g., high external locus of control); followed for a period of 25 years; contacted at least every 6 months; and at each contact, assessed on a variety of psychological, social, and biological factors, including a careful evaluation of women's gynecologic health status at the beginning of the study. These choices should provide the mythical researcher with an important opportunity to test his or her basic hypotheses. They are also likely to offer an empirical base from which to dismiss many of the alternative explanations typically raised in the face of conclusions about psychological etiology of disease.

If this researcher follows the majority of contemporary investigators in health psychology, he or she will eventually reject the longitudinal and prospective options as too demanding of research time and effort (probably after some serious schedule and budget planning). The consequences of the rejection for the field are obvious. References to longitudinal and prospective designs continue to appear more often in discussion or conclusion sections of health psychology manuscripts than in introduction and method sections. Their appearance indicates the authors' reservations about their reported retrospective and "one-shot" results. They also frame the authors' promise to the reader about how they will someday do the definitive study that will answer all the questions left unresolved by the data currently at hand.

The basic aim of this very selective commentary on longitudinal and prospective methods is to encourage the keeping of many of these promises. Both theory and methodology stand to gain from the use of these methods in a way that they cannnot from the more traditional retrospective assessment of subjects at a single point in time. This chapter also seeks, however, to make clear that prospective longitudinal studies do not provide the simple and final solutions to all our questions. Rather, as they remind us of the importance of theory for the selection of research strategies, as they call for conceptual models that are both elaborate and specific, and as they provoke new research questions, the studies referred to here, and the many other longitudinal and prospective studies that they represent, make a distinctive contribution to the development of our field.

The special focus of this chapter is the relevance of prospective longitudinal methods for research on the topic of stress and health. Given the variety and number of studies that currently constitute health psychology, this is a significant as well as necessary restriction of the story that one can tell about these methods. It is also, however, a justifiable focus. Issues of etiology and causal priority emerge as especially salient in the stress area. Typical stress and health hypotheses appear more urgently to call for a turn from single observation and retrospective work than do predictions and exploratory questions in less well-explored areas of health psychology. Literally thousands of studies now exist that suggest some association between stressful life experiences and changes in health. The exact magnitude of this association and its robustness in varying psychosocial and clinical conditions, however, remains unclear. As Kasl (1983) effectively argues in a recent review of stress and illness research, the confusion and inconsistency has in large part to do with stress researchers' failure to take advantage of prospective longitudinal designs. What these methods do offer forms the heart of the chapter. Specific longitudinal and prospective studies, selected from the still small pool of such studies, serve as the basis for pointing out limitations in the earlier stress work. They appear to offer more convincing answers to some stress and stress-resistance questions and to indicate new research directions.

Before these specific prospective and longitudinal issues can be addressed, however, working definitions of these terms are needed. These are provided in the section that immediately follows. There appears to be more than a little inconsistency in the health psychology literature about what constitutes a prospective longitudinal study, especially about what qualifies as prospective. To address this problem, the chapter takes up each of the terms in turn, citing the differences as well as overlap between the two. Traditional areas of psychology provide illustrations of the importance of these methods; speculations on their potential contributions are presented with reference to a variety of topics in health psychology. The reader should be warned at the onset that the chapter seeks to address some basic substantive concerns. It is not a thorough methodological and statistical critique of prospective longitudinal approaches. For this, the reader is referred to other sources. An elaborate description of statistical models that might be brought to longitudinal data and a review of important European longitudinal work appears in an edited collection by Mednick and Baert (1981). For a recent and very sophisticated methodological evaluation of the power and limitations of prospective designs in health research, the reader should consult a chapter by Kessler (1983), a sociologist and survey researcher.

LONGITUDINAL RESEARCH

Longitudinal studies are defined as research that allows the repeated observation of psychological, physical, and other variables within a single group of subjects, over an extended period of time. In the study of phenomena that are thought to involve distinct phases or stages (e.g., aging), they are typically contrasted with cross-sectional studies. The latter involve the observation of different groups of subjects for each of the assumed phases. A longitudinal study of how persons cope with the multiphase process of surgery, for example, would observe the same patients both before and after the surgical procedure. A cross-sectional study would collect data from one set of patients as they prepare for the operation and from a second group that is in a postoperative state. Beyond noting static associations between two or more variables (e.g., a patient's degree of anxiety and the extent of her information seeking), longitudinal studies allow the consideration of change within single variables over time and the study of the ways in which change in one variable influences change in others of a psychological, social, or biological nature. Consider an elaboration of the coping and surgery example. In the current attempt to establish the value of denial as a coping strategy for persons facing such crises (e.g., Cohen & Lazarus, 1973), the ability to follow the same group of patients—from a time prior to surgery through the period immediately following the operation, and to a time at least 6 months in the future— while continuously assessing variables such as information seeking, defensiveness, emotional distress, and actual medical state is essential.

Examples from Developmental and Personality Psychology

Among psychologists, developmentalists have devoted the most attention to the importance of longitudinal designs. Beginning with early studies such as Terman's (1925) on intelligence and gifted children, continuing through landmark work such as that of Kagan and Moss (1962) on the crucial roles played by family relations and parental attitudes in a child's development, and including the recent work by Werner and Smith (1982) on the importance of feelings of self-confidence and coherence for successful coping through childhood, adolescence, and early adulthood, developmental psychologists have demonstrated their dependence on longitudinal studies. This form of research has been critical for them in two basic ways. It allows the identification of (1) constancy as well as variation in individuals' psychological characteristics over time and (2) the interplay between individual (both psychological and biological) and environmental (physical, social, and cultural) influences through the course of development (cf. Brim & Kagan, 1980; Mednick & Baert, 1981).

The appreciation of longitudinal data, however, is not limited to developmentalists. Personality psychologists, still reeling a bit from their debate with social psychologists over the person as opposed to situation determinants of behavior (cf. Maddi, 1984), have come to see the value of longitudinal studies. Many of their basic propositions, seemingly on the way to extinction in the manuscripts of some critics (e.g., Magnusson & Endler, 1977) are supported and revitalized by the appearance of results from long-term personality and behavior studies of sizable groups of individuals (e.g., Olweus, 1978). Data from multidisciplinary longitudinal studies like those instituted approximately 50 years ago at the Fels Research Insitute and the Institute of Human Development at Berkeley have recently come of age. Analyses of reports from subjects seen in early childhood, adolescence, early adulthood, and, more recently, middle and later adulthood make clear that it is possible systematically to measure personality over time and to employ personality constructs as powerful sources of explanation for later behaviors. Among this rich array of results it is possible to draw illustrations that should be of special interest to health psychologists. The reports by Leona Bayer and her colleagues and Mary Cover Jones, both drawing from the Berkeley Growth Study, the Oakland Growth Study, and the Guidance Study, contain important findings about the relationship between personality and health and illness concerns. Leona Bayer et al.

(1981) describes how personality information collected as early as early adolescence is predictive of health in middle age. More specifically, she finds that young adolescents and young adults who show a satisfaction with self, an emotional calm, a dependable rather than rebellious spirit, and a slowness to become excessively aroused grow up to be physically healthier in later life than do young people who do not have these characteristics. In another study, Mary Cover Jones (1981) works with adulthood alcohol abuse as an outcome variable to confirm the results of earlier cross-sectional studies of personality and social adjustment. When compared with adult abstainers and nonproblem drinkers, same-aged problem drinkers lack self-esteem, are more dependent, rebellious, hostile, and self-defeating,, and have conflict-ridden marital and family lives. Even more compelling for personality psychologists are the results of Jones's examination of the longitudinal data on problem drinkers. Here she finds stability in some of the distinguishing characteristics of male drinkers. "In adolescence these men were already significantly differentiated from their peers in being *more* undercontrolled, impulsive, self-indulged, rebellious, negativistic, and harbor deeper feelings of inferiority . . . *less* dependable, giving, and sympathetic" (p. 241). The Bayer and Jones studies offer rebuttals to those social psychologists and other skeptics who question the consistency and predictive power of most personality characteristics. They also offer hope to some health psychologists. Many, although critical of Alexander's (1950) dependence on psychoanalytic formulations and weak research designs, continue to find some of his suggestions about the interplay between early psychological styles, biological constitution, life crises, and later illness worthy of study. The results from Bayer and Jones suggest that one might usefully return to the early psychosomatic ideas and put them to a more rigorous empirical test.

Health psychologists, however, do not only discover specific findings to be of relevance as they evaluate developmental and personality psychologists' use of longitudinal approaches. Promises of methodological and conceptual advances also emerge. For example, longitudinal exercises have led developmental psychologists to identify a number of new and different approaches to collecting data. The elaborated longitudinal designs include longitudinal-sequential, cross-sectional-sequential, and time-lag sequential strategies (e.g., Achenbach, 1978). These are strategies designed specifically with the theoretical concerns and methodological hurdles of developmentalists in mind. They help overcome the confounding effects of variables such as age of subjects, cohort membership, and time of measurement. Noting this, health psychologists might be inspired to develop distinctive methodological strategies that will address some of their idiosyncratic confounds, for example, stage of illness at which subjects are being assessed.

With important conceptual consequences, longitudinal studies have supported the efforts of those developmentalists who employ what is typically called "a life-span developmental perspective." It is still fair to say that this perspective has generated more theoretical speculation than systematic empirical effort. As the results from extensive longitudinal studies (e.g., Werner & Smith, 1982) done from various perspectives come in, however, an empirical base emerges for many of the life-span tenets (cf. Featherman, 1982). Currently receiving support are assumptions such as the importance of studying individuals across the entire life course. The message is that one should not restrict one's examination of development or change to childhood or adolescence. Adulthood, in its early, middle, and late stages, provides numerous opportunities for investigation. In fact, a whole new research field of geronotology has emerged from the life-span focus on the later years of life. A second popular life-span assumption is that change in individuals should be viewed multidisciplinarily. Any developmental study should go beyond individual psychological factors to assess what Reigel (1979) has called inner-biological, cultural-sociological, and outer-physical processes. To explain any instance of change, one needs to understand the relationships among these processes in the lives under study and their reciprocal influences. A third distinguishing tenet or assumption of the life-span perspective involves its promotion of intervention. Researchers within this area are succeeding in an increasingly impressive way to generate more knowledge about how developmental courses at any point in the life cycle from birth to death may be altered, especially in the areas of intelligence for both children and the elderly.

Suggestions from the Life-Span Perspective

There are a number of lessons in all this for the health psychologist. Although there has been little direct interchange between life-span researchers and health psychologists—two notable exceptions are Brim and Ryff (1980) on life events and House and Robbins (1981) in their discussion of aging, stress, and health—there are a number of similarities in their basic orientation toward the study of persons. Certainly, many health psychologists are interested in intervention. In his articles that set out a definition and mission for the new area of psychology, Matarazzo (1982) calls on psychologists to use their theoretical and methodological tools to help persons change those behaviors that are detrimental to health. Another obvious point of overlap has to do with their joint recognition of the importance of the relationship between psychological and biological variables. Given this common ground, it is appropriate to seek suggestions for future health psychology research in the longitudinal emphasis of the life-span investigators.

One suggestion draws on the life-span definition of the entire life course as appropriate subject matter. Unlike the developmental psychologists who needed to be reminded of the existence of life after childhood, health psychologists may benefit from paying more attention to childhood. Given that many of our studies begin with persons who are already ill or showing risk of illness, we tend to enlist middle-age adults as subjects. For many research areas, this may limit our explanatory and intervention power. Take, for example, our work on prevention and the promotion of health-enhancing behavior. Although we have seen some promising results in the short run from our attempts to have persons change behaviors such as smoking, the maintenance of these changes over extended periods of time has proven difficult (e.g., Bernstein & Glasgow, 1979). Certainly, we need to engage in longer-term follow-up studies of our adult subjects in order to understand better the effects of our change techniques (e.g., Pomerleau, 1979). There may also be something to gain, however, by asking about the early life antecedents of those health behaviors that we are attempting to change. Adopting a life-span perspective, we should want to know something about matters such as family norms around smoking, the meaning of cigarettes in subjects' early socialization, the general emphasis on health and health habits in subjects' child-rearing experiences, and the nature of relationships enjoyed with family members who smoked and those who did not. It may be that by considering the place of smoking in the subjects' entire life course, and how all these childhood matters are predictive of later smoking behaviors, health psychologists can significantly improve their efforts to alter what remains a serious health problem (cf. Krantz et al., 1982).

Health psychologists draw other suggestions from the life-span emphasis in longitudinal studies on *multivariate* approaches to human behavior. These call researchers to (1) broaden their understanding of the term multivariate, (2) take this broadened understanding to an assessment of health and illness as continuing and not discrete phenomena, and (3) utilize it to recognize mutual or reciprocal influences among variables. All these potential correctives can be illustrated through reference to health psychology research on patient satisfaction. Appropriate to the increasing concern in contemporary society with the patient as consumer and as active participant in health care, health psychologists have created an active subspecialization devoted to the study of individuals' response to illness and its treatment.

One shortcoming that emerges immediately as one reviews this subspecialization from the perspective defined by life-span longitudinal approaches is the excessively narrow definition of the multivariate by health psychologists. Along with collecting data on psychological and biological variables, life-span researchers gather information on relevant sociocultural conditions. Too often, health psychologists have ignored the latter. More than one commentator on the new field has criticized a bias in health psychology toward an exclusive concern with the individual and a failure to appreciate the contextual determinants of health status and other relevant outcome variables. Although research on patient satisfaction is plentiful, it fails to contain a systematic review of the variety of societal and organization variables that impact on patient reports. Bard et al. (1984), in their review of this literature and its relevance to an understanding of the world of cancer patients, effectively argue that we know very little about the impact of contextual matters. For example, the differences between patients' percep- tions of care in a traditional hospital setting and their perceptions of treat- ment in the newer and "high-tech" settings of the tertiary care institutions remain unspecified. It is certainly worthwhile to continue investigating how factors such as an individual's locus of control or his need for affiliation influence how he perceives his treatment. It will probably be more reveal- ing, however, to consider these variables alongside others. The specific form of treatment the person is undergoing (e.g, a familiar form of cancer surgery as opposed to an experimental chemotherapy procedure), the extent to which the patient and his family have been involved in treatment decisions, the number of unfamiliar health professional specialists who have been called in, all are contextual matters that should have some bearing on patient perception and satisfaction.

Of course, life-span researchers would consider these and other multi- disciplinary concerns over an extended period of time; whereas health psychologists have not. In their review, Bard et al. found the vast majority of studies of patient satisfaction to employ a single observation or data col- lection point. They correctly identify this restriction as the source of much of the inconsistency in the patient satisfaction literature. One would expect that what a patient perceives about her treatment should change as her medical state does. What someone reports when she first learns about her cancer diagnosis should differ from her comments on the experience of chemotherapy, her reflection during remission, and her interpretations of the doctor's news that she has developed a second form of cancer. Illness is not a discrete phenomenon. Developmental psychologists have enjoyed the heuristic benefits of thinking of their outcome variables in terms of stages for many years. Health psychologists interested in patient satisfaction, as well as a number of other health concerns, could benefit substantially from this example. This point is elaborated with regard to stress and illness research in a later section.

A final suggestion to health psychologists from the life-span perspective refers to how they consider the relationships among their variables. Patient satisfaction appears with rare exceptions merely as an outcome variable in health psychology research. It is depicted as the result of the influence of other variables, such as degree of empathy demonstrated by the physician or the extent of information held by the patient about the medical procedure to be instituted. How it, in turn, influences those and other common indepen- dent variables has been relatively neglected. It is fair to say that in both longitudinal and nonlongitudinal work, health psychologists have been preoccupied with unidirectional causal relationships at the expense of mu- tual effects. It may strike some readers that to follow the example of life-span researchers in this matter is to risk opening health psychology to criticisms of soft-headedness (a charge that was brought more than once to the early life-span work). But to ignore the investigation of mutual effects is to miss many of the advantages of longitudinal work. It may be reassuring to point out at this juncture that a group of investigators as empirically rigorous as survey researchers have made the very same claim for longitudinal data (cf. Tanur, 1982).

PROSPECTIVE LONGITUDINAL RESEARCH

Moving to the term *prospective* requires a different form of definition and illustration. Unlike the term longitudinal, the term *prospective* does not appear under its own heading in the entries of social and behavioral science encyclopedias and dictionaries. Instead, one finds reference to it in a significant number of entries on other psychological topics, typically as a way of indicating those studies in an area that have the most scientific respectability. Prospective research offer the possibility of making successful predictions to the nonexperimental psychologist. Drawing from experimental terminology, one assesses independent variables *before* dependent or outcome variables in prospective studies. Prospective is usually defined in terms of what it is not, namely, *retrospective*. Retrospective studies are those that require investigators to rely upon subjects' recollections of their past behavior, or to search out documents in which others' recorded the behaviors of interest as they occurred. A number of biases that are not easily detected can affect these data. For example, all the fallibilities of human memory may contaminate one's results; and, in the use of earlier documents, factors unknown to the present researcher may have influenced the selection of original subjects and variables to be recorded, as well as the current availability of relevant subjects. Prospective studies, on the other hand, allow the investigators to observe the variables they are interested in and the relation ships among them as they actually manifest themselves.

Each of these biases is reviewed in the discussion of stress and illness research. This last bias, however, may be the least obvious and deserves a quick example. Lebovits et al. (1967) provide one in their relatively early demonstration of the advantages of prospective over retrospective approaches for the investigation of relationships between personality and the occurrence of symptomatic life-threatening disease. They found that individuals who survive coronary heart disease differed significantly on a number of scales from the Minnesota Multiphasic Personality Inventory (MMPI) from those who did not survive, that is, those who died between the first and fifth annual examination. Specifically, the nonsurvivors' scores on the F, Hy, PdK, and PtK scales at the first examination when all subjects were free of clinical coronary disease were significantly higher. From this, the authors conclude that survivors of illness do differ, on the variables being investigated, from persons who die before they can be included in a retrospective study. They close with the strong recommendation that any investigations of the influence of personality and behavioral variables on the occurrence of symptomatic life-threatening disease proceed by the prospective method.

In typical usage by health psychologists and others, the term prospective signifies that the authors believe they have come closer to a demonstration of causal priorities among variables than earlier researchers who relied on retrospective methods, and even some longitudinal methods. Exactly how much closer they have come, however, varies from study to study. The elaboration and justification of this slightly cryptic remark for all health psychology would require more pages than are allowed here. This is an appropriate time to begin to shift the discussion to a specific focus on stress and illness research. Although the concern with causality appears in a number of areas within health psychology, it appears to receive the most explicit attention from researchers concerned with psychological etiology of illness. Investigators who seek to document the extent to which psychological and psychosocial variables are risk factors for disease seem to have written the most about prospective methods.

Focus on Stress and Illness Research

At this point in the history of research, it is difficult to justify discussing environmental stressors and their impact on health without simultaneously considering buffers or moderators of stress. The current research topic is *stress resistance*. Researchers are intent on observing individual differences in response to stress and identifying the psychological, social, and biological sources of these differences. For the purposes of this chapter, however, it is profitable to step back a bit in time and consider the models of stress and illness as the psychologists originally found them, that is, models of a direct link between stressful life events and illness onset. Important advantages of prospective methods over retrospective designs emerge as one utilizes them to test the etiological significance of stressful life events taken as the sole independent variable. One might argue that these advantages pale in comparison to those gained from taking moderators or stress resistance into account. Certainly, a major flaw in the early retrospective stress research was its failure to allow for stress resistance. There are other flaws, however, that have to do more with the studies having been retrospective than with the multivariate scope of the research models. These deserve separate consideration.

The Stressful Life Events and Illness Link

The most frequently cited problem in self-report retrospective studies of the link between stressful life events and the onset of illness is the dependence on subjects' recall. Whether one is interviewing persons who recently suffered a heart attack, developed diabetes, or underwent severe depression, the investigator must have serious concerns about the reliability of the information she receives from the patient about the stressful life events that preceded the illness. Brown (1974), a major researcher in the field of stress and psychiatric disorders, convincingly makes this point. Persons who are experiencing a serious illness tend to engage in an "effort after meaning." They search their recent experiences for events that might help explain why this terrible heart attack or cancer happened to them. Accordingly, a good deal is made of recent arguments with one's boss or confrontations with one's children. Persons who are ill may check off more stressful life events on a standard stress test than healthy persons do because, while in hospital, they have been preoccupied with a life review.

There are a number of solid psychological explanations for this biased presentation of stressful life events, drawing from theories as diverse as consistency and defensive displacement. There are also, however, some cogent social and cultural explanations and more technically cognitive grounds for investigator suspicion. At this point in Western society, there are few persons who have not been exposed to the hypothesis that stressful life events cause illness. Relating debilitation of both mental and physical well-being to stress should be common to anyone who attends to health commentaries in the popular media. The stress and illness idea currently has the persuasive power once held by notions of supernatural determination of health and illness. This cultural familiarity undoubtedly influences the retrospective reports of patients. A final explanation for subject bias appears in developmental psychologists' description of the ways in which persons cognitively process information such as that about stressful events. Brim and Ryff (1980) suggest that four fallacies influence the attribution of causality to life events: vividness of events, recency of events, size of events, and simplicity or the tendency to ignore interactions between events.

Adding to the general reasonableness of these concerns is recent empirical proof of the fallibility of retrospective stress reports. For example, Monroe (1982a) compared a traditional retrospective procedure with a concurrent assessment procedure covering shorter recall periods (1 month). Using a large group of working adults, not patients, he found that as many as 60 percent of events may be underreported for a retrospective period as short as 4 months. Even more telling are the studies that do not depend on retrospective subject reports and that overturn seemingly strong conclusions about stress and illness associations. Kasl (1983) cites a number of these prospective "replications" that fail to support the evidence obtained in retrospective case control and cross-sectional studies. Rundall (1978) found in a prospective study of surgical patients that stressful life events had only weak and/or inconsistent association with recovery after surgery. Even the frequently documented connection between increased mortality and widowhood is put into question by at least two prospective projects (Fenwick & Barresi, 1981; Heyman & Giaturco, 1973).

All this appears to point to the crucial importance of assessing subjects' stressful life event experience *before* assessing their illness or symptomatology. Indeed, in the last 5 years, an increasing number of studies have done just that. For example, instead of asking students to complete a stressful life events checklist at the same time that they are reporting their recent moods and physical ailments, many investigators obtain the events data and then wait for a period of about 6 months to assess health status. The field appears to be moving in a better direction. As one reviews these various prospective studies, however, one quickly perceives a need to make distinctions among them. There are studies with viable explanatory power and others that leave room for numerous alternative explanations. Some utilize all the advantages of prospective design and others are what Kasl calls "merely longitudinal" projects. Researchers' attention to *what* is assessed *when* as well as *how long* the assessment goes on, appars to make the crucial difference. To do research that is prospective longitudinal, one has to do more than observe a single group of subjects over an extended period of time. One has also to assess subjects' health status at the onset of the study. Establishing the etiological significance of stressful life events requires investigators to be as accurate as possible about the dating of the onset of illness. At the first data collection point, the investigator needs to know how subjects stand on the outcome variable and its associated biological risk factors.

Without this information, the stress and illness researcher cannot answer skeptics' charges that the observed stress and illness link has to do less with the provocation of illness by stress and more with the consequences of prior illness, or biological risk for illness, on stressful life event reports. This alternative explanation suggests that prior health status may actually influence the occurrence of events, as well as the reporting of events. For example, events such as "trouble with boss" or "increase in arguments with spouse" that occur on most stressful life events checklists may be the consequences of prior symptomatology of either a physical or mental nature. Some researchers have suggested that items that are as susceptible to confounding as these are should be removed from stressful life event tests (e.g., Fairbank & Hough, 1979). Others effectively argue for a less restrictive approach to stress and a more rigid prospective strategy.

Monroe (1982b), for example, uses one form of this strategy in an evaluation of the association between stressful life events and psychological disorder. For what he labels the "true prospective design for onset conditions" segment of his study, he prescreens his 79 working male and female adults on Goldberg's General Health Questionnaire (also his outcome measure). Using the scores on the Goldberg test, he breaks up his sample into initial cases and noncases. At follow-up (the stressful life events lists from the Psychiatric Epidemiology Research Interview and the Goldberg symptom list are completed at the end of each month for 4 months), he analyses the data of 54 initial noncases, 17 (31.5 percent) of whom became cases. In an examination of these subjects combined with all others, there is no significant correlation between stressful life events and psychological disorder. When Monroe considers only the initial noncases, however, a significant correlation emerges between *undesirable* events and symptomatology. His assumption about the importance of prospective prescreening is confirmed.

There are many other interesting findings in this study. These involve main effects of prior symptoms on later disorder, as well as significant interactions of various categories of stressful life events with prior symptoms. Especially noteworthy is the finding that for the initial cases that continue to be cases ($n = 17$), both desirable and neutral ambiguous types of events, but not undesirable events, significantly correlate with follow-up symptoms. By controlling for initial symptoms, Monroe casts doubt on the frequent assumption that psychological distress causes undesirable events. He concludes his paper with a convincing call for obtaining detailed histories of prior incidence of illness in all future stress and illness work. For another version of this directive, the reader is referred again to Kasl's important reappraisal of stress research. To qualify as what Kasl calls "classical prospective cohort study in epidemiology," health psychologists have to start with subjects who are free of the target disease and then follow them long and systematically enough to detect the transition from simple presence of risk factor to disease.

The importance of prescreening is also relevant for prospective studies that include the assessment of stress moderators. Before turning to these, however, we should make another point about how researchers can better conceptualize their outcome variable in prospective longitudinal studies. The distinction between initial cases and noncases—as well as between cases that go into remission, cases that remain cases, noncases that become ill, and noncases that stay healthy—reminds health psychologists of the complexity of the phenomenon that they are trying to predict. To ask only about the etiological significance of stressful life events for illness *onset* is limiting. As Weiner (1977) notes, psychosocial conditions, including event experience, may be associated with the continuation of an illness, its exacerbation, and its improvement. Keeping in mind a model of stages of disease development or health progress suggests a number of hypotheses about the relationship between stress and health status that are yet to be tested.

The Prospective Longitudinal Approach to Stress Resistance

Although the introduction of psychological variables to studies of stressful life events and illness represents a later stage in the development of stress research, the notion of a connection between psychological conditions and illness is by no means a new one. There were speculations on the importance of moods, attitudes, and personality traits for changes in health long before the systematic investigation of the influence of stressful life events or environmental stressors. As a prelude to the examination of psychological factors in interaction with stress, it is appropriate to consider the prospective and longitudinal implications of some of the earlier work on psychological etiology.

Of all the illnesses that investigators have attempted to link directly with psychological risk factors, the one that appears to have captured the most attention while remaining the most empirically elusive is cancer. Since Galen's initial speculation on the susceptibility of those with melancholia to this disease, there have been hundreds of attempts to draw a causal connection. In his review of most of these, Fox (1976) concludes that one can have little confidence in the status of personality, moods, and other internal states as risk factors of cancer. Except for the data on smoking and drinking habits, the evidence for psychological variables is simply not there.

The main problem, according to Fox and other commentators, has to do with the lack of validating or prospective data. The majority of studies have relied on self-report and retrospective case control designs (e.g., Bahnson & Kissen, 1966), comparing persons with cancer with either healthy persons or patients with other diseases. Although investigators conclude that the observed personality differences existed prior to the onset of illness, and that they indeed predisposed persons to cancer, there is substantial basis for alternative inferences. The personality and other psychological information obtained retrospectively from cancer patients is as, if not more, vulnerable to subjective reporting bias than retrospective stressful life event data. Having cancer or facing the threat of a cancer diagnosis is likely to provoke distinctive changes in mood, specific attitudes, and general orientation toward self and the world (e.g., Rosenthal, 1963). The depressive style investigators have commonly observed is likely to be less a cause than a consequence of the illness. The methodological problem is certainly greatest when patients are aware of their disease. Remember Brown's point about patients' efforts after meaning. But even when personality information is collected before subjects know, there is reason to suspect distortion. The study of hopelessness and the onset of cancer of the uterine cervix by Schmale and Iker (1966) exemplifies this problem. They interviewed women after they had received news of an abnormal pap smear, but *before* the results of a diagnostic procedure to establish the presence or absence of cancer were available to either patients or researchers. Without knowing diagnosis, Schmale and Iker used the interview material on personal losses and hopelessness potential to distinguish significantly the eventual patients from the women free of cancer. What we know, however, about the direct effects of primary lesions and metastases on neurologic perceptual, and cognitive functioning makes these conclusions suspect (e.g., Newman & Hansen, 1974). According to Fox, the etiological significance of personality and other psychological variables can only be established through a *truly* prospective study and no one has yet completed this.

Some may want to soften Fox's pessimistic conclusion by referring to the longitudinal studies of Caroline Thomas and her colleagues (e.g., Thomas, 1976). Many (e.g., Engel, 1976) have viewed her 30 years of work as providing prospective empirical proof that psychological characteristics influence susceptibility to cancer and other diseases and death suffered before age 50. Thomas's research is unique in that it involved the collection of psychological data from over 1015 healthy young medical students (the first year classes from 1948 through 1964 were assessed) and a long-term longitudinal following of these men. Thomas had no specific predictions when she initiated this work. She collected a variety of psychological data, gathered information about early family life and child-rearing, and used a number of psychologists tests that were available 40 years ago (e.g., the Rorschach and figure drawing tests). In spite of her lack of initial expectations about relationships between the early psychological patterns and adulthood health records, Thomas finds in her follow-up studies that students who developed serious illnesses or died differ on a number of dimensions from their classmates who remained healthy. Looking back upon what they said about family attitudes and their youthful psychological experiences and styles, Thomas finds that students who developed or died from one of five illness states including cancer (malignant tumor, hypertension, coronary occlusion, mental illness, and suicide) differ from the healthy students with whom they are compared and each other. The latter finding appears to offer some support to Alexander's early speculations about specificity in associations between psychological factors and disease.

Although there is general recognition of the distinctiveness of Thomas's work, a number of telling criticisms have been directed to it. Among these are weak statistical methods, poor choice of testing materials, and difficulties in interpretation of results generated without solid conceptual justification. Most serious, however, for the purposes of this chapter is Fox's claim that the Thomas study looks more like a retrospective exercise than it does a prospective project. He dubs her work *anterospective*. By this he means that although the Thomas studies succeed in eliminating the influence of cancer upon interviews and other tests results, they fail by selecting subjects *because* they have cancer. It is only by choosing subjects on the basis of their standing on the hypothesized personality variable and then going on longitudinally to test success at predicting cancer that one can do a legitimately prospective project (cf. Kasl, 1983).

To find a personality study that meets more of the criteria set out by Fox and Kasl, one has to leave cancer and move to coronary heart disease. The important work of Rosenman and Friedman and their colleagues in the Western Collaborative Group Study (e.g., Rosenman et al., 1975) offers a better prospective model for the health psychologist. Through a prospective, double-blind design, they observed nearly 3500 men on a set of behavioral, social, dietary, biochemical, and clinical variables. All the subjects were determined to be healthy at initial assessment. Among the scoring procedures at the onset of the study was the classification of subjects on the dimension of *type A behavior pattern*, a psychological style consisting of extreme competitiveness and achievement striving; a strong sense of time urgency and impatience; hostility; and aggressiveness. After following subjects for 8½ years, investigators confirm their original predictions. Men classified as type A at onset of the study are twice as likely to develop angina pectoris or myocardial infarction as are men without this psychological pattern, or type B subjects. This significant type A influence remains even when the effects of medically significant variables such as smoking, obesity, and hypertension are partialed out. Reviewing more recent work on type A (cf. Matthews, 1982), one notices that other prospective longitudinal advantages are being met. Most telling for some of the suggestions drawn from the life-span perspective is the current work on the early life experiences and socialization of individuals who show type A pattern as adults (e.g., Matthews). Also relevant and promising are those studies seeking to link changes in type A with organizational and sociocultural changes (cf. Totman, 1979).

With the type A work as background, one is unfortunately disappointed by a review of the research on psychological variables and stress resistance. In an attempt to demonstrate the relevance of psychological questions about stressful life events moderators, investigators appear to have made prospective longitudinal criteria secondary to other methodological requirements. For example, psychologists in the stressful life events field have given more attention to the content of stressful life events lists (and the assignment of stress weights to the events) than they have to the *timing and frequency* of the assessments of events, hypothesized moderators, and health or outcome status. I would like to illustrate the problems with these methodological shortcomings through reference to the stress-resistance work that I know best, namely, my own. Following this discussion, another category of research in stress resistance, that having to do with the moderating power of social support, is reviewed for its prospective longitudinal promise (cf. also Chapter 15 in this volume).

The conceptualization of *hardiness* forms the basis of my research on stress resistance (Kobasa, 1982). Hardiness is a personality style or set of general attitudes toward self and world that express (1) *commitment* to self, work, family, and other areas of involvement, (2) *control* or belief in the ability to influence what occurs in one's life space, and (3) *challenge* or an interest in change and new experiences. The basis proposition in the model is that among persons facing high degrees of stressful life events, those high in hardiness will be significantly less likely to fall ill, either mentally or physically, than those who lack hardiness or who display alienation, powerlessness, and threat in the face of change. Hardiness facilitates a way of perceiving, interpreting, and handling stressful life events that buffers the negative physiological arousal and activation that might be provoked by stress. Hardy individuals are able to (1) keep specific events in perspective, their basic sense of purpose in life allows them to ground events in an understandable and varied life course; (2) know that they have the resources with which to respond to the events; their underlying control allows them to appreciate a well-exercised coping repertoire; and (3) see the stressful events as potential opportunities for change; challenge enables them to see even undesirable events in terms of possility rather than threat.

A number of retrospective studies involving working adults support the hardiness model. Most convincing is the initial study of telephone company executives (Kobasa, 1979)—a research contact that was to continue for the next 9 years. Beginning with a large pool of male middle-and upper-level executives, I was able to identify through questionnaires, 100 executives who reported significantly high levels of stressful life event experience and high levels of physical symptomatology. These high-stress/high-illness executives formed the group one expected to find based on the emphasis on a simple correlation between stressful life event occurrence and illness reports then popular in most stress research. I also, however, found (as predicted) an equal number of executives with comparably high stressful event experiences who were not showing high symptomatology. It was in these high stress/low illness executives that I expected to find higher hardiness. To test this prediction, I had all the executives complete a lengthy personality questionnaire designed to assess all three hardiness components, as well as demographic characteristics, within a few months of their stress and illness assessment. Discriminant function analysis established that high-stress/low-illness executives did differ significantly from high-illness counterparts and that personality made the crucial difference. The hardiness constellation discriminated between those falling sick in the face of stress and those staying healthy, whereas demographic characteristics, such as age, did not. To establish the generalizibility of these findings, other executive subjects from the same company participated in a cross-validation study. The discriminant function coefficients for the hardiness indicators again proved to be significant predictors of health status.

These retrospective results suggested the importance of looking for individual differences in response to stress and the possibility of systematically raising a personality question in stress research. They fell far short, however, of answering questions about psychological etiology and causal priority of variables. They did not permit rejection of the alternative explanation that personality hardiness results from, rather than causes, health in the wake of stressful life events. Consider the situation of the executives in the retrospective study. An executive fills out a questionnaire noting frequent stressful life events at work and home during the last 3 years; he then goes on to engage in a health review from which he may conclude that he is in pretty good shape (low illness). The levels of commitment, control, and challenge that he later tells us about may be more a reflection of the glow that he feels from having remained symptom free in the face of all these pressures than the actual source of his successful coping. Even more significant is the case of the executive who tells us about frequent and serious health problems (e.g., high blood pressure and recurring migraine headaches), as well as significant stress. His low hardiness profile may indicate the blow to his self-esteem that he has suffered because of his weakened physical state, a sign of the psychological debilitation that sometimes accompanies health problems. The alternative explanation points out that he was not alienated, powerless, and threatened by change *before* his bouts with illness.

To address this charge, we had to put the hardiness model to a prospective test. For this, we decided to continue to follow the original executive pool (Kobasa, Maddi, & Kahn, 1982). Two hundred and fifty-nine executives from whom stress, illness, and personality data had been collected in 1975 provided yearly stress and illness reports for the next 2 years. A new hardiness score was created for each subject, from the 1975 data, by creating a composite from the 5 scales (out of the original 15 scales) that appeared on conceptual as well as empirical grounds to be the best indicators of the hardiness construct. These scales were the Work, Self and Powerlessness subscales from the Alienation Test (Maddi et al., 1979), the Rotter Internal Versus External Locus of Control Scale (Rotter et al., 1962), and the Security Scale of the California Life Goals Evaluation Schedule (Hahn, 1966). The intercorrelations among these 5 scales were significant in the expected direction; a principal components factor analysis defines a first factor that is interpretable as hardiness.

We summed executives' follow-up physical symptomatology and illness reports in such a way as to ensure at least 1 month and up to 2 years lag time between self-reports of personality and the onset of illness. Equally crucial to our prospective intentions, we utilized what we knew about executives' health status at the initial assessment in our test of the prediction of later illness. We ran an analysis of covariance with total later illness as the dependent variable; the hardiness component and stressful life event reports entered as independent variables; and executives' illness scores covering the period 1972 to 1975 served as covariate. This last step had the effect of controlling for prior illness. We, thereby, put hardiness to the test of predicting *changes* in executives' illness scores. Table 6.1 presents these results. The earlier hardiness work receives prospective support. Even when prior illness is controlled, stressful life events lead to an increase in

TABLE 6.1.   ANALYSIS OF COVARIANCE ON ILLNESS USING A PROSPECTIVE ESTIMATE OF HARDINESS AND A CONCURRENT ESTIMATE OF STRESSFUL LIFE EVENTS WITH PRIOR ILLNESS CONTROLLED

Classification	M	n	F	df	p
High stressful life events					
Low hardiness	1254.20	64			
High hardiness	552.89	65			
Low stressful life events					
Low hardiness	387.29	65			
High hardiness	368.34	65			
Covariate: Prior illness			65.71	1	.00
Main effect: Stressful life events			13.17	1	.00
Main effect: Hardiness			5.35	1	.02
Interaction: Stress and hardiness			7.84	1	.00

Source: From Kobasa, Maddi, & Kahn, 1982.

illness and hardiness predicts a decrease in illness. A significant stress and hardiness interaction indicates that being hardy is especially important for one's health when one is undergoing an intensely stressful time.

The possibility of confounding plagues most of the moderators that researchers have chosen to include in their stress-resistance studies. For example, reports of perceived social support (the most frequently investigated buffer in the current literature) can easily be contaminated in retrospective studies. The need for prospective designs is especially clear when one is interested in predicting psychological distress. In another interesting paper, Monroe (1983) makes this point well. Utilizing multiple regression techniques and a comparison of retrospective and prospective designs, he finds that what one observes about the relationship between social support and reported distress significantly depends upon the (1) design employed, (2) variables used as controls (notably, prior symptomatology), and (3) type of disorder studied (psychological versus physical). For example, after controlling for prior symptomatology, social support no longer predicts follow-up psychological symptoms. With regard to physical symptoms, however, even after prior physical symptoms are controlled, social support continues to be highly related to outcome. Monroe reviews these and other findings to suggest why so much confusion exists in the work on stress resistance, and to encourage continued prospective longitudinal work.

In a similar vein, Thoits (1982) offers a conceptually broader discussion of the confounding problem in social support studies. In this paper, she appears less concerned with the causal placement of social support in relation to illness outcome than with the relationship between social support and life stress. More specifically, she is troubled by the debate over whether social support has a direct effect on health or an interactive or stress-buffering effect. She directs most of her questions and criticisms to those studies that maintain that social support functions primarily as a buffer or moderator.

After criticizing the lack of clear definitions and invalid operationalizations of social support in published work, she settles on a conceptualization of the term drawn from Kaplan (in this volume). Social support is defined as the extent to which a person's basic needs (for affection, esteem, belonging, identity, etc.) are satisfied through interactions with others. A person's social support system is that subset of others from the total network who provide socioemotional and/or instrumental aid. With this definition in hand, Thoits accuses many social support studies of confounding the direct effects of life events *on* support and interactive effects of life events *with* support. She finds those investigations that measure social support only *after* the stressful life events at issue have already occurred to be especially troubling. To add some empirical force to her charges. Thoits reanalyzes the panel data from the classic study in psychiatric epidemiology by Myers et al. (1974). Her results show that when social support is measured after life events findings are biased in favor of a strong buffering hypothesis.

Thoits concludes that the only valid way of testing the social support buffering hypothesis is through a longitudinal study. In this, investigators will have to obtain measures of social support *before and after* the events have occurred. Social support is measured at times 1 and 2, and the stressful events at issue are those that occurred between times 1 and 2. Her longitudinal model also calls for two assessments of psychological health or distress. For the interaction term for the regression analysis, Thoits finds too much chance of confounding with both the times 1 and 2 measures of social support; she decides instead to focus on the degree to which social support remains stable. Her basic stress-resistance hypothesis, thereby, becomes: The higher the initial level of support is and the greater the degree to which this level persists during the stressful period, the less impact events will have on psychological distress.

Thoits's longitudinal model certainly convinces the reader of the complexity of the relations among social support, stressful life events, and illness (especially when illness is identified with psychological distress). Her closing theoretical comments reinforce the point. She raises additional questions that lead the reader to want to extend the longitudinal model over a greater span of time, adding new variables, and testing out a greater number of direct and interaction effects among these variables. For example, she encourages researchers to ask why it is that stressful life events are distressing. The typical answer refers to the demands for readjustment that events make. Thoits counters with the suggestion that the ability of events to cause distress may have more to do with how they change individuals' social support than with readjustment demands. To resolve matters such as these, health psychologists would have to engage in more extensive and elaborate research designs than is typical for them. Finally, at the very end of her article, Thoits makes the particularly challenging remark that it may very well be preexisting psychopathology that determines individuals' social support levels and their experience of major stressful life events. Social selection may account for what appear to be direct effects of stressful life events and social support, as well as the apparent buffering effects. Even the researcher who is totally committed to a prospective longitudinal design hesitates at the prospect of successfully addressing this alternative explanation. Thoits's note on preexisting psychopathology brings up the serious "third variable" explanation that even the most sophisticated prospected project cannot ignore.

Thoits's model and the current conceptual model for hardiness and health research (depicted in Figure 6.1) make clear that future prospective longitudinal work on stress resistance will proceed successfully only if done with clear theoretical direction. At this point in the hardiness research, significant effects on physical and psychological health have emerged from studies of a number of other stress-resistance resources. These include family medical history (Kobasa et al., 1981), physical exercise (Kobasa, Maddi, & Puccetti, 1982), and perceived social support at home and at work

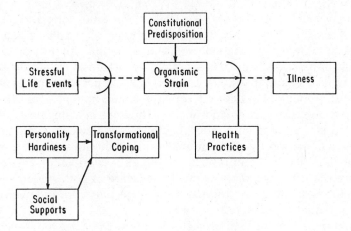

FIGURE 6.1.   Factors affecting health illness status.

(Kobasa & Puccetti, 1983). As independent factors and, more interestingly, in interaction with hardiness, these resources influence whether or not one falls sick following the encounter with stressful life events. At this point in the hardiness research, many questions still remain about these combinations of stress-resistance resources. Much about their effects on each other and on stress and illness experiences *over time* remains to be revealed. For example, I am currently only in the beginning stages of a study on the impact of serious physical illness on hardiness levels. Since the initial theorizing, it has been assumed that hardiness can change over time. The current work is a test of how this might happen and whether illness may be one of the provocations of increase in hardiness. With questions such as these, one has to allow for causal as well as reciprocal effects, main as well as buffering effects. To the longitudinal and prospective data required by these questions, one will have to bring clear predictions based on solid theoretical justifications.

THE LIMITS OF PROSPECTIVE LONGITUDINAL METHODS

In the seventeenth century, the term prospective carried two meanings with special import for this chapter. It referred, on the one hand, to an instrument designed to allow viewers better sight of objects at a distance, an early version of the telescope; and, on the other, to a special glass with supernatural powers that enabled humans to see into mysteries and unknown places, a form of crystal ball. The *Oxford English Dictionary* draws an example of the first reference from *DuMont's Voyages*: "He frequently observ'd what was done in the City from his Seraglio, by the help of some excellent Prospective-Glasses" (p. 2333). For the second, the dictionary draws on Milton: "A Sybil old . . . That . . . in times long and dark Prospective Glass Fore-saw what future days should bring to pass" (p. 2333).

In the contemporary usage of prospective, its dual identify as technical advantage and magical source occasionally reemerges. Prospective longitudinal designs in health psychology substantially better our chances at explanation and prediction and correct some mistaken notions about the interplay of psychosocial factors and health. They are not, however, the easy solution to all our problems. This chapter has reviewed a number of the advantages of prospective longitudinal work. It should also add a warning to researchers about the appeal of the magical connotation of the word *prospective*. Health psychologists need to beware of both underestimating the difficulties of doing longitudinal and prospective work and overestimating the potential of the data they provide.

In initiating a longitudinal project, the investigator has to take seriously the size of the sample to be maintained over an extended period of time. A great deal of interest has been generated in longitudinal survey projects by sociologists and economists. The health psychologist should note, however, that many of the studies cited as uniquely advantageous for psychosocial health questions have extremely large samples. Tanur (1982), for example, associates usefulness with samples of over 50,000. Once subjects are enlisted, the investigator has to worry about keeping them in the study. Attrition has been a serious problem in even the best designed studies (cf. Eichorn et al., 1981). Given this, serious questions arise about the representativeness of the individuals who remain. One suspects an unusual dedication to science in persons who are willing to have so much of their time taken up and their privacy invaded. One might further worry about an unusual interest in interacting with psychologists. Finally, as Kagan and Moss point out, subjects who persist are usually also individuals who have remained geographically close to the research offices. Given what is known about mobility determinants, longitudinal researchers have to note the possible socioeconomic unrepresentativeness of their subjects.

In considering analyses that might be appropriate, the health psychologist needs to avoid being dazzled by the sophistication of new methodological tools and mathematical models that are being developed for longitudinal data sets (cf. Tanur, 1982). Among the most promising are the models that treat time as continuous rather than as discrete. They typically go under the heading of event history analysis (an interesting application of a continuous time model is found in Tuma, et al., 1979). For the type of variables that health psychologists are likely to examine and for studies in which the outcome variable signals a rare occurrence (e.g., a heart attack or the onset of cancer), these models may not be appropriate (cf. Kessler, 1983). It is also important that before taking on these newer methods, one checks that the best possible use has been made of older techniques. Shaffer (1979), for example, points out how most medical and behavioral researchers have not yet utilized analysis of repeated measures over time techniques to their best advantage.

Finally, we need to take care not to be distracted from other requirements of good research. The point has already been made that theorizing and model building have to continue alongside the development of prospective longitudinal methodologies. It is crucial that at the same time that a methodologist such as Kessler develops "instrumental variable" techniques with which to examine longitudinal data and approach the problem of reciprocal causation, theorists such as Lazarus and his colleagues at Berkeley (e.g., Folkman, 1984, Lazarus & Launier, 1978) continue to elaborate their transactional model of the stress, coping, and health process.

There are also other requirements. An especially salient one in this context is sound index construction. The benefits to be derived from prospective longitudinal practices such as measuring stressful life events *before* illness outcome and having a prior measure of health status are dependent upon the use of the right assessment instruments. As health psychologists, we continue to face the problem of having inadequate tools for measuring stress, illness, and the variety of stress buffers as independent and unconfounded factors. A good example of this appears in a paper by Dohrenwend et al. (1984). They demonstrate that each of three commonly used measures of stress is significantly confounded with measures of psychological distress. Only when these measures are unconfounded will we be able to put prospective longitudinal strategies to their best use.

These closing comments are not meant to discourage health psychologists from engaging in prospective longitudinal studies. They are intended as reminders that we work with telescopes and not crystal balls. How well we focus and point the telescope determines how much we can see and discover through it.

References

Achenbach, T. M. (1978). *Research in developmental psychology: Concepts, strategies, and methods.* New York: Free Press.

Alexander, F. (1950). *Psychosomatic medicine.* New York: Norton.

Bahnson, C. B., & Kissen, D. M. (Eds.). (1966). Psychophysiological aspects of cancer. *Annals of the New York Academy of Sciences, 125,* 775–1055.

Bard, M., Myers, L., & Ross, T. (1984). A longitudinal study of patients' perceptions of care. Unpublished manuscript. Memorial Sloan-Kettering Cancer Center.

Bayer, L. M., Whissell-Buechy, D., & Honzik, M. P. (1981). Health in the middle years. In D. H. Eichorn, J. A. Clausen, N. Haan, M. P. Honzik, & P. H. Mussen (Eds.), *Present and past in middle life.* New York: Academic Press.

Bernstein, D. A. & Glasgow, R. E. (1979) Smoking. In O. F. Pomerleau & J. P. Brady (Eds.), *Behavioral medicine; Theory and practice.* Baltimore: Williams & Wilkins.

Brim, O. G., Jr., & Kagan, J. (Eds.). (1980). *Constancy and change in human development.* Cambridge, MA: Harvard University Press.

Brim, O. G., Jr., & Ryff, C. D. (1980). On the properties of life events. In P. B. Bates & O. G. Brim, Jr. (Eds.), *Life-span development and behavior* (Vol. 3). New York: Academic Press.

Brown, G. (1974). Meaning, measurement, and stress of life events. In B. S. Dohrenwend & B. P. Dohrenwend (Eds.), *Stressful life events: Their nature and effects.* New York: Wiley.

Cohen, F. C., & Lazarus, R. S. (1973). Active coping processes, coping disposition and recovery from surgery. *Psychosomatic Medicine, 35,* 375–389.

Dohrenwend, B. S., Dohrenwend, B. P., Dodson, M. & Shrout, P. E. (1984). Symptoms, hassles, social supports, and life events: Problem of confounded measures. *Journal of Abnormal Psychology, 93,* 222–230.

Eichorn, D H., Clausen, J. A., Haan, N., Honzik, M. P., & Mussen, P. H. (Eds.). (1981). *Present and past in middle life.* New York: Academic Press.

Engel, G. L. (1976). The predictive value of psychological variables for disease and death. *Annals of Internal Medicine, 85,* 673–674.

Fairbank, D. T., & Hough, R. L. (1979). Life event classification and the event-illness relationship. *Journal of Human Stress, 5,* 41–47.

Featherman, D. L. (1982). The life-span perspective in social science research. In R. McC. Adams, N. J. Smelser, & D. J. Treiman (Eds.), *Behavioral and social science research: A national resource, Part II.* Washington, DC: National Academy Press.

Fenwick, R. & Barresi, C. M. (1981). Health consequences of marital status change among the elderly: A comparison of cross-sectional and longitudinal analysis. *Journal of Health and Social Behavior, 22,* 106–116.

Folkman, S. (1984). Personal control and stress and coping processes: A theoretical analysis. *Journal of Personality and Social Psychology, 46,* 839–852.

Fox, B. H. (1976). The psychosocial epidemiology of cancer. In J. W. Cullen, B. H. Fox, & R. N. Isom (Eds.), *Cancer; The behavioral dimensions.* New York: Raven Press.

Hahn, M. E. (1966). *California Life Goals Evaluation Schedule.* Palo Alto: Western Psychological Services.

Heyman, D. K., & Giaturco, D. T. (1973). Long-term adaptation by the elderly to bereavement. *Journal of Geronotology, 28,* 359–362.

House, J. S., & Robbins, C. (1981). Age, psychosocial stress, and health. In B. Hess and K. Bond (Eds.), *Leading edges: Recent research on psychosocial aging.* Review essays prepared for the White House Conference on Aging. NIH Publication No. 81-2390.

Jones, M. C. (1981). Middle life drinking patterns: Correlates and antecedents. In D. H. Eichorn, J. A. Clausen, N. Haan, M. P. Honzik, & P. H. Mussen (Eds.), *Present and past in middle life.* New York: Academic Press.

Kagan, J., & Moss, H. A. (1962). *Birth to maturity: A study in human development.* New York: Wiley.

Kasl, S. V. (1983). Pursuing the link between stressful life experiences and disease: A time for reappraisal. In C. L. Cooper (Ed.), *Stress research: Issues for the eighties.* New York: Wiley.

Kessler, R. C. (1983). Methodological issues in the study of psychosocial stress. In H. B. Kaplan (Ed.), *Psychosocial stress: Trends in theory and research.* New York: Academic Press.

Kobasa, S. C. (1979). Stressful life events, personality, and health: An inquiry into hardiness. *Journal of Personality and Social Psychology, 37,* 1–11.

Kobasa, S. C. (1982). The personality and social psychology of stress and health. In G. Sanders & J. Suls (Eds.), *The social psychology of health and illness.* Hillsdale, N. J.: Erlbaum.

Kobasa, S. C., Maddi, S. R., & Courington, S. (1981). Personality and constitution as mediators in the stress-illness relationship. *Journal of Health and Social Behavior, 22,* 368–378.

Kobasa, S. C., Maddi, S. R., & Kahn, S. (1982). Hardiness and health: A prospective study. *Journal of Personality and Social Psychology, 42,* 168–177.

Kobasa, S. C., Maddi, S. R., & Puccetti, M. (1982). Personality and exercise as buffers in the stress-illness relationship. *Journal of Behavioral Medicine, 5,* 391–404.

Kobasa, S. C., & Puccetti, M. C. (1983). Personality and social resources in stress-resistance. *Journal of Personality and Social Psychology, 45,* 839–850.

Krantz, D. S., Glass, D. C., Contrada, R., & Miller, N. E. (1982). Behavior and health: The biobehavioral paradigm. In R. McC. Adams, N, J. Smelser, & D. J. Treiman (Eds.), *Behavioral and social science research: A national resource, Part II.* Washington, DC: National Academy Press.

Lazarus, R. S., & Launier, R. (1978). Stress-related transactions between person and environment. In L. A. Pervin & M. Lewis (Ed.), *Perspectives in interactional psychology.* New York: Plenum Press.

Lebovits, B. Z., Shekelle, R. B. Ostfeld, A. M., & Ogelsby, P. (1967). Prospective and retrospective studies of coronary heart disease. *Psychosomatic Medicine, 29,* 265–272.

Maddi, S. R. (1984). Personology for the 1980s. In R. A. Zucher, J. Aronoff, & A. T. Rabin (Eds.), *Personality and the prediction of behavior.* New York: Academic Press.

Maddi, S. R., Kobasa, S. C., & Hoover, M. (1979). An alienation test. *Journal of Humanistic Psychology, 19,* 73–76.

Magnussen, D., & Endler, N. S. (Eds.). (1977). *Personality at the crossroads: Current issues in interactional psychology.* New York: Wiley.

Matarazzo, J. D. (1982). Behavioral health's challenge to academic, scientific, and professional psychology. *American Psychologist, 37,* 1–14.

Matthews, K. A. (1982). Psychological perspectives on the Type A behavior pattern. *Psychological Bulletin, 91,* 293–323.

Mednick, S. A., & Baert, A. E. III (Eds.). (1981). *Prospective longitudinal research: An empirical basis for the prevention of psychosocial disorders.* Oxford: Oxford University Press.

Monroe, S. M. (1982a). Assessment of life events. *Archives of General Psychiatry, 39,* 610.

Monroe, S. M. (1982b). Life events and disorder: Event-symptom associations and the course of disorder. *Journal of Abnormal Psychology, 91,* 14–24.

Monroe, S. M. (1983). Social support and disorder: Toward an untangling of cause and effect. *American Journal of Community Psychology, 11,* 81–98.

Myers, J. K., Lindenthal, J. J., & Pepper, M. P. (1974). Social class, life events, and psychiatric symptoms. In B.S. Dohrenwend and B. P. Dohrenwend (Eds.), *Stressful life events: Their nature and effects.* New York: Wiley & Sons.

Newman, S. J., & Hansen, H. H. (1974). Frequency, diagnosis, and treatment of brain metastases in 247 consecutive patients with bronchogenic carcinoma. *Cancer, 33,* 492–496.

Olweus, D. (1978) *Aggression in the schools.* New York: Halsted.

Pomerleau, O. F. (1979). Why people smoke: Current psychobiological models. In P. O. Davidson & S. M. Davidson (Eds.), *Behavioral medicine: Changing health life styles.* New York: Brunner/Mazel.

Reigel, K. F. (1979). *Foundations of dialectical psychology.* New York: Academic Press.

Rosenman, R. H., Brand, R. J., Jenkins, C. D., Friedman, M., Straus, R., & Wurm, M. (1975). Coronary heart disease in the Western Collaborative Group Study: Final follow-up experience of 8½ years. *Journal of the American Medical Association, 233,* 872–877.

Rosenthal, I. (1963). Reliability of retrospective reports of adolescence. *Journal of Consulting and Clinical Psychology, 27,* 189–198.

Rotter, J. M., Seeman, M., & Liverant, S. (1962). Internal vs. external locus of control of reinforcement: A major variable in behavior study. In N. F. Washburne (Ed.), *Decision, values and groups.* London: Pergamon.

Rundall, T. G. (1978). Life change and recovery from surgery. *Journal of Health and Social Behavior, 19,* 418–427.

Schmale, A. H., & Iker, H. P. (1966). The effect of hopelessness and the development of cancer. *Psychosomatic Medicine, 28,* 714–721.

Shaffer, J. W. (1979). On the analysis of repeated measures over time in medical, pharmacological, and behavioral research. *Journal of Behavioral Medicine, 2,* 221–238.

Tanur, J. M. (1982). Advances in methods for large-scale surveys and experiments. In R. McM. Adams, N. J. Smelser, & D. J. Treiman (Eds.), *Behavioral and social science research: A national resource Part II.* Washington, DC: National Academy Press.

Terman, L. M. (1925). *Genetic studies of genius, I: Mental traits of a thousand gifted children.* Stanford: Stanford University Press.

Thoits, P. A. (1982). Conceptual, methodological, and theoretical problems in the study of social support as a buffer against life stress. *Journal of Health and Social Behavior, 23,* 145–158.

Thomas, C. B. (1976). Precursors of premature death and disease. *Annals of Internal Medicine, 85,* 653–658.

Totman, R. (1979). *Social causes of illness.* New York: Pantheon.

Tuma, N. B., Hannan, M. T., & Groeneveld, L. P. (1979). Dynamic analysis of event histories. *American Journal of Sociology, 84,* 820–854.

Weiner, H. H. (1977). *Psychobiology and human disease.* New York: Elsevier.

Werner, E. E., & Smith, R. S. (1982). *Vulnerable but invincible: A longitudinal study of resilient children and youth.* New York: McGraw-Hill.

PART **III**

SPECIALIZED ASSESSMENT METHODS

7

Physical, Social, and Inferential Elements of Psychophysiological Measurement

JOHN T. CACIOPPO
RICHARD E. PETTY
BEVERLY MARSHALL-GOODELL

A young man in the third century B.C. was afflicted by inexplicable and debilitating periods of faintness and lassitude. A medical examination proved uninformative, so a physician by the name of Erasistratos monitored the man's bodily signs throughout the course of the day. Erasistratos found that abnormal bodily signs did indeed erupt on several occasions during the

Preparation of this chapter was supported by a University Faculty Scholar Award and by National Science Foundation Grant No. BNS-8217096.

day, and he noticed that the attacks covaried with the appearance of the man's young and attractive stepmother. The youth's mysterious malady was diagnosed as "lovesickness," and separation of the young man and woman relieved the distress (Mesulam & Perry, 1972).

A 5-month-old infant, who showed no abnormalities up to that point, began vomiting shortly after eating. This pattern became fixed, and the infant soon became emaciated. Neither medical or psychological tests were helpful in identifying the cause of the infant's persistent regurgitation. Moreover, interventions such as changes in diet and feeding methods, the administration of antinauseants, and the provision of intensive nursing all proved unsuccessful. At the age of 9 months, the infant was admitted to a hospital weighing only 12 pounds. There, electromyographic (EMG) activity over the infant's perioral region (e.g., chin, throat) was monitored, and clear signs of when the infant was about to vomit were found. Next, the appearance of these subtle physiological signs was used to initiate painful electric shocks to the calf of the infant's leg. When EMG activity over the perioral region decreased, shock was terminated. This intervention proved successful. The frequency of vomiting after meals decreased quickly and disappeared completely by the sixth training session. The infant quickly gained weight and, at last report, is living a normal life (Lang & Melamed, 1969).

The traditional medical examination has proven unable to distinguish neonates who are neurologically normal from those who suffer from mild forms of central nervous system dysfunction. The failure to diagnose and treat these latter neonates increases their likelihood of developing a wide range of developmental disabilities such as mental retardation. In research designed to combat this problem, respiration and heart rate were recorded from a pair of neonates; one was normal and the other had suffered brain-death. The recordings from each neonate were subjected to spectral analysis to determine an index of the vagal tone to the heart. Even when respiration and heart rate did not distinguish these neonates, the index of vagal tone did. The neurologically intact infant showed strong evidence of a relationship between cardiac and respiratory activity (i.e., respiratory sinus arrhythmia), whereas the brain-damaged infant did not. This index of vagal tone may soon prove useful in diagnosing neural pathology in neonates and improve the care given to neonates "at risk" (Porges, in press; Porges et al., 1982).

Psychophysiology refers to the scientific study by nonsurgical means of the interrelationships between psychological processes and physiological systems in humans. Field and laboratory observations using *psychophysiological methods* have made important contributions to our understanding and treatment of a variety of stress-related disorders (cf., Christie & Mellet, 1981; Grings & Dawson, 1978; Krantz et al., 1982; Lang, 1971; Perski et al., 1982). The three cases previously discussed, for example, span more than 2000 years and vary dramatically in the roles assigned to bodily responses, yet they share a common focus on the interactions among physiological, psychological, and behavioral events. In the first and third cases cited earlier, for example, the consequences of the activity of entire systems of cells served as markers of psychobiologic status. In the case of the child who vomited after eating, the bioelectric activity emanating from the muscles in the perioral region were viewed as precursors to the maladaptive behavior and, hence, were used in determining when to administer aversive electrical shocks. In each case, the physiological responses were not viewed as being linked invariantly to a particular psychological or behavioral state, but, rather, they were interpreted within the reigning recording context to gain more information about the status of the organism than was available through verbal inquiries or observational procedures.

The aim of the present chapter is to provide a basis for understanding the methods being developed and used in psychophysiological research. Generally, psychophysiological methods are noninvasive and designed to track either gross bioelectric events (e.g., cardiac activity) or the consequences of gross bioelectric events (e.g., respiratory activity), but they can be employed to produce physiological interventions as well as assessments (e.g., "biofeedback").

In order to provide a broad overview, we have partitioned the chapter into three increasingly abstract levels of analysis. In the first section, we discuss the *physical context* for psychophysiological research. We review the essentials of bioelectric events and the rational behind the instrumentation and procedures used to record these events. Next, we consider the *social context* for psychophysiological research. Psychophysiological experimentation involves human organization, if not interaction, and the act of being a subject in research can alter the very process being investigated. Hence, methods are surveyed that reduce the disruption due to social factors of the events of interest in psychophysiological inquiries. Finally, we consider the *inferential context*, which is important when relating the observed physiological reactions to psychological constructs. This chapter is not intended as an instruction manual for recording various psychophysiological responses, such as electroencephalography (EEG), electrocardiography (EKG), electrodermal activity (EDA), and so forth. The interested reader may wish to see Stern et al. (1980) for an excellent introduction to these recording techniques and consult the relevant chapters in existing reference books for more detail (e.g., Brown, 1972; Coles et al., in press; Greenfield & Sternbach, 1972; Martin & Venables, 1980; Venables & Martin, 1967).

PHYSICAL CONTEXT

Multicellular organisms are constituted by differentiated cells that perform highly specialized and necessarily limited functions. The membrane covering living cells is semipermeable, allowing some biochemicals (e.g., potassium) to enter the intracellular fluid while generally forming a barrier preventing entry by others (e.g., sodium). As a result, there is an ionic gradient, or electrical potential, between the two surfaces of a cell. Maintaining this gradient requires cellular metabolism (i.e., energy), which in turn requires the delivery of cellular fuel and the removal of toxins. Because of the specialization of the cells, no single cell in a multicellular organism could survive without cellular organization and intercellular communication.

Humans possess two major systems for physiological communication and control. The first is the endocrine system, which operates through the release of chemical hormones from glands into the bloodstream. The actions of the endocrine system are comparatively slow and diffuse, at least for hormones released outside the brain. The second, which spans the distances between the receptors (e.g., eyes, proprioceptors) to the brain and back again to peripheral effectors (e.g., muscles, organs), is the nervous system (see Figure 7.1). Although increasing attention is being directed by psychophysiologists toward the endocrine system (e.g., see Carruthers, 1981; Christie & Woodman, 1980), most work by far has concerned the physiological events associated directly with the operation of the nervous system.

Nerve, muscle, and gland cells are somewhat unique in that when they respond to a stimulus, their membrane potentials undergo a series of reversible changes known as *action potentials*. The function of the action potentials in gland and nerve cells is largely communicative. By propagating their changes in biopotentials in the form of action potentials, events acting upon one set of specialized cells are coordinated with those of another. Fortunately, the nature of these electrical changes differ for each type of cell, making it possible to measure independently the electrical activity of a large number of homogeneous cells. The bioelectric signals emanating from groups of these cells have been of interest to psychologists because they are easy to record, harbor information about the organization and functioning of systems of cells, and in some instances reveal reactions to stimuli that are either absent or overlooked in overt behavior.

For example, the human nervous system is formed by a network of heterogeneous cells whose collective actions are responsible for overt behaviors and the maintenance of an internal milieu. In the most general sense, the nervous system transmits information about the external (i.e., environmental) and internal (i.e., organismic) settings in the least possible time to reflexive response mechanisms (e.g., the simple reflex arc of the knee) and/or to integrative neural structures in the brain. These neural structures, in turn, are the source of decisions and instructions to the skeletal muscles to act, or inhibit action, on the external environment and to the viscera and glands to act, or inhibit action, on the internal environment. The incoming information travels along the afferent or sensory pathways, whereas the instructions travel along the efferent or commandatory neural pathways (see Figure 7.1).

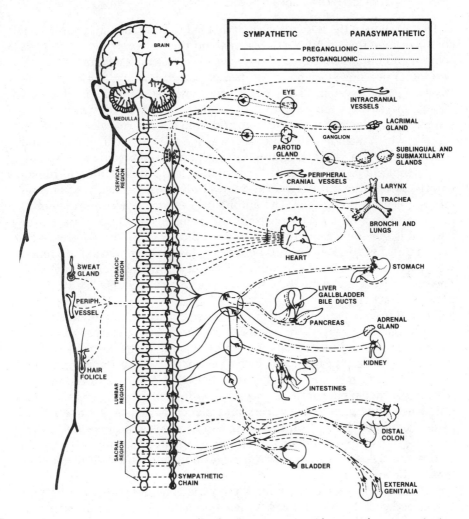

FIGURE 7.1. The human nervous and endocrine systems provide means for communication and control. Components of the nervous system traveling inward from the periphery are called afferents, and components traveling outward are called efferents. These afferents and efferents travel throughout the body to receptors, viscera, glands, and muscles of all types. Endocrine glands located in the central portion of the body secrete their chemical messengers (hormones) directly into the blood stream. Although the human nervous and endocrine systems are usually depicted separately, they are closely related and interact with one another. The hypothalamus, for instance, exerts an influence over the pituitary gland, which in turn affects the other endocrine glands. (Adapted from an original painting by Frank H. Netter, M.D., from *The CIBA Collection of Medical Illustrations*, copyright by CIBA Pharmaceutical Company, Division of CIBA-GEIGY Corporation.)

That portion of the nervous system that falls within the brain and spinal cord is termed the *central nervous system*, and the portion lying outside this column and bulb is called the *peripheral nervous system* (see Figure 7.1). The peripheral nervous system can be further parsed into the *somatic* and *autonomic* nervous system to distinguish those neural components that pertain to the striated muscles from those that pertain to the viscera. The somatic system carries information to and from the external senses (exteroceptors, which includes teleceptors such as the eyes), skeletal muscles, and somatic receptors (proprioceptors) and regulates bodily processes commonly thought to be controlled voluntarily (e.g., skilled muscle movements). The autonomic nervous system is traditionally considered only an output (or efferent) system. The autonomic system carries information to glands and smooth muscles (viscera) and regulates bodily processes over which it is generally more difficult to exert direct, voluntary control (e.g., heart rate). Feedback from these effectors travel along visceral afferents, which are distinguished by definition from the autonomic nervous system. The signals traveling along the visceral afferents are, of course, a function of autonomic activity.

The autonomic nervous system functions primarily to maintain equilibrium (i.e., homeostasis) in the internal environment. Due to clear anatomic, neurochemical, and functional differences, the autonomic nervous system is typically divided yet again into the *sympathetic* and *parasympathetic* nervous systems. The former consists of nerve fibers that originate in the middle portions of the spinal cord (the thoracic and lumbar) and tends to act as a unit when innervating the viscera and glands to which it travels. The parasympathetic branch, on the other hand, consists of nerve fibers that originate in the upper and lower portions (cranial and sacral) of the spinal cord, acts in a specific rather than diffuse fashion, and tends to inhibit rather than excite visceral actions.

Information is transferred along these various neural pathways through specialized cells termed *neurons.* When stimulation of a neuron exceeds a criterion, an electrical impulse in the form of an action potential is transmitted unidirectionally down the neuron. The stimulus operating upon an afferent neuron may have originated in another neuron or a receptor (e.g., the eyes), which transduces information from one form (e.g., light) to a bioelectric signal suitable for processing in the body. The stimulus operating upon an efferent neuron, on the other hand, may terminate at another neuron or at an internal organ or skeletal muscle, where the action potentials are again transformed to perform work of some kind (e.g., muscle contraction, increased heart rate). Finally, stimuli operating upon a neuron can change its synaptic potential, altering the likelihood that further stimulation will evoke an action potential. These bioelectric events are transient residents of the electrically conducting tissues and fluids and provide "an electrochemical diary of neuromuscular functioning" (Stern et al., 1980, p. 29).

The bioelectric signals of interest to psychophysiologists generally range in magnitude from a few microvolts (μV), such as might result from a muscle action potential in a small muscle to a millivolt (mV), such as might result from the ventricular contraction of the heart. Extracting these signals can be difficult because they are part of an electrochemical soup swirling within the individual at any moment in time, and because the person in the laboratory is basked in about 10 volts of electrical "noise" arising from surrounding electrical sources (e.g., lighting, power lines, motors). The task at the physical level, therefore, is to isolate, identify, and accurately gauge specific internal events (e.g., a heart beat).

This task can be partitioned into the following components: (1) detection of the bioelectric events of interest; (2) amplification of these events, in contrast to the surrounding electrical noise, so that these minuscule events can be observed; (3) documentation of these events to allow their inspection for artifacts and subsequent analysis; and (4) quantification and analysis of the components of the physiological events that are of particular interest (cf., McGuigan, 1979, 1983; Muller et al., 1983).

Detecting Bodily Signs

The first component of the task is to obtain a representation of the actions of the underlying physiological system of interest. The specific sensing device used varies depending upon what kind of energy and what amplitude and frequency of a particular type of energy are to be detected. *Electrodes* are used to gauge the biopotentials of nerves, muscles, or gland cells, whereas *transducers* are used to gauge the outcome of these biopotentials. For example, a pair of electrodes could be used to measure the efferent volleys (i.e., muscle action potentials) innervating a muscle, or a transducer could be used to measure the resulting muscular contraction. The relationship between these measures is nonlinear, and which type is preferable depends upon the purpose of the inquiry.

Although it is possible to record the action potentials of a single cell by inserting a microelectrode into it, psychophysiologists generally record from the surface of the skin rather than subcutaneously in part because the former is less invasive and painful, and in part because the aim in psychophysiology is to

> relate some aspect of behavior to the function of large systems of cells which may spread over a considerable area. For instance, we often record the electrical precursors of the beating of the heart (the EKG), the synchronous changes in millions of cortical brain cells (the EEG), or changes in the activity of many motor units in a muscle or muscle group (the EMG) (Stern et al., 1980, p. 30).

It should be noted, however, that recordings of biopotentials from the surface of the body reflect an admixture of temporally and spatially summated electrical events and that the form of the activity that is recorded is influenced by size and location of the electrodes or transducers. For example, even though body tissue and fluids are electrically conductive, the size of bioelectric potentials decreases geometrically as the distance they travel increases. Hence, the location, amplitude, and timing of the specific cellular reactions responsible for surface-recorded biopotentials are indeterminable. These biopotentials can be related, however, to the activity of *systems* of cells, such as muscle groups or organs.

These latter relationships can be determined only if the link between the electrodes and the transient bioelectric signals traveling through the body is generally free of interference. The electrodes, of course, must be constructed of a high-conductivity material to allow transmission of the signal reaching its surface to recording equipment. Less apparent, perhaps, is the need for the electrodes to be constructed of an electrochemically stable compound. Silver-silver chloride, for example, not only conducts electrical signals well (i.e., the signals are not degraded), but it also is less likely than many materials (e.g., platinum or silver) to enter into an electrochemical reaction that produces electrical changes that are indistinguishable from some bioelectric events. Hence, the use of electrodes constructed of electrically unstable compounds can interfere with the clear communication of the underlying bioelectric events of interest.

There are two more components to this link that should be considered: the point of contact on the skin (recording site) and the medium (electrolyte) between the recording site and electrode. The outer layer of skin, particularly when coated by cosmetics or by the dirt and oils that can accrue during the day, does not conduct electrical current well. Hence, the skin must be prepared prior to the application of an electrode to reduce the interference (impedance) introduced by this outer layer of the skin. The exact placement of the electrode and nature of this preparation depends upon the physiological measure that is to be employed. Descriptions of electrode preparation and placements for various measures can be found in reference manuals, such as those by Venables and Martin (1967; Martin & Venables, 1980). Preparation of the skin typically involves abrading the recording site with a course material such as sandpaper or pumice, followed by a cleansing of the site using acetone. When preparing a site for recording low-level bioelectric activity, such as in some electromyographic (EMG) research, attaining low impedance is particularly important. In these instances, a small (e.g., 26 gauge), sterile hypodermic needle can be used to scratch the surface of the skin after the site has been mildly abraded and cleansed. The skin should *not* be penetrated with the needle, but, rather, the needle should only be used to scratch a small "x" at the point on the skin where the electrode is to be placed (i.e., at the recording site).

When recording *exosomatic electrodermal activity* (EDA—e.g., skin conductance level, skin conductance response), the site is neither abraded nor cleansed with acetone, but, instead, it is simply washed using soap and water. The difference in the manner in which the skin is prepared for EMG and EDA recordings is easily understood with a brief explanation. In EMG (and most forms of psychophysiological) recording, the task is to detect the ongoing biopotentials that are being generated within the body. In exosomatic EDA recording, on the other hand, the task is to gauge the electrical conductivity of the skin, which is done by introducing a small current at one electrode and measuring the drop in voltage as the current travels to the nearby electrode. Skin resistance can then be determined by applying Ohm's Law, and skin conductance is calculated by taking the reciprocal of the observed skin resistance (cf. Venables & Christie, 1980). Hence, when exosomatic recordings are to be obtained, the skin should be washed to remove cosmetics, oils, and dirt, but in other respects should be left undisturbed.

The electrolyte is the final component of this link. An electrolyte is simply a solution (usually a gel or paste) that conducts electricity. Some electrolytes have adhesive properties that help hold the electrode in place, but the major function of an electrolyte is to maintain the fidelity of the bioelectric signals that are emanating from the body at the recording site while minimizing the introduction of extraneous signals (e.g., movement of the electrode above the recording site). This is accomplished by rubbing the electrolyte into the skin at the recording site and filling the cavity of the electrode housing with the electrolyte. Care should be taken when injecting the electrolyte into the electrode that air bubbles (which are nonconducting) are not introduced, since the purpose of the electrolyte is to form an uninterrupted, electrically conductive channel between the epidermis and the electrode in the housing. Once the skin and electrode have been prepared, the electrode is placed over the recording site, and its placement secured (e.g., using adhesive collars). It should be noted that the electrolyte can become a carrier of bioelectric signals from a broader area of the body than desired if it is applied outside the boundaries formed by the nonconductive electrode housing and collar. Hence, the electrolyte should be rubbed into a restricted area of the skin.

The purpose of electrodes is to help measure the *differences* in bioelectric potentials, or voltages, at two bodily sites, so electrodes can be conceived as being placed in pairs. In *bipolar* recording, both electrodes are placed over electrically active sites on the body. In *monopolar* recording, in contrast, one electrode is placed at a reference site (e.g., an electrically quiescent site such as the earlobe) and another is (or several others are) placed over the electrically active region(s) of interest. In bipolar recording, it is the electrical difference between electrodes at two active sites that is amplified, whereas in monopolar recording it is the amount of electrical activity relative to an electrically quiet region that is magnified. If the electrical activity within a specific region of the body is of interest, then the electrodes are generally placed close together over this region, and bipolar recordings are obtained. This procedure attenuates the electrical signals emanating from distal regions of the body, and it maximizes the likelihood that those signals from distal regions that *do* travel to the recording site exert a similar impact on both electrodes. This means that the *differences* in biopotentials detected across these electrodes are likely to reflect the underlying cellular activity. On the other hand, monopolar recording can be used to assess the diffuse electrical activity emanating from a broad region of the body, or, much more commonly, to assess the overall electrical activity at particular recording sites. For example, if investigators were interested in comparing the electrical activity from the left versus right frontal lobes of the brain, they could begin by placing an electrode over each frontal lobe (cf. Jasper, 1958). Then, by using a common reference elecrode (e.g., linked sensors on the earlobes) and monopolar recording, two "pairs" of electrodes will have been formed: one to gauge the electrical difference between the electrode over the left frontal lobe and the reference electrode; the second to gauge the electrical difference between the electrode over the right frontal lobe and the refrence electrode. Since the reference electrode is common to the two active electrodes, it is possible to compare the characteristics (e.g., power spectra) of the electrical activity detected on the scalp over these brain regions.

Of course, not all physiological events that are of interest are electrical in nature. Blood pressure, pupillary dilation, skin temperature, and respiratory activity are but a few responses that represent physical *consequences* of bioelectric activity. Transducers are specially designed devices that transform physical energy into electrical energy. One of the most common types of transducers is the *strain gauge*, which consists of an electrical source and an electrical receiver connected by a conductive material (e.g., a tube filled with mercury). The notion is that if a constant electrical current is applied to the conductive material, then differences in electrical conductance reflect changes in the length of (tension on) the electroconductive medium. Strain gauges have been used to measure physiological events ranging from muscular contraction to blood perfusion in a limb to respiratory movements. The designs of the specific recording devices differ depending upon their application, but the underlying principle remains the same.

Other forms of transducers include the *thermistor* and the *photoconduction cell*. Although the electroconductive medium and applications differ across these transducers, the underlying principle governing their use is the same as for strain gauges. Transducers that employ a thermistor consist of an electrical source, an electrical receiver, and a material whose electroconductive properties change as a function of temperature. Hence, when a constant electrical voltage is applied to the conductor, differences in current reflect proximal temperature changes. Finally, transducers that employ a photoconduction cell consist of a light source (e.g., light emitting diode (LED), a photoelectric cell to measure the amount of light received at some other point, and a medium through which the light travels. Typically, the body serves as the medium through which the light travels. For instance, the LED can be placed on one side of a person's finger and the photoelectric cell on the other side of the finger. As blood pulses through the finger, the amount of light that is transmitted through the finger varies. Specifically, since blood absorbs light, the amount of light that is detected by the photoelectric cell is inversely related to the blood perfusion between the light source and the receiver.

Amplifying Bodily Signs

Given the bioelectric signals of interest are being detected, the next task is to magnify these signals so that they can be inspected and recorded. This amplification cannot be done indiscriminantly, however, because irrelevant signals (i.e., electrical interference, or "noise") could potentially be amplifed as well. Indeed, the signal/noise ratio ideally would be improved during amplification, meaning that the bioelectric signals of interest would be amplified, whereas irrelevant electrical signals (whatever their source) would be attenuated. We discussed a few sources of electrical interference in the previous section. For instance, electroconductive gels are used when preparing the skin and attaching electrodes to provide a low impedance, electrochemically stable route along which bioelectric signals can travel. Although placement of a single ground electrode on a subject can be used to prevent ground-loops from developing, the electrical noise emanating from fluorescent lights and dimmers, flickering neon lamps, motor relays, ventilation control systems, and elevators can mask the small bioelectric events of interest in psychophysiological research (cf. Gale & Smith, 1980).

In this section, we consider the problem of magnifying the bioelectric signals of interest, relative to irrelevant signals. Specifically, we briefly discuss three techniques to enhance the signal/noise ratio—(1) employing differential amplifiers to attenuate electrical signals that are common at both sensors at a given recording site, (2) reducing the environmental sources of electrical interference, and (3) conditioning (e.g., filtering) the electrical signal that serves as input to the amplifier.

Two features of amplifiers that should be noted here are their *gain* and their *common-mode rejection ratio*. Gain refers to the ratio of the output to input amplitude. For example, if an input signal is 100 µV (1/10,000 volt) and the output of the amplifier is 1 volt, then the gain for the amplifier would be 10,000. Note that gain is a measure of amplification, and this amplification is indiscriminant. Electrical interference as well as the bioelectric events of interest will be amplified. This is why the second feature of an amplifier, its common-mode rejection ratio, is important.

The common-mode rejection ratio is an index of an amplifier's ability to reject extraneous electrical interference and is an attribute of *differential amplifiers*. A differential amplifier is so named because, rather than simply magnifyng the input signals, it magnifies the *difference* between the two input signals (e.g., from each electrode over a recording site). Theoretically, the electrostatic energy emanating from distal power sources appears at both inputs (e.g., electrodes) simultaneously and, therefore, has no effect on the output of the amplifier. The closer an amplifier is in function to this ideal state, the better will be the common-mode rejection ratio.

In practice, differential amplifiers are not perfect in function, nor do the irrelevant electrical signals necessarily impinge upon both inputs at exactly the same time or in equal quantities. Thus, although differential amplifiers play an important role in psychophysiological recording, low-level bioelectric events can still be lost in the sea of electrostatic noise emanating from external electrical sources unless additional steps are taken to amplilfy the signal relative to the noise.

An obvious and important step is to reduce the electrical interference emanating from external sources. From a strictly physical standpoint, it would be best if psychophysiological recordings were obtained in a chamber miles from any electrical power sources and completely shielded from extraneous electrical signals. Of course, this "ideal" recording environment would be very expensive, inconveniently located, and possibly foreign and intimidating to subjects. Fortunately, a considerable reduction in extraneous electrical interference can be achieved by being cognizant of its possible sources and selecting a recording location that is distant from these sources. For instance, it is seldom necessary to obtain psychophysiological recordings near elevators, workshops, or other heavily instrumented testing rooms or laboratories. The electrical equipment used in the course of research (e.g., electrical motors and relays, fluorescent lighting) can also generate unwanted electrical interference. If substitutes for this equipment cannot be found, it can either be placed in a separate room or shielded and placed at a distance from the subject. For example, it is a simple matter to employ incandescent (or, preferably, battery-powered) rather than fluorescent lighting, and the savings in terms of electrical interference is significant. In sum, then, a judicious selection of a recording location and arrangement of laboratory equipment can be one of the least expensive means of improving psychophysiological recordings.

A third aspect of amplification is signal conditioning, which involves modifying the nature of the input to the amplifier in some manner. A ubiquitous signal-conditioning procedure in a psychophysiological recording is the attenuation (filtering) of unwanted frequencies from the input signal. Filtering unwanted frequencies from the analog input signal can focus amplification much more specifically on the bioelectric signal of interest.

When a person is awake, relaxed, and passively attentive, for example, electrical activity that oscillates about 10 times per second (i.e., 10 Hz) can be recorded on the scalp. These bioelectric oscillations, which are measured using the electroencephalograph (EEG), are termed *alpha waves*. It is possible that a person could display alpha brain waves as slow as 7 or 8 Hz and as fact as 12 or 13 Hz. Hence, if the electrical input includes components at much higher (and/or lower) frequencies (e.g., a 60-Hz component, which can arise from the pervasive alternating current—AC—power lines), then the psychophysiologist interested in monitoring alpha waves benefits from eliminating these irrelevant high-frequency (and/or low-frequency) electrical signals. This is done through the use of filters.

There are four general types of filters: low pass, high pass, bandpass, and notch. A low-pass filter attenuates all electrical signals above a designated frequency. A high-pass filter, in contrast, attenuates all electrical signals below a designated frequency. The combination of low-pass and high-pass filters produces a bandpass filter, which attenuates all but a certain range of electrical signals. The notch filter, which is the complement of the bandpass filter, attenuates all electrical signals within a small, designated range. For example, because a 60-Hz electrical interference emanates from the omnipresent AC power lines and AC-operated equipment, 60-Hz notch filters are common in the amplifiers used in psychophysiological research. These notch filters attenuate the components of the input signal that fall between 58 to 62 Hz and are provided to enable an investigator to reduce the portion of the input signal that is particularly likely to contain irrelevant electrical information. Note, however, that filters are not selective in what is attenuated within the designated frequencies. Electrical impulses of 60 Hz originating from a volley of muscle action potentials are indistinguishable from 60 Hz impulses emanating from an AC power line. Hence, knowledge of the frequency characteristics of the physiological event of interest and the extant electrical noise in a laboratory is essential in psychophysiological recording. The reader may wish to consult the appropriate chapter on the particular psychophysiological measure of interest in Coles et al. (in press), Greenfield and Sternbach (1972), Martin and Venables (1980), or McGuigan (1979).

Filtering is an aspect of signal conditioning that affects the frequency characteristics of the input signal. Unwanted frequency components are simply eliminated. A form of signal conditioning that changes the amplitude (rather than frequency) characteristics is *integration* (cf. Shaw, 1967). The goal in integrating a bioelectric signal is to obtain an index of the *sum* of the various frequency components comprising an electrical signal at any given point in time. There are various types of integrators, but the process typically involves rectifying and summing an input stream representing ongoing bioelectric events to produce a continuous output stream, or integrated signal of these events.

Integration is most often used in electromyography (EMG). The EMG is an extracellular recording of voltage changes, which reflects muscle action potentials as they travel across the muscle fibers. That is, the voltage appearing between the electrodes at any point in time is the algebraic sum of the action potentials of the contracting and recovering muscle fibers between the electrodes. The frequency of these action potentials ranges anywhere from 0 at rest to more than 1000 Hz during contraction. The raw EMG contains information about the amount of energy present within each of a wide range of frequencies over a muscle region across time, whereas the integrated EMG provides a *summary index*, reflecting the total electrical energy recorded over a muscle region across time. This latter information can, of course, be derived from the raw EMG signal, but to extract this information would take a process comparable to integration (e.g., calculating power spectra and summing across frequencies). There are applications in clinical electromyography where the form and frequency of the action potentials per se are of interest (cf. Geddes & Baker, 1968), and hence the raw rather than integrated EMG is necessarily recorded. However, in psychophysiological research, the range and distribution of the frequencies of EMG activity recorded tend to be constant across conditions even when the voltage between the surface electrodes varies (cf. Sokolov, 1972); hence, the integrated EMG is typically employed since it is simpler to quantify and generally as informative as the raw EMG (cf. Cacioppo, Marshall-Goodell, & Dorfman, 1983).

Documenting Bodily Signs

Given the bioelectric signals of interest are being amplified, the next task is to display and store these data. Physiological activity is, of course, continuous. That is, the stream of electrical events emanating from a person's body produces a continuous record of physiological events. Even the "periodic" heart beat is comprised of a never-ending sequence of electrochemical events that cycle in a generally periodic manner (see top panel, Figure 7.2). Accordingly, the amplification of physiological signals yields an analog sequence of physiological events.

Analyses of physiological events are performed on discrete (i.e., digital) rather than analog data, and we will discuss *analog/digital* (A/D) *conversion* in the next section. There are several important reasons, however, for monitoring and storing the analog representations. First, physiological responses not only have characteristic frequency ranges; they also have identifiable waveforms. By monitoring the output of the amplifiers, an experienced observer can easily tell whether there are artifacts in the psychophysiological recording. For example, in the top panel of Figure 7.2, we have presented a typical recording of cardiac activity. Each "spike" (i.e., R-wave) in the recording represents the depolarization of the ventricles of the heart and is what people commonly term the *heart beat*. In the bottom panel of Figure 7.2, we have illustrated cardiac activity recorded in the same manner. The response does not "appear" the same, however, because there are irrelevant electrical signals in the recording. In this particular example, the artifact is attributable to a postural shift by the subject. An investigator may not always know immediately the exact source of an artifact in a psychophysiological recording, but simply knowing that an artifact exists is helpful. At a minimum, the investigator would want this knowledge to eliminate the artifactual portions of the recordings from those that will be digitized and analyzed to study a specific aspect of physiological activity. In addition, the investigator may be able to take steps to locate and eliminate the source of the artifact. For example, if postural adjustments are the source of artifacts, the experimental procedure might be arranged so that postural movements

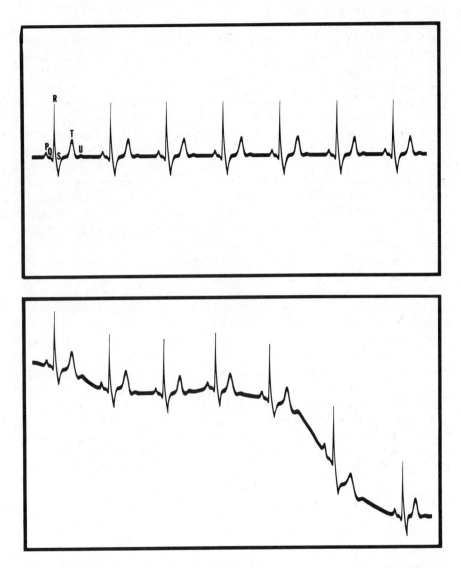

FIGURE 7.2. A recording of the typical EKG is illustrated in the upper panel. A cardiac cycle begins with an impulse from the sinus node, leading to a depolarization of the atria. This is reflected in the *p*-wave (see text). This is followed by a depolarization of the atrioventricular node and a repolarization of the atria. The depolarization of the ventricles follows and is reflected in the *ars* complex of the cardiac cycle. The repolarization of the ventricles is reflected in the *t*-wave, and the after potentials following repolarization of the ventricles are sometimes seen in the *u*-wave of the cardiac cycle. The top panel contains a series of cardiac cycles. In the bottom panel, the appearance of these same physiological events are disturbed by a movement artifact.

were unnecessary, the subject might be asked to avoid unnecessary movements during the study, occasional breaks in the procedure might be provided to allow the subject to make postural adjustments, and the electrodes could be placed at sites that are relatively insensitive to movement artifacts.

Second, by obtaining a continuous record of physiological activity, an investigator can quantify a set of features of the physiological activity that is of interest at one moment and other features that are of interest subsequently. For example, in Figure 7.3 we have illustrated three EMG responses from the surface of the preferred forearm (superficial flexor region) of a person who is performing a task that requires the voluntary contraction of the forearm muscle. The form of this response is complex, and the nature of the research question determines what information is appropriate to extract from this response. In many investigations of EMG activity, the question concerns whether a particular task leads to the firing of more muscle action potentials per unit time in a particular muscular region than does some comparison task. In these instances, a measure of the average amplitude of the envelope formed by the integrated EMG response (i.e., mean amplitude or "energy" per unit time) is a simple and suitable parameter to extract. If the question concerns whether two tasks differed in the overall amount of muscle action potential activity in a particular muscle region that was evoked by the tasks, then the total area (i.e., total energy) formed by the envelope of the response would be the more suitable measure to extract.

In practice, interesting psychophysiological questions are often either not quite so simple or not quite so completely anticipated. For example, the mean amplitudes of the responses displayed in Figure 7.3 are equal, as are the areas bounded by the envelopes of these responses. Having either theoretically anticipated this or learned this in the analysis of the data, an investigator may ask the more general question of whether the two tasks resulted in a particular muscle region being innervated in a different fashion—that is, whether the size and sequence of the muscle action potentials differed between the tasks. Analyses of the *topography* of the IEMG response waveforms, rather than analyses of mean amplitude or the area under the response, bear upon this more general question (cf. Cacioppo, Marshall-Goodell, & Dorfman, 1983). By maintaining permanent documentation of these responses, investigators can systematically extract and analyze information from these responses. Moreover, only by maintaining documentation of the responses can new information be extracted bearing upon questions that arise during the course of exploratory research (cf. Muller et al., 1983).

The two most common methods of securing permanent records are the chart-and-pen recordings (e.g., through the use of a polygraph), and frequency-modulated (FM) tape recordings. A drawback of the former is that, because of the mechanical inertia of chart and pens, high-frequency electrical impulses (e.g., over 75 Hz) are not represented. The importance of this limitation depends upon the frequency characteristics of the responses

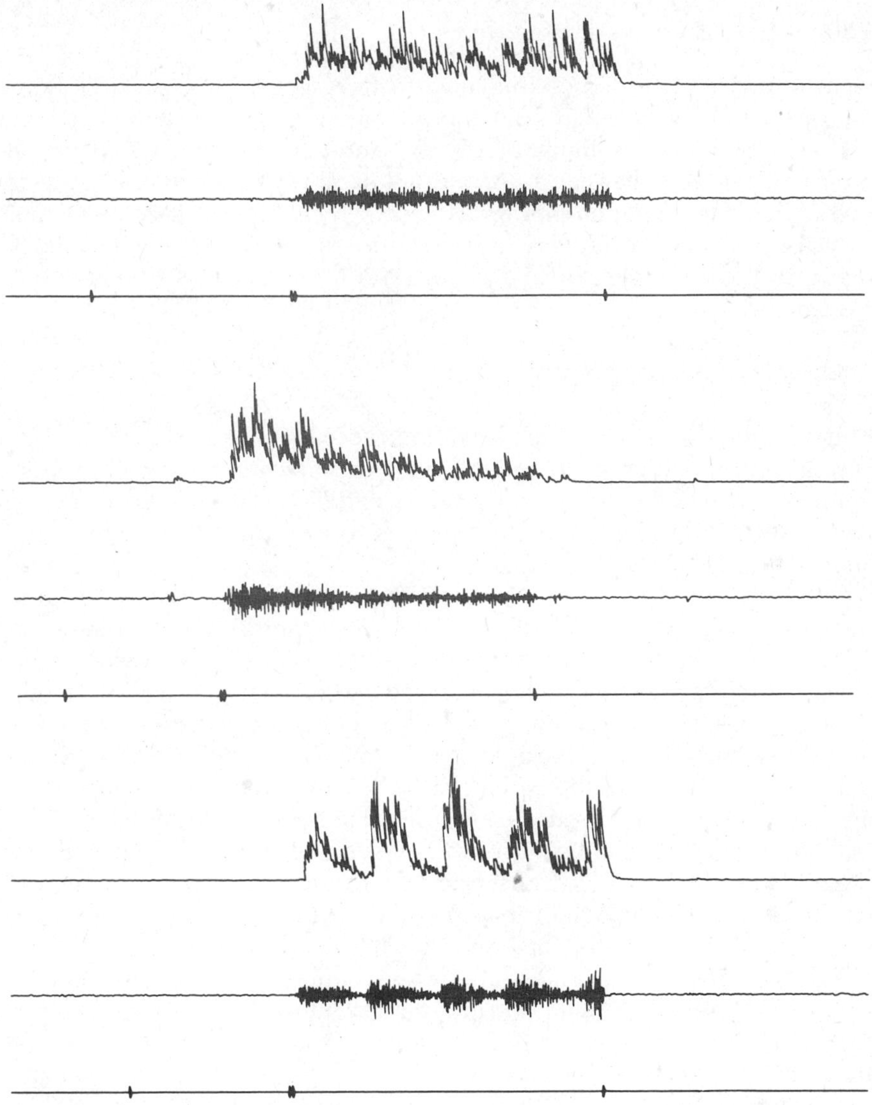

FIGURE 7.3. Three EMG responses produced by various muscular contractions. *Top panel:* A constant level of tension is maintained on a hand dynamometer. *Middle panel:* The tension on the dynamometer is decreased across the trial. *Lower panel:* The tension on the dynamometer is pulsated. The top tracing in each panel represents the integrated EMG response, the middle tracing is the raw EMG recording, and the bottom tracing is the time line. The first mark on the time line designates onset of the baseline, the second mark designates the onset of the task and rcording period, and the final mark designates the termination of the task and recording period. Note that these integrated EMG responses are characterized by approximately equal mean amplitude although the conditions are responsible for the production of each response, but the form of each response is quite different. [Copyright © 1983, The Society for Psychophysiological Research. Reprinted with permission of the publisher from Cacioppo, Marshall-Goodell, & Dorfman, (1983). Skeletomuscular patterning: Topographical analysis of the integrated electromyogram. *Psychophysiology, 20,* 269–283.

being recorded. If the highest frequency of the responses is below 75 Hz, as is the case when measuring electroencephalographic, electrodermal, or cardiac activity, then this limitation of chart-and-pen recordings is of no real import. If, on the other hand, the physiological responses of interest have higher frequency components, as is the case in EMG recording, then either optical or FM tape recorders, which minimize the distortion of the electrical input, would be preferred (cf. Brown, 1972; McGuigan, 1979; Venables & Martin, 1967).

Quantifying Bodily Signs

As the instrumentation and recording procedures in psychophysiology become more standardized, and the experimental control of potent factors in the setting becomes more complete, reproducible chart-and-pen (analog) records of subtle physiological responses to a stimulus are increasingly attainable. The acquisition of comparable analog records of physiological responding is not sufficient, however, for achieving psychophysiological results that are comparable across laboratories or studies, even when dealing strictly within the physical context of the research. As noted earlier, psychophysiological data are not analyzed in their analog form, but, rather, they are digitized and summarized using descriptive statistics, or parameters. The manner (e.g., sampling rate) in which the analog data are digitized, the nature of the parameters (e.g., amplitude, magnitude, variance) extracted from the digital representations of the analog signal, the manner in which a given set of parameters are extracted (e.g., using reciprocals, range-corrections, transformations), and the nature of the inferential statistics employed when analyzing the extracted parameters, each can affect the final results obtained and the conclusions drawn.

For example, we have illustrated three identical waveforms in the left panel of Figure 7.4. In the middle panel of Figure 7.4, we have specified sampling rates (i.e., rates of A/D conversion) that are equal to the fastest frequency in the waveform (i.e., waveform A), twice the fastest frequency component (i.e., waveform B), and three times the fastest component (i.e., waveform C). In the right panel, we have illustrated how the consequent digital arrays for each waveform would appear if treated in analyses as if it *were* the original response. Although waveforms A, B, and C were identical at the outset (e.g., after amplification), the divergent sampling rates have produced dramatically different numeric representations of the physiological response.

Generally speaking, the integrity of a waveform can be retained in a digital array only *if the rate of A/D conversion is at least twice the fastest frequency of interest in the analog signal* (cf. Stearns, 1975). Note that this sampling rate does *not* mean that the digital array can be used in a simple manner to reconstruct the original waveform (e.g., see waveforms B and C in Figure 7.4), but, rather, it indicates that the original waveform can be recovered

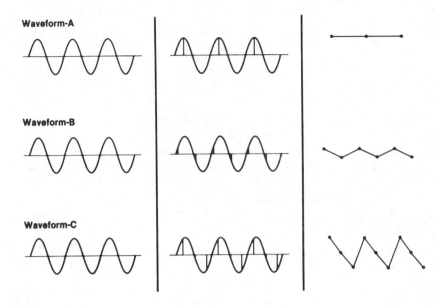

Waveform-A

Waveform-B

Waveform-C

FIGURE 7.4.   Three identical analog signals are illustrated in the left panel. In the middle panel, these signals are reproduced with vertical lines representing analog-to-digital (A/D) conversions. The rate of A/D conversion is equal to the frequency of the fastest component of the analog signal in waveform A in the middle panel, twice the frequency of the fastest component of the analog signal in waveform B of the middle panel, and three times the frequency of the latest component of the analog signal in waveform C in the right panel. The analog signals are reproduced from the digital arrays obtained from the A/D conversions depicted in the middle panel. The waveforms reproduced in the right panel, rather than the original waveforms in the left panel, form the basis for data processing and analysis, thereby illustrating that the rate of A/D conversion is one of several technical factors independent of bioelectric measurement that governs the comparabiity of results across psychophysiological studies. (From Cacioppo, Marshall-Goodell, & Gormezano, 1983.)

from this digital representation. The mathematical procedure that would be used to recover the original waveform is called *convolution*. In many cases for simplicity, parameters are extracted from the digitized values without the process of convolution. As inspection of Figure 7.4 suggests, this procedure, although perhaps not maximally sensitive, is acceptable so long as the sampling rate is more than twice the fastest component of the physiological response of interest.

Computers in psychophysiological research have proven to be an important and powerful tool, particularly when quantifying physiological responses. First, the A/D conversions can be programmed to occur tirelessly and reliably at high speeds if necessary. Second, the experimental control and timing of events can be very specific, simplifying the process of detecting physiological responses elicited by the presentation of an experimental stimulus. Third, the numeric representation of a bioelectric signal and the extraction of parameters from this representation through the use of computers require a formal explication of the procedures (in the form of computer programs), rendering the procedures open for public scrutiny and replication. Fourth, the processing speed of computers has substantially reduced the cost of recording several physiological responses simultaneously, making it more feasible to obtain comprehensive physiological assessments and to study the interrelationships among physiological systems under various testing conditions. Laboratory computers are not absolutely necessary; they simply make the research easier and more precise.

Although the specific parameters that are extracted from a bioelectric recording vary as a function of the physiological system being observed, there are several general classifications that can be discussed. First, bioelectric events can be classified as either event-related or spontaneous. *Event-related* activity is characterized by a stable temporal relationship between a stimulus and the physiological response. For example, Ax (1953) found that when an experimenter's actions frightened subjects, their systolic blood pressure increased; and when the experimenter's actions angered the subjects, the blood pressure increases were even greater than when subjects were made fearful. In another study, the heart rates of 30 individuals were monitored before, during, and after they engaged in public speaking.

> A wide range of speakers addressing audiences of greatly differing sizes was studied. These included medical students and housemen giving factual case histories to small groups of their colleagues, experienced lecturers talking to more critical audiences of up to several hundred people, and television performers appearing "live" before an estimated ten million viewers (Carruthers, 1981, p. 229).

In addition, about 1 hour before speaking, half the subjects ingested a placebo and half ingested a single dose of oxprenolol (a drug that minimizes sympathetic excitation through its competitive inhibition of the beta-adrenergic nerve endings that are found throughout the sympathetic division of the autonomic nervous system). Carruthers (1981) reported that, on average, the maximum heart rate of subjects who ingested the placebo reached 151 beats per minute "usually reaching a peak within a few seconds of the start of the speech and being maintained at only a slightly lower level for most of its duration" (p. 230). In sharp contrast, the maximum heart rate of subjects who ingested the beta-blocking drug was 82 beats per minute. Physiological changes such as the increased blood pressure of angry subjects or the increased heart rates in speakers who had ingested placebos are termed *event-related* because in each case there is a clear and replicable relationship between the presentation of some stimulus (e.g., a set of behaviors emitted by the experimenter, the onset of a public speech) and the consequent physiological activity. The *failure* to find these event-related responses in individuals who ingested a beta-blocking drug indicated something about the physiological mechanism underlying the responses observed in their counterparts: the event-related responses observed in speakers who ingested the placebo were sympathetically mediated.

Spontaneous (or nonspecific) activity refers to physiological events that occur in the absence of a designated or identified stimulus and, as such, represent the complement to event-related responses. If subjects were simply sitting quietly while adapting to the laboratory and a large increase in blood pressure was observed, then this change would be labeled spontaneous. Similarly, if the heart rate of a person waiting quietly to deliver a speech occasionally deviated wildly for no particular reason, these changes in heart rate would be termed spontaneous.

Orthogonal to the classification of a response as spontaneous or event-related is the categorization of physiological activity as phasic or tonic. *Phasic* physiological activity refers to short-term bioelectric events that return to their prior level of activity. When a bioelectric event persists and appears as an adjustment in the level of activity, rather than as a transient shift, then the change in activity is said to be *tonic*. If, for example, a person displayed a sudden but transient rise in blood pressure upon entering an examination room, this change would be classified as event-related (since the change is due to change in setting) *and* phasic (since the change is transient). If, however, a person's blood pressure increased and remained high upon entering an examination room, then the change would be event-related and tonic.

Generally, physiological responses that develop and dissipate within a few seconds are classified as phasic, and those that develop and are maintained for more than 90 seconds are classified as tonic. Although there is no simple rule of thumb that specifies how exactly to distinguish tonic from phasic changes across physiological measures, the time-frame for distinguishing a phasic from a tonic response varies depending upon the latency with which an effector responds to stimulation and the frequency characteristics of the response. For example, responses from the autonomic nervous system have slower latencies and decay more slowly than responses from the central and somatic nervous systems. These differences are quite apparent in the body's reactions to the presentation of a novel or surprising stimulus (e.g., an unexpected sound). The profile of evoked bodily reactions is called an *orienting response*, which was first described by Pavlov (1927). This syndrome of bodily responses includes an increase in high-frequency, low-amplitude EEG activity; a postural orientation to position teleoreceptors (i.e., eyes and ears) toward the stimulus; a cessation of specific muscular activity and an increase in general muscular tonus; vasoconstriction in the limbs; a slowing of heart rate; an increase in skin conductance; and a brief cessation of respiration followed by slower, deeper respiratory activity (Lynn, 1966). These bodily changes are all evoked by the same stimulus (i.e., event-related), are all transient in nature (i.e., phasic), and all act to facilitate the reception of information about the unexpected stimulus. The temporal courses for these changes vary considerably, however. Changes in EEG and somatic activity occur almost the instant the stimulus is presented, whereas changes in the viscera, such as skin conductance, occur more slowly, lagging from about 1 to 5 seconds behind the presentation of the stimulus and taking 6 to 10 seconds to decay. Thus, a longer time-frame can be justified when determining whether a given change in autonomic activity is phasic or tonic than when dealing with changes in central or somatic activity.

Analyses of the tonic or phasic parameters extracted from the recorded psychophysiological data proceed using inferential statistics, such as univariate and multivariate analyses of variance. We consider issues surrounding the analysis of psychophysiological data in a subsequent section. In the next section, however, we first survey issues pertaining to the social context of psychophysiological research.

SOCIAL CONTEXT

Archival, observational, naturalistic, and field studies have primarily been used in psychophysiology to identify empirical problems (e.g., how psychosomatic disorders or hypertension develop). With the advent of portable and telemetric recording devices (e.g., Carruthers et al., 1976), field studies have become more common in tests of the generalizability and limitations of theories. The laboratory, however, remains the predominant research environment because it allows investigators to achieve the necessary control over experimental and confounding variables at a minimum cost.

The laboratory is, of course, a novel setting for most subjects, and the artifacts that can emerge from interactions between the subject and experimenter in investigations of overt behavior (e.g., experimenter bias, demand characteristics) are no less a problem in psychophysiological research (cf. Cacioppo, Marshall-Goodell, & Gormezano, 1983; Christie & Todd, 1975; Gale, 1973; Gale & Smith, 1980). Moreover, references to "electrodes," the presence of electrical instrumentation, cables, and bioelectric sensors, and the obvious scrutiny that subjects undergo can exacerbate the problems of capturing the psychological processes of interest in the laboratory. As Gale and Baker (1981) have noted,

> In psychophysiological studies, experimenter-subject interactions are particularly important since the procedures may involve bodily contact, partial removal of clothing, skin abrasion, touching, and application and removal of electrodes (p. 373).

A few fairly simple procedures can be adopted to reduce the anxiety or quandry that might be created in psychophysiological research. Before subjects agree to participate in the research, they can be given a tour of at least a portion of the laboratory and an explanation of the experimental procedures. We have also found that providing an explanation of the essentials of bioelectric recording and using neutral rather than emotionally laden terminology (e.g., sensors vs. electrodes) reduce subjects' apprehension about participating in the research and increases their involvement in the experimental task per se. Gale and Smith (1980) have suggested that experimenters should be trained to achieve the same level of rapport with subjects as is achieved in psychometric testing. Of course, rapport is of little help if the experimenters are not skilled technicians in the laboratory. If the experimenters appear unknowledgeable about procedures or apparatus, or incompetent in performing their tasks, the subjects may become anxious about their own safety and, consequently, become less attentive to the experimental tasks. Thus, the sensitivity and reliability of the obtained psychophysiological recordings can be improved by training experimenters in the technical aspects of the research and the social aspects of establishing rapport with the subject while remaining objective and detached.

Moreover, the testing room for subjects can be designed to be comfortable and familiar rather than aseptic and intimidating. Most of the wiring and instrumentation need not be placed in the subject's view, and the use of carpeting and furniture can be both functional and consoling. Subjects generally need to avoid unnecessary postural shifts to attenuate error variance due to irrelevant movements or respiratory changes. Developing a procedure that by its nature minimizes movement is preferable to instructional or artificial restraints on subjects' actions. For example, preceding the experimental trials with a period of relaxation and interspersing periods of relaxation throughout the experimental trials may be more desirable to using explicit instructions not to move, for the latter may be distracting, sensitize the subjects to their own proprioception and somatic activity, and/or cause them to adopt a rigid posture.

To reduce the feeling by subjects that they are being scrutinized, the investigator can use a cover story and interesting task, make visual observations unobtrusively (e.g., by hiding the videocamera trained on them), and employ multiple practice trials. (The latter also minimizes practice effects, habituation effect, and any initial confusion or apprehension about the tasks.) Finally, subjects can be interviewed at the completion of the study to determine the effectiveness of the cover story and to learn of their perceptions of the experimental hypotheses, manipulation, and session. The postexperimental interview provides information that is useful in both interpreting the obtained psychophysiological data and developing more effective cover stories and procedures for subsequent research.

Because the interaction between the experimenter and subject is relatively extended and intimate in psychophysiological research, there is a greater opportunity for *experimenter biases* to develop during this interaction. For example, Rosenthal (1966) has argued that an experimenter's expectations regarding the experimental results can bias the data obtained. The notion is that the experimenter's desires are transmitted to the subject by means of unintentional cues (e.g., facial expressions, tone of voice, length of time spent explaining certain points) and that these expectancies influence the subjects' responses. This bias was demonstrated recently in a study on training individuals to relax the muscles in their forehead using EMG bio-feedback (Segreto-Bures & Kotses, 1982). In this study, subjects received either contingent or noncontingent feedback about the level of muscle tension in their forehead. In addition, experimenters were either given no expectancy regarding the outcome or were led to expect that the condition-ing would be easy or difficult to accomplish. The results indicated that when experimenters were given no explicit expectancy, subjects who received contingent EMG feedback learned to relax their forehead more completely than did subjects who received noncontingent feedback. When experi-menters expected that the training would be ineffective, however, no training effect was observed. These results suggest experimenter bias may have been operating, but how? Segreto-Bures and Kotses (1982) also found that the experimenters who expected the training would be easily achieved produced intermediate training results, suggesting that the communication of expectancies to subjects may have distracted subjects from learning to the relatively simple task of using the contingent feedback to relax the muscles in their forehead. These data nicely illustrate that experimenter bias can interfere with the process in which the investigator is really interested, sometimes in ways that are neither completely consistent nor inconsistent with the hypothesis. Fortunately, double-blind testing procedures are easy to employ, especially when the critical experimental instructions are auto-mated or delivered from the control room following the preparation of the subject.

As noted already, subjects may be apprehensive about participating in "electrophysiological" research. Rosenberg (1969) has argued that in many experiments, subjects are apprehensive about being evaluated by experi-menters who are presumably experts in human behavior. This *evaluation apprehension* is likely to be exacerbated by the presence of experimenters who are both socially skilled and technically trained. Rosenberg argues that this evaluation apprehension can lead subjects to distort their behavior in a socially desirable fashion. If an experimenter's behavior or experimental treatment makes subjects especially anxious or aware that they are being observed or evaluated, evaluation apprehension can introduce biases into the obtained data.

In a study of emotional arousal, for example, Cooper and Singer (1956) asked 126 students to rate and rank 20 ethnic and national groups. Of these 126 students, 20 revealed extreme attitudes toward their most liked and disliked groups and served subsequently as subjects in a laboratory ex-periment. Each subject was tested individually by the experimenter, who recorded electrodermal activity as he derogated the most liked group, complimented the most disliked group, derogated a group toward which subjects felt neutral, and complimented a group toward which subjects felt neutral. Cooper and Singer found that the largest electrodermal responses followed derogatory statements about the most liked group and complimen-tary statements about the most disliked group. Cooper and Singer interpreted these results as evidence that the prejudice that subjects harbored toward the national and ethnic groups had a physiological counterpart. If, however, subjects were more apprehensive about their evaluation when they were questioned by the experimenter about groups toward which they felt strongly rather than neutrally, then the difference in electrodermal activity could be due to evaluation apprehension rather than to subjects' prejudice per se (cf. Cacioppo & Sandman, 1981; Petty & Cacioppo, 1983).

A similar source of bias has been noted by Orne (1962), who has argued that many subjects in an experiment try to deduce the true purpose of the experiment. The notion is that the subject wants to modify his or her behavior to conform to what the researcher has hypothesized should occur. Whenever the treatment of the subjects gives them an indication of the experimental hypotheses, then *demand characteristics* are confounded with the experimental manipulation. For example, a series of interesting studies of depression have been conducted in which normal and depressed subjects were asked to engage in emotional imagery (e.g., Schwartz et al., 1976a, 1976b). Electrodes were placed over various facial muscles, and EMG activity was recorded from these muscle regions. (Various recording sites for facial EMG are presented in Figure 7.5.) Schwartz and his colleagues found covert changes in facial EMG activity, with distinctive changes occurring during pleasant versus unpleasant imagery. Specifically, the EMG activity

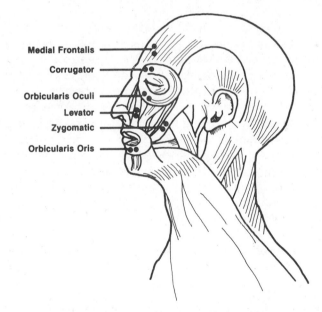

FIGURE 7.5.   Illustrative electrode placements for facial EMG recording. (From Cacioppo, J. T., & Petty, R. E. (1981). Electromyograms as measures of extent affectivity of information processing. *American Psychologist, 36,* 441–456. Copyright 1981 by the American Psychological Association. Reprinted by permission.)

over the corrugator muscle region was greater, and over the zygomatic region was less, during unpleasant than pleasant imagery. Interestingly, depressed subjects exhibited attenuated versions of these changes during pleasant imagery and slightly exaggerated versions during unpleasant imagery. Finally, depressed subjects who showed decreases in the basal level of activity over the corrugator muscle region of the face across a 2-week period also showed improvements in clinical symptoms (Schwartz et al., 1978). Although these studies suggest facial EMG recordings can provide an index of affective state, several authors have argued that demand character-istics could potentially be operating (cf. Fridlund & Izard, 1983). The reason-ing is that the placement of multiple electrodes on a person's face may sensitize that person to the importance of his or her face as a response system. Instructions to imagine a pleasant event, therefore, may artifact-ually induce a subject to use his or her face to express pleasure subtly, whereas instructions to imagine an unpleasant event may cue the subject to express displeasure subtly. (It could also be argued that when clinical populations, who are cognizant of their distress and diagnosis, are asked to engage in emotional imagery, they may be responding in a manner de-signed to please the experimenters.) Although recent evidence suggests that demand characteristics are not *necessary* for facial EMG recording to differen-tiate subtle affective states along an evaluative dimension (Cacioppo et al., 1984; Fridlund et al., 1983), they remain a potential artifact that can bias psychophysiological assessments and research.

In most psychophysiological research, evaluation apprehension and de-mand characteristics can be minimized by employing the following tech-niques: (1) giving the subjects a false hypothesis; (2) employing a cover story emphasizing that the physiological mechanisms being investigated are not subject to voluntary control and that, therefore, their best strategy is simply to relax and attend to the tasks; (3) attaching dummy sensors on areas that lend credence to the cover story (e.g., over the scalp); (4) designing the setting and procedure to minimize the subject's feeling of being scrutinized (see previous discussion); (5) using treatments that are sufficiently absorb-ing to make subjects oblivious to role behavior (i.e., enhancing experimental realism—see Aronson & Carlsmith, 1968); and (6) reducing the apparent status difference between the experimenter and subject through the estab-lishment of rapport. In essence, the nature of the interaction between the experimenter and subject is both a fount of potential biases in psychophysio-logical research and the source of their solutions.

INFERENTIAL CONTEXT

With the application of proper recording procedures in psychophysi-ology, investigators can obtain valid and reliable bioelectric signals that unequivocally reflect the activity of particular effectors (e.g., cardiac activity, blood pressure). In this respect, a psychophysiological measurement strategy can be viewed as differing from those relying upon an individual's ability to verbalize underlying processes (Cacioppo & Petty, in press; Nisbett & Wilson, 1977). However, psychophysiological responses are not linked invariantly to psychological or behavioral states, making the inferential context in which these responses are observed paramount when interpreting their psychological significance. In this section, we briefly review issues involved when examining whether (1) there are reliable differences among conditions; (2) the treatment was necessary to produce the observed effect; (3) the observed effect generalizes to other subjects, times, and settings; and (4) the treatment and observed effects reflect the theoretical constructs of interest. In any experiment, decisions are involved in translating psychological constructs at a conceptual level to operational features of an experimental setting. These four issues listed correspond to Cook and Campbell's (1976) four classes of alternative hypotheses threatening the validity of an experiment: conclusion, internal, external, and construct validity. These issues are not unique to the inferential context of psychophysiological research, but some of the considerations in psychophysiological research are fairly unique.

Consider the issue of *statistical conclusion validity*, which concerns the question whether any true differences among the various conditions in the experiment were obtained. The convention in psychological research is that no difference is accepted as true if a statistical analysis indicates it could have been produced by chance alone more than 5 percent of the time. But what type of statistical analysis should be done? There are no set methods that apply in all cases; however, there are clear decisions that must be made and guidelines available for making them (e.g., see McHugo & Lanzetta, 1983; Muller et al., 1983). For example, although parametric statistical analyses are typically used in psychological research, psychophysiological data often are not distributed normally and have heterogeneous variances across conditions. One option in these instances is to employ nonparametric tests, which make no assumptions about the data distributions, to analyze the data. If parametric tests are used, mathematical transformations can be applied to the psychophysiological data to meet the assumptions of these tests (cf. Johnson & Lubin, 1972; Levy, 1980).

Because there are large differences in physiological responding among individuals and the testing of each individual involves considerable preparation and time, it is often desirable to examine treatment effects within rather than between subjects. The within-subjects examination of treatments can be conceptualized in two different ways.

> The first is the repetition of similar trials so that more stable indices of behavior can be obtained through aggregation or so that changes over time can be observed (e.g., learning, habituation, or extinction). The other is the exposure of single subjects to multiple experimental conditions so that the same subjects appear in both control and treatment cells (McHugo & Lanzetta, 1983, p. 654).

Both procedures help reduce error variance, increase generalizability, and improve replicability.

With the collection of multiple measures from the same individual, however, the decision arises regarding whether to use univariate or multivariate analytic procedures. Multivariate procedures have several advantages over univariate analyses. At the simplest level, they provide protection against making type I errors due to conducting a host of univariate tests on related measures. In addition, multivariate procedures allow one to analyze the configurations of responding, a particularly valuable attribute when studying response syndromes (e.g., reflecting stress or emotion—cf. Fridlund et al., 1984) or the interactions among physiological systems. The major disadvantage of multivariate procedures is that the results of the analysis are constrained by the set of variables obtained. Although it is unlikely, the inclusion or deletion of another psychophysiological measure (or measures) can, in theory, lead to major changes in the weighting of each measure in the multivariate analysis. If, for example, one important measure is embedded in a host of insensitive measures, the multivariate analysis may erroneously yield the conclusion that treatment differences were attributable to chance. Furthermore, even when one measure (e.g., EMG activity over the zygomatic region) within a set of measures is weighted minimally, deletion of one of the measures in the set (e.g., EMG activity over the corrugator region) can drastically change its weighting and "apparent" importance when interpreting the psychophysiological data. The implication is that interpretations of data based upon multivariate analyses can be challenged unless the population of "important" measures are specified and used. Hence, neither univariate nor multivariate analyses are invariably best. Further discussions of the application of multivariate procedures to psychophysiological data can be found in McHugo and Lanzetta (1983), Muller et al. (1983), and Ray and Kimmel (1979).

Internal validity concerns the question of whether or not a specific experimental treatment was responsible for an observed effect. In an early empirical study, for example, Boyd and DiMascio (1954) evaluated a psychotherapeutic interview of a single patient (diagnosed "schizophrenic, paranoid type") using the Bales Interaction Scoring System, and they measured heart rate, GSR, and facial temperature. Boyd and DiMascio reported that positive and negative verbal exchanges increased, whereas neutral exchanges decreased as the interview proceeded. They also noted that skin resistance dropped, heart rate increased then slowed, and facial temperature rose then dropped during the interview. It was suggested that

> At the beginning of the interview sympathetic tension was elevated immediately and was accompanied by profuse "neutral" interaction: as the interview proceeded the patient expressed more feeings (cf. less neutral) and these were accompanied by reduced productivity and sympathetic relaxation (Boyd & DiMascio, 1954, p. 211).

Boyd and DiMascio's (1954) observations are interesting, but no comparison conditions were included to determine what aspects of the interview caused particular physiological and behavioral responses, what aspects were reliable, or what aspects were unique to persons with thought disorders. That is, it is unclear from their observations whether the affective contents of the interview were necessarily related to (e.g., responsible for) the observed physiological changes.

Campbell and Stanley (1963) have outlined eight specific threats to the internal validity of an experiment. These threats all posit that some extraneous causal variable (e.g., nonequivalence of subjects across conditions, a maturation process) is responsible for the observed effects rather than the treatment. Subjects in the comparison conditions should, of course, be treated identically to those in the experimental conditions except for the treatment. If the responses from these conditions are found to differ, then this difference must either be attributed to the treatment, to the fact that the two groups have different kinds of subjects, or to the fact that the treatments were presented to subjects at different points in time during the experimental session. Hence, all the threats to internal validity can be eliminated by employing appropriate comparison conditions (e.g., control groups), randomly assigning subjects to conditions, and presenting the experimental treatments in random sequences.

Even when an experimental design allows an investigator to conclude that a particular treatment was necessary to produce the observed effect, it remains uncertain whether or not the treatment was sufficient. The treatment may only produce the observed difference when certain kinds of subjects are tested, only in the laboratory, only when tested by a same-sex experimenter, only at certain times of the year, and so forth. The question of how generalizable the research findings are is one of *external validity*. Schultz (1969) and Jung (1969) noted, for example, that the vast majority of the individuals serving as subjects in psychological research are young, healthy, male Caucasians who are enrolled in an introductory psychology course. Gale and Baker (1981) echoed the concern that these features characterized the subjects in most psychophysiological research. It is not unreasonable to question whether the interpretations of psychophysiological data based upon the research with these subjects would be informative when trying to interpret the data obtained, for instance, from more anxious or distressed individuals. The external validity of an effect can be assessed only by testing the (conceptual) treatment on a wide variety of subjects, in a wide variety of settings, employing a wide variety of experimental materials.

The question of the external validity of an observed effect is sometimes ignored because it is viewed as the activity of a gadfly rather than a theoretician. In fact, however, investigations of external validity provide an excellent context for obtaining convergent and discriminant validity for theoretical postulates and, in the process, for developing better postulates and theories. Recall that the concept of the orienting response was described in a previous section as a syndrome of bodily reactions (e.g., decreased heart rate, pupillary dilation) that facilitate the perception of an environmental stimulus. The orienting reaction has been observed in animals, infants, children, and adults using stimuli ranging from tones to slides (e.g., see Siddle, in press; Lynn, 1966). The research on individual differences in orienting responses has been particularly informative in light of the impressive generalizability of the orienting reaction. Anxiety neurotics, for example, exhibit smaller orienting responses that habituate more slowly than do normal individuals (cf. Lader, 1975; Lader & Nobel, 1975). In an illustrative experiment, 20 patients suffering from anxiety and 20 normal individuals served as subjects (Lader & Wing, 1966). Skin conductance was measured during a preliminary 10-minute resting period and again when a series of brief loud tones were presented. The subjects suffering from anxiety were characterized by (1) a higher level of skin conductance throughout the study, (2) smaller event-related skin conductance responses to the tone presentations, and (3) a slower habituation of these responses to the repeatedly presented tones. As Grings and Dawson (1978) aptly summarize: "anxiety neurotics give smaller physiological responses to environmental stimuli but they persist in giving these responses despite repeated presentation of the stimuli" (p. 67). Thus, the research on the generalizability of orienting response has improved theories of both the orienting response and anxiety neurotics. It has also suggested a means of gauging the extent of anxiety disorders in individuals and of monitoring therapeutic progress in these individuals.

Thus far, we have discussed issues concerning whether or not a reliable difference exists between treatment groups in psychophysiological research (conclusion validity), whether or not the treatments are necessary to produce an observed effect (internal validity), and what the conditions are under which the treatments will or will not produce an observed effect (external validity). Implicit in these discussions have been the most important theoretical questions: Do the experimental treatments (i.e., operational causal variables) truly represent the theoretical causal variables, and do the operational dependent variables truly represent the theoretical dependent variables? These are questions of *construct validity*. Ideally, alternative theories of observed effects could be eliminated in "crucial experiments" in which the various plausible theories make competing predictions (cf. Petty & Brock, 1981). Unfortunately, crucial experiments are not always possible to conduct, and when conducted they sometimes generate more controversy than they resolve. There simply are not inarguable answers to the questions of construct validity. Some answers are clearly *less* arguable than others, though, so we conclude this chapter with a discussion of construct validity in psychophysiological research.

Experimental treatments delivered in a laboratory setting are complex and unlikely to evoke only one process. Hence, it is always possible that some extraneous causal variable covaries or is confounded with the treatments. Similarly, physiological responses are not invariantly linked to specific psychological processes. Interpretations of the psychological import of physiological responses, therefore, are warranted only to the extent that rival processes have been eliminated either through experimental control (manipulation) or measurement. The problem of determining exactly what a treatment or physiological response *represents* typically generates the most controversy in the interpretation of a psychophysiological experiment. In previous sections, we have discussed methods of eliminating biasing effects such as demand characteristics, experimenter bias, and evaluation apprehension. In the discussion of external validity, we suggested that it is a good idea to repeat the experiment on different groups of subjects, at different times, in different settings, using different operationalizations of the treatments to see if the same results are observed. When the combination of these factors in an experiment are thought to represent the same theoretical factors as observed previously, then this procedure is called *multiple operationalizations*. If comparable results are observed, then attributing these results to the common conceptual variable is more reasonable.

Another method of assessing the validity of a manipulation is to measure its psychological impact directly. For example, let us assume that subjects are presented with either veridical or nonveridical information about the level of the EMG activity over the medial frontalis muscle region in their forehead. Furthermore, assume that the decreases in muscle tension over this region were greater for subjects who received veridical than for those with nonveridical feedback. We can feel more confident in attributing the decline in muscle tension to the feedback if we can be sure that our subjects attended to this feedback. In other words, a question or procedure designed to check on the psychological effectiveness of an experimental manipulation (i.e., a manipulation check) can be particularly useful.

It should be noted that the inclusion of a manipulation check does not require that the psychological impact be *reportable*. Questions can be used as manipulation checks if the treatment was designed to have an impact on a reportable psychological process; otherwise, alternative procedures must be devised. A question asking subjects to rate how "aroused" they feel is appropriate if an experimental treatment (e.g., loud and continuous white noise) is employed to manipulate felt arousal. A more objective measurement (e.g., an aggregated physiological measure) would be more appropriate, however, if the manipulation were employed to alter actual physiological arousal.

By way of summary, consider the use of psychophysiological measurements to help identify processing stages underlying some psychological phenomenon (e.g., speech phobia) when one already has a clearly articulated hypothesis about the sequence of events that transpire between the stimulus and overt responses (cf. Cacioppo & Petty, in press). At the simplest level, an experimental design begins with an experimental and a control condition. The experimental condition represents the presence of some factor and the control condition represents the absence of this factor. The experimental factor might be selected because it is theoretically believed to incorporate stages of a psychological process; the construction of the control condition, on the other hand, is guided theoretically to incorporate $N - 1$ stages of the psychological process and, hence, exert a different impact on reported (e.g., expressed anxiety) or overt behavior (e.g., fluency or rate of speech).

The principle underlying the inclusion of physiological measures in these designs is that the physiological character, or "markers," of the various constituent stages of the underlying psychological process might be deduced through the systematic application of the procedure of *stage deletion*. Thus, this approach is an adaptation of a procedure that is sometimes termed the "subtractive method" (Donder's, 1868, cited by Pachella, 1974). If, for example, differences in the rate or fluency of speech result when individuals perform a task while observed versus unobserved, then the presence of an observer can be conceived as introducing an additional processing stage(s). If a theory including this stage is posited to explain people's speech phobia, then comparison conditions can be constructed and physiological measures obtained to determine the physiological markers of this and each of the accompanying processing stages (cf. Borden, 1980).

When, in a subsequent study, one of these stages is thought to be responsible for the differential impact of two conditions on behavior (e.g., in a study of observed task performances), then analyses of the concomitant physiological activity can again be informative (cf. Cacioppo & Petty, 1983). If the patterns of physiological activity resulting from the isolation of presumably identical stages are dissimilar, then the similarity of the stages is challenged even though there may be similarities between the subsequent behavioral outcomes. The greater the evidence is (from multiple operationalizations) that a particular stage is accompanied by a specific profile of physiological responses across the ranges of the stimuli employed, the more challenging to the theory is the dissimilarity in obtained physiological profiles. If, on the other hand, the patterns of physiological activity resulting from the isolation of presumably identical stages of processing are similar, then convergent evidence is obtained that the same fundamental stage is a part of both processes, although such data do not *prove* that the stages are the same. The more peculiar the physiological profile is to a given stage within a particular experimental context, however, the greater is the value of the convergent evidence conferred. Monitoring phasic changes in skin resistance alone, for example, provides weak convergent evidence for a particular psychological stage (e.g., stress), since it is characteristic of so many divergent stages (e.g., see Schwartz & Shapiro, 1973).

There are two additional concerns that might be mentioned regarding this interpretive framework when investigating an elementary stage of a psychological process. First, it is implicitly assumed that a stage can be inserted or deleted without changing the nature of the other constituent stages. Of course, it is possible that maniplating a factor to insert or delete a processing stage might introduce a completely different processing structure. This problem can be reduced by using multiple operationalizations to insert or delete a stage. If each operational insertion or deletion of a stage differentially alters the processing structure of the task, then no distinctive features attributable to the conceptual processing stage of interest should be observed across operationalizations, and alternative experimental operations and means for isolating the stage would have to be devised.

Parametric studies of a processing stage can also provide important information about the range over which a stage manifests as a particular physiological profile, thereby improving an investigator's ability to generate appropriate comparison conditions and predictions and to draw clear interpretations. A failure to find the same profile of physiological response across a wide range of levels of a stimulus believed to invoke a given processing stage does not in itself indicate whether a new stage is invoked or the old stage manifests differently within the organism at various levels of stimulation. It *does* clearly indicate an important limitation when interpreting the physiological profile obtained in a subsequent study of this processing stage. As Donchin (1982) suggests, "each hypothesis so tested generates predictions for its own specific range of validity. The observed relations may or may not be universally applicable" (p. 460).

CONCLUSION

Psychophysiology is an interdisciplinary science based upon the notion that people's cognitions, emotions, and behaviors are determined by organismic as well as situational factors. The emphasis on physiological processes and their relationships to (e.g., as markers of) psychological states and behavior renders many of the principles and methods emerging from psychophysiology relevant to health psychologists. Indeed, psychophysiologists can already be found in health settings employing procedures ranging, for example, from operant training which teaches patients how to modify selected somatovisceral responses to clinical techniques which assist patients in developing and utilizing social support networks as a means of enhancing their own recuperative powers.

Our aim in this chapter has been to provide an outline of the methods of psychophysiology to enable readers to understand, evaluate, and apply psychophysiological techniques better to problems and issues in the field of health psychology. We began with a discussion of the *physical* context for psychophysiological research and worked our way through discussions of increasingly abstract topics. In the initial section, the essentials of psychophysiological recording were introduced, and issues pertaining to instrumentation and physical sources of artifacts were discussed. Next, we considered the *social* context within which psychophysiological inquiries are made. Procedures for enhancing the validity and reliability of psycho-physiological assessments and for dealing with social sources of artifacts were described briefly. We completed our discussion with an overview of the *inferential* context for psychophysiological research. In this latter section, we dealt explicitly with the problems of relating observed physiological, verbal, and behavioral reactions to psychological constructs and theory. The present survey should make it clear that the value of psychophysiological research is tied inextricably to the logic of the experimental design employed.

ACKNOWLEDGMENTS

The authors gratefully acknowledge the comments of Charles W. Snyder and Barbara L. Andersen on an earlier draft of this chapter.

References

Aronson, E., & Carlsmith, J. M. (1968). Experimentation in social psychology. In G. Lindzey & E. Aronson (Eds.), *The handbook of social psychology* (Vol. 2, 2nd ed). Reading, MA: Addison-Wesley.

Ax, A. F. (1953). The physiological differentiation between anger and fear in humans. *Psychosomatic Medicine, 15*, 433–442.

Borden, R. J. (1980). Audience influence. In P. B. Paulis (Ed.) *Psychology of group influence.* Hillsdale, NJ: Erlbaum.

Boyd, R. W., & DiMascio, A. (1954). Social behavior and autonomic physiology: A socio-physiologic study. *Journal of Nervous and Mental Disorders, 120*, 207–212.

Brown, C. C. (1972). Instruments in psychophysiology. In N. S. Greenfield & R. A. Sternbach (Eds.), *Handbook of psychophysiology.* New York: Holt, Rinehart and Winston.

Cacioppo, J. T., Marshall-Goodell, B., & Dorfman, D. D. (1983). Skeletomuscular patterning: Topographical analysis of the integrated electromyogram. *Psychophysiology, 20*, 269–283.

Cacioppo, J. T., Marshall-Goodell, B., & Gormezano, I. (1983). Social psychophysiology: Bioelectrical measurement, experimental control, and analog/digital data acquisition. In J. T. Cacioppo & R. E. Petty (Eds.), *Social psychophysiology: A sourcebook.* New York: Guilford Press.

Cacioppo, J. T., & Petty, R. E. (1983). *Social psychophysiology: A sourcebook.* New York: Guilford Press.

Cacioppo, J. T., & Petty, R. E. (In press). Social processes. In M. G. H. Coles, E. Donchin, & S. Porges (Eds.), *Psychophysiology: Systems, processes, and applications (Vol. 2).* New York: Guilford Press.

Cacioppo, J. T., Petty, R. E., & Marshall-Goodell, B. (1984). Electromyographic specificity during simple physical and attitudinal tasks: Location and topographical features of integrated EMG responses. *Biological Psychology, 18*, 85–121.

Cacioppo, J. T., & Sandman, C. A. (1981). Psychophysiological functioning, cognitive responding, and attitudes. In R. E. Petty, T. M. Ostrom, & T. C. Brock (Eds.), *Cognitive responses in persuasion.* Hillsdale, NJ: Erlbaum.

Campbell, D. T., & Stanley, J. C. (1963). *Experimental and quasi-experimental designs for research.* Chicago: Rand McNally.

Carruthers, M. (1981). "Field studies": Emotion and beta-blockade. In M. J. Christie & P. G. Mellett (Eds.), *Foundations of psychosomatics.* Chichester: Wiley.

Carruthers, M., Arguelles, A., & Masovich, A. (1976). Man in transit: Biochemical and physiological changes during intercontinental flights. *Lancet, 1*, 977−981.

Christie, M. J., & Mellett, P. G. (1981). *Foundations of psychosomatics.* Chichester: Wiley.

Christie, M. J., & Todd, J. L. (1975). Experimenter-subject-situational interactions. In P. H. Venables & M. J. Christie (Eds.), *Research in psychophysiology.* London: Wiley.

Christie, M. J., & Woodman, D. D. (1980). Biochemical methods. In I. Martin & P. H. Venables (Eds.), *Techniques in psychophysiology.* Chichester: Wiley.

Coles, M., Donchin, E., & Porges, S. (Eds.) (In press). *Psychophysiology: Systems, processes, and applications.* (Vol. 2). New York: Guilford Press.

Cook, T. D., & Campbell, D. T. (1976). The design and conduct of quasi-experiments and true experiments in field settings. In M. Dunnette (Ed.), *Handbook of industrial and organizational psychology.* Chicago: Rand McNally.

Cooper, J. B., & Singer, D. N. (1956). The role of emotion in prejudice. *Journal of Social Psychology, 44*, 241−247.

Donchin, E. (1982). The relevance of dissociations and the irrelevance of dissociationism: A reply to Schwartz and Pritchard. *Psychophysiology, 19*, 457−463.

Fridlund, A. J., Cottam, G. L., & Fowler, S. C. (1982). In search of the general tension factor: Tensional patterning during auditory stimulation. *Psychophysiology, 19*, 136−145.

Fridlund, A. J., & Izard, C. E. (1983). Electromyographic studies of facial expressions of emotions and patterns of emotion. In J. T. Cacioppo & R. E. Petty (Eds.), *Social psychophysiology: A sourcebook.* New York: Guilford Press.

Fridlund, A. J., Schwartz, G. E., & Fowler, S. C. (1984). Pattern recognition of self-reported emotional state from multiple-site facial EMG activity during affective imagery. *Psychophysiology, 21*, 622−637.

Gale, A. (1973). The psychophysiology of individual differences: Studies of extraversion and the EEG. In P. Kline (Ed.), *New approaches in psychological measurements.* London: Wiley.

Gale, A., & Baker, S. (1981). *In vivo* or *in vitro*? Some effects of laboratory experiments, with particular reference to the psychophysiology experiment. In M. J. Christie & P. G. Mellett (Eds.), *Foundations of psychosomatics.* Chichester: Wiley.

Gale, A., & Smith, D. (1980). On setting up a psychophysiological laboratory. In I. Martin & P. Venables (Eds.), *Techniques in psychophysiology.* Chichester: Wiley.

Geddes, L. A., & Baker, L. E. (1968). *Principles of applied biomedical instrumentation* (2nd ed.). New York: Wiley.

Greenfield, N. S., & Sternbach, R. A. (1972). *Handbook of psychophysiology.* New York: Holt, Rinehart and Winston.

Grings, W. W., & Dawson, M. E. (1978). *Emotions and bodily responses: A psychophysiological approach.* New York: Academic Press.

Jasper, H. H. (1958). The ten-twenty electrode system of the international federation. *Electroencephalography and Clinical Neurophysiology, 10*, 371−375.

Johnson, L. C., & Lubin, A. (1972). On planning psychophysiological experiments. In N. S. Greenfield & R. A. Sternbach (Eds.), *Handbook of psychophysiology.* New York: Holt, Rinehart and Winston.

Jung, J. (1969). Current practices and problems in use of college students for psychological research. *Canadian Psychologist, 10*, 280−290.

Krantz, D. S., Glass, D. C., Schaeffer, M. A., & Davia, J. E. (1982). Behavior patterns in coronary disease: A critical evaluation. In J. T. Cacioppo & R. E. Petty (Eds.), *Perspectives in cardiovascular psychophysiology.* New York: Guilford Press.

Lader, M. (1975). The psychophysiology of anxious and depressed patients. In D. C. Fowles (Ed), *Clinical applications of psychophysiology.* New York: Columbia University Press.

Lader, M. H., & Nobel, P. (1975). The effective disorders. In P. H. Venables & M. J. Christie (Eds.), *Research in psychophysiology.* New York: Wiley.

Lader, M. H., & Wing, L. (1966). Physiological measures, sedative drugs, and morbid anxiety. (Maudsley Monograph #14). London: Oxford University Press.

Lang, P. J. (1971). The application of psychophysiological methods to the study of psychotherapy and behavior modification. In A. E. Bergin & S. L. Garfield (Eds.), *Handbook of psychotherapy and behavior change.* New York: Wiley.

Lang, P. J., & Melamed, B. G. (1969). Avoidance conditioning therapy of an infant with chronic ruminative vomiting. *Journal of Abnormal Psychology, 74,* 1–8.

Levy, A. B. (1980). Measurement units in psychophysiology. In I. Martin & P. Venables (Eds.), *Techniques in psychophysiology.* Chichester: Wiley.

Lynn, R. (1966). *Attention, arousal, and the orientation reaction.* Oxford: Pergamon.

Martin, I., & Venables, P. H. (Eds.). (1980). *Techniques in psychophysiology.* Chichester: Wiley.

McGuigan, F. J. (1979). *Psychophysiological measurement of covert behavior: A guide for the laboratory.* New York: Wiley.

McGuigan, F. J. (1983). Fundamentals of psychophysiological measurement. In J. T. Cacioppo & R. E. Petty (Eds.), *Social psychophysiology: A sourcebook.* New York: Guilford Press.

McHugo, G., & Lanzetta, J. T. (1983). Methodological decisions in social psychophysiology. In J. T. Cacioppo & R. E. Petty (Eds.), *Social psychophysiology: A sourcebook.* New York: Guilford Press.

Mesulam, M., & Perry, J. (1972). The diagnosis of lovesickness: Experimental psychophysiology without the polygraph. *Psychophysiology, 9,* 54–55.

Muller, K. E., Otto, D. A., & Benignus, V. A. (1983). Design and analysis issues and strategies in psychophysiological research. *Psychophysiology, 20,* 212–218.

Nisbett, R. E., & Wilson, T. D. (1977). Telling more than we can know: Verbal reports on mental processes. *Psychological Review, 84,* 231–259.

Orne, M. T. (1962). On the social psychology of the psychological experiment: With particular reference to demand characteristics and their implications. *American Psychologist, 17,* 776–783.

Pachella, R. G. (1974). The interpretation of reaction time in information-processing research. In B. Y. Kantowitz (Ed.), *Human information processes: Tutorials in performance and cognition.* Hillsdale, NJ: Erlbaum.

Pavlov, I. P. (1927). *Conditioned reflexes.* New York: Oxford University Press.

Perski, A., Engel, B. T., & McCroskery, J. H. (1982). The modification of elicited cardiovascular responses by operant conditioning of heart rate. In J. T. Cacioppo & R. E. Petty (Eds.), *Perspectives in cardiovascular psychophysiology.* New York: Guilford Press.

Petty, R. E., & Brock, T. C. (1981). Thought disruption and persuasion: Assessing the validity of attitude change experiments. In R. E. Petty, T. M. Ostrom, & T. C. Brock (Eds.), *Cognitive responses in persuasion.* Hillsdale, NJ: Erlbaum.

Petty, R. E., & Cacioppo, J. T. (1983). The role of bodily responses in attitude measurement and change. In J. T. Cacioppo & R. E. Petty (Eds.), *Social psychophysiology: A sourcebook.* New York: Guilford Press.

Porges, S. W. (In press). Heart rate patterns in neonates: A potential diagnostic window to the brain. In T. Field & A. Sostek (Eds.), *Infants born at risk: Physiological and perceptual processes.* New York: Grune & Stratton.

Porges, S. W., McCabe, P. M., & Yongue, B. G. (1982). Respiratory-heart rate interactions: Psychophysiological implications for pathophysiology and behavior. In J. T. Cacioppo & R. E. Petty (Eds.), *Perspectives in cardiovascular psychophysiology.* New York: Guilford Press.

Ray, R. L., & Kimmel, H. D. (1979). Utilization of psychophysiological indices in behavioral assessment: Some methodological issues. *Journal of Behavioral Assessment, 1,* 107–122.

Rosenberg, M. J. (1969). The conditions and consequences of evaluation apprehension. In R. Rosenthal & R. L. Rosnow (Eds.), *Artifact and behavioral research.* New York: Academic Press.

Rosenthal, R. (1966). *Experimenter affects and behavioral research*. New York: Appleton-Century-Crofts.

Schultz, D. P. (1969). The human subject in psychological research. *Psychological Bulletin, 72,* 214–228.

Schwartz, G. E., Fair, P. L., Mandel, M. R., Salt, P., Mieske, M., & Klerman, G. L. (1978). Facial electromyography in the assessment of improvement in depression. *Psychosomatic Medicine, 40,* 355–360.

Schwartz, G. E., Fair, P. L., Salt, P., Mandel, M. R., & Klerman, G. L. (1976a). Facial expressions and imagery in depression: An electromyographic study. *Psychosomatic Medicine, 36,* 337–347.

Schwartz, G. E., Fair, P. L., Salt, P., Mandel, M. R. & Klerman, G. L. (1976b). Facial muscle patterning to affective imagery in depressed and non-depressed subjects. *Science, 192,* 489–491.

Schwartz, G. E., & Shapiro, D. (1973). Social psychophysiology. In W. F.Prokasy & D. C. Raskin (Eds.), *Electrodermal activity in psychological research*. New York: Academic Press.

Segreto-Bures, J., & Kotses, H. (1982). The experimenter expectancy affects in frontal EMG conditioning. *Psychophysiology, 19,* 467–471.

Shaw, J. C. (1967). Quantification of biological signals using integration techniques. In P. H. Venables & I. Martin (Eds.), *A manual of psychophysiological methods*. Amsterdam: North Holland Publishing.

Siddle, D. A. T. (In press). *The orienting response*. London: Wiley.

Sokolov, A. N. (1972). *Inner speech and thought*. New York: Plenum Press.

Stearns, S. D. (1975). *Digital signal analysis*. Rochelle Park, NJ: Hayden.

Stern, R. M., Ray, W. J., & Davis, C. M. (1980). *Psychophysiological recording*. New York: Oxford University Press.

Venables, P. H., & Christie, M. J. (1980). Electrodermal activity In I. Martin & P. H. Venables (Eds.), *Techniques in psychophysiology*. Chichester: Wiley.

Venables, P. H., & Martin, I. (Eds.), (1967). *A manual of psychophysiological methods*. Amsterdam: North Holland Publishing.

8

The Use of Psychodiagnostic Questionnaires in Predicting Risk Factors and Health Outcomes

CATHERINE J. GREEN

The movement toward more psychologically oriented medical care reflects an increased focus on the interrelationship of mind and body. Researchers and clinicians posit a variety of salient issues, generally addressing only those that they consider of import and leading to a literature

Portions of this chapter were abridged from Green, C. "Psychological Assessment in Medical Settings," in Millon, T., Green, C. and Meagher R. (Eds.), *Handbook of Clinical Health Psychology*. New York: Plenum, 1982. By permission.

replete with studies that lack shared conceptual frameworks and present conflicting results. Within this confused morass of data there resides the patient and his or her medical problem. Clearly there exists one or some number of relationships among the patient, his or her feelings, and his or her health status. Our task is the elucidation of these relationships. As Sir William Osler stated: "It is more important to know what kind of man has a disease than to know what kind of disease a man has." Osler's statement seems as apt today as when it was first formulated. Assessment in clinical health psychology should be designed to appraise the relationship of emotional factors and physical disease mechanisms within specific individuals. This chapter will address the use of objective psychodiagnostic instruments to obtain this vital information.

PSYCHOLOGICAL ANALYSIS IN MEDICAL SETTINGS

In traditional medicine, the goal of clinical diagnosis is the identification of the ongoing disease process and the formulation of a plan to deal with the disease. When psychosocial factors are added to the medical symptomatology, the patient cannot be seen simply as a vessel, so to speak, who carries a group of predictable or constant symptoms available for evaluation. Rather, the psychosocial events and the patient's premorbid personality covary to create a changing constellation. Under these circumstances clinical analysis must not only systematically evaluate these varied elements, but it must also elucidate their interrelationships and dynamic flow. Current behaviors and attitudes should be interpreted in conjunction with the physical aspects of the presenting problem. The premorbid background of the patient must be delineated in an effort to clarify the historical context or pattern of the syndrome. Moreover, personality and environmental circumstances must be appraised to optimize therapeutic recommendations. Ultimately, the goal of psychological assessment is the development of a preventive or remedial plan.

As in other settings, problems occur when this assessment relies solely on the evaluation skills and impressions of the clinician involved. Clinicians often see what they anticipate. It is unlikely that the data obtained will be at variance with these expectancies. Moreover, questions likely to get unanticipated information are rarely asked. It is in this regard that objective psychological assessment is so important; these tools serve to standardize clinical evaluations and to ensure comprehensive coverage. Moreover, it seeks to appraise the patient's present status within the context of the past and within his or her larger social framework or environment, including both current physical and psychosocial stressors. Although the clinician evaluates a patient caught at one point of time, it is necessary to trace the sequence of events preceding and leading to that point. This knowledge allows the formulation of a remedial plan that is based on understanding the interface between the patient's illness and the resources available to manage the problem successfully.

Clinical psychological analysis with medical patients is both an abbreviated and more extensive evaluation than for the psychiatric patient as characterized by Millon (1969). The first task is the description of the current clinical picture. The presenting medical problem is often the most obvious aspect of this picture. However, it often serves as a precipitant of difficulties of a more extensive, or long-lasting nature. The impact of this physical problem must be evaluated in both its effects on the physiology of the individual and the impact upon the patient's emotions and those who surround the patient. Throughout the evaluation process various levels are observed including the overt behaviors, stated reports of feelings along with the inferred intrapsychic processes, as well as the biophysical processes.

As stated earlier, the patient is caught at one point in time and yet the analysis must consider and attempt to elucidate the developmental influences on the presenting problems. Here again the physical and emotional, along with current stressors, may be relevant to etiology. This information, combined with the clinical picture, allows for the construction of a clinical syndrome. Rather than labeling, the effort now is to clarify the complex interactive roles of medical concerns, the feelings of the patient, and the reactions of individuals surrounding the patient. This hopefully will assist in prognosis and the formulation of therapeutic management. All these issues must be evaluated to assess a patient optimally; however, psychological assessment in medical settings did not generally assume so comprehensive an approach.

ASSESSMENT TRENDS IN MEDICAL SETTINGS

Initially, psychologists employed traditional psychometric instruments that could answer specific questions regarding problems of psychopathology, but often did not illuminate questions posed in requests for nonpsychiatric psychological services. New instruments designed to assess the general medical patient developed very slowly, many by clinicians unfamiliar with psychometric theory. Consequently, these new tests often were poorly grounded in theory and gave minimal evidence of validity or reliability. The following sections of this chapter will serve as a guide to the evaluation and use of selected objective and self-report instruments. These tools have been chosen because of the ease with which they can be employed in medical settings. Although the list is by no means exhaustive, it does encompass a variety of approaches, theoretical stances, and issues found significant for medical patients.

The instruments selected will be evaluated in terms of general psychological test criteria and their relevance to medical-psychological issues specified. If an instrument fails to meet general psychometric consideration, its value as a medical diagnostic instrument is seriously compromised.

GENERAL CRITERIA FOR TEST EVAULATION

The first criterion for evaluating a psychometric instrument is whether it addresses a characteristic relevant to a target population, is tailored to gauge some specific trait or behavior through the parsimonious use of questions, and displays simplicity of administration and economy of time. Brevity, clarity, and minimal intrusiveness maximize client compliance and minimize fatigue.

Although different methods have been employed in the development of the following tests, the same criteria of test construction must be applied. These include (1) evaluating reliability or the test's ability to yield consistent results from one set of measures to another and the extent to which the obtained test scores are free from such internal defects as will produce errors of measurement inherent in the items and their standardization (test-retest, reliability across forms of the test, and internal consistency); (2) evaluating validity, which measures the degree to which a test measures what it purports to measure when compared with accepted criteria (construct, content, and empirical); and (3) evaluating the completeness of the manual and instructions for interpretation.

Further evaluation criteria must be applied to those instruments that are utilized in medical settings. First, there are the behaviors, traits, and attitudes relevant to the individual. Another major criterion relates to the predictive value of the instrument. What is the likelihood of illness occurring in an individual who is otherwise asymptomatic?

The following sections utilize these criteria in evaluating a number of instruments.

RESEARCH INSTRUMENTS

State-Trait Anxiety Inventory (STAI)

This inventory was originally developed as a research instrument for investigating anxiety in normal adults (Speilberger et al., 1970) and is composed of two questionnaires of similar format, one asking the subject to indicate how he or she feels *right now*, the other, how the individual *generally* feels. The subject choices are either "almost never," "sometimes," "often," or "almost always." This instrument was specifically developed to evaluate feelings of tension, nervousness, worry, and apprehension. It was posited by the test developers that it could serve as either a clinical tool for evaluating anxiety proneness or, in the case of state scores, the evaluation of the level of anxiety or anxiety change.

The STAI was designed to be self-administered and may be given individually or in groups; complete instructions are printed on the test form. Subjects respond to each STAI item by rating themselves on a 4-point scale; most patients require 20 minutes or more to complete the form. Templates and machine scoring are available.

The normative sample, or those individuals to whom the test subjects are to be compared, are composed of college students or varied groups of psychiatric and medical patients. Although a variety of student groups were utilized in various stages of construction, the normative samples are extremely narrow in scope, including very few noncollege or clinical populations. Given the difference between male and female responses on this inventory with high school and college samples, it would be unwise to view the medical sample as an adequate comparison group.

Interpretation is straightforward; higher scores on A-trait indicate higher levels of anxiety proneness. High A-state scores are conceptualized as transitory or characterized by subjective or consciously perceived feelings of apprehension. The instrument is not intended to be used for individual evaluation, but, rather, for assessment of group differences.

As expected, the test-retest reliability (reliability of instrument administered twice to the same group of individuals) for anxiety as a state was low; .20 to .40 regardless of the time elapsed. Trait anxiety test-retest was higher, at about .80. Content validity (estimated by evaluating the relevance of the test items, individually and as a whole) and empirical validity (obtained by comparing to some external criterion measure of the trait assessed) of the instrument are two critical issues. Scores obtained on these inventories have not been compared fully to nontest evaluations of anxiety, although hypothetical conditions data were employed in item selections. The STAI was built on the assumption that the initial item pool covered the full domain of anxiety and that further selection on the basis of internal consistency would not distort this circumstance.

Even though the STAI was not designed for individual prediction, anxiety is a central component of patients' reaction in medical settings. Researchers may utilize this instrument to examine anxiety and how it relates to the medical problem under study. For example, the effectiveness of various forms of presurgical instruction might be examined. One could logically evaluate the effectiveness of specific preparatory approaches in relation to the anxiety of the patient (along with other relevant variables). Another area of application is in the study of phobialike reactions that are seen to have a strong relationship to anxiety. In medical settings, this reaction may be seen when patients are diagnosed as having a serious, but not necessarily life-threatening, medical problem such as heart disease. A reasonable question would address the role of state and trait anxiety in the development of cardiac invalidism in a group of patients with coronary heart disease. These are just a few examples of medical research applications of the STAI.

Although it is possible to see how both state and trait anxiety can contribute to the development and difficulties of disease, the STAI's limited focus on one aspect of the individual would cause it to be of limited value in assessing the complex interrelationships of the individual, his or her interaction with the family, and his or her reaction to illness.

Life Experiences Survey (LES)

The Life Experiences Survey, developed by Sarason et al. (1978), was formulated to assess an individual's perception of the life stresses experienced during the preceding 12 months. The notion that life stresses lead to an increase in the frequency of illness is well established in the medical literature. Holmes and Rahe (1967) were the first to address this issue in their early Schedule of Recent Experience (SRE), an objective self-report measure of significant events in the respondent's life. They posited that each life event, regardless of its positive or negative impact, requires adaptive coping on the part of the individual. Events were chosen for the SRE because their advent required adaptation on the part of the individual. Standardized weights were then determined for each event, reflecting the amount of social readjustment they appeared to require. This absolutist approach to events contrasts with that of Lazarus (1977) who states that it is the individual's perception of the meaning of the event that is of critical importance.

Sarason et al. developed the LES as a means of gauging both the occurrence of an event and its perceived significance. The 57-item LES self-report inventory has two sections. The first, completed by all respondents, contains 47 specific events plus three blank spaces where individuals can add unlisted events. These events cover a wide range of experiences. The second section is designed primarily to use with students. In both sections, the respondent is asked to indicate which events were experienced during the past year, and, in addition: (1) whether they viewed the event as positive or negative on a 7-point scale, and (2) the perceived impact of the event at its time of occurrence, on a 7-point scale.

The inventory is self-administered. Respondents are asked to check which events have occurred, when in the last year they took place, and then indicate the type and extent of impact the event may have had. The LES takes 20 to 25 minutes to complete.

A positive change score is obtained by summing the impact ratings of events designated as positive; negative change scores are derived by summing the impact of negative events. The total change is the sum of these.

LES items were chosen to represent life changes frequently experienced by individuals in the general population. Of the 57 items, 34 are similar in content to those of the SRE. Specific items were reworded so as to be applicable to both male and female respondents. No further details are given as to the development of the item pool.

According to the authors, a stressful event calls for adaptation, and adaptation rests in part on the individual's perception of the event. It is also assumed that this level of adaptive behavior will be related to illness events. Although efforts were made to be representative, it was impossible to tap the entire domain of potentially significant life events. Leaving a section of blanks to be filled in addresses this problem, but recall is likely to be a less adequate process than recognition as a means of identifying events.

There is no indication that external criteria were utilized in constructing the instrument, even though numerous correlational studies were employed to evaluate the relationship between LES scores and relevant personality indices. It is hoped that a formal manual, when published, will address a number of these issues.

Test-retest data with two samples show that positive change scores correlate between .19 and .53 for 5 to 6 weeks, whereas negative scores correlated .56 and .88, and total change scores .63 and .64, respectively.

LES scores were correlated with a number of other instruments. Negative scores correlated .29 with trait anxiety on the STAI and .46 with state; an almost zero correlation was found between positive scores and state or trait anxiety. Crowne-Marlowe Social Desirability correlations were also in the zero range, suggesting that the LES is free of social desirability bias. Employing the Psychological Screening Inventory, investigators found correlations of .20 between neuroticism and negative LES scores and a correlation of .28 between extraversion and positive LES scores. From these data it would appear that personal maladjustment is marginally associated with negative change scores. No studies were reported on the relationship of these scores and illness onset, the posited sequel to life stress.

This instrument proposes to address the issue of life events only. It is presumed that these have an impact on the incidence of illness and psychological difficulties. Although no construct-validity studies have been reported on the efficacy of this instrument in making such predictions, research (Yunik, 1979) indicates that negative weighted events tend to have a high correlation with future illness; negative impact scores correlated .42 with the total number of illness problems reported. On the basis of this preliminary study, it appears that the LES may prove to be useful in predicting illness behavior. Looking directly at the individual's perceptions of life stressors, it may highlight an "at risk" population which may serve as an intervention focus.

As we examine the recent life events literature, a question that emerges is whether there is an increase in illness alone or if we are really seeing an increase in illness and help-seeking "illness behavior". A study designed to evaluate this could divide high LES subjects into a "no treatment" group and a group that received support and attention. Medical help-seeking and illness could then be evaluated in both groups to delineate further the nature of both the physical and psychological processes.

SINGLE-DIMENSION INSTRUMENTS

The following instruments were developed for use in the assessment of single traits either between groups or in an individual.

Internal-External Scale (I-E Scale)

The effects of reward or reinforcement on behavior depends to some measure on whether or not the individual perceives a causal relationship between his or her own behavior and the reward. The I-E Scale was developed to measure the degree to which an individual feels that reinforcement is or is not contingent upon his or her own action.

Brought to its final form by Rotter et al. (1961), the I-E Scale is composed of 29 items in which the respondent selects which of two statements is more strongly believed. Twenty-three of the items refer directly to the subject's "externality"; six serve as filler in an effort to disguise the intent of the instrument somewhat. The authors see this as an instrument suitable to measure group differences; it is not meant to be used for individual or clinical prediction. No specific population was targeted and items are applicable to many life settings. No manual has been written for the I-E Scale and users must rely on the 1966 monograph for information on construction and utilization of the instrument.

Self-report instructions for the I-E Scale are printed at the top of the questionnaire and geared to an upper high school reading level. Subjects are told to select which of a pair of statements is more strongly believed. The testee is admonished to select the one that seems to be more true rather than the one he or she thinks should be chosen or wishes to be true. The 29 items are usually completed in 15 to 20 minutes.

Scoring is accomplished by totaling the number of "external" responses. One monograph appendix provides a frequency distribution for male and female samples of university undergraduates; no statment is made regarding the generalizability of this distribution or its applicability to other samples or populations.

Means and standard deviations are reported for a number of samples; full distributions are not described and no attempt is made to present a set of norms. Users are encouraged to create their own local norms. Regarding interpretation, the higher the score is, the more reinforcement is seen to be the product of luck, chance, or the control of others.

The I-E Scale evolved through a number of developmental stages. The first instrument developed by Phares (1957) was composed of 26 items selected a priori, with 13 stated as external attitudes and 13 as internal. Following this, James (1957) developed a test employing Phares's most successful items, building the total to 26 by adding several filler items as well. Subsequently, researchers sought to broaden the test by developing a series of subscales. A 100-item scale was analyzed and reduced back to 60 items. Control for social desirability bias was considered and a forced-choice format was instituted. Item analyses showed that the subscales failed to generate separate predictions. A series of further construction steps sought to reduce the instrument's social desirability and to improve its internal consistency. The final 29-item scale is composed of 23 real and 6 filler items.

At no point does it appear that considerations of empirical validity entered into the construction of the instrument. Subsequent to the construction stage, it was found that correlation between interviewer ratings of externality and the I-E scale score were in the .60 range. Having gone through a sequence of construction steps, the I-E is internally consistent and reliable. There is some question, however, as to what the instrument is really measuring and whether, in fact, it adequately covers the domain specified. The absence of normative data is a serious problem, forcing users of the instrument to make their own judgments as to the meaning of given scores. These concerns appear more serious in light of the research literature, since many studies find that the instrument fails to predict expected behaviors consistent with the measured construct (Lambley & Silbowitz, 1973; Marston, 1969).

Internal consistency (KR20) ranges from .69 to .73, whereas test-retest reliability at 1 to 2 months ranges from .49 to .83. Significant efforts had been made to reduce the relationship between the I-E Scale and social desirability. This appears to have been accomplished. In one study the correlation between the I-E Scale and Taylor Manifest Anxiety Scale was .24; in another, the correlation was .00 (Efran, 1963). Nonquestionnaire "projectives" correlated modestly with the I-E Scale scores (Adams-Webber, 1963), and Cardi (1962) found a significant correlation between a semistructured interview measure of locus of control and the I-E Scale.

The I-E Scale evaluates a single concept, internality-externality. Although this construct is an appealing one, the instrument makes no effort or claim to tap any of the vast number of other variables that relate to health behaviors. Its value as a group measure only effectively eliminates it as a tool for individual prediction and global approach to locus of control.

Although internality-externality, as measured by the I-E scale, may account for only a small part of the variance in patient behavior, responsibility for self is a cornerstone of most medical treatment, and certainly all long-term treatment. Its importance compels the researcher to continue to address this issue. New studies might employ other instruments along with the I-E Scale to tap the internality-externality dimension. For example, compliance with an exercise regimen for heart patients might look at I-E along with personality and beliefs about health in an attempt to elucidate further the complex of feelings, thoughts, and behaviors that contribute to this specific type of compliance. Often a variety of treatment approaches are possible for a given medical problem. A study might attempt to match specific treatments for patients to their perceived sense of control as measured by the I-E Scale while controlling for depression or other variables deemed salient with a specific population.

Other researchers, in an attempt to overcome the weakness of the I-E scale have developed scales specific to the assessment of locus of control among medical patients. The Multidimensional Health Locus of Control Scales (MHLC) (Wallston et al., 1978) are among the most widely utilized. These three scales are modeled after Levenson's I, P, and C Scales (Levenson, 1973; 1981) and each consist of six items using a 6-point, Likert response format. These scales grew in part from the earlier Health Locus of Control Scale (Wallston et al., 1976) which included both internally and externally worded items.

The MHLC scales include the PHLC Scale which evaluates the beliefs that the individual's health is largely determined by powerful other people such as doctors or friends. The second of the two external scales is CHLC. This scale measures the degree to which a person believes that health or illness is a matter of chance, fate, or luck. These scales are not combined, but are evaluated separately. The final scale, the IHLC Scale measures health internality or the degree to which individual's believe that internal factors are responsible for health and illness. These scales seem to be statistically independent and have proven more internally consistent (Wallston & Wallston, 1981) than the HLC.

A variety of research studies have been completed utilizing either the HLC or MHLC and are reported in some detail by Wallston and Wallston (1982). Although results are often conflicting or disappointing, this is clearly an area and set of scales that would benefit from further attention.

Symptom Check List-90 (SCL 90)

This 90-item self-report symptom inventory was based on the Hopkins Checklist and designed to reflect psychological symptom patterns of psychiatric patients. Derogatis (1977), one of the test developers, suggests that it also has utility for assessment of medical patients. Each item is rated on a 5-point scale of distress from "not at all" to "extremely." These responses are then interpreted along nine primary symptom dimensions: somatization, obsessive-compulsive, interpersonal sensitivity, depression, anxiety, hostility, phobic anxiety, paranoid ideation, psychoticism. In addition, three global indices of distress are calculated: global severity, positive symptom distress index, positive symptom total. The SCL-90 is intended as a measure of current psychiatric symptom states and is designed to be interpreted on three levels. The first level is the global, and the "global severity index" (GSI) is employed as the gauge. The primary symptom dimensions address the patient's level of psychopathology. Individual items are used to relate the presence or absence of specific symptoms.

Instructions are simple and written on the test form. There is a note that asks the patient to record how much discomfort a particular problem has caused during the last X number of days. Most patients take 20 to 30 minutes to complete the task.

Scoring requires either templates or transferring the 90-item scores from the test paper to profile sheet, where scores are summed to arrived at distress scores for each of the nine symptom dimensions. The global severity index, positive symptom total, and symptom distress index are also calculated. Raw scores are transformed into T-scores utilizing nonpsychiatric patient norms.

The nonpsychiatric normative group (females, $N = 480$; males, $N = 493$) was a stratified random sample that was balanced to be broadly representative of the general population and drawn from one county in a mid-Atlantic state. No determination was made as to the subjects' status as medical patients. Brief descriptions of the clinical significance of each scale and global indices are provided. The GSI is considered an indicator of overall distress, whereas the nine primary symptom dimensions provide a profile of the patient's status in psychological terms. Discrete symptoms may also be noted. Small sample profiles are provided as guides.

The SCL-90, constructed to serve as a checklist of psychiatric symptomatology, was developed through a combination of clinical/rational and empirical/analytic procedures. The clinical/rational method involves the development of items that are intended to reflect specific psychological symptom patterns of psychiatric patients and that are based on clinical experience and observation. The empirical/analytic procedures involve a variety of structural assessments as well as validation approaches utilized in the development of this instrument. The original item pool was drawn from the Hopkins Symptom Checklist (Derogatis et al., 1974a, 1974b) which, in turn, can be traced back to the Cornell Medical Index (CMI) item pool (Wider, 1948). Neither the method of developing new items nor the method for the initial reduction of the Hopkins checklist is detailed in the manual. Internal consistency (referring to the extent to which the results obtained throughout the test are consistent when administered once) ranged from .77 to .90. These high measures may indicate the homogeneity of scale dimensions, but closer examination suggests that they may be the product of several items restating the same emotion or behavior in slightly different words. One week of test-retest reliability ranges from .78 to .90.

The SCL-90 includes both medical and psychiatric symptoms but is geared primarily to the level and nature of current psychopathology. Although a brief cataloging of psychiatric distress is of value, the majority of individuals without psychiatric problems will vary along such a narrow band of differences that the results are likely to be of minimal value.

Furthermore, the information obtained from the SCL-90 is unlikely to contribute very much to the development of a program for enhancing the satisfaction of the individual, providing no information for ways in which circumstances might be altered. Turning to other criteria, the SCL-90 does not attempt to gauge prognosis or probably occurrence of later illness; rather, it calculates the presence of current feelings and behaviors. Its major utility in management of individuals is in relation to serious psychiatric complications, a factor of little relevance with most medical populations. The problems of utilizing a test developed for psychiatric patients in a nonpsychiatric setting is a serious one. Even a well-designed psychiatric instrument is likely to provide information that is distorted when applied to a general health-oriented population. Problems arise because of the unsuitability of norms, the questionable relevance of clinical signs, and the consequent inapplicability of interpretations.

There are, however, problems where the difference between defining the difficulty as medical and psychiatric rests more in the patients' willingness to acknowledge psychological problems than in the degree of physical involvement. Sexual dysfunction is a prominent example of this. The SCL-90 might allow the researcher or clinician to evaluate these patients in relation to both psychiatric and general medical patients. Here the SCL-90 may serve as a reasonable, brief tool to acquire critical assessment of patients' distress in relation to psychological symptom patterns.

Beck Depression Inventory (BDI)

The Beck Depression Inventory (Beck, 1972) is an instrument that seeks to approximate clinical judgments of depression intensity. Efforts were made also to differentiate clearly depressed from nondepressed psychiatric patients. It should be noted that the inventory was designed for research purposes and conceived as appropriate for discriminating levels of depression only in psychiatric populations. The inventory is composed of 21 multiple choice items reflecting specific behavioral signs of depression which were weighted in severity from 0 to 3.

Originally designed to be administered by a trained interviewer who read each statement and asked the patient to select the statement that fit best, the instrument is now often presented as a self-administered inventory. No information is given regarding the possible impact upon norms and scores of this modification to a self-administered format.

The total score is obtained by adding the weighted values for each response endorsed by the patient. No attempt is made to transform raw scores. Scores of 0 to 9 are considered normal, the 10 to 15 range is seen as representing mild depression, 16 to 19 as mild to moderate severity, 20 to 29 as moderate to severe, and 30 to 63 as severe depression.

Two patient samples were utilized in the development of the inventory.

Both groups of patients were drawn from routine admissions to the psychiatric outpatient department of a university hospital and to the psychiatric outpatient department and psychiatric inpatient service of a metropolitan hospital.

The test developer sought to develop explicit rather than inferred behavioral criteria for evaluating depression. To accomplish this, experimenters selected items from the literature and clinical experience. Each subcategory describes a specific behavioral manifestation of depression and consists of a graded series of self-evaluative statements. The items were chosen on the basis of their relationship to overt behavioral manisfestations of depression and do not reflect a particular theory regarding etiology or any viewpoint concerning the psychological processes underlying depression.

Test-retest was not employed in the traditional manner due to the assumption that change would be occurring and this would significantly alter the interpretation of results. Indirect methods were utilized to assess change scores over time; in general, total depression scores tended to parallel clinical changes.

Concurrent validity indicating the extent of the test's agreement with other criteria measuring similar psychological operations or traits was addressed by comparing scores with clinical assessment of levels of depression (correlations between test scores and clinical judgments averaged .66). It is of some note that prediction of clinical change was accurate in 85 percent of the cases.

The total depression score seeks only to address level of severity among psychiatric patients, having been developed expressly for this purpose. It can serve a function with other individuals in this regard if clinical levels of depression are suspected. It is unlikely to prove sensitive to the more moderate levels of dysphoria which, although affecting an individual's work effectiveness and satisfaction, would not be categorized as clinical depression.

The BDI has been used for both research and clinical purposes. Although depression is not a prominent component of all medical problems, it can be a significant factor for specific individuals and is commonly seen in certain patient populations. When depression is suspected the BDI serves as a brief, reasonably nonintrusive assessment measure. Certain groups, such as patients who have had their first myocardial infarction, are often seen to have elevated BDI scores (Kolitz, 1983). Routine screening with the BDI would allow rapid identification of patients in whom depression appears to be a significant issue and allow for expeditious and focused intervention. Furthermore, research studies on medical patients frequently include the BDI as a brief, reactive marker of depression over time. This application would be useful in evaluating treatment that, in part, is expected to alleviate depression, as well as in evaluating the natural evolution of depression over time in a population with a long-term or chronic illness.

Jenkins Activity Survey (JAS)

The Jenkins Activity Survey (Form C), developed by Jenkins et al. (1979), is the latest version of a 52-item self-report questionnaire designed to measure the type A behavior pattern. This pattern is characterized by extreme competitiveness, striving for achievement, aggressiveness, self-imposed responsibility, impatience, haste, restlessness, and feelings of being challenged and being pressed for time. The behavior pattern is not conceived as a personality trait or a standard reaction to a challenging situation, but, rather, the reaction of predisposed persons to a situation that challenges them. A large body of research has been built around the significance of this pattern in the development and persistence of coronary heart disease. Although the instrument is actively marketed to be utilized for individual diagnostic assessment, the test developers recommend that the instrument be used primarily for research into group differences, and, given the multifactorial pathogenesis of CHD, they state that the test should not be used by itself to predict individual risk. The instrument proposes to tap three factors within type A: speed and impatience, job involvement, and hard-driving-competition.

The JAS is easily administered and the majority of subjects complete the instrument in 15 to 20 minutes. Each response is assigned numerical points based on the product of the item regression weight and the optimal scaling weight for that response. The sum of the points for all items constitute the raw score. Hand-scoring templates are available, but machine scoring is encouraged.

Normative data are based on a 2588 male sample drawn exclusively from individuals in middle- and upper-echelon jobs. One serious flaw in this area of evaluation is the total absence of female subjects in both the development and normative stages of test construction. This further compounds the rather narrow socioeconomic group that was employed in the normative population.

Previous to this instrument, Rosenman et al., (1964) designed a structured interview protocol to assess the type A behavior pattern. Items for the JAS were derived from this interview, as well as from Jenkins's observations of interview behavior and the theory of type A behavior. A major flaw in the development sequence of the JAS was the use of discriminant function as the prime tool of scale construction. Each successive form of the test was changed substantially insofar as specific item content. Without adequate data on cross-validation, items were dropped, whereas others, retained on the basis of discriminant utility, had to be dropped later when new samples were employed. Discriminant function analysis can always be made to separate construction sample groups, but these discriminations may not hold up on cross-validation.

Test-retest reliabilities at 4- to 6-month intervals ran from .65 to .82 on the four factors, with internal consistency ranging from .73 to .85.

Turning to validity, the construct underlying the test has some intuitive logic as well as empirical support. Initially developed to maximize its correlation with the structured interview, the JAS attempts to adhere closely to its major features. As development progressed, however, particularly in later stages, it became uncertain as to whether the original type A domain was still being fully addressed; that is, the items selected and the factors produced may have become a product of statistical manipulation and sample idiosyncracies. Each step in the construction phase appeared to move the instrument farther away from the original base in the structured interview.

The developers recommend that the instrument be used primarily for research into group differences. It has been employed as a predictor of CHD, with some success, although recent literature shows that it does not improve on the predictive accuracy of the structured interview itself (Brand et al., in press.) The instrument does not propose to provide information on the progress and management of ongoing disease processes.

The JAS is directed at the examination of type A behavior. In spite of some difficulties with the instrument, it has been used to assign individuals to preventive intervention groups. Another application would be in regard to studies on whether patients diagnosed as having coronary heart disease pursue treatment, and, if so, what kind of treatment. Given the methodological problems of the instrument and its focus on only one aspect of functioning, other indices of the individuals' moods, health beliefs, and coping style should be utilized to elucidate the answers to such research questions.

PERSONALITY/COPING STYLE INVENTORIES

The following instruments deal with the realm of personality functioning rather than with single traits or dimensions. They represent different conceptions of personality and different development procedures. The instruments included are the 16 Personality Factor Inventory, the Minnesota Multiphasic Personality Inventory, and the Millon Behavioral Health Inventory.

The 16 Personality Factor Inventory (16PF)

The 16 PF (Cattell et al., 1970), one of the oldest personality tests currently in use, was first published in 1949. It is composed of a multidimensional set of 16 scales arranged in omnibus form. If the supplement is used, it seeks to tap 23 personality dimensions. The most commonly used form, comprised of 187 trichotomous items, is designed to measure what Cattell terms "source traits" rather than syndromes. The traits evaluated are said to have withstood critical examination of over 30 years of factor-analytic research. Since the scales are seen as factorially pure, there is no item overlap; consequently, each scale score is gauged by responses to between only 10 and 13 items.

A paper-and-pencil self-report inventory, the 16PF takes generally less than 45 minutes for the subject to complete and requires no assistance from the individual administering the test. Hand-scoring templates, as well as machine-scoring and computer-generated narratives, are available. Raw scores are transformed into sten or standard ten scores for the 16 traits. A variety of normative samples have been developed over the years. Standardization of the instrument involved a sample of 15,000 normal adults; however, it is unclear from the manual as to the nature and size of the original construction samples.

The traits are viewed as bipolar and scores are evaluated in terms of their location on the trait continuum. A variety of publications are available to help in interpreting scores (Karson & O'Dell, 1976), including a book specifically addressing the issue of the medical patient (Krug, 1977).

A significant body of literature has been developed utilizing the 16PF; nevertheless, the meaning of these results is often unclear. Regarding initial construction, Rorer (1972) states that the scales are of indeterminate origin and unknown significance. Data gathered in support of the instrument often employ samples selected in an unknown way and the manual is not very specific as to which form, developmental stage, or population was employed in many of the reported studies. One of the continuing difficulties in evaluating this instrument is the atypical manner in which data are presented in the handbook (Cattell et al., 1970). Although large quantities of data are presented, they are not comparable to standard psychometric evaluation techniques.

Test-retest reliabilities are reported to be in the .70 to .90 range short term, and drop to .50 to .80 at 2 months. Split-half reliabilities used to assess internal consistency by dividing the whole test into two halves that should be equivalent, or nearly so, have indicated considerable within-factor heterogeneity. There is a high likelihood that several of the supposedly pure factors subsume a number of different traits. This finding is especially troublesome since the instrument rests on the factorial purity of the 16 traits. No effort is made to provide correlation data in the manual with instruments purported to measure similar traits. Furthermore, the factoring method that Cattell has used is but one of many available, each of which might have produced different results. Correlations between identical scales on different forms of the test are sometimes very low, ranging from .15 to .82; in fact, some scales correlate more highly with other scales than with their matched scales. This puts into question the meaning and reliability of these scales; at the very least, it makes comparison across forms impossible.

The 16PF has been proposed as suitable for assessing the personality of normal individuals. If valid, it may actually be more suitable with so-called normals than with general psychiatric populations for whom it has also been claimed to be useful.

In reviewing this instrument, one is left with a sense of the considerable methodological sophistication of its constructors. At the same time, one is struck by the idiosyncratic conception of personality and the reluctance to compare this instrument and its results with anything other than itself. The use of esoteric proofs and the absence of more widely employed techniques seriously hamper the outsider in efforts to evaluate the instrument. These deficits and idiosyncrasies seriously compromise the confidence one may have in the 16PF's construct validity and consequent usefulness.

In spite of these problems, the 16PF has been widely used with a variety of populations. Developed to evaluate the "normal" personality, its use was encouraged with medical patients. For those clinicians familiar and comfortable with this instrument, the information on patients' profiles may be of some value. In contrast to the instruments presented earlier, the 16PF proposes to look at the full spectrum of the normal personality and therefore would provide information across a wider range than would single-dimension instruments.

Minnesota Multiphasic Personality Inventory (MMPI)

The MMPI is an empirically derived instrument that was constructed by Hathaway and McKinley in 1939 to serve as an objective aid in a psychiatric case workup and as a tool for determining the severity of specific psychiatric conditions. In its original development the MMPI had little to do with personality traits. As stated by Dahlstrom et al., (1972), the MMPI was developed and validated as a psychiatric nosologic categorizing device leading to dichotomous discriminations between psychiatric patients and normals. They wrote,

> Although the content covered in the MMPI item pool included by far a larger array of personological topics than in any other instrument available, subsequent studies have indicated that—while some areas of emotional maladjustment may be over-represented (Block, 1965)—items referring to values, to primary group relationships, and to mood, temperament, and various special attitudes are probably too scarce to provide a well-balanced coverage of the domain of personality (see Schofield, 1966, p. 6).

The 566-item true-false questionnaire has 10 basic clinical scales: hypochondriasis, depression, hysteria, psychopathic deviance, male sexual introversion, paranoia, psychasthenia, schizophrenia, hypomania, and social introversion, along with the following validity scales: cannot say, lie scale, confusion scale or straight validity, K or suppressor factor.

The test was developed so that those 16 years old or above with 6 years of schooling would be able to complete the inventory. The instrument takes an average of 1.5 hours to complete, although there are no limits to the time allotted to complete the inventory.

Hand scoring templates are available, as is machine scoring: Scores are often transformed into profiles. Raw scores are converted to T-scores with separate norms for males and females. Unfortunately, T-score scaling assumes a normal distribution of the trait, an unlikely assumption given the highly variable prevalence rates of the syndromes involved.

The original normative group was drawn from samples of Minnesota adults with separate male and female groups. Most lived in rural or semi-rural areas, worked in skilled or semiskilled trades, and had an eighth grade education. The test itself has not been renormed since this 1940 sample, although such efforts are currently under way.

Originally, only single-scale elevations were interpreted. Over the years extensive clinical data have led to its increased utility. A number of code-books have been written to aid in profile interpretations. (Gilberstadt & Duker, 1965; Good & Brantner, 1974; Lachar, 1974; Marks & Seeman, 1963).

Construction criterion groups were selected from adult psychiatric clinics and wards of the University of Minnesota hospitals; "normal" subjects were families and visitors of the patients. Items were selected for inclusion in a scale based on their capacity to discriminate between normals and each of the criterion groups. No effort was made at that time to examine scale overlap or to develop a ratinale for item selection. Cross-validation samples were employed to evaluate the stability of the obtained separation and the generality of initial scale findings. Of the 550 items (16 are repeated), 351 are utilized in scoring the initial 10 clinical scales.

The MMPI is without doubt the most thoroughly researched personality instrument available. One problem in evaluating the inventory is that its manual has not been updated since 1967, and vast quantities of information on the test's empirical utililty and validation reside in hundreds of journal articles often beyond the reach of all but the most diligent students. However, a significant amount of data is published concisely in the two-volume handbook (Dahlstrom et al., 1972).

Test-retest reliability in one sample at 3 to 4 days ranged from .56 to .88, with the majority in the low .80s. Psychiatric patients show 1 week test-retest ranging from .59 to .86, with the majority in the high .70s. At 1 year, test-retest correlations drop to the range of .36 to .72. Test-retest can be difficult to interpret because it is not possible to discriminate real change from reliability error, particularly in the case of psychiatric patients undergoing treatment over extended periods of time. Kuder-Richardson internal consistency estimates are reported on a sample employing the KR21 formula. These ranged from .36 to .93, with a median of .70.

Validity data are best summarized in the MMPI Handbook (Dahlstrom et al., 1972).

As one reads through reviews of the MMPI chronologically, one is struck by the changing response of those describing the test. Reviews such as that of Benton and Probst in 1945 state that there is a signficant agreement on ratings and test scores on only psychopathic deviate, paranoia, and schizophrenia, but not on the other scales. Schmidt (1945) wrote that psychiatric patients can be distinguished from normals, but it is difficult to distinguish among different abnormal populations. Rotter (1945), in his review, thoughtfully notes that reliability and validity are dependent upon the reliabililty and validity of the criterion disease groups themselves, which appear to have been much less than might be desired. For example, those diagnosed as belonging to one disease group were more likely than not to have their highest score on a scale other than the expected one. Ellis (1959) stated that the individual diagnostic utililty of the instrument was still in question but that it was useful for purposes of group discrimination. Adcock (1965) noted that the instrument failed to demonstrate discriminative validity regarding those who do and do not need help in a normal population. He went on to indicate that most clinicians assume the validity of the instrument rather than evaluate it as critically as one should. This acceptance often led to misinterpretations of the meaning of scores. Lingoes (1965) continued in his review to mention difficulties in discriminating among groups of psychiatric patients.

Undoubtedly, the best instrument of its generation, the MMPI, has assumed an almost mystical impregnability as a function of its age. For its time and purpose, its excellence of construction was unmatched.

The MMPI has been employed in a variety of health applications with some equivocal results. Most frequently, it has been used to differentiate psychosomatic from organic disease, to delineate psychological factors associated with psychosomatic disorders, and to predict the outcome of surgery or recovery from illness (Dahlstrom et al., 1972). As Butcher and Owens (1978) note, however, the MMPI does not appear to differentiate successfully psychosomatic types with the commonly noted 1-3/3-1 elevation of organic disease (Schwartz et al., 1972). Although utilized in a number of studies with medical patients, the MMPI appears to serve as an aid only if psychiatric issues are prominent. Of course, psychiatric issues are sometimes a serious concern in regard to an individual medical patient. Here the clinician may find MMPI data of real value. This is particularly true if the clinician has extensive experience in the utilization of the MMPI with patients having the specific medical problem in question. Since this instrument is appropriate only when psychiatric problems are a significant component of the patient's problem, it would not be suitable for addressing the degree of distress either co-occurrent or consequent to a medical problem. For example, although the MMPI could serve to evaluate the level of clinical depression in an oncology patient referred for his or her failure to comply with needed medical treatment, it would not be suitable in research on dysphoria in newly diagnosed diabetes. Both the intensity range and issues addressed by the MMPI would be inappropriate when applied to the analysis of psychological mediators of illness or disease.

Million Behavior Health Inventory (MBHI)

The MBHI was developed specifically with medical-behavioral decision-making issues in mind (Millon et al., 1982). A major goal in constructing the MBHI was to keep the total number of items comprising the inventory small enough to encourage its use in all types of diagnostic and treatment settings, yet large enough to permit the assessment of a wide range of clinically relevant behaviors. Geared to an eighth grade reading level, it contains 150 items.

Diagnostic instruments such as the MBHI have increased usefulness if they are linked systematically to a comprehensive clinical theory or are anchored to empirical validation data gathered in their construction (Loevinger, 1957). The eight basic "coping styles" comprising the first scales of the MBHI are derived from a theory of personality (Millon, 1969). The six "psychogenic attitude" scales were developed to reflect psychosocial stressors found in the research literature to be significant precipitators or exacerbators of physical illness. The final six scales comprising the present form were empirically derived for the MBHI either to appraise the extent to which emotional factors complicate particular psychosomatic ailments or to predict psychological complications associated with a number of diseases.

Self-administered, with instructions printed on the questionnaire, the inventory can be completed by the great majority of individuals in 20 to 25 minutes. Multiple-keyed, the test is best machine scored, computer synthesized, and interpreted. The raw scores on the 20 scales are transformed into base-ratio scores. These conversions were determined by known or estimated prevalence data to maximize correct classifications, as argued by Meehl & Rosen (1955).

Norms for the MBHI are based on several groups of nonclinical and numerous samples of medical patients involved in diagnosis, treatment, or follow-up. The nonclinical groups involved in the construction phases of test development consisted of subjects drawn from several settings (e.g., colleges, health maintenance organizations, nursing schools, medical schools, factories, etc.) and was composed of 212 males and 240 females; the test construction patient group, drawn from diverse clinical population (e.g., surgical clinics, pain centers, dialysis units, cancer programs, etc.) consisted of 1194 persons, of which 130 males and 170 females were selected as a representative cross section for purposes of developing construction norms. An additional series of patient populations comprised of 437 males and 482 females were involved in development and cross-validation of the six empirically derived scales. Hence, there was a total of 2113 patients and 452 nonclinical individuals used to validate the instrument.

Interpretation is based on both profile configurations and single-scale elevations. The first eight scales, the *basic coping styles*, characterize individuals regarding interpersonal and personality traits. For most individuals, these characteristics blend with other features in a configural pattern of several scales.

The *psychogenic attitude* scales represent the personal feelings and perceptions of the person regarding different aspects of psychological stress presumed to increase psychosomatic susceptibility or to aggravate the course of a disease already present. Scores are gauged by comparing these attitudes to those expressed by a cross section of both healthy and physically ill adults of the same sex. Some details concerning these six scales may be useful.

The "chronic tension" scale gauges level of stress, a factor that has repeatedly been found to relate to the incidence of a variety of diseases. More specifically, qualitative studies of chronic stress, such as persistent job tensions or marital problems, have been carried out with particular reference to their impact on heart disease, often addressed as type A-type B behavior (Friedman & Rosenman, 1974; Gersten et al., 1976; Jenkins, 1976; Rahe, 1977). Constantly on the go, type A individuals live under considerable self-imposed pressure and have trouble relaxing. Frequently endorsed for certain aspects of this behavior, such individuals are often found in positions of responsibility and are well targeted for preventive intervention.

The "recent stress' scale addresses the patients' perception of events in the recent past that were experienced as stressful. This is a phenomenological assessment similar to the Social Readjustment Rating Scale (Holmes & Rahe, 1967) and (the Life Experience Survey Sarason et al., 1978). High scorers on this scale are assumed to have an increased susceptibility to serious illness for the year following test administration. Recent marked changes in their life predicts a significantly higher incidence of poor physical and psychological health than that found in the population at large (Andrew, 1970; Rahe & Arthur, 1968; Yunik, 1979). Identifying patterns of susceptibility is of particular importance in health settings where preventive interventions may prove both beneficial and cost effective.

The "premorbid pessimism" scale represents a dispositional attitude of helplessness-hopelessness that has been implicated in the appearance or exacerbation of a variety of diseases such as multiple sclerosis, ulcerative colitis, and cancer (Mei-Tal et al., 1970; Paull & Hislop, 1974; Schmale, 1972; Stavraky et al., 1968). It differs from other "depression" indices by noting characterological tendencies toward viewing the world in a negative manner. High scorers on this scale are disposed to interpret life as a series of troubles and misfortunes and are likely to intensify the discomforts they experience with real physical and psychological difficulties (Levine, 1980; Yunik, 1980). Again, this scale is of particular salience in identifying individuals whose personal life and health may suffer as a consequence of these feelings.

The "future despair" scale focuses on the individual's willingness to plan and look forward to the future (Engel, 1968; Wright, 1960). This is more likely than the previous scale to tap the person's response to current difficulties and circumstances rather than a general or lifelong tendency to view things negatively. High scorers do not look forward to a productive future life and view medical difficulties as seriously distressing and potentially life-threatening.

"Social alienation" looks at the level of familial and friendship support, both real and perceived, that appears to relate to the impact of various life stressors (Cobb, 1977; Rabkin & Streuning, 1976). This sense of aloneness had been detailed in sociological literature (Berkman, 1967; Comstock & Partridge, 1972; Moss, 1977; Parkes, Benjamin & Fitzgerald, 1969). High scorers are prone to physical and psychological ailments. A poor adjustment to hospitalization is also common. These individuals perceive low levels of family and social support and may not seek medical assistance until illness is extremely discomforting. Being able to target these individuals would allow the development of alternative support systems for them.

All the above stressors seem to be significantly modulated upward or downward by the preoccupations and fear that individuals may express about their physical state, a characteristic addressed in the "somatic anxiety" scale. Studies of what may be called somatic anxiety reflect the general concerns that people have about their bodies (Lipsitt, 1970; Lowy, 1977; Lucente & Fleck, 1972; Mechanic & Volkart, 1960). High scorers on this scale tend to be hypochondriacal and susceptible to various minor illnesses. They experience an abnormal amount of fear concerning bodily functioning and are likely to overreact to the discomforts of surgery and hospitalization (Green et al., 1980). Such preoccupations often lead patients to excessive searching for medical treatment.

The next set of three scales was derived empirically. They have been labeled the *psychosomatic correlates* scales and are designed for use only with individuals who have previously been medically diagnosed as exhibiting one of the following specific disease syndromes: allergy, gastrointestinal problems, or cardiovascular difficulties. The scores of each scale gauge the extent to which the person's responses are similar to comparable diagnosed patients whose illness has been judged substantially psychosomatic or whose course has been complicated by emotional or social factors.

The last three of the empirically derived scales—labeled *prognostic indices*—seek to identify future treatment problems or difficulties that may arise in the course of the individual's illness. The scores of each scale, "pain treatment responsivity;" "life-threatening reactivity": and "emotional vulnerability," gauge the extent to which the person's responses are similar to patients whose course of illness or treatment has been more complicated and unsatisfactory than is typical.

The MBHI was developed following procedures recommended by Loevinger (1957) and Jackson (1970), in that validation was an ongoing process involved in all the phases of test construction, rather than a procedure for assessing or corroborating the instrument's accuracy following completion.

The three aspects of this validation procedure are labeled theoretical-substantive, internal-structural, and external-criterion.

Theoretical-substantive Validation Stage. Over 1000 items were gathered from numerous sources, including other psychological tests and abnormal and personality tests, and some were written specifically for item pool purposes. Items were developed so as to cover the full range of characteristics to be tapped by both the personality and psychogenic scales. At this stage the number of items in the personality-style scales ranged from 60 to 135. The psychogenic-attitude scale items ranged in number from 37 to 57. The item set for the 6 empirically derived scales was drawn entirely from the final pool based on the 14 personality and psychogenic scales; they were not subject to initial theoretical-substantive analysis. Items were balanced at this stage so that approximately half of them could be answered in order that the response "true" would signify the style or attitude, and half in order that the response would be "false"; balance of this type was built in to attempt to correct for "acquiescent" bias (Jackson & Messick, 1960).

Items were deleted according to the following general criteria: too complicated for patient understanding, obvious social desirablility bias, lack of clarity in phrasing, probable extreme endorsement frequency. Items were retained if they exemplified the traits of the scale for which they were written, and efforts were made to cover the full range of behaviors and attitudes typified by a given scale. To achieve this, researchers asked 10 health professionals, with knowledge of personality theory and experience with psychological traits among medical patients, independently to sort these items into their theoretically appropriate personality and psychogenic categories. The criteria for inclusion required that the item be sorted into the "correct" scale by at least seven of the judges.

Internal-structural Validation Stage. To accord with the theoretical model, items should give evidence not only of substantial within-scale homogeneity but also of selective overlap with theoretically related scales. Item and scale overlap within the MBHI was both expected and constructed in line with theoretical considerations: This contrasts with other instruments, such as the MMPI, where overlap among items on different scales is solely a function of empirically obtained covariations. A detailed explanation of this rationale may be found in the Millon Clinical Multiaxial Inventory (MCMI) manual (Millon, 1977).

According to the theory underlying both the MCMI (Millon, 1969) and the MBHI, no personality style or psychogenic attitude is likely to consist of entirely homogeneous and discrete psychological dimensions. Rather, these styles and attitudes comprise complex characteristics, as well as having distinctive features sharing many traits. Items are expected to exhibit their strongest but not their only association with the specific scale for which they were developed. The ultimate test of an item's or scale's efficiency is not statistical, but instead, is discriminatory or predictive; procedures that enhance high item-scale homogeneity through studies of internal consistency are the best methods for optimizing, rather than maximizing, discriminations among scales.

The initial items had been chosen in accord with theoretical-substantive validation data and were reduced on grounds of preliminary internal consistency and structural validation to the 289 "best." This 289-item "personality" form was administered to over 2500 persons in a variety of settings, somewhat over half being students at urban universities; medical populations were not included in this evaluation phase.

Several procedures were followed after this form had been administered to these subjects. Most importantly, item-scale homogeneities were again calculated using measures of internal consistency; additionally, true and false endorsement frequencies were obtained. Point-biserial correlations (corrected for overlap) were calculated between each personality scale. To maximize scale homogeneity, investigators retained for further evaluation only items that showed their highest correlation with the scale to which they were originally assigned. With few exceptions, items showing a correlation below .30 were eliminated. The median biserial correlation for all items for all personality scales was .47. The final number of items retained for inclusion in the MBHI from the provisional 289-item inventory was 64; these comprised the core group of coping-style items for the final 150-item inventory.

Items for the six psychogenic attitude scales were developed on theoretical-substantive grounds, following the development of the core 64 personality items. Lists of approximately 35 to 60 items were developed for each of the six scales on the basis of previous research by other investigators into the characteristics to be measured. These item lists were then rated by clinicians with experience in assessing the effects of psychological influences upon physical illness. Only items "correctly" placed by more than 75 percent of the raters were considered for inclusion in the inventory. Efforts were made to include some representation of the several diverse traits comprising each scale. By this procedure, 83 items in total were added to the core group of 64 personality items; an additional 3 "correction" items were also included, resulting in a final form of 150 items.

External-criterion Stage. The final 150-item form of the inventory was administered in a large number of medical settings in order to develop a series of empirically derived scales. The central idea behind this step, both as a construction approach and as a method of validation, is that items comprising a test scale should be selected on the basis of their empirically verified association with a significant and relevant criterion measure. The procedure by which this association is gauged is also direct. Preliminary items are administered to two groups of subjects who differ on the criterion measure. The "criterion" group exhibits the trait with which the item is to be associated, whereas the "comparision" group does not. In the case of the MBHI, all subjects were patients with a given diagnosis, but they varied according to clinical judgments regarding the degree to which various psychological or social complications were involved. After administration, true-false endorsement frequencies obtained with each group were calculated on every item. Items that differentiated the criterion group statistically from the comparison group were judged "externally valid." This was the approach followed in attempting to construct empirical scales that would either identify (correlate) or predict (prognose) certain clinically relevant criteria.

Point-biserial correlations between each of the 150 items and all scales were recalculated and reexamined. Items that showed high correlations (usually .30 or more) with any scale other than a theoretically incompatible one were added as items to that scale.

A central factor in the evaluation of any psychological instrument is whether the results obtained with it are reliable. It is particularly difficult to address this question with instruments designed to measure personality traits; it is even more difficult when attitudes that may reflect transient or situational concerns are being appraised. Change is inevitable in these states. Thus, low test-retest reliabilities may be a function of changing circumstances rather than intrinsic measurement errors.

At 4½ months the coping style scales showed reasonably high test-retest reliabilities, with most in the range of .77 to .88 and a mean of .82. The psychogenic attitude scales also show high reliabilities, averaging around .85, as do the empirically derived scales, at about .80, with the single exception of emotional vulnerability. KR20s were calculated as the optimal method for addressing internal consistency. The KR20 coefficients for all scales ranged from .66 to .90, with a median of .83.

Correlational data have been obtained employing a variety of different and often homogeneous patient and nonpatient samples. Among the inventories used were the MMPI, the SCL-90, I-E Scale, Beck's Depression Inventory, the Personal Orientation Inventory, the Life Events Survey, the Webber-Johansson Temperament Survey, and the California Personality Inventory, which are reported at length in the MBHI manual (Millon et al., 1982).

The MBHI addresses interpersonal style, attitudes shown to be significant to the management of health concerns, likelihood of psychological components of medical problems, and specific prognostic issues. It uses this information to make probabalistic statements about the individual's behavior in relation to illness, its management, and health care personnel. Directly addressing specified disease processes and their management, the manual provides the basis for making recommendations across a variety of medical problems regarding the likelihood of illness occurring and probable progress as well as optimal management of the disease process.

The MBHI can be used for both research and purposes of individual prediction. For example, the effect of coping styles on outcome and patient management is readily studied with the MBHI. It serves to predict successfully behaviors such as isolation, hostility toward health personnel, and excessive complaining and emotionality. It also shows significant value as a clinical tool. Detailing the patients' style of relating to the world, attitudes toward their specific medical problems and health care personnel, the MBHI provides a framework in which to establish treatment plans. Further, information obtained from scores on the psychogenic attitude scales allow the clinician to evaluate the patients' level of concern across a wide and salient range of issues.

A case report is presented to illustrate how the MBHI can be used with medical patients to elucidate difficulties and enhance treatment.

The Treatment of George C.

George C. was an obese 54-year-old divorced bookkeeper with a long history of multiple medical complaints. He had demonstrated a pattern of frequent illness resulting in his seeking medical attention and repeated evaluation for a wide variety of medical problems. His cardiovascular difficulties were long-standing, with a history of elevated cholesterol levels, hypertension, and angina. Furthermore, his father died of myocardial infarction at the age of 47, and his older brother suffered a heart attack at 58. In fact, it was his brother's attack that initially brought George to his internist, complaining of increased angina and generalized anxiety over his health.

A stress test and other diagnostic evaluations indicated moderate blockage, with good function in spite of this blockage. Surgery was not recommended at that time, but an exercise and diet regimen were established. George began his diet and exercise program; however, within 1 year he had gained 15 additional pounds, partly in response to the stresses of his second divorce. Hospitalized 6 months later, he was diagnosed as having a mild heart attack, and, subsequently, was reevaluated for coronary bypass surgery. Surgery was recommended and completed at this time.

George had not changed his set, expectancies, or characteristic life patterns when he donned the patient's gown. Rather, his entire set of past experiences, current fears, and beliefs of the future colored aspects of his enactment of the patient role. Following the levels of analysis described in the beginning of this chapter, we look first at the patient's overt behaviors. George, although worried about health and fearful of heart disease had proven noncompliant. Although willing to seek the physician's evaluation, he chose, when stressed, to discontinue a necessary diet and exercise regimen. He had stated that he was upset and worried, but it appeared that the focus was largely on medical problems. One can only conjecture that perhaps his failing marriage figured prominently in precipitating his worried and fearful state. In fact, it might have been his anticipated loss of emotional support that caused him to seek attention and reassurance, as if employing the health care system to replace his wife in the event of his loss. While all this was occurring, George's body was reacting to the stressors along a variety of biophysical pathways leading to an increased risk of disease.

The results of the MBHI taken by the patient early in his hospitalization are seen in Figure 8.1, and a brief abstract from the MBHI computer interpretive report follows.

This patient is characteristically tense, exhibits an undercurrent of sadness and anger, and is occasionally moody, anxious and irritable taking a pessimistic and negative outlook on life. Vigilant about what others think, he is watchful for fear of being hurt. There is an inclination to react to events in a

```
              REPORT FOR:  George C.                    SEX:   M              AGE:  54

ID NUMBER:                                    DATE:

CODE.

*****************************************************************************************
SCALES       * SCORE   *          PROFILE OF BR SCORES           *
             *RAW BR  *     35    60       75           85        100    DIMENSIONS
********+***+****+****+                                                   INTROVERSIVE
        1    12   13   XXX
                                                                         INHIBITED
        2    19   82   XXXXXXXXXXXXXXXXXXXXXXXXXXXXXXXXX
                                                                         COOPERATIVE
BASIC   3    19   52   XXXXXXXXXX
                                                                         SOCIABLE
        4    21   22   XXXXX
                                                                         CONFIDENT
STYLE   5    19   32   XXXXXXX
                                                                         FORCEFUL
        6    17   70   XXXXXXXXXXXXXXXXXXX
                                                                         RESPECTFUL
        7    25   43   XXXXXXXXX
                                                                         SENSITIVE
        8    21   79   XXXXXXXXXXXXXXXXXXXXXXXXXXXX
********+***+****+****+                                                   CHRONIC TENSION
        A    20   70   XXXXXXXXXXXXXXXXXXX
                                                                         RECENT STRESS
PSYCHO- B    13   72   XXXXXXXXXXXXXXXXXXXX
                                                                         PREMORB PESSIMISM
GENIC   C    30   87   XXXXXXXXXXXXXXXXXXXXXXXXXXXXXXXXXXXXXXX
                                                                         FUTURE DESPAIR
ATTI-   D    24   76   XXXXXXXXXXXXXXXXXXXXXXXXXX
                                                                         SOCIAL ALIENATION
TUDES   E    19   76   XXXXXXXXXXXXXXXXXXXXXXXXX
                                                                         SOMATIC ANXIETY
        F    27   90   XXXXXXXXXXXXXXXXXXXXXXXXXXXXXXXXXXXXXXXXXX
********+***+****+****+                                                   ALLERGIC INCLIN
PSYCHO- MM   16   81   XXXXXXXXXXXXXXXXXXXXXXXXXXXXXXXX
                                                                         GASTRO SUSCEPTBL
SOMATIC NN   10   70   XXXXXXXXXXXXXXXXXXX
                                                                         CARDIO  TENDENCY
        OO   22   85   XXXXXXXXXXXXXXXXXXXXXXXXXXXXXXXXXXXXX
********+***+****+****+                                                   PAIN TREAT RESPON
PROG-   PP   11   59   XXXXXXXXXXX
                                                                         LIFE-THREAT REACT
NOSTIC  QQ   12   69   XXXXXXXXXXXXXXXXXXX
                                                                         EMOTIONAL VULNER
        RR    7   80   XXXXXXXXXXXXXXXXXXXXXXXXXXXXXX
********+***+****+****+
```

FIGURE 8.1.   MHBI Profile of Geroge C.

somewhat unpredictable manner, with anger and disappointment expressed at one time, usually followed with apologies for being so emotional the next. This emotionality and angry vigilance is both physically and psychologically upsetting, and may dispose him to psychosomatic discomforts and ailments. In regard to illness he may be almost exhibitionistic when describing his symptoms, complaining at great length about an ever widening variety of discomforts, appearing at times to enjoy the role of being ill.

Characteristically negative and inclined to view life as difficult, the patient appears even more negative and distressed than usual, seeing the past as full of misfortunes about which nothing can be done. These attitudes are likely to complicate the course of an illness and its treatment. Further, he views the future as especially problematic. Anticipating that the future will not be productive, but complicated by personal difficulties and worsening medical problems, the patient feels unable to cope well or even to make an effort to do so. The patient reports far less emotional support from friends and family than is typical. In addition to characteristic emotional complaints, this patient is deeply pre-occupied with physical health concerns. Anxious over even minor discomforts, he may become very upset by any change in symptoms, which are invariably assumed to be for the worse. Health care personnel, alert to these excessive concerns, should allay anxiety, but retain focus on the real medical issues. If faced with major surgery, there is a chance, albeit small, that this patient will briefly display depression or disorientation.

Patients such as these tend to be as erratic in their relations with doctors as they are with others, alternately engaging and distancing to the exasperation of professionals. He may be inclined to collect doctors and medicaitons, shopping about, rarely satisfied with the results of any treatment or with the expertise of all professionals, combining a variety of treatments and medications without consultation or supervision. Sensitive to negative suggestions or exasperation on the part of health professionals, he will become easily upset or angered. It is likely that his cardiovascular complaints are greatly affected by his characteristic hypersensitivity to stress.

The MBHI report clearly indicated that George's health preoccupations were an integral part of a long standing pattern of cranky unhappiness and that seeking to change this pattern significantly was unrealistic. Efforts were directed, rather, to minimize the impact of this characteristic stance upon both the patient and his level of functioning.

When first hospitalized, George's anxiety led him to question his doctor and nurses frequently about any number of minor concerns. The instinct of the clinician is to provide detailed information to patients in response to these inquiries. However, what would occur at that point is that the patient would distort or misconstrue what was said, increasing his anxiety as well as his questioning. When an individual such as this patient is asking the doctor to tell him what will happen, he is actually requesting reassurance that everything will be all right. Sensitized to this possibility, the physician provided George with information about the nature of his illness and the surgical procedure while concurrently providing strong statments of support and confidence in the attending physician. This met the patient's need to trust, and however briefly, to comply with the demands he faced.

Post-operative Course and Long-term Follow-up.   The patient's surgery was successfully completed although he was briefly disoriented in surgical intensive care. All health care personnel had been encouraged to be particularly patient in allaying George's concerns. Due to his depression and life stresses, a psychologist was called in for both presurgical counseling and postsurgical follow-up. Anxious and fearful, George required encouragement to become active following his surgery. Provided with a forum in which to examine his fears, the patient was able to complete his postsurgical recovery successfully, albeit with checkered progress. The counseling process focused on long-term compliance. George continued to see the psychologist well into his outpatient rehabilitation program. Anticipating that the return to work would be difficult, George and his therapist developed strategies for his return, detailing his work schedule, a means of maintaining his new fitness regimen, and how and when he might share information regarding his medical status with coworkers. Three and one half years later, George remains active, is employed, and continues his diet and exercise program, with occasional lapses. Although he still expresses concerns and difficulties regarding interpersonal relationships, he senses that he is in command of his life, and particularly his physical well-being.

CONCLUSION

The process of evaluating the medical patient is currently evolving from a strictly medical-diagnostic approach to one encompassing the presenting symptoms along with events, actions, reactions, and personality interactions in an ever-changing presentation. Psychologists employing interview and diagnostic testing contribute to this evaluation by delineating psychosocial aspects of the patient's life as well as by developing diagnostic and prognostic statements.

This review of self-report inventories provides the practitioner with an overview of the state of the art. Ranging from simple checklists to single-trait assessments and multidimensional personality inventories, these instruments provide a variety of diagnostic options for the clinician. Unfortunately, even within this selected group, construction and post construction validation results have often proved disappointing. It is critical that the clinician utilizing a given instrument demonstrate caution in both application and interpretation. Employing tests developed and normed with psychiatric populations may fit old habits and be expedient, but only rarely have such instruments proven useful in nonpsychiatric health studies. Psychological assessment utilized in this fashion is new and instruments must be carefully evaluated regarding not only their construction, but also their suitability to provide answers to diagnostic and decision-making requirements.

References

Adams-Webber, J. (1963). *Perceived locus of control of moral sanctions*. Unpublished Master's thesis, Ohio State University.

Adcock, C. J. (1965). *Review of the MMCI*; In Oscar Buros (Ed.), *The 6th Mental Measurements Yearbook*. Highland Park, NJ: Gryphon Press.

Andrew, J. M. (1970). Recovery from surgery, with and without preparatory instruction, for three coping styles. *Journal of Personality and Social Psychology, 15*, 223–226.

Beck, A. T. (1972). *Depression: Causes and treatment*. (p. 186–207). Philadelphia: University of Pennsylvania Press.

Benton, A. L., & Probst, K. A. (1945). A comparison of psychiatric ratings with MMPI scores. *Journal of Abnormal and Social Psychology, 41*, 75–78.

Berkman, P. L. (1967). Spouseless motherhood, psychological stress, and physical morbidity. *Journal of Health and Social Behavior, 10*, 323–334.

Brand, R. J., Rosenman, R., Jenkins, C., Stoltz, R., & Zyzanski, S. (In press). Comparison of coronary heart disease prediction in the VCGS using the structures interview and the JAS assessments of the coronary-prone Type A behavior pattern. *Journal of Chronic Disease*.

Butcher, J. N., & Owens, P. L. (1978). Objective personality inventories: Recent research and some contemporary issues. In B. Wolman (Ed.), *Clinical diagnosis of mental disorders: A handbook*. New York: Plenum Press.

Cardi, M. (1962). An examination of internal versus external control in relation to academic failures. Unpublished Master's thesis. Ohio State University.

Catell, R. B., Eber, H. W., & Tatsouoka, M. M. (1970). *Handbook for the Sixteen Personality Factor Questionnaire (16PF)*. Champaign, IL: Institute for Personality and Ability Testing.

Cobb, S. (1977). Epilogue: Meditation on psychosomatic medicine. In Z. J. Lipowski, D. R. Lipsitt, & P. C. Whybrow (Eds.), *Psychosomatic medicine: Current trends and clinical applications*. New York: Oxford Press.

Comstock, G. W., & Partridge, K. B. (1972). Church attendance and health. *Journal of Chronic Disease, 25*, 665–672.

Dahlstrom, W. G., Welsh, G. S., & Dahlstrom, L. E. (1972). *An MMPI Handbook* (Vols. 1, II). Minneapolis: University of Minnesota Press.

Derogatis, L. R. (1977). *SCL-90-R (Revised Version Manual-1)*. Baltimore.

Derogatis, L. R., Abeloff, M., & McBeth, C. (1977). Cancer patients with their physicians in the perception of psychological symptoms. *Psychosomatics, 17*, 197–201.

Derogatis, L. R., Lipman, R. S., Rickels, K., Uhlenhuth, E. H., & Covi, L. (1974a). The Hopkins Symptom Checklist (HSCL): A self-report symptom inventory. *Behavioral Science, 19*, 1–15.

Derogatis, L. R., Lipman, R. S., Rickels, K., Uhlenhuth, E. H., & Covi. L. (1974b). The Hopkins Symptom Checklist (HSCL): A measure of primary symptom dimension. In P. Pichot (Ed.), *Psychological measurements in psychopharmacology*. Basel: Karger.

Efran, J. S. *Some personality determinants of memory for success and failure*. Unpublished doctoral dissertation, Ohio State University, 1963.

Ellis, A. (1959). *Review of the MMPI*; In Oscar Buros (Ed.), *5th Mental Measurements Yearbook*. Highland Park, NJ: Gryphon Press, (pp. 166–167).

Engel, G. L. (1968). A life setting conducive to illness: The given-up-giving-up complex. *Bulletin of the Menninger Clinic, 32,* 355–365.

Friedman, M., & Rosenman, R. H. (1974). *Type A behavior and your heart.* New York: Knopf.

Gersten, J. C., Frii, S. R., L& Lengner, T. S. (1976). Life dissatisfactions, job dissatisfaction and illness of married men over time. *American Journal of Epidemiology, 103,* 333–341.

Gilberstadt, H., & Duker, J. (1965). *A handbook for clinical and actuarial MMPI interpretation.* Philadelphia: Saunders.

Good, P., & Brantner, J. A. (1974). *Practical guide to the MMPI.* Minneapolis: University of Minnesota Press.

Green, C., Meagher, R., & Millon, T. (1980). The management of the "problem" patient in the milieu setting. Paper presented at the Society of Behavioral Medicine Meetings, New York, November.

Hathaway, S. R., & McKinley, J. C. (1967). *The Minnesota Multiphasic Personality Inventory Manual.* New York: Psychological Corp.

Head, R. (1979). *The impact of personality on the relationship between life events and depression.* Unpublished Doctoral dissertation, University of Miami.

Holmes, T. H., & Rahe, R. (1967). The social readjustment rating scale. *Journal of Psychosomatic Research, 11,* 213.

Jackson, D. N. (1970). A sequential system for personality scale development. In C. D. Spielberger (Ed.), *Current topics in clinical and community psychology.* (Vol. 2). New York: Academic Press.

Jackson, D. N., & Messick, S. (1960). Acquiescence and desirability as response determinants in the MMPI. *Educational and psychological measurement, 21,* 771–790.

James, W. H. (1957). *Internal versus external control of reinforcement as a basic variable in learning theory.* Unpublished doctoral dissertation. Ohio State University.

Jenkins, C. D. (1976). Psychological and social precursors of coronary disease. *New England Journal of Medicine. 284(6),* 307–317.

Jenkins, C. D. Zyzanski, S. J., & Rosenman, R. H. (1979). *Jenkins Activity Survey Manual.* New York: Psychological Corp.

Karson, S., & O'Dell, J. (1976). *Clinical use of the 16PF.* Champaign, IL: Institute for Personality and Ability Testing.

Kolitz, S. (1983). *The effect of personality style and depression upon the physical and emotional recuperation of patients who have sustained a first MI.* Unpublished Second Year Project. University of Miami.

Krug, S. E. (1977). *Psychological assessment in medicine.* Champaign, IL: Institute for Personality and Ability Testing.

Lachar, D. (1974). *The MMPI: Clinical assessment and automated interpretation.* Los Angeles: Western Psychological Services.

Lambley, P., & Silbowitz, M. (1973). Rotter's Internal-external scale and prediction of suicide contemplators among students. *Psychological Report, 33,* 585–586.

Lazarus, R. (1977). Cognitive and coping processes in emotion. In A. Monat & R. Lazarus (Eds.), *Stress and Coping.* New York: Columbia University Press.

Levenson, H. (1973). Multidimensional locus of control in psychiatric patients. *Journal of Consulting and Clinical Psychology, 41,* 397–404.

Levenson, H. (1981). Differentiating among internality, powerful others, and chance. In H. Lefcourt (Ed.), *Research with the locus of control construct.* (Vol. 1). New York: Academic Press.

Levine, R. (1979). *The impact of personality style upon emotional distress, morale and return to work in two groups of coronary bypass surgery patients.* Unpublished master's thesis, University of Miami.

Lingoes, J. C. (1965). *Review of the MMPI*; In Oscar Buros (Ed.), *6th Mental Measurements Yearbook* (pp. 316–317). Highland Park, NJ: Gryphon Press.

Lipsitt, D. R. (1970). Medical and psychological characteristics of "crocks." *International Journal of Psychiatry in Medicine, 1*, 15–25.

Loevinger, J. (1957). Objective tests as instruments of psychological theory. *Psychological Reports, 3*, 635–694.

Lowy, F. H. (1977). Management of the persistent somatizer. In Z. J. Lipowski, D. R. Lipsitt, & P. C. Whybrow, (Eds.), *Psychosomatic medicine: Current trends and clinical applications.* New York: Oxford Press.

Lucente, F. E., & Fleck, S. (1972). A study of hospitalization anxiety in 408 medical and surgical patients. *Psychosomatic Medicine, 34*, 304–312.

Marks, PJ., & Seeman, W. (1963). *The actuarial description of abnormal personality.* Baltimore: Williams & Wilkins.

Marston, M. (1969). Compliance with medical regimen as a form of risk taking in patients with myocardial infarctions. *Dissertation Abstracts International, 30*, 2151A–2152A.

Mechanic, D., & Volkart, E. H. (1961). Stress, illness behavior and the sick role. *American Sociological Review, 26*, 51–58.

Meehl, P. E., & Rosen, A. (1955). Antecedent probability and the efficiency of psychometric signs, patterns or cutting scores. *Psychological Bulletin, 52*, 194–216.

Mei-Tal, V., Meyerowitz, S., & Engel, G. L. (1970). The role of psychological process in a somatic disorder: Multiple sclerosis. 1. The emotions of illness onset and exacerbation. *Psychosomatic medicine, 32*, 67–86.

Millon, T. (1969). *Modern Psychopathology,* Philadelphia: Saunders.

Millon. T. (1982). *Millon Clinical Multiaxial Inventory Manual.* (2nd ed). Minneapolis: National Computer Systems.

Millon, T., Green, C., & Meagher, R. (1982). *Millon Behavioral Health Inventory Manual.* Minneapolis: National Computer Systems.

Moss, E. (1977). Biosocial resonation: A conceptual model of the links between social behavior and physical illness. In Z. J. Lipowski, D. R. Lipsitt, & P. C. Whybrow (Eds.), *Psychosomatic medicine: Current trends and clinical application.* New York: Oxford Press.

Osler, W. (1971). In W. P. D. Wrightsman (Ed.), *The emergence of scientific medicine.* Edinburgh: Oliver & Boyd.

Parkes, M., Benjamin, B., & Fitzgerald, R. G. (1969). Broken heart: A statistical study of incrased mortality among widowers. *British Medical Journal, 1*, 740–743.

Paull, A. & Hislop I. G. (1974). Etiologic factors in ulcerative colitis: Birth, death and symbolic equivalents. *International Journal of Psychiatry in Medicine, 5*, 57–64.

Phares, E. J. (1957). Expectancy changes in skill and chance situation. *Journal of Abnormal and Social Psychology, 54*, 339–342.

Rabkin, J. C., & Struening, E. L. (1976). Life events, stress and illness. *Science, 194*, 1013–1020.

Rahe, R. H. (1977). Subjects' recent life changes and their near future illness susceptibility. *Advances in Psychosomatic Medicine, 8*, 2–19.

Rahe, R. H. & Arthur, R. J. (1968). Life change patterns surrounding illness experience. *Journal of Psychosomatic Research, 11*, 341–345.

Rorer, L. G. (1972). *Review of the 16PE*; In Oscar Buros (Ed.), *7th Mental Measurements Yearbook.* Highland Park, NJ: Gryphon Press.

Rosenman, R. H., Friedman, M., Strau, R., Wurm, M., Kostichek, R., Hahn, W., & Werthessen, N. T. (1964). A predictive study of coronary heart disease: The Western Collaborative Group Study. *Journal of the American Medical Association, 189*, 15–22.

Rotter, J. B. (1945). *Review of the MMPI*; In Oscar Buros (Ed.), *3rd Mental Measurements Yearbook.* Highland Park, NJ: Gryphon Press.

Rotter, J. B. (1966). Generalized expectancies for internal versus external control of reinforcement. *Psychological Monograph, 80*,(1), 1−28.

Rotter, J. B., Liverant, S., & Crowne, D. P. (1961). The growth and extinction expectancies in chance controlled and skilled tests. *Journal of Psychology, 52,* 161−177.

Sarason, I. G., Johnson, J. H., & Siegel, J. M. (1978). Assessing the impact of life changes. *Journal of Consulting and Clinical Psychology, 46,* 932−946.

Schmale, A. H. (1972). Giving up as a final common pathway to changes in health. In Z. J. Lipowski (Ed.), *Psychological aspects of physical illness.* Basel, Switzerland: Karger.

Schmidt. H. O. (1945). Test profiles as a diagnostic aid: The MMPI. *Journal of Applied Psychology, 29,* 115−131.

Schofield, W. (1966). Clinical and counseling psychology: Some perspectives. *American Psychology, 11,* 122−131.

Schwartz, M. S., Osborne, D., & Krupp, N. E. (1972). Moderating effects of age and sex on the association of medical diagnoses and 1-3/3-1 MMPI profile *Journal of Clinical Psychology, 28,* 502−505.

Spielberger, C. D. Gorsush, R. L., & Lushene, R. (1970). *The State-Trait Anxiety Inventory Manual.* Palo Alto, CA: Consulting Psychologists Press.

Stavraky, K. M., Buck, C. N., Lott, J. S., & Wanklin, J. M. (1968). Psychological factors in the outcome of human cancer. *Journal of Psychosomatic Research, 12,* 251−259.

Wallston, K. A., & Wallston, B. S. (1981). Health locus of control scales. In H. Lefcourt (Ed.), *Research with the locus of control construct* (Vol. 1). New York: Academic Press.

Wallston, K. A., & Wallston, B. S. (1982). Who is responsible for your health? The construct of health locus of control. In G. S. Sanders & J. Suls (Eds.), *Social psychology of health and illness.* Hillsdale, NJ: Erlbaum.

Wallston, K. A., Wallston, B. S., & DeVellis, R. (1978). Development of the Multidimensional Health Locus of Control (MHLC) Scales. *Health Education Monographs, 6,* 161−170.

Wallston, B. S., Wallston, K. A., Kaplan, C. D., & Maides, S. A. (1976). Development and validation of the health locus of control scale. *Journal of Consulting and Clinical Psychology, 44,* 580−585.

Wider, A. (1948). *The Cornell Medical Index.* New York: Psychological Corp.

Wright, B. A. (1960). *Physical disability:* A psychological approach. New York: Harper & Row.

Yunik, S. (1980). *The relationship of personality variables and stressful life events to the onset of physical illness.* Unpublished doctoral dissertation, University of Miami.

9

Assessment in Health Psychology: A Cognitive-Behavioral Perspective

Dennis C. Turk
Robert D. Kerns

Health, disease, and illness are ambiguous concepts that vary in subjective meaning and experience. For example, it has frequently been observed that whether or not an individual seeks medical care often has little to do with his or her objective physical condition (e.g., Mechanic, 1968; Meichenbaum & Turk, 1982; Zola, 1966). Most individuals experience clinically significant symptoms of one kind or another during the major portion

Preparation of this chapter was supported in part by a Veterans Administration Merit Review Grant.

of their lives. Yet, according to White, et al. (1961), less than one third of the people who report experiencing illness episodes consult physicians. As Janis and Rodin (1979) recently noted, "A person's health-seeking behavior is to a great extent based on his or her peception of a bodily state, rather than on the body's true physical condition" (p. 488). Pennebaker (1982) has reported on an extensive program of research supporting the importance of subjective perceptions and appraisals and defines symptoms as "the awareness of some aspect of internal states." The important role of subjective interpretation and meaning can be noted along the entire health-disease (illness) continuum. The following examples are presented to support this proposition.

Harris and Guten (1979) surveyed over 800 individuals from the general population and noted that the majority of those contacted reported that they performed some behavior or set of behaviors to protect, promote, or maintain their health, from eating a balanced diet to having regular medical checkups. Interestingly, the "health-protective behaviors" that were reported by these subjects have not been consistently and objectively demonstrated to be effective. Yet they are performed with an expectancy that they will produce some beneficial outcome. Moreover, little association was reported between performance of one health-protective behavior and another. People seem to have some relatively idiosyncratic criteria that they employ in deciding what behaviors should be performed for health protection. At the present time little is known as to the nature of the relevant criteria people employ, although several recent studies have begun to investigate this area (e.g., Lau & Hartman, 1983; Turk, Rudy, & Salovey 1984).

It has been suggested that the mere presence of stressful events or stimuli may be less significant in the etiology of disease than in the manner in which these stimuli are interpreted (e.g., Rabkin & Struening, 1976; Turk, Meichenbaum, & Genest, 1983). For example, migraine headaches have been described as resulting from prolonged, excessively stressful situations. Henryk-Gutt and Rees (1973), however, found that the life stresses to which migraine suffers and headache-free individuals are exposed are practically identical. Katz et al. (1970) assessed 17-hydroxycorticosteroid ("stress hormone") levels in women several days before breast tumor biopsies were performed and noted that the patients evidenced a broad range of stress responses, despite the fact that they were confronted with the same objective stressors—biopsies and potential diagnosis of breast cancer. It has been suggested that both physiological and psychological stressors have a final common pathway, the *perception of threat* (Lazarus, 1966; Mason, 1971).

Significant individual differences have been reported among patients responding to aversive medical diagnostic procedures (e.g., Kendall et al. 1979), adherence to programs for health risk reduction (e.g., DiMatteo & DiNicola, 1982), acute illnesses (e.g., Cassel, 1976), chronic illnesses, (e.g., Turk, 1979), and terminal illnesses (e.g., Weisman, 1979). Hypotheses to explain these individual differences have intrigued health care professionals for a long time. The examples presented were selected to underscore the importance of psychological mediating factors in defining health, interpreting symptoms, and responding to various medical procedures and medical conditions.

A first step to understanding differential responding to what might appear to be similar stimuli is the development of adequate assessment procedures. From the examples presented it is apparent that the development and validation of assessment procedures must focus on two primary goals: (1) the need for inceasingly sensitive strategies designed to delineate further individual and/or group differences and (2) the need to develop strategies designed to evaluate factors that potentially mediate or contribute to these differences in responding. Individuals' cognitive appraisals of relevant stimuli, including their idiosyncratic *beliefs, attitudes,* and *interpretations* are essential targets in addressing both these goals.

Before examining recent developments in the assessment literature addressing health-related issues, we will present a brief discussion of the cognitive-behavioral perspective that serves as the basis for many of these developments. This discussion will be followed by an overview of the purposes and goals of cognitive-behavioral assessment. Finally, we will present the general types of cognitive-behavioral assessment strategies with more detailed description and critique of specific strategies that serve as models for future developments.

COGNITIVE-BEHAVIORAL PERSPECTIVE

Individuals are constantly being inundated with a wide array of information from both internal and external sources. People not only respond to available stimuli and observe the consequences of their behavior, but also actively select from the information present and transform and categorize stimuli in idiosyncratic fashions, thereby partially determining some of the stimuli that impinge upon them. The objective environment is only one determinant of what people attend to, perceive, feel, think, and how they behave. By altering the immediate environment, selectively attending to stimuli, attributing meaning, interpreting information, generating expectancies, creating self-inducements, and assigning conditional incentives, people influence both their internal and external environments and their behavior (Turk, Meichenbaum, & Genest, 1983). The experience generated by behavior also contribute to what individuals think, feel, and do, which in turn affect subsequent behavior. A continuous reciprocal transaction between the individual and his or her environment determines what that individual thinks, feels, and does (Bandura, 1978). From a cognitive-behavioral perspective, assessment of individuals' responses, whether they are related to health maintenance, the presence of physical symptoms or adjustments to stress, disease, or medical diagnosis or treatment, must focus on cognitive, affective, behavioral, environmental, and physiological factors and their interactions.

As has been suggested, one hallmark of the cognitive-behavioral perspective is the fundamental assumption that individuals' conceptual and affective systems are intrinsically involved with health, disease, and illness. These conceptual systems include the patient's (1) values, beliefs, and goals regarding the maintenance of health, prevention of disease, and responses to symptoms and diseases (i.e., illness behavior, Kasl & Cobb, 1966; Mechanic, 1968); (2) information about diseases, risk behaviors, health-protective behaviors; (3) perceived self-competence or self-efficacy based largely on prior experience; and (4) role expectations and sets of action plans for responding to situational demands and internal states (Pennebaker, 1982; Turk, Meichenbaum, & Genest, 1983). Such cognitive and affective factors not only contribute to the patient's responses to disease, but also influence the ways people define health and illness; respond to symptoms, treatment, and incapacity; and utilize the health care system (Jones et al., 1981; Leventhal et al., 1980; Turk, Meichenbaum, & Genest, 1983).

The behaviors that individuals perform in response to conceptions of health, disease, and illness will also influence the environment and responses from others that may reinforce existing conceptualizations and behavior. For example, the patient who has a chronic medical condition may become hypervigilant to bodily sensations and seek attention from health care providers and significant others. The preoccupation with symptoms may elicit a variety of responses from others (e.g., reinforcing sick-role behaviors) and may confirm the individual's conception of him or herself as sick. Reinforcement of sick-role behaviors may result in continued performance of the behaviors, potentially even in the absence of sensory phenomena in order to obtain positive reinforcement or to avoid undesirable activities (e.g., Fordyce, 1976).

There are several additional characteristics that define the cognitive-behavioral perspective on assessment. These are related to two levels of assessment—assessment of *groups* of patients or individuals and assessment of *an individual.*

Assessment of Groups of Individuals

Intervention strategies developed within the context of the cognitive-behavioral perspective emerge from a theoretical understanding and empirical base of information about the target problem, its topography and associated variables, and a hypothesized model to describe the problem's development and maintenance. Although individual differences are presumed to be operating, both in terms of describing the problem and in evaluating response to intervention, a *nomothetic* approach to assessment is most often the rule rather than the exception.

Cognitive-behavioral analysis of groups of individuals in relation to a specific response, whether the analysis is for the purpose of describing the response or in manipulating the response (e.g., changing the response via the application of some treatment protocol), has many advantages over idiographic approaches, at least in the early phases of hypothesis testing. Perhaps most importantly, methods of empirical validation of behavioral constructs, factors involved in the development and maintenance of problematic behaviors, treatment efficacy, and so forth, are better developed and more widely accepted when group data are presented.

Assessment of groups of individuals are conducted for several purposes: (1) to identify mediators of a specific response; (2) to evaluate the efficacy of specific interventions for individuals with similar targeted problems; and (3) to evaluate not only whether interventions succeed, but also *how* they may have had their effects. Subsequently, through group designs incorporating a single comprehensive assessment approach, characteristics of groups of individuals who either fail or succeed in a particular intervention, or who conform or fail to conform to a particular descriptive model, can be identified. Such analyses can, therefore, lead to refinement of treatment strategies or theoretical models for some subset of the original group. Eventually, such a process can lead to a clearer understanding of individual differences, and, in the case of response change, this process can lead to optimal treatment decision making and planning. To paraphrase Paul's (1966) often cited statement, we note that this process should help establish what mediational factors, for what individual or group of individuals, delivered in what manner, by whom, will result in what types of effects, and for what reasons.

Assessment can serve an important heuristic, hypothesis-generating function that may lead to clarification of understanding and the modification of intervention programs. Once hypotheses are developed, they can be subjected to more formal tests.

Consider some examples of studies that have examined potentially important mediational factors across a variety of health-relevant situations (see also Kendall & Turk, 1984; Turk, Meichenbaum, & Genest 1983). Klein et al. (1965) found that among a sample of myocardial infaction patients, the subjective meaning of the heart attack was an important determinant of the degree of disability. An important consideration for these patients was how their medical condition was going to affect their roles as providers, parents, husbands, as well as their activities (Zborowski, 1969, identified similar concerns among a group of chronic pain patients). In another study with cardiac patients, Davis (1967) reported that farm workers suffering from a variety of cardiac diseases, reported some of the following beliefs that were attributed to their nonadherence to medical regimen: "If you wait long enough you can get over any illness," "Ilness and trouble is one way God shows displeasure," "Some of the old fashion remedies are better than the things you get in a drug store," "You need to give your body some rest from medicine once in a while otherwise your body becomes dependent on it."

Failure to consider such beliefs may account for the low levels of adherence to medical regimens frequently reported in the literature (Leventhal et al., 1983; Turk et al., (in press).

One area in which psychological mediating factors appear to be important is that of risk-related beheviors such as obesity, smoking, and alcohol abuse. In several studies obese clients have been asked to monitor weight-relevant thoughts and feelings (e.g., Leon et al., 1977; Mahoney, 1975; Sjoberg & Persson, 1979). Mahoney (1975) classified weight-relevent thoughts into five categories: (1) thoughts about pounds lost (e.g., "I've starved myself and I've only lost 2 pounds"), (2) thoughts about capabilities (e.g., I just don't have the willpower"), (3) excuses (e.g., "If I didn't have so much pressure at my job, I would lose weight"), (4) standard setting (e.g., "Well I blew it with that doughnut—my day is shot"), and (5) thoughts about actual food.

Sjoberg and Persson (1979) attempted to identify the conditions under which thoughts and feelings lead to deviations from weight control regimens. They reported that, in the majority of cases, episodes of overeating were preceded by maladaptive and distorted thinking, for example, "An extra sandwich now helps me to eat less later," or "I've already lost a lot of weight so I can indulge myself this once." Sjoberg and Persson also noted a "domino effect" such that initial backsliding often resulted in complete relapse. Leon et al. (1977) asked people on diets to record what they did to avoid overeating when they had the urge to eat. Two patterns were identified; namely, active behaviors that served as distractors from eating (e.g., doing the laundry) and covert activities such as visualizations of positive and negative self-images.

Individuals engage in smoking behavior for diverse reasons (e.g., social approval, to cope with negative affect), each tied to a variety of discriminative stimuli (e.g., social situations, after meals, driving a car). To examine the variety of covert processes related to smoking and maintenance of smoking cessation, several studies have asked successful and unsuccessful "quitters" to report on the nature of their smoking-related thoughts and coping techniques (e.g., Perri et al., 1977; Sjoberg & Johnson, 1978).

Sjoberg and Johnson (1978) noted the presence of both positive and negative moods preceding abstinent smokers' relapse as well as distorted reasoning similar to that identified for obese subjects: "I've been doing so well, I'll treat myself to just one cigarette." Relapsed smokers reported fatalistic attitudes about the results of treatment and a low sense of self-efficacy related to their repeated failures to quit—"Once a smoker, always a smoker." Best (1980) noted that at the 6-month follow-up in a smoking cessation study, 55 percent of the reasons given for relapse were related to coping with stress, five times more common than any other reasons given.

The mediational factors identified in samples of smokers and obese individuals are similar to those identified for relapse following an alcohol abuse program. Especially noted have been statements of low self-efficacy, use of alcohol to cope with stress, and the domino effect or what has been labeled the "abstinence violation effect"—one slip is viewed as an indicant of treatment failure with subsequent full-blown relapse (Marlatt & Gordon, 1980). These observations suggest that approaches for smoking reduction, obesity, and alcohol abuse might be more effective if the treatment were modified or supplemented by inclusion of approaches to modify clients thoughts and feelings, thus enabling the individual to develop alternative coping skills to deal with high-risk-of-relapse situations (e.g., social situations, after meals, while driving) and other particularly stressful situations.

Many intervention programs geared toward helping different groups of medical patients are based on some theoretical conceptions of problems that confront patient groups. For example, there is an a priori assumption that patients who have had breast cancer will suffer from depression and body image distortion. Recent research suggest that these assumptions are unfounded and that, although some patients may be depressed and experience distress related to distorted body image, the percentages of patients with these problems are relatively small (Peters-Golden, 1982; Worden & Weisman, 1977). Examining the specific and major concerns of patients (rather than relying on a priori theoretical assumptions) would facilitate tailoring interventions to the exact clinical needs of patients as well as the clarifiying the concerns of patients, in general (e.g., Turk et al., 1980).

These studies underscore the utility of obtaining information about internal states and mediating factors directly from the population of interest, although the degree to which such self-reports are veridical is yet unclear. The important point is that they serve a heuristic function by raising hypotheses that may be more directly evaluated in other research. We will discuss the utility of self-report data later in this chapter.

Assessment of Individuals

The major role of assessment of individual patients in the fostering of optimal decision making—decision making related to initial treatment planning and decision making throughout the intervention process. At the individual level, assessment instruments or procedures are geared toward acquiring information about specific aspects of the patient that will be useful in refining treatment plans beyond what can be derived from information about group norms. All questions and assessment procedures should be geared toward improving decision making. Assessment continues throughout treatment so that modifications in the plan or therapeutic goals can be implemented as indicated rather than adhered to as a rigid treatment protocol.

Examples may help emphasize this point about tailoring a relatively standard treatment protocol to meet the specific needs of an individual patient. In the chronic pain literature, both operant (Fordyce, 1976) and cognitive-behavioral (Turk, Meichenbaum, & Genest, 1983) models of pain and pain treatment have been proposed. Treatment strategies based on these models have been demonstrated to be effective (see recent reviews by Kerns et al., 1983; and Turner & Chapman, 1982); but, to date, no study has directly compared the efficacy of these two approaches.

In our Pain Management Program at the West Haven VA Medical Center, we commonly identify patients who, on the basis of a comprehensive, multidimensional cognitive-behavioral assessment protocol (Holzman, 1982), appear to be preferentially suited for a treatment that emphasizes one or more specific aspects of a more standard treatment regimen. One of our low back pain patients who emitted a high frequency of "pain behaviors" (e.g., grimacing, bracing, moaning) in the presence of his overly solicitous spouse appeared to be ideally suited for an operantly-oriented treatment. Additional assessment strategies were incorporated into the general assessment protocol to refine further the analysis of this particular patient's responses. Ultimately, the treatment protocol emphasized teaching the spouse about operant conditioning and the importance of consistent reinforcement of "well behaviors" (e.g., increased social activity, increased statements of well-being) in the context of a more general pain treatment approach.

As a function of the detailed pain assessment protocol, another of our pain patients was identified as clinically depressed, despite participation in frequent "reinforcing" activities. By means of careful interviewing and particular attention to maladaptive self-statements regarding her pain problem and her activities, a pattern of negative self-statements and catastrophic rumination was elicited. Cognitive distortions, stimuli provoking these cognitions, and potential alternative cognitive responses became the primary targets for futher assessment and intervention. In both these cases, a variety of cognitive, affective, and behavioral factors were incorporated in the treatment, but the relative emphasis varied as a function of their specific problem and mediating variables. It is important to note the decisions regarding these treatment refinements were based on theoretical assumptions and clinical validation. Empirical validation of the appropriateness of these decisions remains to be demonstrated.

Another feature of the cognitive-behavioral perspective is the focus on patient collaboration. That is, the patient is not viewed as a passive object about whom the therapist or investigator tries to uncover information, but, rather, is viewed as an active agent in the assessment process. The patient is viewed as someone who has access to certain information that is relevant for the problem but that is unavilable to the therapist from any other source. A variety of assessment strategies are incorporated in the process, not merely to engage the patient (so as to gain excessive amounts of information), but also in order to facilitate accurate and reliable information-gathering, to improve the specificity or precision of the information, to increase the patient's motivation and efficacy in relation to treatment, and to foster the patient's understanding of the problematic responses and variables that potentially mediate them.

A hallmark of cognitive-behavioral assessment is the use of observation techniques, and, in particular, self-observation techniques that permit the identification and examination of internal events. The inclusion of self-monitoring strategies has the benefit of fostering an increased perception of collaboration. The patient can observe his or her own feelings, thoughts, and behaviors in the natural environment rather than rely exclusively on retrospective reporting. For example, in the case of a cigarette smoker seeking help to stop smoking, the individual can be asked to monitor thoughts and feelings at the time of an urge to smoke, the salient environmental cues associated with the urge, whether he or she smoked the cigarette, how he or she felt, and how others responded. The inclusion of such a self-monitoring procedure clearly increases the sense of involvement of the individual in the assessment process and likely increases the utility of the information derived from the process.

Another important characteristic of the cognitive-behavioral approach is the emphasis placed on the interrelationship between assessment and treatment. Consistent with models of treatment that emphasize a collaborative problem-solving approach, assessment is conducted throughout the treatment process. Although the first few meetings with the therapist may be labeled as the "assessment phase," the patient is told that a primary goal of the assessment process is to clarify the factors related to the problem for both the therapist and the patient. In other words, the educative emphasis of the assessment process is explicitly described to the patient. The entire assessment process, its goals and functions, the types of information to be gathered, the format for collection of the information, and a conceptual framework emphasizing a cognitive social learning perspective, is presented to the patient before beginning the process. Subsequently, each "treatment" session incorporates a reevaluation and reconceptualization component in the ongoing change process.

This educative process is reinforced merely as a function of the types of questions asked and variety of tasks in which the individual becomes engaged during the assessment process. For example, asking the patient to indicate what factors exacerbate or reduce his or her problem implicitly suggests that the problem is subject to various controlling factors. Asking a patient to monitor thoughts and feelings that may influence or be influenced by symptoms, or asking a patient to describe the circumstances surrounding the performance of some risk-related behavior or relapse (e.g., smoking), begins to lead the patient to identify environmental events that are instigators. Asking the patient to monitor others' responses begins to raise the importance of environmental influences in the maintenance of symptomatic behaviors. These illustrations are only to make the point that a key characteristic of the cognitive-behavioral perspective is the use of assessment information provided by the patient to facilitate a reconceptualization of a problem away from being inexplicable and uncontrollable to being subject to specific thoughts, feelings, behaviors, and socioenvironmental characteristics (Turk & Kerns, 1983; Turk, Meichenbaum & Genest, 1983).

Misunderstandings About the Cognitive-Behavioral Perspective

The cognitive-behavioral perspective is not wedded to any specific assessment techniques. All assessment instruments have flaws and no one technique is likely to be sufficiently sensitive or comprehensive enough to examine the nature of patients' thoughts, feelings, behaviors, and socioenvironmental circumstances. The cognitive-behavioral apparach is one that encourages "converging operations," that is, multiple approaches to examining similar constructs (Meichenbaum & Butler, 1979).

The term cognitive-behavioral is unfortunately deceptive and has led to much confusion. It is important to differentiate between the techniques employed to change behavior and the processes that mediate the behavior (Bandura, 1978). Both cognitive and behavioral techniques are employed to acquire information about factors that mediate behavior. Much of overt behavior, however, is believed to be determined by cognitive and affective structures and processes (Turk & Salovey, in press (a); Turk & Speers, 1983a).

A criticism that is frequently leveled at the cognitive-behavioral perspective is that it ignores or minimizes the important role of affect. From our perspective, affect and cognition are intricately associated, with cognition mediating affect and vice versa. For example, the patient's mood state can influence what is attended to and, consequently, what is learned and stored, and, moreover, the individual's mood state can influence what information is retrieved from memory (e.g., Bower, 1981). Cognitive factors may conversely influence mood state. For example, when an individual appraises a stimulus as threatening to him or her and judges the coping resources available as inadequate, he or she is likely to become aroused and experience dysphoric mood and distress (Lazarus & Launier, 1978). Thus, although the term cognitive-behavioral does not include the word *affect*, it subsumes affect within cognitive structures that are postulated to have both ideational and affective content (Turk & Speers, 1983a).

COGNITIVE-BEHAVIORAL ASSESSMENT STRATEGIES IN HEALTH PSYCHOLOGY

Thus far we have presented a perspective for evaluating individuals and groups with respect to health and illness variables. We have in particular emphasized the importance of the assessment of cognitive and affective variables in the context of a comprehensive and multidimensional analysis of behavior. Specific aspects of the cognitive-behavioral perspective designed to improve the reliability and validity of assessment data, some of the roles and functions of the assessment process, and examples of its potential utility have been presented. In the subsequent pages we will discuss some of the general categories of assessment strategies used to assess cognitive and affective variables and give details of a subset of these strategies in order to provide models for future developments in the health assessment literature. We begin this section with comments on the reliance on self-report data in assessing cognitions and close with some recommendations for refinement of these techniques.

Use of Self-report Data

The majority of approaches to the assessment of internal cognitive and affective processes rely on patient's or subject's self-reports (for an exception, see Cacioppo et al., in this volume). The validity of self-reports has been challenged since at least the 1700s by Hume among others. It is not our purpose to review the lengthy debate that has raged since that time. For some recent discussion of the relevant issues that have been raised, see papers by Ericsson and Simon (1980), Genest and Turk (1981), Lieberman (1979), and Nisbett and Wilson (1977).

Briefly, the arguments center around the accuracy of subjective reports of internal states. Self-reports are challenged because they may be incomplete, reactive to environmental influence (i.e., demand characteristics, social desirability, evaluation apprehension), idiosyncratic and uninterpretable, and possibly merely post hoc rationalizations. Moreover, self-reports may be confounded by investigator bias in the interpretation of the reported data (e.g., Turk & Salovey, in press (b); Turk & Speers, 1983a).

After examining potential confounds, the reader may wonder whether there is any reason to continue reading this chapter. There are at least two reasons why we believe wholesale rejection of self-reports is unwarranted. First, none of the alternative assessment procedures available has proven to be completely satisfactory and unproblematic. For example, the validity of projective techniques has been seriously challenged (Mischel, 1968); the ecological validity of analog role-playing tasks has been called into question (e.g., Bellack et al., 1978); methodological problems in behavioral observations have been acknowledged, as has the construct validity of various behavioral observation systems (Turk, Wack, & Kerns, in press; Wildman & Erickson, 1977), some physiological measurements have been reported to be unreliable (Russo et al., 1980) and less accurate than self-reports (Hilgard, 1969); and biochemical assays have inherent limitations, as do archival approaches (McGrath, 1982). In fact, Mischel (1973) has noted that clinicians guided by concepts about underlying genotypic dispositons have not been able to predict behavior better than have the patient's or subject's self-reports.

The second reason why we believe self-reports should be retained is that they may be the only techniques, or the best ones available, to obtain information that is inaccessible by alternative types of measurement (e.g., appraisal of symptom meaning). Self-reports can clarify the individual's idiosyncratic perceptions. Furthermore, the use of self-reports may bring to light information that might otherwise be overlooked and stimulate health care providers and investigators to generate new hypotheses and ask different questions (Genest & Turk, 1981). For example, in a recent study examining the strategies used by individuals who successfully quit smoking, DiClemente and Prochaska (1982) found that "self-liberation"—a strong commitment reviewed on a day-to-day basis—was rated as the most important strategy related to maintenance. This commitment is given limited attention in the therapeutic research literature (Prochaska, 1979; see earlier discussion of thoughts of substance abusers). Such results provide important information that may lead to modification of therapeutic interventions; yet without self-report data it may never have come to the health care provider's attention.

A wide array of self-report procedures have been developed to assess internal states and beliefs: interviews, paper-and-pencil inventories, projectives techniques, thought listing, thought sampling, expectancy ratings, "think aloud" techniques, videotape reconstructions, and self-monitoring (see for detailed reviews of these techniques Kendall & Hollon, 1981; Merluzzi et al., 1981). In the area of health psychology, however, most investigators have relied on interviews, paper-and-pencil inventories, and questionnaires. We will briefly review some relevant approaches by using traditional techniques, and will then focus on less frequently employed strategies in health psychology.

Interviews

Interviewing is probably the oldest and most frequently employed assessment strategy in the medical and the mental health fields. In most clinical contexts, the interview is indispensable, as both a source of information and a process of providing support to the patient.

Typically, the interview represents the initial contact between the patient and the therapist. The most frequent opening statment made by the interviewer regardless of theoretical orientation or training is likely to be "tell me about your problem" or some variant. Depending on the specific goals of the interviewer, the nature of the presenting problem, what information is available from other sources, and the theoretical orientation of the interviewer, the interview proceeds with varying degrees of structure, specificity, and focus. In many ways the cognitive-behavioral interview is similar to most commonly employed interview styles. Differences primarily involve the relative emphasis on specification and quantification in cognitive-behavioral interviewing. To those relying on alternative conceptual frameworks, the cognitive-behavioral (and behavioral) interview may appear relatively structured. The focus of the interview and its relative structure, however, are likely to be a function of the specific purpose or goal of the assessment process and specific characteristics of the patient and interviewer, rather than primarily related to the theoretical orientation of the interviewer. (For a detailed discussion of the behavioral interview the reader is encouraged to refer to Haynes, 1978).

The cognitive-behavioral interview has several important functions and goals. First, it is designed to identify and specify potential target behaviors. In this context, most clinicians and investigators emphasize the importance of the interview for surveying possible problem areas. It is the rare individual who has his or her problem(s) neatly outlined and appropriately targeted upon presenting to the health care professional for the first time. Thus, it is incumbent upon the interviewer to remain open to a wide range of potential targets for further analysis rather than to focus prematurely on the patient's "presenting complaint." Many clinicians espouse the importance of remaining relatively unstructured and primarily reflective in attempting to review possible problem areas in order to minimize possible interviewer bias in considering and/or interpreting the problem areas (cf. Turk & Salovey, in press (b); Turk & Speers, 1983a). This view is particularly emphasized in the case where multiple problem areas are to be assessed or when the problem is unspecified prior to the interview. On the other hand, a prearranged structure for the interview directed by the interviewer is more commonly used in conjunction with specific intervention programs (e.g., pain management program, marital dysfunction or sexual dysfunction treatment program). In this case, the opportunity to elicit potentially relevant information about other areas of functioning is sacrificed for increased specificity of the data when formulating behavioral hypotheses and interventions.

We should emphasize at this point that specific cognitions themselves may be identified as targets for further analysis and potential intervention. For example, prior to cardiac catheterization, a patient's repertoire of cognitive distraction strategies or maladaptive thoughts may be assessed (e.g., Kendall et al., 1979). In the case of the cigarette smoker entering a smoking cessation program, the participants' "urges" to smoke may become a primary target for intervention. Thus, it is important for the interviewer to attend not only to the individuals' reports of overt motoric behavior but also to their internal processes.

The cognitive-behavioral interview departs from the nonbehavioral (i.e., traditional) interview in terms of its emphasis on specification of the topography of each problem identified. Consistent with the cognitive-behavioral perspective, the interviewer focuses on the patient's reports of specific cognitions, behaviors, affects, and physiological responses that precede, accompany, and follow the target behaviors, as well as the environmental conditions associated with the response. The interviewer is careful to focus on the temporal association of these cognitive, affective, and behavioral events; their specificity versus generalizability across situations; the frequency of their occurrence; and so forth. In this process, the interviewer continues to generate and test hypotheses concerning each problem behavior and possible controlling variables.

The cognitive-behavioral interviewer also attempts to establish potential alternative behaviors, appropriate goals for the patient, and possible reinforcers for these alternatives. The interviewer attempts to elicit a range of behavioral and cognitive alternatives and environmental and self-reinforcers. The interviewer attends to this function of the assessment process with the same specificity that has been described for identification of target behaviors and their topography. The opportunity to explore these possibilities in a supportive and problem-solving manner may take place more efficiently and with greater success by means of a well-constructed interview than by using other assessment strategies.

It is both interesting and disappointing to note the relative lack of attention that has been paid to the careful psychometric development of cognitive-behavioral interviews (or almost any interview format for that matter), especially in light of its crucial role within most clinical assessment contexts. This inattention is at least partly related to the desire to rely on the interview's relatively unstructured, open-ended nature in order to generate hypotheses, probe for details, and clarify important points not available when using other standardized assessment strategies.

Most structured interviews have been forthcoming in recent years that were associated with attempts to assess specific problem areas and empirically derived constructs. With increased structure has come the opportunity to attend to issues of reliability and validity. Two specific structured interview strategies will be reviewed as models for future developments in the health psychology assessment literature.

A particularly innovative demonstration of the utility of structured interviews with medical patients is provided by Gordon and his colleagues (1980). Gordon et al. noted that, although it had frequently been reported that cancer patients were distressed, no systematic means for identifying their specific problems and concerns existed. Thus, the content of intervention programs tended to be limited by the a priori assumptions regarding relevant issues held by health care providers. Gordon et al. (1980) developed a structured procedure to survey patients' cancer-related psychosocial problems that could become the targets of intervention.

Problem-oriented clinical interviews were conducted with a large number of cancer patients to elicit patient relevant information concerning the range of problems that might be encountered in living with cancer. The interview assessed the presence of 122 psychosocial problems originally identified by another sample of cancer patients. The psychosocial problems covered in the interview focused on 13 areas of life functioning: physical discomort, medical treatment, medical service, mobility, housework, vocation, finances, family, social concerns, worry regarding the disease, affect, body image, and communication. The patients were asked not only to report on the presence of the problems but also to rate their severity.

The information collected during the interview was used to identify specific patient concerns, to determine the priority of intervention (i.e., problems with the highest weights), and to evaluate the effectiveness of a psychosocial intervention program. The interrelationship between assessment and intervention advocated by the cognitive-behavioral perspective is readily apparent in this study.

The results reported by Gordon et al. (1980) suggest that the intervention was quite successful in improving cancer patients adjustment to living with their disease. These results, thus, validate both the assessment methodology and the treatment approach employed. As Gordon et al. note,

> The type of assessment emphasized in this study has two additional benefits: (a) It provides patients with opportunities to respond to questions that are relevant to their daily functioning, concerns that are not systematically addressed by conventional mechanisms of health care service delivery, and (b) it provides a vehicle for focusing the efforts of the oncology counselor on the specific concerns of the patient. Review of these assessments alerted the counselor to the particular problems of concern to the patient. This information was utilized when intervening with the patient. Thus, it suggested that this form of systematic behavioral assessment provides an approach to diagnosis and intervention that is more closely allied with efficient cost-effective treatment than a method that merely labels the patient "anxious," "depressed," "hysterical" and so forth. Although such descriptions may provide useful information to the oncology counselor, the level of inference that they evoke is often several steps removed from the concrete concerns of the patient; they are, therefore, not as useful therapeutically (pp. 757–758).

Another important example of a structured interview with clinical research applications in health psychology is the interview developed by Rosenman, Friedman, and their colleagues to assess a pattern of behavior now known to be a risk factor for coronary heart disease (Rosenman, 1978). In the 1950s, the type A coronary-prone behavior pattern was described by Friedman and Rosenman based on their observations of the behavior of heart-diseased patients in their private practice. The major factors of the behavior pattern include extremes of aggressiveness, easily aroused hostility, a sense of time urgency, and competitive achievement striving (Rosenman, 1978). The construct is further defined as a set of overt behaviors that are elicited from vulnerable individuals by a series of appropriately challenging stimuli. Thus, by definition, the most theoretically consistent means of eliciting the behavior pattern may be the interview format rather than a paper-and-pencil measure.

The Structured Interview, as its name connotes, consists of a standard set of questions in which individuals are asked how they typically respond to a variety of situations that often elicit impatience, competitiveness, and hostility from type A individuals (Rosenman, 1978). For example, individuals are asked about their reactions when waiting in long lines, how often they find themselves doing two things at once, and whether others view them as competitive. Also incorporated in the interview are a set of questions that are presented in a manner designed to elicit speech characteristics consistent with the type A construct, such as a pressured pace, interruptions, and a tone of annoyance. These special characteristics are incorporated in the scoring as are the individual's self-reports. Scoring of the Structured Interview results in the classification of individuals into one of four categories: type A, type A2, X, and type B. The type B individual represents the absence of type A characteristics, and the individual who prospectively has been demonstrated to have the lowest risk among the four groups for the development of coronary heart disease, independent of all other major risk factors (e.g., hypertension, hypercholesterolemia, cigarette smoking, gender, family history).

The Structured Interview is important in several respects. The interview was developed to assess a specific behavioral construct with potentially important heuristic and clinical implications. The interview content is internally consistent with the behavioral characteristics of the construct it attempts to assess. As already noted, the interview incorporates adequate samples of the individual's response to a variety of provocative environmental stimuli both within and outside the context of the interview itself. That is, rather than relying on the individual's self-reports about his or her characteristic response to certain situations as other paper-and-pencil measures of the construct must (e.g., the Jenkins Activity Survey; Jenkins et al., 1967), the Structured Interview additionally incorporates and, in fact, emphasizes the interviewer's observation of the interviewee during the questioning and the *in vivo* presentation of provocative stimulus conditions. The incorporation of these "behavior analog" or "experimental" conditions has the potentially important asset of improving the reliability, content validity, and overall construct validity of the measurement technique.

In fact, both interscorer agreement in classifying subjects by the Structured Interview and test-retest reliability have been demonstrated to be quite high (Jenkins et al., 1968; Jenkins et al., 1974). The predictive validity of the Structured Interview has been demonstrated in prospective studies, and in the Western Collaborative Group Study was found to be a stronger predictor of subsequent coronary heart disease than the Jenkins Activity Survey (Blumental et al., 1975; Brand et al., 1976; Zyzanski et al., 1976). The establishment of the psychometric properties of the measure have clearly facilitated research in the area of the type A behavior patterns and fostered the widespread acceptance of type A as an independent risk factor for coronary heart disease. (For a comprehensive review of the type A literature and research related to use of the Structured Interview, readers are encouraged to refer to a recent paper by Matthews, 1982).

One additional point seems important to mention. Rosenman and his colleagues have paid particular attention to the need to control the use of the Structured Interview in clinical and research settings. These investigators have established an exceptionally well-organized process for training others in the reliable use of the interview. Emphasis on thorough training seems crucial in order to perform the interview reliably and code the behavioral aspects of the interviewer-interviewee interaction. Attention to possibilities of observer drift and bias that would jeopardize the validity of the assessment strategy should serve as a model for others interested in the development of such interactional, structured, and standardized assessment strategies. Unfortunately, emphasis on training limits the widespread use of the technique and its potential utility as a clinically valid instrument to assess type A behavior.

Questionnaires and Traditional Psychological Instruments

Perhaps because of their ease in administration, face validity, and/or availability, investigators and clinicians have relied heavily on questionnaires. The questionnaires that have been utilized most frequently can be categorized along three related general dimensions: (1) general population psychological measures versus health specific measures; (2) standardized measures versus measures developed for specific studies; and (3) personal (traitlike) measures versus situation specific (state) measures. Table. 9.1 lists some of the more frequently employed instruments representing these three dimensions.

Historically, psychological assessment in health areas has been associated with the tradition of psychosomatic medicine, that is, conceptually linked to the view that particular personality characteristics may be causally associated with the development of medical problems such as asthma, tuberculosis, and peptic ulcers. From this perspective, attempts have been made to employ traditional psychometric instruments, often developed for use in mental health or psychiatric settings, to differentiate groups of individuals who manifested specific diseases. Although these instruments could address specific questions regarding personality and psychopathology, they suffer from two serious drawbacks. First, they often do not directly address specific problems of medical patients that have been raised by other health care providers (e.g., problems of behavioral management). Secondly, although the traditional instruments were often psychometrically sound they were usually not developed on a relevant normative sample (e.g., relevant medical groups).

By and large, early attempts to use traditional psychological assessment instruments with specific medical populations have proven to be unsatisfactory. For example, recent papers have documented the failure to identify specific personality traits associated with hypertension (e.g., Goldstein, 1981), bronchial asthma (Alexander, 1981), cancer (Barofsky, 1981), diabetes (Turk & Speers, 1983b), and substance abuse (e.g., Schwartz & Graham, 1978; Sobell & Sobell, 1977). Moreover, the ability of general measures of personality or psychopathology to identify which patients would respond to different types of treatment or to differentiate organic from functional (i.e., psychogenic) problems has been challenged (e.g., Bradley et al., 1981; Cox et al., 1978).

Disillusionment with traditional instruments has resulted in two trends in assessment. First, a number of investigators have attempted to develop

TABLE 9.1. THREE DIMENSIONS OF QUESTIONNAIRES

	A	B	C	D
	Personal (Trait) Measures		Situation Specific (State) Measures	
	Standardized Measures	Measures Developed for Specific Studies	Standardized Measures	Measures Developed for Specific Studies
General population psychological measures	Minnesota Multiphasic Personality Inventory (Hathaway & McKinley, 1951)	General Cognitive Error Questionnaire (Lefebvre, 1981)	Profile of Mood States (McNair et al., 1971)	Face Valid Mood Ratings (e.g., Wilson, 1981)
	Beck Depression Inventory (Beck et al., 1961)	Modified Subjective Probability Questionnaire (Lewinsohn et al., 1981)	Anxiety Inventory A-State (Spielberger et al. 1970)	
	Anxiety Inventory-A-Trait (Spielberger et al., 1970)	Cognitive Events Schedule (Zeiss et al., 1979)	Depression Adjective Check Lists (Lubin, 1965)	
	Internal-external Locus of Control (Rotter, 1966)		Ways of Coping Scale (Folkman & Lazarus, 1980)	

Health-specific measures	Health Locus of Control Scale (Wallston & Wallston, 1981)	Low Back Pain-Cognitive Error Questionnaire (Lefebvre, 1981)	Dental Anxiety Scale (Corah, 1969)	Face Valid Recovery Ratings (e.g., Wilson, 1981)
	Illness Behavior Questionnaire (Pilowsky & Spence, 1975)	Health Opinion Survey (Krantz, Baum, & Wideman, 1980)	Sexual Interaction Inventory (LoPiccolo & Steger, 1974)	Self-report of Perceived Physical Symptoms (Pennebaker et al., 1982)
	Behavioral Health Inventory (Millon et al., 1982)		McGill Pain Questionnaire (Melzack, 1975)	Catheterization Self-Statement Inventory (Kendall et al., 1979)
	Jenkins Activity Survey (Jenkins et al., 1974)		Sickness Impact Profile (Bergner et al., 1976)	Pretreatment Confidence Questionnaire (Condiotte & Lichtenstein, 1981)

general assessment instruments that are specifically designed for use with medical population samples (e.g., *Sickness Impact Profile*, Bergner, et al., 1976; *Millon Behavioral Health Inventory*, Millon, et al., 1982; *Illness Behavior Inventory*, Pilowsky & Spence, 1975) and to examine health-relevant individual differences (e.g., Health Opinion Survey, Krantz, et al., 1980; *Multidimensional Health Locus of Control*, Wallston, et al., 1978). A second trend, one that has complemented the first, has been a number of attempts to develop relatively specific, high fidelity instruments designed to focus on very specific symptoms or situations (e.g., *Cardiac Catheterization Self-Statments Inventory*, Kendall et al., 1979; *Low Back Pain-Cognitive Error Questionnaire*, Lefebvre, 1981; *McGill Pain Questionnaire*, Melzack, 1975). The more general health-related instruments have received a good deal of attention recently and thus we will not consider them here (cf. Green, 1982, in this volume; Reeder, et al., 1976; Wallston & Wallston, 1981; Ward & Lindeman, 1978). Rather, we will examine some of the more specific instruments that are most consistent with the cognitive-behavioral perspective. The examples presented are not exhaustive, but, instead, illustrate a variety of approaches.

Coping with Stress.   As noted earlier, ways in which individuals appraise and cope with stress may be more important in the development of illness than the quantity or type of stress (e.g., Lazarus, 1966; Meichenbaum & Turk, 1982). From the transactional view of stress proposed by Lazarus (1966; Lazarus & Launier, 1978), assimilated within the cognitive-behavioral perspective, stress is viewed as a process involving a changing set of threats and demands that extend over time. This view may be contrasted with the view of stress as a relatively static event (e.g., Holmes & Rahe, 1967). The importance of considering stress as a process can be readily observed when we consider the changing threats and demands that confront individuals with chronic illness and disabilities (Turk, 1979; Turk et al., 1980).

Viewing stress as extending over time also leads to consideration of changing responses made by the individual to the associated threats and demands. That is, unlike earlier attempts to identify relatively enduring personality characteristics related to coping, as is true of measures categorized in columns A and B in Table 9.1 (for a review of this approach see Moos, 1974), the transactional view emphasizes that individuals likely employ different coping responses to deal with changing demands. Thus, rather than relying on specific techniques associated with a personality disposition (e.g., repressors-sensitizers, copers-avoiders), the transactional model suggests that at certain times an individual might rely more heavily on some types of coping strategies and at other times, or in other situations, he or she might use other alternatives. The shift in strategy utilization is hypothesized to occur in conjunction with changing situational demands.

Recently, several instruments have been developed to assess the ways that individuals cope with changing demands (e.g., Berman & Turk, 1981;

Folkman & Lazarus, 1980; Pearlin & Schooler, 1978; Stone & Neale, in press). One instrument that has received considerable attention is the Ways of Coping Scale developed by Folkman and Lazarus (1980).

The Ways of Coping Scale consists of a list of 68 cognitive and behavioral strategies that an individual might use when confronted with a specific threatening episode or stimulus. The items are classified within two general categories: (1) problem-focused and (2) emotion-focused. The problem-focused category includes items that describe problem-solving efforts and behavioral strategies for altering or minimizing the source of stress (e.g., "Made a plan of action and followed it," "Drew on past experiences, you were in a similar situation before"). The emotion-focused category includes items that describe palliative cognitive efforts to minimize emotional distress (e.g., "Let your feelings out somehow," "Told yourself things that helped you to feel better"). An important characteristic of the Ways of Coping Scale is that subjects' responses are linked to specific situations rather than viewed as coping efforts resulting from a more general personality style. In this approach, the coping techniques employed with a range of problems can be examined in order to look for both patterns of coping and idiosyncratic or problem-specific responding.

To our knowledge, the Ways of Coping Scale has as yet not been examined with regard to a specific illness population, but it does seem to have promise. For example, it would be of interest to use the Ways of Coping Scale in conjunction with the psychosocial problems of cancer patients described by Gordon et al. (1980) to identify the individual patient's ways of coping with various problems identified.

Recently, Tobin et al., (1982) have developed a variation of the Ways of Coping Scale that employs a similar format but with some different items. Preliminary factor analyses reported by Tobin et al. suggest that five factors characterize their Coping Strategies Inventory: (1) self-denigration (e.g., "I blamed myself"); (2) avoidance (e.g., "I hoped that if I waited long enough things would turn out ok"); (3) problem-centered (e.g., "I made a plan of action and followed it"); (4) social-centered (e.g., "I talked with someone about how I was feeling"); and (5) cognitive restructuring (e.g., "When I reorganized the way I looked at the situations, things did not look so bad"). The Coping Strategies Inventory is currently being used by Holroyd and his students to examine coping responses of headache patients (personal communication), and in our laboratory, we are using this inventory to examine the association between psychophysiological reactivity to a personally relevant stressful event and coping responses in a sample of chronic pain patients.

Cognitive Appraisal of Events.   In addition to an interest in the assessment of the use of specific strategies in response to stressful situations, investigators interested in the assessment of cognitive variables, presumed to mediate the coping response, have focused on individual's cognitive appraisals of the stressful stimulus. Theoretically, the processes of cognitive appraisal of provocative stimuli and the initiation of some coping response may be inextricably linked. This seems particulary evident, for example, in a study by Katz et al. (1970) that demonstrated that one of the most common ways that women "coped" with the threat of breast cancer, having discovered breast lumps, was to fail to evaluate the lumps as an indicator of a possible problem, an evaluative process characteristically referred to as *avoidance* or *denial*. Such an appraisal process, in this example among many others, led to a poor behavioral coping response, that is, a delay in seeking medical examination.

A variety of cognitive variables potentially related to both the appraisal process and use of particular coping strategies have already been mentioned for their importance in addressing issues of health and illness (e.g., symptom appraisal, attributions of causality, attributions of control and predictability, expectations of recovery). Most commonly, investigators have relied on instruments developed for specific studies rather than on previously standardized, but more general and hence less sensitive, measures of the appraisal process. For the purpose of the present chapter, we can do little more than allude to developments in this important area. An example of the application of one particularly relevant construct, that is, cognitive distortion to a specific health problem, will help demonstrate potential applications and utility of this line of investigation.

Cognitive approaches to the treatment of depression have received considerable attention in the clinical and research literatures (e.g. Beck, 1976; Beck et al., 1979). Beck suggests that distorted cognitions and beliefs are essential in the production and maintenance of depression. He suggests that depressed individuals are characterized by faulty information processing reflected by errors of logic so that they seem systematically to misinterpret or distort the meaning of events in order to construe themselves, their world, and their experiences in a negative way. According to Beck's conceptualization, differences in the type and frequency of cognitive errors and cognitive distortions should differentiate depressed individuals from nondepressed individuals.

Independent descriptions of the cognitive processes of depressed persons and pain patients have been reported to be strikingly similar (Lefebvre, 1981). Lefebvre developed two cognitive error questionnaries, one general and one specific to low back pain patients. The general cognitive error questionnaire was designed specifically to assess general life experiences (GEN CEQ) and the second cognitive error questionnaire (LBP CEQ) was designed to assess the limitations of and problems experienced by chronic back pain patients. Each questionnaire consists of brief vignettes followed by a dysphoric cognition about the vignette. Subjects were asked to reach each vignette and the accompanying cognitions and rate how likely it would be that they would have had that thought in a similar situation (5-point scale ranging from "almost like I would think" to "not at all like I would think").

The following is an example of a vignette from the general CEQ: "You are a manager in a small business firm. You have to fire one of your employees who has been doing a terrible job. You have been putting off this decision for days and you think to yourself, 'I just know that when I fire her, she is going to raise hell and will sue the company.' "

An example from the LBP CEQ is: "You work at a job where you have to sit all day. The other day, your back was really sore at the end of the day. Driving home from work, you found yourself thinking, 'If this keeps up, I'll be crippled and won't be able to work or even walk.' "

The cognitions that follow the vignettes reflect one of four types of cognitive errors described by Beck et al. (1979): "(a) catastrophizing: anticipating that the outcome of an experience will be catastrophic or misinterpreting an event as a catastrophe, (b) overgeneralization: assuming that the outcome of one experience applied to the same experience in the future or to even slightly similar experiences, (c) personalization: taking personal responsibility for negative events or interpreting such events as having a personal meaning, and (4) selective abstraction: selectively attending to negative aspects of experience" (Lefebvre, 1981, p. 518).

Self-efficacy Scales. According to Bandura (1977), changes in behavior are directly associated with modification of underlying beliefs and expectancies. He suggests that the two particularly important beliefs are: (1) the belief that the procedure will be effective in bringing about the desired change ("outcome efficacy") and (2) the conviction that one can successfully execute the requisite behavior to produce the desired change ("self-efficacy").

Self-efficacy expectations are assessed by means of a questionnaire procedure specifically designed for the target problem. In the original study where self-efficacy scales were employed with a population of snake phobic subjects, Bandura and Adams (1977) developed a procedure whereby subjects had to indicate whether or not they expected to be able to perform each of a set of tasks graded in difficulty (e.g., "look at a snake through a wire cage," "touch a snake with your bare hand"). Subjects also rated their confidence in how they could complete each of the tasks on a scale ranging from "not at all certain" to "complete certainty." The responses were then scored for *level* (how many tasks subjects felt they could perform) and *strength* (based on the average confidence score per task) of perceived self-efficacy expectations. Bandura and Adams (1977) reported that efficacy expectations were excellent predictors of the subjects' actual performance. Although the items in the behavioral performance list will vary, the self-efficacy methodology is applicable across a wide variety of behaviors.

The assessment of efficacy expectations should be valuable in the investigation of the role of cognitive factors in behavior change. To the extent that cognitive factors mediate behavior change, as is postulated in the cognitive-behavioral perspective, successful interventions should be associated with an increase in efficacy expectations related to the individual's ability to perform adaptive or avoid the performance of maladaptive behaviors. Moreover, the degree, strength, and generality of these altered expectations should predict the maintenance of treatment gains (Bandura, 1977). Recently, several studies have employed the self-efficacy methodology described earlier in several health relevant contexts: smoking cessation (e.g., Chamblis & Murray, 1979a; Condiotte & Lichtenstein, 1981); weight control (Chamblis & Murray, 1979b); and treatment of chronic pain (Turk et al., 1980).

To illustrate the application and utility of self-efficacy methodology, we will consider the recent study conducted by Condiotte and Lichtenstein (1981). These authors developed an efficacy expectation scale (i.e., Pretreatment Confidence Questionnaire) that subjects completed prior to a treatment for smoking cessation, at the conclusion of treatment, and at a 3-month follow-up. The authors reported that treatment success was highly correlated with participants' increased perceptions of self-efficacy. Higher levels of self-efficacy at the completion of treatment were predictive of greater maintenance of abstinence. Furthermore, measurement of posttreatment self-efficacy made possible accurate predictions of the circumstances when and where relapse would occur. That is, the data presented showed an high correspondence between clusters of smoking situations in which relapse was experienced and low degrees of self-efficacy specifically for those situations. Condiotte and Lichtenstein concluded:

"For the clinician involved in the treatment of addictive disorders, the ability to predict, through the use of a low-cost instrument, the specific situations in which clients might encounter great difficulty remaining abstinent might be invaluable. Self-efficacy assessment during the course of treatment could be used to identify the areas toward which the greatest therapeutic effort should be addressed (p. 657).

Problem Specific Self-Statement Inventories.   Meichenbaum (1977) has emphasized the importance of individuals' self-statements or "internal dialogues" during stressful situations. The therapeutic effectiveness of interventions especially designed to modify presumed maladaptive self-statements or self-talk have been reported in a number of papers (e.g., Kendall et al., 1979; Langer et al., 1975). As Kendall and Korgeski (1979) have noted, however, without adequate assessment of self-statments it is impossible to confirm the presence of such self-statements, whether the self-statement contributed to the problem, or whether the interventions succeeded because of modification of self-statments or via some other active mechanisms.

Kendall and his colleagues (1979) developed a specific self-statement inventory for evaluating the role of maladaptive self-statements in production of arousal and distress during in an aversive cardiac catheterization procedure. These investigators constructed a 20-item self-statement inventory with items asking specifically about patients' thoughts and feelings during the catheterization procedure. The inventory included 10 positive and 10 negative statements that another sample of patients had indicated emitting when they were exposed to the catheterization procedure. Positive self-statements included verbalizations viewed as facilitating coping behavior during the catheterization (e.g., "I was thinking that the procedure could save my life.") Negative self-statements were verbalizations viewed as likely to inhibit more favorable coping behavior during the catheterization (e.g., "I kept thinking that the procedure might cause complications that might never go away." "I was listening and expecting them to say something bad about my heart.") Patients were asked to indicate to what extent each of these positive and negative self-statements were characteristic of their thoughts during the procedure. Kendall et al. (1979) found that the patients' negative self-statement scores were correlated with both physicians' and technicians' ratings of patient adjustment during the procedure. The more frequent the negative thoughts were, the poorer was the adjustment.

Self-monitoring

In addition to the use of interviews and self-report inventories described earlier, the next most frequently employed assessment procedure in cognitive-behavioral assessment is self-monitoring. Self-monitoring is usually employed by having patients record specific aspects of overt or covert behavior. In cognitive-behavioral assessment, in contrast to the use of self-monitoring in more traditional behavioral assessment, patients frequently will be asked to record the thoughts, feelings, and images that precede, accompany, and follow a target behavior.

Self-monitoring has been employed for several purposes.

1. It has been used to obtain baseline frequencies of target behaviors, including covert behaviors, and to explicate the functional relationship of the target behaviors to environmental and internal antecedents and consequents of the behavior. Thus, by attempting to identify thoughts, feelings, and environmental events that surround the target behavior, self-monitoring may be useful in identifying controlling variables.

2. It has been used as a treatment technique designed to bring about behavioral change. That is, many maladaptive behaviors are performed in a seemingly automatic or involuntary fashion. Requiring patients to monitor the performance of such behaviors may serve to "deautomatize" the performance of these behaviors and assist the patient in perceiving control in relation to them. Related to the observation that self-monitoring may lead to desired changes in the targeted behavior, self-monitoring had been employed to enhance self-efficacy. For example, pain patients may keep charts of their

physical activities (e.g., Fordyce, 1976), thus providing the patients the opportunity to attend to their progress.

3. It may be used in the evaluation of treatment programs. As target behaviors are monitored in relation to other observed internal or environmental events, attributions about the mediators of behavior change may be validated. Alterations in treatment strategies may be implemented on the basis of data collected by means of ongoing self-monitoring.

Self-monitoring has a number of advantages over alternative assessment approaches. However, there are also a number of major disadvantages. On the side of advantages, self-monitoring is less expensive and more convenient than the use of trained observers to assess target behaviors. Additionally, the presence of observers may be extremely reactive and may influence the performance of behaviors. Moreover, in many instances the target behaviors may be unobservable because of privacy (e.g., sexual behavior) or because the relevant variables are covert (e.g., thoughts, feelings, images, urges). Kazdin (1974) has pointed out that self-monitoring may produce a more representative sample of data than is possible by observers. External observers have access to only a sample of incidents in an individual's life. Self-monitoring has the advantage of providing a "motion picture" of the target problems in contrast to the "snapshot" available through the use of paper-and-pencil inventories and other static, standardized instruments. Finally, self-monitoring has an advantage over interviews in that it is less reliant on retrospective reporting.

There are at least two major disadvantages to self-monitoring. As noted, self-monitoring may be useful in the modification of target behaviors. Thus, it is likely to be reactive. The simple task of asking a patient to monitor the occurrence of some behavior may alter its frequency or topography, thus providing an erroneous portrait of the problem. Related to the issue of reactivity is the more general question of reliability and validity of the procedure. Do patients or subjects who are asked to record certain behaviors at specific times actually carry out the task in the prescribed manner? There has been much debate as to the accuracy of self-monitoring data. Thoresen and Mahoney (1974) have suggested that the assumption that individuals will be consistent and accurate in their self-reports is naive and not supported by available data. Other investigators have reported that when significant others are used to make ratings of overt behavior there is a high enough association between the patient and significant other monitoring data to warrant the continued use of self-monitoring, at least in some circumstances (e.g., Blanchard et al., 1981). When covert events are the target of self-monitoring, of course, it is impossible to assess the accuracy of the patient's report.

A number of attempts have been made in an effort to improve the accuracy of patients' self-monitoring (cf. Ciminero et al., 1977; Kazdin,

1974). As a minimum set of requirements, self-monitoring must be relatively easy to implement, reasonably brief, and not excessively intrusive. The target behaviors that are to be monitored should be as concrete as possible. Patients need to be carefully instructed in how to self-monitor. Self-recording forms can be made portable and small enough to fit in a pocket or purse. Salient cues can be placed in appropriate locations to serve as reminders to monitor (e.g., a piece of colored tape on a watch, on the telephone). Times of recording may be associated with well-rehearsed or frequent behaviors (e.g., at meal times, when brushing one's teeth). Mechanical counters have been developed that can be attached to a watch or a belt and, thus, may be relatively unobstrusive.

Depending upon the behavior examined, self-monitoring may involve event sampling (i.e., the number of responses/unit time), duration of behavior (e.g., when the behavior occurs at a relatively low frequency but is discrete such as headaches or angina episodes), and time sampling (i.e., frequency of behavioral occurrence during a specified period of time). Thus, individuals may be asked simply to indicate each time he or she engaged in a specific behavior (e.g., smoked a cigarette), whether they engaged in a specific behavior during a specified period of time (e.g., between breakfast and lunch), or how long the target behavior lasted (e.g., an episode of angina may last from a few seconds to more than 20 minutes).

To supplement abbreviated self-monitoring as previously described, investigators may incorporate and use patient diaries or more extended assessment of behaviors to assess behaviors over a restricted time period (e.g., a day or week). This is particularly possible during self-monitoring of less frequent behaviors. For example, Deyo et al., (1983) asked arthritis patients to complete the Sickness Impact Profile (SIP; Bergner et al., 1976) for the day preceding clinic visits. The Sickness Impact Profile consists of 136 items describing specific dysfunctional behaviors that are grouped together into 12 categories: mobility/ambulation, body care, movement, social interaction, communication, emotional behavior, alertness, eating, work, sleep/rest, household management, and recreational and pastimes. The respondents were asked to indicate whether or not each item described a dysfunction they experienced *that day* because of their illness. The authors reported that scores on the SIP showed high correlations with physiological parameters of arthritis (e.g., hematocrit levels, sedimentation rate, and anatomic stage).

In our own work, we have asked chronic pain patients and their spouses to complete daily diaries regarding the occurrence of severe pain episodes; thoughts and feelings that preceded, accompanied, and followed the episode; characteristics of the situation (e.g., who is present, where, time; what they did during the episode; and how effective their behaviors were in alleviating distress) (Turk & Kerns, 1983; Turk, Meichenbaum, & Genest, 1983). We have found that the information from these diaries provides valuable information that can be incorporated into the treatment process.

Roghmann and Haggerty (1972) have also reported on the utility of semistructured diaries to examine a wide range of everyday events related to health. They argue that interviews may be adequate to identify important events such as hospitalization or deaths in the family but are less useful in obtaining information about everyday medical complaints such as use of over-the-counter medications, minor physical complaints, and so forth. Roghmann and Haggerty used a health diary with a large community sample and concluded that this approach was both an efficient and reliable source of information.

Other Cognitive Assessment Procedures

In addition to applications of the more common assessment techniques already reviewed, cognitive-behavioral assessment is greatly concerned with the ongoing process of thoughts and feelings that surround a specific target behavior. A number of "process" assessment procedures other than self-monitoring have been developed, but these have received relatively little attention in health psychology. We will, therefore, briefly describe some of the process approaches and speculate as to how they might be employed in assessment in health-related areas. (For more extensive reviews and analyses of these cognitive assessment techniques, see recent volumes edited by Kendall & Hollon, 1981; Merluzzi et al., 1981).

Thought Listing.   Much of coping is anticipatory in nature. Examples of anticipatory coping responses include the thoughts and feelings experienced by individuals prior to exposure to aversive or stressful events such as surgery, dental treatment, childbirth, or cancer chemotherapy. The nature of these thoughts and feelings prior to the aversive event are likely to influence the nature of the actual experience and the patient's responses during the event (Chaves & Brown, 1978; Genest et al., 1977). At the present time, little is known about the nature of these thoughts and feelings or the association between them and the actual experiences of the patient. It should be noted that the Kendall et al. (1979) catheterization questionnaire described earlier was one attempt to examine relevant thoughts and feelings, but these were retrospective rather than prospective accounts.

Thought listing may be a useful procedure to employ to acquire preliminary information about patients' relevant covert processes. Simply put, thought listing involves asking patients to list the thoughts and feelings they experience prior to exposure to some event (e.g., surgery, endoscopic examination, laser photocoagulation). These prospective covert processes would then be categorized along some relevant dimensions and then correlated with various dependent measures (e.g., subjective distress, objective signs of distress). Subsequent investigations could be explicitly designed to modify those maladaptive covert events to determine the effect on behaviors during the noxious event (cf. Turk & Genest, 1979 for a review of such studies.)

Thought listing may also be used in a retrospective manner, that is, immediately following a relevant episode. Although this strategy has been used less frequently in this manner, it may be an important first step in the development of more standardized, self-statement inventories (e.g., Kendall et al., 1979).

Thought Sampling and "Think Aloud" Strategies.   Thought sampling and think aloud procedures are variants of thought listing. Rather than having patients report upon their thoughts and feelings in anticipation of distress as is typically the case in the use of thought listing, or retrospectively as in the case of self-statement inventories (e.g., Kendall et al., 1979), these two approaches attempt to assess covert processes during the actual aversive situation. Thus, patients might be asked to provide a continuous monologue of their thoughts and feelings *during* a situation such as a physical examination, a blood pressure test, cast removal, and so forth. This information should serve the heuristic function of permitting examination of the *in vivo* relations among thoughts, feelings, and behaviors (e.g., tensing, flinching, coughing, gagging). In procedures of longer duration, thought sampling might be employed instead of the continuous monologue approach to think aloud. Thought sampling involves a request that the patient provide lists of thoughts that occur at a specified time during a prolonged process. For example, this approach might be employed with patients undergoing renal dialysis, or during the process of labor and childbirth.

Reconstructive Techniques.   Instead of sampling or concurrently collecting covert behaviors, attempts have been made to have subjects reconstruct a train of cognitions and to comment upon this reconstruction, thereby providing additional clarification (Meichenbaum, 1977; Smye, 1978). Reconstructive techniques, therefore, provide somewhat of a compromise between process measures and retrospective strategies. The two reconstructive techniques that have been employed most frequently are imagery reconstruction and videotape reconstruction.

Imagery reconstruction involves asking patients to describe a target situation and then to imagine the situation in as much detail as possible while providing a continuous monologue of the thoughts and feelings that they can reconstruct. We have used this approach clinically with our chronic pain patients. An example may serve to underscore the utility of this approach.

One of our migraine headache patients provided the following reconstruction of her thoughts and feelings during her most recent migraine epidode.

> For hours and hours, God will it (pain) ever end? How much longer do I have
> to live this way? I have outlived my capabilities . . . the hours are endless and I

am alone. I wish someone would take a scalpel and cut that artery . . . How long will it be until I am sent to a mental institution? Migraines are not fatal, doctors do not care. You live through one only to be struck with another in a few days. I am incapable of everything I used to do. . . . (Turk, Meichenbaum, Genest, 1983, p. 207).

From this reconstruction it is obvious that the patient feels helpless, views her situation as hopeless, and appraises her situation as one of inevitable deterioration. We would expect that such thoughts and feelings might exacerbate her symptoms and would likely influence her communication with her family and health care providers. Such information may be of use within the therapeutic process and would likely not have been available through other assessment means.

A second way in which reconstructions have been employed is with the use of videotapes. Usually, patients' experience in a structured analog situation is videotaped and then they are asked to view the videotape and provide a continuous monologue of their thoughts and feelings that coincide with the picture of them on the screen.

In one study (Genest et al., 1977), subjects were videotaped while being exposed to a laboratory pain induction procedure (i.e., the cold pressor test). Subjects were subsequently shown the videotapes of themselves with their hands emersed in the ice water tank and asked to reconstruct their thoughts and feelings using the tape as a cue. Different cognitions were found to be characteristic of the high and low tolerant subjects. Those in the high tolerant group seemed to feel that they could use coping strategies to affect the aversive sensations and their power to persevere despite the pain. Those in the low tolerant group viewed themselves as less competent to cope with the situation and were more likely to "catastrophize," reporting negative self-referent thoughts and vivid aversive images.

Spanos et al., (1979) identified a similar classification of participants in their study of laboratory pain and indicated that procedures to modify the maladaptive thinking pattern resulted in longer tolerance for the aversive sensations. Chaves and Brown (1978) identified a set of similar covert responses from patients immediately following dental treatment. One subgroup reported vivid negative thoughts and images, whereas a second subgroup reported more frequent thoughts related to perceptions of self-control and positive coping.

Whether such attempts to reconstruct or experience aversive events are successful in eliciting the covert responses, whether they are accurate, and whether they are a representative sample of responses that would be emitted in a similar situation are important issues. Additionally, it remains to be demonstrated how reliability and accuracy of these procedures can be increased and if the videotapes add to the imagery approach. Nevertheless, it is plausible that these procedures may perform a valuable function both clinically and in generating hypotheses that have heuristic significance.

CONCLUDING COMMENTS

We began by suggesting that the cognitive-behavioral approach to assessment in health psychology is more tied to a perspective on human functioning that emphasizes the interrelationship among thoughts, feelings, behaviors, and socioenvironmental variables than to any specific assessment technique. This perspective emphasizes the importance of a comprehensive, multidimensional assessment of many areas of human functioning that are likely to be related to health-relevant issues. From the standpoint of clinical assessment, the process that we would advocate includes a number of purposes and goals.

1. Evaluation of the descriptive characteristics of the target behavior emphasizing situational characteristics and quantification.
2. Evaluation of the physiological, emotional, cognitive, and behavioral responses that occur in the presence of the target behavior.
3. Evaluation of the individual's perception of the target behavior and what its means to him or her.
4. Evaluation of the impact of the target behavior on different aspects of the patient's life (e.g., vocational, social, marital, as well as physiological).
5. Evaluation of the adaptive and maladaptive mechanisms and responses used to appraise and cope with the target problem (Turk & Kerns, 1983).

Obviously, what we are advocating is a comprehensive evaluation of the individual's entire life situation as well as characteristics of the target problem per se. Health problems do not occur in a vacuum and need to be assessed in the more general context of the patient's life. Some of the information required can be obtained by interviews with the patient and significant others, some by paper-and-pencil inventories, some by self or other observations, and some by a variety of innovative cognitive assessment strategies. Each specific technique has limitations and advantages. For these, and a variety of other reasons discussed, we emphasized the need for the application of a method for converging operations.

We view assessment as a process of problem solving that utilizes a variety of data collection procedures and sources. Data from multiple sources are integrated in the generation and confirmation of hypotheses about the individual or groups of individuals and their target problems and in the evaluation of treatment efficacy. Methods for data collection should meet at least four criteria: (1) They must provide information about cognitive, emotional, behavioral, and socioenvironmental aspects of the target problem; (2) they must be quantifiable so that they can be treated statistically; (3) they must be sensitive enough to detect small changes in the target behavior; and

(4) to the extent possible, they should meet the basic psychometric properties of reliability, validity, and utility (Turk & Kerns, 1983).

The present chapter emphasized the importance of the development of cognitive-behavioral asssment strategies in order to advance our empirically derived understanding of a wide range of health- and illness-related issues. The development and application of many of these strategies is still in its infancy, with the majority of published studies relying on general, rather than specific, and unvalidated assessment techniques. Examples of recent advances in the literature that may serve as models for future development of cognitive-behavioral assessment strategies in health psychology were presented. We would like to end this discussion with a plea for continued attention to the need to develop psychometrically sound, comprehensive, converging, and efficient strategies for assessment within the cognitive-behavioral perspective in health psychology. Only after such instruments and procedures are developed can we hope to identify relevant cognitive factors that contribute to the individual's health and illness behaviors.

References

Alexander, A. B. (1981). Behavioral approaches in the treatment of bronchial asthma. In C. K. Prokop & L. A. Bradley (Eds.), *Medical psychology: Contributions to behavioral medicine*. New York: Academic Press.

Bandura, A. (1977). Self-efficacy: Toward a unifying theory of behavioral change. *Psychological Review, 84*, 191–215.

Bandura, A. (1978). The self-system in reciprocal determinism. *American Psychologist, 33*, 344–359.

Bandura, A., & Adams, H. E. (1977). Analysis of self-efficacy theory of behavioral change. *Cognitive Therapy and Research, 1*, 287–308.

Barofsky, I. (1981). Issues and approaches to the psychosocial assessment of the cancer patient. In C. K. Prokop & L. A. Bradley (Eds.), *Medical psychology: Contributions to behavioral medicine*. New York: Academic Press.

Beck, A. T. (1976). *Cognitive therapy and emotional disorders*. New York: International Universities Press.

Beck, A. T., Rush, A. J., Shaw, B.F., & Emery, G. (1979). *Cognitive therapy of depression*. New York: Guilford Press.

Beck, A. T., Ward, C. H., Mendelson, M., Mock, J., & Erbaugh, J. (1961). An inventory for measuring depression. *Archives of General Psychiatry, 4*, 561–571.

Bellack, A. S., Hersen, M., & Turner, S. M. (1978). Role-play tests for the assessing social skills: Are they valid? *Behavior Therapy, 9*, 168–189.

Bergner, M., Bobbitt, R. A., Pollard, W. E., et al. (1976). The Sickness Impact Profile: Validation of a health status measure. *Medical Care, 14*, 56–78.

Berman, W. H., & Turk, D. C. (1981). Adaptation to divorce: Problems and coping strategies. *Journal of Marriage and the Family, 46*, 179–189.

Best, J. A. (1980). Mass media, self-management, and smoking modification. In P. O. Davidson & S. M. Davidson (Eds.), *Behavioral medicine: Changing health life styles*. New York: Brunner/Mazel.

Blanchard, E. B., Andrasik, F., Neff, D. F., Jurish, S. E, & O'Keefe, D. M. (1981). Social validation of the headache diary. *Behavior Therapy, 12,* 711−715.

Blumenthal, J. A., Williams, R. B., Kong, Y., Thompson, L. W., Jenkins, C. D., & Rosenman, R. H. (1975). Coronary-prone behavior and angiographically documented coronary disease. *Psychosomatic Medicine, 37,* 75−79.

Bower, G. H. (1981). Mood and memory. *American Psychologist, 36,* 129−148.

Bradley, L. A., Prokop, C. K., Gentry, W. D., Van Der Heide, L. H., & Prieto, E. J. (1981). Assessment of chronic pain. In C. K. Prokop & L. A. Bradley (Eds.), *Medical psychology: Contributions to behavioral medicine.* New York: Academic Press.

Brand, R. J., Rosenman, R. H., Sholtz, R. I. & Friedman, M. (1976). Multivariate prediction of coronary heart disease in the Western Collaborative Group Study compared to the findings of the Framingham Study. *Circulation, 53,* 348−355.

Cassel, J. (1976). The contribution of the social environment to host resistance. *American Journal of Epidemiology, 104,* 107−123.

Chamblis, C., & Murray, E. J. (1979a). Cognitive procedures for smoking reduction: Symptom versus efficacy attribution. *Cognitive Therapy and Research, 3,* 91−96.

Chamblis, C., & Murray, E. J. (1979b). *Efficacy attribution, locus of control and weight loss.* Unpublished manuscript, University of Miami: Miami.

Chaves, J. G., & Brown, J. M. (1978). *Self-generated strategies for the control of pain and stress.* Paper presented at the annual meeting of the American Psychological Association, Toronto, Canada.

Ciminero, A. R., Nelson, R. O., & Lipinski, D. P. (1977). Self-monitoring procedures. In A. R. Ciminero, K. S. Calhoun, & H. E. Adams (Eds.), *Handbook of behavioral assessment.* New York: Wiley.

Condiotte, M. M., & Lichtenstein, E. (1981). Self-efficacy and relapse in smoking cessation programs. *Journal of Consulting and Clinical Psychology, 49,* 648−658.

Corah, N. L. (1969). Development of a dental anxiety scale. *Journal of Dental Research, 48,* 396.

Cox, G. B., Chapman, C. R., & Black, R. G. (1978). The MMPI and chronic pain: The diagnosis of psychogenic pain. *Journal of Behavioral Medicine, 1,* 437−443.

Davis, M. S. (1967). Predicting non-compliant behavior. *Journal of Health and Social Behavior, 8,* 265−271.

Deyo, R. A., Inui, T. S., Leininger, J. D., & Overman, S. S. (1983). Measuring functional outcomes in chronic disease: A comparison of traditional scales and a self-administered health status questionnaire in patients with rheumatoid arthritis. *Medical Care, 21,* 180−192.

DiClemente, C. C., & Prochaska, J. O. (1982). Self-change and therapy change of smoking behavior: A comparison of processes of change in cessation and maintenance. *Addictive Behaviors, 7,* 133−142.

DiMatteo, M. R., & DiNicola, D. D. (1982). *Achieving patient compliance: The psychology of the medical practitioner's role.* New York: Pergamon Press.

Ericsson, K. A., & Simon, H. A. (1980). Verbal reports as data. *Psychological Review, 87,* 215−251.

Folkman, S., & Lazarus, R. S. (1980). An analysis of coping in a middle-aged community sample. *Journal of Health and Social Behavior, 21,* 219−239.

Fordyce, W. E. (1976). *Behavioral methods for chronic pain and illness.* St. Louis: Mosby.

Genest, M., Meichenbaum, D., & Turk, D. C. (1977). *A Cognitive-Behavioral Approach to the Management of Pain.* Paper presented at the 11th annual convention of the Association for the Advancement of Behavior Therapy, Atlanta.

Genest, M., & Turk, D. C. (1981). "Think aloud" procedures to assess cognitions. In T. V. Merluzzi, C. R. Glass, & M. Genest (Eds.). *Cognitive assessment.* New York: Guilford Press.

Goldstein, I. B. (1981). Assessment of hypertension. In C. K. Prokop & L. A. Bradley (Eds.), *Medical psychology: Contributions to behavioral medicine.* New York: Academic Press.

Gordon, W. A., Freidenbergs, I., Diller, L., Hibbard, M., Wolf, C., Levine, L., Lipkins, R., Ezrachi, O., & Lucido, D. (1980). Efficacy of psychosocial intervention with cancer patients. *Journal of Consulting and Clinical Psychology, 48,* 743–759.

Green, C. J. (1982). Psychological assessment in medical settings. In T. Millon, C. Green, & R. Meagher (Eds.), *Handbook of clinical health psychology.* New York: Plenum Press.

Harris, D. M., & Guten, S. (1979). Health-protective behavior: An exploratory study. *Journal of Health and Social Behavior, 20,* 17–29.

Hathaway, S. R., & McKinley, J. C. (1951). *The Minnesota Multiphasic Personality Inventory Manual.* New York: Psychological Corp.

Haynes, S. M. (1978). *Principles of behavioral assessment.* New York: Gardner Press.

Henryk-Gutt, R., & Rees, W. L. (1973). Psychological aspects of migraine. *Journal of Psychosomatic Research, 17,* 141–153.

Hilgard, E. R. (1969). Pain as a puzzle for psychology and physiology. *American Psychologist, 24,* 103–113.

Holmes, T. H., & Rahe, R. H. (1967). The social readjustment rating scale. *Journal of Psychosomatic Research, 11,* 213–218.

Holzman, A. D. (1982). *Cognitive-behavioral methods in the management of chronic pain: Issues in assessment.* Paper presented at the annual meeting of the American Pain Society, Miami.

Janis, I. L., & Rodin J. (1979). Attribution, control and decision making: Social psychology and health care. In G. Stone, F. Cohen, & N. Adler (Eds.), *Health psychology.* San Francisco: Jossey-Bass.

Jenkins, C. D., Rosenman, R. H., & Friedman, M. (1967). Development of an objective psychological test for the determination of the coronary-prone behavior pattern in employed men. *Journal of Chronic Diseases, 20,* 371–379.

Jenkins, C. D., Rosenman, R. H., & Friedman, M. (1968). Replicability of rating the coronary-prone behavior pattern. *British Journal of Prevention and Sociological Medicine, 22,* 16–22.

Jenkins, C. D., Rosenman, R. H., & Zyzanski, S. (1974). Prediction of clinical coronary heart disease by a test for coronary-prone behavior pattern. *New England Journal of Medicine, 290,* 1272–1275.

Jones, R. A. Wiese, H. J., Moore, R. W., & Haley, J. V. (1981). On the perceived meaning of symptoms. *Medical Care, 19,* 710–717.

Kasl, S. V., & Cobb, S. (1966). Health behavior, illness behavior and sick-role behavior. I. Health and illness behavior. *Archives of Environmental Health, 12,* 246–266.

Katz, J. L., Weiner, H., Gallagher, T. G., & Hellman, L. (1970). Stress, distress and ego defenses. *Archives of General Psychiatry, 23,* 131–142.

Kazdin, A. E. (1974). Self-monitoring and behavior change. In M. J. Mahoney & C. E. Thoresen (Eds.), *Self-control: Power to the person.* Monterey: Brooks/Cole.

Kendall, P. C., & Hollon, S. D. (Eds.). (1981). *Assessment strategies for cognitive-behavioral interventions.* New York: Academic Press.

Kendall, P. C., & Korgeski, G. P. (1979). Assessment and cognitive-behavioral interventions. *Cognitive Therapy and Research, 3,* 1–21.

Kendall, P. C., & Turk, D. C. (1984). Cognitive-behavioral strategies and health enhancement. In J. Matarazzo, N. E. Miller, S. M. Weiss, J. A. Herd, & S. M. Weiss (Eds.), *Behavioral health: A handbook of health enhancement and disease prevention.* New York: Wiley.

Kendall, P.C., Williams, L., Pechacek, T. F., Graham, L. E., Shisslak, C., & Herzoff, N. (1979). Cognitive-behavioral and patient education interventions in cardiac catheterization procedures: The Palo Alto medical psychology project. *Journal of Consulting and Clinical Psychology, 47,* 49–58.

Kerns, R. D., Turk, D. C., & Holzman, A. D. (1983). Psychological treatment for chronic pain: A selective review. *Clinical Psychology Review, 3,* 15–26.

Klein, R. F., Dean, A., & Willson, M. L. (1965). The physician and post-myocardial infarction invalidism. *Journal of the American Medical Association, 194*, 123–128.

Krantz, D. S., Baum, A., Wideman, M. V. (1980). Assessment of preferences for self-treatment and information in health care. *Journal of Personality and Social Psychology, 39*, 977–990.

Langer, E. J., Janis, I. L., & Wolfer, J. A. (1975). Reduction of psychological stress in surgical patients. *Journal of Experimental Social Psychology, 1*, 155–165.

Lau, R. R. & Hartman, K. (1983). Common sense representation of common illnesses. *Health Psychology, 2*, 167–186.

Lazarus, R. S. (1966). *Psychological stress and the coping process.* New York: McGraw-Hill.

Lazarus, R. S., & Launier, R. (1978). Stress-related transactions between person and environment. In L. A. Pervin & M. Lewis (Eds.) *Perspectives in interactional psychology.* New York: Plenum Press.

Lefebvre, M. F. (1981). Cognitive distortion and cognitive errors in depressed psychiatric and low back pain patients. *Journal of Consulting and Clinical Psychology, 49*, 517–525.

Leon, G. R., Roth, L., & Hewitt, M. I. (1977). Eating patterns, satiety, and self-control behavior of obese persons during weight reduction. *Obesity and Bariatric Medicine, 6*, 172–181.

Leventhal, H., Meyer, D., & Nerenz, D. (1980). The common sense representation of illness danger. In S. Rachman (Ed.), *Medical psychology* Vol. 2. London: Pergamon Press.

Leventhal, H., Nerenz, D., & Leventhal, E. (1983). Illness and dehumanizing environments. In J. Singer & A. Baum (Eds.), *Advances in environmental psychology.* Hillsdale, NJ: Erlbaum.

Lewinsohn, P. M., Steinmetz, J. L., Larson D. W., & Franklin, J. (1981). Depression-related cognitions: Antecedent or consequence. *Journal of Abnormal Psychology, 90*, 213–219.

Lieberman, D. A. (1979). Behaviorism and the mind: A (limited) call for a return to introspection. *American Psychologist, 34*, 319–333.

LoPiccolo, J., & Steger, J. C. (1974). The sexual interaction inventory: A new instrument for assessment of sexual dysfunction. *Archives of Sexual Behavior, 3*, 585–595.

Lubin, B. (1965). Adjective checklists for measurement of depression. *Archives of General Psychiatry, 12*, 57–67.

Mahoney, M. J. (1975). The obese eating style: Bites, beliefs and behavior modification. *Addictive Behaviors, 1*, 47–53.

Marlatt, G. A., & Gordon, J. R. (1980). Determinants of relapse: Implications for the maintenance of behavior change. In P. O. Davidson & S. M. Davidson (Eds.), *Behavioral medicine: Changing health life styles.* New York: Brunner/Mazel.

Mason, J. W. (1971). A re-evaluation of the concept of "non-specificity" in stress theory. *Journal of Psychiatric Research, 8*, 323–333.

Matthews, K. (1982). Psychological perspectives on the type A behavior pattern. *Psychological Bulletin, 91*, 293–323.

McGrath, J. E. (1982). Methodological problems in research on stress. In H. W. Krohne & L. Laux (Eds.), *Achievement, stress, and anxiety.* Washington, DC: Hemisphere.

McNair, D. M., Lorr, M., & Droppleman, L. F. (1971). *Profile of mood states.* San Diego: Educational and Industrial Testing Service.

Mechanic, D. (1968). *Medical sociology.* New York: Free Press.

Meichenbaum, D. H. (1977). *Cognitive-behavior modification: An integrative approach.* New York: Plenum Press.

Meichenbaum, D. H., & Butler, L. (1979). Cognitive ethology: Addressing the streams of cognition and emotion. In K. Blankstein, P. Pliner, & J. Polivy (Eds.), *Advances in the study of communication and affect (Vol. 6). Assessment and modification of emotional behavior.* New York: Plenum Press.

Meichenbaum, D. H., & Turk, D. C. (1982). Stress, coping, and disease: A cognitive-behavioral perspective. In R. W. J. Neufeld (Ed.), *Psychological stress and psychopathology*. New York: McGraw-Hill.

Melzack, R. (1975). The McGill Pain Questionnaire: Major properties and scoring methods, *Pain, 1*, 277–299.

Merluzzi, T. V., Glass, C. R., & Genest, M. (Eds.). (1981). *Cognitive assessment*. New York: Guilford Press.

Millon, T., Green, C., & Meagher, R. (1982). *Millon Behavioral Health Inventory Manual*. Minneapolis: National Computer Systems.

Mischel, W. (1968). *Personality and assessment*. New York: Wiley.

Mischel, W. (1973). Toward a cognitive social learning reconceptualization of personality. *Psychological Review, 80*, 252–283.

Moos, R. H. (1974). Psychological techniques in the assessment of adaptive behavior. In G. V. Coelho, D. A. Hamburg, & J. E. Adams (Eds.), *Coping and adaptation*. New York: Basic Books.

Nisbett. R. E., & Wilson, T. D. (1977). Telling more than we can know: Verbal reports on mental processes. *Psychological Review, 84*, 231–259.

Paul, G. L. (1966). *Insight vs. desensitization in psychotherapy: An experiment in anxiety reduction*. Stanford, CA: Stanford University Press.

Pearlin, L. I., & Schooler, C. (1978). The structure of coping. *Journal of Health and Social Behavior, 19*, 2–21.

Pennebaker, J. W. (1982). *The psychology of physical symptoms*. New York: Springer-Verlag.

Pennebaker, J. W., Gonder-Frederick, L., Stewart, H., Elfman, L., & Skelton, J. A. (1982). Physical symptoms associated with blood pressure. *Psychophysiology, 19*, 201–210.

Perri, M. G., Richards, C. S., & Schultheis, K. R. (1977). Behavioral self-control and smoking reduction. A study of self-initiated attempts to reduce smoking. *Behavior Therapy, 8*, 360–365.

Peters-Golden, H. (1982). Breast cancer: Varied perceptions of social support in the illness experience. *Social Science and Medicine, 16*, 483–491.

Pilowsky, I., & Spence, N.D. (1975). Patterns of illness behavior in patients with intractable pain. *Journal of Psychosomatic Research, 19*, 279–288.

Prochaska, J. O. (1979). *Systems of psychotherapy: A transtheoretical analysis*. Homewood, ILL: Dorsey Press.

Rabkin, J. G., & Struening, E. L. (1976). Life events, stress and illness. *Science, 194*, 1013–1020.

Reeder, L. G., Ramacher, L., & Gorelnik, S. (1976). *Handbook of scales and indices of health behavior*. Pacific Palisades, CA: Goodyear Publishing.

Roghmann, K. J. & Haggerty, R. J. (1972). The diary as a research instrument in the study of health and illness behavior: Experiences with a random sample of young families. *Medical Care, 10*, 143–163.

Rosenman, R. (1978). The interview method of assessment of the coronary-prone behavior pattern. In T. M. Dembroski, S. M. Weiss, J. L. Shields, S. G. Haynes, & M. Feinleib (Eds.), *Coronary-prone behavior*. New York: Springer-Verlag.

Rotter, J. B. (1966). Generalized expectancies for internal versus external control of reinforcement. *Psychological Monographs: General and applied, 80* (1, Whole No. 609).

Russo, D. C., Bird, P. L., & Masek, B. J. (1980). Assessment issues in behavioral medicine. *Behavioral Assessment, 2*, 1–18.

Schwartz, M. F., & Graham, J. R. (1978). Construct validity of the MacAndrew Alcoholism Scale. *Journal of Consulting and Clinical Psychology, 47*, 1090–1095.

Sjoberg, L., & Johnson, T. (1978). Trying to give up smoking: A study of volitional breakdowns. *Addictive Behaviors, 3*, 139–164.

Sjoberg, L., & Persson, L. O. (1979). A study of attempts by obese patients to regulate eating. *Addictive Behaviors, 4*, 349–359.

Smye, M. D. (1978). Behavioral and cognitive assessment through role-playing. *Psychology, 15,* 35–48.

Sobell, L. C., & Sobell, M. B. (1977). Alcohol problems. In R. B. Williams, Jr., & W. D. Gentry (Eds.), *Behavioral approaches to medical treatment.* Cambridge, MA: Ballinger.

Spanos, N. P., Radtke-Bodorik, H. L., Ferguson, J. D., & Jones, B. (1979). The effects of hypnotic susceptibility, suggestions for analgesia, and the utilization of cognitive strategies on the reduction of pain. *Journal of Abnormal Psychology, 88,* 282–292.

Spielberger, C., Gorsuch, R., & Lushene, N. (1970). *Manual for the State-Trait Anxiety Inventory.* Palo Alto, CA: Consulting Psychologists Press.

Stone, A. A., & Neale, J. M. (In press). A new measure of daily coping: Development and preliminary results. *Journal of Personality and Social Psychology.*

Thoresen, C. E., & Mahoney, M. J. (1974). *Behavioral self-control.* New York: Holt, Rinehart and Winston.

Tobin, D. L., Holroyd, K., & Reynolds, R. (1982). *The assessment of coping: Psychometric development of the Coping Strategies Inventory.* Paper presented at the annual convention of the Association for the Advancement of Behavior Therapy, Anaheim, CA.

Turk, D. C. (1979). Factors influencing the adaptive process with chronic illness. In I. G. Sarason & C. D. Spielberger (Eds.), *Stress and anxiety* (Vol. 6), Washington, DC: Hemisphere.

Turk, D. C. & Genest, M. (1979). Regulation of pain: The application of cognitive and behavioral techniques for prevention and remediation. In P. C. Kendall & S. D. Hollon (Eds.), *Cognitive-behavioral interventions: Theory, research and procedures.* New York: Academic Press.

Turk, D. C., & Kerns, R. D. (1983). Conceptual issues in the assessment of clinical pain. *International Journal of Psychiatry in Medicine, 13,* 57–68.

Turk, D. C., & Kerns, R. D., Bowen, W. & Rennert, K. (1980). *An outpatient cognitive-behavioral group approach for the management of chronic pain.* Paper presented at the annual meeting of the American Pain Society, New York.

Turk, D. C., Meichenbaum, D., & Genest, M. (1983). *Pain and behavioral medicine: A cognitive-behavioral perspective.* New York: Guilford Press.

Turk, D. C., Rudy, T. E., & Salovey, P. (1984). Health protection: Attitudes and behaviors of college students, teachers, and LPNs. *Health Psychology, 3,* 189–210.

Turk, D. C. & Salovey, P. (In press (a)). Cognitive structures, cognitive processes, and cognitive-behavior modification. I. Client issues. *Cognitive Therapy and Research.*

Turk, D. C., & Salovey, P. (In press (b)). Cognitive structures, cognitive processes, and cognitive-behavior modification. II. Judgments and inferences of clinicians. *Cognitive Therapy and Research.*

Turk, D. C., Salovey, P., & Litt, M. D. (In press). A cognitive-behavioral perspective on adherence. In K. E. Gerber & A. M. Nehemkis (Eds.), *Compliance—The dilemma of the chronically ill.* New York: Springer.

Turk, D. C., Sobel, H. J., Follick, M. J., & Youkilis, H. D. (1980). A sequential criterion analysis for assessing coping with chronic illness. *Journal of Human Stress, 6,* 35–40.

Turk, D. C., & Speers, M. A. (1983a). Cognitive schemata and cognitive processes in cognitive-behavioral interventions: Going beyond the information given. In P. C. Kendall (Ed.), *Advances in cognitive-behavioral research and therapy* (Vol. 2). New York: Academic Press.

Turk, D. C., & Speers, M. A. (1983b). Diabetes mellitus: A cognitive-functional analysis of stress. In T. Burish & L. A. Bradley (Eds.), *Coping with chronic disease.* New York: Academic Press.

Turk, D. C., Wack, J. T., & Kerns, R. D. (in press). An empirical examination of the "pain behavior" construct. *Journal of Behavioral Medicine.*

Turner, J. A., & Chapman, C. R. (1982). Psychological interventions for chronic pain: A critical review. *Pain, 12,* 23–46.

Wallston, K. A., Wallston, B. S. (1981). Health locus of control scales. In H. Lefcourt (Ed.), *Research with the locus of control construct* (Vol. 1). *Assessment methods.* New York: Academic Press.

Wallston, K. A., Wallston, B. S. & DeVellis, R. (1978). Development of the multidimensional health locus of control (MHLC) scales. *Health Education Monographs, 6,* 161–170.

Ward, M. J., & Lindeman, C. A. (Eds.) (1978). *Instruments for measuring nursing practice and other health care variables* (Vol. 1). Hyattsville, MD.: Department of Health, Education, and Welfare, Publication No. HRA 78-53.

Weisman, A. D. (1979). *Coping with cancer.* New York: McGraw-Hill.

White, K. L., Williams, F., & Greenberg, B. G. (1961). The ecology of medical care. *New England Journal of Medicine, 265,* 885–892.

Wildman, B. G., & Erickson, M. T. (1977). Methodological problems in behavioral observation. In J. D. Cone & R. P. Hawkins (Eds.), *Behavioral assessment: New directions in clinical psychology.* New York: Brunner/Mazel.

Wilson, J. F. (1981). Behavioral preparation for surgery: Benefit or harm. *Journal of Behavioral Medicine, 4,* 79–102.

Worden, J. W., & Weisman, A. D. (1977). The fallacy in post-mastectomy depression. *American Journal of the Medical Sciences, 273,* 165–175.

Zborowski, M. (1969). *People in pain.* San Francisco: Jossey-Bass.

Zeiss, A. M., Lewinsohn, P. M. & Munoz, R. F. (1979). Nonspecific improvement effects in depression using interpersonal skills training, pleasant activity schedules, or cognitive training. *Journal of Consulting and Clinical Psychology, 47,* 427–539.

Zola, I. (1966). Culture and symptoms: An analysis of patients presenting complaints. *American Sociological Review, 31,* 615–630.

Zyzanski, S. J., Jenkins, C. D., Ryan, T. J., Flessas, A., & Everest, M. (1976). Psychological correlates of coronary angiographic findings. *Archives of Internal Medicine, 136,* 1234–1237.

10

Taxonomic Methods in Health Psychology

ERIK E. FILSINGER
PAUL KAROLY

to help people cope better means that we also have to take into account the *classes* (or groups) of persons who can profit from a particular coping strategy, as well as the *classes* of situational contexts mediating adaptational outcomes. (F. Cohen & R. S. Lazarus, 1983)

classifications of disease are usually based on a combination of "characters" (symptoms, signs, and test results), no single character being both sufficient and necessary to every member of the group, yet the group as a whole possessing a certain unity. (D. N. Baron & P. M. Fraser, 1968)

An examination of the health-oriented journals most likely to receive submissions from the psychological community (including *Health Psychology*, the *Journal of Behavioral Medicine, Psychosomatic Medicine, Social Science and Medicine, Journal of Health and Social Behavior,* among others; cf. Swencionis, 1982) reveals, not surprisingly, a preference for statistical treatments of data that is identical to that manifested by social scientists working in their "home" fields. Although our purpose in this chapter is not to suggest that correlational methods, the ANOVA, MANOVA, and the like are inappropriate to questions currently being addressed, we intend to introduce the reader to a family of numerical taxonomy procedures whose potential relevance to health psychology is currently underappreciated. We believe that the methods discussed in this chapter can be of enormous assistance to a discipline in its nascent stages, when questions of classification—the identification of "natural clusters" of people at risk for an illness or who may be particularly fit (or unfit) for certain treatments—are most salient. As the quotations at the beginning of the chapter indicate, the concerns of social scientists and medical scientists converge in the search for relatively homogeneous subgroups with underlying attributes that permit ready prediction, clinical manipulation, and ethical control.

Consider, for example, "psychosomatic" research in the area of asthma. The search for that "certain unity" that Baron and Fraser (1968) mention has been ongoing for many years as it relates to the so-called "asthma personality." Noting that asthma was originally viewed as a psychological disorder (before allergic components were scientifically measurable), Franz Alexander (1950) discussed an emotional etiology for this problem.

> The nuclear psychodynamic factor is a conflict centering in an excessive unresolved dependence upon the mother. As a defense against this infantile fixation, all kinds of personality traits may develop . . . aggressive, ambitious, argumentative persons, daredevils, and also hypersensitive, aesthetic types (pp. 133–134).

More recently, Stern (1981) demonstrated how unity can be overlayed upon diversity in his account of parental rejection as an etiologic foundation of asthma. Citing both rejection and overprotection as themes in the parent-child relationship, Stern (1981) suggested that there are actually three forms of rejection (hostility, perfectionism, and compensatory overprotection) that may be played out singly or in combination and that impact negatively upon the child.

It perhaps goes without saying that neither the classical psychosomatic "hypothesis" of Alexander nor the newer version of Stern has led to many diagnostic or therapeutic advances in asthma. Yet the attempt to discern regularities in complex patterns of behavior among asthmatics is both logical and scientifically sound. However, in place of armchair categorization a method is needed for allocating patients to subgroups on an empirical basis. This is precisely what Robert Kinsman and his colleagues (Kinsman et al., 1982; Kinsman et al., 1973; Kinsman et al., 1974) have attempted to do for adult asthmatics and what Lebowitz et al. (1981) have described for adolescent asthmatics using the logic and procedures of cluster analysis. The success of these researchers is a testament to the value of the methods that will be the focus of the present chapter.

A SHORT HISTORY OF CLASSIFICATION IN PSYCHOLOGY

Interest in various classification systems has existed in the social sciences for many years, certainly prior to the emergence of scientific psychology. Eysenck and Eysenck (1969) trace the four personality types of Hippocrites and Galen (based on body humours) through to the foundations of modern psychology in Wundt's reworking of a scheme by Immanuel Kant. Cattell (1946) lists many of the other influential typologies in the history of psychology, including those of Freud, Adler, McDougall, James, Jung, and Sheldon. It has been suggested (Bolz, 1977) that we have witnessed the decline of these classical typologies because of their scientific inadequacy. The preceding frameworks were overambitious in their attempt at global coverage, oversimplified in their models, and overextended in their attempt to account for every personality configuration. Bolz further suggests that, "Most often the reason for the inadequacy was that many of these schemes were arm-chair inventions without empirical foundation" (1977, p. 270). Interestingly, the major diagnostic tool used in contemporary psychopathology, the DSM-III, remains a typology constructed largely in the arm-chair (Skinner & Blashfield, 1982).

Empirical, or numerical, approaches to creating typologies are of recent origin, Blashfield (1980) evaluated the impact of three major originators of numerical typology in psychology—Tryon, Ward, and Johnson (the name of Raymond B. Cattell should, in our opinion, also be added)—and concluded that, although each has developed a following, the followers of each have tended not to be aware of the work of the others. In the 1950s, investigators interested in empirical classification tended to work in relative isolation (dare we say, in clusters), but the advent of high-speed computers has spread the word to new generations of behavioral and social scientists—groups that have shown growing dissatisfaction with traditional (so-called rationally based) techniques of diagnosis and clinical case identification.

Although multivariate procedures for creating new classification systems are increasingly popular, the newer methodologies have yet to make a significant impact on the domain in which they are most often being applied—psychiatric (psychological) diagnosis. Skinner (1981) has suggested that cluster analysis methods have been used merely in a global descriptive fashion. "Too often," Skinner notes, "a clustering algorithm has been applied to a convenient data set as an end in itself" (1981, p. 69). A central aspect of this problem appears to be the dynamic contrast between communication as a value versus prediction. In order to communicate about a patient, clinicians have tended to prefer familiar concepts, organized in a relatively simple system. Historically, such systems have not had high predictive value. On the other hand, techniques like cluster analysis tend to lead to complex organizational schemes with good predictive value, but not necessarily meaningful or relevant to everyday clinical practice. Methods such as cluster analysis also depend upon the gathering of data on hundreds of patients using structured instruments and the allocation of equal weights to the various measures, practices not common to the clinical case study model (Skinner & Blashfield, 1982).

As has been noted, health psychology has a short history, one marked by the enthusiastic application of psychological theory and methodology to the problems of health promotion, risk reduction, life-style influence, and the explication of personal and social factors in health and illness. The aims of the empirical taxonomy approach are seen to be highly compatible with the general objectives of the health psychology field in establishing for itself a firm conceptual and classificatory foundation. The five specific purposes of clustering techniques, recently outlined by Lorr (1983), can be readily applied to a variety of extant and emerging health psychology interests. These purposes are:

1. To identify natural clusters within a set of individuals (e.g., individuals prone to autoimmune disorders) when there is reason to believe that several homogeneous subtypes might be discernible
2. To erect a useful (descriptive and predictive) conceptual model for classifying entities (e.g., type A individuals)
3. To generate new hypotheses by discovering unsuspected clusters
4. To test hypothesized classes that are believed to be present within groups of as yet unclassified individuals
5. To identify homogeneous subgroups of people whose pattern (profile) of attributes will be useful in prediction (e.g., relating psychological "hardiness" to reduced risk of disease)

THE LOGIC OF NUMERICAL TAXONOMY AND CLUSTER ANALYSIS

A *taxon*, as first discussed by Aristotle, is a class, group, or set of objects (entities, people) belonging together because of their equivalence or similarity on some basic dimension or common factor. Whereas early philsophers sought to explain the relationships between natural phenomena on the basis of arbitrary abstract "essences" (common factors), the French botanist Adanson (1927–1806) is credited (by Sneath & Sokal, 1973) with the idea that objects in nature can be grouped on the basis of physical similarities among multiple characteristics (the so-called polythetic system; to be discussed later).

Several distinct terms are used to describe the processes involved in the meaningful organization of information about objects in the environment. The terms *assignment* or *identification* are used to describe the process of fitting a new (or unclassified) object into an already existing class of objects. Psychiatric diagnosis is, thus, an act of identification (Blashfield & Draguns, 1976). *Classification*, on the other hand, refers to the process of discovering the best means of grouping objects together when no prior format is available. In many cases, the goal of classification is to permit subsequent assignment of newly discovered objects. *Systematics* refers to the scientific study of the kinds of individuals or objects in an environment and the relationships among them. And, finally, *taxonomy* refers to the theoretical study of classification, including its assumptions, techniques, and rules. Taxonomy is sometimes referred to as *botryology* (from the Greek word *botryus* meaning "resembling a cluster of grapes"). When the process of classification is based upon mathematical manipulation of quantitative data, the field is called numerical taxonomy (cf. Good, 1977; Gordon, 1981; Sneath & Sokal, 1973).

The concept of *type*, as used within numerical taxonomy, refers to an explanatory concept invented by an investigator in order to make sense of an empirically derived cluster. Typing of this sort helps to facilitate communication and reduce the complexity of a data base (Lorr, 1983). Clearly, the use of such reasoning is predicted upon a philosophy of knowledge sometimes called Aristotelian and can be contrasted with another broad approach to understanding labeled Galilean.

A Galilean perspective on science tends to be the basis of much current research in psychology (cf. Cattell et al., 1966). The Galilean approach focuses on the relationships (or covariation) between variables. An example of such an approach from physics is Boyle's law, which states that the pressure of a gas varies inversely with its volume. The variable *pressure* is related to the variable *volume* through the rule of inverse covariation. A health psychology hypothesis of a similar form would be the assertion that, all else being equal, the individual's risk for a stress-related illness varies inversely with the availability of social support (with support being seen as causally prior). In each case, a uniformity in nature is being stated in terms of a relationship between variables. Measurement consists of ordering the units along a continuum involving more or less of an attribute.

In contrast, the Aristotelian system of seeing order in nature is built upon classification and identification.

> It is natural that having achieved a recognition of types, men took pride in using them, and it sufficed to place an individual in a type in order to "explain" why he had such and such properties. "He is a dog; therefore, you may anticipate that he will bite." It fitted the syllogistic form: "All men are mortal. Aristotle is a man. Therefore, Aristotle will die." The gain in prediction here comes with the act of first recognizing to what type the given individual belongs. (Cattell et al., 1966, p. 289).

Measurement of the units of analysis consists in establishing their particular value on several relevant attributes. However, rather than discovering the laws of covariation between variables, the units are grouped together so that units that have similar values on the attributes constitute a *class*, that is, a type. The typological approach emphasizes prediction based upon knowledge of the type that particular entity happens to be and of the behaviors known to be associated with that type of entity. For example, much of what is known about the plant and animal kingdoms is stored within taxonomic classifications. Once a plant is properly identified, all the information that is stored about the family, genus, and species is readily available (Blackwelder, 1966).

Much of our working knowledge of the world is based upon classification. In order to conduct his experiments, the chemist must first have a classification of his compounds (Mayr, 1969). Identifying harmful organisms, for example, cholera bacteria versus normal gastrointestinal bacteria, requires accurate identification. The chemical compound and the cholera bacteria do not possess a "degree" of something that covaries with some other property; rather, it is the totality of the entity that carries the unique identity for which it is known. It is that uniqueness that is important for understanding the functioning of entities (Crowson, 1970).

The appealing aspects of the typological approach lie directly in contrast to the variable-oriented approach. When a type represents a grouping of the entities being observed, it places the emphasis upon the functional unity of the entity. The entity is specified by the particular combination of values that it possesses on several variables. In other words, the typological approach stresses that what is important for the functioning of the organism is the unique combination of characteristics that the organism possesses. In contrast, the variable-oriented approach does not focus on the entity, but, rather, focuses upon the variables. The entities merely serve the purpose of obtaining measurement on the variables. Relatively speaking, it is the typological approach that preserves the unity of the organism (cf. also Karoly's discussion of property versus transition theories in Chapter 1).

Because the typological contrasts with the variable-oriented approach, the conceptualizations of scientific utility that fit the latter approach do not necessarily fit the scientific logic of the typological approach. The basis of scientific utility for the variable-oriented investigator is prediction. Information about the world is cataloged in terms of covariation. In terms of causality, a change in X will lead to a corresponding change in Y. When we manipulate X or see a "natural" change in X, we can be reasonably sure that the corresponding change in Y will occur. These general rules for covariation hold even when causality is not being directly addressed and, instead, the researcher is seeking to establish the rule for covariation between two or more variables.

In contrast, the scientific utility of the typological approach consists primarily in the classification, cataloging, and identifiction of entities. The organizing power of a typology is of great importance (Sneath & Sokal, 1973). Once a name is given to a type, that name serves as an index for information retrieval. Identification of an unclassified entity as being a member of a class retrieves all the information about that class as being potentially applicable to that entity. Some classification schemes do a better job of information storage than do others. If a library stored its books on the basis of color and weight, it is doubtful that many scholars would find it useful. Hempel (1952; 1965), as well as a number of taxonomists (e.g.,

Blackwelder, 1966; Carmichael et al., 1968; Crowson, 1965; 1970; Mayr, 1969; Ross, 1974), makes the distinction between such "artificial" classifications and the more desirable "natural" classifications. This point will be elaborated subsequently.

Armchair Versus Empirical Types.   Most of the classical typologies in psychology and philosophy have been constructed through the process of observing certain descriptive regularities in the world that are believed to lead to greater understanding of the phenomena under investigation (McKinney, 1966). In fact, the actual construction of the typology takes place within the observer's head. That approach to constructing typologies will be referred to as the *armchair method*.

The ancient classification of temperamental types, which was amplified by Wundt, illustrates the classical approach to types of people. The temperamental types were (1) the sanquine temperament (nonemotional and changeable), (2) the melancholic temperament (emotional and unchangeable), (3) the choleric temperament (emotional and changeable), and (4) the phlegmatic temperament (nonemotional and unchangeable).

Jung's introverted and extroverted personalities were also of the armchair variety (Bolz, 1977). Research has shown that the two aspects of personality form a continuum rather than coalescing into polar types (Eysenck & Eysenck, 1969).

The major problem with the armchair method is that the theoretician can bias his or her product in the direction of preconceived values and relationships. The result can be a classification system that will make great logical sense (or have intuitive appeal) but that is both low in reliability and of doubtful validity.

Monothetic Versus Polythetic Typologies.   In order to clarify further the nature of a numerical taxonomy approach, we must characterize the relationship between the values that N individuals possess on n variables. That is, for all levels of measurement, persons can be assigned a number representing their value on each of n variables, yielding an N by n data matrix. Table 10.1 is a simplified data matrix with the labels "high" and "low" substituting for individual subjects' scores on the chosen variables.

It is readily seen that individuals possessing the same values on all classifying variables can be presumed to constitute a type. In Table 10.1, subjects 1, 2, and 3 are of one type (high scores on the first two, and low scores are the second two variables) and subjects 4, 5, and 6 are another type. It can also be seen that the arrangement of the variables (columns) can be switched (e.g., 4 and 1 can be interchanged) but that operation will not affect the fact that subjects 1, 2, and 3 "belong together" as do 4, 5, and 6.

Typologies that are characterized by the fact that all the individuals belonging to a type share the same values on the variables are labeled "monothetic typologies". In "polythetic typologies" (the invention of

TABLE 10.1.   ILLUSTRATIVE IDEALIZED DATA MATRIX

		Variables				
		1	2	3	4	. . . *n*
	1	High	High	Low	Low	
	2	High	High	Low	Low	
Persons	3	High	High	Low	Low	
(entities)	4	Low	Low	Low	Low	
	5	Low	Low	Low	Low	
	6	Low	Low	Low	Low	
	.					
	.					
	.					
	N					

Adanson), the individuals (entities) may be grouped into a type on the basis of their having similar profiles but not having identical values on all variables. As we shall see, determining how to classify patterns of scores (numbers, rather than summary labels like high, medium, and low) as "similar" is a critical element of cluster analysis.

The polythetic types have several strengths compared to monothetic types. Perhaps the most important stems from the fact that many of the profiles in a polythetic system are basically the same, differing in only a few values. Similar profiles would likely "function" similarly. Although there are many possible varieties of profiles in a polythetic system, not all will occur (because not all logical possibilities will occur in nature). Most of the statistics referred to as cluster analysis yield polythetic types.

Justification for Numerical Taxonomy

Of primary importance in the determination of whether or not a typology is justified is the joint distribution of the variables. If the distribution is unimodal and continuous, a typology is not justified (cf. Cattell, 1946; 1952). An example of such a distribution is the multivariate normal distribution. On the other hand, the joint distribution may be multimodal. In such cases, the distribution has been called a "species distribution" (Cattell, 1946; 1952; Cattell et al., 1966). Each mode is a "species," and the species represents the types. At this basic level, the justification for a typology has to do with no more than a distributional property. This distributional requirement connects with a frequently used definition of an empirical type, that is, a dense set of points in the data hyperspace separated by regions of relative sparsity (Everitt, 1974, p. 43). Note that the number of variables (*n*) determines the configuration of the hyperspace (or *n*-dimensional space). With more than three variables, it is extremely difficult (if not impossible) to visualize what the regions in the space might look like. Visualization problems notwithstanding, each type can be described by a unique combination of values on variables for the individual. Knowledge of these profiles may add to a scientific understanding not afforded when merely examining the variables separately. Parsimony of the description can be achieved when the profiles fall into groups based upon their similarity, that is, types.

Recently, a theory of data analysis with regard to classification has been offered under the rubric of the "mixture model" (Blashfield, 1976; Day, 1969; Fleiss & Zubin, 1969). Such a theory is needed to guide the research because there is no mathematically exact way of defining a cluster. As a result, it is difficult to determine whether a cluster analysis is imposing a structure on the data or locating the actual structure of the data.

Under the mixture model, the assumption is made that the actual structure of the data is such that the sample contains subsamples of several different populations. The task of cluster analysis is to locate the different subsamples and identify the individuals as belonging to their respective populations. It is assumed that each separate population is unimodal. Therefore, the modes in the multivariate distribution are a likely starting point in locating the respective populations. The logic of most cluster analysis algorithms is merely an attempt to capitalize on the dense grouping of the individuals at the modes. The algorithms "search the data space" for similar individuals, since similarity, as defined by closeness in data space, will produce dense portions interpretable as types.

Artificial Versus Natural Typologies. A classification is useful to the extent that it leads to distinctions between types on additional characteristics. This is the property of systematic import: "To be scientifically useful a concept must lend itself to the formulation of general laws or theoretical principles that reflect uniformities in the subject matter under study, and thus provide the basis for explanation, prediction, and generally scientific understanding" (Hempel, 1956, p. 146). Cattell et al. (1966) use the term "functional emergents" to refer to types that have the quality of systematic import. Denoting its ability to access a degree of uniformity in the world, we can call a classification that has systematic import a "natural classification" (e.g., Carmichael et al., 1968). In other words, a classification that predicts characteristics other than those used to derive it can be called natural. As will be seen subsequently, this feature is directly related to validation of a typology. In contrast, a classification that references only those differences associated with its derivation is called an "artificial classification." It should be noted, however, that not everyone shares this view (Fleiss & Zubin, 1969).

It is useful, therefore, to construct types that uncover fundamental underlying differences. Within health psychology these fundamental differences might be differential responses to treatments. The use of cluster analysis to identify types of depressives illustrates this point. Overall and his colleagues (1966) employed inverse (Q) factor analysis to derive an empirically based typology of depression. The types they uncovered were labeled retarded, hostile, and anxious. Despite methodological criticisms of the use of inverse factor analysis, Overall's depressive typology has generally been supported in other empirical typologies (Blashfield & Morey, 1979). The anxious type responds best to major and minor tranquilizers, whereas the retarded type responds best to tricyclic antidepressants. In contrast, the hostile depressive type showed no drug effects superior to that brought on by a placebo. Raskin et al. (1972) have supported the type by drug response interaction. Yet, despite the mounting evidence that traditional (armchair) diagnoses are inaccurate relative to empirical typologies, the work in numerical taxonomy has had relatively little impact on clinical practice (Skinner & Blashfield, 1982). Nevertheless, the typologies discovered within recent years have demonstrated their scientific value and deserve to be called natural classifications.

BASICS OF CLUSTER ANALYSIS

Cluster analysis does not refer to one standard statistical procedure. Instead, there are many different clustering strategies (well over a hundred), each somewhat unique. In addition, cluster analysis can be thought of as involving a number of steps. Within each step a decision must be made among a wide variety of alternatives. In order to handle this diversity, several authors have chosen to reference each of the decision points and their available alternatives (Anderberg, 1973; Everitt, 1974; Sneath & Sokal, 1973). Selecting from among the lists, we have chosen to discuss six major decisions: choice of units, choice of variables, choice of similarity/dissimilarity coefficients, choice of clustering procedures, the problem of validation, and the process of interpretation.

Choice of Data Units

Classifications can be attempted using entire populations, if the populations are readily identifiable and small enough to manage. When classification is not done on the entire population, some thought is needed with regard to the nature of the sample drawn and the population to which the study is to be generalized. Interestingly, it is not unusual for presentations concerning cluster analysis to omit a discussion of the data unit (e.g., Bailey, 1975; Everitt, 1974).

When a sample is drawn, it should be basically representative of the larger population. Anderberg (1973) makes the point, however, that randomization is not always desirable. Small or rare groups could become lost among the larger ones. If it is suspected that such groups exist, it may be legitimate to oversample their members. If the type is present and identified, it can be described accurately without reference to its proportion in the population, since types are usually described by their means. Under- or overrepresentation in the sample will not necessarily affect the estimation of the type's population means in a way that would necessarily invalidate the results.

A related point, made by Sneath and Sokal (1973), is that the selection of individuals for a classification involves an initial screening of individuals as fitting the issue being considered. If someone is not included because he or she does not possess some initially screened criteria, the typology is being delimited. For example, if a cluster analysis of depression were conducted only on diagnosed depressives, it is conceivable that some individuals who might form a depressive cluster would not be included, and the type would be lost. It is to the credit of researchers in the area of depression that efforts are made to include individuals who do not possess the classic characteristics (Blashfield & Morey, 1979). For example, Overall and his colleagues (1966) included subjects who had not been primarily diagnosed as depressive.

Choice of Variables

Conceptual Sphere.   It is usual in natural and biological, but not in behavioral science taxonomy for the conceptual sphere to include everything having to do with the individual organisms around which they can potentially be classified. As Everitt (1980) has noted,

> the initial choice of variables is itself a classification of the data which has no mathematical or statistical guidelines, and which reflects the investigator's judgment of relevance for the purpose of the classication . . . (p. 9).

In human studies, a choice of a problem area is needed to provide the conceptual sphere. In contemporary health psychology, for example, physical and psychological symptoms or illness correlates, modes of coping, hypothesized predictors of help seeking or medical compliance, and stressful life events of various kinds have recently provided some of the conceptual spheres.

Once the conceptual sphere has been established, it is important to obtain measures representative of its contents. If the sphere is thought of in geometric terms, the conceptual space should be measured in a way that does not overrepresent some areas and/or entirely miss other areas. In other words, the conceptual space must be adequately sampled by the measures employed. Moreover, the measures should have both relevance to the particular problem and be capable of discriminating between individuals (Bailey, 1975; Sneath & Sokal, 1973). Anderberg (1973) suggests that good discriminators could conceivably be irrelevant; therefore, caution should always be employed. There is general agreement that variables that are the same for all clusters should not be selected.

Number of Variables.   Determination of the proper number of variables needed to assess the conceptual space in order to develop a useful taxonomy is a moot point. Sneath and Sokal (1973) note that there is no universally valid answer to this question. They suggest a rough guideline of no less than 60 characters in biological taxonomy. However, that figure is much higher than is typically employed in psychology.

Additional considerations should be kept in mind. When large numbers of variables are used, estimates of similarity seem to occur that appear to follow a principle of inertia or marginal utility. That is, "as more and more characters are added, it takes an increasingly large number of characters with quite different phenetic information to alter appreciably a given estimate of phenetic similarity" (Sneath & Sokal, 1973, p. 107). The "proper" number of variables is probably the number that fully accesses the distinguishing features of the conceptual sphere and that should preferably be dictated by a theoretical framework (Bailey, 1975).

Inadmissible Characters.   Sneath and Sokal (1973) provide a list of the variables that should not be used in a classification. This list includes: meaningless characters, logically correlated characters, partially logically correlated characters, invariant characters, and empirically correlated characters. Meaningless characters are those that do not reflect the inherent nature of the individual. Correlated variables include those that are redundant because one necessarily follows from the other or because they covary with each other. Invariant variables add no useful information for distinguishing between or among the hypothesized types.

Scaling and Weighting.   Factor analysis has been suggested as a way to reduce the correlation among variables, but some writers (e.g., Sneath & Sokal, 1973) cast doubt on the utility of the approach. They argue that factor analysis seldom yields groups of variables that are intuitively as meaningful as the variables themselves. In addition, factor analysis adds another step in the process. The results may not justify the time and energy devoted to it.

Problems also exist in attempting to determine the weights to be assigned to each factor. The question of weighting of variables has always been controversial (Everitt, 1974; 1980). Sneath and Sokal (1973) argue that each variable should be weighted equally. Frequently, distance coefficients are used to assess similarity (see subsequent discussion); so that if one were to measure characteristics such as height and weight in feet and pounds, respectively, the scaling would be affected by the comparative unit increase. A man who is 1 pound lighter and 1 foot shorter than man B would probably be put in the same taxon with man B, whereas someone who was 10 pounds lighter and 0.1 foot shorter than man B would not be placed with him, even though he is obviously similar to B in many ways. It may, therefore, be advisable to standardize the variables to zero mean and unit variance. With that transformation no one variable will distort the joint distribution of individuals in a way that misrepresents their similarity. Again, it should be noted that it has been argued that standarization may dilute the best discriminators (Fleiss & Zubin, 1969).

The nature of the univariate distribution of the individual variables does not markedly affect numerical taxonomy. In fact, the univariate distribution contains the seeds of the larger multivariate distribution's distinguishing characteristics. A variable may be skewed, multimodally or normally distributed, or have some other distributional property, and, in combination with the other variables, it will still be useful in determining the taxa. Attempts to normalize the data, for example, log transformations, are therefore not necessary (Sneath & Sokal, 1973).

Estimation of Taxonomic Resemblance

Most clustering techniques begin with calculation of a similarity matrix, and many statistics are available for computing the similarity/dissimilarity of the units of analysis (individuals). Because of the wide variety of techniques available, the following discussion is not exhaustive (with only the more familiar options being described). Statistical presentations of cluster analysis should be read when choosing a coefficient (Anderberg, 1973; Everitt, 1974, 1980; Sneath & Sokal, 1973). Four types of similarity measures will be considered: coefficients of association, correlation coefficients, distance metrics, and information statistics.

Coefficients of Association.   When qualitative data with two or more categories are being used, it is possible to calculate a variety of coefficients that use the information that two individuals do or do not possess the same characteristics. In general, these similarity coefficients are based upon the number of variables possessed by both objects $[n(11)]$, the number possessed by one or the other object $[n(10), n(01)]$, and the number of negative matches, or those characteristics possessed by neither object $[n(00)]$. One such similarity coefficient is the simple matching coefficient (SMC). SMC $= [n(11) + n(00)] / [n(10) + n(01) + n(11) + n(00)]$.

One problem with the SMC is that negative matches are counted as similarity. This may not always make sense, for instance, neither Jack nor Joe have wings—does that make them similar? One solution is to use a coefficient that does not use negative matches, for example $n(11)/ [n(01) + n(10) + n(11)]$. Ultimately, the choice of including negative matches rests with the informed researcher (Sneath & Sokal, 1973).

Other coefficients of association for qualitative data include Jaccard's coefficient, Yule's Q, and Phi (Bailey, 1975; Lorr, 1983). For cases where the data involve different numbers of categories for different variables, Gower's method has been recommended (Everitt, 1974; 1980).

The strength of the coefficients of association is their simplicity. In fact, Sneath and Sokal (1973) suggest the use of a dummy variable approach to reduce complex variables so as to permit coefficients of association to be employed.

Correlation Coefficients.   For quantitative data, a Pearsonian product-moment correlation can be calculated between two individuals across the set of variables. This has been called a Q-correlation (Cattell, 1946). As a measure of similarity, it has been argued that Q-correlations represent the slope between values on variables (Skinner, 1979). To the extent that this is true, the shape of the profile of the two individuals becomes a predominant concern.

Skinner (1979) has argued that the similarity of slopes between variables fits with the notion of a psychiatric syndrome. He further argues that the elevation of the values on the variables indicates the severity of the syndrome. For those reasons Skinner has perhaps been the leading advocate in psychology of correlation coefficients to measure similarity. Several authors, however, have been critical of the Q-correlation (Everitt, 1974; Fleiss & Zubin, 1969; Sneath & Sokal, 1973). One difficulty is the interpretation of the correlation coefficient. In terms of similarity between individuals, a correlation of "0" is not particularly meaningful. Although it does refer to independence, a correlation of "−1" means maximal difference.

A second criticism relates to the fact that slope and not elevation is tapped. A high correlation implies a linear relationship, not sameness of scores. Since a correlation coefficient is a measure of covariation, two individuals who have similar slope profiles but only one of which has a high score profile would correlate strongly although the mathematical value of their scores is dissimilar. In contrast, a third individual who has basically high scores, but not in the exact relative position to each other as the pattern exhibited by the first high scoring individual, probably would not correlate highly with him although the two are similar in the responses given for each variable. Everitt (1974, p. 56) provides an example, demonstrating that the slopes do not even have to be parallel to have a high correlation, but merely must be linearly related. It is possible for parallel profiles to have a lower correlation than do linear, nonparallel profiles.

Additional arguments against the Q-correlation include the fact that seldom are the variables on which it is based randomly drawn from a known population of variables (Bailey, 1975). As a result, the variables are not independent from each other (as individuals in a sample should be for meeting the parametric assumptions in the normal usage of correlations between two variables). In addition, the correlation coefficient does not meet the criteria to be a metric (Sneath & Sokal, 1973, p. 139).

Distance Metrics.   Because cluster analysis involves finding groups of individuals in multidimensional space, it is relatively easy to conceive of the variables as the spatial dimensions, thus providing a framework for calculating similarity between individuals plotted in that space. Elementary geometry brings Euclidean distance to mind as a way of calculating distance between individuals in multidimensional space. This approach has intuitive appeal, since the only way individuals can be plotted near to each other is for them to have similar scores on the variables. In terms of the data structure of individuals plotted in the variable space, a cluster can be thought of as a region of dense points separated by sparser regions where fewer individuals are located.

Distance coefficients have the additional advantage of having an easily interpretable zero point. "$D = 0$ if and only if two objects are identical in value on all variables" (Bailey, 1975, p. 68).

Several different distance coefficients are available, however, each with slightly different properties. The simplest form is Euclidean distance:

$$d_{ij} = \left\{ \sum_{k=1}^{P} (X_{ik} - X_{jk})^2 \right\}^{1/2}$$

where i and j are points and X_{ik} is the value on the kth variable for the ith individual (Everitt, 1974). Squared distance is sometimes used.
Average distance,

$$d_{av} = (d_{ij}^2/N)^{1/2}$$

where N equals the number of variables, may be preferable to d_{ij} because d_{ij} increases with the N.

Everitt (1974) advises standardizing each variable to preserve relative distance. The problem is that with raw data, changes in the scales of the same variable, for example, from feet to inches, can drastically affect Euclidean distances.

Sneath and Sokal (1973) also mention Pearson's coefficient of racial likeness. A related distance coefficient, the Mahalanobis (1936)D^2 is offered by Bailey (1975) and Everitt (1974) as having some desirable characteristics. Bailey (1975) suggests its use when the entities have variance within them, for instance, cities. Everitt (1974) points out that the Mahalanobis D^2 takes into account the correlation between the variables. This allows the typologist to relax the criteria for selecting uncorrelated variables. For certain forms of research, for example, within families, this may be a desirable feature because important measures are very likely to be correlated, such as husband and wife marital adjustment.

Other distance metrics include Cattell's coefficient of pattern similarity (Cattell et al., 1966) and the city-block metric (Sneath & Sokal, 1973).

Information Theory-based Metrics.   Jardine and Sibson (1971) prefer similarity measures derived from information theory and statistical notions of entropy and information. This strategy can bypass the calculation of a similarity matrix as the fusion of clusters proceeds based on minimizing the change in the information statistic.

Clustering Procedures

The basic goal of a cluster analysis is to reveal what is hoped to be a "type structure" by putting together similar individuals and separating dissimilar ones. There are a number of ways of doing this (Anderberg, 1973; Bailey, 1975; Cormack, 1971; Everitt, 1974, 1980). The approaches are grouped in our discussion under the following labels: hierarchical agglomerative, divisive, optimization/partitioning, density search, clumping, and inverse factor analysis. Somewhat greater detail will be given to the more popular approaches, for example, hierarchical agglomerative. Within each approach there are a variety of specific techniques. Often these techniques are referenced under different names by different writers. Where possible, the alernative names will be mentioned.

Hierarchical Agglomerative Techniques.   If the sample is viewed as having N clusters, each cluster being an individual, the researcher could start by putting together the two most similar individuals and labeling this pair as a new cluster. From the $N - 1$ clusters at that point, the most similar clusters could be grouped together into a new cluster. The process could continue until the last two clusters are finally merged into one cluster that contains the whole sample. At some point, the researcher will decide what is the proper number of clusters. That decision will be discussed later. The approach of successively grouping individuals is referred to as the *hierarchical agglomerative procedure*. A number of decision rules, or algorithms, exist for choosing the merger at each stage. Each takes its initial values from the similarity/ dissimilarity matrix.

In *single linkage*, also known as nearest neighbor, two clusters are defined as most similar if any two individuals between them are more similar to each other than any other possible combination of between-cluster individuals. Where $d(x, y)$ and $d(y, z)$ represent the distances between the nearest pairs, the single linkage algorithm is

$$d([x, y], z) = min \ [d(x, z), d(y, z)]$$

In other words, the single shortest link decides which prospective merger will take place.

A contrasting algorithm is *complete linkage*, or the farthest-neighbor method. At each stage in the agglomerative process, calculations are made between clusters so that clusters are merged when the distances between the farthest members of the comparative clusters are the smallest, or

$$d([x, y], z) = max \ [d(x, z), d(y, z)]$$

In contrast to the two techniques just mentioned that take into account only the nearest or fai thest pairs of individuals, respectively, a number of algorithms are based upon the relationship of all the members in any two clusters. These algorithms, therefore, use more information to obtain a merger. The *centroid method* uses the centroids (means as the variables) of the groups to calculate the respective distances. The group average method measures distance as the average of the distances between all pairs of individuals in separate clusters. In fact, there are weighted and unweighted variants of each. Weighting refers to giving the latest possible entrant into a merger more importance. This may be useful when the clusters are of unequal size and the researcher does not wish to lose an important, but rare, type. Certain psychiatric syndromes might fit this logic.

Ward's technique (Ward, 1963) merges clusters where the error sum of squares (ESS) caused by the respective possible fusions is a minimum. The ESS is defined as the total sum of squared deviations of every individual from the centroid of its parent cluster.

Lance and Williams (1967) have provided a generalized approach to the hierarchical agglomerative techniques by showing that all of them fit a recurrence formula but differ in the values given to parameters of the formula. Their own technique, the *flexible-beta*, allows the researcher to select parameter values.

In the procedures just discussed, the clustering proceeds from the case where each entity is a cluster through successive mergers until the final point where all entities have merged into one cluster. This structure, graphically, looks like a tree and is called a dendogram.

A consideration in a numerical taxonomy is choosing the cluster solution that most adequately reflects the distributional properties and the underlying type structure of the data. The researcher has to decide what number of clusters best represents that data structure. As in factor analysis, certain solutions do a better job at this than do others.

One basic principle in the hierarchical agglomerative techniques is that at each successive agglomeration some information is being lost. This loss can be assessed through a measure of the variation in the data at each number of clusters. The variation will increase as more and more individuals are admitted who are not close to the mean of the cluster. At some point, relatively dissimilar clusters are forced together. When this happens, there is a large jump in the variance as compared to the preceding increases. This jump would be a signal to back up one step and pick the solution prior to the jump as the most likely correct number of clusters (Filsinger, 1980). This procedure is analogous to the scree test for determining the proper number of factors in factor analysis (Cattell, 1966).

Hierarchical Divisive. In a sense, the divisive techniques do the same thing as the hierarchical agglomerative approaches. The difference is that the divisive techniques begin with one cluster to which the whole sample belongs and then begin to divide the sample into subgroups, making a new division at each point. A polythetic-monothetic distinction can be made among these techniques.

The polythetic divisive strategies (Everitt, 1974) take all the information on the variables into account. For example, the technique described by McNaughton-Smith and his colleagues (1964) involves the use of average Euclidean distance to locate the most distant entity within a cluster. The distances between the splinter group and the main group are found for each individual. When the difference between those distances is positive, the individual goes to the splinter group; when negative, to the main group. The process is then repeated for the two clusters.

The automatic interaction detector (Sonquist & Morgan, 1963) can be used in divisive clustering as a monothetic method. That is, splits are made based upon values on one variable so that the new groups share that value. Each split is determined by considering the reduction in the unexplained variance in a dependent variable of interest, for example, recovery rate.

As Everitt (1974) points out, "a set of n individuals can be divided into two subsets in 2^{n-1} ways, . . ." (p. 18). Even for a sample of 100, this figure is mind-boggling. Each of the methods just discussed shortcut the procedure. However, the initial divisions determine later possibilities. An error due to the chance configuration of the data could lead to important types being split somewhere in the process. Because of their complexitiy, Bailey (1975) suggests that the divisive techniques developed to date are primarily of theoretical interest.

The possibility of using the automatic interaction detector to match possible types to outcome measures sounds appealing, but the risk of only optimizing within a given data set (rather than finding naturally occurring types with real differences) should give some caution to its use in classification.

Optimizing/Partitioning. Another approach to grouping the most similar individuals is to start with a given solution and to relocate an individual from one cluster to another if a statistic is optimized. Often trace W or similar measures of "within-group" dispersion are used (Everitt, 1974). In the covariance matrix, the diagonal represents the within-group variances. If the sum of these is minimized, the clusters are of greater similarity.

According to Everitt (1974), the partitioning techniques involve three different steps: a method of initiating clusters, a method for assigning individuals to these clusters, and a method for reallocating them to other clusters on a best-fit basis.

Although a number of procedures are available to the researcher for specifying the number of clusters and assigning individuals to those clusters, the most unique aspect of these approaches is the reallocation on a best-fit basis. These procedures are called *relocation*, or optimization procedures, since they iteratively relocate individuals until a minimization of the statistic is obtained. Unfortunately, this technique runs into the problem of the local optimum of the statistic. It is of great importance, therefore, that the initial solution is a reasonably good one.

One way to handle this problem to the mutual benefit of each approach is to enter the final solution from an alternative strategy (e.g., a hierarchical agglomerative solution) as the initial solution in a relocation routine. This is perhaps superior to the hierarchical routine alone, in that its final solution is partially determined by initial merges that may place individuals in clusters that do not represent their greatest similarity. The relocation technique would theoretically produce a solution that properly places these individuals. For example, Filsinger (1980) used a relocation procedure to improve a mode analysis in his study of various types of cognitive styles.

Density Search Methods.   The intuitive definition of a natural cluster is that it is a dense set of points separated from other dense sets of points. Everitt (1974) provides an overview of these procedures. Mode analysis (Wishart, 1969) will serve as an example.

Mode analysis searches for natural subgroupings of the data by estimating disjoint density surfaces in the sample distribution (Wishart, 1969). The number of points corresponding to other entities within a given radius R of each entity is counted. If there are parameter K or more other points within the density threshold or radius R, the entity is considered "dense." If there are less than K entities within radius R, the entity is considered "nondense." The linkage parameter K is chosen as a function of the sample size (Wishart, 1970).

Other density search techniques include the *taxometric map* (TAXMAP) (Carmichael et al., 1968) and the *Cartet count* method (Cattell & Coulter, 1966).

Clumping.   Up to this point, the solutions of a cluster analysis produces mutually exclusive clusters. In some areas of investigation it may make sense to have overlapping clusters because it is felt that naturally some individuals belong to more than one type.

In general, these techniques seek to split the sample into two groups such that a cohesion function between the groups is minimized. The solution is then enhanced by iteratively reallocating individuals between the groups. A different starting point is then instituted and a new bifurcation is begun. One problem with these techniques is that because of starting at a number of different points, it is very possible to find repeatably the same cluster in different passes (Everitt, 1974).

Q-factor Analysis.   Regular R-factor analysis proceeds to find dimensions within a matrix formed by the correlation of the variables. In Q-factor analysis, dimensions are sought within the correlation of the individuals across the variables. Psychologists have been among the few users of this technique for clustering (cf. Skinner, 1979,; Tryon & Bailey, 1970). Outside psychology, most taxonomists have not looked upon it with much favor.

Combination Approaches.   In psychology, a number of statisticians have attempted to develop approaches that combine a dimensional search in the data set (similar to factor analysis) at the same time as they attempt to locate individual patterns. Tucker (1966) has offered a model for individualized learning curves. Skinner (1979) has developed a combinational approach of locating factors and then finding clusters based on those dimensions. Tryon and Bailey's (1970) approach clusters variables and then clusters individuals on those clusters of variables. Most of these combinational approaches are intuitively appealing but have not garnered a large following. To some extent this is due to the complexity of the statistical and mathematical assumptions and calculations involved.

Evaluation of Procedures.   Since the various algorithms frequently produce different clustering solutions, some comparisons need to be made. Single linkage has the undesirable property of chaining. This means that clusters developed by linking groups with the closest two individuals can produce serpentine chains through the data space. It has already been mentioned that single linkage and complete linkage may not take into account all the information available.

In general, the hierarchical approaches can be criticized for not allowing reallocation of individuals between clusters. Thus, there is no correcting for a poor initial agglomeration (or division). Optimization techniques face the problem of local optima; that is, although the next move might not optimize the solution, an increase might be necessary before continuing to narrow the criteria.

Although the various techniques have been compared to theoretical criteria (e.g., Fisher & Van Ness, 1971), perhaps the best evidence as to the relative merit of each comes from evaluating their performance on data sets with known distributional properties. Blashfield (1976) conducted tests of various algorithms on Monte Carlo data sets with various mixtures of multivariate normal populations. On easy data sets, that is, where the separate distributions were rather distinct, all the techniques performed adequately. However, when the mixtures became more similar and over-lapped to a greater extent, Ward's method performed best in producing groups with memberships corresponding to those of the input populations.

Milligan (1981) has reviewed the Monte Carlo studies and also suggests that Ward's method leads to the best recoveries. He cautions, however, that this may be in part due to the contrived Monte Carlo data sets. The reader is advised to know the research area in question well enough to know if the ideal solution is a minimum variance type of solution.

Validation

Unfortunately, even basically proven algorithms give different solutions (cf. Everitt, 1974, p. 67−68; Cormack, 1971). It is therefore necessary to determine to what degree the solution has imposed a structure upon the data set. This is the question of the validity of the clustering solution.

Blashfield et al. (1978) classified group validation efforts under three categories: statistical, data manipulation, or graphical analysis. The statistical measures include: (1) cophenetic measures, which compare the similarity matrix in the original data with that produced by the clustering; (2) variance measures, which focus on the homogeneity of the clusters; (3) interpoint distance measures, which measure the proximity of one cluster's members versus other cluster's members; and (4) maximum likelihood estimates of the parameters of the mixture model of the data.

Although the exact procedures of validation would require a detailed discussion, a few general statements can be made. Even though different techniques are available for checking the validity of the solution, the use of a number of them for combined inference is preferable to dependence upon just one. A relatively simple technique is to use different clustering algorithms and then to compare the solutions. Some intelligent decision is needed to pick the comparison algorithms. Those algorithms that best fit the chosen clustering criterion are preferable. Single linkage, for example, does not perform well in data sets where the types overlap (Blashfield, 1976). Ideally, the membership of individuals in taxa produced by one algorithm should match the membership given by a second algorithm.

A discriminant analysis or multivariate analysis of variance could be performed on the groups. The result should indicate significant differences. On the other hand, all the algorithms make an effort to produce dissimilarity between the clusters, so any algorithm could potentially produce significantly different clusters from artificial dissections of the data (Anderberg, 1973). In other words, a clustering solution with significant differences is very likely and cannot be taken as conclusive evidence. This technique probably should not be used as the sole validation procedure.

A cross-validation design can be employed where the initial sample is randomly split and separate cluster analyses are performed on each. The outcomes should not be significantly different. This can be tested by taking the discriminant functions from the first random half and applying them to the second half to see if the individuals in the second half can be correctly placed by the first discriminant functions into their respective taxa as defined by the second half results. Further, any given group can be randomly split. The two halves should not be significantly different.

Interpretation of the Results

A given group can be described in terms of its centroid. (The centroid being the series of means on the variables used as a basis for the classification). Groups can be interpreted in two ways, both of which are necessary in order to understand the results. The groups can be taken individually and the particular combination of means, or the profile, within any one cluster will give the picture of its nature. Second, the groups can be compared with each other. Contrasts and comparisons indicate the distinguishing characteristics of each.

ILLUSTRATIONS OF CLUSTER ANALYSIS FROM HEALTH PSYCHOLOGY

Cluster analysis has been used in a number of studies related to health psychology. What follows is a series of brief descriptions of a small selection of these studies. The selection was based on an attempt to demonstrate the range of techniques and issues addressed while also pointing out the strengths and the weaknesses of those efforts. Because each study has unique features, the descriptions do not necessarily follow a common outline for the analysis of issues.

Medicine

The typological approach has frequently been used as a diagnostic tool in medicine. Baron and Fraser (1968) used cluster analysis to diagnose liver diseases such as infectious hepatitis, alcoholic cirrhosis, and extrahepatic biliary obstruction. When the authors removed nonspecific histologic characters (which did not contribute to a differential diagnosis), the cluster analysis produced types that corresponded quite closely to the clinical assessment of the diseases. The Baron and Fraser article provides an illustration of the principle that the quality of the information is more important than the quantity of the information and that, in fact, more information does not necessarily improve the classification of the units under analysis (cf. Sneath & Sokal, 1973).

Alcoholism

Against a background of both armchair and empirical typologies of alcoholics, Finney and Moos (1979) attempted to extend the cluster analysis-derived typologies to the issues of differential etiology, prognoses, and type by treatment interaction. They did this by drawing their sample from several different treatment programs and including sociodemographic, social psychological, and social environmental variables.

The cluster analysis is not described in detail and is referenced by citing the computer program used (but not the explicit algorithm). It appears that a hierarchical agglomerative technique was chosen using Euclidean distance as the dissimilarity coefficient. A 10-cluster solution was chosen without explanation as to the choice of the number of clusters. In addition, two small clusters of those 10 "were merged with those from a larger cluster having a similar profile, leaving a final set of eight types" (p. 29).

The labeling of the types was in terms of the level of social competence (high and low), level of resources (high, medium, and low), or family press (present or not), for example, type 5: high social competence and low resources, and type 8: high social competence and family press. This naming strategy suggests a cross tabulation of several categorical variables and does not perhaps do full justice to the assumed species distribution.

The types were compared on additional background, outcome, and patient-treatment congruence variables. Moderate support was found for the prognostic utility of the typology and for the patient-treatment congruence questions. This second issue suggests that certain types of patients select, or are selected for, certain types of treatment.

Aphasia

In an attempt to develop an empirical typology of aphasia from data on 206 subjects diagnosed as either aphasic or brain-damaged, Crockett and his colleagues (1981) used a combination of factor analysis and cluster analysis. Principal component factor analysis was used to derive the basic dimensions of the Neurosensory Comprehensive Examination for Aphasia (Spreen & Benton, 1977). The factor scores from those dimensions were cluster analyzed using the hierarchical grouping analysis, not a well-known procedure that would make an exact replication difficult for those not having access to the particular computing program. The decision as to the number of clusters was empircally based on the points of discontinuity in the cumulative within-group error term (a scree test) and on the percentage of total variability ascribed to each solution. Both criteria pointed to a five-cluster solution. A reanalysis using only the aphasic subjects supported the typology.

The substantive interpretation of the types suggested that the types were arranged based on the severity of impairment. The nonaphasic brain-damaged subjects fell into the two least impaired types along with the less impaired medically diagnosed aphasics. The other three types were exclusively medically diagnosed aphasics but differed in the extent of impairment. The authors suggest that only the most severely impaired type represented "a salient feature type of aphasic disorder" (p. 91).

The two primary conclusions that the authors have drawn relate to the uniqueness of aphasia and the specificity of the impairment. That two types contained both medically diagnosed aphasics and other brain-damaged subjects suggests that, at least for lower levels of impairment, aphasics may not be unique or medical diagnosis may be imperfect. The fact that only 6.3 percent of the subjects were found in a type with specific impairment (for reading skills) suggests that most aphasics suffer from general impairment.

If the findings had merely pointed to the level of impairment as being important, a cluster analysis would not necessarily have been justified.

Linear models of data analysis would have been sufficient. However, the unique cluster that represented the specific feature type of aphasia might well have been missed because it was related in an essentially nonlinear manner to the others.

Minimal Brain Dysfunction

Crinella (1973) presented an empirical typology that was designed to help clarify the problematic classification of minimal brain dysfunction (MBD). The investigator used 53 children who either had verified brain lesions ($n = 19$) or were clinically suspected of MBD ($n = 34$). Again, this practice of including some subjects who would not be classified as possessing minimal brain damage strengthens the typology by showing the extent of the uniqueness of the cluster of characteristics associated with the dysfunction. The subjects were administered an extensive battery of neuropsychologic tests. The resulting 90 test variables were factor analyzed to reduce the number of classificatory dimensions. The 16 rotated factors were used to derive factor scores for each subject. Employing these factor scores, Crinella used Cattell's r coefficient to calculate profile similarity among the subjects and employed Thurstone's multiple group method to derive clusters. The clusters were lettered A through H rather than substantively named. The types did show a number of MBD children who were not behaviorally different from children with brain lesions. In addition, several types were found that consisted primarily of either the brain-lesioned children or the MBD children. The brain-lesioned children who were located within the predominantly MBD types were analyzed in order to develop hypotheses as to the possible organic origins of the MBD syndromes. A unitary MBD syndrome was clearly contraindicated.

Dementia

Ballinger et al. (1982) used Ward's agglomerative technique to cluster analyze a variety of ratings (35 binary attributes) on 100 elderly "demented" patients from a psychiatric ward. Of interest was the fact that attention was paid to those characteristics that were invariant across subjects. That is, variables where fewer than 5 percent or greater than 95 percent of the subjects displayed the characteristics were not used in the cluster analysis. Many of these characteristics were classic exemplars of dementia, for example, intellectual impairment, confusion, phobias, obsessions, and compulsions. This decision had interesting implications for taxonomy. It meant that some of the most important characteristics for distinguishing dementia from other disorders were not employed. As assumption was made that the typology would occur within a larger type defined a priori. On the other hand, this decision follows guidelines for taxonomy suggested by Sneath and Sokal (1973) that invariant characteristics should not be used. However, the Sneath and Sokal suggestion was offered in the context of differentiating species. The Ballinger et al. decision maximized differences between types.

Ballinger also chose an eight-cluster solution because it offered "the best clinical interpretation" (p. 258). It is not clear from that decision rule that the types chosen represented a basic structure of the data in terms of a multi-modal distribution. The scree test rule offers some suggestion of this and could have been employed.

Seven additional characteristics not included in the cluster analysis, such as sex, age, and dead at follow-up, were used to describe the clusters further. Unfortunately, the authors did not report whether or not the types were significantly different for these additional characteristics (and would have helped validate the solution). The authors do comment that the empirical types correspond to clinical experience. However, the outcome is not surprising, given the fact that clinical meaningfulness was used as the criterion for selecting the clustering solution.

CONCLUSIONS

The purpose of this chapter was to introduce the reader to the logic and basic procedures of taxonomic grouping via cluster analysis. If health psychology is to benefit from the lessons of clinical and personality psychology, then the assumption of "patient homogeneity" should be put aside, along with the tendency to "force fit" people into preconceived (and often ill-conceived) categories. In attempting to sort out the complexities of human disease perceptions, coping strategies, environmental reactions, health schemata, responses to chronic pain, drug responsivity, beliefs about medical treatment, psychophysiological reactivity, or patterns of illness-related self-management of thought, affect, and action, we can assume that we face what statisticians call the "mixture problem" (cf. Lorr, 1983). That is, we confront samples of individuals from diverse subpopulations, many of whom superficially resemble one another, to the point that they are lumped under a single rubric—for example, hypochondriac, good coper, coronary prone, bad medical risk, overexcitable, ulcer personality, and the like. However, if clinicians are, in fact, seeing several distinct populations of persons, then progress in diagnosis, treatment design, and clinical prediction would be greatly aided by methods designed to identify empirical types. The methods discussed in this chapter represent one such avenue for the improvement of classification in contemporary health psychology.

Interested readers will, alas, be quite unable to conduct cluster analytic studies solely on the basis of the material presented here. Indeed, because of the ever-increasing availability of new and powerful multivariate data analytic techniques, the student/researcher must first gain familiarity with a number of potential data reduction methods—including factor analysis, multidimensional scaling, as well as cluster analysis (cf. Cleary, 1983). Only after a thoughtful consideration of the substantive issues being researched and of the available methods should an individual proceed to apply any particular method (or set of methods).

It has been noted that cluster analytic techniques have not yet caught on among behavioral scientists. Obviously, we feel particularly hopeful about their potential for clarifying classificatory issues in health psychology/ behavioral medicine. However, given the number of decisional crossroads in the conduct of a taxonomic study, good cluster analytic studies will always require knowledge, patience, and sensitivity to one's data. These are not the ingredients of which "quick and dirty" experiments are made.

References

Alexander, F. (1950). *Psychosomatic medicine*. New York: Norton.

Anderberg, M. R. (1973). *Cluster analysis for applications*. New York: Academic Press.

Bailey, K. D. (1975). Cluster analysis. In D. R. Heise (Eds.), *Sociological methodology, 1975*. San Francisco: Jossey-Bass.

Ballinger, B. R., Reid, A. H., & Heather, B. B. (1982). Cluster analysis of symptoms in elderly demented patients. *British Journal of Psychiatry, 140,* 257–262.

Baron, D. N., & Fraser, P. M. (1968). Medical applications of taxonomic methods. *British Medical Bulletin, 24,* 236–240.

Blackwelder, R. A. (1966). *Taxonomy: A text and reference book*. New York: Wiley.

Blashfield, R. K. (1976). Mixture model tests of cluster analysis: Accuracy of four hierarchical agglomerative methods. *Psychological Bulletin, 83,* 377–388.

Blashfield, R. K. (1980). The growth of cluster analysis: Tryon, Ward, and Johnson. *Multivariate Behavioral Research, 15,* 439–458.

Blashfield, R. K., Aldenderfer, M. S., & Morey, L. C. (1978). *Cluster analysis literature on validation*. Paper presented at the Annual Meeting of the Classification Society, Clemson, May.

Blashfield, R. K., & Draguns, J. G. (1976). Evaluative criteria for psychiatric classification. *Journal of Abnormal Psychology, 85,* 140–150.

Blashfield, R. K. & Morey, L. C. (1979). The classification of depression through cluster analysis. *Comprehensive Psychiatry, 20,* 516–527.

Bolz, C. R. (1977). Typological theory and research. In R. B. Cattell & R. M. Dreger (Eds.), *Handbook of modern personality theory*. Washington, DC: Hemisphere.

Carmichael, J. W., George, J. A. & Julius, R. S. (1968). Finding natural clusters. *Systematic Zoology, 17,* 144–150.

Cattell, R. B. (1946). *Description and measurement of personality*. London: Harrap.

Cattell, R. B. (1952). *Factor analysis: An introduction and manual for the psychologist and social scientist*. New York: Harper & Row.

Cattell, R. B. (1966). The scree test for the number of factors. *Multivariate Behavioral Research, 1,* 245–276.

Cattell, R. B. & Coulter, M. A. (1966). Principles of behavioral taxonomy and the mathematical basis of the taxonomy computer program. *British Journal of Mathematical and Statistical Psychology, 19,* 237–269.

Cattell, R. B., Coulter, M. A. & Tsujioka, B. (1966). The taxonometric recognition of types and functional emergents. In R. B. Cattell (Ed.), *Handbook of multivariate experimental psychology*. Chicago: Rand McNally.

Cleary, P. D. (1983). Multivariate analysis: Basic approaches to health data. In D. Mechanic (Ed.), *Handbook of health, health care, and the health professions*. New York: Free Press.

Cohen, F., & Lazarus, R. S. (1983). Coping and adaptation in health and illness. In D. Mechanic (Ed.), *Handbook of health, health care, and the health professions*. New York: Free Press.

Cormack, R. M. (1971). A review of classification. *Journal of the Royal Statistical Society, 134*, 321–367.

Crinella, F. M. (1973). Identification of brain dysfunction syndromes in children through profile analyses: Patterns associated with so-called "minimal brain dysfunction." *Journal of Abnormal Psychology, 82*, 33–45.

Crockett, D., Clark, C., Spreen, O. & Klonoff, H. (1981). Severity of impairment of specific types of aphasia: An empirical investigation. *Cortex, 17*, 83–96.

Crowson, R. A. (1965). Classification, statistics, and phylogemy. *Systematic Zoology, 14*, 144–148.

Crowson, R. A. (1970). *Classification and biology*. New York: Atherton Press.

Day, N. E. (1969). Estimating the components of a mixture of normal distributions. *Biometrika, 56*, 463–474.

Everitt, B. (1974). *Cluster Analysis*. London: Heinemann.

Everitt, B. (1980). *Cluster Analysis*. (2nd ed.). London: Heinemann (Halsted Press).

Eysenck, H. J., & Eysenck, S. B. G. (1969). *Personality structure and measurement*. London: Routledge & Kegan Paul.

Filsinger, E. E. (1980). A numerical typology of cognitive styles based on college students' beliefs about societal institutions. *Representative Research in Social Psychology, 11*, 122–138.

Finney, J. W., & Moos, R. H. (1979). Treatment and outcome for empirical subtypes of alcoholic patients. *Journal of Consulting and Clinical Psychology, 47*, 25–38.

Fisher, L., & Van Ness, J. W. (1971). Admissible clustering procedures. *Biometrika, 58*, 91–104.

Fleiss, J. L., & Zubin, J. (1969). On the methods and theory of clustering. *Multivariate Behavioral Research, 4*, 235–250.

Good, I. J. (1977). The botryology of botryology. In J. Van Ryzin (Ed.), *Classification and clustering*. New York: Academic Press.

Gordon, A. D. (1981). *Classification*. London: Chapman & Hall.

Hempel, C. G. (1952). *Fundamentals of concept formation in empirical science*. Chicago: University of Chicago Press.

Hempel, C. G. (1965). *Aspects of scientific explanation*. New York: Free Press.

Jardine, N., & Sibson, R. (1971). *Mathematical taxonomy*. New York: Wiley.

Kinsman, R. A., Dirks, J. F., & Jones, N. F. (1982). Psychomaintenance of chronic physical illness. In T. Millon, C. Green, & R. Meagher (Eds.), *Handbook of clinical health psychology*. New York: Plenum Press.

Kinsman, R. A., Luparello, T. J., O'Banion, K., & Spector, S. L. (1973). Multidimensional analysis of the subjective symptomatology of asthma. *Psychosomatic Medicine, 35*, 250–267.

Kinsman, R. A. Spector, S. L., Schucard, D. W., & Luparello, T. J. (1974). Observations on patterns of subjective symptomatology of asthma. *Psychosomatic Medicine, 36*, 129–143.

Lance, G. N., & Williams, W. T. (1967). A general theory of classificatory sorting strategies. I: Hierarchical systems: *Computer Journal, 9*, 373–380.

Lebowitz, M. D., Thompson, H. C. & Strunk, R. C. (1981). Subjective psychological symptoms in outpatient asthmatic adolescents. *Journal of Behavioral Medicine, 4*, 439–449.

Lorr, M. (1983). *Cluster analysis for social scientists*. San Francisco: Jossey-Bass.

Mahalanobis, P. C. (1936). On the generalized distance in statistics. *Proceedings of the National Institute of Science of Calcutta, 12*, 49–55.

Mayr, E. (1969). *Principles of systematic zoology*. New York: McGraw-Hill.

McKinney, J. C. (1966). *Constructive typology and social theory*. New York: Appleton-Century-Crofts.

McNaughton-Smith, P., Williams, W. T., Dale, N. B., & Mockett, L. G. (1964). Dissimilarity analysis. *Nature, 202,* 1034–1035.

Milligan, G. W. (1981). A review of Monte Carlo tests of cluster analysis. *Multivariate Behavioral Research, 16,* 379–407.

Overall, J. E., Hollister, L. E., Johnson, M., et al. (1966). Nosology of depression and differential response to drugs. *Journal of the American Medical Association, 195,* 946–950.

Raskin, A., Schulterbrandt, J. G., Boothe, H., et al. (1972). Some suggestions for selecting appropriate depression subgroups for biochemical studies. In T. Williams (Ed.), *Recent advances in the psychobiology of depressive illness*. Washington, DC: U.S. Government Printing Office.

Ross, H. H. (1974). *Biological systematics*. Reading, MA: Addison-Wesley.

Skinner, H. A. (1979). Dimensions and clusters: A hybrid approach to classification. *Applied Psychological Measurement, 3,* 327–341.

Skinner, H. A. (1981). Toward the integraton of classification theory and methods. *Journal of Abnormal Psychology, 90,* 68–87.

Skinner, H. A., & Blashfield, R. K. (1982). Increasing the impact of cluster analysis research: The case of psychiatric classification. *Journal of Consulting and Clinical Psychology, 50,* 727–735.

Sneath, P. H. A. & Sokal, R. R. (1973). *Numerical taxonomy*. San Francisco: Freeman.

Sonquist, J. A., & Morgan, J. N. (1963). Problems in the analysis of survey data, and a proposal. *Journal of the American Statistical Association, 58,* 415–435.

Spreen, O., & Benton, A. (1977). Neurosensory center comprehensive examination of aphasia. Neuropsychological Laboratory, University of Victoria, Victoria, Canada.

Stern, A. (1981). *Asthma and emotion*. New York: Gardner Press.

Swencionis, C. (1982). Journals relevant to health psychology. *Health Psychology, 1,* 307–313.

Tryon, R. C. & Bailey, D. E. (1970). *Cluster analysis*. New York: McGraw-Hill.

Tucker, L. R. (1966). Learning theory and the multivariate experiment: Illustration by determination of generalized learning curves. In R. B. Cattell (Ed.), *Handbook of multivariate experimental psychology*. Chicago: Rand McNally.

Ward, J. H. (1963). Hierarchical grouping to optimize and objective function. *Journal of the American Statistical Association, 58,* 236–244.

Wishart, D. (1969). Mode analysis. In A. J. Cole (Ed.), *Numerical taxonomy*. New York: Academic Press.

Wishart, D. (1970). *Cluster IA: User Manual*. Fife, Scotland: University of Saint Andrews.

PART IV

SPECIAL TARGETS OF ASSESSMENT

11

The Measurement of Medical Compliance in the Treatment of Disease

PATRICIA A. CLUSS
LEONARD H. EPSTEIN

INTRODUCTION

Importance of the Compliance Problem

It is often assumed that improvement in patients' clinical state is a correlate of our increasing knowledge of the etiology and course of diseases and of the medical community's expanding ability to make clear and accu-

The research presented in this paper was supported in part by a Mellon Fellowship awarded to Patricia Cluss.

rate diagnoses. The current availability of oral medications for an increasing number of medical and psychiatric disorders places an additional emphasis on concise diagnosis and prescription by the physician of an adequate course of therapy for patients.

Until fairly recently, however, little attention has been focused on the aftermath of the receipt of a prescription by the patient. In earlier days, medical treatment was, by necessity, performed by medical personnel in treatment facilities and accurate medication intake was assured. With our increasing ability to prescribe outpatient regimens, however, compliance has often simply been assumed.

The effectiveness of treatment for a chronic disease depends upon both the efficacy of treatment and the rate of patient adherence or compliance to the treatment. Most clinical outcome research is designed to find better treatments; that is, treatments that provide better evidence of their efficacy for a target problem. Although this research must continue, more research in compliance is needed to maximize treatment effectiveness. Research in compliance is also important, since, in some cases, treatment results may have as much to do with quality of adherence as with the specific pharmacologic effect of the treatment itself.

Unfortunately, the level of adherence to most treatment regimens for chronic disease is quite low. Bergman and Werner in 1963 were among the first to indicate that patient noncompliance with prescribed regimens was a major health problem. Their data showed that, of a total of 70 outpatient children prescribed a 10-day regimen of penicillin, 56 percent had stopped taking the drug by day 3 of the regimen and that a full 82 percent were noncompliant by day 9.

Consequences of noncompliance to prescribed medical treatment may be grave, including exacerbation of disability and progression of the disease (Stewart & Cluff, 1972), more frequent medical emergencies, and unnecessary prescriptions of more potent and/or toxic drugs (Norell, 1979) and, ultimately, failure of treatment (Dixon et al., 1957; Hogarty, et al., 1973; Sackett et al., 1975). Hogarty et al. (1973), for example, found that of schizophrenics taking chlorpromazine or placebo, fully one half of all relapsers in both groups were noncompliant and had ceased taking medication prior to relapse.

Since the initial studies on compliance several decades ago, research in this area has proliferated. In their definitive work on compliance in health care, Haynes and coworkers (1979) compiled a reference list of 537 original articles on compliance which will be used to summarize the amount of research done in selected areas of compliance. The largest group of studies on adherence (217 or 40 percent) are descriptive studies in which a single patient group was studied at one point in time and comparisons were made between compliers and noncompliers.

There is a dearth, however, of well-controlled treatment research attempting to develop and evaluate methods of increasing compliance and assessing the effect of increased compliance on clinical status. Only 17 percent of the studies noted by Haynes et al. (1979) met their criteria for a well-controlled randomized trial, whereas even fewer (34 studies or 6 percent of the total) involved a random sample, including attention to an adequate number of demographic variables. Only one study of the 537 (Hogarty et al., 1973) received a top rating according to Haynes and his colleagues' stringent criteria for both design and sample characteristics.

Focus of the Chapter

The main purpose of this chapter is to review general issues in the area of compliance research, such as the problems of adequately defining compliance and setting goals for adequate compliant behavior, issues of data interpretation and prediction of adherent behavior, as well as other important considerations in the measurement of compliance.

DEFINITION OF COMPLIANCE

Strict Versus Broad Definitions

Compliance (or adherence) has been defined in many different ways with definitions ranging from very strict to very loose interpretations of the term. Haynes (1979), for example, defines compliance as, "the extent to which a person's behavior (in terms of taking medications, following diets, or executing lifestyle changes) coincides with medical or health advice" (p. 2−3). Others add to this definition by including as components of compliance knowledge of the correct name of the medication, attendance at follow-up appointments (Becker et al. 1972; Nessman et al. 1980), and failure to fill prescriptions (Becker et al., 1972; Haggerty & Roghmann, 1972). Compliance with medication-taking according to various definitions may include omission of doses, taking medication for the wrong reason, errors in dosage or timing of sequence, and discontinuing therapy before the end of the recommended course (e.g., Blackwell, 1973; Haggerty & Roghmann, 1972).

Relative Frequencies of Medication-taking Errors

Studies of the relative frequencies of several of these medication-taking errors have demonstrated conflicting results. Boyd et al. (1974), for example, found that the most frequent error in outpatients was that of improper dosing intervals, occurring at least once on over half of all prescriptions, followed by premature discontinuation of medication, forgetting of doses, and intentional omission of medication in that order.

Other investigators (Schwartz et al., 1962), however, have shown omission of medication to be the most frequently occurring error among elderly, chronically ill patients, followed by inaccurate knowledge, errors in incorrect dosage, and, finally, improper timing or sequence of medication, with the latter occurring only one fifth as frequently as omission of doses. The increased incidence of errors of omission in this study may be due to the geriatric sample, since memory loss is a typical problem of the elderly.

Because of the difficulty of comparison among studies utilizing such disparate definitions of compliance, a recent trend has been to distinguish between *medication errors*, or mistakes in dosage or timing, in which failure to comply may be due to the patient's lack of understanding regarding some aspect of the regimen, and *true noncompliance*, or an actual omission of doses (Gordis, 1979; Stewart & Cluff, 1972).

Formula for Adherence and the Need for Specificity of Measurement

Adherence may be determined by the following formula (Feinstein, 1974).

$$\text{Percent adherence} = \frac{\text{number of doses taken by patient}}{\text{number of doses prescribed for the patient}} \times 100$$

Taken this way, adherence may vary from 0 to 100 percent. The ability to make knowledgeable assessments of the percentage of pills taken is based in large part on the measurement technology available. The ideal situation would be to be able to measure medication intake *directly*, so a patient would be considered compliant only if a dose were taken within the time interval specified by the drug regimen.

This specificity of measurement has been performed in only one published account. Norell (1979), in studying compliance of glaucoma patients to eye drops, developed an automatic eyedropper that provided continuous measurement of when and how many times the dropper was used. More often, however, the actual dose is not measured, but, rather, the total number of doses taken are inferred indirectly from the observation of pills remaining as compared to those prescribed (Gordis, 1979).

Haynes (1979) notes that, as an additional problem in defining compliance, some investigators choose to report actual compliance rates (number of treatment units taken divided by the number of units prescribed), whereas others report as their compliance rate the percentage of patients judged compliant according to some predetermined standard. It is, therefore, important when attempting to assess the significance of individual studies to determine the precise definition of compliance used by the investigator. If the study focuses specifically on omission errors in medication regimens, the reader must also determine whether reported compliance rates are the mean percentage of individual patients' ingestion of medication (dosage-centered) or the total percentage of the sample that reached a predetermined compliance cutoff point (sample-centered).

RANGE OF COMPLIANCE: A REVIEW

Range of Compliance Other Than Medication-taking Errors

Of primary interest in initial investigations of compliance was the determination of the scope and generality of noncompliance, often in an attempt to alert the medical community to this problem. As mentioned earlier, 40 percent or more of all literature in the area is specifically concerned with this issue. The range of compliance appears to be affected by several factors which will be described subsequently. Sackett and Snow (1979) have reviewed those studies that met their inclusion criteria and have reported compliance ranges by category. Although this chapter focuses on compliance to medication regimens, the results of research into other types of noncompliance in the health care system will be explored briefly. Table 11.1 summarizes Sackett and Snow's (1979) review of compliance rates in studies of nonmedication-taking errors.

Sackett and Snow (1979) first looked at studies investigating compliance with scheduled appointments and found differential rates of adherence for patients who initiated appointments themselves as compared with appointments scheduled for the patient by a health professional. Overall adherence to scheduled appointments was an average of 53 percent, with individual results ranging from 10 to 84 percent. When initiated by a health professional, however, scheduled appointments were kept by patients an average of only 51 percent of the time; when scheduled by the patient him- or herself, attendance at appointments rose to a mean of 74 percent.

TABLE 11.1.   COMPLIANCE RATES OTHER THAN MEDICATION ERRORS

Type of Study	No. of Studies	Range of Compliance (%)	Mean (%)
Appointment-keeping	15	10−84	53
Initiated by professional	13	10−84	51
Initiated by patient	2	71−77	74
Children	6	32−84	58
Adults	9	10−77	51
Prevention	8	10−65	43
Management/cure	7	55−84	69
Adherence to diet	3	8−70	34

Adapted from Sackett & Snow (1979, pp. 15−16, 20).

There are several other ways in which to look at compliance rates based on these appointment-keeping studies. Dividing studies into those that investigated appointments made by or for adults (including adolescents) as compared with those made for children shows that the range of compliance for adult attendance is 10 to 71 percent with a mean of 51 percent, whereas for children the range is 32 to 84 percent, with an average of 58 percent attendance. It was also found that adherence to appointments for prevention of disease (e.g., gynecologic, breast cancer, Tay-Sachs, or hypertension screening), was only 43 percent (range: 10 to 65 percent), whereas for appointments that were necessary for management or cure of an already-diagnosed disease, appointment adherence rose to a mean of 69 percent (range: 60 to 84 percent).

Sackett and Snow (1979) next looked at compliance to regimens involving changes in health habits, such as diet, smoking, or seat belt use. In general, compliance rates to "life-style" regimens are quite variable and often quite bad. Research in this area generally does not stress behavior changes made by patients with chronic illness. A growing body of literature is developing, however, on intervention with noncompliance for nonpharmacologic treatments in chronic disease. For example, programs to promote dietary changes in hemodialysis patients with kidney disease (Cummings et al., 1981; Magrab & Papadopoulou, 1977) and with phenylketonuria (Fox & Roseen, 1977) have been developed.

Range of Compliance in the Medication Compliance Literature

When looking at research specifically focusing on medication compliance, researchers find that differential rates seem to occur depending on whether the regimen is short-term or intended to continue for longer periods of time. Table 11.2 summarizes short- and long-term compliance rate data. With short-term regimens, many investigators have studied children receiving 10-day prescriptions of penicillin for streptococcal pharyngitis and otitis media. In these diseases it is crucial for the prevention of reoccurrence that patients continue taking medication for the entire 10 days of the regimen whether or not they have become asymptomatic before that time.

As mentioned earlier, Bergman and Werner (1963) found that by day 9, 82 percent of their sample had discontinued taking medication. Other investigators (Charney et al, 1967) found that 44 percent of their pediatric sample failed to complete the 10-day regimen. Becker et al. (1972) report that 50 percent of the children they studied were continuing to take penicillin by the fifth day.

A higher rate of adherence, 66 percent, was found by Mohler et al. (1956) when they assessed compliance simply through self-report. Although most of the patients in compliance studies are outpatients at health care clinics, Leistyna and Macaulay (1966) studied pediatric patients seen in private

TABLE 11.2.   COMPLIANCE RATES TO MEDICATION REGIMENS

Type of Study	No. of Studies	Range of Compliance (%)	Mean (%)
Short-term regimens	4	60–78	70
For prevention	2	60–64	62
For treatment/cure	2	77–78	79
Long-term regimens	14	33–94	56
For prevention	5	33–94	57
For treatment/cure	9	41–69	54

Adapted from Sackett & Snow (1979, pp. 16–18).

practice and found that 89 percent of these children complied with the full 10-day regimen. Sackett and Snow (1974) estimate that the mean adherence rate for short-term treatment regimens is 78 percent, whereas for short-term preventive regimens the adherence rate is 62 percent.

Patients prescribed medication regimens for long periods of time for prophylaxis or for chronic diseases appear, according to Sackett and Snow's data, to be less compliant than those on short-term regimens. In the studies reviewed by them, the range of compliance for long-term preventive regimens was 33 to 94 percent, with a mean of 57 percent; for long-term treatment regimens, the range was 41 to 69 percent, with a mean compliance rate of 54 percent.

A study of children and adolescents on long-term antistreptococcal prophylaxis for rheumatic fever, for example, identified only 36 percent of the sample as adequate compliers (Gordis et al., 1969). Many investigations of long-term treatment of tuberculosis have been undertaken, with different researchers assessing adherence to PAS and isoniazid therapy. Reported compliance in several of these studies has been 50 percent (Dixon et al., 1957), 55 percent (Hecht, 1974), 69 percent when those considered unreliable were excluded from the sample (Moulding et al., 1970), 82.8 percent (Moulding, 1961), and even 89 percent, if patients who took only 50 percent or more of the prescribed amount were identified as compliers (Berry et al., 1962).

The levels of adherence reported may vary as a function of the problem, patient population, and method of assessing adherence; thus, it is difficult to define an average level of adherence. An estimate of adherence can be obtained from studying adherence patterns in the control or untreated, groups of randomized clinical trials. Study of these groups has the advantage of having large numbers of carefully selected patients measured over common intervals using common methods. In addition, the methods of measuring adherence in these studies are usually more intricate and sophisticated than is possible for practitioners.

The Problem of Under- or Overestimation of Compliance Rates in Research

Although well-controlled, randomized research designs are necessary in order to provide accurate, generalizable results in the compliance literature, the rigorous sample selection processes made necessary by such designs may cause results to be underestimates of the compliance problem in the general population. Samples studied in randomized trials must meet entrance criteria that may intentionally or naturally weed out persons who are not interested in complying to the medical regimen.

It is important to mention, however, that compliance may be *overestimated* in a large majority of all investigations due to other sample selection problems. Most studies include in their sample only those patients who are willing to participate in a research project. It is reasonable to assume that this subgroup of volunteers may be different in motivational or other characteristics, making them more likely to comply as a group than others who are not willing to participate.

Nessman et al. (1980) in their study of patient-operated hypertension groups found, for example, that their experimental group showed an increase in compliance from 38 to 88 percent over the course of the study and achieved some of the best diastolic blood pressure results in the compliance literature (24 of 26 subjects in control at end of treatment). From an initial pool of 500 possible subjects, however, these investigators were able to recruit only 52 to participate in the study, indicating that some motivational self-selection process was operating that could be expected to bias outcome in the direciton of increased compliance.

Even those investigators who have used as their sample *all* patients being seen in a clinic or practice at a given time for a specific disease or disorder have, by this cross-sectional method, weeded out those grossly noncompliant patients who began treatment at an earlier time, immediately discontinued treatment and never returned. Sackett and Snow (1979) discuss the crucial need for following an "inception cohort"—all members of a group of patients just beginning a therapeutic regimen—and for measuring compliance of both dropouts and "survivors" in determining final compliance rates. They note that, although this method is time-consuming and expensive, a more time-efficient alternative would be to track down and include in a cross-sectional sample done at a point in time all patients (whose names can be obtained from medical records) who were seen initially for the target disease but who discontinued treatment on their own.

Only 12 percent or 62 of the studies reviewed by Haynes et al., (1979), however, employed such an inception cohort as their sample. The overall ranges of compliance as estimated from a majority of investigations in the literature, therefore, must be considered overestimates.

In summary, then, results of investigations focusing on different types of compliance patterns have demonstrated overall mean rates of adherence to be 54 percent with appointment-keeping, 34 percent with dietary and other nonmedication regimens, 78 percent with short-term regimens of medication, and 56 percent with medication prescribed over long periods of time. Overall rate of compliance including all these types of studies was determined to be 54 percent (Sackett & Snow, 1979).

SETTING GOALS FOR COMPLIANT BEHAVIOR

The Need for Establishing Relevant Criteria for Compliance Goals

The need to establish criteria for the setting of compliance goals necessary to achieve a clinical response to the treatment regimen has been considered by only a few researchers. Eighty percent compliance is a standard cutoff point used by many investigators as an acceptable goal. Indeed, hypertensives who consume a minimum of 80 percent of their prescribed medication generally are found to exhibit systematic decreases in blood pressure levels (Sackett & Snow, 1979).

For other disorders, however, an 80 percent rate of compliance may be unnecessary. Gordis (1979), for example, reports that pediatric patients on oral penicillin prophylaxis for rheumatic fever need comply with their regimens only a minimum of one third of the time in order to reduce significantly the risk of contacting streptococcal infection. Researchers who arbitrarily set a higher standard for compliant behavior that is unrelated to treatment goals unnecesarily label a portion of their patients as noncompliant.

In a study of hypertensives, for example, Nessman et al. (1980) defined compliant behavior in part as taking 100 percent of the prescribed hypertension medication and had to report that neither their experimental nor their control group was compliant according to that standard. The experimental group, however, was 88 percent compliant, significantly decreased their pretreatment blood pressures, and had 24 of 26 members achieving the therapeutic goal of a diastolic blood pressure less than 90 mm Hg. These results are excellent and occurred in an experimental goup that was "noncompliant" according to investigator standards.

The opposite side of the problem occurs when compliance standards are set below what is necessary for attainment of therapeutic goals. By setting 75 percent pill ingestion as the standard for hypertensives' compliant behavior, for example, it was possible to label significantly more of the experimental group members as compliant than those in a control group (Inui et al., 1976). It is unknown, however, what proportion of the compliant group in this study attained the usual standard therapeutic goal of diastolic blood pressure at or equal to 90 mm Hg.

Thus, compliance should be related to minimally acceptable levels of medication intake that produce the desired clinical response. Setting a standard of 50 percent intake as compliant would be too low for hypertension, but possibly higher than necessary for prophylactic penicillin use. Berry and coworkers (1962) suggest that 50 percent compliance with an isoniazid regimen for long-term management of tuberculosis may be satisfactory.

Rates of compliance, instead of being determined by the percentage of pills taken, may be set as a minimum serum concentration of the prescribed drug. Gibberd and colleagues (1970), for example, report that epilepsy patients with serum phenytoin concentrations of less than 10 μg/ml may continue to suffer from uncontrolled seizures. Likewise, Eney and Goldstein (1976) report that serum concentrations of theophylline necessary for adequate control of chronic asthma range from 10 to 20 μg/ml. When serum concentrations are used to measure compliance, adherence may be estimated by repeated sampling of the marker, and a distribution of percentage of times the patient was adherent or within acceptable levels can be developed (Gordis et al., 1969).

What is clear from this group of studies is that more attention must be focused in compliance research on the question of adequate standards for adherence behavior linked empirically and clinically to treatment goals. This is an important "first step" in developing meaningful research that is both methodologically and therapeutically accurate, but it is a step that has been ignored by many researchers in the field.

PREDICTING COMPLIANCE: FACTORS THAT AFFECT COMPLIANCE

Range of Factors That Have Been Studied

Haynes and his colleagues (1979) identified 230 factors that have been studied in relationship to compliance. Among these factors there were 27 that have been studied at least 10 times. Only 7 of these factors were found to have positive correlations with measures of compliance in at least one half of the times studied. These factors are (1) patient compliance with other aspects of the regimen, (2) whether the patient is receiving other treatment for the same condition, (3) influence of the family, (4) family stability, the patient's perception (5) of the disease as serious, (6) of his or her personal susceptibility to disease, and (7) of the efficacy of therapy.

Four factors were found to have negative correlations with compliance in at least half of the studies reviewed: (1) the duration of therapy, (2) the number of concurrent drugs or treatments, (3) side effects, (4) and family size. Factors often thought to be associated with compliance such as diagnosis, severity, and duration of the disease; knowledge about the disease and/or treatment; sex; education; socioeconomic status; race; and ethnic background have been found in the majority of studies to show no correlation with measures of compliance.

The Health Belief Model as It Applies to the Problem of Adherence

Three of the seven factors that have repeatedly shown positive correlations with compliance behavior deal specifically with the patient's perception of illness and therapy. These patient perceptions are part of the health belief model of illness-related behavior formulated originally by Rosenstock (1966) to predict the liklihood of patients engaging in health or illness behaviors.

Assumptions of the Model.   This model contains three basic assumptions: (1) the patient's subjective readiness to engage in preventive health behaviors, including the perceived seriousness of the disease and the patient's perceived personal susceptibility; (2) the evaluation on the part of the patient of the feasibility and possible effectiveness of carrying out the recommended health behaviors; (3) the cue to action that must occur in order to stimulate health-related behaviors (Rosenstock, 1966).

This model was later reformulated (Becker, 1979) to include contributions from expectancy theory and compliance to recommended therapeutic regimens. The major emphasis in this reformulation is on subjective factors such as general health motivations, perceptions of susceptibility, faith in medical care, and patient beliefs regarding the doctor-patient relationship, with the implication that predictions of compliance might be possible from a knowledge of the patient's health beliefs (Becker & Maiman, 1975).

Difficulty of Predicting Compliance from the Health Belief Model.   Positive correlations have been found between health beliefs and concurrent compliance status, but prospective studies have often failed to find an association between health beliefs at the initiation of therapy and later compliance to regimen (Rosenstock, 1966). Becker and associates (1977), however, in a prospective study, found certain health behaviors to be useful in explaining and predicting mothers' adherence to a diet regimen prescribed for their children and in predicting attendance at future appointments scheduled for the child. Haefner and Kirscht (1970), likewise, found that health beliefs of personal susceptibility and benefits of treatment could be modified significantly through the viewing of health-related films. Subjects in the experimental groups who had altered beliefs were significantly more likely to have had a doctor checkup 8 months later (a recommended medical action in the film they had seen) in the absence of symptoms of illness than the control group who had not seen the films.

In contrast, Taylor (1979) reports the results of a prospective study dealing specifically with medication compliance in hyptertension. His data dispute the assumption that compliance is largely determined or caused by a patient's health beliefs, but, rather, show that such beliefs assessed before the implementation of drug treatment for hypertension do not predict medication compliance 6 months later. Health beliefs measured 6 months after initiation of the regimen, however, were associated with concurrent compliance and with compliance at 12 months, suggesting a bidirectionality in the relationship between health beliefs and compliance in which the patient's experience with compliance or noncompliance in the early stages of treatment affect the patient's health beliefs, as well as the reverse occurring.

These results indicate that investigating patients' health beliefs at the *beginning* of treatment may be useless for predicting noncompliance with a proposed medication regimen and, thus, for identifying a subgroup of patients appropriate for treatment intervention aimed at increasing compliance during the course of therapy. Taylor (1979) notes that only 15 percent of the variance in compliance is explained even by correlating health behaviors at a later time in treatment with concurrent compliance behavior. Fifty-two percent of the variance can be explained, however, simply by asking the patient at initiation of treatment to estimate his or her own compliance, despite the possible inaccuracies of this method of assessment.

In addition, partial correlation techniques showed that after patient estimates of compliance were accounted for, assessment of health beliefs added little information to knowledge of compliance. Likewise, Cummings et al. (1981) failed to find significant relationships between components of the health belief model and outcome for hemodialysis patients.

The most appropriate use of the health belief model may not be to predict compliance, but, rather, to develop a better understanding of why people do or do not comply. Based on specific reasons for noncompliance, this should be an important goal of future research. Global noncompliance factors must be translated into more specific and operational terms that lend themselves to continuous behavioral assessment and to individualized behavioral treatments. Since reasons for noncompliance may vary within a group of patients, it is not all that surprising that correlations across the group do not relate to outcome. If the components of the health belief model are truly mechanisms for compliance, then treatments must be developed that alter the specific mechanisms for subgroups of the population, with effects on outcome measured.

METHODS OF ASSESSING COMPLIANCE

Introduction

The assessment of compliance is based on the development of methods for accurate measurement of the amount of medication ingested by the patient. Indirect methods such as patient self-report, pill count or volume measure, and physician estimates of compliance generally are not expensive or time-consuming but are subject to inaccuracy and/or falsification. More objective methods including blood and urine assays may be more accurate but are often expensive, unavailable, or simply unreliable in long-term assessment. This section will review the different methods currently available for assessing medication compliance and will address the advantages and disadvantages of each.

Indirect Methods

Self-reports.   The most obvious method of indirect assessment is to ask the patient if he or she has taken the prescribed amount of medication. This method was employed by many earlier researchers and is still, occasionally, used alone today (e.g., Mohler et al., 1956; Schwartz et al., 1962; Taylor, 1979). Other investigators include the report of another family member in order to increase accuracy (e.g., Hogarty et al., 1973). The major problem with this method is that many patients simply overreport self-administration of oral medication (Bergman & Werner, 1963; Gordis et al., 1969). Gordis and colleagues (1969), for example, found that 82 percent of the pediatric patients in their sample claimed to have followed their penicillin regimens accurately, whereas only 58 percent were shown to have penicillin present in a urine sample on the day of a clinic visit. Relying on compliance reports of the mothers of these children would have done little to increase the accuracy, since 88 percent of the mothers reported compliance, whereas only 68 percent of the urine assays matched with maternal report showed the presence of penicillin.

When patients admitted to being noncompliers in this study, however, they were indeed found by urine assay to have been noncompliant with the regimen. This accuracy of self-report of those who claim to be noncompliers has been demonstrated by other researchers as well (e.g., Lund et al., 1964; Malahy, 1966). There is some indication also that patients who identify themselves as noncompliant are most likely to respond to interventions aimed at increasing adherence (Lund et al., 1964). If the goal of assessment, therefore, is to identify in a patient sample a subgroup that is likely to be most amenable to compliance improving strategies, then the self-report method may be adequate. Where the risks of noncompliance to those who misrepresent themselves as compliers is great, however, more accurate techniques are necessary.

Therapeutic Outcome.   Reliance on therapeutic outcome as the measure of medication compliance is another indirect assessment method. Takala and coworkers (1979), for example, categorized hypertensive patients as compliant or noncompliant based on a decrease in blood pressure during the course of their study. Therapeutic outcome, however, may be mediated in part by factors other than adherence to regimen, including environmental factors such as socioeconomic level and changes in the amount of external stressors (Gordis, 1979). Therefore, although it is important to determine empirically derived goals for compliant behavior based on desired therapeutic outcome, categorizing individual patients on the basis of clinical outcome may be misleading.

There are numerous examples of the inadequacy of using outcome to determine compliance. After 6 months, Sackett (1979) showed that 35 percent of a sample of previously uncontrolled hypertensives were now in control and that the rate of adherence was twice that of nonadherence (23 versus 12 percent) for these patients. Thus, 12 percent were in control without being adherent. In addition, another 34 percent was adherent, but uncontrolled. Likewise, in two studies to be reported in greater length later, one half of the patients who showed a poor clinical response were classified as adherers (Hogerty et al., 1973; the Coronary Drug Project Research Group, 1960).

Physician Estimates.   A third assessment method often used clinically but that shows questionable validity is that of physician estimates of the compliance of his or her patients. Caron and Roth (1971) found that medical residents could not accurately estimate levels of compliance with antacid regimen in their patients any better than chance. Even when statistical analysis was limited to those patients whom the physicians felt they could identify correctly, their estimates continued to be inaccurate. Others have found similar results with physicians (Charney et al., 1967; Davis, 1968) and other health workers.

Pill and Bottle Counts.   A more potentially accurate indirect assessment method is that of pill or bottle counts. In each of these methods the amount of remaining medication is compared with the amount that would have remained had the patient consumed the medication with complete accuracy.

In addition to being ineffective for monitoring patterns of noncompliance that may be clinically relevant (Gordis, 1979), this method is subject to falsification by the patient who may simply throw away any unconsumed medication. Investigators employing the pill count method which has been announced to patients in advance or which is obvious to the patient may report unusually high rates of compliance without addressing the possibility that patients may have discarded unused medication to avoid detection as noncompliers. Other investigators have made unannounced pill counts or have gone to great lengths to ensure that patients were unaware of the assessment technique (Boyd et al., 1974; Haynes et al., 1976; Linkewich et al., 1974; Sharpe & Mikeal, 1974).

Roth et al. (1970) investigated the correlation between bottle counts of compliance and a more direct method of assessment (serum assay). They found the bottle count to be moderately accurate ($r = .80$) over a 12-month to a 2-year period. Accuracy was considerably less, however, when a correlation was determined over a shorter period of time ($r = .64$), when the period between bottle counts exceeded 35 days ($r = .53$), and when the individual bottle counts were compared with each corresponding serum level ($r = .51$).

In addition, 10 patients (10 percent of the total sample) appeared to be consistent noncompliers who consumed less antacid than would have been indicated by simple reliance on bottle counts alone. The correlation for this group between bottle count and serum assay was only $r = .22$, indicating that within a sample the compliance of a subgroup of "irregular" patients might be significantly overrated if bottle counts were the only method of assessment.

Bergman and Werner's data (1963), likewise, indicate that 18 percent of their pediatric sample was rated compliant by pill count on day 8 of a penicillin regimen, whereas only 8 percent were shown to have penicillin present in a urine specimen.

Finally, Leistyna and Macaulay (1966) discuss one additional problem with accurate assessment by volume measure of a liquid prescription medication. Most bottle counts performed are based on the expected amount of consumption if the patient had taken the prescribed number of teaspoons of the medication. These investigators examined the household teaspoons used to dispense penicillin to subjects in their pediatric sample and found that they measured volumes varying from 2.8 to 4.2 cc. Leistyna and Macaulay (1966) took these variations into account when analyzing results of bottle counts from their sample, but few other researchers have followed suit, bringing increasingly into question the accuracy of bottle counts in assessing compliance.

It is clear then that although pill and bottle counts are a simple and inexpensive means of assessing the amount of medication consumed by patients, ease of falsification and lack of standardized liquid measures might result in inaccurate judgments of compliance and noncompliance.

Mechanical Methods.   Several researchers have developed mechanical devices that make a record of the number and time sequence of pills removed from prescription bottles. Moulding and coworkers (1970) developed a complicated "medication monitor" which dispensed medication and recorded on photographic film the regularity with which pills were removed. Patients, however, were aware of the purpose of this dispenser and could easily have removed pills without actually consuming them.

Norell (1979) developed a less obtrusive-looking medication monitor for liquid pilocarpine drops for patients with chronic simple glaucoma. Patients were not aware of the mechanics or purpose of the monitor that recorded the date and hour each time the eyedrop bottle was opened. Very accurate assessment of use of the eyedropper was possible, including patterning and sequencing of medication use as well as errors of omission.

However, as technically sophisticated as these methods may be, they do not actually measure medication use, but, rather, measure use of the medication dispenser. There is no way to detect patients who remove and discard the medication without using it appropriately. Thus, these methods may offer little advantage over pill counts. Indirect methods of assessing compliance, then, in general, limit the accuracy of researchers and clinicians attempting to evaluate adherence to medical regimens chiefly because there is no way of knowing whether medicine removed from bottles or vials has been consumed. Other methods are needed that base compliance on actual ingestion of the drug.

Direct Methods

Blood/Serum Assays.   An extremely accurate method of assessing whether patients have recently ingested medication is to obtain a blood sample and perform a serum assay for concentration of the drug in the blood. Serum drug level of diphenylhydantoin (Gibberd et al., 1970; Lund et al., 1964) and ethosuximide (Roth et al., 1970) in patients with epilepsy has been measured, as has the theophylline level in chronic asthmatics (Eney & Goldstein, 1976).

Attention must be focused in performing serum assays, however, on the timing of blood-drawing from patients, since drugs may show wide variations in rate of absorption and metabolism. Any drug that gives steady-state serum levels could theoretically be measured for compliance by blood assays (Haynes, 1979). In practice, however, assay procedures for all drugs are not available, and those that are may be prohibitively expensive and/or time-consuming.

Urine Assay or Inspection.   A similarly direct test for recent drug ingestion is the urine assay for detection of excreted medication or drug metabolite. This method has been used often in assessing compliance to penicillin regimens in which adequate levels of the drug in the urine will inhibit growth of *Sarcina lutea* microbes on paper filter strips (e.g. Becker et al., 1972; Bergman & Werner, 1963; Charney et al., 1967; Colcher & Bass, 1972; Gordis et al., 1969; Leistyna & Macaulay, 1966; Sherwin et al., 1973). Urine assay techniques have also been employed in tuberculosis patients who had been prescribed phenylaminosalicylic acid (Dixon et al., 1957).

Prior patient knowledge of an upcoming request for a urine or blood sample may cause overestimation of compliance by this detection method, since generally noncompliant patients may ingest several doses of medication immediately prior to the expected request. For this reason, unannounced requests for specimens at doctors' visits and during unannounced home visits have been scheduled by many investigators to collect urine specimens on a more random schedule. Charney et al. (1967), however, found no differences with the accuracy of results based on unannounced requests at the doctor's office as compared to requests for urine specimens to be collected at home and brought to the office.

Haynes (1979) notes that of crucial importance to investigators employing urine or serum tests is the knowledge of the absorption and excretion pattern of the target drug since such patterns vary considerably. A test performed before or beyond the point that the agent could be present in the urine might cause inaccurate labeling of true compliers as noncompliers.

Tracer and Marker Methods.   Another method of testing for adherence based on drug ingestion is the addition of a tracer "tag" to the medication that may permit accurate evaluation of compliance. Although this method is typically used in conjunction with urine detection methods, it has been on occasion employed in investigations using blood assays (Roth et al., 1970).

Agents used as tracers must be nontoxic (pharmacologically and chemically inert), unaffected by the physical and chemical properties of the urine, and freely excreted (Haynes, 1979; Porter, 1969). Examples of tracer substances that have been employed are riboflavin (vitamin B_2) which fluoresces in the urine under ultraviolet light (Berry et al., 1962; Hobby & Deuschle, 1959; Veterans Administration Cooperative Study Group, 1970); phenolsulfonphthalein (phenol red or PSP), a pH indicator that develops a bright violet color in the urine when an alkaline reagent is added (Ryan et al., 1962): and phenazopyridine, a drug that produces a bright red-orange urine discoloration by itself (Epstein & Masek, 1978).

Tracers can be used in one of two ways. In the first method, a tag can be added to all the medication and adherence established by the proportion of tests that contain the tracer. On the other hand, tracers may be added to only a portion of the total doses. This is known as the *marked item* or *marker* method of measuring medication compliance. In this method, marked pills are packaged either as a known proportion of total pills in the bottle or vial or in a particular known random order within the medication supply. In the first case, the measure of compliance compares the total number of marked items observed to the number provided. A sample of this technique is a series of studies done in our laboratory to develop an accurate home assessment technique for parent determination of children's medication compliance (Cluss et al., submitted for publication). A riboflavin (vitamin B_2) tracer was used in this instance to determine, in part, whether lay adults were able to detect B_2 fluorescence in urine samples, the quantity of B_2 that must be ingested by children for adults to detect fluorescence, and whether compliance, determined by adults with inexpensive "black light" equipment, discriminated among chronically ill children with specific clinical symptoms.

In the first study in this series, designed to determine whether relatively untrained adults could detect fluorescence in urine samples, six healthy adults collected urine samples at bedtime and in the morning after bedtime ingestion of riboflavin in varying dose amounts or ingestion of a similarly colored placebo. They were instructed in the use of an inexpensive black light to determine fluorescence of urine in a darkened room and were asked to judge fluorescence or nonfluorescence of their own sample. These adults made 24 of 33 possible accurate judgments, thus showing 73 percent accuracy ($X_1^2 = 6.82$, $p < .025$).

In the second study in the series, these results were extended to include lay judgments of the fluorescence of children's urine. Six healthy children, ages 7 to 12, took an evening urine sample, then ingested 10 mg of riboflavin at bedtime, and collected a first morning urine sample. Adults then judged fluorescence/nonfluorescence of the samples and were correct in their judgments 88 percent of the time ($X_1^2 = 56.8$, $p < .001$).

The next study refined this technique and attempted to determine whether ingestion by children of 10 mg of riboflavin at bedtime was enough to cause fluorescence of their urine beyond the following 24-hour period. The five children in this study took 10 mg of B_2 at bedtime on days 1 and 3 of the study and no B_2 on days 2 and 4. They collected urine samples on the morning following each of these days and 10 adults again judged fluorescence of the samples. Only 1 of the 20 samples showed "spillover" of fluorescence on a day that was preceded by no ingestion of riboflavin, and adults accurately assessed the presence or absence of B_2 in the samples 94 percent of the time ($X_1^2 = 69.34$, $p < .001$).

The last study in the series was a validation study using the B_2 marker method to determine if chronically ill children's medication compliance, judged by adults using the black light as described, discriminated between subjects with differing clinical symptoms. Twenty-two chronic asthmatic children between the ages of 7 and 12 had vitamin B_2 added as a marker to bedtime doses of their daily theophylline regimen for 2 weeks. A similarly colored B_2 placebo was added to daytime theophylline doses. Subjects collected first morning urine samples and kept a daily asthma diary, recording asthma symptoms experienced during the 2-week study period. They also monitored lung functioning at home (peak expiratory flow rate) and kept a record of daily lung function readings.

Adult raters judged fluorescence of urine samples at the end of the 2-week period and subjects were divided into a compliant ($\geq$ 80 percent of urines fluorescent) group and a noncompliant ($<$ 80 percent fluorescent urines) group. Theophylline compliance in this sample as determined by urine fluorescence ranged from a minimum of .50 to a maximum of 1.00 ($\overline{X} = .77 \pm .16$). Designating 80 percent fluorescence as the compliance cutoff point enabled investigators to divide the sample evenly; it should be noted, however, that no clinically relevant theophylline compliance cutoff point has as yet been determined in the asthma literature.

With the sample divided into compliant and noncompliant subgroups as noted previously, t tests or chi-square tests of significance were run on the following measures: sex, age, number of wheezing days experienced during the 2-week period, number of asthma attacks during the same period, variability of daily peak flow rates, lowest peak flow (PEFR) score recorded, and whether or not the child was wheezing during the visit to our office at the end of the study. Results are shown in Figure 11.1.

Tests showed no difference between groups on the variables of sex ($X_1^2 = 0.0$, $p > .05$) and age ($t_{20} = 1.26$, $p > .05$)). A t test on the number of asthma attacks showed no differences between groups ($t_{19} = 1.64$, $p > .05$)

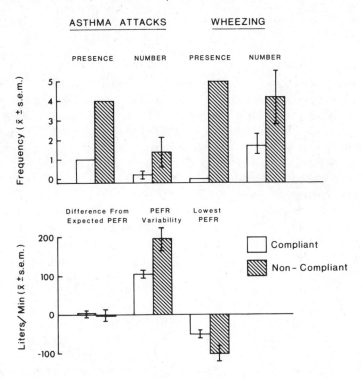

FIGURE 11.1. Comparisons of asthma attack, wheezing, and peak expiratory flow rate (PEFR) variables for compliant and noncompliant asthmatic children. All comparisons are significant at at least $p < .05$ level except for the number of asthma attacks and difference from expected PEFR at rest.

during the 2-week period assessed. Only 5 of the 22 subjects actually experienced any attacks at all, however, and 4 of those children were noncompliant. Chi-square analysis (using Yates's correction for small numbers) showed that the noncompliant subjects were significantly more likely to have suffered at least one asthma attack during that time than their compliant peers ($X_1^2 = 4.73$, $p < .05$).

The number of wheezing days reported on the asthma diary was also significantly higher for the noncompliant group than for the group that had been compliant to their theophylline regimens during assessment ($t_{19} = 2.10$, $p < .05$).

A mean peak flow score for each subject was determined from the 2-week self-monitoring data and an "expected" peak flow score was obtained according to the formula determined by Polgar and Promadhat (1971). This formula was developed by measuring the lung functioning of a sample of nonasthmatic children and is partially based on the child's height. Using this formula, the researcher could develop a deviation score independent of height for each child in our sample. There was little difference, however, between the compliant and noncompliant groups, respectively, on this measure ($\bar{X}$ = 1.64, 1.27), and the t test results were nonsignificant (t_{20} = .26, p = > .05).

Two-week peak flow recordings were also used to obtain a variability score for each subject, which was determined by subtracting the child's lowest recorded score during that period from the highest reading. This measure indicates the amount of variability in lung functioning that occurred during that time. Analyses showed that the children in the compliant group had peak flow rates that varied an average of 106.36 l/min, whereas those in the noncompliant group varied significantly more at $\bar{X}$ = 195.90 l/min (t_{20} = 3.04, $p < .01$).

Although the preceding analysis indicated that noncompliant children's PEFR scores varied significantly more than that of the other group, a related question was whether this variability included lung functioning scores that were lower than those recorded by compliant subjects. Again, to control for the child's size, each child's expected PEFR score (Polgar & Promadhat, 1971) was subtracted from the lowest PEFR reading recorded during the 2 weeks of monitoring, and a t test between the groups was calculated on this measure. Results indicated that noncompliant subjects had significantly lower recorded PEFR scores than their more compliant peers (t_{20} = 2.14, p = < .05).

The final variable analyzed was whether the subject was wheezing when he or she returned to our office at the completion of the screening period. Of 22 children in the sample, 17 were not wheezing at that visit and 5 were. All 5 of the wheezing children were later determined by the urine fluorescence method to have been noncompliant during the preceding 2 weeks. Not one compliant child was noted by the blind rater to be evidencing signs of wheezing. This result shows a significant difference between these two groups (X^2_1 = 4.14, $p < .05$) as determined by the B_2 marker method of compliance assessment. This series of studies with chronic asthmatic children shows that a riboflavin marker method such as the one described may be useful in discriminating between groups of chronically ill subjects with differing symptom pictures.

In addition to the preceding method, marked items may also be packaged in a particular order and compliance assessed by experimenter or patient examination of the urine and by comparison of days when the tracer should have appeared in the urine with days when it was actually present. This method allows a more fine-grained analysis of patient compliance patterns than simply marking a proportion of doses with the tracer.

Epstein and Masek (1978), for example, provided subjects with a supply of vitamin C, some of which contained phenazopyridine as a marked item tracer. The marked items were placed in a known order within the pill supply, so that a tracer was to turn up, for example, on Tuesday morning and Friday afternoon of 1 week. Comparison of the times the tracers did appear provided an estimate of compliance. Epstein et al., (1981) used the marked item technique to determine adherence to urine testing in juvenile diabetes. The children were provided a supply of reagent tablets that contained a known number of marked items, which in this case were similar-appearing tablets that did not react with the urine/water solution. Adherence was established by comparing the known number of marked items with the number reported.

In summary, then, many methods, both direct and indirect, are available as techniques for assessing patient adherence to medication regimens. The researcher or clinician interested in assessing compliance must choose a method considering both the practicality and the data regarding validity of each method and must do so keeping in mind his or her goal for the assessment.

Investigators who make use of two or more of these methods (e.g., Epstein, 1979; Hecht, 1974; Sackett et al., 1975) have the opportunity not only to compare estimates of compliance across techniques, but also to be more confident of the results obtained than are those employing one method alone.

THE RELATIONSHIP OF COMPLIANCE TO CLINICAL OUTCOME

Introduction

One major surprise in the adherence literature is the often poor relationship between adherence and outcome (Epstein & Cluss, 1982). Once the scope of the problem of noncompliance was recognized, it became common to attribute poor clinical outcome to the noncompliance of patients. However, in several adherence treatment studies, some patients who were adherent were still symptomatic and some patients who were not adherent were under clinical control. For example, in the Sackett et al. (1975) investigation, 57 percent of the patients took 80 percent or more of their medication, whereas only 40 percent of these patients had diastolic blood pressures below 90 mm Hg. Of the 43 percent who were not adherent, 28 percent were in clinical control. Likewise, in the Sherwin et al. (1973) investigation, 53 of 70 (76 percent) patients were adherent, whereas only 30 of these 53 (57 percent) were in control. The remaining 43 percent who had been compliant to the medication regimens were not in control.

Results Suggesting the Need for Cautious Interpretation

Two interesting patterns of results demonstrate the need for caution in assuming a linear relationship between adherence to active medication and therapeutic outcome.

First, adherence itself may have an effect statistically independent of the effect of the medication being consumed. If adherence and clinical outcome are highly correlated, then, in a drug outcome study, it would be expected that patients who were adherers would have better treatment effects than patients who were nonadherers. Patients who were not adherent might be expected to show equal or slightly better results than patients on placebo, depending on the percent of medication intake used to separate adherers from nonadherers. Similarly, adherers to the medication regimen would be expected to show superior results to all patients on placebo, and no differences between adherers and nonadherers to placebo would be expected.

The results of two studies suggest a statistical main effect for adherence on clinical status regardless of whether patients were taking placebo or active medication. The first of these studies, the Coronary Drug Project (1980), was designed to compare the effects of lipid-lowering drugs on secondary prevention of coronary heart disease. No main effect was found in this study for clofibrate versus placebo (18 versus 19.5 percent mortality), but adherers showed a significantly lower mortality rate (16.2 percent) than nonadherers (24.8 percent).

Within placebo and drug conditions, this effect was highly significant (both less than .0001). Patients who adhere to placebo and show improvement in clinical status are obviously responding to something other than the pharmacologic effects of the drug. However, since the drug itself in this case was not effective, it might be assumed that the effect for adherence was an artifact of the absence of a true drug effect and would not occur in the presence of an active drug whose efficacy was demonstrated.

This, apparently, is not the case, however. In one of the best designed (Haynes et al., 1979) adherence studies to date, Hogarty et al., (1973) showed that schizophrenics who adhere to either medication or placebo show lower relapse rates than schizophrenics who do not adhere to their prescribed dosages. In this study, patients were stabilized on chlorpromazine and then assigned to one of four groups varying drug/placebo and major role therapy/no major role therapy in a 2 X 2 design. The overall results showed a clear main effect for chlorpromazine, with 31 percent of drug patients, compared to 67 percent of placebo patients, relapsing in 12 months ($p < .001$). However, when adherence rates are examined for relapsers and nonrelapsers, patterns remarkably similar to those of the Coronary Drug Project (1980) appear.

Over 80 percent of the patients who do not relapse are adherers, regardless of whether they took the drug or placebo. Likewise, when relapsers are considered separately, about one half are adherers and one half are nonadherers. Thus, when patients adhered, they had a reduced probability of relapse, whether or not they were provided with the active drug. When the Coronary Drug Project (1980) data are presented in this fashion, the patterns are very similar, although the role of adherence is not so strong. There were approximately twice as many surviving patients who did not adhere in the Coronary Drug Project (1980) than those who do not relapse and did not adhere in the Collaborative Group Study (1973): 30 versus 15 percent.

It should be noted, however, that long-term follow-up of subjects in the Collaborative Group Study (1973) showed the continued superiority of chlorpromazine over placebo. By the end of 2 years ther were few placebo patients who had not relapsed, presumably whether or not they were adherent.

Within two large, well-controlled clinical trials, main effects of adherence have been demonstrated over 6-month and 5-year intervals. This is interesting in light of the marked differences in patient populations, characteristics of the disease, mechanisms of the drugs used, and actual effects of the drugs.

Efficacy of the Pharmacologic Agent.   The second caution to be considered in attempting to determine the relationship between adherence and outcome is the efficacy of the pharmacologic agent involved in the treatment. The attribution of poor treatment results to noncompliance would certainly be misleading in instances in which the drug itself was ineffective.

Hogarty, et al., (1979), for example, studied schizophrenics taking a neuroleptic (fluphenazine) either orally or by injection and found no difference in relapse rates between those taking tablets and those administered the drug parenterally. Relapse in the parenteral group certainly cannot be attributed to noncompliance, but, rather, to the fact that the drug itself was less than completely effective.

Thus, it can be seen from this review that both adherence itself, independent of drug treatment, may have an influence on clinical outcome and also that blind attribution of poor treatment results to poor compliance may be an overestimation of the importance of adherence, especially in cases in which the efficacy of the drug treatment in a clinical trial has yet to be established. In the first instance, it may be that the actual *act of adhering* to a treatment regimen, which often involves modifying old habits in order to meet daily, well-defined goals, may increase feelings of well-being and confidence in the patient's abilities to cope with chronic disease. Reduction of the psychological side effects of chronic illness such as anxiety, depression, and dependence on others may cause improvements in the patient's clinical status, perhaps by encouraging the patient to make other health-related changes that had not been undertaken previously. It may be, however, that some third factor, as yet to be established, is operating that independently affects adherence behaviors as well as other cognitive, behavioral, or physiological health factors influencing disease outcome.

One of the major contributions of future compliance research may be to assess more directly the effects of pharmacologic treatment. Development of techniques that will assure adequate adherence to the prescribed regimen will enable drug researchers to rule out noncompliance as a variable influencing treatment outcome. An additional contribution of adherence research will be to improve the clinical response of noncompliant patients to pharmacologic treatments with proven efficacy. Designs for addressing both these issues will be explored in the next section.

THE DESIGN OF OUTCOME RESEARCH IN COMPLIANCE

Research in medicine compliance may vary in both the independent and dependent variables studied. The purpose of the present section is to identify the combinations of variables that may be studied and the types of conclusions that can and cannot be made from each design.

In general, there are two classes of dependent variables in compliance research: compliance behavior, which can be measured in a wide variety of ways, as previously stated; and outcome, which relates to the physiological effect of the treatment on a disease process. Independent variables may involve the study of medication efficacy by assigning subjects to medication or placebo groups and/or treatment programs designed to improve compliance, comparing treatment to appropriate attention placebo groups.

Designs utilizing various combinations of these independent and dependent variables are differentially effective for investigating research questions in this area and have implications for the types of conclusions that can be drawn from results. Variations of these independent and dependent variables can be seen in Figures 11.2 and 11.3.

Independent Variables

This section is designed to present possibilities for studying the behavioral/pharmacologic effects of treatments in medicine compliance re-

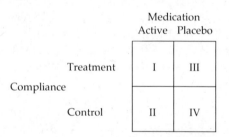

FIGURE 11.2.   Independent variables in medicine compliance research.

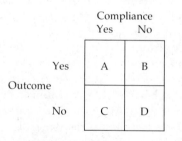

FIGURE 11.3.   Dependent variables in medicine compliance research.

search. There are several basic components of outcome research that are assumed and that must be followed as part of good, basic research design: Subjects will be randomized to groups; sample size will be sufficient to generate fair tests of treatments; clear criteria for subject selection will be used; subjects who are representative of the general clinical population with the disorder will be chosen; the treatment protocol will be spelled out; and patients will be followed up. The appropriate control groups are medication placebo or attention placebo controls, depending upon the type of question under investigation.

1. The first design that will be discussed is appropriate for testing efficacy of medication. It includes the comparison of active medication versus placebo under standard care conditions. This involves comparison of groups II and IV from Figure 11.2. Of course, comparison of groups I and III also provides a comparison of medication versus placebo, but results will be confounded by the addition of an experimental treatment for compliance to regimen. Adherence rates in this case are likely to be higher than if the medication is provided based upon standard care.

2. The second design is a test of experimental versus control treatments for patients who are also prescribed medication. This is a standard design in clinical studies designed to improve compliance. In this case, compliance would be targeted as a mediator through increased drug ingestion for physiological improvement in the disorder. As mentioned in previous sections, however, such a relationship cannot always be assumed. This design compares groups I and II.

3. The third design is a comparison of groups III and IV that are not provided an active medicine, but compliance behavior itself is being targeted and measured. This is a design for *basic* research in compliance where the goal is to alter medication-taking behavior itself. In this design, changes in outcome are not expected nor are they important. This comparison is appropriate for basic research in compliance because results cannot be confounded by the degree of efficacy of the drug.

4. Finally, the interaction between medicine and adherence can be studied. This factorial design provides testing both medicine versus placebo and experimental treatment versus control, as well as the interaction between medication and adherence.

Dependent Variables

There are three ways people have determined effects in medicine compliance studies. These are shown as A, B, and C in Figure 11.3. Since D is the absence of measuring either compliance or outcome, D is not a possible alternative in compliance research.

The first type of measurement is exclusively measurement of compliance with no physiological end points (cell C). This level of analysis seems appropriate only for basic research in nonclinical populations since improvement in outcome is presumed to be of primary importance in clinical research with patient groups. The second type of measurement is measurement of end point alone, without measuring compliance (cell B). Although end points are often used to estimate compliance, there is sufficient data to question the validity of such a practice. Thus, we do *not* consider research that does not measure compliance to be compliance research.

Finally, research may measure both compliance and outcome. This is the preferred level of analysis for all but basic research in compliance. This is the only design in which the effect of compliance as a mediator of outcome can be studied.

It is important to mention that studies are designed by, in effect, merging the cells from Figures 11.2 and 11.3. A study of medication efficacy alone, for example, would compare groups II and IV from Figure 11.2 and use as dependent variables either cell A, B, or C from Figure 11.3. The optimal design would compare active medication versus placebo and measure both compliance behavior and physiological outcome (cell A), allowing for the determination of main effects of drug efficacy as well as for the independent effects of the act of compliance. Comparing groups II and III and measuring only outcome, but not compliance (cell B), would be an adequate test of drug efficacy although the effect of compliance would remain unknown. As previously mentioned, designs employing only measures of outcome and not adherence are not considered to fall within the realm of compliance research.

To complete the possibilities, investigators could study groups II and III by measuring compliance behavior alone with no outcome measure (cell C). As discussed, however, since compliance to the regimen does not always correlate with improvement in the disorder, drug efficacy could not be established in this manner.

It is, therefore, important when designing studies within the area of health research to choose first from the cells in Figure 11.2 the cell comparisons that will be most useful for answering the specific questions being addressed and then to select from Figure 11.3 the combination of dependent variables most appropriate for the Figure 11.2 variables under study.

CONCLUSION

We have seen that the measurement of medication compliance in the treatment of disease is a multifaceted issue. Accurate assessment of compliance behavior may be difficult and information gathered from compliance studies may be biased depending upon the measurement technique employed. Compliance itself is not a unidimensional behavior but appears to be situation-specific with regard to contingencies impinging upon the regimen and patients' perceptions of the regimen and their control over it.

It has also been shown that compliance may not be linearly related to clinical outcome and that adherent behavior alone may have an impact that is independent of medication efficacy. The studies showing evidence for these findings underscore the necessity for developing and choosing accurate compliance assessment techniques and for including them in well-designed adherence outcome research strategies, that is, those that have given consideration to appropriate comparisons and contrasts from among the available independent and dependent variables.

Although literally hundreds of studies have been carried out in the area of compliance research, only a small percentage of them have been methodologically sound in terms of measurement techniques and design characteristics. Increased attention to these considerations is necessary for more valid results to be obtained on medication compliance.

References

Becker, M. (1979). Understanding patient compliance: The contribution of attitudes and other psychosocial factors. In S. T. Cohen (Ed.), *New directions in patient compliance*. Lexington, MA: Heath.

Becker, M., Drachman, R., & Kirscht, J. (1972). Predicting mothers' compliance with pediatric medical regimens. *Journal of Pediatrics, 81,* 843–854.

Becker, M., & Maiman, L. (1975). Sociobehavioral determinants of compliance with health and medical care recommendation. *Medical Care, 13,* 10–24.

Becker, M., Maiman, L., Kirscht, J., Haefner, D., & Drachman, R. (1977). A test of the health belief model in obesity. *Journal of Health and Social Behavior, 18,* 348–366.

Bergman, A., & Werner, R. (1963). Failure of children to receive penicillin by mouth. *New England Journal of Medicine, 268,* 1334–1338.

Berry, D., Ross, A., Huempfner, H., & Deuschle, K. (1962). Self-medication behavior as measured by urine chemical tests in domiciliary tuberculosis patients. *American Review of Respiratory Disease, 86,* 1–7.

Blackwell, B. (1973). Drug therapy: Patient compliance. *New England Journal of Medicine, 289,* 249–252.

Boyd, J., Covington, T., Stanaszek, W., & Coussons, R. (1974). Drug defaulting Part II: Analysis of noncompliance problems. *American Journal of Hospital Pharmacy, 31,* 485–494.

Caron, H., & Roth, H. (1971). Objective assessment of cooperation with an ulcer diet: Relation to antacid intake and to assigned physician. *American Journal of Medical Science, 261,* 61–66.

Charney, E., Bynum, R., Eldredge, D., Frank, D., MacWhinney, J., McNabb, N., Scheiner, A., Sumpter, E., & Iker, H. (1967). How well do patients take oral penicillin? A collaborated study in private practice. *Pediatrics, 40,* 188–195.

Cluss, P., Epstein, L., Galvis, S., Fireman, P., & Friday, G. A riboflavin tracer method for assessment of medication compliance in children. Article submitted for publication.

Colcher, I., & Bass, J. (1972). Penicillin treatment of a streptococcal pharyngitis: A comparison of schedules and the role of specific counseling. *Journal of the American Medical Association, 222,* 657–659.

The Coronary Drug Project Research Group. (1980). Influence of adherence to treatment and response of cholesterol on mortality in the Coronary Drug Project. *New England Journal of Medicine, 303,* 1038–1041.

Cummings, K., Becker, M., Kirscht, J., & Levin, N. (1981). Intervention strategies to improve compliance with medical regimens by ambulatory hemodialysis patients. *Journal of Behavioral Medicine, 4,* 111–128.

Davis, M. (1968). Physiologic, psychological and demographic factors in patient compliance with doctor's orders. *Medical Care, 6,* 115–122.

Dixon, W., Stradling, P., & Wootton, I. (1957). Outpatient PAS therapy. *Lancet, 2,* 871–872.

Eney, R., & Goldstein, E. (1976). Compliance of chronic asthmatics with oral administration of theophylline as measured by serum and salivary measures. *Pediatrics, 57,* 513–517.

Epstein, L., Beck, S., Figueroa, J., Farkas, G., Kazdin, A., Daneman, S., & Becker, D. (1981). The effects of targeting improvements in urine glucose on metabolic control in children with insulin dependent diabetes. *Journal of Applied Behavior Analysis, 14,* 365–376.

Epstein, L., & Cluss, P. (1982). A behavioral medicine perspective on adherence to long-term medical regimens. *Journal of Consulting and Clinical Psychology, 50,* 950–971.

Epstein, L., & Masek, B. (1978). Behavioral control of medicine compliance. *Journal of Applied Behavior Analysis, 11,* 1–10.

Feinstein, A. (1974). Biostatistical problems in compliance bias. *Clinical Pharmacology & Therapeutics, 16,* 846–857.

Fox, R., & Roseen, D. (1977). A parent administered token economy for dietary regulation of phenylketonuria. *Journal of Behavior Therapy and Experimental Psychiatry, 8,* 441–443.

Gibberd, F., Dunne, J., Handley, A., & Hazelman, B. (1970). Supervision of epileptic patients taking phenytoin. *British Medical Journal, 1,* 147–149.

Gordis, L. (1979). Conceptual and methodological problems in measuring patient compliance. In R. B. Haynes, D. Taylor, & D. Sackett (Eds.), *Compliance in health care,* (pp. 23–48). Baltimore: Johns Hopkins Press.

Gordis, L., Markowitz, M., & Lilianfeld, A. (1969). The inaccuracy in using interviews to estimate patient reliability in taking medications at home. *Medical Care, 7,* 49–54.

Haefner, D., & Kirscht, J. (1970), Motivational and behavioral effects of modifying health belief. *Public Health Reports, 85,* 478–484.

Haggerty, R., & Roghmann, K. (1972). Noncompliance and self-medication: Two neglected aspects of pediatric pharmacology. *Symposium on Pediatric Pharmacology, 19,* 101–115.

Haynes. R. (1979). Introduction. In R. Haynes, D. Taylor, & P. Sackett (Eds.), *Compliance in health care.* Baltimore: Johns Hopkins Press.

Haynes, R., Gibson, E., Hackett, B., Sackett, D., Taylor, D., Roberts, R., & Johnson, A. (1976). Improvement of medication compliance in uncontrolled hypertension. *Lancet, 1,* 1265–1268.

Haynes, R., Taylor, D., & Sackett, D. (Eds.) (1979). *Compliance in health care.* Baltimore: Johns Hopkins Press.

Hecht, A. (1974). Improving medication compliance by teaching patients. *Nursing Forum, 13,* 112–129.

Hobby, G., & Dueschle, K. (1959). The use of riboflavin as an indicator of isoniazid ingestion in self-medicated patients. *American Review of Respiratory Disease, 80,* 415–423.

Hogarty, G., Goldberg, S., & The Collaborative Study Group. (1973). Drug and sociotherapy in the aftercare of schizophrenic patients: One year relapse rates. *Archives of General Psychiatry, 28,* 54–64.

Hogarty, G., Schooler, N., Ulrich, R., Mussare, F., Ferro, P., & Herron, E. (1979). Fluphenazine and social therapy in the aftercare of schizophrenic patients. *Archives of General Psychiatry, 36,* 1283–1294.

Inui, T., Yourtee, E., & Williamson, J. (1976). Improved outcomes in hypertension after physician tutorials. *Annals of Internal Medicine, 84,* 646–651.

Leistyna, J., & Macaulay, J. (1966). Therapy of streptococcal infections: Do pediatric patients receive prescribed oral medication? *American Journal of Disease of Childhood, 111,* 22–26.

Linkewich, J., Catalano, R., & Flack, H. (1974). The effect of packaging and instruction on outpatient compliance with medication regimens. *Drug Intelligence and Clinical Pharmacy, 8,* 10–15.

Lund, M., Jorgenson, R., & Kuhl, V. (1964). Serum diphenylhdantoin (phenytoin) in ambulant patients with epilepsy. *Epilepsia, 5,* 51–58.

Magrab, P., & Papadopoulou, Z. (1977). The effect of a token economy on dietary compliance for children on hemodialysis. *Journal of Applied Behavior Analysis, 10,* 573–578.

Malahy, B. (1966). The effect of instruction and labeling on the number of medication errors made by patients at home. *American Journal of Hospital Pharmacy, 23,* 283–292.

Mohler, D., Wallin, D., Dreyfus, E., & Bakst, H. (1956). Studies in the home treatment of streptococcal disease. *New England Journal of Medicine, 254,* 45–50.

Moulding, T. (1961). Preliminary use of the pill calendar as a method of improving the self-administration of drugs. *American Review of Respiratory Disease, 84,* 284–287.

Moulding, R., Onstad, G., Sbarbaro, J. (1970). Supervision of outpatient drug therapy with the medication monitor. *Annals of Internal Medicine, 73,* 559–564.

Nessman, D., Carnahan, J., & Nugent, C. (1980). Increasing compliance: Patient operated hypertension groups. *Archives of Internal Medicine, 140,* 1427–1430.

Norell, S. (1979). Improving medication compliance: A randomized clinical trial. *British Medical Journal, 2,* 1031–1033.

Polgar, G., & Promadhat, V. (1971). *Pulmonary function testing in children.* Phildelphia: Saunders.

Porter, A. (1969). Drug defaulting in a general practice. *British Medical Journal, 1,* 218–222.

Rosenstock, I. (1966). Why people use health services. *Milbank Memorial Fund Quarterly, 44,* 94–127.

Roth, H., Caron, H., & Hsi, B. (1970). Measuring intake of a prescribed medication: A bottle count and a tracer technique compared. *Clinical Pharmacological and Therapeutics, 2,* 228–237.

Ryan, W., Carver, M., & Haller, J. (1962). Phenosulfonphthalein as an index of drug ingestion. *American Journal of Pharmacy, 134,* 168–171.

Sackett, D. (1979). A compliance practicum for the busy practitioner. In R. Haynes, D. Taylor, & D. Sackett (Eds.), *Compliance in health care* (pp. 286–294). Baltimore: Johns Hopkins Press.

Sackett, D., Haynes, R., Gibson, E., Hackett, B., Taylor, D., Roberts, R., & Johnson, A. (1975). Randomized clinical trial of strategies for improving medication compliance in primary hypertension. *Lancet, 1,* 1205–1207.

Sackett, D., & Snow, J. (1979). The magnitude of compliance and noncompliance. In R. Haynes, D. Taylor, & D. Sackett (Eds.), *Compliance in health care* (pp. 11–22). Baltimore: Johns Hopkins Press.

Schwartz, D., Wang, M., Zeitz, L., & Goss, M. (1962). Medication errors made by elderly, chronically ill patients. *American Journal of Public Health, 52,* 2018–2029.

Sharpe, T., & Mikeal, R. (1974). Patient compliance with antibiotic regimens. *American Journal of Hospital Pharmacy, 31,* 479–484.

Sherwin, A., Robb, J., & Lechter, M. (1973). Improved control of epilepsy by monitoring plasma ethosuximide. *Archives of Neurology, 28,* 178–181.

Stewart, R., & Cluff, L. (1972),. A review of medication errors and compliance in ambulant patients. *Clinical Pharmacology and Therapeutics, 13,* 463–468.

Takala, J., Niemela, N., Rosti, J., & Sievers, K. (1979). Improving compliance with therapeutic regimens in hypertensive patients in a community helath center. *Circulation, 59,* 540–543.

Taylor, D. (1979). A test of the health belief model in hypertension. In R. Haynes, D. Taylor, & D. Sackett (Eds.), *Compliance in health care* (pp. 103–109). Baltimore: Johns Hopkins Press.

Veterans Administration Cooperative Study Group on Antihypertensive Agents. (1970). Effects of treatment on morbidity in hypertension: Results in patients with diastolic blood pressure averaging 90 through 114 mm Hg. *Journal of the American Medical Association, 213,* 1143–1152.

12

Evaluating Social Resources in Community and Health Care Contexts

RUDOLF H. MOOS

The development of behavioral medicine has sparked renewed interest in the role of social ecological factors in health and health-related behavior. There is growing concern about the ways in which psychosocial and biological factors interact to determine the natural history and outcome of treatment of disease. By emphasizing the active role of the individual in the etiology, management, and prevention of illness, behavioral medicine has taken a valuable step beyond the biomedical model. As a field, however, it has tended to neglect psychological and personality factors and to limit

Preparation of the manuscript was supported by NIAAA Grant AA02863, NIMH Grant MH28177, Veterans Administration Medical and Health Services Research Funds, NIH Multipurpose Arthritis Center Grant AM20610, and the John D. and Catherine T. MacArthur Foundation.

itself to a somewhat restricted perspective on social and environmental factors. The biopsychosocial model being applied to health psychology can help to overcome the unsatisfactory mind-body dualism that besets behavioral medicine and foster the eventual integration of biobehavioral and psychosocial approaches.

Building on an ecological perspective in psychosomatic medicine, the biopsychosocial orientation involves an interdisciplinary systems orientation to health care. This contextual, multicausal approach provides a conceptual framework that enables clinicians to consider biological, psychological, and environmental information about a patient, to make "diagnoses" in all three domains, and to develop treatment recommendations that encompass all three areas. Although this integrated systems approach is complex, it provides a realistic perspective that can inform researchers and clinicians about the determinants and effects of psychosocial factors (Engel, 1980; Schwartz, 1982).

The trend toward systems approaches in behavioral medicine and health psychology highlights the value of considering social environmental factors in research and clinical work with both individual patients and health care programs. As Warner (1982) has noted, patients' memberships in such social systems as family and work groups can influence their mood and behavior. Stress and resource factors characteristic of such systems are implicated in health maintenance behavior, initiation and continuation of contact with the health care system, compliance with treatment regimens, and individual adjustment to the onset and progression of illness and the process of recovery. These factors can also affect health risk behaviors such as smoking, alcohol abuse, and overeating that leads to obesity, as well as the probability of relapse after treatment of these disorders (Moos & Finney, 1983).

At the social systems or health care program level, social resources and stressors are involved in the development of the physician-patient relationship, the characteristics of hospital settings and their effects on patients, and the organization of the work environment and its impact on health care staff. Each of these sets of factors can influence patient recovery and morale. A general conceptual framework can provide a context for the subsequent overview of measurement procedures and findings in these areas.

AN INTEGRATED CONCEPTUAL FRAMEWORK

The framework shown in Figure 12.1 depicts the major sets of factors that influence health and health-related behavior. In general, the framework follows the biopsychosocial model in considering aspects of an illness such as its timing and stage, personal factors such as sociodemographic characteristics and coping styles, and environmental factors such as life stressors and resources. Personal and environmental factors affect each other as well as the likelihood that the individual will seek and utilize medical care and the quantity and quality of such care. The treatment selected and received by the individual acts in conjunction with pretreatment characteristics to affect the subsequent status of the personal and environmental system, and, finally, health and health-related outcome criteria. In turn, such outcomes can affect the status of the personal and environmental system as well as the characteristics and quality of the health care program.

Illness-related Factors

Illness-related factors include the type and location of symptoms— whether painful, disfiguring, disabling, or in a body region vested with special importance like the heart or reproductive organs. Such factors are a major component in defining the nature of the tasks patients and others face and, consequently, of the social resources they need and receive. For instance, fears of contagion and the myth that some patients "deserve" their illness may make it difficult to provide effective support to cancer patients. In addition, different organs and functions may have a psychological significance (see section on the personal system) and lead to a need for support that has little to do with biological factors related to survival. An injury to the face or amputation of a breast can have greater psychological impact on a woman than severe hypertension actively threatening her life.

The Personal System

The personal system includes such demographic characteristics as age, gender, and socioeconomic status, as well as cognitive and emotional development, ego strength and self-esteem, and previous illness experiences. These factors influence the meaning that a physical symptom or illness episode carries for an individual and affect the health care and social resources available to meet the situation (see Figure 12.1). For instance, the enforced dependency associated with serious illness may be particularly threatening to men because they are less likely to develop and maintain the social resources that can provide needed long-term support. Personal factors also include coping skills such as appraising and reappraising a stressor, dealing with reality-oriented tasks and problems, and handling the emotions aroused by a health crisis. An individual's social resources can influence the selection and effectiveness of these coping strategies.

The Environmental System

Features of the physical and social environment affect the development and initial reaction to an illness, the adaptive tasks patients must face, and the choice and outcome of the coping skills they utilize. Life stressors and resources emerge from the relationships of patients and their families, the features of their work settings, the social conditions in the wider community, and sociocultural norms and expectations. Social resources can help individuals to anticipate and confront stressful situations, foster successful tension management, and strengthen an overall sense of coherence and self-esteem. Although most researchers have conceptualized stressors and social resources as independent domains, a more unified conceptual framework considers these domains in conjunction with one another. For instance, many of life events that have been related to the onset and course of illness (especially "exit" events such as separation or divorce, and the death of a family member) involve a significant loss of social resources.

The Health Care System

The framework considers both the quantity and quality of the treatment that the patient selects and receives. The emphasis here is primarily on the characteristics of health care programs and hospital settings, although interpersonal relationships with health care providers are important, too. Health care settings are a significant source of stress for many patients, as summarized by Norman Cousins's (1979) conviction that "a hospital is no place for a person who is seriously ill." However, such settings can be designed to meet the needs of acute and chronic patients as well as of family members and health care staff (Moos, 1982). The following sections focus on two sets of factors in the model: (1) the environmental system, with particular emphasis on social network resources and (2) the quality of the social environment in health care settings.

CONCEPTIONS OF SOCIAL NETWORK RESOURCES

Current conceptions of social network resources are derived from three related areas: social network analysis, research on maternal separation and attachment behavior, and crisis theory and related ideas about the characteristics of helpful or therapeutic relationships.

The historical roots of social network analysis can be traced to the ecological perspective that emerged from psychological field theory over 50 years ago. Sociometric analysis emanated from Moreno's (1934) attempts to describe the "psychological geography" of groups and communities by examining the relationships between individuals. He developed sociometric procedures by which individuals report actual or desired interactions with each other. The resulting data are arranged into a sociogram, which depicts the positions of individuals and their interactions in a pattern of social structure. The related approach of social network analysis developed from attempts by social anthropologists to understand patterns of interaction that were not based on membership in kinship and institutional groups. Such networks may provide access to varied types of information and resources (such as health care) and exert normative pressure to seek a certain type of care.

Basic behavioral research on the effects of maternal death or separation, which began with Spitz's (1946) observations of marasmus among institutionalized infants, led Bowlby to formulate his theory of the centrality of the maternal bond and attachment behavior. This theory was initially applied to the mother-infant relationship but was later extended to encompass the phenomenon of social bonding among adults (Bowlby, 1973). The majority of adults develop strong reciprocal attachments with specific individuals whom they seek out preferentially when under stress and who tend to provide the needed comfort and support.

These developments are linked to a third strand of more clinically oriented research, which was pioneered by Lindemann (1979) and Caplan (1964). Trained in the tradition of Gestalt psychology, Lindemann believed that individuals were influenced by a web of social forces. He saw effective utilization of the existing social field as enhancing individual adaptation in crisis situations. Since an individual is thought to be especially susceptible to influence during a life crisis, the outcome of the crisis may depend in part on the support available from significant personal relationships. A related line of work has attempted to identify the most important factors involved in therapeutic or helping relationships (Rogers, 1951).

These intellectual traditions have spawned a diversity of concepts and measures of social network resources. The term *social network resources* is used here to refer to indices developed from network analysis techniques, as well as to measures of social connectedness based on factors such as membership in social and community groups and the quality of contacts with friends and relatives. This usage is employed as a convenient way of referring to a diverse set of measures that have in common an attempt to assess the characteristics of social relationships (see Moos & Mitchell, 1982). In general, existing measures in this area can be divided into indices of the structure and function of social network resources (see Table 12.1).

The Structure of Social Network Resources

The simplest measurement strategy is to tap the presence or absence of specific interpersonal relationships (such as the availability of a spouse or confidant) or general social ties (such as religious affiliation) that typically provide sources of support. Thus, for example, married status has been used as an index of the availability of a reciprocal social attachment. Some investigators have constructed more general indices of social ties that combine different sources of social contacts, such as marriage, close friends and relatives, church membership, and group associations (Berkman & Syme, 1979; Holahan & Moos, 1982).

A more comprehensive approach involves conducting a detailed assessment of the structure of an individual's social network. The procedure

TABLE 12.1.   INDICES OF SOCIAL NETWORK
RESOURCES

The structure of social network resources
  Social connectedness indices
    Married status
    Religious affiliation
    Group associations
    Presence of friends and relatives
  Social network indices
    Size and density
    Frequency of contacts
    Duration of relationships
    Proximity and similarity of network members
The function of social network resources
  Indices of specific exchanges or functions
    Social companionship
    Emotional support
    Cognitive guidance and advice
    Material aid and services
    Social regulation
  Indices of the quality of social relationships
    Intensity and valence
    Reciprocity
    Multidimensionality
    Overall degree of cohesion or "supportiveness"

includes constructing a list of network members by, for example, asking respondents to name "important" or "significant" individuals with whom they have been in contact recently. Respondents then rate each relationship (linkage) on dimensions such as the frequency of contact, the duration of the relationship, proximity or how close the respondent lives to the network member, and homogeneity or the similarity of the respondent and network member on sociodemographic and personal factors. The resulting information can be used to characterize the entire network or subsets of it (such as family and nonfamily relationships). Other structural factors include the size and density (the extent to which individuals in a network know and contact one another independently of the focal individual) of a portion or of the overall network.

The Function of Social Network Resources

A complete social network analysis includes an examination of the function and content of exchanges. At least five types of interpersonal exchanges or resources have been identified: (1) social companionship, (2) emotional support, (3) information and guidance, (4) tangible aid and services, and (5) social regulation, that is, an expectation to maintain daily routines and responsibility for other persons, such as dependent children or ill family members (Moos & Mitchell, 1982).

Only a few measures include separate indices of these kinds of exchanges. Schaefer et al. (1981) used a questionnaire that tapped tangible, informational, and emotional support. In completing the Psychosocial Kinship Inventory, respondents rate the degree of emotional and tangible support provided by each network member (Pattison et al., 1979). An alternative assessment strategy is to ask respondents to identify individuals who provide (or would provide) such exchanges or resources. For instance, the Social Support Questionnaire asks respondents to list up to nine people to whom they can turn for each of 27 types of support and to indicate how satisfied they are with such support (Sarason et al., 1983). The provision of these exchanges is likely to be related to other aspects of network linkages (relationships) such as their intensity, reciprocity, or mutuality.

The proliferation of specific indices has led some investigators to develop measures of the overall perceived quality of either one designated relationship or a set or relationships that stem from one source, such as family members or friends (e.g., see Procidano & Heller, 1983; Turner et al., in press). A related approach is to focus separately on affectionally close relationships or attachment bonds and on social integration or membership in a network of persons who share common concerns and values. The Interview Schedule for Social Interaction (ISSI) obtains four main indices that tap the presence and perceived adequacy of attachment and social integration (Henderson et al., 1981). The social integration dimension was formed by combining indices of three "provisions" of relationships (friendship, reassurance of worth, and sense of reliable alliance).

A set of conceptually integrated measures taps the perceived quality of family, work, and social group settings. The Family Environment Scale (FES) assesses three domains of factors that characterize family settings: (1) the quality of interpersonal relationships; (2) the emphasis on personal growth goals such as involvement in cultural and recreational activities and concern about ethical and religious issues; and (3) system maintenance factors used as the extent of family organization. Thus, the FES covers the supportiveness of family relationships (cohesion and expressiveness), aspects of social connectedness or integration (intellectual and recreational orientation, religious concern), and social regulation (organization). An index of potentially problematic family interactions (conflict) is also included (Moos & Moos, 1981).

The Work Environment Scale (WES) is conceptually similar to the FES in that it measures the same three underlying domains: the relationship domain (involvement, peer cohesion, and supervisor support), the personal growth or goal orientation domain (autonomy, task orientation, and work pressure), and the system maintenance domain (clarity, control, innovation, and physical comfort). These dimensions cover major sources of work stress (such as high work pressure and lack of autonomy), as well as interpersonal resources (such as supervisor support) that may buffer the effects of such stress (Moos, 1981c; see also Moos, 1981b). Since these scales have parallel forms that ask individuals about their actual and preferred situation, they can be used to obtain information about the availability and adequacy (the difference between actual and preferred) of social network resources.

This overview can serve as a guide in classifying the measurement strategies employed by different investigators. Although different aspects of the structure and functions of social relationships have been linked to indices of physical health and health risk behavior, the specific measures used have varied widely. Since a critical review and comparative assessment of available measurement procedures is not yet possible, a selected overview is presented to illustrate the range of current applications.

SOCIAL NETWORK RESOURCES AND HEALTH OUTCOMES

Development and Recovery from Myocardial Infarction (MI)

Several studies have linked social resources in work and family settings to the development of illness and adequacy of rehabilitation among men with angina pectoris or myocardial infarction (MI). One prospective study found that family problems were associated with the development of angina or a first MI in the subsequent 5-year interval. Men who felt that they had poor relationships with their supervisors at work were more likely to experience an MI. Incidence rates were somewhat lower among more religious men and men who perceived more love and support from their wives. Spousal support was related to a reduced risk of angina even in the presence of high-risk factors (such as high systolic or diastolic blood pressure and high serum cholesterol) (Medalie & Goldbourt, 1976; Medalie et al., 1973). Although they used different measurement procedures, Theorell et al. (1975) also found that increased work responsibility and dissatisfaction with aspects of work and family settings predicted the probability of MI in a subsequent 12- to 15-month interval.

The availability of psychosocial resources from family and work associates is predictive of better social and emotional functioning among men who are long-term survivors of an initial MI (Croog & Levine, 1982). These resources may also help the wives of such men. Finlayson (1976) asked wives of MI survivors to identify those individuals with whom they discussed problems or difficulties related to their husband's illness. Families in which wives used fewer sources of network support and where such sources were predominantly restricted to families of origin of either or both spouses tended to experience less favorable rehabilitation outcomes. Adult children were a particularly valuable source of support for wives of manual workers, perhaps because such children were more educated and facilitated changes in family roles and the effective use of health and other services.

Adaptation to Breast Cancer and Long-term Illness

Bloom (1982) interviewed women at varying lengths of time after surgery for breast cancer and related measures of social contact and family cohesion (FES) to three indices of psychosocial outcome. Both the lack of availability and perceived adequacy of support were linked to greater reliance on accommodative or emotion-focused coping (such as smoking, eating, and drinking more), which, in turn, was related to poorer adaptation. In a longitudinal study, Spiegel et al. (1983) found that high family expressiveness and low conflict were predictive of better adjustment among women with metastatic breast cancer. Family cohesion and expressiveness have also been linked to "self-care agency" (motivation and reported behavior involved in self-care) among diabetic adults (Brugge, 1981), as well as predictively to successful long-term rehabilitation among hemodialysis patients (Dimond, 1979). These findings held even after the "effect" of the patient's initial health status was controlled.

The importance of both the type and quality of a relationship was emphasized in a recent study of more than 650 postmastectomy patients. Social support was indexed by married status, by the presence of a person in whom a woman could confide during her illness and recovery, and by her perceptions of the quality of her marriage. Married women were somewhat less depressed than unmarried women, whereas married women who confided in their husbands had much lower rates of depression than those who did not. These findings suggest that the quality of the spousal relationship is as important as the fact of marriage. Women who had a male confidant but were unmarried showed higher rates of depression than married women who confided in their husbands. Thus, intimacy may have stronger protective effects when it is in the context of a long-term formal social tie (Bauman et al., 1982).

Some evidence suggests that the perceived quality or adequacy of relationships is more strongly linked to the outcome of rehabilitation than is the quantity or availability of such relationships. In a study of men hospitalized after automobile accidents, Porritt (1979) asked each patient about the availability of help from different sources (such as spouse, parents, siblings, and friends). If help was available, the respondent rated the individual who was the source of support on three dimensions derived from Rogers's (1951) theory of interpersonal relationships: empathic understanding, respect, and constructive genuineness. Although the availability of support was unrelated to later work adjustment, morale, or physical health status, the perceived quality of support was associated with better outcome on these indices.

Chronic Conditions Among Children and Adolescents

Family social resources seem to foreshadow better adaptation among families of children with such chronic illnesses as anorexia, diabetes, autism, and cerebral palsy (e.g., see Bristol, in press; McCubbin et al., 1982). One study compared two matched groups of juvenile anorexia patients, one with and one without the syndrome of bulimia. The family environment of bulimics was characterized by more conflict and less cohesion and organization than the nonbulimic anorectic families. These findings were consistent with evidence of greater affective instability and behavioral deviance among the bulimic patients (Strober, 1981). Family interpersonal resources have also been related to the degree of metabolic control among diabetic youth. As compared with adolescents in good and fair metabolic control, those in poor metabolic control saw their families as high in conflict and low in cohesion. The mothers of the adolescents in poor control saw the family as less expressive and less encouraging of independent behavior (Anderson et al., 1981).

Family social relationships may reflect the results of an illness as well as contribute to it. In this regard, Breslau (1983) compared over 300 families of children who had a serious disability (such as cystic fibrosis or cerebral palsy) with a representative group of control families in which the children were not disabled. The presence of a disabled child was related to lower family cohesion (as indexed by FES cohesion and conflict) and less family social connectedness (as indexed by FES intellectual-cultural and active-recreational orientation). The two family process factors (lack of cohesion and external stimulation) reduced the mother's feelings of mastery and increased her personal distress. These connections were stronger for black than for white families, probably because black families had fewer economic resources to deal with the concomitants of child disability.

Morbidity and Mortality Among Community Groups

The structure and function of social network resources have been linked to indices of morbidity and mortality among community (nonpatient) groups. For example, in an examination of job milieu factors that contributed to outbreaks of mass "psychogenic" illness in eight work settings, Schmitt and Fitzgerald (1982) found that more physical symptoms were reported in settings characterized by high work pressure, lack of clarity and organization, and less support from peers and supervisors. La Rocco and his colleagues (1980) conducted a study of men in 23 occupations in which they measured the perceived presence of psychological and tangible support from three sources: supervisor; coworkers; and wife, family, and friends. Only job-related sources of support (supervisors and coworkers) were related to less experience of job strain. However, complaints of physical and emotional symptoms (more general health outcomes that are not specifically job related) were affected by all three sources of support. Specifically, men who were under high job stress and reported high social resources complained of fewer symptoms than men under stress without such resources.

Our own studies with the FES and WES among a representative group of community families have shown that employed men and women who perceive more family and work support and nonemployed women who perceive more family support report fewer psychosomatic symptoms and less depression (Holahan & Moos, 1982). Decreases in the supportiveness of work and family settings were generally related to increases in psychosomatic symptoms and depression among both men and women over a 1-year period. Family support was somewhat more important for women, whereas work support was somewhat more important for men (Holahan & Moos, 1981). However, high stress in a married woman's job setting was associated with her husband's reports of less positive family relationships and complaints of more physical symptoms (Billings & Moos, 1981). Factors such as lack of family expressiveness, high family organization and control, and greater spouse disagreement about the family milieu have also been related to elevated health service utilization rates (Weimer et al., 1983).

In a longitudinal study, Gersten and her associates (1976) interviewed a random sample of women twice at 5-year intervals in regard to their husbands' job satisfaction and to spouses' quarrels, lack of free time or participation in social activities, and dissatisfaction with the marriage. Both job and marital satisfaction were concurrently and predictively related to the husbands' physical health status; spouses' quarrels and their lack of participation in social activities also predicted the husbands' subsequent health status. Some of the concurrent relationships remained significant after controlling for sociodemographic and mental health factors, and in the longitudinal analyses, reports of spouses' quarrels were linked to poorer physical health status among husbands 5 years later.

Indices of social resources have shown long-term predictive relationships to the subsequent development of serious illness and to mortality rates. One prospective study of a cohort of former medical students found that men who later developed cancer had reported as youngsters a greater lack of closeness to their parents as compared to the reports of their healthy classmates (Thomas et al., 1979). Berkman and Syme (1979) constructed an index composed of four sources of social contact (marriage, contacts with close friends and relatives, church membership, and informal and formal group associations). Higher levels of each of these four sources predicted subsequent 9-year mortality rates; the more intimate ties of marriage and contact with friends and relatives were stronger predictors than were the ties of church and group membership. These associations were independent of self-reported physical health status at the time of the initial survey; socioeconomic status; health practices such as smoking, alcoholic beverage consumption, obesity, and physical activity; and use of preventive health services.

Person-Environment Congruence

The foregoing studies have examined the effects of social resources without considering the personal characteristics or preferences of the recipients of the support. However, the conceptual framework presented earlier suggests that the impact of the provision of support may depend on the individual recipient. In this regard, Chesney and her colleagues (1981) have shown that peer cohesion may have more positive effects on individuals with a type A than on those with a type B behavior pattern. Since type A's tend to be more extroverted than type B's, it is possible that a type A individual is congruent in a cohesive work setting, whereas a more introverted type B individual may experience such a setting as aversive.

Some recent findings have focused on stressful life events, personal "hardiness" (as assessed by indices of commitment, control, and challenge), and perceived family and work support among men business executives. High perceived support from supervisors was related to less physical illness among men who experienced more stressful events (most of which were job related). With family support, on the other hand, the findings varied according to the level of hardiness of the individual. Executives who were low in hardiness and who were located in more cohesive families showed higher illness scores, particularly when they experienced more stress. The authors suggest that high family support during periods of high stress may contribute to a vulnerable man's alienation from his job and thus to his illness. Alternatively, family members may provide more support for less healthy men, especially when they are under high stress (Kobasa & Puccetti, in press).

Conceptual and Methodological Issues

The foregoing studies highlight the consistent linkages between indices of the structure and function of social network resources and health-related criteria. The findings are robust in that they generalize across different measurement procedures, patient and community groups, and diverse functioning and outcome variables.

Perceptual Bias and Prospective Findings. Two methodological issues need to be addressed in interpreting this body of research: (1) the reliance on individuals' perceptions of their social resources and (2) the possibility that prodromal signs of physical illness precede and affect the reduction of social resources. Perceptions of social resources can provide a biased picture (typically negatively biased) in that physically ill (especially depressed) individuals may see fewer resources than objectively exist. Such a bias could result in spurious relationships between lack of social resources and physical illness. The saliency of this issue is heightened by the idea that the concept of social support cannot be reduced to either the "objective" availability of resources or network capacity or potential. Instead, the central issue is the individual's perception or appraisal of the availability and adequacy of social bonds (Henderson et al., 1981; Turner et al., in press).

Negative perceptual biases do not appear to be so strong as some investigators have suspected. When individuals report on the perceived quality of different sources of social support, the relationships among the measures are relatively low (Funch & Mettlin, 1982; Gersten et al., 1976; La Rocco et al., 1980). Moreover, the ill spouse and the healthy spouse in a family show reasonably high agreement on the characteristics of their marital relationship and the family environment. More importantly, when disagreements do occur, the healthy spouse is just as likely to perceive the quality of support more negatively than the ill spouse and vice versa (Billings et al., 1983).

A second line of evidence stems from studies that have related the perceptions of social resources of one or more persons in a setting to the physical health status of other persons in that setting. As noted earlier, Gersten and her colleagues (1976) found that wives' perceptions of marital and job dissatisfaction were linked to their husbands' physical health status. Alfredsson et al.,(1982) identified the psychosocial characteristics of each of 118 occupations on the basis of an interview survey of over 3800 Swedish working men. Occupations characterized by monotony, low potential for growth and low personal control, and hectic or rushed work tempo were associated with excess MI among individuals other than the interview respondents. Thus, the relationships between lack of social resources and physical illness are not necessarily dependent on the ill individual's negative perceptual set.

With regard to the second issue, several studies have identified prospective connections between indices of social resources obtained at one time interval and measures of physical and psychological adaptation obtained between 1 and 8 years later (e.g., see Croog & Levine, 1982; Gersten et al., 1976; Medalie & Goldbourt, 1976; Theorell et al., 1975), as well as more than 20 years later (Thomas et al., 1979). Related evidence from a prospective life course study of men begun when they were in college showed that indices of poor psychological adjustment (which tapped aspects of lack of social resources such as an unhappy marriage, job dissatisfaction, and lack of recreational activities) were associated with a deterioration in physical health during a subsequent 8-year interval. Ratings of strengths in the childhood environment (such as family cohesion) based on data gathered during the college years were associated with better maintenance of physical health as assessed more than 30 years later (Vaillant, 1979). Taken together, this body of research provides reasonably convincing evidence of relationships between social network resources and health.

Developing Expanded Measures of Social Network Resources. One conceptual issue involves the definition and measurement of social network resources. For example, can the supportiveness of a relationship be assessed adequately by a single dimension of perceived quality, or is it necessary to distinguish among different types of exchanges or functions of the relationship? Schaefer et al. (1981) found that emotional and informational support were positively related to each other but were essentially unrelated to tangible support. Lack of tangible support and emotional support were independently related to depression and negative morale, whereas informational support was associated with positive morale. Such evidence points to the potential value of distinguishing among different types of exchanges or functions.

Measures of social resources also need to encompass patients' and family members' perceptions of the support they receive from physicians and other health care personnel. One recent study that focused on short-term recovery from surgery among breast cancer patients tapped both social support (from spouse, children, relatives, and friends) and professional support (such as ability to talk with physicians). Social and professional support were only moderately related to each other and each was independently linked to fewer complaints of negative affect and better postsurgical psychological adjustment (Funch & Mettlin, 1982). Other studies have shown that surgeons, nurses, spouses, and fellow patients may provide different types of support (Ray & Fitzgibbon, 1979) and that informational and emotional support received from a nurse can enhance partner support and thereby increase adherence to a medical regimen for hypertension (Caplan et al., 1980).

Aside from considering more varied sources of social network resources, existing measures might be broadened to tap more than just the cohesion or degree of support involved in interpersonal relationships. One point involves the value of assessing the problematic aspects of social ties (such as competition and conflict), as well as the potential negative concomitants of what are typically seen as social resources. For example, cohesive relationships can place undue pressure on individuals to conform to normative expectations or foster collective rejection and scapegoating. Another issue is that the impact of qualities such as cohesion depend in part on other characteristics of the overall context of a relationship. Thus, for example, family cohesion is likely to have different effects on health care compliance among adolescents depending upon whether it occurs in a context of independence or organization.

Psychosocial Mechanisms.   Just as social network resources have been assessed in terms of their structure and function, posited psychological mechanisms involve the effects of social integration and social interaction (Antonucci & Depner, 1982). Social integration effects stem from the existence of social relationships and are assumed to promote well-being through their influence on self-definition, a sense of identity, and continuity of meaning. Social interaction effects stem from specific types of exchanges and the manner in which they have positive impacts on well-being. For instance, informational support may help an individual to forestall a health crisis by providing access to the details of a new method of treatment. Network members can help an individual appraise or reappraise the consequences of an acute health crisis in the most positive light. Tangible support and other kinds of supportive exchanges can also have preventive effects (help to forestall a crisis), insulating effects (help to make a crisis less threatening), or buffering effects (help to reduce the impact of a crisis that is appraised as threatening). In formulating new measures of social network resources, investigators would do well to consider the potential role of these mediating mechanisms.

SOCIAL RESOURCES IN HEALTH CARE SETTINGS

Considerable research has focused on the relationships between health care practitioners and their patients and on the organizational factors that affect the delivery of health care. However, relatively few studies have examined the characteristics of specific health care settings or their effects on patients and staff. There is almost no work on the social environments of outpatient settings such as medical clinics, and most of the research on hospital environments has identified their stressful rather than their supportive aspects. For instance, the Hospital Stress Rating Scale (HSRS) taps stress due to the unfamiliarity of the surroundings (unusual smells, strange machines, strangers sleeping in the same room), loss of independence (eating at different times than usual, wearing a hospital gown, being assisted with bathing), and lack of information. Scales such as the HSRS can help to identify stressful hospital settings as well as high-risk patients (Volicer et al., 1977).

Although there are an infinite number of environmental variables, it is useful to consider health care settings in terms of four major domains: physical and architectural factors, policy and program factors, suprapersonal factors, and social-environmental factors (Moos,1979). Although all four of these domains can mutually affect one another, the social environment is the key mechanism by which the influence of the other domains is transmitted—that is, the impact of architectural, organizational, and suprapersonal factors is channeled primarily through the type of social climate they help to create. For example, program size (an organizational factor) affects patients and staff by fostering a more rigidly structured and less cohesive social environment.

The Social Climate of Health Care Settings

Accordingly, some of our own research has involved the development of scales to assess the social environments of psychiatric and substance abuse programs (Moos, 1974) and residential health care facilities for older people (Moos & Lemke, 1984). These scales are conceptually parallel to the assessment procedures described earlier (the FES and WES) in that they tap the same three underlying domains. For example, the Ward Atmosphere Scale (WAS) and the Community-Oriented Programs Environment Scale (COPES) assess the quality of interpersonal relationships among patients and staff (involvement, staff support, spontaneity), the goals toward which the program is oriented (autonomy, practical orientation, personal problem orientation, and the cathartic expression of anger), and how well the program is structured (organization, clarity, staff control).

These scales have been used to describe the characteristics and effects of hospital-based (WAS) and community-based (COPES) treatment settings (Moos, 1974; Moos et al., 1979). In brief, this work suggests that certain aspects of support may affect psychiatric and substance abuse patients differentially, depending upon their level of disturbance. Specifically, less disturbed patients do better in programs that emphasize involvement and spontaneity, whereas more disturbed patients need a well-structured setting that insulates them from too much interpersonal stimulation. Moreover, the effectiveness of health care staff may be a function of the match between their orientation toward treatment and the social environment of the program in which they are located. Psychiatric aides who believe in being kind and benevolent to patients tend to be more effective in programs that stress the quality of interpersonal relationships. Aides who feel that interpersonal factors are relatively unimportant in mental illness tend to be more effective in well-organized and structured programs (Boyle, 1979).

The WAS and COPES have been adapted for use in medical settings such as hemodialysis and oncology units. For instance, Rhodes (1981) found that patients and staff perceived the quality of the relationships on a dialysis unit similarly but that staff saw more emphasis on treatment program goals of personal problem orientation and the open expression of anger. In comparison to nondepressed patients, depressed patients saw the unit environment somewhat more negatively, indicating that they may filter out positive factors to maintain a biased perceptual set of their treatment program and/or that they are treated more negatively by unit staff. Alexy (1981–1982) examined the compatibility of patients', staff's, and family members' perceptions of the actual and preferred treatment milieu of an adolescent oncology unit. All three groups saw the need for some changes, particularly in aspects of interpersonal relationships such as support and spontaneity.

These measures of health care settings provide an index of the viability of new methods of delivering health services (Greenwood et al., 1980). In one relevant study with the WAS, some patients with multiple disabilities were exposed to an integrated team-oriented rehabilitation program, whereas others were given "standard" treatment. The fact that patients in the enriched program perceived more support from staff and other patients, more concern with their personal problems and feelings, and less staff effort to maintain control suggested that the program was implemented as intended (Crisler & Settles, 1979). A similar line of reasoning was used by Steiner (1982) to show that a therapeutic community milieu could be developed on an adolescent psychosomatic unit that combined a medical with a psychiatric treatment orientation.

The Multiphasic Environment Assessment Procedure (MEAP)

My colleagues and I employed the conceptualization of the four environmental domains described earlier to guide us in developing a Multiphasic Environmental Assessment Procedure (MEAP) to assess such geriatric health care programs as skilled nursing and nursing home facilities and residential care settings. The MEAP consists of four main instruments, the content of which follows the conceptual organization of the four environmental domains. For example, the Physical and Architectural Features Checklist (PAF) taps physical resources such as social-recreational aids, prosthetic and orientational aids, and safety features, whereas the Policy and Program Information Form (POLIF) covers program resources such as policy clarity, resident choice and control, and provisions for privacy. The Sheltered Care Environment Scale (SCES) assesses residents' and staff members' perceptions of the facility social environment on dimensions such as cohesion, conflict, and organization (Moos & Lemke, 1984).

Such comprehensive environmental assessment procedures enable researchers to examine the environment as a dynamic system and to identify the factors that foster cohesion and support. After using data from the MEAP gathered on 90 sheltered care settings to address this issue, we found that cohesion among residents was more likely to develop in settings with more physical amenities (such as attractive decorations in the halls), better social-recreational aids (such as lounges furnished for casual conversation), and more available personal space. Such settings also tended to have policies that provided their residents with broader personal choice and more opportunity to participate in facility governance. In turn, residents in more cohesive settings were more involved in facility-based and community-based activities and showed less use of health and daily living assistance services. Architectural and policy factors can enhance the development of supportive social environments that, in turn, can foster aspects of health-related functioning among older persons (Moos & Igra, 1980).

Information and Control as Social Resources

One salient aspect of hospital settings involves the relative lack of information and control afforded to patients. As Taylor (1979) has emphasized, individuals forfeit control over virtually every task they customarily perform when they enter a hospital. She believes that the loss of control depersonalizes patients and that they often react by either becoming depressed and helpless or exhibiting anger and resistance. The provision of information and the creation of an active role for hospitalized patients and their family members thus may enhance the treatment and recovery process.

In an unusually well-designed study that addressed this issue, Skipper

and Leonard (1968) randomly assigned children hospitalized for a tonsillectomy to a control group (regular hospital routine) or an experimental group
in which a special nurse tried to create a supportive atmosphere and to
communicate information to the child's mother. The study was double-
blind in that neither the mother nor the nursing staff knew which children
were in the control or experimental group. The intervention was effective in
reducing the experimental group mothers' appraisal of the degree of stress
and enabling them to adapt more successfully to the hospitalization and
operation. Moreover, children in the experimental group showed lowered
temperature, pulse rate, and blood pressure; less disturbed sleep and fear of
doctors and nurses; and a quicker period of recovery. Thus, by reducing a
mother's stress and changing her definition of the hospital situation, the
provision of information and support by health care staff can reduce a child's
stress and hasten recovery from surgery. Similar benefits may stem from the
presence of a supportive lay woman companion during labor and the delivery of a baby (Sosa et al., 1980).

Together with the trend toward humanizing health care, such findings
have led to attempts to involve patients more actively in the treatment
process. Davis (1980) described some of the conditions that may enhance
patient participation in long-term rehabilitation for conditions such as brain
and spinal cord injury. These conditions include increased staff-patient
interaction, explicit staff expectations for patients, ongoing opportunities
for information exchange among staff, patient, and family, shared staff
decision-making concerning patients, and autonomy of function among
nonphysician staff.

In an attempt to measure these factors, Schulman (1979) constructed an
Active Patient Orientation (APO) scale that covers patients' perceptions of
how much they are encouraged to be actively involved in the treatment
process and the extent to which they see illness management as collaborative and medical resources as provided in a useful manner. Hypertensive
patients who were afforded a high degree of APO were more likely to have
their blood pressure under control and to exhibit positive cognitive and
behavioral responses to illness management. Moreover, Schulman (1979)
found that the level of APO could be increased significantly by changing the
system of routine clinic care.

Personal control can be fostered by allowing residents to determine their
daily routine and take responsibility for some aspects of facility programs
and policies. To tap these factors, we developed measures that cover the
flexibility of policies regulating residents' daily activities (policy choice) and
how actively residents participate in running the facility (resident control).
Higher levels of choice and control were associated with a more cohesive
social environment and more activity among residents. Women residents
reacted more positively than men to the provision of choice over daily
activities, whereas more functionally able residents reacted more positively
to the provision of control over facility policies (Moos, 1981a).

These findings indicate that individual characteristics such as gender and current personal resources can affect residents' reactions to environment opportunities and demands. Similarly, Marone and Desiderato (1982) noted that male psychiatric patients oriented toward internal control perceived the treatment setting as better organized and clearer with regard to expectations as well as higher on autonomy and personal problem orientation. They argue that such positive perceptions are fostered by internally oriented patients' active involvement in the functioning of the unit. However, externally oriented patients desired minimal participation in program operation and felt that treatment plans should be formulated by professional staff and not by their peers. Consequently, when such patients are allowed to shape their own medical care, they may perceive the treatment process as disorganized and unclear.

The Work Environments of Health Care Staff

Health care settings provide a work environment for staff as well as a treatment or living environment for patients. Although these two facets of the environment serve different functions, they are closely related. For instance, staff who feel little support from peers or supervisors and who are unclear about their job and role performance expectations may find it difficult to establish a supportive clear treatment environment. The press of required activities can lead staff to use less time-consuming methods of care that reinforce passive dependent behavior of patients. Conversely, staff attention and positive expectations are powerful resources that facilitate patient functioning by enhancing cognitive and social stimulation and setting standards for acceptable behavior. Available evidence indicates that staff morale and performance are partly a function of the organization of care, the degree of difficulty involved in providing services, and the amount of support and autonomy afforded staff (Cherniss, 1980).

A small but growing body of research is focusing on work-related stressors and resources among health care staff (Caldwell & Weiner, 1981). For example, in a study that used the Work Environment Scale (WES) to characterize general medical and intensive care unit work settings, Mohl and his colleagues (1982) concluded that high levels of supervisor support tended to reduce the level of stress among staff. In comparison to nonhealth care work settings, employees in health care report significantly less supervisor support and clarity in their work milieus. Health care settings are also rated as somewhat less involving and cohesive, as allowing less autonomy, and as characterized by more work pressure and supervisor control (Moos, 1981a). However, a well-managed quality assurance program can enhance the supportiveness of health care work environments (Sinclair & Frankel, 1982).

Future research can profitably focus on the development of setting-specific methods to tap work-related stressors and social resources among health care staff. In addition, we need an expanded framework to help conceptualize the links between the structure of health care programs and patient outcomes. For instance, a recent model developed in facilities for long-term mental patients suggests that better patient functioning at intake is related to greater staff and patient participation in treatment decisions and higher staff morale, which in turn foster more individualized patient management practices and ultimately better patient functioning (Holland et al., 1981).

IMPLICATIONS FOR RESEARCH AND PRACTICE

Information about the determinants and effects of social resources can be used to improve the provision of health care services. Such information can help to formulate clinical case descriptions and interventions and to design and change health care settings. It may also be of value in implementing an expanded conceptual paradigm (see Figure 12.1) for assessing and evaluating health care programs.

Developing Clinical Formulations and Interventions

A social ecological framework such as the one presented here can improve the completeness and accuracy of clinical case descriptions and enhance plans for treatment and counseling. For example, we have used semistructured interviews and structured questionnaires to understand the social ecological environment of a 15-year-old adolescent girl who was being counseled for academic difficulties. The girl experienced considerable stress because of her parents' demand for academic achievement in conjunction with their inability to provide a supportive family climate. These problems stemmed in part from her parents' involvement in responsible but highly stressful jobs that took precedence over their daughter's emotional needs. Thus, stressors in her parents' work settings indirectly influenced the girls' functioning by reducing the quality of family social resources (Moos & Fuhr, 1982). Information of this type can help to identify high-risk family and work settings and to develop strategies to modify them (Fuhr et al., 1981).

Practitioners can be taught to use such assessment procedures to understand the personal and environmental factors involved in adaptation. The FES has been incorporated in a training program to aid student clinicians in evaluating marital and family systems (Cromwell & Keeney), 1979). The scale has also been used to help nurses understand the family context in which patients develop symptoms (Eichel, 1978). The framework of three underlying domains of social climate factors can clarify the salient dimensions of family and treatment settings and help clinicians and other health care professionals utilize information about social ecological factors in research and practice.

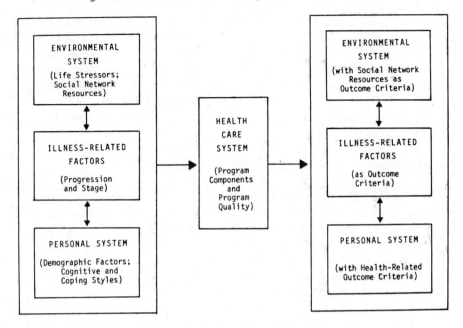

FIGURE 12.1.   A conceptual framework that considers the role of social resources in health and illness.

Monitoring and Improving Health Care Settings

Information derived from environmental assessment procedures can be used to describe and improve health care programs. Such information provides useful feedback to staff members, increasing communication among them and anchoring their perceptions in a normative framework. Moreover, these procedures may serve as useful tools in program modification by identifying potential areas for change and monitoring the results of change efforts. Knowledge about the "determinants" of social stressors and resources can specify directions in which change is likely to occur and indicate the types of settings that are most amenable to change. A focus on all four domains may help to ensure that changes in one domain are compatible with program functioning and to develop integrated strategies that involve related dimensions from different domains (Moos et al., 1983).

In an example of this type of change study, we used the WES to help ameliorate work stress among staff in an intensive care unit for treatment of serious burns. Unit staff were showing dysfunctional reactions (such as mild depression and physical and emotional withdrawal from patients) that seemed to be attributable to work pressure, confusion about unit policies, and lack of personal autonomy and of support from supervisors. Staff were assessed and provided with feedback on the WES results and on the discrepancies between their actual and preferred work milieu. Target areas for change were identified and a liaison psychiatrist worked with unit staff to formulate and implement changes. Staff felt that the actual work setting improved on several dimensions after the intervention period, as shown, for example, by greater involvement and staff cohesion as well as by increases in program clarity and autonomy and decreases in work pressure. Thus, a consultation program can help make health care work environments more satisfactory for their employees (Koran et al., 1983).

Environmental Assessment and Evaluation Research

Environmental assessment procedures can play a valuable role in implementing a process-oriented framework for evaluating health care programs. Until recently, more evaluation researchers were guided by an idealized paradigm in which individuals were assessed, assigned to treatment (or control) conditions, and then reevaluated at follow-up to identify treatment-related changes in their behavior and adaptation. Current trends in health psychology and evaluation research have led to a two-pronged expansion of this "summative" paradigm.

Since intervention programs typically are neither implemented as planned nor delivered to recipients in a fixed, standard manner, one area of development involves monitoring the adequacy of treatment implementation. As noted earlier, measures of the social environments of health care settings can provide information about the degree to which a new program has actually been operationalized. When the treatment is being delivered as intended, the relationship between specific treatment components (including the quality of the social environment) and treatment outcome can be explored. At this point, the evaluator can help clinicians to reorient the program and concentrate its resources on those components that are associated with better outcome.

Evaluators are also realizing that extratreatment factors such as life stressors and social network resources can affect the relative benefits of health care programs. In an evaluation of a group of alcoholism treatment programs, for example, we found that patients' environmental stressors and coping resources had as strong an influence on their posttreatment adaptation as did the treatment itself. Information about these life context factors can help to understand how health care programs (especially the psychosocial components) exert their effects, to monitor the process of relapse and recovery, and to guide the reformulation of treatment approaches (Moos & Finney, 1983).

FUTURE DIRECTIONS

Social resources in community and health care contexts affect health and health-related adaptation. More refined concepts and measures of social resources are needed at both the individual and the program level in order to explore the specific connections and psychosocial mechanisms that mediate such relationships. The complexity of stress and coping phenomena has been generally recognized, but empirical work has not adequately reflected the interrelated, multicausal nature of the processes involved. The findings presented here emphasize the interdependence of stressors and resources and the fact that the effects of social resources on health may be moderated by other factors such as the degree of structure and goal orientation in a setting. Such considerations highlight the value of assessing interpersonal resources in light of a conceptual framework that encompasses a broad array of environmental factors.

Ultimately, cross-disciplinary collaborative research is needed to explore the connections between social factors and physiological and biochemical indicators that can affect disease directly. In this regard, social factors (such as marital and job strain) can influence disease processes by affecting endogenous psychological factors such as depression, which may predict increased cancer risk and is hypothesized to affect the immune system. Alternatively, social factors can affect illness indirectly, by, for example, changing health risk behaviors such as smoking and drinking patterns (Fox, 1982). With improved measurement procedures and an expanded evaluation framework, it should eventually be possible to specify the biopsychosocial mechanisms by which social resources exert their influence. Enhanced knowledge in this area has important implications for primary as well as for secondary and tertiary prevention.

References

Alexy, W. (1981–1982). Perceptions of ward atmosphere on an oncology unit. *International Journal of Psychiatry in Medicine, 11,* 331–340.

Alfredsson, L., Karasek, R., & Theorell, T. (1982). Myocardial infarction risk and psychosocial work environment: An analysis of the male Swedish working force. *Social Science and Medicine, 16A,* 463–467.

Anderson, B., Miller, J. P., Auslander, W., & Santiago, J. (1981). Family characteristics of diabetic adolescents: Relationship to metabolic control. *Diabetes Care, 4,* 586–594.

Antonucci, T., & Depner, C. (1982). Social support and informal helping relationships. In T. A. Wills (Ed.), *Basic processes in helping relationships.* New York: Academic Press.

Bauman, L., Rogers, T., & Metzger, L. (1982). An empirical specification of the concept of social support. Presented at the American Sociological Association Convention, San Francisco, CA.

Berkman, L., & Syme, S. (1979). Social networks, host resistance and mortality: A nine-year follow-up study of Alameda County residents. *American Journal of Epidemiology, 109,* 186–204.

Billings, A., Cronkite, R., & Moos, R. (1983). Social-environmental factors in unipolar depression: Comparisons of depressed patients and nondepressed controls. *Journal of Abnormal Psychology, 92,* 119–133.

Billings, A., & Moos, R. (1981). The role of coping responses and social resources in attenuating the stress of life events. *Journal of Behavioral Medicine, 4,* 157–189.

Bloom, J. (1982). Social support, accommodation to stress, and adjustment to breast cancer. *Social Science and Medicine, 16A,* 1329–1338.

Bowlby, J. (1973). *Attachment and loss,* Vol. 2. *Separation: Anxiety and anger.* London: Hogarth Press.

Boyle, W. (1979). Predicting and producing effective psychiatric aids. Doctoral dissertation, Department of Psychology, St. John's University, New York: *Dissertation Abstracts International, 1980, 41*(1-B), 341.

Breslau, N. (1983). Family care of disabled children: Effects on siblings and mothers. In L. Rubin, G. Thompson, & R. Bilenker (Eds.), *Comprehensive management of cerebral palsy.* New York: Grune & Stratton.

Bristol, M. (In press). Family resources and successful adaptation to autistic children. In E. Schopler & G. Mesibov (Eds.), *The effects of autism on the family.* New York: Plenum Press.

Brugge, P. (1981). The relationship between family as a social support system, health status, and exercise of self-care agency in the adult with a chronic illness. Doctoral dissertation, School of Nursing, Wayne State University, Detroit, MI: *Dissertation Abstracts International, 1981, 42*(11-B), 4361.

Caldwell, T., & Weiner, M. F. (1981). Stresses and coping in ICU nursing, I. A review. *General Hospital Psychiatry, 3,* 119–127.

Caplan, G. (1964). *Principles of preventive psychiatry.* New York: Basic Books.

Caplan, R. D., Van Harrison, R., Wellons, R. V., & French, J. R. P. (1980). *Social support and patient adherence.* Institute for Social Research, University of Michigan, Ann Arbor, MI.

Cherniss, C. (1980). *Professional burnout in human service organizations.* New York: Praeger.

Chesney, M., Sevelius, G., Black, G., Ward, M., Swan, G., & Rosenman, R. (1981). Work environment, type A behavior and coronary heart disease risk factors. *Journal of Occupational Medicine, 23,* 551–555.

Cousins, N. (1979). *Anatomy of an illness as perceived by the patient.* New York: Norton.

Crisler, J., & Settles, R. (1979). An integrated rehabilitation team effort in providing services for multiple disability clients. *Journal of Rehabilitation, 45,* 34–38.

Cromwell, R., & Keeney, B. (1979). Diagnosing marital and family systems: A training model. *Family Coordinator, 28,* 101–108.

Croog, S., & Levine, S. (1982). *Life after a heart attack: Social and psychological factors eight years later.* New York: Human Sciences Press.

Davis, M. Z. (1980). The organizational, interactional and care-oriented conditions for patient participation in continuity of care: A framework for staff intervention. *Social Science and Medicine, 14A,* 39–47.

Dimond, M. (1979). Social support and adaptation to chronic illness: The case of maintenance hemodialysis. *Research in Nursing and Health, 2,* 101–108.

Eichel, E. (1978). Assessment with a family focus. *Journal of Psychiatric Nursing and Mental Health Services, 16,* 11–15.

Engel, G. L. (1980). The clinical application of the biopsychosocial model. *American Journal of Psychiatry, 137,* 535–544.

Finlayson, A. (1976). Social networks as coping resources: Lay help and consultation patterns used by women in husbands' post-infarction career. *Social Science and Medicine, 10A,* 97–103.

Fox, B. (1982). Endogenous psychosocial factors in cross-national cancer incidence. In J. R. Eiser (Ed.), *Social psychology and behavioral medicine.* New York: Wiley.

Fuhr, R., Moos, R., & Dishotsky, N. (1981). The use of family assessment and feedback in ongoing family therapy. *American Journal of Family Therapy, 9,* 24–36.

Funch, D. P., & Mettlin, C. (1982). The role of support in relation to recovery from breast surgery. *Social Science and Medicine, 16A,* 91–98.

Gersten, J. C., Frii, S. R., & Langner, T. S. (1976). Life dissatisfactions, job dissatisfaction and illness of married men over time. *American Journal of Epidemiology, 103,* 333–341.

Greenwood, R., Marr, J., Roessler, R., & Rowland, P. (1980). The social climate of a rehabilitation center: Implications for oganizational development. *Journal of Rehabilitation Administration, 4,* 20–24.

Henderson, S., Byrne, D. G., & Duncan-Jones, P. (1981). *Neurosis and the social environment.* Sydney, Australia: Academic Press.

Holahan, C. J., & Moos, R. (1981). Social support and psychological distress: A longitudinal analysis. *Journal of Abnormal Psychology, 90,* 365–370.

Holahan, C. J., & Moos, R. (1982). Social support and adjustment: Predictive benefits of social climate indices. *American Journal of Community Psychology, 10,* 403–415.

Holland, T. P., Konick, A., Buffum, W., Smith, M. K., & Petchers, M. (1981). Institutional structure and resident outcomes. *Journal of Health and Social Behavior, 22,* 433–444.

Kobasa, S. C., & Puccetti, M. C. (In press). Personality and social resources in stress-resistance. *Journal of Personality and Social Psychology.*

Koran, L., Moos, R., Moos, B., & Zasslow, M. (1983). Changing hospital work environments: An example of a burn unit. *General Hospital Psychiatry, 5,* 7–13.

La Rocco, J., House, J., & French, J. (1980). Social support, occupational stress, and health. *Journal of Health and Social Behavior, 21,* 202–218.

Lindemann, E. (1979). *Beyond grief: Studies in crisis intervention.* New York: Jason Aronson.

Marone, J., & Desiderato, O. (1982). Effects of locus of control on perceived hospital environment. *Journal of Clinical Psychology, 38,* 555–561.

McCubbin, H., Nevin, R., Cauble, A., Larsen, A., Comeau, J., & Patterson, J. (1982). Family coping with chronic illness: The case of cerebral palsy. In H. McCubbin, A. Cauble, & J. Patterson (Eds.), *Family stress, coping, and social support.* Springfield, IL: Thomas.

Medalie, J. H., & Goldbourt, V. (1976). Angina pectoris among 10,000 men: II. Psychosocial and other risk factors as evidenced by a multivariate analysis of a five year incidence study. *American Journal of Medicine, 60,* 910–921.

Medalie, J. H., Kahn, H. A., Neufeld, H. N., Riss, E., & Goldbourt, V. (1973). Five year myocardial infarction incidence—II. Association of single variables to age and birthplace. *Journal of Chronic Disease, 26,* 329–349.

Mohl, P., Denny, N., Mote, T., & Coldwater, C. (1982). Hospital unit stressors that affect nurses: Primary task versus social factors. *Psychosomatics, 23,* 366–374.

Moos, R. (1974). *Evaluating treatment environments.* New York: Wiley.

Moos, R. (1979). Social-ecological perspectives on health. In G. Stone, F. Cohen, & N. Adler (Eds.), *Health psychology: A handbook.* San Francisco: Jossey-Bass.

Moos, R. (1981a). Environmental choice and control in community care settings for older people. *Journal of Applied Social Psychology, 11,* 23–43.

Moos, R. (1981b). *Group Environment Scale manual.* Palo Alto, CA: Consulting Psychologists Press.

Moos, R. (1981c). *Work Environment Scale manual.* Palo Alto, CA: Consulting Psychologists Press.

Moos, R. (1982). Coping with acute health crises. In T. Millon, C. Green, & R. Meagher (Eds.), *Handbook of health care clinical psychology,* New York: Plenum Press.

Moos, R., Clayton, J., & Max, W. (1979). *The Social Climate Scales: An annotated bibliography.* Palo Alto, CA: Consulting Psychologists Press.

Moos, R., & Finney, J. (1983). The expanding scope of alcoholism treatment evaluation. *American Psychologist.*

Moos, R., & Fuhr, R. (1982). The clinical use of social-environmental concepts: The case of an adolescent girl. *American Journal of Orthopsychiatry, 52,* 111–122.

Moos, R., & Igra, A. (1980). Determinants of the social environment of sheltered care settings. *Journal of Health and Social Behavior, 21,* 88–98.

Moos, R., & Lemke, S. (1984). Supportive residential settings for older people. In I. Altman, J. Wohlwill, & P. Lawton (Eds.), *Human behavior and the environment: The elderly and the physical environment.* New York: Plenum Press.

Moos, R., Lemke, S., & Clayton, J. (1983). Comprehensive assessment of residential care settings: A means of facilitating program evaluation and change. *Interdisciplinary Topics in Gerontology, 17,* 69–83.

Moos, R., & Mitchell, R. (1982). Social network resources and adaptation: A conceptual framework. In T. A. Wills (Ed.), *Basic processes in helping relationships.* New York: Academic Press.

Moos, R., & Moos, B. (1981). *Family Environment Scale manual.* Palo Alto, CA: Consulting Psychologists Press.

Moreno, J. (1934). *Who shall survive.* Washington, DC.: Nervous and Mental Disease Publishing.

Pattison, E., Llamas, R., & Hurd, G. (1979). Social network mediation of anxiety. *Psychiatric Annals, 9,* 56–67.

Porritt, D. (1979). Social support in crisis: Quantity or quality? *Social Science and Medicine, 13A,* 715–721.

Procidano, M., & Heller, K. (1983). Measures of perceived social support from friends and from family: Three validation studies. *American Journal of Community Psychology, 11,* 1–24.

Ray, C. J., & Fitzgibbon, G. (1979). Socially mediated reduction of stress in surgical patients. In D. J. Oborne, M. M. Grunneberg, & J. R. Eiser (Eds.), *Research in Psychology in Medicine* (Vol. 2). London: Academic Press.

Rhodes, L. (1981). Social climate perception and depression of patients and staff in a chronic hemodialysis unit. *Journal of Nervous and Mental Disease, 169,* 169–175.

Rogers, C. R. (1951). *Client-centered therapy.* Boston: Houghton Mifflin.

Sarason, I. G., Levine, H. M., Basham, R. B., & Sarason, B. R. (1983). Assessing social support: The social support questionnaire. *Journal of Personality and Social Psychology, 44,* 127–139.

Schaefer, C., Coyne, J. C., & Lazarus, R. S. (1981). The health-related functions of social support. *Journal of Behavioral Medicine, 4,* 381–406.

Schmitt, N., & Fitzgerald, M. (1982). Mass psychogenic illness: Individual and aggregate data. In M. Colligan, J. Pennebaker, & L. Murphy (Eds.), *Mass psychogenic illness: A social psychological analysis.* Hillsdale, NJ: Erlbaum.

Schulman, B. A. (1979). Active patient orientation and outcomes in hypertensive treatment. *Medical Care, 17,* 267–280.

Schwartz, G. E. (1982). Testing the biopsychosocial model: The ultimate challenge facing behavioral medicine? *Journal of Consulting and Clinical Psychology, 50,* 1040–1053.

Sinclair, C., & Frankel, M. (1982). The effect of quality assurance activities on the quality of mental health services. *Quality Review Bulletin, 8,* 7–15.

Skipper, J. K., & Leonard, R. C. (1968). Children, stress, and hospitalization: A field experiment. *Journal of Health and Social Behavior, 9,* 275–287.

Sosa, R. Kennell, J., Klaus, M., Robertson, S., & Urrutia, J. (1980). The effect of a supportive companion on perinatal problems, length of labor, and mother-infant interaction. *New England Journal of Medicine, 303,* 597–600.

Spiegel, D., Bloom, J., & Gottheil, E. (1983). Family environment as a predictor of adjustment to metastatic carcinoma. *Journal of Psychosocial Oncology.*

Spitz, R. (1946). The smiling response: A contribution to the ontogenesis of social relations. *Genetic Psychology Monographs, 34,* 57–125.

Steiner, R. H. (1982). The sociotherapeutic environment of a child psychosomatic ward. *Child Psychiatry and Human Development, 13,* 71–78.

Strober, M. (1981). The significance of bulimia in juvenile anorexia nervosa: An exploration of possible etiologic factors. *International Journal of Eating Disorders, 1,* 28–43.

Taylor, S. E. (1979). Hospital patient behavior: Reactance, helplessness, or control? *Journal of Social Issues, 35,* 156–184.

Theorell, T., Lind, E., & Floderus, B. (1975). The relationship of disturbing life changes and emotions to the early development of myocardial infarction and other serious illness. *International Journal of Epidemiology, 4,* 281–293.

Thomas, C. B., Duszynski, K. R., & Shaffer, J. W. (1979). Family attitudes reported in youth as potential predictors of cancer. *Psychosomatic Medicine, 41,* 287–302.

Turner, J., Frankel, B. G., & Levin, D. (In press). Social support: Conceptualization, measurement and implications for mental health. In J. R. Greenley (Ed.), *Research in Community and Mental Health* (Vol. 3). Greenwich, CT: JAI Press.

Vaillant, G. E. (1979). Natural history of male psychologic health: Effects of mental health on physical health. *New England Journal of Medicine, 30,* 1249–1254.

Volicer, B. J., Isenberg, M. A., & Burns, M. W. (1977). Medical-surgical differences in hospital stress factors. *Journal of Human Stress, 3,* 3–13.

Warner, R. (1982). The psychologist as social systems consultant. In T. Millon, C. Green, & R. Meagher (Eds.), *Handbook of clinical health psychology.* New York: Academic Press.

Weimer, S., Hatcher, C., & Gould, E. (1983). Family characteristics in high and low health care utilization. *General Hospital Psychiatry, 5,* 55–61.

13

The Assessment of Pain: Concepts and Procedures

PAUL KAROLY

INTRODUCTION

The most pervasive symptom in medical practice, the most frequently stated "cause" of disability, and the single most compelling force
underlying an individual's choice to seek or avoid medical care, pain
(particularly chronic pain), is a focal point in the contemporary health
sciences (cf. Melzack & Wall, 1983; Weisenberg, 1977). In recent years it has
been estimated that 35 percent of Americans suffer from chronic (prolonged)
pain, with over 50 million "partially or completely disabled for periods
ranging from a few days per year to permanently" (Bonica, 1980, pp. 381–
382). The cost of pain, in terms of workdays lost, health care and insurance
expenses, rehabilitation efforts and the like, is enormous, estimated in
monetary terms by Bonica at one tenth the national budget. The cost in
human despair is as vast as it is immeasurable.

Yet, despite the importance of pain as a social, personal, and medical problem, basic research is still in its nascent stages. That we should know more than we now do (particularly in view of the long-standing interest in the subject of pain) is not a reasonable position to take—lest we wish to second-guess history. But we can probably do better in our logical assault than to argue, as some current commentators have, that (1) the best way to measure pain is simply to ask people how much hurt they feel; (2) because pain is a subjective state, it is, by definition, not subject to measurement or quantification; or (3) despite the fact that pain measurement is an inexact science, certain medical procedures, drugs, or forms of rehabilitation have been "proven" to be either effective or ineffective as pain treatments.

The "facts" about pain are often disturbing ones. Pain has no consensual definition across the varied health disciplines charged with its management and control. Findings based on research conducted with animals or human volunteers experiencing controlled, laboratory-based presentations of "noxious stimulation" bear no clear relationship to the experience of "clinical" pain. The treatment of pain syndromes is extremely varied—ranging from the use of pharmocologic agents, surgery, electric implants, and hypnosis to group therapy, biofeedback, relaxation training, and cognitive restructuring (cf. Chapman & Wyckoff, 1981; Crue et al., 1980; Stewart, 1977; Turk et al., 1983). In an era when laypersons have been taught to identify "medical science" with finely calibrated biomechanical devices and carefully controlled research, the absence of a coherent approach to the topic of pain is lamentable (perhaps tragic).

Psychologists and other nonmedically trained investigators have, in the last 30 to 40 years, played a major role in providing increasingly sturdy underpinnings for the study of pain in its acute and chronic forms. Methods have been developed that transcend, supplement, and/or upgrade the verbal descriptions of the pain experience and that permit the analysis of its relationship to a multiplex of antecedents and consequences. Further, artificial definitional boundaries are being gradually eliminated, thus widening the scope of investigatory efforts. The present chapter is intended as an overview of the major contemporary strategies of pain assessment that have emerged in the context of today's expansive and heuristic biopsychosocial perspective on health and illness (cf. Engel, 1977; Pelletier, 1977). First, however, an examination will be made of the pain concept as it is currently articulated by advocates of an interdisciplinary, multidimensional strategy.

The Pain Experience: A Multidimensional Approach

Pain is neither a unitary phenomenon nor does it bear a direct, one-to-one relationship to tissue damage and/or sensory arousal. These two assertions, simple as they may appear, have not come forth without considerable and heated debate. Historically, conceptions of pain have had a decidedly dualistic and reductionist complexion, with theorists separating pain perception and its neurological conductivity from consequent subjective reports and behavioral responses and assuming little or no voluntary modulation over the "purely" or "fundamentally" biophysical nature of the process. Whether arguing for specific sensory receptors and/or specific pain pathways or for complex central nervous system mediation (so-called pattern, central summation, or sensory interaction theories), pain investigators nonetheless "embodied" pain, although leaving the disembodied "mind" to play a more or less reactive or secondary role (Melzack, 1973; Schneider & Karoly, 1983; Weisenberg, 1977). Contemporary conceptualizers, guided by the provocative gate-control theory (Melzack & Wall, 1965, 1983), have introduced an egalitarian and nondeterministic mode of analysis into the field—components may be separate, but they are all part of the system; and the assignment of causal priority is seen as downright defamatory.

The phenomenon of pain can profitably be approached both horizontally (as a stochastic temporal progression) and vertically (as an information-processing system, yielding a variety of possible "outputs").

Urban (1982) articulated the structure of the former perspective when he suggested that

> pain behavior may be viewed as the end stage of a progression: *nociception* becoming *pain* leading to *suffering* resulting in *pain behavior* (p. 430, italics added).

Of course, it really makes more sense to think, not in terms of an "end stage," but in terms of a cyclical process, wherein recognizably different categories of pain (perception, suffering, pain behavior, etc.) occur in what Melzack and Wall (1983) term a "loose association" (i.e., probabilistically). Further, it is important to insert into the causal cycle the role of environmental events (including the responses of relevant others that may signal, reinforce, facilitate, or inhibit the pain sequence). Thus, the pain message moves on a trackless yet often decipherable path.

Stopping the action of the pain sequence figuratively at a particular point of interest allows us then to conduct a vertical analysis. Here the insights of the still developing, yet comprehensive, gate-control theory will be of immeasurable assistance. Prior to the advent of multicomponent "systems" approaches, the search for an adequate account of why a patient was experiencing a particular level of pain and emitting pain behaviors might have involved attempts to determine: (1) the stimulus source, (2) the nature of the sensory induction (mechanical, thermal, electrical, or chemical), and (3) the individual's sensation threshold and pain tolerance limits. Such an approach would have proven to be very limited, particularly in the analysis of chronic, clinical pain of unknown origin. Whether dealing with acute or chronic pain, however, the mechanistic stance that dominated (still dominates?) medicine and physiology would fail to reliably link identifiable patterns of sensory transmission to repeatable patterns of action, thought, and feeling (Melzack & Wall, 1983). The fact that nervous system causes do not lead, in a straightforward manner, to psychological effects may be disappointing, but it does not mean that the assessment enterprise is doomed to be a hit-and-miss affair. By taking what was formerly error variance or noise and reframing such factors as legitimate targets of measurement, contemporary theorists like Fordyce (1973), Melzack (1973), Sternbach (1968, 1974a), Chapman (1980), and others have helped to make the inherent uncertainty of prediction in medicine less daunting (cf. also Bursztajn et al., 1981). Of course, the reader should be aware that there are still those who believe that the direct link between sensory transmission and pain experience remains to be discovered—and that, once it is, all current work will be of historical interest only.

The Gate-Control Model and Nonlocality. The reader will probably recall being asked (usually in a high school science class) if a tree falling in a forest will make a sound if no one is there to hear it. The point of the question was to stimulate thinking in relativistic rather than absolutistic terms. A sound, by definition, requires not only the physical production of a signal via disturbance of air molecules but a sensing device (an ear) that, in essence, completes the circuit. Hence, no receiver, no sound. The presence of a sensate organism determines (according to one definition of sound) the reality of the existence of sound. Later on, in college, more elaborate examples of the relative nature of reality may have been encountered (e.g., Heisenberg's principle or the paradox of Schrödinger's cat). Although such examples are usually confined to the study of physics, the underlying theme is applicable to phenomena in other fields—such as pain perception.

For example, we might ask whether a person stuck by a pin while under hypnosis really feels pain, even though he acts as if he does not. Does a patient under the influence of morphine still feel pain although he may appear to be relaxed, even elated? Can a person with no left arm feel pain emanating from a so-called "phantom limb"? The traditional (absolute, mechanistic, deterministic) view of pain perception would answer "yes" to the first two questions and "no" to the third. The new model or paradigm, epitomized by the gate-control theory, would have us first examine the larger system in which a nervous impulse, traveling from a sense organ to the brain, is but a part. To say that pain exists or does not exist irrespective of other things occurring in the system is to simplify a highly complex and indeterminate set of relationships. A principle of quantum theory, called *nonlocality*, states that a "system cannot be analyzed into parts whose basic properties do not depend on the . . . whole system" (Bohm & Hiley, 1975). Pain may well not be there if a person does not notice it (despite all external evidence to the contrary). And, similarly, pain from a nonexistent arm may well be "real" pain. What follows is a brief outline of the theoretical rationale underlying these assertions concerning the nature of pain.

First, needing to account for such robust clinical phenomena as phantom limb pain, summation (wherein mild stimulation can, over time, trigger a pain response), the spread of trigger zones from pathologic to nonpathologic areas of the body, the persistence of pain after healing of injured tissue, and the high degree of specialization in central nervous system pathways and fiber activity, Melzack and Wall, in 1965, proposed a theory that integrated psychological and physiological factors in the explanation of pain perception. In addition to highlighting the nature of sensory transmission via small diameter fibers (A-delta and C) and large diameter sensory fibers (A-beta) and the role of the spinal cord as a transmission site, the model also postulated a key role for the descending fibers from the brain to the cord. The perception of pain thus became a complex interactive product of afferent sensory activity and central (cognitive) processes. Neither the physical nor the higher-order cognitive activities are preeminent. Just as quantum physics accepts the Heisenberg principle that a moving particle is partly in one place and partly in another, pain researchers were given permission by Melzack and Wall to view pain as a psychophysiological process, partly sensation, partly emotion, partly cognitive evaluation, and partly behavioral response, but not a unitary something reducible to a "pure" sensory experience.

The precise nature of the interactive process centered at the spinal cord is not yet clear; and Melzack and Wall's theory is best viewed as a developing framework, one that builds upon emergent literatures in medicine, physiology, and psychology.

In the original formulation (Melzack & Casey, 1968, Melzack & Wall, 1965), a modulating mechanism was proposed that influenced the transmission of signals carried along small diameter neural fibers to the dorsal horns of the spinal cord (so-named because a view of the spinal cord in transverse section reveals an H-shaped gray structure, with the posterior or dorsal sections resembling horns) where they then activate transmission (T) cells that project the signal to the brain. The theory proposed that when the firing of the dorsal horn T-cells exceeded a critical level a pain action system would be triggered involving several different areas of the brain subserving sensory-discriminative, affective-motivational, and cognitive-evaluational functions (all of which interact and project to the motor system). The location of the important modulating mechanism was said to be at the level of the spinal cord. The small diameter fibers (S-fibers) that typically signal pain not only activate T-cells but also send projections to an area of the dorsal horns known as the *substantia gelatinosa* of Rolando (SG) which presumably facilitates transmission from the S-fibers to the T-cells. The key to the gating mechanism is in the relative activity of the S-fibers and large diameter (L) fibers, both of which project to the SG and the T-cells. Simply put, the activity in large diameter cells tends to inhibit transmission (closing the gate), whereas activity on the S-fibers facilitates transmission of the pain signal (opening the gate to the T-cells and the higher cortical centers). Because both large and small diameter cells project to the substantia gelatinosa, and because the SG influences T-cells, it is considered the prime physiological site of the pain gating mechanism. Melzack and Wall (1965) also postulated a specialized system of large diameter fibers, called the central control trigger, which descends from the cerebral cortex to influence the spinal modulation process. Therefore, brain activities that deal with conscious, information-processing (attention, emotion, memory, etc.) were hypothesized to exert control over sensory messages, augmenting or reducing felt pain.

One of the most important aspects of the gate-control model is its provision of a conceptual framework from which to understand multiple, interacting influences on pain and upon which clinicians can base multicomponent treatments for pain (especially of the long-standing, chronic type). Among the forces reputedly acting upon T-cell transmission are: phasic (periodic) sensory inputs (such as injury or short-term noxious stimulation), tonic (prolonged) sensory inputs (such as scar tissue), phasic downflow from the brain (attention, anxiety, expectancy, etc.), tonic downflow from the brain (so-called "personality" or "style" variables, cultural conditioning, values, etc.) and inputs due to autonomic nervous system activity, among other factors (Melzack & Wall, 1983).

For psychologists, another key aspect of the gate-control model is its recognition of the role of central organizational and control processes. Pain signals, like other classes of input, compete for a share of the brain's limited information-processing capacity. Whereas the arousal potential of a second-degree burn seems potentially greater than that of a distant car horn, the psychophysical properties of so-called nociceptive stimuli do not completely determine figural conscious experience. The meaning or significance (acquired or intrinsic) and the collative properties (e.g., novelty, surprisingness, complexity, ambiguity, and so on) of stimuli also contribute, along with sensory phenomena, to organismic arousal (Martindale, 1981). Control of "figure ground transitions" thus becomes very critical to psychologically based pain treatment programs (Chapman, 1980).

In the years since the gate-control model was first articulated, new data and challenges to old assumptions have been put forward. In 1983, Melzack and Wall offered the gate-control theory "Mark II"; a revision of the earlier model. The modifications are more or less neurophysiologic in nature, including the existence of excitatory as well as inhibitory cells in the SG, the possibility that inhibition of T-cells can be presynaptic, postsynaptic, or both, and the inclusion of another inhibitory system extending downward from the brainstem (from areas called the periaqueductal grey and the nucleus raphe magnus). However, the basic thrust of the gate-control model remains unchanged, particularly its promulgation of a unified systems-oriented approach to the analysis of pain phenomena.

The existence of a heuristically potent model of pain is of inestimable value to contemporary investigators. However, the fields of pain management and pain measurement are not without problems, some of which the gate-control model may (inadvertently) be supporting.

For example, physiological explanations, which are basically reductionistic, tend to give the greatest weight to sensory "first causes." The gate-control model also places heavy emphasis upon the cutaneous, peripheral receptor sites where stimulation is first transduced into the nerve messages that are gated (or not gated) in the region of the dorsal horns. The complex, interactive processes that modulate pain appear less likely to be invoked in discussions of acute pain (which is, therefore, left to be dealt with in more or less traditional, "medicalistic" ways). Comparatively fewer psychologically based interventions have been designed for acute pain relative to chronic pain problems; and there are fewer well-controlled studies on the efficacy of the former (cf. Turk et al., 1983).

The gate-control model has not led to the emergence of an entirely new worldview or paradigm in the fields of pain measurement and treatment. Although perhaps opening the door to different professions, the gate-control model has not yet served as an impetus to genuine interdisciplinary cooperation among distinct scientific groups. Furthermore, clinicians (whether physicians, nurses, or psychologists) and researchers (within the same disciplines as just noted) rarely collaborate (cf., Crue et al., 1980).

In the absence of a singular theory of pain that clearly elucidates the mechanisms of both acute and chronic pain or that permits the ready integration of laboratory-based and clinical observations, the pain measurement and pain treatment enterprises remain fractionated, existing as separate islands or colonies under a single, but remote jurisdiction. Research and practice are highly pragmatic undertakings, such that no one questions an investigator's integrity if he or she takes a biochemical, physiological, or purely psychological route to greater understanding of pain. Only the legitimacy of the investigative method and the usefulness of the results appear to matter.

ASSESSING THE PAIN CONTEXT

The Definitional Dilemma

The International Association for the Study of Pain issued the following definition of pain several years ago.

> an unpleasant sensory and emotional experience associated with actual or potential tissue damage, or described in terms of such damage (IASP Subcommittee on Taxonomy, 1979, p. 250).

This definition has been said to have "great merit" because of its explicit recognition of the variable relationship between perceived pain and injury and its acknowledgment of the emotional dimension (Melzack & Wall, 1983). However, Melzack and Wall (1983) fault the use of the term "unpleasant" because it does not go far enough toward elucidating the complexity of the experience of pain. Based upon their own empirical analyses of patients' verbal descriptions of pain, these investigators suggest that a complete definition must include not only a sensory and affective, but also an evaluative dimension that

> reflects the capacity of the brain to evaluate the importance or urgency of the overall situation . . . based not only on sensory and affective qualities, but also upon previous experiences, capacity to judge outcome, and the meaning of the situation (Melzack & Wall, 1983, p. 71).

It is my contention that, although the definitions of Merskey (the chairman of the IASP Taxonomy committee) and Melzack and Wall reflect multidimensionality, it is nontheless a constrained multidimensionality. Pain remains mainly *an immediate or short-term emotional reaction to sensory experience*, if you agree with Plutchik's (1980) definition of an emotion as

> an inferred complex sequence of reactions to a stimulus, and includes cognitive evaluations, subjective changes, autonomic and neural arousal, impulses to action, and behavior designed to have an effect upon the stimulus that initiated the complex sequence (p. 361).

To be perfectly consistent with the spirit of the gate-control model, with a reciprocal determinist view of human action (cf. Bandura, 1978), and with the relativist philosophy of quantum indeterminacy, (1) no single aspect of the pain experience (sensory, emotive, cognitive, behavioral, or physiochemical) should be considered primary, but, rather, the pain context should be the fundamental unit; (2) the mode of the inquiry or measurement theory should always be considered as part of the pain context; (3) the environment (social and/or inanimate) should be examined, not just as an antecedent or consequence of a pain event or episode, but as an essential component of the mind-body-setting interaction (the smallest unit of study in a "biopsychosocial" model of human adaptation); and (4) the temporal perspective must not be limited to the short-term past or the present, since the adaptive implications of pain may be future-oriented. The specific dimension (within the extended sequence of actions and reactions that defines the pain context) that an investigator selects to assess should be determined solely by the nature of the referral or experimental question and not by convenience or convention (i.e., standard practice or the way it was done in the latest issue of the *Journal of Abnormal Psychology*).

Although the proposed framework would appear to be complicating an already complex construct (e.g., adding long-term cognitive organizational and interpersonal elements to the "sensory-emotive essence" of pain), the pain context view is seen as a necessary corrective to a self-limiting reductionist mode of approach (cf. also Elton et al., 1983).

Traditionally, the most common reason for measuring pain is to make a differential medical diagnosis. To accomplish this goal, physicians typically require answers to three seemingly simple questions: Where does it hurt? What does the hurt feel like (penetrating versus surface, sharp versus dull, confined versus radiating, thermal properties, etc.)? How long has it been there (e.g., acute versus chronic, steady versus recurrent)? Despite the problems of unreliability and the personal idiosyncracies of patients' pain reporting, physicians have been quite successful in assigning patients to treatments on the basis of what is not strictly measurement at all, but, rather, nominal scaling (cf. Bradley, et al., 1981). Therefore, it can be asserted that the first stage(s) of clinical pain assessment almost always involves non-quantifiable categorical judgments, first by patients (in deciding whether they are distressed enough to see a doctor), and then by physicians, in classifying pain into acute versus chronic types and in delineating its biological substrates (e.g., benign versus malignant). Nominal scaling in pain assessment will be discussed later, but now it is time to articulate more fully the dimensions of the so-called pain context and the various considerations involved in reliably measuring pain (i.e., in assigning the right numbers to the right objects in accordance with a set of rules).

A Heuristic

When a clinician or researcher is ready to assess pain, it is suggested that, in place of the pain sensation, pain symptom, or pain reaction, the focus be upon the multilevel pain context. In addition, assessment should be guided by an appreciation of factors beyond the target response that determines how pain will be quantified and to what use the derived data can most meaningfully be put. The key elements involved in such an assessment enterprise are outlined in Table 13.1.

Focal Pain Dimensions.   The six aspects of pain listed in the left-hand column should be noncontroversial, as the list includes the immediate products of both the unpleasant sensation and what Beecher (1959) called the reactive component, as well as the extended processes that derive from the actions of the central nervous system (particularly the higher centers) and that produce the complex patterns of intrapsychic and social adaptation characteristic of many chronic pain patients. Although most pain classification systems acknowledge the variety of pain experiences, few appear to cover the range of attributes listed. Pain has been discussed (Sanders, 1979) as a trimodal cluster of gross motor, cognitive, and physiological responses, as a three-dimensional experience, divisible into sensory, affective, and evaluative qualities (Melzack & Wall, 1983), and in terms of stimulus dimensions, reaction dimensions, and modalities of expression (Moitoza & Espin, 1980). It is not clear where the verbal, sensory, or interpersonal dimensions fit into Sanders' model, or whether Melzack and Wall's basic definition gives

TABLE 13.1. KEY ELEMENTS IN PAIN (SYMPTOM) CONTEXT ASSESSMENT

Focal Pain Dimensions or Response Levels in the Pain Context	Source(s) of Information Regarding Focal Dimensions	Fundamental Assessment Parameters
A. Sensory-discriminative/somatic perception e.g., intensity, duration, threshold, tolerance, thermal qualities, location, etc.	Client (patient): direct Client; indirect Client/interviewer/test interpreter	I. Measurement context Naturalistic Laboratory (simulational) Clinic
B. Neurophysiologic—autonomic-biochemical (e.g., brain wave activity, heart rate, GSR, endorphin assay, etc.)	Observer-informant (doctor, nurse, family member, friend, trained observer)	II. Unit of Study Person (mind × body) Interaction between persons Person × environment interaction
C. Motivational/affective (e.g., anxiety, anger, depression, resentment, loss of reinforcer, effectiveness, etc.)	Biochemical assays Biomechanical devices	III. Unit of observation Discrete responses (digital) Continuous responses (analog)
D. Behavioral (verbal-motoric) (e.g., asking for medication; "uptime" vs. "downtime"; avoidance of exercise; pain complaints; invalidism, etc.)	Medical records/ Medical history/ other archival sources	IV. Scaling level Nominal Ordinal Interval Ratio
E. Lifestyle impact/quality of life/interpersonal (e.g., marital distress, litigation, changes in sexual patterns, vocational changes, etc.)		V. Analytic Focus Single index within focal dimension Multiple indices within focal dimension

F. Information-processing/central control (e.g., attentional focus, problem-solving skills; self-perceptions, expectancies of future outcomes, coping styles, health beliefs, standard setting, etc.)

   Multiple indices across multiple dimensions

VI. Unit of measurement
   Responses (singular or aggregated)
   Instrumental acts (singular or aggregated)
   Attributions about acts or responses (ratings, rankings, interview answers, questionnaire responses, etc.)

VII. Mode of analysis
   Descriptive (steady states, analysis of system properties)
   Predictive (analysis of covariations, modeling of relationships)
   Functional (analysis of causal sequences, conditional probabilities, transitional phenomena)

VIII. Clinical-evaluative referent
   Self-referenced (idiographic)
   Norm-referenced (nomothetic)
   Caretaker-referenced
   Clinician-referenced

IX. Temporal referent
   Remote past
   Recent past
   Present
   Projected future

sufficient expression to long-term adaptations to noxious sensory arousal. Finally, Moitoza and Espin's definition seems to blend the "what" and the "how" of pain assessment. Nevertheless, it is clear that all modern commentators have been attempting to broaden the definition so as to enrich research and treatment possibilities. The focal dimensions listed in Table 13.1 are entirely consistent with the dominant trend in research and clinical interventive studies to focus upon the somatic, psychological, and behavioral activation aspects of pain and the short- and long-term modulating influences (particularly in chronic conditions).

An exhaustive listing of the sensory-discriminative aspects associated with various pain states would be difficult. However, at the head of any tabulation would appear the intensity dimension. Both somatosensory and negative affective qualities are reflected in the person's report of "how much it hurts" when the measurement is of reactions to experimentally induced pain. Intensity reports given by patients with pain due to injury or disease (medically confirmed or not) are, however, indicative of cognitive-evaluational (or meaning) components associated with the processing of pain-relevant information, as well as of sensory and emotional qualities. Despite the complex roles played by cultural conditioning, expectancies, current social contingencies, and the like in determining a person's answer to the question, "How much does it hurt?" that question is still perhaps the most asked in pain assessment work.

In addition to intensity, other sensory aspects of interest include the threshold of pain detectability (a controversial topic, as we shall later see), body location, thermal properties, apparent depth of the sensation (e.g., on the skin surface or visceral), degree of pressure and type (dull, throbbing, aching, etc.), temporal dimensions (brief, steady, episodic), tolerance (or upper threshold), and the temporal and spatial patterning of stability and change. Finally, pain sensations have been categorized as fast (epicritic) and slow (protopathic), and linked to different sensory pathways and fiber types.

Neurophysiologic, biochemical, autonomic, and central nervous system components of various pain states have also been the object of study, for diagnostic and treatment purposes. For some pain assessors, the attempt to tap into the pain transmission network (anywhere from the level of the peripheral sensory neuron to the thalamus and the cerebral cortex) by means of electrical recording, thermograph, or biochemical assay represents the only "objective" means of analysis. If by objective is meant uncontaminated by the personal actions, thoughts, or biases of the subject, this is problematic. If, however, the bias of the observer (pain assessor) is to be kept minimal, then this level of analysis may well be the most pristine. It is important to bear in mind, however, that the neurophysiology and biochemistry of pain (as complex response systems) are no less variable and plastic than the other five focal dimensions. What may be unique about the chemistry and physiology of pain is (1) the fact that medical and surgical interventions are almost exclusively concerned with this aspect of pain; (2) the fact that information is transmitted via "hard-wired," integrated and specialized systems with evolutionary significance; (3) that both pain suppression (inhibition) and expression are innately involved; and (4) that the nature of the physiologic and biochemical aspects of pain are often defined (operationally) by the instruments or procedures used to measure them (cf. Kelly, 1981; Melzack & Wall, 1983, Chapters 5–8).

Briefly, to defend against the view that this second pain dimension should actually be taken as the superordinate explanatory and interventive emphasis, I shall simply reiterate the levels-of-analysis rationale stated earlier, that the investigator's specific question in the interactional context of pain dictates the appropriate target. Pain at the "tissue level" is no more basic than pain at the perceptual, verbal, behavioral, or cognitive level, notwithstanding the "high tech" nature of its measurement (cf. also Peele, 1981).

There can be no doubt that pain involves affective elements, with implications for the motivational (goal-directed) state of the patient. A major advance in pain assessment is associated with the position that emotionality and its attendant approach/avoidance tendencies can be viewed as an element of pain rather than a psychological correlate or psychiatric overlay. It is not clear, however, that this advance is disseminated much beyond textbook discussions, for it is still commonplace for physicians to refer patients with "pain of unknown origin" to psychiatrists or to specialty pain clinics, along with a bleak prognosis and an eagerness on the part of the patients to prove that "The pain isn't just in my head, Doc." This writer has witnessed the withholding of analgesics from severely (third-degree) burned children based on the position that the cries, contortions, and grimaces of these youngsters could only be indicative of "anxiety," rather than of true pain, since the nerve endings ("pain receptors") had been destroyed. I have also witnessed psychologists collude with physicians by arguing that elevations on the MMPI Hysteria and Hypochondriasis scales of chronic pain patients helped to confirm the psychopathologic rather than pathophysiologic nature of the presenting complaints.

It has been noted that as many as 50 percent of the patients in a psychiatric facility report experiencing some pain and that they do so to a greater extent in winter than in summer (Spear, 1967). Clearly, then, it is up to the pain context assessor to find the most parsimonious explanation for patients' emotional expression (as well as for their behavioral, cognitive, and interpersonal expression). This may be aided through a consideration of information sources and assessment parameters, to be discussed in upcoming sections of this chapter.

The fourth focal pain element, verbal motoric expression, is a common target for so-called behavioral pain assessment. To some extent, of course, verbal expression is an essential ingredient across all pain levels with the exception of level B (see Table 13.1). However, pain complaints along with nonverbal posturing, impaired motor functioning, pain medication intake, psychomotor slowing, proportion of daily sleeping, sitting, standing, and walking time, exercise time, and the like have been used as practical and verifiable indices of pain (Fordyce, 1978; Keefe et al., 1982). A number of investigators have cautioned, however, that exclusive reliance on level D measures is unwarranted, because (1) it is often difficult to distinguish pain behaviors from coping efforts (Turk et al., 1983) and (2) a singular behavioral focus ignores the potential contribution of the other pain levels (cf. Bradley et al., 1981). The word *potential* in the preceding sentence is critical, because (as will be discussed further subsequently) there is no logical or scientific reason to prefer two, three, or more assessment levels to one. An assessor can employ converging measures only when there is a reasonably well-articulated entity upon which to converge. In some cases, then, the verbal-motoric level may be the only one within which a clinician-assessor may wish to operate.

Levels E and F are the least often discussed in the literature on measurement. This neglect is not suprising inasmuch as in health psychology (as in other areas) the trend is toward operationalizing terms as strictly as possible in order to avoid conceptual drift and weak prediction. The interpersonal and life-style impacts of a chronic pain disorder are, it is generally reasoned, better conceived as consequences rather than as focal components. Similarly, individuals' long-term processing of pain (their understanding or implicit theory of pain, the way they integrate the facts of being chronically ill into their self-schema, their ability to self-regulate actions, emotions, and beliefs concerning pain, etc.) would appear to represent secondary considerations. Although such positions are not without merit, I contend that chronic pain (despite the advances of the last 30 years) is still an "open concept." As Meehl (1978) has argued, some theoretical concepts should be considered open due to the "indefinite extensibility of our provisional list of operational indicators of the construct" and because such constructs are better defined in context (by their role in a nomological network), rather than by their "inner nature." In view of the findings suggesting that only half the chronic pain patients currently receiving treatment derived from "body-centered" models are being relieved of their suffering, it would appear that, at least provisionally, a biopsychosocial model, incorporating levels A through F, should be accorded serious attention.

Sources of Information.   Our knowledge of pain is constrained not only by where we look but by who (or what) does the looking (the data source). In medical practice all or nearly all seven of the sources listed in column two of Table 13.1 are accessible, yet only a subset are typically employed. A similar statement can be made about research in pain, both laboratory-based and clinical. This is probably as it should be, since the various sources are not all relevant to every question a pain assessor may wish to address. The data sources are listed here because, rather than being left as implicit aspects of pain assessment, they should be kept clearly in mind when making decisions about the design of data gathering and intervention programs.

A discussion of specific methods for pinpointing pain targets will be presented later in this chapter. At present it is important simply to highlight some issues bearing on the extraction of data on subjective states.

The patient is the only source of information about pain at levels A and B and a prime source for levels C and F. To some, this would imply that a good deal of the knowledge available about the pain experience (excluding level B) will be of limited scientific value because of its essentially "introspective" or self-report nature—which, of course, denotes a lack of experimental control and external verifiability, and a basic unreliability. However, as Ericsson and Simon (1980) note, the process of making psychophysical judgments is quite different from what we ordinarily understand as "introspective." The subjects' attention is more readily directed at pain sensations; the sensations are themselves naturally compelling of attentional focus; the memory is usually short-term (particularly with ongoing pain), leaving little room for distortion or retrieval bias; and the judgments are usually being referenced by a personally meaningful standard of comfort or painlessness.

Indirect measurement of a patient is even less problematic than a "tell me how you feel" approach insofar as measurement bias is concerned. Individuals can inform the pain assessor about the status and processes of their felt pain by what they do, not just by what they say. Pain can affect behavioral and cognitive efficiency, for example; and such effects can be gauged by performance decrements in these realms. Pain can also affect the pursuit of one's personal goals. Change in goal-directedness can be assessed by examining response patterns before and after the advent of the pain problem or by carefully observing current activities, particularly the relationship between the patient and his or her goal objects as indexed by the following verb classes (suggested by Klinger et al., 1981): getting, keeping, restoring, doing, abandoning, avoiding (ignoring), preventing, escaping, attacking, or exploring. Changes in the indirect indices noted can usually be attributed to genuine pain process changes rather than to unreliability (measurement error) or to intentional distortion.

Interview-based and test-derived data on pain should be viewed as composite indices, the result of an interaction between the patient and interviewer (or the patient and tester). Most interview protocols that deal with pain are structured or semistructured, and the findings that emerge from them are, to a degree, dependent upon the interviewer's skill and theoretical commitments. As we shall see, interview data can be invaluable in pain assessment. But, it is important to remind the reader that information derived from the nonverbal/verbal exchange between patient and interviewer contains a unique source of variance—that due to the professional training of the clinician.

Informant data, also potentially valuable, may contain all manner of bias—such as that due to inadequate sampling, memory distortion, the quality of the informant-patient relationship, and the like. However, individuals can be trained to be reasonably accurate observers, particularly when judging discrete categories of events according to a preset schedule (Wildman & Erickson, 1977).

The remaining sources of data will be discussed in the section on pain assessment procedures.

Fundamental Assessment Parameters.   The dimensions listed in the third column of Table 13.1 represent the how of pain assessment, but on a metameasurement level. That is, these aspects of assessment are the implicit foundations of the specific methods most often used to measure pain (e.g., via self-report, pain diary, EMG recording, or biochemical assay). Because these dimensions are often unstated, their impact on the outcome of pain measurement frequently goes unnoticed. In this way, assessors generalize their successes and their failures without adequate appreciation of the so-called "provincial" nature of their data base. As Fiske (1978) noted, observations are always tied to time, place, observer, and purpose. The nine facets of pain measurement presented in Table 13.1 should be considered fully by anyone seriously interested in making generalizable statements about the nature of pain in groups or in individuals.

As is the case in other measurement domains, pain can be most thoroughly and reliably assessed under artificial conditions. Laboratory methods of pain scaling, although far from infallible, yield data that are believed to be less contaminated by fluctuating background conditions and person variables than data taken (by the pain sufferer or others) in the natural environment. A distinction between the laboratory and clinic is made in Table 13.1 in order to highlight the fact there is a middle ground between the highly constrained atmospheres of a laboratory for pain induction and the patient's home environment, namely, the clinician's consulting room. Interview data are typically obtained in a hospital, clinic, or private practitioner's office where the cues and contingencies (quite different from those of the lab or real world) should be taken into account when evaluating the quality of the data. Of course, there is no reason (except the "either or" quality of most assessment) to confine the measurement context to only one of the three listed locales.

In most pain analyses, the unit of study is the person. Hardly a profound statement, the preceding is also a deceptively simple one. Instead of locating the pain exclusively inside the patient, it is asserted from within our temporally extended transactional framework that an alternate unit of study can well include the exchange between a chronic pain sufferer and his or her social and inanimate environment. Whether it is described ("pain at work is worse than pain at home") or functionally analyzed ("an arthritic patient's inability to stand is directly, linearly related to the occurrence of sympathetic reactions received from family members"), the interactional unit of study may shed some new light on the assessment of the traditional pain response levels and the prediction of the outcome of treatment programs.

The unit of observation in research is defined as that part of the ongoing behavior stream used for any given observation (Fiske, 1978). In the study of pain, as in most other areas of psychology, the units most often employed are decontextualized prior to their entry into a data analytic program. That is, whether described as an event or a specific reaction, pain experience, revealed via interview, questionnaire, and even ongoing behavioral observation, is actually a summary of interactional events, with time, place, social demands, situational constraints, and subjective reactions all "pooled" (or as Fiske, 1978, says "blurred") for the purpose of reducing them to a level that can be manipulated statistically. Chapman (1976) makes a similar point in his discussion of pain "attributes":

> A unidimensional measure determined by multiple attributes is likely to yield inconsistent experimental outcomes when it is compared across laboratories, and such measurements are characterized by low precision. The question . . . has rarely been considered by algesiologists (p. 348).

Another often implicit assessment parameter is the scaling level achieved in pain measurement. At the preliminary stages, pain assessment is usually categorical (the nominal level), and appropriately so. But a good deal of the more advanced analyses of pain responding are predicated upon measurement at the ordinal and interval levels, and sometimes at the ratio level. Measurement theory cautions that correct (valid) interpretations of the effects of various manipulations (drugs, surgery, psychotherapy, etc.) requires that we know clearly the meaning of the numbers denoting our dependent variables. The concern is not whether we can perform various statistical operations on certain types of scaled numbers (since "the numbers do not know where they come from"; Gaito, 1980), but, for instance, whether we can logically conclude that drug X is twice as potent as drug Y because X reduced a pain rating level by 10 units as compared to 5 units for Y, or whether one form of therapy is significantly better than another because of statistically significant prepost changes in favor of one intervention on an empirically keyed "invalidism" scale. As was the case for the measurement context, there is no logical reason for measurement of pain to be confined to just one facet, or, in this case, to one metric scale.

The analytic focus of pain assessment here refers to the assessor's decision to examine either one or several focal pain dimensions and to index them either singly or with multiple measures. The decision about focal levels is usually a deliberate one, tied very directly to the purposes of the pain assessment. Questions of pain severity tend to direct the focus to the sensory/somatic dimension. Questions about the mental health implications of chronic pain tend to direct attention to levels C and D. Questions bearing on vocational rehabilitation usually suggest looking at E and F. In most clinical contexts, where time and money are prime considerations, single measures within levels are employed. On the other hand, in research, multiple indices are often used because a more complete picture is thereby attainable (and, of course, if one measure fails to achieve statistical significance, it is wise to have a backup or two).

The unit of measurement in psychology is typically a response, be it behavioral, cognitive, attitudinal, or physiological; covert or overt, directly observed, inferred, or recollected. On occasion, chains of responses, cues, and reinforcers are assessed in order to clarify the process of goal attainment or motivational disruption. But, in all cases, the unit must be capable of being coded and transformed into a number (for later analysis). For many of the focal pain dimensions, the units being applied appear to be face valid, technically sound, and reliable. However, in the more topographically complex domains involving behavioral transactions between individuals or cognitive transactions within persons, it would behoove the pain assessor to pay heed to his or her measurement units (cf. also Fiske, 1978).

Modes of pain analysis differ, as do the other parameters, as a function of one's assessment objectives. Description, prediction, and functional analysis all have important roles in clarifying certain aspects of the chronic pain experience. However, it is necessary that the assessor not confuse a descriptive with a predictive or functional requirement. For example, a clinician may wish to ascertain a patient's ability to cope with an upcoming and unavoidable stressful event, which is likely to exacerbate perceptions of pain and magnify familial discord. Or, a clinician may want to gauge a patient's potential for postsurgical noncompliance. The administration of an "ego strength" scale (or battery of coping skills measures) or a measure of trust in physicians, a health values survey, a locus of control index, and the like will, in most cases, not yield much beyond a partial description of the patient's current psychological orientation toward health and illness. On the other hand, asking patients to record, in real time, their daily experiences with life events of all sorts, their thoughts upon encountering them, their emotional reactions, the role of significant others, and the like, and then subjecting these data to a sequence analysis (Notarius, 1981) may yield information of predictive significance (see Turk and Kern's chapter, in this volume).

An issue implicit in the preceding discussion is the selection of an anchoring point for one's measurement operations. The final entries in column three of Table 13.1 (VIII and IX) are aspects that also bear upon this issue. Where, for example, do we establish the clinical-evaluative referent when any pain reaction is assessed? How much pain is too much? What are "tolerable" limits? On what basis are dimensional weights assigned to elements in a regression equation with pain behaviors, vocational outcome, or treatment response as criteria? The use of standardized instruments suggests a so-called norm-referenced model. On the other hand, in attempts to modify the response patterns, values, or cognitive appraisals of pain patients, do we really care how patients compare to a normative sample (often from a different social, racial, or economic background)? In many instances, we may need to rely upon the "standards" set by peers, parents, school officials, and other caretaker groups, as well as those of pain experts in clinical settings. Since the tasks of adapting to pain are ultimately person-centered, although variability in pain responding and in sensory arousal before, during, and after treatment is the cornerstone of process measurement, the use of self-referenced assessment should doubtless see wider application (cf. Chassan, 1979 for a discussion of statistical considerations in the "intensive," within-person design; and Chapter 1, in the present volume, for a discussion of idiographic assessment).

Finally, the temporal referent in pain assessment deserves to be made explicit. It has been argued that "our perceptions of health events, such as pain, are tied to our perception of time . . . and our perception of time influences the degree that we believe ourselves to be healthy" (Dossey, 1982, p. 46). This holds for pain assessors as well as for pain patients. Simply put: The assessor's time frame should match the referral question.

To summarize the rationale behind the preceding model, I again point to the fact that, despite the vast amount of literature on pain and its assessment, a great deal remains implicit. Certain methods are brought to bear on certain assessment questions because the investigator has presumably chosen the appropriate measurement model. Unfortunately, very few writings on pain assessment attempt explicitly to link questions to methods via intervening models of measurement. Usually, pain assessors discuss the questions of greatest interest to them and the methods they most often employ. Perhaps for this reason, much of the research seems to involve assessment by convention or convenience. The pain context approach to measurement was, therefore, proposed to provide at least one way of organizing an assessment enterprise. The investigator was urged to consider what level of pain he or she is interested in gauging, who or what is providing the data, and how the data are structured by often implicit decisions about basic parameters of research.

Having offered a tentative measurement model, my next task is to employ it as the link between assessment questions (what one may want to know about chronic pain) and available procedures. I shall, therefore, address questions and procedures next.

A SURVEY OF ASSESSMENT OBJECTIVES

Those who have sought to operationalize the concept of pain and to draw sharp distinctions between pain per se and its consequences (e.g., pain complaints, medication abuse, interpersonal distancing, and the like) have, I believe, inadvertently narrowed the legitimate targets of assessment via premature boundary making. Comprehensive assessment, in these systems, typically involves diagnosis (identification of the medical or neuro-physiologic nature of the pain problem), the gauging of pain severity, the search for possible intrapsychic mediators of treatment effectiveness, and the identification of controlling variables (cues and contingencies) in the patient's environment (cf. Bradley et al., 1981; Keefe et al., 1982). Although these objectives are extremely important and logistically complex, they tend to revolve around the short-term sensory and behavioral aspects of pain, reflecting a concern "more with the assessment of the phenomena rather than the phenomena" (Turk & Kerns, 1983). A larger set of basic questions is suggested by the pain context approach; and Table 13.2 provides a summary of these pain assessment purposes.

Some Thoughts on the Role of "Readiness" Factors

It has already been noted that a primary assessment question has to do with the medical nature of the pain problem and its status as either acute (less than 6 months duration and self-limiting) or chronic (longer than 6 months, progressive, episodic, and/or traumatic). An equally critical concern, in the early stages of assessment, is the degree of the patient's readiness for pain treatment(s). This may be a categorical judgment, not subject to strict quantification; but it is one whose significance should not be underestimated.

TABLE 13.2.　FUNDAMENTAL OBJECTIVES (PURPOSES) IN CHRONIC PAIN ASSESSMENT

1. Categorization of the pain problem (e.g., acute vs. chronic)
2. Determination of patient readiness for treatment
3. Prioritizing the foci of intervention
4. Evaluating the effectiveness of the patient's coping mechanisms
5. Evaluating the situational predictors and/or intrapsychic mediators of pain reactivity
6. Differentiating the situational from the sensory antecedents of pain
7. Quantifying the disruptiveness of the pain problem
8. Forecasting the impact of the pain problem on future adaptation
9. Suggesting possible negative "side effects" of successful treatment
10. Designing suitable intervention(s)
11. Evaluating the short- and long-term effectiveness of intervention(s) and proposing necessary programmatic alterations
12. Assessing the degree of posttreatment life-style modification
13. Evaluating the level(s) of patient self-management of pain
14. Assessing the nature and adjustive impact of the patient's implicit pain theory (schema, script, model)
15. Assessing consumer satisfaction with pain treatment programs
16. Regulating the patient's use of pain medications

Many of the celebrated pain treatment programs are selective of the patients admitted into their setting. Patients involved in litigation, or whose primary concern is the retention of their workmen's compensation, are often excluded. Similarly, patients who are not sufficiently committed to the inpatient program to attend for 3, 4, or more weeks or who do not agree to involve their families or to provide follow-up data are denied admission. Although most of the over 800 pain clinics in the United States cannot ethically or financially justify such exclusionary regulations (perhaps explaining their marginal success rates), the need to engage in some form of "readiness screening" remains a valid element in the pain assessment process.

Francis J. Keefe and his colleagues (Keefe & Brown, 1982; Keefe et al., 1982) propose an intriguing developmental (stage) model of adaptation to pain, which relates quite directly to the readiness question. According to these authors, three stages can be discerned in the life course of the chronic pain patient: the acute stage (0 to 2 months after the first appearance of symptoms), the prechronic (2 to 6 months), and the chronic (6 months to 2 years, plus) stages. During the acute stage, the pain patient is motivated to seek help—but is not inclined to see the assistance coming from psychological avenues. Rather, a medical cure is anticipated. During this period the patient is hopeful, although periodically anxious and/or depressed. When pain lingers, the patient enters stage 2 (prechronic), wherein withdrawal from doctors and pain medication(s) takes place. This is a period when a "self-help" perspective emerges, in reaction to the disappointment with medical help. Keefe and his colleagues suggest that active and passive coping efforts occur during this stage. Patients are motivated to get back to "business as usual" during this time; and, if they can, without worsening their pain by pushing themselves too much, they may not progress into stage 3. If, on the other hand, patients push too much, experiencing severe episodes of pain that result in increased use of medications, hospitalizations, leaves of absence from work, family sympathy, and the onslaught of attorneys seeking compensation, then the stage is set for a chronic pain stance. During the chronic period (during which time many hospital or clinic-based pain professionals come in contact with patients), passivity, depression, antimedical and psychological attitudes, drug dependence, hopelessness, reliance upon insurance monies or other forms of disability payment, and "doctor shopping" characterize the patient. Furthermore, many patients find their way to pain clinics at this stage because they have been referred by physicians who can no longer handle their demands (for surgery, new medications, more tests, etc.) or by relatives who likewise feel compelled to get these patients out of their hair. Many patients are motivated to resist help, either passively or actively, simply to spite the referral agents whose motives and attitudes are usually quite obvious. Neither assessment nor therapy can proceed under these conditions. The clinician's task is the overcoming of resistance, negative expectations about the treatment context, and anger at the referral sources. The reader is referred to Turk et al. (1983) who discuss, in detail, the initial phase of patient contact and methods for overcoming resistance and building a therapeutic partnership.

Patients may not be ready to undertake a thorough treatment/assessment program for reasons other than those just noted. Among the most often discussed (but least investigated) negative prognostic indicators is the patient's general psychological adjustment. Clinics and private practitioners routinely administer instruments such as the MMPI, 16PF, or the Rorschach to determine those premorbid personality characteristics of the patient that might interfere with obtaining a "true picture" of the pain problem. It has been noted that neurotic patients tend to portray their pain in a more exaggerated, intense, diffuse, and dramatic manner (Dubuisson & Melzack, 1976) or as more burdensome (McCreary & Turner, 1983). Similarly, patients with diagnosable lesions ("with an organic cause for pain") are said to possess fewer predisposing psychological precipitants than patients without detectable lesions, suggesting a tenuous causal link between psychological factors and real (organic) pain (Mersky & Boyd, 1978). In addition to their use of questionable statistics and dualistic thinking, those who have sought to divide pain patients along broad psychopathological lines have generally failed to offer diagnosis-specific treatment recommendations. Indeed, it has not been demonstrated via a controlled experiment that patients who show somatic preoccupation or hysterical tendencies are less amenable to comprehensive (multimodal) treatments than patients with normal MMPI profiles.

Thus, I shall argue that process or style variables may be more important as readiness mediators than are static trait conceptions. Although the use of the MMPI (or similar instruments) to downgrade the importance of some patients' pain complaints or to distinguish functional from organic etiology is not warranted, the use of psychological tests (including the MMPI) as well as behavioral analyses to predict differential response to specific types of treatment, to distinguish situational from sensory antecedents of pain responding, or to evaluate short- and long-term consequences of therapeutic intervention are certainly worthy objectives (see also Bradley, et al., 1981 for a detailed discussion of related assessment issues).

Although space limitations preclude a discussion here of all the assessment objectives listed in Table 13.2, one key topic is deserving of further consideration. Points 13 and 14 represent particularly important, yet relatively neglected, process dimensions in pain assessment—aspects of measurement and intervention closely tied to the inherently covert nature of nociception and to the goals of long-term maintenance and generalization of coping strategies for patients with chronic, benign pain. Both points focus upon the need to identify, train, and evaluate central mediation mechanisms presumed responsible for the self-management of pain. To help return to pain patients a measure of perceived and actual control over their lives, clinicians must be able to conceptualize the self-management process and assess its major facets. The self-management perspective may also offer a means of integrating assessment goals and pain context measurement levels.

A Potentially Integrative Level: The Self-Management of Pain Adaptation

The time has come to move beyond the recognition of pain as a complex phenomenon toward a model that links the sensory-neurophysiology of pain with the multifaceted psychology underlying the process. Despite the widespread and important work in which psychologists are currently engaged with respect to the alleviation of chronic pain, the field of pain treatment is being carried out in parallel universes—surgical and pharmacologic interventions directed at short-circuiting neural pathways on the one side, and cognitive-behavioral programs aimed at altering verbal-motor and interpersonal modes of pain/stress expression on the other. No matter how compatible the two approaches may appear (and there are differing opinions on this point), the study of pain adaptation currently proceeds as if adjustment occurs along distinct, but coextensive paths, one for the sensory-affective and nervous system and another for the person (cf. Zajonc, 1980, for a defense of this view).

Reasoned discussions of how psychological factors might influence or mediate the physiology of pain are not uncommon, however.

> Psychological methods of reducing stress and pain share a common feature—they decrease anxiety, depression, tension, and perceived lack of control. Anxiety, tension, depression, and perceived incontrollability appear to exacerbate a variety of somatic symptoms and the perception of pain. These psychological variables have been shown to modulate the production of stress hormones, neurotransmitters and autonomic arousal, including increased muscle tension (Turk, et al., 1983, p. 351).

Unfortunately, a major difficulty with current views of how psychology and neurophysiology interact is the relative neglect of the central coordination or transduction process involved. Although theorists discuss the notion that pain is "a function of the whole individual" (cf. Melzack & Wall, 1983), pain experience and the pain action system are nonetheless reactive ("triggered when the integrated firing level of the dorsal horn T-cells reaches or exceeds a critical level"; Melzack and Wall, 1983, p. 241). Despite the acknowledgment that central control can occur at the earliest levels of sensory transmission, psychological mechanisms are almost always seen as responses to the prevailing motivational state of the person that is the result of reticular arousal plus sensory transmission. Why does such a viewpoint suffer "difficulties"? First, whether described as an S-R or S-O-R model, it cannot account for flexibility or variability in pain expressivity in response to fluctuating situational demands or cues. The behavior of pain patients (particularly those with chronic pain) is not uniform. From this fact, we can extract the conclusion that the motivational-action patterns of chronic pain patients are not readily predictable habits triggered by singular motivational states (cf. Bindra, 1979). Second, the dominant view about the relationship between sensory and psychological (reactive) components of pain addresses mainly the products of the interaction, rather than the processes involved. As Turk and Kerns (1983) have noted,

> If pain is the interaction of sensory processing and psychological variables, then there is a need to study these interactions and not just each component separately. How does cognition influence sensory processing? How does affect relate to sensory stimuli? How do affect and cognition and sensory processing covary? (p. 60).

The process of *transduction* in pain remains elusive, as does the process of translating the nonmaterial (psychological) into the physiological (and vice versa) in other areas of psychobiologic study. As Weiner (1977) notes, it is a problem that has long puzzled philosophers and one that scientists have generally sought to conceptualize in linear and nonspecific terms.

An alternate model, proposed for its heuristic value (and not because it resolves the mind-body problem), is one that presumes that the pain experience (like other complex experiences) is internally regulated in a closed-loop system organized so that the flow of information within it serves the purpose of keeping momentary input within the range of a preset (but not invariant) standard. The foregoing are the essential assumptions of what is variously called control theory, cybernetics, information theory, general systems theory, feedback theory, adaptation-level theory, and so on (cf. Ashby, 1952; Carver & Scheier, 1981; Kanfer & Karoly, 1972; Karoly & Kanfer, 1982; Powers, 1973; and a brief discussion in Chapter 1 of the present volume).

Powers (1973), for example, would argue that between the first-order input signals, arising in the sensory nerve endings, and an individual's organized verbal-motor output there is a hierarchically organized system of reference levels, with each successive level specifying the reference value for the next lower one.

The most primitive level involves intensity readings. These provide the input for second-order perceptual signals, which create sensations. Sensations input into third-order configurations which, in turn, input into fourth-order transition control functions. Fourth-order control should be particularly important in defining pain experience, because it is at this level that a person will perceive differences in bodily sensations as a function of time. The fifth order of control consists of systems for detecting sequences of lower-order quantities. These first five levels represent the reality with which the higher nervous centers must deal. The next higher levels can be considered psychological or subjective, whereas the first five denoted analogs of physical reality (Powers, 1973). It is interesting that, within control theory, sensory aspects of pain can still be looked upon as "first causes" (as they are in most contemporary accounts, including the gate-control model) but not necessarily as basic—because the meaning has not yet been added. Sixth-order control involves control of relationships. Seventh-order control involves the execution of programs (planned relationships). Eighth-order systems detect and control principles (a set of programs aimed at keeping certain facts true). To control yourself in accordance with principles may require the kind of flexibility in behavioral program enactment that linear S-R principles cannot explain. Finally, consistent with the pain context model articulated earlier, the ninth-order level is called the systems level. It is necessary to postulate this ninth level because individuals must, on occasion, choose among alternative, sometimes incompatible, principles. At the ninth level there may be the person's sense of self (identity, self-schema, etc.) or the person's social image, allegiance to which may require alterations at the lower levels of behavior and perception.

The preceding summary of control theory (admittedly brief) should offer the pain assessor some valuable perspectives because it is process-oriented, content-specific, nonreductionistic (emphasizing neither sensations nor cognitions), nonlinear (assuming negative feedback loops within levels), and person-centered (rather than reactive). Built upon the sensory realities of pain, the control theory perspective suggests some propositions about higher-level processes. Consider the following, which I offer as part of a first approximation to a self-management model of chronic pain adaptation.

> Individuals with chronic pain may seek to instantiate either of three central (systems or principle level) motives: to control the display of pain, to cope with pain in order to achieve various instrumental objectives and maintain self-esteem, or to inhibit (suppress) pain perception. The motives vary with the patient's situational appraisal.
>
> The central motives influence not only how patients behave, but also how they interpret first-order and second-order signals (i.e., how they feel and think about themselves).
>
> Individuals with chronic pain may disregulate (fail to act in accordance with program, principle, or system level reference standards) if they are unable to access the relevant standards, if the standards are structurally vague or imprecise, or if their attention is focused upon irrelevant perceptual signals.
>
> A pain patient who is acting in a disorganized fashion (who seems emotional, hypersensitive, fearful, or unpredictable) is not necessarily "out of control" or showing an absence of regulation (system breakdown) but, rather, could be operating in the service of the pain display motive.

The introduction of the three central motives highlights the complexity of the pain management process. Regulatory goals, varying from not feeling (signal suppression), to managing the pain input in a productive way (pain modulation), to controlling the expression of one's subjective reaction to unpleasant sensory states (control of pain display) yield diverse products, all of which are legitimate targets of analysis from a control theory perspective. The hypothesized existence of these three regulatory goals leads also to the framing of another proposition:

The pain modulation system is disregulated by both too little and too much awareness of noxious sensory input.

The disruptive effectives of too much pain may not appear to be in need of comment. For as Chapman (1980) aptly notes,

A characteristic of pain and the other aversive senses (itch, vertigo, etc.) is that these modalities often demonstrate a unique ability to captivate attention. Aversive interoceptive sensory input intrudes like an alarm bell into normal waking consciousness, interrupting and disturbing the ongoing activity and mental preoccupation of the perceiver (p. 114).

However, many clinicians lose sight of the fact that pain can overwhelm information-processing and problem-solving activities. This author was reminded of this fact by a patient who, when advised to concentrate on relaxing as a means of reducing pain, pointed out that if he could concentrate well enough to relax, he would not have to relax!

On the other hand, the role of too little pain awareness as a disruptive factor in pain regulation might not be readily apparent. A statement of how the awareness mechanism might operate is, however, a straightforward derivative of a control theory model. Specifically, if a person's objective is to control how he or she appears to others or to modulate the pain sensation so as to be able to work productively, either goal can be said to serve as the internal reference (standard) against which input (perceptual signals) are compared. Any behaviors enacted in the environment are motivated primarily to ensure a match between the standard and the reference signal—that is, behavior serves the function of controlling perception (Powers, 1973). If pain is interfering with goals, it must be detected, for it is the input signal that makes possible the sequence of matching and subsequent corrective action. Control theory, therefore, posits a basic incompatibility between the signal suppression motive and the other two control motives. Patients who only want their pain to go away, who are motivated to blunt or dampen the pain signal, cannot effectively control their self-presentation or put into effect various coping mechanisms cued by the presence of pain (cf. also Schwartz, 1982). It has already been noted that a patient with an acute illness view may not be ready to undertake a program of pain/stress management training. The foregoing discussion offers yet another mechanism for explaining how a pain patient's "agenda" (not to feel the hurt, to be on drugs, to hope for the "magic pill") can be a roadblock to his or her learning how to cope effectively.

The fundamental message for the pain assessor that comes out of this discussion of self-management of pain is that the measurement of the content and structural properties of a patient's regulatory motives (standards, reference levels) and ninth-order value systems is an essential ingredient in a comprehensive assessment program.

A SURVEY OF ASSESSMENT STRATEGIES AND PROCEDURES

Although it is probably obvious that unidimensional, one-shot, atheoretical approaches to pain measurement provide little worthwhile data to the assessor, the exact formulas for "comprehensive," "integrated," "multimodal," "interactional," "multifaceted," or "broad-band" assessment programs have not been readily forthcoming. The material presented thus far in this chapter was meant to serve as an organizing framework: to give the reader a conceptual basis for making informed choices among the many measurement techniques currently available (and often presented without benefit of annotation.) From the material presented thus far, the reader should, by now, have developed a healthy skepticism about simplistic approaches to complex issues. Hopefully, statements like "Brain evoked potentials are the only objective means of assessing pain," or "Self-reports tell you nothing about a patient's real pain," would be greeted with suspicion.

What many introductions to pain assessment do is a bit like introducing two unknown candidates for political office by informing the reader (the voter) merely that one is a Democrat and the other a Republican. We might, in fact, know a lot about the two candidates simply because there are a host of characteristics associated with each of the two major political parties (just as there are important attributes associated with each of the major pain assessment modes). You would not, of course, know enough to vote for either candidate. And, indeed, the analogy holds for descriptions of pain assessment—that is, knowing all there is to know about the ins-and-outs of behavioral observation, physiologic recording, or cross-modality matching, for example, does not prepare you to select one or the other in an actual clinical situation. Keeping the pain context model in mind, however, should aid in the evaluation of the techniques to be described later (i.e., so you can "vote wisely" when the time comes). The presentation will also cross-reference the foregoing discussion, so that the reader can evoke a three-dimensional pain facet by pain assessment objective by measurement mode matrix as an overall guide to understanding.

A simple alphabetical listing of possible measurement modalities will

probably not suffice for our didactic purposes. Several alternative organizational schemes have, however, been suggested to introduce specific measurement strategies. We can, for example, distinguish between controlled,
laboratory-based methods and naturalistic (clinical) procedures. Unfortunately, this sort of distinction breaks down when we note that controlled
procedures can also be employed with clinical patients, depending upon our
specific objectives. On the other hand, the experimental and clinical study of
pain are quite distinct in terms of what they are able to reveal about the pain
experience (Beecher, 1959; Elton et al., 1983; Schneider & Karoly, 1983). We
can also link assessment procedures to specific types of pain, for example,
chronic disease pain, acute (injury) pain, pain induced by therapeutic procedures, and psychogenic pain (Beales, 1982). This method has clinical
validity, but does not, however, preserve the fine distinctions of the pain
context model. An interesting basis for distinguishing among assessment
methods is Chapman's (1976) division of quantitative approaches according
to the following scheme: measurement of events, measurement of objects,
and subjective estimations (cf. also Bradley et al., 1981).

Chapman's (1976) definition of events is quite broad, consisting of "behaviors" at the "level of the receptor, the nervous system, or the organism as
a whole" which tend to reflect responses to noxious stimulation (p. 349).
Pain tolerance, as indexed by how long a period of time a person will bear
the discomfort of heat, cold, or pressure, is listed by Chapman as an example
of a pain event. Other pain events include verbal pain complaints, the
number of medications requested (in a hospital context), and the degree of
mobility (cf. Bradley et al., 1981). Object measurement, on the other hand,
involves gauging abstract attributes (usually of people) in an indirect manner. Pain sensitivity (e.g., threshold) is an example of a pain object measure,
because it supposedly reflects the operation of a neurologic structure or
process characteristic of the human subject. Finally, the most abstract level
of assessment deals with subjective estimations—the assignment of numbers by individuals to their own internal pain states. A typical procedure
involves the use of graphic or visual analog scales (cf., Huskisson, 1974).

It is helpful to think of pain assessment as varying along a continuum of
concrete to abstract measurement operations. Numbers generated by event
and object assessment are believed by Chapman to be scalable at the interval
or ratio levels, whereas subjective pain estimates are typically nominal in
nature (and sometimes ordinal). The scaling level of pain data is represented
in Table 13.1 and has been previously discussed. Although in my opinion
scalability does not seem like the best vehicle for neatly differentiating
assessment methods, Chapman's notion of concreteness-abstractness is an
important one for the following reason: Almost any pain response, be it
overt, covert, physiological, linguistic, or paralinguistic, can be thought of
as an event, an object, or a subjective response, depending upon the assessor's purpose. For example, if your patient immerses his hand in a cold
water bath (the cold pressor test), you can observe the point at which he says

"It's cold," the point at which he removes his hand after trying to keep it submerged for as long as possible, and you can note the rating (on a 1 to 10 scale) he assigns to the aversiveness of the experience. Chapman's (1976) system would have us view the hand withdrawal as the most objective test, because it is an *event* in response to noxious stimulation. The point at which the patient indicates "It's cold" is seen as being at the next level of abstractness (it is an *object* measurement). And, the rating of aversiveness is considered the most abstract (a *subjective estimate*). But, is the abstract quality of a measure truly inherent in the measure itself, or does it attach to the use to which the measure is put? If one wanted to do a functional analysis of a patient's pain responding, could not the subjective estimate (if reliable) serve as the dependent measure? Similarly, the event measure (tolerance time) could be correlated with other, more indirect indices, to assist in describing the abstract attributes of the patient. Descriptive, predictive, or functional analytic uses of data, then, are the keys to deciphering the objectivity-subjectivity of contemporary pain assessment methodologies.

The organizational scheme most in keeping with the pain context approach is ultimately the pain context approach! Thus, if we cross the six focal pain dimensions with the seven sources of pain data (see Table 13.1), a list of 42 assessment methods results—a somewhat unwieldly organizing procedure. However, many of the cells are empty because they represent illogical combinations (e.g., biochemical assays of behavior patterns) or currently nonexistent technologies (bioelectronic monitoring of pain-related information processing). Keeping in mind that medical screening is always necessary along with whatever disorder-specific measurements seem warranted, and that the assessment questions ultimately dictate which methods are most cost effective, the following 10 pain assessment strategies seem to efficiently summarize the complexity of a multifaceted, relativistic approach.

A. Interview procedures
B. Standardized psychometric instruments
C. Pain-specific self-evaluations, estimates, and recordings
D. Event-specific self- and other evaluations, estimates, and recordings
E. Psychophysical pain scaling: controlled nociceptive stimulation
F. Psychophysical pain scaling: magnitude estimation
G. Direct external observation methods
H. Biophysical and biochemical event recording (laboratory-based and telemetric)
I. Cognitive-behavioral-physiologic simulations and skills assessments
J. Unobtrusive measures of pain products/consequences

These methods can, and should be, employed in various combinations, depending upon the assessment purposes and relevant contextual constraints (e.g., time, facilities, patient cooperation).

Interview Methods in Pain Assessment

The clinical interview, perhaps the most common method for gathering information, involves the pain patient along with key informants (family, friends, coworkers) as data sources, aided and facilitated by the interviewer-clinician. Although traditional psychodiagnostic interviewing is often guided by a relatively explicit classificatory system (e.g., the DSM-III or the research diagnostic criteria), no such frameworks exist in the area of pain assessment. However, over the years, skilled practitioners have evolved clinically sound and conceptually grounded methods for screening pain patients, consultation with medical referral sources, medical history taking, assessment of premorbid functioning (before the injury or medical problem antedating the current pain, if these are present), and the like. Excellent discussions of initial diagnostic interview procedures with pain patients can be found in Turk et al. (1983, Chapter 9 and Appendices C and D) and Johnson (1977).

Within the current pain context framework, it is suggested that the interview be employed to gather background and referral information necessary to place all the other pain data in perspective. The interview is also particularly suited for the collection of life-style impact information, motivational data, and (as a minilaboratory) indices of information processing.

First, unlike the experimenter, the clinician is prepared to assess the patient's reasons for being in a hospital or clinic context and the "time-line" of the pain problem. The "story" told a few weeks after an on-the-job injury when some form of financial compensation is in the balance is not likely to resemble the narrative provided by the same patient seen in a pain clinic setting, 6 years and six operations after the initial trauma (see Keefe et al., 1982).

Because of the variations in patients' experience of pain, in their willingness and ability to report accurately their subjective states to a helping professional, and in their expectations of the possible consequences of pain reporting, the assessor should try to work within at least a semistructured data collection framework. The interview can be broken down into focused phases such as: (1) assessment of premorbid adjustment; (2) an elicitation of the patient's understanding of the pain problem (its causes and meaning); (3) an assessment of the patient's general level of medical sophistication and knowledge; (4) a determination of the dimensional qualities of the perceived pain; (5) an assessment of the pain chronology (including precipitating factors, exacerbating factors, variations in pain experience as a function of time, place, and interpersonal events); (6) a description of behavioral, cognitive, and emotional reactions to a pain episode; and (7) a discussion of the patient's typical modes of coping with pain (during which it is helpful to offer a list of "common" reactions/coping responses to pain in order to forestall reluctant reporting of reaction patterns perceived by the patient to be "silly," "undignified," "undesirable," or "unman(woman)ly"). The assessor should seek to contextualize further the coping analysis by including questions about mediating factors such as: Does this (coping method) work if you are _____ (tired, medicated, angry, distracted, anxious, etc.)? In addition, the assessor should seek to determine the degree to which the pain and/or the pain coping efforts interfere with the "normal" conduct of the patient's life.

The interview is a particularly rich source of information about the lifestyle impacts and interpersonal factors in pain. Both the pain patient and significant others in his or her home and work environments can provide data about prepain and postpain patterns of family interaction, marital satisfaction, vocational performance, recreational activities, exercise, and the like (cf. Armentrout et al., 1982). The doctor-patient relationship should not be forgotten in the quest for data (Jacox, 1977). Indeed, Sternbach (1974b) has written about the specific strategies used by pain patients to manipulate their physicians, many of which can be discerned even in the early diagnostic sessions.

A motivational analysis of the pain patient would center on the extent to which control over the "pain experience" is perceived as internal or external and the implications of such perceptions (attributions). Many chronic pain patients reject (at least outwardly) any suggestion of a "psychological component" to their illness, thus limiting their willingness to work to manage their thoughts, feelings, or behaviors. The desire for the "magic pill" or the expectation of the "surgical breakthrough" can certainly retard the process of therapeutic change and patients' mastery over their disorders (Karoly, 1980). Although the assessment of motives is often assigned to paper-and-pencil measures, the pain assessor should use the interview as a first line of data acquisition about the patient's ongoing pattern of expectancies, attributions, plans, needs, beliefs, and commitments.

Standardized (Norm-referenced) Psychometric Tests

The assumption that individuals possess relatively enduring styles of pain perception/reaction and that a set of predictable correlates (emotional responses, coping or defense mechanisms, causal attributions, etc.) tends to accompany chronic pain provide the major justification for the use of psychological tests in clinical pain assessment (cf. Elton et al., 1983; Keefe, 1982; Viernstein, 1982; Weisenberg, 1977). Psychological attributes are sought that, when accurately assessed, can be used to aid in diagnosis and in the prediction of treatment outcome. Assessment of the psychological dimensions of pain also has basic research as a rationale.

By far the most often used psychodiagnostic instrument in pain studies has been the MMPI. Because so-called "neuropsychiatric complications" can result from various painful medical disorders, such as severe body burns or back injuries (cf. Andreasen, 1974; McCreary et al., 1977), and because pain may be associated with psychiatric conditions (Pilowsky, 1978), there seems to be good justification for the use of the MMPI in pain assessment. Yet, a number of recent reviews of the MMPI literature suggest that the utility of the instrument cannot be assumed. Inconsistent findings and methodological problems have been noted (Bradley, et al., 1981; Keefe, 1982; Turk et al., 1983; Viernstein, 1982). The MMPI, when applied to the task of distinguishing organic from functional (psychogenic) pain or to the prediction of treatment outcome with heterogeneous patient samples, does not perform well. The use of short-form versions of the MMPI is also questionable (Bradley et al., 1981). However, attempts to avoid the patient homogeneity assumption (i.e., that all pain patients with the classic "conversion V profile" are the same) and the use of multivariate test procedures have yielded promising findings. Bradley et al. (1978) and Armentrout et al. (1982) employed cluster analytic methods (see Chapter 10, in this volume) and discriminant analysis to identify empirically several subgroups of pain patients based upon MMPI scores. Three subpopulations, a basically normal (no T-score elevations above 70), a hypochondriasis, and a high pathology group, were identified and shown to differ in terms of the life-style impact of their pain problem.

The Pain Apperception Test (PAT) of Petrovich (1957) and Petrie's (1967) kinesthetic approximation (block) task are two other assessment procedures that have been widely used (although not as systematically as has the MMPI) in the clinical pain literature. Petrie's method of identifying augmenters and reducers has not been experimentally validated (Elton et al., 1983). The PAT has been found to correlate with some MMPI subscales; but its concurrent validity remains suspect (Ziesat & Gentry, 1978). The developers of a new pain apperception test, the Melbourne Pain Apperception Film (MPAF), although reporting some correlations between MPAF scores and measures of pain threshold and tolerance, nonetheless conclude that as far as apperception tests are concerned "there is no strong evidence to support their use as clinical measures of pain reactivity" (Elton et al., 1983, p. 30).

Perhaps the most promising of the newer psychometric devices is the Millon Behavioral Health Inventory (Millon et al., 1979), developed as the "first general-purpose instrument of a psychological nature designed for use in a wide range of medical settings" (Millon et al., 1979, p. 537). The MBHI contains, in addition to its scales assessing personality styles and attitudes relevant to illness, a specific prognostic index tapping pain treatment responsivity. Interested readers should consult Green's chapter in the present volume and a recent version of the MBHI test manual. It should be noted here that the validation of this instrument is only in its nascent stages.

Pain-Specific Self-Evaluations, Estimates, and Recordings

Quantitative and qualitative clinical assessments of individual pain patterns for use in descriptive analyses, treatment planning, and treatment outcome evaluation have generally relied upon self-evaluative responses, self-ratings (or estimates), and self-monitoring records. Considerable time and effort have been devoted to the development of procedures whereby a patient's subjective pain state can be reliably translated into a single numerical score (usually reflecting the intensity of felt pain) that can then be used to assess the efficacy of drug treatment, surgical intervention, physiotherapy, psychological therapy, or their combination. Such a pursuit is consistent with a linear and univariate medical world view—but may do a serious disservice to the patient, whose experiences associated with pain are doubtless more complex and multicausal.

The use of numerical intensity ratings, anchored by verbal descriptors, is perhaps the oldest "scientific" pain measurement method (Huskisson, 1974; Noordenbos, 1959). Assigning the numbers 1 through 4 to pain levels indicative of "mild," "moderate," "severe," and "agonizing" pain does not constitute interval scale measurement, but, rather, is a "disguised nominal scale" approach. The sensitivity of numerical scales is also a serious drawback, for

> Between the limits of "agonizing pain" and "no pain" there are only three points, and it is difficult to think of any other intermediate description. A patient with slight pain has only one possible grade of improvement— complete relief, which is seldom achieved by simple analgesics in chronic pain (Huskisson, 1974, p. 1128).

A number of attempts have been made, over the years, to improve the sensitivity of simple self-rating scales (be they numerical or verbal). Instead of multiple measures of perceived intensity, some investigators have assessed pain relief (leaving the patient to do the mental arithmetic necessary to distinguish pretreatment from posttreatment pain). Or, rather than calculating raw pain scores, some researchers examine changes in pain ratings over time, peak effects, or the proportion of time over which relief is reported (or the proportion of patients reporting relief). None of these methods is totally satisfactory (cf. Lutterbeck & Triay, 1972).

The so-called visual analog scale was also proposed as an alternative to the simple numeric rating. This procedure involves an unmarked 10-cm line anchored only at the ends ("no pain" to "pain as bad as it could be"), allowing patients numerous points to express their subjective perceptions. Since the distribution of scores on the visual analog scale is often non-normal, the use of arcsin transformations is recommended (Huskisson, 1974). The procedure has the advantage of simplicity (allowing for its use with children as young as 5) and a consistently high correlation with verbal scales (Bradley et al., 1981). Its unidimensionality and the need to assume equality of intervals represent its enduring disadvantages (Keefe, 1982).

It is important to remember that pain does not have to be assessed unilaterally or simplistically. Even intensity ratings can be made in the context of a broad-based assessment plan. Such a plan would involve the acceptance of a self-referenced (idiographic) perspective on measurement and of a multimodal (converging operations) strategy.

Turk et al. (1983), for example, ask their pain patients to self-monitor the intensity of their discomfort between therapy sessions, following a format suggested by Budzynski et al. (1973). The pain intensity cards list the hours of the day and a 6-point scale of pain for each (with each point "explained" by a verbal descriptor). Problems with the use of the cards are anticipated and discussed in detail. Even hints for remembering to carry the cards are provided. The researcher-clinicians use the data provided by the intensity cards to conduct functional analyses of their patients' pain problems and to monitor the course of treatment.

Reading and Newton (1978) developed a card sort procedure for assessing different qualities of pain experience, modeled after M. B. Shapiro's "personal questionnaire" method of idiographic analysis (cf. Neufeld, 1977, Chapter 3). After identifying commonly used pain adjectives and determining "the amount of pain each word suggested on 5-point scales," the authors grouped the adjectives into four categories—sensory, affective, temporal, and evaluative—and pain levels within categories. The card sort procedure itself involves about 5 minutes of time, during which pain patients are required to select one word from a triad of pain descriptors varying in intensity. The test contains 10 triads (or a total of 30 cards), 4 sensory, 2 affective, 1 temporal, and 3 evaluative. Reading and Newton (1978) present data on the test's reliability and validity and discuss its clinical advantages (e.g., ease of administration, built-in reliability check, minimal response bias potential, flexibility of purpose).

A more well-known and widely used verbal descriptor approach (which is likewise multidimensional in nature) is Melzack's (1975) McGill Pain Questionnaire (MPQ). Like a number of other critics of pain assessment methods, Melzack wanted to transcend unscalable numbers and unidimensional reliance upon intensity by elevating the "language of pain" to a quantifiable level. Malzack and Torgerson (1971) began their empirical specification of pain qualities by asking subjects to classify 102 words taken from the clinical literature on pain. The words were subdivided into 3 major classes—sensory, affective, and evaluative—and 16 subclasses. Then groups of physicians, students, and pain patients assigned intensity values to the words. As Melzack (1975) states,

> Because of the high degree of agreement on the intensity relationships among pain descriptions by subjects who have different cultural, socio-economic, and educational backgrounds, a pain questionnaire was developed as an experimental tool . . . (p. 279).

After adding four descriptor classes to the original 16 (because "many patients found certain key words to be absent"), Melzack (1975) administered his MPQ to 297 patients with various painful medical disorders (including arthritis, cancer, and menstrual-related, dental-related, postsurgical, and obstetric pain). Four types of data were derived from the MPQ: a pain rating index based upon a sum of scale values across categories [the PRI(S)]; a pain rating index based upon a ranking of scale values [the PRI(R)]; the number of words chosen (NWC), and the number-word combination chosen as the indicator of overall pain intensity (the PPI).

Melzack (1975) reported high correlations between the PRI(S) and the PRI(R) and suggested using the rank method due to its ease of computation. The NWC also correlated strongly with the PRI (correlations in the .80s or .90s). On the other hand, the correlations between the PPI and the NWC and PRI are in the .30s and .40s, suggesting that "a large part of the variance of the PPI may be determined by factors other than those indicated by the descriptors" (p. 285). Melzack also investigated patient consistency in subclass selection by analyzing data from 10 patients who completed the MPQ several times in a 3- to 7-day period. The consistency of descriptor subclass selection varied between 50 to 100 percent, with a mean of 70.3 percent.

A number of investigations have been published since the introduction of the MPQ. In their recent review, Bradley et al. (1981) noted that, although the reliability and validity of the instrument are in the acceptable range, there have been doubts raised about (1) the ability of the MPQ to discriminate among organic versus functional groups, (2) the factor structure of the MPQ, and (3) the cross-cultural applicability of the instrument. Of these, only the latter appears to be a serious concern. In this regard, it can be noted that adaptations of the MPQ for various cultural groups have been reported (e.g., Ketovuori & Pontinen's Finnish version, 1981). Keefe's (1982) analysis of the MPQ is somewhat less enthusiastic. His conclusion, that the use of category scaling introduces bias by "imposing response constraints," touches upon the key issues of calibration and sensitivity of subjective scaling—toward whose resolution various psychophysical procedures (to be discussed) have been developed.

Another basic issue in the domain of pain-specific self-ratings has to do with their comprehensiveness. The MPQ, card sort, visual analog scale, and the like all tend to focus upon the sensory and emotional qualities of pain. Although they do look beyond "intensity" as a basic dimension, they nonetheless stay very close to feeling states in pain. Should we not also be examining pain-produced judgment processes, meaning states, and motive changes? Based upon the discussion in the first part of this chapter, we might be inclined to ask our pain patients to tell us not only where, when, and how much they hurt, but also whether they expect their rated pain to interfere with the day's goals or assigned tasks, whether they have altered or will alter their performance standards in response to their pain, and to assign causal responsibility for the felt pain. Such pain-specific ratings may well inform us about the unique role that pain plays in the lives of our patients.

Perhaps the most reasonable approach to comprehensiveness is the multifaceted pain diary or pain chart, wherein the sort of information just noted can be collected. Simple pain records that are small in size and unobtrusive have the very desirable feature of becoming part of the patient's daily routine—that is, these forms will be used consistently. Records that require the patient to rate pain (on a numerical, verbal descriptor, or visual analog scale), plus a few additional setting factors (e.g., time of day, location, presence or absence of significant others, medication taken, etc.), may eventually lose whatever reactive effects they engender, thus yielding reasonably accurate perceptual accounts of daily pain experience. Within the present classificatory system, however, such recordings constitute mixed pain-specific and event-specific measurement (the latter to be discussed in greater detail subsequently). At present, I would like to make a plea for more informative pain-specific self-evaluations. If pain ratings are made on a daily basis for a period of weeks or months (a very realistic requirement of clinic patients; less so of "research subjects"), then patients can alternate using simple formats and more complex ones. The latter might involve the adaptation of common "cognitive assessments" such as pain thought listing, expectancies of pain relief, current concerns, and the like (cf. Merluzzi et al., 1981).

The comparative clinical value and cost effectiveness of the several self-rating methods discussed in this section are not easy to calculate based upon the available data. Each of the procedures has obvious advantages and disadvantages. If a quick, reproducible index of pain intensity is needed, the visual analog scale may be most appropriate. If data on the evaluative and affective aspects of pain are desired, in addition to that touching upon sensory dimensions, then some variant of verbal descriptor analysis (the MPQ or card sort) may be employed. Psychological meaning may be assessed by more intensive analyses of pain diaries. These methods may be employed in combination with one another (and with other techniques discussed in this section). Woodforde and Mersky (1972), for example, compared the data generated by an analog scale, clinical self-labeling, laboratory-induced (pressure) pain, and a cross-modality matching procedure (the latter being a thymometric method wherein pain intensity is matched to sounds produced by an audiometer; cf. Peck, 1967). The correlation between the clinical description and the 10-cm analog scale was quite high (.83), whereas the induced pain (pressure algometer) and verbal descriptor data were negatively correlated ($-.27$). Ohnhaus and Adler (1975) compared the verbal rating and visual analog methods in a study on the effects of analgesics on pain. The two measures were highly related ($r = .81$), although the authors interpreted the verbal scale data as less sensitive. Similarly, Reading (1980), comparing the visual analog, numerical scale, and verbal descriptor methods in the assessment of childbirth-related (episiotomy) pain, found that the degree of the intermethod relationship varied over two testing occasions (becoming higher on the second day, when within-method variability was lower). Finally, Kremer et al., (1981), examining visual analog, verbal (adjectival), and numerical scale methods, found intercorrelations of between .59 and .86, a preference for the verbal scales (indeed, 11 percent of the chronic pain group could not complete a visual scale), and no support for the view that pain reports are differentially influenced by patient sex, psychological variables, or etiology of the pain problem (malignant versus nonmalignant). However, depressed/anxious patients tended to report higher pain intensities overall as compared to nondepressed/nonanxious subjects.

Given the small numbers of subjects in the various comparative studies, and the setting and population differences, firm conclusions cannot be drawn. However, it would appear that some cross-method convergence does occur. Clinicians need not include all the pain-specific self-rating methods in their patient studies but should select one on the basis of the assessment purpose and patient preference. Diary data have rarely been compared to the simpler procedures. If comprehensiveness can be obtained without sacrificing reliability and patient compliance, it would be preferable to employ the more broad-based (meaning centered) daily pain diary approach.

Event-specific Self- and Other Evaluations, Estimates, and Recordings

This brief section is included to remind the assessor that aspects of the pain experience other than pain per se may occupy important roles in the overall evaluation of the patient. Consider, for example, psychosocial variables such as family patterning, cultural heritage, social class, quality and availability of social supports, and the sorts of environmental dimensions discussed by Moos and Winett in the present volume.

Intrapsychic perceptions, evaluations, estimates, and monitoring operations that touch upon antecedents, correlates, or consequences of chronic pain can provide data to the assessor bearing upon many of the important questions outlined in Table 13.2. If these dimensions are stable and cross-situationally consistent, it would appear appropriate, using Chapman's (1976) terminology, to refer to them as *object-specific*. For example, if low self-esteem were found to be a result of a persistent pain condition, then the self-esteem measure would be object-specific. However, except for predictive and diagnostic purposes, the assumption of stable attributes is not necessary from a conceptual standpoint. Indeed, both pain and its associated experiential elements might best be viewed as events, thus allowing for the possibility of change and necessitating continued assessment.

For example, in the interest of treatment evaluation, relapse prevention, medication regulation, or life-style impact measurement, the assessor may wish to track the relationship between pain and *general mood*. Anxiety, hostility, frustration, and depression are the most often discussed mood/motivational accompaniments of chronic pain (Sternbach, 1974a). Few studies have, however, sought to examine the relationship between mood and pain perception over prolonged periods. Shacham, et al. (1983) collected mood and pain data from 95 cancer patients over an 18-week period. The Profile of Mood States (POMs) was completed and four pain ratings— intensity, least pain, worst pain, degree of interference with daily activities— using a 100-mm visual analog scale, were taken at five interviews during the 18-week investigation. The researchers found that, in general, pain and negative mood states were positively correlated, but the correlations were of relatively small magnitude. These patterns were assessed by both *within-subject* and *interindividual* (cross-sectional) *methods*. In cancer, high levels of pain are accompanied by only mild emotional distress (as reported by patients themselves). Of course, the possibility that patients may deny their degree of upset or underreport certain behavioral patterns suggests that, in addition to event-specific *self*-ratings, event-specific *observer* (informant) *ratings* of a patient's activities, apparent mood states, quality of social relationships, and so on should be obtained. Turk et al. (1983) have described a "significant other pain diary" approach as well as issues in training informants to collect pain and event-specific data.

Psychophysical Pain Scaling: Controlled Nociceptive Stimulation

Although the patient's pain intensity estimate remains the cornerstone of clinical assessment (for it is the amount of hurt that usually brings the patient to the doctor and the reduction of that hurt, via medication, surgery, hypnosis, or other interventions, that constitutes the treatment goal), there has been much energy expended over the 30 years in the development of *ways to enhance the reliability of the pain report*. Even numerical reports of subjective pain experience have been assumed to be "loaded with psychiatric and cultural overlay" (Sternbach et al., 1974). But, if pain is viewed as a kind of sensory input and the individual is assumed to be capable of judging the presence or absence of a sensory signal and/or its relative value, then it should be possible to employ the methods of *psychophysics* to assist in the assessment of pain perception. Psychophysics asks the fundamental question, "When the stimulus increases, precisely how does the sensation grow?" (Stevens, 1972). This question would appear to be relevant to the problem of pain perception.

Apart from the application of psychophysical methods to pain intensity measurement, assessors have generally relied upon categorical forms of scaling. Verbal description of one's experience, whether it be via questionnaire, card sort, or the marking of a point on a line between two extreme statements, does not provide for direct estimates of the relationship between the induction of the noxious stimulation and the subjective or felt magnitude of pain. A turning point in the *quantitative* approach to pain assessment came when Hardy et al. (1952) and their associates applied radiant heat stimulation to human subjects and formulated rules for relating stimulus magnitude to subjective report (Wolff, 1980). The science of experimental pain measurement—algesimetry—came under attack by Henry Beecher (1959), who felt that the kind of pain "induced" in the laboratory bore no relationship to "clinical pain." The history of the induced versus clinical pain debate need not concern us, here. Suffice it to say that, due to the sophistication of modern signal detection theory and magnitude estimation methods, a sharp distinction between laboratory-based and clinical methods is now infrequently made—even to the point that pain is induced experimentally in clinical pain patients in order to quantify their patterns of interoceptive judgment.

It is sometimes said that, in science, knowledge is knowledge of relationships. The key to appreciating the psychophysical scaling approach to pain is in understanding that: (1) the relationship between stimulus input and perceived magnitude is the assessment target and (2) the experimenter controls the quantitative variation in the stimulus.

> In its most fundamental sense, the subjective judgment is intended to provide a basis for assessing a subject's ability to perceive a quantifiable external stimulus or to tell the difference between stimuli. In practice, the subject judges stimuli delivered at variable levels, and the accuracy of his performance, scored from verbal reports, is used as a measure of sensory ability (Chapman, 1980, p. 125).

According to S. S. Stevens (1972), judgments along "prothetic continua" (those having to do with intensity, degree, or amount) can be said to relate to actual stimulation in accordance with a *power law*, written as:

$$\Psi = KS^n$$

where Ψ is the perceived (subjective) magnitude, K is a constant, and S is a physical stimulus raised to some power n. Stevens and his colleagues performed experiments with a variety of judgment continua—loudness, brightness, roughness, hardness, and the like—and derived estimates of the exponent n. The value of n for *thermal pain* was, for example, assessed by Stevens to be 1.0, meaning that a doubling of the amount of heat applied to the skin would result in a doubling of the perceived painfulness of the stimulus. However, other modes of induction (cold, pressure, etc.) yield different exponents.

It should be apparent that the nature of the nociceptive stimulus and the method ot its induction are important considerations, along with the nature of the judgment, in any psychophysical study of pain. Over the years, a number of "rules" for controlled pain induction studies have been discussed. These include the need to employ several types of nociceptive stimuli (e.g., heat, cold, pressure, electrical stimulation, chemical stimulation, etc.), the need to apply the stimuli to different body locations and tissue depths, the need to employ safe levels of stimulation, the need to employ methods that are readily replicated, and the need to choose laboratory inductions of pain that mirror the clinical patterns (Elton et al., 1983; Wolff, 1980; Wolff, et al., 1976).

The nature of the pain response parameter(s) is also important. Because much of the early work on pain quantification was intensity-centered, it was predicated upon the existence and measurability of a point above which afferent stimulation produces a "sensation of pain" and below which no such sensation is noted. This point was called the *pain threshold*. In his classic text, *The Human Senses*, Geldard (1973) notes that Hardy's radiant heat method for the assessment of pain thresholds "revealed remarkably little variation from person to person, or from day to day in the same person" (pp. 320–321). However, contemporary investigators have tended to criticize the threshold measure because (1) it has not always been shown to be invariant within subjects; (2) clear-cut dose-response relationships between powerful analgesics and threshold indices have not been found; (3) it is based upon the assumption that pain is a pure sensation, readily mapped onto a singular stimulus continuum; and (4) it bears little relevance to the dynamics of clinical pain (Chapman, 1974; Grossberg & Grant, 1978; Wolff, 1980).

Another historically important psychophysical unit is the just noticeable difference (or JND). In pain assessment, this was articulated as the Dol scale (Hardy et al., 1952). Although its originators claimed that individuals could make a 21-step discrimination, from no pain to excruciating pain, others have not found the approach useful (Wolff, 1980).

According to Wolff, there are three pain parameters that yield useful information (in addition to the two parameters generated by signal detection analyses, to be discussed subsequently). The three are: pain tolerance, the drug request point, and the pain sensitivity range (the arithmetic difference between the pain threshold and the pain tolerance point). In terms of stability, or "resistance to modulation by external or internal conditions or stimulation," the pain sensitivity range is considered best. Wolff (1980), therefore, recommends the threshold, drug request point, and pain tolerance indices for studies of the effects of analgesics, cultural factors, or various treatments, whereas the pain sensitivity range "is a good predictor of a given individual's ability to endure pain" (p. 181).

Despite Wolff's (1980) endorsement, many investigators feel that the classical psychophysical approach to pain yields inconsistent results (particularly in analgesic assays) because such measures as threshold and tolerance are influenced by social, emotional, attitudinal, and attentional factors in addition to the sensory. In the context of debates over the utility of familiar psychophysical methods, an approach known as signal detection theory (or sensory decision theory; both abbreviated as SDT) has appeared on the scene.

The importance of SDT methods lies in their acceptance of the psychological as well as sensory nature of pain. The model assumes that individuals can reliably detect high levels of stimulation (mechanical, thermal, electrical, or chemical), as well as the absence of any stimulation. However, when attempting to judge the presence or absence of a weak stimulus (near the so-called threshold level), the sensate human confronts a statistical decision. Errors in perceptual judgment are, in part, related to the fact that there is a natural and continual background of "internal noise" derived from spontaneous nervous system activity, within which any given external stimulus will be embedded. The individual, therefore, has to decide or distinguish between effects due solely to a background noise component (conceptualized as a normally distributed probability density function) and the effects due to a signal plus noise function (also presumed to be a Gaussian distribution). Note that there is no signal alone (without noise) because sensitivity to stimulation is always limited by the background of neural firing. The noise and the signal-plus-noise curves are said to overlap when a *weak stimulus* is involved. It is also assumed that there may be some cost or benefit (or other external situational constraint) operating to influence the judge's willingness to report a detection of a signal.

Given this hypothetical model of sensation and perception, two distinct measures are derivable: (1) one reflecting the sensitivity or ability of the individual to separate accurately noise from signal-plus-noise (in this case, the signal is pain) and (2) a measure reflecting a response criterion for acknowledging the existence of a signal. The first measure, called d' (dee prime), is defined as the separation between the means of the noise distribution and the signal-plus-noise distribution (both distributions assumed to have equal variances), with higher numbers suggesting greater sensory discriminatory ability. The second measure, called beta (sometimes labeled L_x or C_x), is a response bias measure and can be conceptualized as a cutoff point based on a subjectively held decision rule (or likelihood ratio) relating the judged probability of a signal being present (located in the signal-plus-noise distribution) to the judged probability of no signal (located in the noise distribution). Where the cutoff value is set "depends upon the willingness of the observer to tolerate errors in order to maximize correct responses" (Dember & Warm, 1979, p. 68). Signal detection theory, thus, offers the possibility that pain assessors can apportion their patients' pain reports into a sensory component and a strategic component.

Since W. Crawford Clark's (1969) first use of SDT methods to show that a placebo analgesic affects response bias rather than pain sensitivity, a large number of studies have been published applying the methodology to pain perception. The typical experiment involves presenting subjects with a large number of trials in which a noxious stimulus (heat, cold, electric shock, etc.) is presented at low, moderate, and high intensities and during which no stimulus is presented (blank trials). A subject, on any given trial, can either correctly detect a signal—a hit—report a signal when none was present—a false alarm—report no signal when one was present—a miss—or report no signal when, in fact, no signal was present—a correct rejection. If, on alternate days, subjects are given an analgesic drug (or a placebo, or are hypnotized and told not to feel pain, or are "treated" in some other way), then it should be possible to evaluate the effects of the experimental treatment on both pain sensitivity and response bias. It is also common to employ the SDT method with distinct groups of subjects (normal, acute pain, or chronic pain) and to compare their patterns of reactivity. Specifically, when hit rate and false alarm rates are examined (misses and correct rejections provide redundant information with these) in concert with different types of instructions to subjects (designed to impact on where they set their criterion level, either conservatively or leniently), then a plot, called a *receiver operating characteristic* (ROC) curve, can provide the necessary data on sensory sensitivity and response bias (see Chapman, 1980; Clark, 1969; Dember & Warm, 1979; and Rollman, 1976 for further details on the use of SDT methods in pain research).

Clearly, the application of signal detection methods to pain measurement was motivated by a desire to quantify precisely the individual's characteristic mode of perceiving pain signals and to separate the effects of emotional and cognitive-evaluative biases from pure sensory effects. Early enthusiasm for SDT approaches has now apparently been replaced with caution and concern for the ecological validity of these laboratory-based pain assessments. Among the questions or criticisms raised about SDT research in pain are the following: (1) SDT procedures applied to pain perception deviate from the standard practice in a number of ways, such as the frequent unequal noise and signal-plus-noise distribution variances; the absence of true blank trials (no pain stimuli); the fact that, rather than examining the presence or absence of a weak stimulus, pain studies involve various levels of suprathreshold stimulation; the fact that attentional and motivational factors can influence the estimate of d'; (2) SDT procedures are as dependent as other methods upon the subject's verbal responses; and (3) the fact that the experimenter can control the levels and presentation rates of various forms of noxious stimulation does not guarantee that the perceptual data so derived will mirror the person's characteristic manner of perceiving and reacting to internally generated pain in the extralaboratory environment. Both the pain context model and a large body of data on symptom perception (cf. Pennebaker, 1982) suggest that situational, affective, and cognitive factors strongly influence the perception of bodily signals. Responses to controlled nociceptive stimulation may be extremely informative about general processes, when "all else is equal." However, as Chapman (1980) noted,

> Like the classical approaches, SDT suffers from the weakness of being an oversimplification of the complex perceptual experience. . . . As in many other areas of psychophysical research, the results obtained are meaningful only in the context of the experimental design employed (pp. 130–131).

Psychophysical Pain Scaling: Magnitude Estimation

Although SDT methods are (theoretically) concerned with the discrimination between adjacent levels of discomfort or pain measured by random presentation of blank trials and precisely controlled pain trials, the techniques of magnitude scaling would appear to offer greater flexibility to the pain assessor—including the very desirable option of dispensing with the controlled delivery of noxious stimulation—in the context of seeking to scale perceptual judgments relative to an arbitrary standard. Whereas subjects in signal detection studies must detect whether or not the signal is present (e.g., a just noticeable amount of pain), subjects in magnitude estimation studies judge the amount of a test stimulus *in proportion to a standard* or *modulus*, presented early in the testing session.

An "ideal" pain measurement procedure would, according to Gracely and Dubner (1981), possess the following attributes:

1. Be relatively free of the biases that inhere in psychophysical methods
2. Be capable of providing data on the accuracy and reliability of a subject's performance
3. Be useful for clinical as well as experimental research
4. Be capable of distinguishing the sensory and affective qualities of pain
5. Allow for reliable comparison between the clinical and experimental pain assessment.

It has been proposed (Gracely & Dubner, 1981; Gracely et al., 1978a, b) that the procedure known as *cross-modality matching* can be used to scale (quantify) in a bias-free manner and to verify the verbal descriptors of the sensory intensity and unpleasantness dimensions of pain. The scaled descriptors can then be used to assess the effects of various pain treatments or to compare the pain experience of different groups of patients.

The cross-modality matching paradigm assumes that the power law (previously discussed) is valid for many perceptual dimensions. The exponents derived for any sensory dimension are assumed to be "truly characteristic" across settings (unlike the SDT parameters that are dimensionless numbers). Thus,

any two quantitative response measures with established exponents could be used to judge a sensory continuum and the validity of the derived ratio scale confirmed by obtaining a close match between the theoretical and empirically obtained ratios *between the two response measures* (Lodge, 1981, p. 28).

If we were validating a magnitude scale of apparent pain intensity or unpleasantness, we might ask subjects to match a set of verbal descriptors (such as those collected by Melzack and Torgerson, 1971) to a loudness dimension (e.g., sound pressure, SP) and the force of a hand grip (HG) using an audiometer in the first case and a hand dynamometer in the second. The first response (loudness setting or handgrip force) to each word could serve as the reference, with all subsequent responses made in response to it. Or, the subject could be instructed to start with a particular verbal descriptor (e.g., moderate pain) and begin the relative comparisons from this standard. As Lodge (1981) points out,

> Because both magnitude response modalities are matched to the same set of stimuli, they are brought into a functional relationship on the principle of equivalence—objects equal to the same object are equal to each other (p. 29).

Since the characteristic exponent for loudness (sound pressure) is .67 and for the force of a handgrip is 1.7, the characteristic ratio between the two should be .39. The subject's impression of pain descriptors matched to loudness and to handgrip force should preserve the expected relationship. If the empirically derived slope approximates the expected, then it is said that the magnitude scale has been criterion validated. Tursky et al. (1982) have described in detail how they utilize the cross-modality matching procedure as part of their multidimensional *Pain Perception Profile*. Readers should consult this paper and the writings of R. H. Gracely and colleagues (e.g., Gracely, et al., 1978a, b) for further information about ratio scaling methods. Particularly noteworthy in the Tursky procedure is the fact that scaled pain descriptors are entered as data in a daily pain diary which assesses many other aspects of the pain experience and relates these to the quantified, bias-free estimates of intensity, unpleasantness, or feeling state. The most discussed drawbacks of the magnitude estimation procedures are that some patients cannot grasp the concept of proportional judgment and that the methods are seen as impractical for everyday clinical use (cf. Philips & Hunter, 1982).

Direct External Observation Methods

A fundamental distrust of any measure requiring subjective judgment on the part of the pain patient coupled with the belief that internal reactions to supposed nociceptive experience is less informative clinically than behavioral (overt) responding has led to a good deal of research on the assessment of "pain behaviors" (e.g., Fordyce, 1973; 1976).

Direct observation of behaviors of pain patients in natural settings is "generally considered the most fundamental, objective, and valid method of behavioral assessment" (Keefe, et al., 1982). Note that the authors are not proposing direct observation as the most valid or objective measure overall—but, only within the realm of behavioral assessment.

A good example of how careful observational procedures can elucidate chronic pain patterns is provided by Keefe and Block (1982). The authors noted that although behavioral assessment of certain categories of pain behavior, such as the amount of time pain patients spend standing or walking (called *uptime*; Sanders, 1980) or the amount of medication they ingest, has been undertaken, less systematic attention has been devoted to measurement of motor behaviors that routinely accompany chronic pain and that may elicit *caregiving responses* which reinforce patient dependency. The motor behaviors in question include guarded movement, bracing, rubbing, grimacing, and sighing. Each of these five responses was given a behavioral definition, and trained observers were used to determine their frequency in low back pain patients. In a series of four experiments, Keefe and Block (1982) demonstrated that (1) these *concomitant behaviors* could be reliably observed, (2) the frequency of these behaviors correlated with self-report of pain intensity, (3) the frequcney of these behaviors decreased from intake to discharge (with the exception of "grimacing"), (4) even untrained observers' ratings correlated with the coded categories, and (5) concomitant behaviors were not characteristic of normal or depressed subjects.

The importance of precise behavioral specification of verbal and motor pain reponses notwithstanding, there is a danger in any failure to recognize that pain actions are subject to distortion and that the degree of apparent pain behavior may be confounded with efforts at coping.

> How pain behaviors are defined, and whether they should be viewed as inappropriate and thus the focus of change, is a major issue that has not been addressed sufficiently (Turk et al., 1983, p. 211).

Biophysical and Biochemical Event Recording

The pain context model acknowledges that, without reducing pain to its neural or biochemical "essences," the pain assessor can examine the neurophysiologic dimensions of pain in the effort to appreciate its nature fully.

Because of its status as an emotional response, pain has been examined from the perspective of autonomic (sympathetic and parasympathetic) activation or arousal. Indeed, the gate-control model, which is characterized by its integration of physiological and psychological levels of analysis, notes the importance of the reciprocal connection between the reticular formation and the limbic system and their role in pain processes. Thus, it is not surprising that investigators have sought to link naturally occurring and laboratory-induced pain to such indices as skin conductance, heart rate, blood pressure, and the like (cf., Craig & Neidermayer, 1974; Hilgard & Hilgard, 1983; Melzack & Wall, 1983). Autonomic indicators are notoriously difficult to pin down, even in the laboratory. None of the traditional measures has proven consistently reliable in the laboratory. Their use in the natural environment is, therefore, rarely recommended (Chapman, 1980; Elton et al., 1983).

Central nervous system measures, particularly cortical-evoked potentials, have been receiving a good deal of attention in recent years. For example, Lavine et al. (1976) examined cortical-average-evoked responses (AERs) in a group of normal subjects exposed to electrical stimulation (shock) to the forearm. Subjects reported different perceived discomfort associated with higher shock intensities, and, most importantly, showed an orderly shock intensity—AER amplitude function. Lavine et al. (1976) also found that music (so-called auditory analgesia) produced a decrease in the AER-amplitude-intensity slope, suggesting the usefulness of the AER in the study of central pain control mechanisms. Chapman (1980) and his colleagues have also explored the relationship between laboratory-induced pain (electrical tooth pulp stimulation) and evoked potentials. The intensity-amplitude function is essentially linear, although the latencies of the evoked potential waves appear unaffected by painful stimulation. Chapman (1980) has suggested that SDT methods and evoked potential procedures may be converging in their assessment of a complex perceptual process involving orienting to and evaluating noxious stimulation (cf. also Pritchard, 1981).

Investigators have long been interested in the biochemistry of pain. Recent research on the endorphins (particularly beta endorphin), enkephalins, and substance P, has sparked renewed investigatory efforts toward clarifying the role of neurotransmitters in pain. Terenius (1980), in reviewing the use of biochemical methods of assessment in chronic pain, notes that two lines of study have emerged: attempts to objectify pain severity via biochemical assay methods and attempts at differential diagnosis of pain. The area of biochemical analysis is relatively new, but promising (e.g., cerebrospinal fluid assays of chronic patients suggest inadequate endorphin activation). Causal inferences remain difficult to draw and the validity of molecular biochemical analyses remains limited by the relative imprecision with which the criterion events (pain status) are assessed.

Cognitive-Behavioral-Physiologic Simulations and Skills Assessments

This next-to-last assessment approach is, of course, the most difficult to detail, for it is intended to represent an amalgam of assessment strategies. The goals of this hybrid category are, however, clearly distinct from those just articulated. Essentially, category I represents methods that focus not upon objectifying pain as a sensory-emotive event (as in methods E, F, G, and H) but upon contextualizing pain as a multilayered transactional process. To avoid relegating this last statement to the status of "intellectual junk food" (all packaging and no substance), we must elaborate and illustrate it, albeit in an abbreviated manner.

One good way to flesh out this multifaceted model is by noting the questions it suggests, such as: Why are some chronic pain patients better able than other to cope with the sensory, emotional, and evaluative consequences of their disorder? How does pain impact upon a patient's long and short-term life plans? In what ways does chronic pain alter an individual's efficiency in problem solving or in general information processing? Do chronic pain patients organize their memories of themselves and their interactions in dysfunctional ways? Under conditions of stress, how do pain patients differ from healthy individuals in terms of their self-appraisals, expectancies, and self-regulatory strategies? Can assessors determine how best to match pain patients to various interventions (psychological, pharmocologic, surgical, etc.)? Do chronic and acute pain patients differ in their theories of illness (in general) or of pain (in particular)? Can the three central motives postulated earlier in this chapter be assessed, and, if so, can they be functionally linked to adjustive outcome(s)?

These are but a few of the clinically important questions that are engendered by an interactionist, biopsychosocial perspective on pain—one that exists in sharp contrast to the unidimensional perspectives that are currently preeminent in the field. Efforts to address the sorts of questions listed earlier will surely be stifled by premature commitments to singular assessment strategies and/or data analytic modes. Although it is certainly important to know *what* a pain patient is feeling and *where*, it is equally important to know *how* the feelings are being labeled, stored, organized, and used in the *process* of adaptation/maladaptation. In my opinion, pain assessors have been overly concerned with quantifying a patient's *degree of hurt* and the behavioral or bodily correlates of the sensory experience. For a large number of chronic pain patients, no therapeutic intervention is likely significantly to dampen the "hurtfulness" directly. However, by helping patients reorganize their understanding of themselves and their pain, psychologists may be able to facilitate the kind of pervasive life-style modification necessary to move patients from the status of dependent and angry denizens of the medical system to a reasonable level of independent functioning and psychological well-being (determined, of course, on the basis of each patient's premorbid adjustment).

How can we accurately assess a pain patient's understanding of his or her pain, his or her illness theories, coping repertoires, information-processing styles, self-regulatory abilities, and the like? Space limitations preclude anything more than a cursory illustration of potential methods. However, readers are urged to consult the volumes by Kendall and Hollon (1981), Merluzzi et al. (1981), and Pope and Singer (1978) for further discussions of so-called cognitive-behavioral assessment modalities, as well as the chapters by Turk and Kerns and Leventhal and Nerenz, in the present volume.

I shall illustrate a broad-spectrum assessment approach by referencing two promising measurement paradigms, none of which has seen widespread application in pain research.

Wack and Turk's (1984) Latent Structure Analysis.   Recognizing that pain coping strategies have typically been derived on the basis of investigators' "intuitive notions" about the ways people in pain seek to cope with the experience, Wack and Turk (1984) suggested that the failure to discover differentially effective methods may be due, in part, to the one-sided reliance upon the researcher's perspective. An examination of subjects' perceptions about the relationship (similarity) among coping strategies would permit the "derivation of a classification system of strategies" based upon subjects' cognitive organizational schemas. It should be noted that the context for their analysis was laboratory-induced pain rather than clinical pain (however, see Copp, 1974, for an informal analysis of clinic patients' perceptions).

Wack and Turk (1984) presented a list of 30 coping strategies (generated in several previous experimental pain studies) to a group of 32 student volunteers who sorted them on the basis of similarity. The group similarity matrix was then subjected to a multidimensional scaling analysis and a cluster analysis. A three-dimensional solution emerged (and was essentially replicated in a second experiment using different subjects, different coping strategies, and a different multidimensional scaling program). The three dimensions to emerge were: sensation acknowledgment versus sensation avoidance, coping relevant strategies versus irrelevant, and active behavioral versus cognitive-imaginal strategies. Clearly, such an approach could be of use in clinical contexts (particularly with the SINDSCAL scaling procedure, available in the SAS system, which is based upon a matrix of similarities for *each subject*).

Davison, Robins, and Johnson's (1983) Articulated Thoughts Paradigm. Although the previous paradigm potentially gives us a glimpse into the group and/or individual's cognitive ecology, it does not provide much insight into the transactional process of pain management. However, a procedure recently described by Davison et al. (1983) might be called upon to serve such a function. These investigators were interested in the assessment of spontaneous thoughts in the context of complex events. Rather than utilizing naturalistically based methods (such as cued thought sampling), the investigators opted for greater control over, or knowledge of, the stimulus configurations toward which individuals were responding. Hence, an audio recording of a conversation is used to stimulate a complex event. The tape is played for a brief time (15 to 25 seconds), followed by a 30-second silent interval, during which subjects say what they are thinking and feeling. Various stress-provoking versus neutral tapes are presented, a subject's verbalizations are recorded and subsequently content analyzed. Davison et al. (1983) report on a 25-category coding scheme for the classification of "articulated thoughts."

Consider, now, how such a procedure might be adapted for pain assessments. First, chronic versus acute pain sufferers could be studied or patients with the same pain disorder (e.g., migraines, TMJ pain, low back pain, etc.) but with differing patterns of adjustment, medication use, workdays missed, and so on, or pain could be induced via standard laboratory methods (e.g., the cold pressor task, electrical stimulation, the submaximum effort tourniquet technique, etc.). Tape recordings of personally meaningful events could be simulated and presented to the pain subjects, whose task would be to talk aloud (not only about their self-relevant thoughts, but also their coping thoughts) and rate their emotional states. Alternatively, subjects with real or induced pain could be assigned complex information-processing tasks while listening to neutral or stressful tapes, and an assessment made of their comparative cognitive efficiency. In all cases, subjects would be asked to make periodic ratings of their pain level and other relevant bodily symptoms. To assess the interpersonal aspects of pain, investigators could require subjects to listen to various conversational opening lines and to react verbally to the taped speaker, with the goal of assessing the impact of pain upon the adequacy of social responding. Finally, subjects could be instructed in various methods for the self-regulation of pain and placed into the expanded articulated thoughts paradigm to assess the effects of training on the varied response parameters noted.

Although we have barely begun to examine the complex cognitive-behavioral-emotional-physiological relationships in everyday pain experience, the need to enlarge upon our current assessment focus is a critical one—and it should be addressed in the coming years by careful, innovative investigators willing to conduct complex, multifaceted studies in both the laboratory and the clinic.

Unobtrusive Measures of Pain Products and Consequences

This final category of pain assessment is by far the least often employed. However, it is one that deserves at least brief discussion. It is, in fact, the one procedure or strategy that best epitomizes the *pain context* view—for it is predicated on the assumption that an individual with a chronic pain problem leaves his or her "mark" on the environment(s) that he or she occupies.

Webb et al. (1981) describe a variety of so-called nonreactive measures available to researchers in the social sciences who would take the trouble to search them out. Physical trace measures can be divided into two types: natural erosion and natural accretion data. Such potentially informative bits of information about people are described by Webb et al. (1981) as consisting of:

> those pieces of data not specifically produced for the purpose of comparison and inference but available to be exploited opportunistically by the alert investigator (p. 5).

Examples of erosion measures in the pain arena are: the wear on a patient's cane (particularly after a physician has advised the patient that it is not needed), the wear on patients' shoes (particularly if a spouse can tell us how often the shoes are worn and their date of purchase), the wear on patients' home exercise equipment (again requiring additional data, such as about who else uses the equipment and how often). Accretion measures might include: an examination of a pain patient's personal library or borrowed books (e.g., is the patient reading about retirement and/or lawsuits or about medical news and alternative careers?), an examination of the setting on a patient's alarm clock, or an examination of the collection of medications in a pain patient's medicine cabinet. It should, of course, be noted that patient consent is required for any survey of private or public physical trace data or archival records, by either the clinician or an informant.

A FINAL NOTE

Although no attempt will be made to summarize the contents of this chapter, nonetheless it is fitting that I try to address what may be the reader's main complaint—namely, that pain assessment has been made to appear inordinately complicated.

In fact, my intention was not to complicate matters, but, rather, to hint at the *inherent complexity* of the human experience of pain and to suggest that our conceptual and assessment models must be as finely textured as the process we are seeking to unravel. The tentative organizing framework presented in this chapter was built upon the collective wisdom of numerous theoreticians, researchers, and clinicians. If it proves useful, practically and heuristically, then it will demonstrate that sensible blind men, communicating openly, can indeed describe an elephant—even one as indescribable as pain.

References

Andreasen, N. J. C. (1974). Neuropsychiatric complications in burn patients. *International Journal of Psychiatry in Medicine, 5,* 161–171.

Armentrout, D. P., Moore, J. E., Parker, J. C., Hewett, J. E., & Feltz, C. (1982). Pain-patient MMPI subgroups: The psychological dimensions of pain. *Journal of Behavioral Medicine, 5,* 201–211.

Ashby, W. R. (1952). *Design for a brain.* New York: Wiley.

Bandura, A. (1978). The self-system in reciprocal determinism. *American Psychologist, 33,* 344–359.

Beales, J. G. (1982). The assessment and management of pain in children. In P. Karoly, J. J. Steffen, & D. J. O'Grady (Eds.), *Child health psychology: Concepts and issues.* New York: Pergamon Press.

Beecher, H. K. (1959). *Measurement of subjective responses: Quantitative effects of drugs.* New York: Oxford University Press.

Bindra, D. (1979). *Motivation, the brain, and psychological theory.* Paper presented at American Psychological Association Meetings. New York.

Bohm, D., & Hiley, B. (1975). On the intuitive understanding of nonlocality as implied by quantum theory. *Foundations of Physics, 5,* 94−101.

Bonica, J. J. (1980). Conclusion. In J. J. Bonica (Ed.), *Pain.* New York: Raven Press.

Bradley, L. A., Prokop, C. K., Gentry, W. D., Van der Heide, L. H., & Prieto, E. J. (1981). Assessment of chronic pain. In C. K. Prokop & L. A. Bradley (Eds.), *Medical psychology.* New York: Academic Press.

Bradley, L. A., Prokop, C. K., Margolis, R., & Gentry, W. D. (1978). Multivariate analysis of the MMPI profiles of low back pain patients. *Journal of Behavioral Medicine, 1,* 253−272.

Budzynski, T. H., Stoyva, J. M., Adler, C. S., & Mullaney, D. J. (1973). EMG biofeedback and tension headache: A controlled outcome study. *Seminars in Psychiatry, 5,* 397−410.

Bursztajn, H., Feinbloom, R. I., Hamm, R. M., & Brodsky, A. (1981). *Medical choices, medical chances.* New York: Delta/Seymour Lawrence.

Carver, C. S., & Scheier, M. F. (1981). *Attention and self-regulation: A control-theory approach to human behavior.* New York: Springer-Verlag.

Chapman, C. R. (1974). An alternative to threshold assessment in the study of pain. In J. J. Bonica (Ed.), *Advances in Neurology.* New York: Raven Press.

Chapman, C. R. (1976). Measurement of pain: Problems and issues. In J. J. Bonica & D. Albe-Fessard (Eds.), *Advances in pain research and therapy* (Vol. 1). New York: Raven Press.

Chapman, C. R. (1980). Pain and perception: Comparison of sensory decision theory and evoked potential methods. In J. J. Bonica (Ed.), *Pain.* New York: Raven Press.

Chapman, C. R., & Wyckoff, M. (1981). The problem of pain: A psychobiological perspective. In S. N. Haynes & L. Gannon (Eds.), *Psychosomatic disorders.* New York: Praeger.

Chassan, J. B. (1979). *Research design in clinical psychology and psychiatry* (2nd ed.). New York: Irvington.

Clark, W. C. (1969). Sensory-decision theory analysis of the placebo effect on the criterion for pain and thermal sensitivity (d'). *Journal of Abnormal Psychology, 74,* 363−371.

Copp, L. A. (1974). The spectrum of suffering. *American Journal of Nursing, 74,* 491−495.

Craig, K. D., & Neidermayer, H. (1974). Autonomic correlates of pain thresholds influenced by social modeling. *Journal of Personality and Social Psychology, 29,* 246−252.

Crue, B. L., Kenton, B., Carregal, E. J. A., & Pinsky, J. J. (1980). The continuing crisis in pain research. In W. L. Smith, H. Mersky, & S. C. Gross (Eds.), *Pain: Meaning and management.* New York: SP Medical & Scientific Books.

Davison, G. C., Robins, C., & Johnson, M. K. (1983). Articulated thoughts during simulated situations: A paradigm for studying cognition in emotion and behavior. *Cognitive Therapy and Research, 7,* 17−40.

Dember, W. N., & Warm, J. S. (1979). *Psychology of perception* (2nd ed.). New York: Holt, Rinehart and Winston.

Dossey, L. (1982). *Space, time, and medicine.* Boulder, CO: Shambhala.

Dubuisson, D., & Melzack, R. (1976). Classification of clinical pain descriptions by multiple group discriminant analysis. *Experimental Neurology, 51,* 480−487.

Elton, D., Stanley, G., & Burrows, G. (1983). *Psychological control of pain.* Sydney: Grune & Stratton.

Engel, G. L. (1977). The need for a new medical model: A challenge to biomedicine. *Science, 196,* 129−136.

Ericksson, K. A., & Simon, H. A. (1980). Verbal reports as data. *Psychological Review, 87,* 215−251.

Fiske, D. (1978). Cosmopolitan constructs and provincial observations: Some prescriptions for a chronically ill specialty. In H. London (Ed.), *Personality: A new look at metatheories.* Washington, DC: Hemisphere.

Fordyce, W. E. (1973). An operant conditioning model for managing chronic pain. *Postgraduate Medicine, 53*, 123–128.

Fordyce, W. E. (1976). *Behavioral methods for chronic pain and illness.* St. Louis: Mosby.

Fordyce, W. E. (1978). Learning processes in pain. In R. A. Sternbach (Ed.), *The psychology of pain.* New York: Raven Press.

Gaito, J. (1980). Measurement scales and statistics: Resurgence of an old misconception. *Psychological Bulletin, 87*, 564–567.

Geldard, F. (1973). *The human senses.* New York: Wiley.

Gracely, R. H., & Dubner, R. (1981). Pain assessment in humans—a reply to Hall. *Pain, 11*, 109–120.

Gracely, E. H., McGrath, P., & Dubner, R. (1978a). Ratio scales of sensory and affective verbal pain descriptors. *Pain, 5*, 5–18.

Gracely, R. H., McGrath, P., & Dubner, R. (1978b). Validity and sensitivity of ratio scales of sensory and affective verbal pain descriptors: Manipulation of affect by diazepam. *Pain, 5*, 19–29.

Grossberg, J. M., & Grant, B. F. (1978). Clinical psychophysics: Applications of ratio scaling and signal detection methods to research on pain, fear, drugs, and medical decision making. *Psychological Bulletin, 85*, 1154–1176.

Hardy, J. D., Wolff, H. G., & Goodell, H. (1952). *Pain sensations and reactions.* Baltimore, MD: Williams & Wilkins.

Hilgard, E. R., & Hilgard, J. (1983). *Hypnosis in the relief of pain* (2nd ed.). Los Altos, CA: Kaufmann.

Huskisson, E. C. (1974). Measurement of pain. *Lancet, 2*, 1127–1131.

International Association for the Study of Pain, Subcommittee on Taxonomy (1979). Pain terms: A list with definitions and notes on usage. *Pain, 6*, 249–252.

Jacox, A. K. (Ed.). (1977). *Pain: A source book for nurses and other health professionals.* Boston: Little, Brown.

Johnson, M. (1977). Assessment of clinical pain. In A. K. Jacox (Ed.), *Pain: A source book for nurses and other health professionals.* Boston: Little, Brown.

Kanfer, F. H., & Karoly, P. (1972). Self-control: A behavioristic excursion into the lion's den. *Behavior Therapy, 3*, 398–416.

Karoly, P. (1980). Person variables in therapeutic change and development. In P. Karoly & J. J. Steffen (Eds.), *Improving the long-term effects of psychotherapy.* New York: Gardner Press.

Karoly, P., & Kanfer, F. H., (Eds.). (1982). *Self-management and behavior change: From theory to practice.* New York: Pergamon Press.

Keefe, F. J. (1982). Behavioral assessment and treatment of chronic pain. Current status and future directions. *Journal of Consulting and Clinical Psychology, 50*, 896–911.

Keefe, F. J., & Block, A. R. (1982). Development of an observation method for assessing pain behavior in chronic low back pain patients. *Behavior Therapy, 13*, 363–375.

Keefe, F. J., & Brown, C. (1982). Behavioral treatment of chronic pain. In P. Boudewyns & F. J. Keefe (Eds.), *Behavioral medicine in general medicine practice.* Menlo Park, CA: Addison-Wesley.

Keefe, F. J., Brown, C., Scott, D. S., & Ziesat, H. (1982). Behavioral assessment of chronic pain. In F. J. Keefe & J. A. Blumenthal (Eds.), *Assessment strategies in behavioral medicine.* New York: Grune & Stratton.

Kelly, D. D. (1981). Somatic sensory system IV: Central representations of pain and analgesia. In E. R. Kandel & J. H. Schwartz (Eds.), *Principles of neural science.* New York: Elsevier.

Kendall, P. C., & Hollon, S. D. (1981). *Assessment strategies for cognitive-behavioral interventions.* New York: Academic Press.

Ketovuori, H., & Pontinen, P. J. (1981). A pain vocabulary in Finnish—the Finnish Pain Questionnaire. *Pain, 11,* 247–253.

Klinger, E., Barta, S. G., & Maxeiner, M. E. (1981). Current concerns: Assessing therapeutically relevant motivation. In P. C. Kendall & S. D. Hollon (Eds.), *Assessment strategies for cognitive-behavioral interventions.* New York: Academic Press.

Kremer, E., Atkinson, J. H., & Ignelzi, R. J. (1981). Measurement of pain: Patient preference does not confound pain measurement. *Pain, 10,* 241–248.

Lavine, R., Buchsbaum, M. S., & Poncy, M. (1976). Auditory analgesia: Somatosensory evoked response and subjective pain rating. *Psychophysiology, 13,* 140–148.

Lodge, M. (1981). *Magnitude scaling.* Beverly Hills: Sage.

Lutterbeck, P. M., & Triay, S. H. (1972). Measurement of analgesic activity in man. *International Journal of Clinical Pharmacology,* 315–319.

Martindale, C. (1981). *Cognition and consciousness.* Homewood, IL: Dorsey Press.

McCreary, C., & Turner, J. (1983). Psychological disorder and pain description. *Health Psychology, 2,* 1–10.

McCreary, C., Turner, J., & Dawson, E. (1977). Principal dimensions of the pain experience and psychological disturbance in chronic low back pain patients. *Pain, 11,* 85–92.

Meehl, P. E. (1978). Theoretical risks and tabular asterisks: Sir Karl, Sir Ronald, and the slow progress of soft psychology. *Journal of Consulting and Clinical Psychology, 46,* 806–834.

Melzack, R. (1973). *The puzzle of pain.* New York: Basic Books.

Melzack, R. (1975). The McGill Pain Questionnaire: Major properties and scoring methods. *Pain, 1,* 277–299.

Melzack, R., & Casey, K. L. (1968). Sensory, motivational, and central control determinants of pain: A new conceptual model. In D. Kenshalo (Ed.), *The skin senses.* Springfield, IL: Thomas.

Melzack, R., & Torgerson, W. S. (1971). On the language of pain. *Anesthesiology, 34,* 50–59.

Melzack, R., & Wall, P. D. (1965). Pain mechanisms: A new theory. *Science, 150,* 971–979.

Melzack, R., & Wall, P. D. (1983). *The challenge of pain.* New York: Basic Books.

Merluzzi, T. V., Glass, C. R., & Genest, M. (Eds.). (1981). *Cognitive assessment.* New York: Guilford Press.

Mersky, H., & Boyd, D. B. (1978). Emotional adjustment and chronic pain. *Pain, 5,* 173–178.

Millon, T., Green, C. J., and Meagher, R. (1979). The MBHI: A new inventory for the psychodiagnostician in medical settings. *Professional Psychology, 10,* 529–539.

Moitoza, E., & Espin, O. M. (1980). *Pain.* In R. H. Woody (Ed.), *Encyclopedia of clinical assessment,* (Vol. 2). San Francisco: Jossey-Bass.

Neufeld, R. W. (1977). *Clinical quantitative methods.* New York: Grune & Stratton.

Noordenbos, W. (1959). *Pain.* Amsterdam: Elsevier.

Notarius, C. I. (1981). Assessing sequential dependency in cognitive performance data. In T. V. Merluzzi, C. R. Glass, & M. Genest (Eds.), *Cognitive assessment.* New York: Guilford Press.

Ohnhaus, E. E., & Adler, R. (1975). Methodological problems in the measurement of pain: A comparison between the verbal rating scale and the visual analogue scale. *Pain, 1,* 379–384.

Peck, R. E. (1967). A precise technique for the measurement of pain. *Headache, 2,* 189–194.

Peele, S. (1981). Reductionism in the psychology of the eighties: Can biochemistry eliminate addiction, mental illness, and pain? *American Psychologist, 36,* 807–818.

Pelletier, K. R. (1977). *Mind as healer, mind as slayer.* New York: Dell.

Pennebaker, J. (1982). *The psychology of physical symptoms.* New York: Springer-Verlag.

Petrie, A. (1967). *Individuality in pain and suffering.* Chicago: University of Chicago Press.

Petrovich, D. V. (1957). The pain apperception test: A preliminary report. *Journal of Psychology, 44,* 339–346.

Philips, H. C., & Hunter, M. (1982). A laboratory technique for the assessment of pain behavior. *Journal of Behavioral Medicine, 5,* 283–294.

Pilowsky, I. (1978). Pain as abnormal illness behaviour. *Journal of Human Stress, 4,* 22–27.

Plutchik, R. (1980). *Emotion: A psychoevolutionary synthesis.* New York: Harper & Row.

Pope, K., & Singer, J. (Eds.) (1978). *The stream of consciousness.* New York: Plenum Press.

Powers, W. T. (1973). *Behavior: The control of perception.* Chicago: Aldine.

Pritchard, W. S. (1981). Psychophysiology of P300. *Psychological Bulletin, 89,* 506–540.

Reading, A. E. (1980). A comparison of pain rating scales. *Journal of Psychosomatic Research, 24,* 119–124.

Reading, A. E., & Newton, J. R. (1978). A card sort method of pain assessment. *Journal of Psychosomatic Research, 22,* 503–512.

Rollman, G. B. (1976). Signal detection theory assessment of pain modulation: A critique. In J. J. Bonica & D. Albe-Fessard (Eds.), *Advances in pain research and therapy* (Vol. 1). New York: Raven Press.

Sanders, S. (1979). Behavioral assessment and treatment of clinical pain: Appraisal of current status. In M. Hersen, R. Eisler, & P. M. Miller (Eds.), *Progress in behavior modification* (Vol. 8). New York: Academic Press.

Sanders, S. (1980). Toward a practical instrument for the automatic measurement of "uptime" in chronic pain patients. *Pain, 9,* 103–109.

Schneider, F., & Karoly, P. (1983). Conceptions of the pain experience: The emergence of multidimensional models and their implications for contemporary clinical practice. *Clinical Psychology Review, 3,* 61–86.

Schwartz, G. E. (1982). Testing the biopsychosocial model: The ultimate challenge facing behavioral medicine? *Journal of Consulting and Clinical Psychology, 50,* 1040–1053.

Shacham, S., Reinhardt, L. C., Raubertas, R. F., & Cleeland, C. S. (1983). Emotional states and pain: Intraindividual and interindividual measures of association. *Journal of Behavioral Medicine, 6,* 405–419.

Spear, F. G. (1967). Pain in psychiatric patients. *Journal of Psychosomatic Research, 11,* 187–193.

Sternbach, R. A. (1968). *Pain: A psychophysiological analysis.* New York: Academic Press.

Sternbach, R. A. (1974a). *Pain patients: Traits and treatment.* New York: Academic Press.

Sternbach, R. A. (1974b). Varieties of pain games. In J. J. Bonica (Ed.), *Advances in neurology* (Vol. 4). New York: Raven Press.

Sternbach, R. A., Murphy, R. W., Timmermans, G., Greenhoot, J. H., & Akeson, W. H. (1974). Measuring the severity of clinical pain. In J. J. Bonica (Ed.), *Advances in neurology* (Vol. 4). New York: Raven Press.

Stevens, S. S. (1972). *Psychophysics and social scaling.* Morristown, NJ: General Learning Press.

Stewart, M. L. (1977). Measurement of clinical pain. In A. K. Jacox (Ed.), *Pain: A source book for nurses and other health professionals.* Boston: Little, Brown.

Terenius, L. Y. (1980). Biochemical assessment of chronic pain. In H. W. Kosterlitz & L. Y. Terenius (Eds.), *Pain and society.* Weinheim: Verlag Chemie GmbH.

Turk, D. C., & Kerns, R. D. (1983). Conceptual issues in the assessment of clinical pain. *International Journal of Psychiatry in Medicine, 13,* 57–68.

Turk, D. C., Meichenbaum, D., & Genest, M. (Eds.), (1983). *Pain and behavioral medicine.* New York: Guilford Press.

Tursky, B., Jamner, L. D., & Friedman, R. (1982). The pain perception profile: A psychophysical approach to the assessment of pain report. *Behavior Therapy, 13,* 376–394.

Urban, B. J. (1982). Therapeutic aspects in chronic pain: Modulation of nociception, alleviation of suffering, and behavioral analysis. *Behavior Therapy, 13*, 430–437.

Viernstein, M. C. (1982). Psychological testing for chronic pain patients. In N. H. Hendler, D. M. Long, & T. N. Wise (Eds.), *Diagnosis and treatment of chronic pain.* Boston: Wright.

Wack, J. T., & Turk, D. C. (1984). Latent structure of strategies used to cope with nociceptive stimulation. *Health Psychology, 3*, 27–43.

Webb, E. J., Campbell, D. T., Schwartz, R. D. Sechrest, L., & Grove, J. B. (1981). *Nonreactive measures in the social sciences.* Boston: Houghton Mifflin.

Weiner, H. (1977). *Psychobiology and human disease.* New York: Elsevier.

Weisenberg, M. (1977). Pain and pain control. *Psychological Bulletin, 84*, 1008–1044.

Wildman, B. G., & Erickson, M. T. (1977). Methodological problems in behavioral observation. In J. D. Cone & R. P. Hawkins (Eds.), *Behavioral Assessment.* New York: Brunner/Mazel.

Wolff, B. B. (1980). Measurement of human pain. In J. J. Bonica (Ed.), *Pain.* New York: Raven Press.

Wolff, B. B., Kantor, T. G., & Cohen, P. (1976). Laboratory pain induction methods for human analgesic assays. In J. J. Bonica & D. Albe-Fossard (Eds.), *Advances in pain research and therapy* (Vol. 1). New York: Raven Press.

Woodforde, J. M., & Mersky, H. (1972). Some relationships between subjective measures of pain. *Journal of Psychosomatic Research, 16*, 173–178.

Zajonc, R. B. (1980). Feeling and thinking: Preferences need no inferences. *American Psychologist, 35*, 151–175.

Ziesat, H. A. & Gentry, W. D. (1978). The pain apperception test: An investigation of concurrent validity. *Journal of Clinical Psychology, 34*, 786–789.

14

The Assessment of
Illness Cognition

HOWARD LEVENTHAL
DAVID. R. NERENZ

For the past 5 years we have been studying the ways in which patients conceptualize or represent illness threats. Our basic goals at the start were threefold: (1) to draw, or "picture," the models patients generate of illness threats, that is, to describe their content and organization; (2) to show how patients' representations affected their plans and responses for coping with these illness threats; and (3) to develop a model of the information-processing system that generated patient representations of illness and plans for coping.

In pursuing these goals, we have studied: (1) patients who have just entered or are already continuing in treatment for high blood pressure

Preparation of this report was supported by the National Institutes of Health and the National Institute of Aging grants CA26235, HL24543, and AG03501.

We would like to thank David Steele for his comments at the early stages of this project.

517

(Meyer et al., 1984); (2) patients receiving chemotherapy to prevent recurrence or to control existing lymphatic or breast malignancies (Nerenz, 1979; Nerenz et al., 1982; Ringler, 1981; (3) patients seeking care for minor medical emergencies (Safer et al., 1979) and for mental or emotional problems (Mosbach et al., 1984); (4) people suffering from diabetic retinopathy (Espenshade, 1984) and (5) samples of well persons of varying ages (E. Leventhal, 1984). Our data have been obtained by interviews using both open-ended questions and closed-ended rating scales and checklists and by self-administered questionnaires and diaries. We have accumulated much useful data, although not without the pain of a good many mistakes. Our goal in this chapter will be to describe the various strategies and methods we have used to assess illness cognition and to present our ideas about when each method should be used and how best to use it.

Although we will discuss the specific advantages and pitfalls of different methods for the study of illness cognition, we will not present a cookbook for studying these and similar cognitive-behavioral problems. The reason we cannot construct a simple cookbook is that methods for asking questions and for coding and analyzing answers are highly dependent upon theory and prior knowledge. What you ask, how you ask, and how you code and analyze your data are determined by your conceptualization of the cognitive and behavior phenomena under study, and this is dependent upon prior knowledge (Bandura, 1977; Ericksson & Simon, 1980; Nelson, 1983; Nelson & Hayes, 1979). Research is an iterative process: We formulate and test an hypothesis, refine our concepts and measures, and test our hypothesis once again. The purpose of a good method is to generate the data needed to determine the closeness of fit and to close the gap between our conceptualization of a behavioral process and the thoughts, feelings, and actions of our human subjects. Hence, we must begin with a theory about the way people represent illnesses.

A THEORY OF ILLNESS COGNITION

We will outline as briefly as possible the basic assumptions and concepts in our model of illness cognition. In ideal circumstances we would present the history of the interaction of our ideas, methods, and data. Such a reconstruction, however, is difficult, given the erratic course of the development of ideas, the failings of memory, and the limitations of space; moreover, it would be tedious. Thus, we will present our theoretical ideas simply, turn to general methodological issues, and then discuss specific strategies and methods for the assessment of illness cognition.

Basic Processes in Illness Cognition

A number of basic assumptions about the human organism shaped our approach to the study of cognition. They were as follows:

1. People are active problem solvers, not passive responders (Kelly, 1955), and their behavior is directed by their perceptions and interpretations of specific situational stimuli (Lewin, 1935). Thus, experience and behavior are not created *de novo* with each stimulus, but reflect an interaction of environmental events and a knowledge base that consists of both cognitive and emotional memory schemata (Leventhal, 1980; 1984). We have referred to the individual's construction of perceptions and reactions to illness threats as "common-sense models of illness" (Leventhal et al., 1980).

2. A substantial portion of the cognitive-processing system and the knowledge base that give rise to commonsense models of illness are not directly observable. We observe the output of the system in speech and action (overt behavior; physiological response) at specific points in time.

3. Behavior is episodic in organization. There is a specific time frame, a beginning and an end, to the process of constructing a representation of and responding to a specific (illness) problem. The representation in any episode is constantly updated as new information is processed.

4. Both situational and individual factors are involved in the production of experience and behavior. Thus, although successive episodes will reflect prior episodes, the impact of unique situational factors and variation in the availability of individual schemata can lead to wide variation in commonsense models. This necessarily generates difficulties for prediction over situations and time (see Nelson, 1983).

The Structure and Content of Commonsense Models of Illness

We believe that an individual cannot formulate structural models of the mind without specifying *content*. It is essential, therefore, to identify classes of content variables and specific variables within these classes (Janis, 1982b). Failure to confront the content of situations and behavior is akin to developing structural models of molecules and atoms without having first identified elements (Leventhal, 1982b; 1974). Although this may seem obvious, there is a tradition of cognitive and social-psychological theory that proceeds in the opposite direction and attempts to describe structure independent of any known (or knowable) content. For example, social psychologists developed "balance theories" to describe attitude formation and change (Rosenberg & Abelson, 1960; Peak, 1958) without specifying particular classes and subtypes of elements that were or were not in balanced relationships. More recent cognitive models use the concepts such as *script* or *schema* (Abelson, 1981; Bower et al, 1979), again failing to specify particular classes or types of script and schemata. When these content-free concepts are used to account for substantive findings in fields such as judgment or person perception, the explanations take on an air of prayerful, but insubstantial, incantation.

So-called explanations become little more than explanations by naming. Thus, in order to develop a model of the cognitive processes underlying illness behavior, we have first sought to identify the cognitive and behavioral contents that make up these processes. Indeed, one of our basic assumptions is that we can identify stable and universal elements in the content of illness cognition because illness is intrinsic to the human condition.

Stages in Processing. The commonsense model activated for a behavioral episode appears to be the product of an underlying control system that can be divided into three components or stages, the organization of which is sometimes directly visible in the organization of experience and behavior. The three stages or divisions of the process are as follows.

1. **Problem Representations.** The representation of a problem involves a set of attributes that identify or specify the features of the problem and goals for action.
2. **Action Plan.** The set of coping responses perceived as relevant to the problem representation. This consists of a set of specific behaviors and expectations respecting their effectiveness or impact on the problem as currently defined.
3. **Appraisal Process.** A set of rules for comparing the pre- and post-action relationships between the organism and goal states. The appaisal process evaluates whether movement has occurred toward or away from specified goals.

Variables Within Stages. Within each state we can define and discover specific attributes or content variables, and specific processes. We focus here on the representation of the illness itself.

Illness representations are multidimensional and the dimensions are in turn multilevel—that is, they are defined in both *abstract* and *concrete* terms. This is a critical factor in the study of illness cognition and in the understanding of behavior during illness episodes. We have tentatively identified four attributes that seem common to many illness representations.

1. **Identity.** Variables that identify the presence or absence of the illness. Illnesses can be identified abstractly by labels (cancer, heart attack, etc.) and concretely by signs (sores or bleeding) and symptoms (pain, nausea, headache, or tiredness).
2. **Consequence.** The perceived physical, social, and economic consequences of the disease and its felt emotional consequences (e.g., shame or despair).
3. **Causes.** The perceived causes of the disease, for example, genetic factors, environmental pathogens (viruses, bacteria, or toxic wastes),

an individual's own behavior, (smoking, poor diet, lack of rest), stress, interpersonal influence, or bad luck.

4. **Time Line.**   The perceived time frame for the development and duration of the illness threat. A time frame is implicit in every attribute of the representation, every action plan and every action.

These four attributes have been the major ones uncovered in our work. Lau and Hartmann (1983) have added curability or controllability to the list. Although this factor clearly belongs within commonsense models, it is debatable whether it should be defined as an attribute of the illness representation or a summary of expectations with respect to coping (response effectiveness and self-effectance).

There are also many subprocesses within the representation stage. One of these is the process of interpretation or what Lazarus (1966) has called *primary appraisal*. In interpretation, the attributes of the representation are generated by the interaction of stimuli and features of the individual's memory schemata. Different types of schemata may be involved in interpretation (Leventhal & Nerenz, 1983). For example, sensations from the body, such as pain in the gut, may combine automatically (without conscious interpretive effort) with a perceptual schema that includes intense emotional reactions, such as perceiving oneself as emaciated and dying of cancer (Leventhal, 1980; 1982a; 1984). Deliberative reflection may suppress these frightening images by relabeling the pain as something less threatening. Although a respondent is likely to be aware of his or her active efforts to suppress fear and find a benign definition to a threatening symptom, he or she is less likely to be aware of the initial automatic process that gave rise to the fearful interpretation of cancer. These issues are clearly important for the development of methods for studying illness representations.

STRATEGIES AND METHODS FOR STUDYING ILLNESS REPRESENTATIONS

The methods used to study illness representations depend upon the state of our knowledge at the time the study is initiated. The less we know about the problem, the more our methods should be oriented toward discovery. The more we know about the problem, the more our methods should be oriented toward verification and refinement (Nunnally, 1978). Research is an iterative process with its initial stages oriented toward the discovery or uncovering and defining of important content variables and describing their possible relationships to one another.

Many investigators pay insufficient attention to the discovery process. All too often, new phenomena and new areas of study are used as convenient stages for playing out old themes. As Silver and Wortman (1980) suggest, theoretical concepts and operations such as causal attributions (Kelley, 1971), internal control (Rotter, 1966), and social comparison (Festinger, 1954) are borrowed from studies of college students and applied to the behavior of patients without first assessing whether the theoretical concept is appropriate to the setting, or if operations standardized in the laboratory tap the concept in the new setting. For example, readiness to yield control to technical expertise might reflect high rather than low levels of internal control in a hospital where the patient cannot perform the actions needed to control a serious disease threat. Applying the control concept in a naïve way without considering the specifics of situations can lead to meaningless data. There is a progression, therefore, from opening a problem, that is, from discovery, to confirmation or testing hypotheses formulated during the discovery process. Our discussion will be organized around these two phases of the research process.

METHODS FOR DISCOVERY

Framing the Research Question

How do we go about discovering the attributes of illness representations? Can we systematize the steps? Indeed, why did we seek to study commonsense models or illness cognition?

The decision to study commonsense models of illness and, more specifically, to focus on how people *represent* illness threats was determined primarily by prior data, although personal observations and intuition played a role. Earlier work on fear-arousing communications (Leventhal, 1970) had shown that fear arousal led to temporary, and not to long-term, changes in attitudes, intentions, and behavior. By adding action instructions, that is, a plan specifying the cues for action and the specific steps to take to cope with the fear-arousing information, we succeeded in generating long-term behavioral change (Leventhal et al., 1965; Leventhal, et al., 1966; Leventhal, et al., 1967). Plans alone, however, were insufficient to generate action. Knowing what to do and when to do it did not lead to action if a clear view of specific attributes of the health threat was lacking. Since the degree to which the warning message aroused fear was irrelevant to long-term action, it was clear that what our subjects had learned about the threat was essential in promoting their use of the plans. Thus, the warning messages describing the threat did two things: (1) they stimulated a temporary state of fear, and (2) they defined a health threat or problem. If the combination of threat perception and a plan maintained action over the long term in the fear communication studies, it seemed possible that we had a key to the more generic problem of the maintenance of therapeutic change, a problem that is central to smoking withdrawal (Hunt & Bespalec, 1974; Leventhal & Cleary, 1980), diet or weight control (Dunbar & Stunkard, 1979; Mahoney & Mahoney, 1976), exercise maintenance (Dishman, 1982), and medication compliance (Leventhal, et al., 1984; see also Kirschenbaum & Tomarken, 1983, for an excellent review). Even with valuable insight, we felt we knew little of how people actually acquired knowledge about illness threats and generated internal representations of those threats.

Beginning Discovery. There were at least four ways of undertaking research in this new problem area: (1) using available theory; (2) developing a map of the domain via pilot research and/or open-ended data collection; (3) defining attributes using factor analytic and scaling methodologies; and (4) following a focused hunch. We will discuss each of these approaches, the considerations that led us to adopt and/or reject them, and the consequences of using them.

1. *Using Available Theory.* The first question we asked was whether available theoretical models and methods would help us to understand how people perceive illness threats. We evaluated each theory with respect to the following criteria.

    a. Does the theory seem to fit the domain under consideration? Specifically, does it seem to capture the *content*, *process*, and *structure* of the domain?

    b. Does the theory suggest methods likely to uncover new variables and discover new and important relationships between variables?

    c. Does the theory do a very good job in accounting for outcomes in the domain in which it has been developed?

Two types of theory were clearly applicable to our question: the health belief model (Becker, 1974; Rosenstock, 1974) and social learning theory (Bandura, 1969). The health belief model appeared to be the most relevant. It is a decision model in which motivation to act is a product of the probability of negative consequences (perceived vulnerability or revulnerability to disease) times the severity of these consequences. The specific action chosen is the sum of the perceived effectiveness less the perceived barriers for each of the behaviors available for problem solving, the behavior with the largest sum being chosen (Hochbaum, 1958). The word *equation* is clearly similar to the formal model of need achievement and fear of failure developed by Atkinson (1957).

We decided not to use the health belief formulation for the following reasons (see Leventhal et al., 1983, for more detail). First, it assumed people reacted to illness threats in terms of perceived vulnerability and perceived severity, and it assessed these variables by direct questioning (Becker et al., 1977). It was our judgment that these variables do not adequately describe how people see or define illness threats. Thus, we did not believe that subjects store knowledge or think of disease threats in these specific terms. We expected their knowledge to be more concrete and situationally specific (e.g., an image of a cripple recalled prior to surgery [Janis, 1958]), and categorical rather than probabilistic (I am or am not vulnerable to cancer).

Thus, we did not see a match between the variables in the model and the attributes of illness cognition.

We were also concerned that the method of the health belief model relied on a type of direct questioning that stimulated reasoning, that is, retrieval and *inferences* from prior experience, rather than reporting feelings or experiences of the moment (Ericksson & Simon, 1980). Consider, for example, the processes that might be involved in answering the following two questions: (1) How likely is it that you will get cancer in your lifetime? and (2) What thoughts come to your mind when you think about cancer? The first asks you to review facts about cancer and your history and to make an inference from these facts. The second asks for current thoughts.

Because many of the attributes of illness cognition are processed automatically, we felt that to tap the product of this concrete thinking it would be necessary to ask questions specific to the type of episodic information that would run through the subject's mind when he or she was thinking about an illness or was ready to act to prevent or cure it. Thus, rather than acting when their perceived vulnerability reached a threshold of 80 or 90 on a 100-point probability scale, we expected subjects to respond to symptoms they felt might be cancer or to the death from cancer of a friend or family member. These more concrete perceptions and pieces of knowledge would be the instigators to action. They might also instigate thinking that would lead the respondent to conceptualize him- or herself as vulnerable, but we could not count on that and needed to ask our questions so that this self-reflective abstracting step was not required.

We were also concerned that using a decision-theory approach would lead to the type of research where we would add new variables to the decision equation to improve its fit (e.g., Wallston & Wallston, 1982) and miss the concrete thoughts and emotional reactions underlying the subject's performance. We believed it essential, therefore, that our first methods formulate the variables to match their actual representation in the head of the respondents. We could then *reformulate* and reshape our concepts with repeated study. These biases were reinforced by the relatively meager amounts of variance accounted for in studies using the health belief model (Leventhal et al., 1983).

The decision to reject social learning theory was a bit more complex. First, the earliest and most advanced versions of social learning models such as Rotter's (1954; 1966) had many of the same problems as the health belief model: It was an expectancy times value model that did not provide any clear methods for the conceptualization and appraisal of expectancies and values in a new domain. Other models, such as Bandura's (1969), seemed to conceptualize the organism as reactive rather than as active and dealt with the external variables of reinforcement and modeling, which presumably regulated behavior, but did not at that time discuss the mechanisms by which modeling or reinforcement operated. Thus, neither the cognitive nor the behavioristic version of social learning theory seemed adequate to the process of discovering the critical attributes of illness cognition.

2. *Developing a Map via Pilot and Open-ended Data Collection.*   The second way to initiate discovery, developing a map of the domain, is often the most attractive in a new area of investigation, as well it might be. There is a great merit to simply going out and asking questions and observing! How do people talk about imagined and actual threats? How do they describe the environments that lead them to think about illness? What cues do they identify? Do the cues differ for potential and current illness, for fatal versus minor illness? And, how do they act to prevent and control illness? Do the cues that stimulate action differ from those that do not? The list of questions can be expanded virtually without end! Investigators new to an area also can do well by positioning themselves in settings where people make health decisions and by watching how different environmental messages affect thinking and action.

Although all these activities form an important part of the investigator's education, they do not generate the type of data likely to excite journal editors and reviewers. The very features that make the open-ended approach attractive for investigation of a new problem area are the sources of its major traps and pitfalls. In short, it is far easier to collect vivid descriptions of how patients feel and act when learning they have cancer than it is to know what to do with these descriptions once they are collected. Verbal, expressive, and overt responses must be coded. Coders and coding must be reliable, and this is not always easy to achieve. The relationships between different response categories must be determined to see which codes or variables are independent and which are indicators of a common variable. A common solution to this problem is to use exploratory factorial methods to determine which codes are indicators of a common latent or underlying variable (see Nunnally, 1978). When we adopt this approach, some of the obtained covariance will reflect a common latent factor, some may reflect relationships between latent factors, and some may be specific to the sample under study. Unfortunately, it is difficult to determine whether the covariance reflects a single factor or related factors if we have no theoretical basis in beginning our data reduction! We could, for example, factor only those items we wrote to measure the perceived causes, or, we could factor the entire item pool. The factors we get depend on the item we choose for the analysis, which is a theoretical as well as an empirical decision. The dilemma emphasizes the interactive nature of research at the very earliest level: The writing of items and the formation of code categories are heavily influenced by theory.

Although there are established, cookbook procedures for ensuring reliability and independence of codes, the major barrier to successful management of data, therefore, is deciding how to code in the first place. This is an issue of validity; that is, what are the best, the most valid, code categories. For better or worse, the choice of coding schemes is theoretical as much as it is empirical. The same data can be coded in different ways, and each way of coding reflects a difference in theoretical perspective. The adequacy of the theory will depend upon its ability to provide summary code categories that then relate to one another informatively; that is, in ways that account for substantial amounts of variance and that are intellectually and aesthetically satisfying (see Kaplan, 1964).

The possibility of multiple coding offers opportunities, since we could code the data in two different ways to see which gives us greater insight into people's representations of illness threats. Although multiple, comparative coding is possible and could be the basis of a strong study that allows us to compare alternative models, there are serious limitations to conducting such an exercise on a first data set. The most obvious is that it is time-consuming. Coding data takes a good deal of time. Coding data twice in different ways takes more time and multiple persons to keep the two coding operations independent. More important, however, is that comparisons between two coding systems for a common data set are unlikely to be equally "fair" to each system, since the data may not contain the material critical for adequate (reliable and valid) coding of the variables from one of the two theories and may even omit the data needed to code one or more predictors, moderators, or criterion variables important for one of the two approaches. For example, in one of our early studies of patient compliance to hypertension medication, we asked about and coded two types of independent variables: use of body symptoms and belief that a person's own health behaviors were responsible for high blood pressure. Although the former predicted medication compliance, the latter did not, suggesting that causal beliefs were irrelevant for adaptation to this chronic disease. This conclusion, however, was both premature and incorrect. Causal beliefs did not predict medication usage, but they did predict making efforts to control hypertension through smoking cessation and weight loss. We had not measured this latter criterion in our first study, although we fortunately did in our second (Steele, et al., 1984). An important lesson to be learned from this series of studies is that the frame of reference or theory being used to guide interview and questionnaire construction is likely to be represented in the data collection instruments and to fare better in a race against an alternative perspective or theory that was less salient at the time the exploratory study was designed. And, this is true whether the frame of reference is made explicit or allowed to remain implicit.

The lesson, therefore, is simple. Data collection and coding is heavily theory dependent. This is a fact of life that we cannot escape! If possible, we would have long since been replaced by one or another statistical program.

3. *Discovery Through Scaling and Factor Analysis.* Statistical procedures such as factor analysis and multidimensional scaling (MDS) offer a third way for discovering the content attributes of a domain. Factor analysis requires a series of initial guesses as to the nature of these attributes in order to write items to tap the potential attributes. The statistical method is then used to investigate the interdependencies among the items or to define the dimensionality of the item space. Each dimension is presumed to define a latent variable responsible for item covariation. It is also important

to note that factor analysis is inherently an iterative procedure. Thus, the initial solution should be cross validated on a second sample, and, more important, the second test should include new items designed to measure more precisely the core of the latent variables as well as items designed to test the boundaries of these latent variables and to probe for new latent factors.

Because factor analysis requires both asking many specific questions and repeating this on several samples to define clearly those factors, we felt it was not the best tool to use to begin the exploration of illness cognition. We wished neither to put words into the mouths of our subjects nor first to conduct several studies refining measures of independent and mediating variables prior to using these measures as predictors. [We should point out that LISREL (Joreskog & Sorbom, 1981; Long, 1983) is designed both to factor the predictor and criterion variables and to depict the relationships among the latent variables underlying the predictor and criterion measures.] We have, however, made use of multidimensional scaling (MDS) which is the most open of the discovery techniques, since it does not require that subjects address a series of questions about a specific illness or medical procedure. The subject's task is to compare and judge the similarity between pairs of elements drawn from the set of elements that define the knowledge domain of interest to the investigator (Shepard et al., 1972). In our studies the pairs consisted of every possible pair from a set of 20 illness labels. The statistical program examines the similarity judgments and generates the set of underlying dimensions needed to regenerate the similarity space. The technique makes virtually no suggestions as to the attributes to be used to compare the illnesses and is presumed to draw upon the respondent's own knowledge base.

Although MDS is an attractive procedure, it does have several shortcomings. First, the investigator must generate a set of elements, in this instance disease labels, that represent the domain and are familiar to respondents. The selection of elements, particularly the omission of an important subset, can lead us to overlook an important dimension. Second, the dimensions must be labeled! Typically, this is done by having the (same or other) subjects rate each disease label on a large number of rating scales and examine the correlation of the ratings with the MDS dimensions. The procedure has all the virtues and faults of factor analysis: We must now suggest attributes for ratings and face the problem that several scales will relate to each dimensions. Thus, the dimension names are somewhat arbitrary, as is our understanding of them.

Third, MDS is merely a procedure, and the context (subjects, whether they are ill or well, the instructions) under which it is conducted can influence the solutions. For example, we found that changes in the instructions altered the dimensions. In one instance we asked subjects to compare the diseases with respect to symptoms and found a robust first dimension that was different from that generated under other instructions and that could *not* be labeled (Penrod et al., 1982a; 1982b). We also found that older respondents had great difficulty with the procedure. It seemed that the mathematical model underlying the procedure—diseases lie in a continuous space defined by similarity—did not mesh with the model in the minds of our respondents: They saw illnesses as either the same or different and unique points! Thus, they made graded judgments for only a small number of the comparisions.

Finally, the procedure is extremely time-consuming, making it virtually impossible to assess other variables. This latter problem made the technique virtually unusable in our clinical settings. Using college students, however, we were able to generate MDS solutions that generated virtually the same basic dimensions found with open-ended interviewing in our patient samples (Linz et al., 1982). The dimensions were that of cause (external infections versus internal change), duration of time line (acute versus chronic conditions), and severity or consequences. The identity factor, labels and symptoms, could not emerge as a dimension since they were represented in the elements that comprised the space. Although it is satisfying to note that MDS did yield similar dimensions, its practical limitations and the nature of its product, a set of potential dimensions but *no* instrument for their more rapid assessment, suggest a technique of highly limited utility.

4. *The Focused Hunch.*   We decided to initiate our work on the basis of a focused hunch, that is, a simple hypothesis that could serve as an entry point to the study of commonsense models of illness. The hypothesis was that individuals would feel motivated to engage in health-protective actions when they noticed concrete body symptoms or sensations that could be interpreted as warning signs of future or current disease threats (Leventhal, 1975). There were two sets of factors that led to this hypothesis. One was clinical observation of the type discussed earlier; the other was data from our laboratory studies on the reduction of pain distress through sensation monitoring (Johnson, 1975; Leventhal & Johnson, 1983). The clinical observations were introduced by several members of our research team (e.g., Jean Johnson, Elaine Leventhal, Tom Jackson) who were persuaded that patients placed substantial emphasis on symptomatology. Indeed, the medical encounter typically focuses on the exchange of information about body sensations or signs and symptoms.

Data from our laboratory represented the second influence. We had found that providing subjects with information about the concrete sensations they would experience during noxious stimulation (Johnson, 1975; Leventhal et al., 1979) and noxious medical procedures (Johnson and Leventhal, 1974) facilitated their adaptation to these procedures and led to substantial reductions in reported distress, even though the participants did not necessarily think the procedures were helpful (Ahles et al., 1983). These observations led us to focus on the symptomatic aspect of illness representations and to formulate the hypothesis that the concrete component of illness representations, that is, their symptoms and signs, may play a very important role in affecting emotional reactions and behavior in contrast to relatively abstract messages warning of potential harm.

Designing the Investigation.   Having chosen a focus, that is, the role of bodily sensations and symptoms in generating the representation that guides coping behavior, we were faced with the vast range of issues of designing a study. How could we obtain data to show that symptoms and sensations play a key role in generating a representation of an illness? What types of coping behaviors could we observe that would reflect the representation? Who should we observe, and when should we make observations to obtain data on the workings of commonsense models of illness?

Each of these questions subsumes many other questions, and students new to the study of illness cognition will spend much time making a multitude of decisions that they have neither faced nor heard of during their past professional education. For better or worse, many of these decisions are made for us, as circumstances often dictate whom we will study and how to go about it. Although decisions forced by circumstances are often less than optimal, they are less stressful since they do not require excessive cogitation (see Janis, 1982a).

Subject Selection.   Selection of subjects in the study of illness cognition means much more than simply choosing to study old or young people, students or lawyers, and so forth: It means selecting a disease or illness. This is an extremely important step, because each illness and its treatment has its characteristic "natural history" which may vary by patient subgroups. Let us examine each of these two issues in turn.

1. *The Disease and Its Attributes.*   Diseases vary with respect to their initiating agent, the period of incubation or promotion, the way they manifest clinically (specific types of signs and symptoms), their duration, likelihood of cure and of recurrence, as well as their possible postillness disabilities that can last for different periods of time. Choosing a disease, therefore, means making one or more illness attributes salient at the potential expense of others. The issue is very similar to that of "known groups" methodology where the investigator compares neurotics to normals, or salespersons to secretaries, to obtain data relevant to the way anxiety or extroversions-introversion contributes to performance (Eysenck, 1970).

The first two populations we chose for study were hypertensives and cancer patients. The selection meant that we had groups differing in the severity of disease—cancer patients are, as a rule, substantially more ill than patients who are in treatment in primary care clinics for hypertension—and groups differing in the degree to which the diseases were symptomatic. Thus, two of our key attributes, consequences and identity, differed across these populations, and we could see if their illness representations differed drastically and/or if some attributes of illness cognition were important regardless of the nature of the disease.

Hypertension is especially interesting since it is presumably an asymptomatic condition: Virtually no studies show consistent association between the disorder and symptoms, whether this is measured on a between-subject or a within-subject basis (see Pennebaker, 1982; Baumann & Leventhal, in press). Would patients with this disorder report symptoms? If the answer to this question was yes, it would be powerful evidence for the operation of an underlying illness schema in which the identity of illness is both abstract (the label, hypertension) and concrete (the symptom of blood pressure). By contrast, about half the first sample of cancer patients that we studied (Leventhal, et al., 1984) were highly symptomatic: They had disseminated breast cancer.

2. *Categories of Patients Within Disease Groupings.*   No category of patients is homogeneous: Hypertension and hypertensives vary in the causes and nature of their disease and its treatment history; cancer patients may have different types of cancer and different prognoses. These differences pose the second major challenge of design. Should they be allowed to vary freely, introducing a host of unknown sources of variance into our data? Should they be strictly controlled by studying only one type of hypertensive or one type of cancer or patients with a common history? Or, can we take advantage of the variety and use it to introduce "controlled variation" on one or another important aspect of commonsense models and representations of illness?

We have always tried to use the third approach in our study designs. In both the hypertensive and cancer studies we could identify and isolate natural subgroups whose history would lead to alternate ways of perceiving the illness, its course, and its treatment. These subgroups were often based upon differences in history, that is, where the patients were with respect to the course of the disease. For example, in our studies of hypertension, we divided our subjects into those *new* to treatment; those who entered treatment at least 6 months in the past and *continued* in treatment; and those who had entered treatment, dropped for more than 6 months, and *reentered* treatment for any number of reasons. Comparisons among the *newly* treated, *continuing* treated, and *reentry* groups were expected to show differences in the representation of the disease—those new to treatment would be less socialized to the medical system and less likely to hold a symptomatic view and more likely to expect a cure; those who continued would be more accepting of the chronic nature of the disease and the need for continued treatment (Meyer et al., in press). The reentry group should have been least likely to hold to a medically accepted definition of the disease. The groups served, therefore, as a means of validating the basic measures of the representation of the disease.

The cancer patients were divided on different lines. We studied women with breast cancer and men and women with lymphoma. Our breast cancer samples were further divided into those in treatment for metastatic disease and those receiving chemotherapy as an adjunct to successful surgery.

These groups permitted a variety of contrasts: The lymphoma patient is more likely to view the disease as *acute* or *cyclic* (i.e., as susceptible to cure); the breast patient, particularly the metastatic patient, is more likely to view the disease as *chronic*. The three groups also differ in the availability of signs and symptoms to identify or define their condition and to monitor the effectiveness of treatment: Approximately two thirds of the lymphoma patients have palpable (cancerous) lymph nodes that permit direct monitoring of the disease. The metastatic treatment patients are also likely to have signs and symptoms of disease, whereas the adjuvant patients are free of detectable cancer. Thus, the informational base for the disease differs across groups as do the expectations they bring to treatment.

Identifying group differences is critical to the conduct of a field study, because many of the processes and hypotheses under test involve variables that cannot be directly measured. We cannot directly measure the differences in the automatic processing of symptoms by adjuvant and metastatic treatment patients, since these processes occur instantly upon perception of symptoms or side effects of treatment. However, we can expect the groups to differ in the way they perceive the signs and symptoms of breast cancer and its treatment, for the two groups of patients bring very different expectations to treatment—the adjuvant expecting "cures" and a prolonged cancer-free existence; the metastatic hoping at best for the disease to be checked.

Using "naturally" appearing groups to validate various measures of illness representation greatly enhances the power of illness cognition studies: It introduces a form of natural experimentation into what is otherwise a descriptive process. The procedure is common to epidemiologic research (Lilienfeld & Lilienfeld, 1980), but it is encumbent upon investigators to demonstrate the validity of their groupings by direct assessment of some of the attitudes and beliefs presumed to differentiate these groups and to affect their commonsense models (representations, coping strategies, and appraisals of outcomes) of illness.

Mapping the Study.   Perhaps the most critical step in the design process is developing a (series of) flowchart(s) to depict the basic independent and dependent variables under study and to spell out the various intervening variables and pathways by which they are presumed to operate. Although this step is the *most basic* in study design and would precede that of subject selection in an investigation that was purely theory driven, our reality was that subject selection came first: This is likely to be the case with most studies, particularly when the behavioral investigator is new to a problem area and is working with a medical collaborator whose specific interests play a major role in the selection of a population.

The study map reflects both the investigator's theory and the features of the disease and patient population under study. For example, our study map of the breast cancer cases was drawn in two sections, one for metastatic treatment cases and one for adjuvant treatment cases. The map began with the disease, its symptoms, the treatment, the side effects of the drugs, the interpretations that may be given these side effects, the coping responses that they might stimulate, the possible outcomes of coping and their appraisals, and the resultant experience of emotional distress about treatment, about cancer, and disruptions in daily activities.

The map defines the set of variables to be measured. It also defines the key dependent variables and the potential confounds. Reality has taught us that the investigator can never exhaust the map. Each new study informs us of an as yet unassessed variable, often a suspected confound that may be responsible for the relationships we have attributed to some "more interesting" psychological process but that now seems explainable by some "trivial" but potentially impactful aspect of the disease or treatment. The map also defines the analysis. It does so at several levels, including suggestions for scale construction (what items to include in a factor analysis), as well as the more laborious task of defining causal pathways for computing regression models. The map makes a critical contribution to the latter step, as it points to potential nonlinear relationships, which may require transformations of key variables or the use of dummy variables, and it points to possible interactions, which need to be entered as terms in the regression model.

Finally, the map provides the basic framework for the construction and initial evaluation of items. Both the novice and expert may find it easier to imagine themselves in an interview setting to begin item construction. But investigators cannot develop a reasonable set of items (or a study) in this way. The items must tap the concepts in the map as well as other things likely to be reported by the respondent. And, each concept should be given a reasonable chance; that is, the questions or scales used to measure different variables, independent, dependent, and mediating, should be equally reliable and valid. If they are not, differences in the strength of association between predictors and criteria may reflect differences in scale reliability of the predictors rather than differences in the psychological processes. Thus, no interview can be constructed or evaluated without disassembling it and classifying its items (and codes) in the appropriate "boxes" of the map.

Developing the Instruments

With a map in hand, the investigator is ready to develop instruments to assess his or her constructs. But, should items be written to measure the independent variables, the mediators, or the dependent measures? Enthusiasm for the investigator's theory would likely encourage him or her to begin with independent variables and various mediators, but we believe this is in error. It is best to start with dependent measures. Unfortunately, we have not always followed this sound advice. Beginning with dependent measures is wise in that it provides us with the opportunity to review carefully what we are trying to predict! Thus, first we turn to the properties of the

criterion and the situational events immediately surrounding and controlling it.

The Dependent Variables.   There are at least four reasons to start with
the dependent variable, and a discussion of each follows.

1. *Selecting the Appropriate Response Attribute.*   There are many attributes
that can be abstracted from a behavior (Nunnally, 1978). Each may reveal
different properties of the behavior and be relevant to different theoretical
and practical issues. Consider for a moment the main criterion in our
hypertension studies, medication compliance. Apart from the many ways
we might obtain compliance data, for example, from blood levels of medication, through pill counts, to verbal reports (Dunbar, 1980), we were faced
with deciding whether to determine if patients took all, only some, or none of
their medication, and if they did miss their medication, was it only rarely, or
frequently. More important, we needed to know if they were missing
according to some pattern. If the behavior is regulated by the patient's
representation of the disorder, it is possible that medication taking will show
specific patterns that could be detected by some indicators, but not others.
For example, one woman in our first study reported taking her medication
when her legs were swollen during her menstrual period. She used "water
pills (Diazides) only at that time. But, she used twice the recommended
dosage when taking the pills and always needed refills at the recommended
time. Had our measure been a pill count at the pharmacy (a presumably
"hard" measure in comparison to "soft" verbal report), we would have
never detected this pattern of pill usage. A self-regulation model demanded
that we assess patterns until experience proved it unnecessary to do so.

Other important properties of the response are its duration and threshold
effects. Some dependent measures are extended over time, whereas others
are not. Use of antihypertension medication is typically a life-long affair and
measures of compliance must be spread over a sufficiently long time to
evaluate whether usage is indeed long term. Our second study (Steele et al.,
1984) examined medication usage over a 9-month treatment period and also
used a 6-month delayed follow-up. The final measures were taken, therefore, fully 17 months after exposure to the compliance intervention which
was run in the first and second months of the study. Long-term follow-ups
place severe restrictions on the investigator, since it takes time, effort, and
money to keep a sample intact. Moreover, when studying the determinants
of a long-lasting behavior, we can surmise that the maintenance of the action
may depend upon a multitude of factors external to the treatment and
investigative setting. This may lead us to rethink the map and ask whether
we have considered all the appropriate independent and mediating factors
or given short shrift to a variety of aspects of the social context, such as
whether the patient is single or married, in an intact household with adequate resources and supports, or in a socially disintegrated or disintegrating
situation.

Our cancer studies posed quite a different set of problems for measuring medication usage. Although treatment lasts for several months (or even 1 to 2 years), it typically ends in a finite period of time for the adjuvant cases and is discontinued for metastatic treatment patients if they do not show improvement. Compliance to cancer chemotherapy is, therefore, largely under the control of the treatment system: The patient is on a protocol calling for a certain number of drugs at specified dosages, and the social pressures and threat of death are sufficiently strong to ensure very high rates of compliance—indicators such as discontinuing treatment or partial use of at home medication were of no use. The only indicators we could obtain were reports in the medical records as to whether the patient was receiving only part of the medication prescribed by the original treatment regimen. These measures, then, had to be qualified by ascertaining the reasons for medication reduction to be sure the decision to reduce was under the control of the patient and not due to medical complications. Such reasons were hard to verify, since we did not actually observe and/or record these negotiations in encounters between the patient and the oncologist.

2. *Alternative Modes of Assessment.* As the compliance discussion suggests, alternative modes of assessment may be found for the same variable, such as self-reports in interview, medical records, interviews and ratings from physicians and/or nurses, and similar ratings from interviewers and study team members. Not surprisingly, alternative measures are not always highly correlated. The lack of association may reflect the fact that different variables affect different measures. The threshold issue mentioned in the prior section is one example. In our second study of compliance with hypertension medication, our independent variables (e.g., symptom monitoring) predicted compliance as measured by verbal report. Unfortunately, however, we noticed that, unlike our first study, symptom monitoring did not predict blood pressure control. Before rejecting our data as invalid, our medical collaborator pointed out that we could not find associations of monitoring with blood pressure since nearly all the patients were taking over 80 percent of their medication, a threshold of compliance above which we are unlikely to see blood pressure variation. The high levels of reported compliance and the high levels of blood pressure control created a ceiling effect, preventing us from seeing an effect of monitoring on blood pressure.

It is clearly advantageous to have access to a variety of measures to establish a valid criterion. Aside from the threshold problem discussed earlier, which was only a problem in a sample with very good compliance, *both* an objective indicator of pressure and a good self-report measure provide a superior index of the behavioral criteria than either one alone. In our cancer studies, we faced a somewhat different set of issues. One key dependent measure was the amount of distress and life disruption caused by treatment. What alternative methods could we find for assessing distress and disruption? An obvious technique was ratings by our interviewers, who had contact with the patient for 1 to 2 hours and could assess the degree to which the patient was distressed about the treatment and the cancer. But, these interviewer ratings, or similar ratings made by nurses, doctors, and family members, were dependent upon observations of many similar behaviors that patients would include in self-reports. Thus, if a patient complained of nausea and vomiting and protested about the inability to manage daily tasks, the complaints and protest would very likely affect the interviewer or staff assessments. Unless the rater is specifically instructed to use behavioral indicators that are not part of the patient's self-reporting system, the ratings will not provide a truly independent assessment.

We have adopted three strategies to obtain an effective measure of distress in our studies of cancer patients. First, we have used self-report ratings that require differentiating between distress and upset over cancer and distress and upset over chemotherapy. This seemingly small addition is important because the patient has to consider the meaning and sources of distress in greater detail. Empirically, different variables predict distress in the two types of measure. Second, we have used interviewer and staff ratings (the latter only occasionally) as a partially independent source of evidence of adjustment of our patients to treatment. Third, we have taken self-reports on different schedules: Ratings of distress and disruption due to treatment at each monthly chemotherapy treatment and ratings of moods on diaries completed day by day in each treatment cycle. Correspondence between day by day ratings and monthly ratings will increase our confidence that we have an adequate measure of distress and disruption of daily activities due to chemotherapy.

3. *Alternative Criteria.*   Beginning with dependent variables in operationalizing the map provides the opportunity to consider alternative criteria. Practical, that is, real world questions, are typically vague: For example, "How do people adjust to cancer or cancer chemotherapy?" "Can we get people to take medications to control their blood pressure?" Terms such as *adjustment* and phrases such as *control their blood pressure* seem simple, but they encompass a wide range of potential behavioral criteria. Adjustment could mean not becoming emotionally upset, being able to continue everyday activities, maintaining closeness with family and friends, quitting a bad job, and so forth. Controlling blood pressure could mean taking medication, losing weight, quitting smoking, and making a variety of dietary and life situation changes. Some of these changes might prove as effective as medication in reducing blood pressure and are potentially important criteria. However, their effectiveness (and value as an intervention outcome measure) will depend upon the initial values of these alternative factors and the history of the disease.

For example, weight loss could be an important behavioral criterion since it can lower blood pressure, but only in obese subjects! Failure to define the subgroup in which weight loss is relevant would do little more than create confusion, because the two criteria—weight loss and blood pressure—would be poorly related in a heterogeneous group of hypertensives. Similarly, changes in life-style for stress reduction would more likely relate to changes in blood pressure for subjects early in the disease history, that is, in the dynamic stage. Patients with stable elevations may be less responsive to these changes (Steptoe, 1983). It should be emphasized that all the additions, substitutions, and subtractions (Hayes-Bautista, 1976) made by patients to "treat" a disorder are legitimate and important to study: If we know a patient has lost weight and quit smoking, it may help explain why he or she is "failing" to take medication as prescribed. Moreover, it is important to make these assessments regardless of the patient's weight or history of disease so as to understand the patient's commonsense model of disease and treatment.

The patient's commonsense model need not recognize the conditions limiting the effectiveness of self-treatment; it is the investigator who must define subgroups of patients to detect the impact of behavioral change on disease outcome.

As mentioned earlier, our first hypertension study focused upon medication taking and ignored a host of alternative criterion variables such as quitting smoking and changing diet to reduce salt intake or lose weight. Our results showed that variables such as perceived control over the causes of the disease had absolutely no effect on medication compliance (Silver & Wortman, 1980). These independent variables did, however, predict compliance to quitting smoking, salt reduction, weight control, and so on, which were included as measures in our second study. Factors more clearly under the control of the subject were indeed changed when the subject perceived these variables as causal. Our patients seemed quite reasonable: What was unreasonable about our initial effort was failure to consider the range of measures that a person might take to deal with a disease. In short, our investigative commonsense did not match the commonsense of our subjects!

4. *Biases in Questioning.* The nuts and bolts of question writing have been covered in numerous informative volumes and articles, for example, Cannell, et al. (1977), Bradburn, Sudman, and associates (1979), Gallup (1978), Kahn and Cannell (1957), Sudman and Bradburn (1982), which the reader should consult. We will focus here on a few issues we encountered in asking questions about dependent measures in our two studies.

a. *Good respondent bias.* No more fatal way can be used to ask about medication compliance than a direct question such as, "Do you take your hypertension medication?" Although many respondents will undoubtedly respond honestly and report misses, even the honest respondent who has missed on several occasions is likely to say yes as he or she *does* take (at least some) of his or her medication. In opening questions on this topic, our strategy has been to communicate that we expect people to be less than perfect compliers. Indeed, we even expect them to experiment with their medication taking! Our opening item might be, "Many people miss their medications from time to time. Does this ever happen to you? When? How much do you miss?"

An item to probe the pattern of misses might begin, "A professor I know told me he varied his medication to see how little he really needed. Have you ever done anything like that? When did you do it? For how long? What did you decide was best?"

The approach, therefore, recognized misses; in the first instance, a more or less random pattern and in the second a deliberate pattern to evaluate the effects of self-prescribing. The problems with assessing compliance with cancer chemotherapy medication were vastly different since people simply did not miss medications. Our questions focused, therefore, on whether people ever wished they could quit or if they intended to quit and when and why? The data, however, proved of limited value.

b. *Temporal biases.* The measurement of emotional distress and disruption due to cancer chemotherapy seemed simpler, at least initially. We devised items such as "How much distress did you feel from the chemotherapy during the past cycle?" A 10-point scale accompanied this and similar items. We soon discovered, however, that our respondents had a problem in selecting a referent for the item. A treatment cycle lasts 4 weeks. Did our question refer to the average for the 4-week period, the average for the 2 weeks on medication, the average for the 2 days when injections were given, or the worst period during those days? Despite these ambiguities, people answered the questions and the answers seemed orderly: They changed over time and related in meaningful ways to predictors. Our diary data showed, however, very substantial fluctuations in negative emotional reactions from day to day, with distress being high on days of injection and tapering off in the days following. We have decided, thus, to modify our question strategy and to ask about the *worst* distress level (presumably tapping that experience the day of the injection), the number of "bad" days, (presumably the 3 or 4 days postinjection when there is still emotional upset), and the average upset during those worst days. Although many decisions are still left to the patient (e.g., what is a bad day, how many were bad), this more differentiated set of items to measure both distress and life disruption from chemotheapy should provide still more useful information than do single items. The issue of the referent of questions and the time span referred to appears in many other areas; one good example is the measurement of life satisfaction.

To someone inexperienced with research in the medical setting, attention to so many details in question asking may seem to border on the trivial; why not ask all the questions and see which work best? Unfortunately, access to patients is difficult and patient time is scarce. The investigator has to get as much information as possible in the least possible time with the least possible upset to the respondent. After all, the patient's primary goal is to complete treatment, not to complete your study. It is critical, therefore, to use the minimum number of items to get the most information and the most essential information in as little time as possible. One value in meeting this goal is that it ensures that items are worded so as to mesh better with the patient's experience: They are, then, easy to answer! The demand is yet more severe when the investigator is operating with a multivariate map and has many variables to assess.

Independent and Mediating Variables.   Although we should typically begin with measure of the dependent variable(s), we must be careful not to devote all our time and effort to its assessment at the expense of our independent and mediating variables. One area in which this has happened is in the assessment of smoking and other so-called addictive behaviors (NIDA Report, 1978; 1981). The goal of this care and attention is often to increase the reliability of the measure rather than to find out something in particular about the pattern or development of the behavior. Increased reliability is seen as important for testing hypotheses.

Although a more reliable criterion provides some insurance against a nonsignificant probability test, achieving it at the expense of the reliability of the predictor (independent and mediating) variables can be most unfortunate, because unreliability in the predictor side of the equation will reduce estimated beta weights in addition to affecting the value of the significance tests (Pedhazur, 1982). A less reliable criterion does not affect the estimated size of the relationships between it and the predictors. There is a definite disadvantage, therefore, in trying to locate predictors and determine their relative importance (for which the size of the beta weights is important) and leaving too little interview time for adequate assessment of a set of multiple predictors.

We have no special nostrums to offer to resolve this problem. The single most important, and the most painful, to the investigator (and the one seemingly least appreciated by journal editors), is to conduct repeated investigations, moving from a broad map of the domain to successively more focused and refined pictures of specific subsets of variables. The problem here, however, is that a clear picture of the relationship between a specific subset of factors and a criterion may require measuring a substantial number of moderating and contextual factors to be sure simply that the investigator is in the "right place" (appropriate subsample at the appropriate phase of illness and treatment) in the system of variables to see the specific relationships under study. In short, it may take a substantial number of items to measure the conditions limiting a relationship.

1. *Assessing the Representation.* The assessment of illness cognition requires developing items to measure the attributes of the representation, coping, and the appraisal of coping outcomes. We have used various types of questions to assess the attributes of illness representation, and our experience in measuring the symptomatic and temporal aspects will probably be of

greatest interest, although we will comment briefly on the assessment of consequences and causes.

In our first study (Meyer et al., in press) of hypertensive patients, we allowed the patient to define the attributes he or she used to determine if blood pressure was elevated: Hence we used an open-ended approach. But we began our questioning with a very direct agree-disagree item, asking patients if they agreed that, "People can't tell if their blood pressure is elevated?" Of the respondents in the study, 80 percent agreed that people could not tell, and in response to the item that followed (What about you? Can you tell when your blood pressure is high?"), fully 88 percent of continuing treatment patients responded, "Yes," they could tell. We then asked, "How can you tell?" and obtained a list of symptoms and signs such as headache, face flushed, heart beat, and so on that seem to characterize the symptoms reported by people thinking they have elevated blood pressure.

Our juxtaposition of a closed and open question producing two such discrepant replies was fortunate, since it persuaded us that patients must truly believe they can use symptoms to monitor variations in blood pressure. Our aim was to allow the patients to define the representation rather than suggesting specific attributes for them to respond to. We have also used an open-ended approach in asking patients how they monitor the progress of cancer chemotherapy treatment.

The open-ended approach to questions seems to be preferred for addressing patient perception because it appears to avoid suggesting attributes that may be of interest to the investigator but are of little concern to the patient. In our judgment, this type of question is to be recommended at the opening phases of study when we would not know what signs or symptoms to ask about or use for a self-report checklist. There is reason to doubt, however, that it is an adequate resolution to the problem of getting at the patient's representation rather than that of the investigator. Although the patient's response is clearly still his or hers, it is also the response of the moment or the most available reply that is stimulated by the question. Thus, the probe, "How can you tell" might be more likely to key symptom responses than is some other way of asking, such as, "How could your wife tell if your blood pressure was elevated?" The latter would likely evoke responses suggesting that overt behaviors are signs of hypertension. (Robinson, 1971). There is little we can do about such biases other than to use alternative approaches (if there is time) to evaluate the salience or availability of the response, independent of the specific question content.

It is also important to remember that the most salient or available response at the moment is not necessarily representative of the most available response at other moments. If the patient has just completed an encounter with the physician and been asked about symptoms, he or she might be strongly biased to discuss symptoms. Not all attributes important in controlling behavior will be salient at a given instance and some attributes may be difficult to report on because they are implicit and have never been consciously considered. For example, assessing the temporal aspects of the representation has proven extremely difficult. The first problem is that time is an element of all the attributes: The disease has a duration, its symptoms have duration, the causes have duration, the consequences have duration, as does the treatment and the process of rehabilitation. Patients may not recognize which of these items is being addressed in a time question, and/or if they do recognize which item, they may never have thought about this issue or realized they had implicit thoughts about it.

The preceding issues and their deeper meaning did not become clear to us until we moved from very general open questions, which dominated our early studies and pilot interviewing, to more specific ways of directly assessing representation attributes. We found, for example, that checklists of symptoms and signs were quite adequate for detecting the identity attribute for patients with hypertension or cancer. Responses to open and checklist items were reasonably well correlated ($r = .50$ and above). Although the checklists elicited more responding, the relative proportion of checks for specific symptoms did not differ from that observed in the open-ended items, and the two types of questions related in the same way to other variables, including the important criterion of medication compliance (symptom-monitoring patients are less likely to be compliant).

More direct probing of the temporal factors created more difficulties, however. We attempted to assess temporal ideas through direct questions, scales using hours and days as response terms, and bar graphs, where the subject marked the elevation of blood pressure on a chart that used a separate bar for each day, beginning with the day when the patient first began to take (or stopped taking) medication. It became clear, first, that many patients had not explicitly thought about the time it took for them to become hypertensive, the time it took for the medications to be effective, and the time it would take for their blood pressure to rise if they stopped taking medication. It was also apparent, however, that they had many implicit beliefs that they did not wish to make explicit because the implications of these beliefs were often unpleasant! Patients did not care to acknowledge that their blood pressure would rise as soon as they stopped medication, nor did they care to acknowledge that it may have taken them some time to become hypertensive (implying that they had been unable to tell that their pressures were elevated and had been untreated and "at risk" for an unknown and possibly very long time). Indeed, some of the methods we were using for assessment might be better employed as components in an intervention designed to alter rather than to assess cognitions.

2. *Assessing Coping and Evaluation.*   We can readily distinguish two contrasting approaches to the assessment of coping and evaluation of coping outcomes: (1) a testing-oriented approach and (2) a situationally oriented assessment. Testing approaches begin with specific coping strategies in mind and prepare items to assess each one. For example, Lazarus and his

associates (Lazarus, 1966; DeLongis, et al., 1982), Billings and Moos (1981; 1982; 1984), and Pearlin and his associates (1981; Pearlin & Schooler, 1978) have used checklists designed to assess specific types of coping processes, including problem-oriented processes such as information gathering, direct manipulation of situational factors, and a variety of so-called cognitive and emotionally focused coping strategies (such as reinterpretation of the meaning of situations, discharge of emotion, etc.), designed to alter the individual's internal appraisal system and emotional state. The scales devised to assess these factors can vary in length from as few as 4 or 5 items (typical of the Pearlin et al. studies) to 20 or even more items (typical of many of the Lazarus studies).

Such scales can be effective if they indeed define and exhaust the major forms of coping used to deal with specific problems. However, if the scales overlook the key responses, the picture they present will be distorted. Even if no specific category of coping is overlooked, the scales do not give a highly specific picture of the coping *process*, since the items are necessarily written to be general. Thus, we may find that people "search for information" and "attempt to directly manipulate" their relationships with children while learning nothing about precisely what actions they have been taking.

Both to avoid overlooking specific coping tactics and to obtain information on the specific ways patients coped with particular aspects of their illness and treatments, we followed a strategy more similar to that advocated by the behaviorally oriented investigators (Goldfried & D'Zurilla, 1969; Meichenbaum & Turk, 1976; Turk et al., 1980) and asked, specifically, what people did to deal with treatment and illness problems and then asked how they evaluated the outcomes of these coping responses. For example, our cancer patients were asked the following sequence of questions: (1) "Have you had any problems with (list of specific side effects reported by patients in prior study)?" (2) For each item responded to positively, "When did it start?" (3) "How long did it last?" (4) "When (the specific side effect) happened, did you try to do anything about it?" (5) (If yes) "What did you do?" (6) "Did that help?" (7) "When you try to control the side effects, do you expect to make the side effects: (list read to patients) Go away completely—to—Or, do you do it, even though you don't think it will work?"

This specific set of questions allowed us to identify precisely what people did for each disturbing aspect of chemotherapy and to evaluate its effectiveness. Such data have two major advantages over that provided by the scale approach. First, they provide an exhaustive listing of the things that people actually do to control a specific problem and allow us to see differences in the specific actions performed to handle problems with different attributes. In short, they let us see if the "same" score for a type of coping, for example, emotional coping, problem coping, information collection, and so on, is truly the same. Second, they provide a specific set of suggestions for coping interventions targeted to specific problems with specific expectations for success and failure.

This second way of assessing coping removes some of the aura of "romance" from the study of coping. Rather than leading to generalized statements that people make internal adjustments to specific classes of situation, for instance, they readjust their expectations and detach with age, or they focus on emotion coping to deal with illness (Folkman & Lazarus, 1980), we find that *people do very mundane things* because the situations they confront give every appearance of constraining their behavior in fairly simple and direct ways. If we feel tired, we rest. If we feel nauseous, we drink something. If that does not work, we do something else. If none of these work, we just wait for things to improve.

In our judgment, a much truer picture of adaptation to cancer treatment arises from the preceding, rather banal sequence of coping responses used to deal with the rather specific and banal aspects of cancer treatment such as nausea and tiredness, than the picture derived from the more abstract statements generated by "coping scales." More importantly, the rather mundane picture shows the close connection between coping and representation, giving us insight into why coping failures do *not* lead to horrendous outcomes such as learned helplessness, long-lasting aggressive reactance, and so forth (Silver & Wortman, 1980). The horrors anticipated by some theories of coping fail to materialize because the coping sequence is indeed *episodic*, and tuned to the demands of the treatment at that moment.

Of course, coping is nested in a larger context of illness and treatment expectations and these generic contextual factors (the longer term outlook for the treatment and disease), along with contextual factors that are intermediate in nature (the fact that episodes of nausea do clear up, the fact that treatment will stop), do affect the meaning of coping. For example, for many patients, later episodes in treatment will likely be improvements over early ones. We can see, therefore, how more generalized attitudes of hope arise from the sequence of specific experiences with treatment and how hope can be dashed by the occurrence of unexpected and unwanted setbacks that make clear the disease is taking over and threatening the individual's existence (Taylor, 1983).

Structuring the Interview.   We have covered mapping and assessment of the basic components of commonsense illness models (representation, coping, and appraisal) with respect to the earliest phase of research, the initiation of a new investigation. The final topic to be discussed in this section involves putting the interview together, the final step prior to pilot testing and revision.

As already mentioned, there are two starting points for writing interview items: (1) sitting down and imagining what it would be like to ask a patient questions about his or her illness and (2) a taking the map of the problem variables and writing questions to fit each of its conceptual "boxes." Effective questionnaire construction requires both perspectives, since the investigator moves back and forth from one to the other with two products emerging: (1) An interview ready for use and (2) a chart with the items nested under each of the concepts. The chart allows a visual examination of (a) the number of items per concept; (b) the overlap in items by concept— this raises key questions about the independence of the concepts; and (c) the overlap in the codes—if the items are similar, or not distinguishable, there should be different codes, meaning different aspects of behavior are being measured under each item.

Once the questionnaire has been fully charted and assembled for active use, it is time to examine its overall structure and ask questions such as,

1. Do the first items fit the patient's expectations? The interview should open so as to confirm the patient's expectation that he or she is participating in a study of how people view and adapt to their illness and its treatment.

2. Are the first items relatively direct and easy to answer? It seems wise to begin with questions that are readily answerable to avoid discouraging the respondent. Questions can become more difficult, with appropriate explanation that not all the items will be easy to answer or that the patient's opinion is being sought. We have found questions on the representation of the disease to be easy to answer and nonthreatening.

3. Does the interview flow smoothly? A good interview should be highly specific and focused, yet, it should flow more or less like a conversation.

4. Are the separate sections distinctly defined to avoid contamination from one to the other? We have found it important to demarcate clearly certain topics from the rest of the interview. The items on compliance are often placed toward the end of the interview and preceded by an introduction to mark the beginning of a new section. For example, the interviewer introduced the items on willingness to comply with cancer chemotherapy with the following statement: "I'd like to ask you some questions about your feelings about chemotherapy." A somewhat longer statement was used to set off the compliance items in the hypertension work. Setting off a section has several signficant functions. One is to make clear the importance of the questions. Also, it breaks off the thought and avoids suggestions that answers to the prior section are relevant to the current topic. We do not wish to suggest to patients that using symptoms or having acute time lines affects their coping; we want to analyze associations between the two sets of factors measured as independently as possible.

STUDIES TO CONFIRM RELATIONSHIPS

Our discussion of mapping, assessment of criterion or dependent measures, and various independent and mediating variables that make up the commonsense model of illness, and the assembly of the interviews, was aimed at the initial stage of investigation, when relatively little is known about the problem area and investigations are exploratory in character. A number of changes occur as we move to *confirmatory* studies where replication and hypothesis testing are of primary importance along with testing and rejecting potential causal hypotheses from among a set of alternatives. These will include changes in measurement tools, typically moving to more refined measures; increased specification of the conditions needed to obtain specific effects, and changes in experimental design, including movement toward longitudinal and experimental investigations. All these changes assume increased precision in theory and increasingly precise specification of the study map. We discuss each of these issues briefly beginning with the last, increased precision in theory.

Increased Precision in Theory

Although the study of commonsense models of illness began as an attempt to perceive illness and treatment as the patient would see it, there is as yet no limit in sight regarding the degree to which the approach can be further differentiated and made increasingly precise. We can specify three ways in which we are attempting to increase the precision of our theoretical analysis. First, we can try to confirm relationships between the variables we have defined in our initial studies. An example here is our effort to replicate the relationship found with hypertensive patients between symptom monitoring and failure to comply with medical conditions, using patients with diabetes (Espenshade, 1984). We are also examining whether the temporal perceptions of cancer, for example, its perception as an acute (short-lasting and curable), cyclic (treatable but likely to recur), or chronic condition relate to worry and depressive feelings about the disease. In addition, we are seeking to confirm the finding that distress during chemotherapy treatment is increased by unsuccessful, active coping. More complex hypotheses can be tested involving contingent relationships between two factors and a third one. For example, do failures of active coping lead to different degrees of distress and depressive affect if failure occurs within different perceptions for the time frames (acute or chronic) of the disease? Elaborate hypotheses of this sort are unlikely to be tested in initial investigations.

A second direction for development involves the analysis of specific attributes of the commonsense illness model. For example, we have suggested that symptoms form an important part of the identity of an illness. But, are all symptoms equally significant, or are there symptoms that have a high probability of conveying a specific meaning? For example, we have found that symptoms such as tiredness and weakness are more likely to be associated with worry about cancer than more specific symptoms such as nausea and vomiting, mouth sores, or hair loss. Not that the latter symptoms are not distressing: They are! But the emotional upset they create is usually an upset about treatment and not worry about disease. We are also exploring the contribution of such vague, systemic cues to broader self-evaluations, such as feeling old.

A third type of specification involves time. Investigators studying topics such as stress and coping are convinced of the importance of conducting longitudinal investigations under the assumption that longitudinal data are more likely to give insight into causal networks. This may or may not be true. A relationship, for example, between ability to cope with side effects in a first chemotherapy cycle and distress in the sixth cycle may be evidence *against* the interpretation that failure to cope is a cause of distress if it is clear that the temporal lag between the two measures is too great for one to be a necessary consequent of the other. At the least, other variables may have to intervene in order for us to accept causation over such long time spans.

Changes in Experimental Design

As theory becomes more precise we can expect more precision in experimental design: That is, increased precision in the framework for data collection in addition to increased precision in the construction of the map used to generate a specific interview. The changes are of two types. First, as we more fully specify the variables, the relationships among them, and the time order of these relationships, we can profit from a repeat measure or longitudinal design. But, as mentioned earlier, it is important to consider the temporal relationships between variables in selecting times for assessment and deciding what factors to include at each of these observation points.

The second way of increasing the specificity of design is to conduct a randomized trial, or a true experiment in which one or more of the common sense model variables is manipulated at the outset of a treatment procedure. Experiments in the natural setting, however, are likely to combine and confound several factors in the cross-treatment comparison rather than focus on a single variable. This is particularly the case if the randomized trial is the first of a series of such trials, since the investigator's goal is to obtain a meaningful (clinically as well as statistically) effect, and not merely to evaluate the impact of a particular variable. But although a clinical experiment may lack the elegance of the laboratory study in which one or two variables are manipulated with "surgical" precision, it can compensate for this by including a composite set of assessment devices to evaluate the "causal" paths within each of the conditions studied.

For example, we have recently begun an intervention study comparing three types of preparation for cancer chemotherapy. The control condition uses a slide and tape show of the standard booklet, "Chemotherapy and

You," used for patient preparation in a large number of oncology units. Three such programs were prepared, shown before each of the first, second, and third cycle of treatment. The intermediate condition in the study specifies the problems we might encounter with particular aspects of treatment and cancer, for example, information overload, waiting at the clinic, injections, nausea, tiredness, and changes in relationships in the family, and also lists the type of coping responses patients have reported using in each of these problem areas. The third treatment uses the same material as the second but adds information designed to create a perspective for looking at oneself in relation to cancer and treatment. This is a metatheory in which the patient is urged to look at him or herself as an experimenter and to take care to define and redefine goals, to try different coping responses, to evaluate coping responses as poor or good, and to regard him or herself as a successful problem solver for discarding inadequate coping as well as accepting effective coping.

It is clear that these conditions confound multiple factors that can be uncorrelated in later studies, if the initial study shows a meaningful (clinically and theoretically) treatment effect. The map for the multivariate assessment examines whether patients actually perform the recommended responses, what they thought about and how they looked at themselves while doing so, and a variety of other factors related to the representation, coping, and appraisal of cancer and chemotherapy. If our treatment was effective for the reasons anticipated, it should produce a substantial treatment difference (the fully prepared patients being less distressed with treatment and showing generalization of effective performance to other, nontreatment areas of life), and the within-condition paths, assessed by multivariate methods, should show that changes in the perception of problems are dependent upon self-perception as an active experimenter.

Changes in Assessment

The increased precision of questions and design is accompanied by increased precision in measurement. This is of two kinds: (1) Specific scales are used to assess factors such as emotional state and self effectance. (2) Single items are used, where possible, to measure particular variables. These seemingly contradictory trends are part and parcel of improvements in measurement. It is not always an improvement to have a reliable scale and to discard items that are not coherent with the set (Nelson, 1983). Single items may in fact measure important, single aspects of illness perception and coping. Not all variables are latent: Indeed, we might argue that as knowledge increases, we would move away from using multiple indicators of latent factors toward the use of single items that directly assess theoretically critical variables. An interesting example of this has been reported in the stress literature. Collins et al. (1983) found that a single item was pivotal and did as good a job in predicting stress responses to the Three Mile Island accident as did a nearly 40-item-long denial scale! Virtually everyone who answered any of the scale items said "Yes" to the pivotal item that directly assessed denial! If the concept is clear to the respondent and assesses something directly available to his or her experience, single-scaled items may do as well or better than a set of items made vague by the need to avoid repetition of what is indeed a single, clear experience. If this sounds impossible, just think how awkward it might be to show a subject a blue patch and to ask a series of nonrepetitious questions to find out what color he or she is seeing!

Finally, as studies advance it is likely the investigator will still have to use a fairly large number of items to assess various contextual factors that define subgroups within which, or define the conditions under which, a relationship will hold between two variables of theoretical interest. Although this problem is present even at the first step of initiating studies, it may actually become more serious as the investigator looks at more and more subtle effects that can only be reproduced with highly filtered sets of subjects and contextual factors.

CONCLUSION

We have looked at the study of commonsense models of illness, describing some of the methods appropriate to the initiation of research in this domain and ending by looking at some of the changes in the research process as it moves to the replication and verification of new and more subtle hypotheses. Although our discussion treated initiation and verification as two types of study, they actually are two ends of a rather ill-defined continuum, most studies falling somewhere in between. Indeed, the requirement that research begin with a theoretical map suggests that verification is built into the study of commonsense models of illness becoming in time a rich area of cognitive research, which might then take the more theoretical title of the study of illness cognition.

Three types of changes were outlined in the movement from the initiation of research to the verification of theory: (1) greater specificity in testing hypotheses about the association between the variables; (2) the analysis of components of specific attributes within the model, such as the analysis of the identity or symptom component of the representation; (3) more precise specification of the expected relationships that would define a functional or causal relationship between variables and the development of hypotheses respecting contingent relationships, that is, variable X relating to Y only in the presence of factors A, B, and/or C.

Each increase in theoretical precision means an increase in precision in design and measurement. As in epidemiologic research, where there is a natural sequence between retrospective studies based on the method of matched cases, followed by prospective studies in increasingly well-defined subsamples of the population, followed in turn by natural experiments and clinical trials, there is a similar and equally natural progression in the study of commonsense illness models. This progression begins with cross-sectional studies and makes use of naturally appearing groups as a way of validating measures of independent variables and finding relationships between these variables and various performance criteria. The studies next move to repeated measure designs with multiple measures taken at multiple points in time. With careful attention to the temporal aspect of relationships between predictors and outcomes, such designs can give a clearer picture of causal pathways from environmental inputs to representations and from representations to coping and appraisal. The repeated measure design can also provide insight as to how the appraisal of coping feeds back to alter the environment, the representation, and subsequent coping. Finally, the investigator of illness cognition can undertake clinical trials in which a specific set of variables is manipulated with the aim of producing a clinically significant effect in patients' representations, coping, and appraisals. The investigator can then analyze the causal paths for such effects by using multiple measures and a multivariate analysis within conditions, as well as making cross-condition comparisons.

With respect to assessment itself, we placed major emphasis upon asking questions that match and, therefore, map the subjects' perceptual experience and interpretations of their illness and treatments. Questions should tap what the patients now see, hear, and do, and what they have seen, heard, and done, and not require complex inferences about what may have caused them to see and hear specific things or what in their past caused them to act the way they did. We also emphasized the value of multiple measures and multiple criteria, with due warning to avoid assuming all measures would or *should* be associated, and discussed some of the merits and demerits of scale construction versus single items well tuned to the patients' view of his or her illness. We believe that the diligent application of these methods of assessment and suggestions for design can lead to the development of a broadly based and "deep" picture of the social and cognitive processes involved in behavior during illness and add to our basic understanding of human perception, emotion, and thought.

Finally, we must note the importance of various contextual factors that both modify the relationship between variables and that may be the source of specific illness cognition variables. Mass media and books by cancer patients; the local culture of the family and the medical care system, the latter including the attitudes, preparatory communications and explanations (verbal and nonverbal) by doctors and nurses; and the availability, condition, and openness of other patients as points of comparison are the information base, along with the patient's private experience of the disease and its treatment, from which patients construct their illness representations and coping and appraisal patterns. Until we understand how such factors impact on moment-by-moment representations, coping and appraisal, we will have only a partial understanding of illness cognition. Their study requires methods that we have not discovered.

It is appropriate to end by questioning one of our earlier assumptions. How stable are the processes of illness cognition? Can we expect studying them will develop our understanding of the basic processes of the mind in the same way that neurophysiologic study can grant us insight into specific organic structures and the chemical processes that underlie perception, feelings, thought, and action? The question can be put somewhat differently: "Will the study of illness cognition evolve into an increasingly complete and accurate picture of the mind in a body and social context, or will there be revolutions in our thinking where what has been done will prove little more than reflections of an ill-conceived theory to be replaced by new data, facts, and laws that are reflections of a hopefully better conceived theory?" We can do little more than offer a guess as to the correct answer to this clash between gradualism and revolution (Kuhn, 1962). Given that illness cognition and illness representations in particular are functions of interactions among individual biology, disease agents and disease, and cultural ideas about disease and treatment, we can expect both stability and change in representations and, therefore, stability and change in coping and appraisal. The actual substance or content of representations is likely to show substantial variation across cultures and over time within cultures, although we believe the broader outlines will be stable, that is, people will respond to concrete symptoms as well as labels and will have beliefs about duration (acuteness-chronicity), causes, and consequences. Coping and appraisal may prove to be more highly culture specific, although here too there is similarity as we move from the shaman and religious healer to the modern-day biomedical wonder worker.

The greatest hope for stability may lie, however, in our picture of mental processes; that is, how the mind assembles a representation, how it puts a coping plan into place, and how it engages in appraisals that reevaluate the coping responses, the representation, or the self. The dynamics of sequential coping processes may also prove stable if we can identify the moderating conditions that structure these sequences.

There is no need, however, to answer these questions now. If the past is a useful predictor of the future (see Whiting & Child, 1953), there is reason to guess that the study of illness cognition both within and across cultures will enrich psychological science and provide as stable a view of mental process as we can hope to get.

References

Abelson, R. P. (1981). Psychological status of the script concept. *American Psychologist, 36*, 715–729.

Ahles, T. A., Blanchard, E. B., & Leventhal, H. (1983). Cognitive control of pain: Attention to the sensory aspects of the cold pressor stimulus. *Cognitive Therapy and Research, 7*, 159–178.

Atkinson, J. W. (1957). Motivational determinants of risk-taking behavior. *Psychological Review, 64*, 359–372.

Bandura, A. (1969). *Principles of behavior modification.* New York: Holt, Rinehart and Winston.

Bandura, A. (1977). Self efficacy: Toward a unifying theory of behavioral change. *Psychological Review, 84*, 191–215.

Baumann, L. J., & Leventhal, H. (In press). "I can tell when my blood pressure is up: Can't I?" *Health Psychology.*

Becker, M. H. (1974). *The health belief model and personal health behavior.* Thorofave, NJ: Slack.

Becker, M. H., Maiman, L. A., Kirscht, J. P., Haefner, D. P., & Drachman, R. H. (1977). The health belief model and prediction of dietary compliance: A field experiment. *Journal of Health and Social Behavior, 18*, 348–366.

Billings, A. G., & Moos, R. H. (1981). The role of coping responses and social resources in attenuating the stress of life events. *Journal of Behavioral Medicine, 4*, 139–157.

Billings, A. C., & Moos, R. H. (1982). Stressful life events and symptoms: A longitudinal model. *Health Psychology, 1*, 99–117.

Billings, A. G., & Moos, R. H. (1984). Coping, stress, and social resources among adults with unipolar depression. *Journal of Personality and Social Psychology, 46*, 877–891.

Bower, G. H., Black, J. B., & Turner, T. J. (1979). Scripts in memory for test. *Cognitive Psychology, 11*, 77–220.

Bradburn, N. M., Sudman, S., & Associates. (1979). *Improving Interview Method and Questionnaire Design.* San Francisco: Jossey-Boss.

Cannell, C. F., Marquis, K. H., & Laurent, A. (1977). *A Summary of Studies of Interviewing Methodology.* Vital and Health Statistics, Series 2, No. 69, Rockville, MD: National Center for Health Statistics.

Collins, D. L., Baum, A., & Singer, J. E. (1983). Coping with chronic stress at Three Mile Island: Psychological and biochemical evidence. *Health Psychology, 2*, 149–166.

De Longis, A., Coyne, J. C., Dakof, G., Folkman, S., & Lazarus, R. S. (1982). Relationship of daily hassles, uplifts and major life events to health status. *Health Psychology, 1*, 119–136.

Dishman, R. K. (1982). Compliance/adherence in health related exercise. *Health Psychology, 3*, 237–267.

Dunbar, J. M. (1980). Assessment of medication compliance: A review. In R. B. Haynes, M. E. Mattson, T. U. Engebretson Jr. (Eds.), *Patient compliance to prescribed antihypertensive medication regimens: A report to the National Heart, Lung and Blood Institute.* Bethesda, MD: U.S. Department of Health and Human Services, Public Health Service, National Institutes of Health, NIH Publication No. 81–2102.

Dunbar, J. M., & Stunkard, A. J. (1979). Adherence to diet and drug regimens. In R. Levy, B. Rifkind, B. Dennis, & N. Ernst (Eds.), *Nutrition, lipids and coronary disease.* New York: Raven Press.

Ericksson, K. A., & Simon, H. A. (1980). Verbal reports as data. *Psychological Review, 87*, 215–251.

Espenshade, J. E. (1984). Diabetics' response to evaluation for retinopathy. Unpublished master's thesis, University of Wisconsin, Madison.

Eysenck, H. J. (1970). *The structure of human personality.* London: Methuen.

Festinger, L. (1954). A theory of social comparison processes. *Human Relations, 7*, 117–140.

Folkman, S., & Lazarus, R. S. (1980). An analysis of coping in a middle aged community sample. *Journal of Health and Social Behavior, 21*, 219–239.

Gallup, G. H. (1978). *The Gallup Poll: Public Opinion, 1972–1977.* Wilmington, DE: Scholarly Resources.

Goldfried, M., & D'Zurilla, T. (1969). A behavior-analytic model for assessing competence. In

C. Spielberger (Ed.), *Current topics in clinical and community psychology*. New York: Academic Press.

Hayes-Bautista, D. E. (1976). Modifying the treatment: Patient compliance, patient control and medical care. *Social Science and Medicine, 10*, 233–238.

Hochbaum, G. M. (1958). Public participation in medical screening programs, socio-psychological study. U.S. Department of Health Education and Welfare. Public Health Service Publications No. 572.

Hunt, W. A., & Bespalec, D. A. (1974). An evaluation of current methods of modifying smoking behavior. *Journal of Clinical Psychology, 30*, 431–438.

Janis, I. L. (1958). *Psychological stress*. New York: Wiley.

Janis, I. L. (Ed). (1982a). *Counseling on personal decisions: Theory and research on short-term helping relationships*. New Haven: Yale University Press.

Janis, I. L. (1982b). *Stress attitudes and decisions*. New York: Praeger Prints.

Johnson, J. E. (1975). Stress reduction through sensation information. In I. C. Sarason & C. D. Spielberger (Eds.), *Stress and anxiety* (Vol 2). Washington,DC: Hemisphere.

Johnson, J. E., & Leventhal, H. (1974). Effects of accurate expectations and behavioral instructions on reactions during a noxious medical examination. *Journal of Personality and Social Psychology, 29*, 710–718.

Joreskog, K. G., & Sorbom, D. (1981). LISREL V. User's Guide. Chicago: National Educational Resources.

Kahn, R. L., & Cannell, C. F. (1957). *The dynamics of interviewing: Theory, technique, and cases*. New York: Wiley.

Kaplan, A. (1964). *The conduct of inquiry*. San Francisco: Chandler.

Kelley, H. H. (1971). Attribution in social interaction. In E. E. Jones et al. (Eds.), *Attribution: Perceiving the causes of behavior*. Morristown, NJ: General Learning Press.

Kelly, G. A. (1955). *The psychology of personal constructs*. New York: Norton.

Kirschenbaum, D. S., & Tomarken, A. J. (1983). On facing the generalization problem: The study of self-regulatory failure. In P. C. Kendall (Ed.), *Advances in cognitive-behavioral research and theory* (Vol. 1). New York: Academic Press.

Kuhn, T. (1962). *The structure of scientific revolutions*. Chicago: University of Chicago Press.

Lau, R. R., & Hartmann, K. A. (1983). Common sense representations of common illnesses. *Health Psychology, 2*, 167–185.

Lazarus, R. (1966). *Psychological stress and the coping process*. New York: McGraw-Hill.

Leventhal, E. (1984). A self-definitional approach to determining the beginning of the aging process. *Research on Aging, 6*, (1), 119–135.

Leventhal, H. (1970). Findings and theory in the study of fear communications. In L. Berkowitz (Ed.), *Advances in experimental social psychology*. New York: Academic Press.

Leventhal, H. (1974). Attitudes: Their nature, growth and change. In C. Nemeth (Ed.), *Social Psychology*. Chicago: Rand McNally.

Leventhal, H. (1975). The consequences of depersonalization during illness and treatment. In J. Howard & A. Strauss (Eds.), *Humanizing health care*. New York: Wiley.

Leventhal, H. (1980). Toward a comprehensive theory of emotion. In L. Berkowitz (Ed.), *Advances in experimental social psychology* (Vol. 13). New York: Academic Press.

Leventhal, H. (1982a). The integration of emotion and cognition: A view from the perceptual motor theory of emotion. In M. Clarke & S. Fiske (Eds.), *The Seventeenth Annual Carnegie Symposium on Cognition*. Hillsdale, NJ: Erlbaum.

Leventhal, H. (1984). A perceptual motor theory of emotion. In L. Berkowitz (Ed.), *Advances in experimental social psychology*. New York: Academic Press.

Leventhal, H. (1982b). Behavioral medicine: Psychology in health care. In D. Mechanic (Ed.), *Handbook of Health, Health care and Health Professions*. New York: Free Press.

Leventhal, H., Brown, D., Shacham, S., & Engquist, G. (1979). Effect of preparatory information about sensations, threat of pain and attention on cold pressor distress. *Journal of Personality and Social Psychology, 37*, 688–714.

Leventhal, H., & Cleary, P. D. (1980). The smoking problem: A review of the research and theory in behavioral risk modification. *Psychological Bulletin, 88*, 370–405.

Leventhal, H., Easterling, D. V., Ringler, K. E., Nerenz, D., & Love, R. R. (1984). Adaptation to chemotherapy in patients with breast cancer. Manuscript in preparation, University of Wisconsin, Madison.

Leventhal, H., & Johnson, J. E. (1983). Laboratory and field experimentation: Development of a theory of self-regulation. In R. Leonard & P. Woolridge (Eds.), *Behavioral science and nursing theory*. St. Louis: Mosby.

Leventhal, H., Jones, S., & Trembly, G. (1966). Sex differences in attitude and behavior change under conditions of fear and specific instructions. *Journal of Experimental Social Psychology, 2*, 387–399.

Leventhal, H., Meyer, D., & Nerenz, D. (1980). The common sense representation of illness danger. In S. Rachman (Ed.), *Medical Psychology* (Vol. 2). New York, Pergamon Press.

Leventhal, H., & Nerenz, D. (1983). A model for stress research with some implications for the control of stress disorders. In D. Meichenbaum & M. Jaremko (Eds.), *Stress prevention and management: A cognitive behavioral approach*. New York: Plenum Press.

Leventhal, H., Safer, M., & Panagis, D. M. (1983). The impact of communications on the self-regulation of health beliefs, decisions, and behavior. *Health Education Quarterly, 10*, 3–29.

Leventhal, H., Singer, R. P., & Jones, S. (1965). Effects of fear and specificity of recommendations upon attitudes and behavior. *Journal of Personality and Social Psychology, 2*, 20–29.

Leventhal, H., Watts, J. C., & Pagano, F. (1967). Effects of fear and instruction on how to cope with danger. *Journal of Personality and Social Psychology, 6*, 313–321.

Leventhal, H., Zimmerman, R., & Gutmann, M. (1984). Compliance: A self-regulation perspective . In D. Gentry (Ed.), *Handbook of behavioral medicine*. New York: Guilford Press.

Lewin, K. (1935). *A dynamic theory of personality*. New York: McGraw-Hill.

Lilienfeld, A. M., & Lilienfeld, D. E. (1980). *Foundations of epidemiology* (2nd ed.). New York: Oxford University Press.

Linz, D., Siverhus, S., & Penrod, S. (1982). Chronicity, causation, severity, responsibility and emotion: The structure of illness cognition. APA, Washington, DC.

Long, J. S. (1983). *Covariance structure models: An introduction to LISREL*. Beverly Hills, CA: Sage.

Mahoney, M. J., & Mahoney, K. (1976). *Permanent weight control*. New York: Norton.

Meichenbaum, D., & Turk, D. (1976). The cognitive-behavioral management of anxiety, anger and pain. In P. Davidson (Ed.), *Behavioral management of anxiety, anger and pain*. New York: Brunner/Mazel.

Meyer, D., Leventhal, H., Gutmann, M. (1984). Common-sense models of illness: The example of hypertension. Manuscript submitted for publication, University of Wisconsin, Madison.

Meyer, D. L., Leventhal, H., & Gutmann, M. (In press). Symptoms in hypertension: How patients evaluate and treat them. *New England Journal of Medicine*.

Mosbach, P., Leventhal, H., Safer, M., & Cleary, P. (1984). Factors associated with delay in seeking care for mental health problems. Manuscript in preparation, University of Wisconsin, Madison.

National Institute on Drug Abuse. (1978). Compatability in Survey Research on Drugs. Technical Paper, DHEW No. (ADM) 78-750.

National Institute on Drug Abuse. (1981). Assessing Marijuana Consequence: Selected Questionnaire Items. Reseach Issues 28 DHHS No. (ADM) 81–1150.

Nelson, R. O. (1983). Behavioral assessment: Past, present, and future. *Behavioral Assessment*, 5, 195–206.

Nelson, R. O., & Hayes, S. C. (1979). Some current dimensions of behavioral assessment. *Behavioral Assessment*, 1, 1–16.

Nerenz, D. R. (1979). Control of Emotional Distress in Cancer chemotherapy. Unpublished doctoral dissertation, University of Wisconsin, Madison.

Nerenz, D. R., Leventhal, H., & Love, R. R. (1982). Factors contributing to emotional distress during cancer chemotherapy. *Cancer*, 50, 1020–1027.

Nunnally, J. C. (1978). *Psychometric theory* (2nd ed.). New York: McGraw-Hill.

Pearlin, L. I., Lieberman, M. A., Menaghan, E. G., & Mullan, J. T. (1981). The stress process. *Journal of Health and Social Behavior*, 22, 337–356.

Pearlin, L. I., & Schooler, C. (1978). The structure of coping. *Journal of Health and Social Behavior*, 19, 2–21.

Pedhazur, E. J. (1982). *Multiple regression in behavioral research: Explanation and prediction*. New York: Holt, Rinehart and Winston.

Pennebaker, J. (1982). *The psychology of physical symptoms*. New York: Springer.

Peak, H. (1958). Psychological structure and person perception. In R. Tagiuri & L. Petrullo (Eds.), *Person perception and interpersonal behavior*. Stanford, CA: Stanford University Press.

Penrod, S., Linz, D., & Leventhal, H. (1982a). Assessing patient physician communication difficulties: Pinpointing differences in conceptions of disease. 20th International Congress of Applied Psychology, Edinburgh, Scotland.

Penrod, S., Linz, D., & Leventhal, H. (1982b). The cognitive organization of disease among lay persons. 20th International Congress of Applied Psychology, Edinburgh, Scotland.

Ringler, K. E. (1981). Processes of coping with cancer chemotherapy. Unpublished doctoral dissertation, University of Wisconsin, Madison.

Robinson, D. (1971). The process of becoming ill. London: Routledge & Kegan Paul.

Rosenberg, M. J., & Abelson, R. P. (1960). An analysis of cognitive balancing. In M. J. Rosenberg et al. (Eds.), *Attitude organization and change*. New Haven, CT: Yale University Press.

Rosenstock, I. M. (1974). The health belief model and preventive health behavior. *Health Education Monographs*, 2, 354–386.

Rotter, J. B. (1954). *Social learning and clinical psychology*. New York: Prentice-Hall.

Rotter, J. B. (1966). Generalized expectancies for internal vs. external control of reinforcement. *Psychology Monograph*, 80, Whole No. 609.

Safer, M. A., Tharps, Q., Jackson, T., & Leventhal, H. (1979). Determinants of three stages of delay in seeking care at a medical clinic. *Medical Care*, 17, 11–29.

Shepard, R. N., Romney, A. L., & Nerlove, S. B. (1972). *Multidimensional scaling: theory and applications in the behavioral sciences*. New York: Seminar Press.

Silver, R. L., & Wortman, C. B. (1980). Coping with undesirable life events. In J. Garber & M. E. P. Seligman (Eds.), *Human helplessness*. New York: Academic Press.

Steele, D., Gutmann, M., Leventhal, H., Esterling, D. V., & Jackson, T. (1984). A longitudinal treatment study of hypertension. Manuscript in preparation, University of Wisconsin, Madison.

Steptoe A. (1983). Stress, helplessness and control: The implications of laboratory studies. *Journal of Psychosomatic Research*, 27, 361–367.

Sudman, S., & Bradburn, N. M. (1982). *Asking questions: A practical guide to questionnaire design.* San Francisco: Jossey-Boss.

Taylor, S. E. (1983). Adjustment to threatening events: A theory of cognitive-adaptation. *American Psychologist, 38,* 1161–1173.

Turk, D., Sobel, H., Follick, M., & Youkilis, H. (1980). A sequential criterion analysis for assessing coping with chronic illness. *Journal of Human Stress, 6,* 35–40.

Wallston, K., & Wallston, B. (1982). Who is responsible for your health? The construct of health locus of control. In G. Sanders & J. Suls (Eds.), *Social psychology of health and illness.* Hillsdale, NJ: Erlbaum.

Whiting, J. W. M., & Child, I. (1953). Child training and personality. New Haven: Yale University Press.

15

Assessment of Life Stress Events

IRWIN N. SANDLER
ROBERT T. GUENTHER

The proposition that social stress is causally related to the onset and progress of physical illness has been an important focus of research over the past several decades. The roots of this proposition can be traced to the work of early pioneers such as Cannon (1929), Meyer (Lief, 1948), and Selye (1956). Considerable research has been done to explore this proposition empirically, often generating exciting results (Elliot & Eisdorfer, 1982; Schmale, 1972; Glass, 1977; Zegans, 1982). We will not attempt to review this voluminous research, but will assume that the reader has agreed that studying the role of social stress in the etiology of physical illness is a practically important and theoretically interesting endeavor. Our purpose is to review one assessment strategy that has played an important role in this research, the assessment of life stress events.

The task of life stress event assessment is an ambitious one—to quantify the amount of stress that is derived from people's interactions in their

555

environment. To accomplish this task, we need to find a way to identify the stress-producing transactions, to quantify how much stress they each produce, and to develop procedures to summate these different experiences to determine an overall stress level for the person. Not surprisingly, the history of life event assessment methodology has included many creative advances as well as a few serious mistakes.

The early efforts to assess life stress events empirically essentially translated Adolph Meyer's "life chart of significant experiences" into a list on which subjects could easily check off whether the 43 identified significant events had occurred during the recent past (Rahe et al., 1964). This simple approach was then made somewhat more complicated by *life event scaling* studies that attempted to identify the differential amount of stress involved in each event (Holmes & Rahe, 1967). Life event scaling was based on the theoretical notion that a single event property, the amount of change and readjustment, was responsible for the stressful impact of events. Over the past 20 years considerable debate has been generated over alternative approaches to assessing life events and quantifying their stress-engendering properties. Over a dozen serious critical reviews have been published of the life stress event methodology (Brown & Harris, 1978; Cleary, 1981; Dohrenwend & Dohrenwend, 1978; Hurst, 1979; Monroe, 1982a; Neugebauer, 1982; Paykel, 1983; Perkins, 1982; Rabkin & Struening, 1976; Sandler, 1979; Sarason et al., 1975; Tausig, 1982; Tennant et al., 1981; Thoits, 1983; Zimmerman, 1983). These reviews have criticized the methodology on grounds of content of the items (e.g., lack of representativeness, vague wording, confounding with illness measures), the reliability and validity of subject reports, the method of data collection (checklist versus structured interview), and the attributes of stress being assessed (e.g., change versus undesirability). Current methodologies have changed in response to such criticisms, so that there are currently many different life event scales in use. The purpose of this chapter is to review the developments and criticisms of life event assessment strategy.

The review is organized along conceptual lines, in accordance with a broadly accepted model of life stress processes. The intention is to help the reader place the different criticisms and alternative methodologies within the context of a stress model, to promote a better informed future use of the life stress approach. Since the chapter focuses on placing life event methodology in the context of a stress model, we have chosen studies that best enable us to illustrate our conceptual points and have not attended particularly to studies that use physical health indicators as the dependent variables.

DEFINITIONAL ISSUES: LIFE EVENTS AND THE STRESS MODEL

A basic problem in the assessment of life stress events is the failure of researchers to place their measures consistently within a theoretical frame-

work. A guiding theoretical framework is particularly important in reviewing the life events assessment methodology, where it is necessary to
compare one life event methodology with another. It may be, for example,
that different measures of life events operationalize different aspects of a
stress model so that simply comparing one measure with another may make
no theoretical sense. Illustratively, as will be described later, Horwitz et al.
(1977) developed a presumptive stress score to assess the current stressful
effects of events while accounting for the decay in stress effects over time.
The inclusion of the time dimension here is an important theoretical statement, which would be completely ignored by studies that simply compare
the effects of the presumptive stress score with other event scores. Furthermore, it is difficult to decide what psychometric properties an event scale
should possess without a theoretical model of the construct being assessed!
For example, Neugebauer (1981) points out the difficulty of deciding on an
appropriate test of life event scale reliability in the absence of a theoretical
model of the construct.

Thus, this review will initially treat the basic conceptual issues by (1)
discussing the nature of the general construct being measured by life events
scales, and (2) outlining different aspects of the overall construct that are
assessed by different scales.

A good part of the conceptual problems in life stress events research can
be traced to the lack of consensually agreed-upon definition of the term
stress. Reviewers of the definitional issue point out that the term has been
applied to a wide range of behavioral phenomena (McGrath, 1970; Appley &
Trumbull, 1967): the stimulus situation (e.g., heat, cold, noise, electric
shock), response patterns (e.g., physiological, cognitive, and behavioral),
and person-environment interactions (e.g., perceptions of threat or excess
demands). McGrath (1970) proposed that one useful approach to the definitional issue is to consider stress not as a single phenomenon but as a series
of phenomena that occur over time and include environmental stimulation,
perception, and interpretation of the stimulus by the person as well as the
responses of the person to the perceived stimulus. This model of the stress
process is presented in Figure 15.1. Events are a product of an ongoing
life context, including continuing conditions, and of a person who possesses
unique values, a history, personality, physical and psychological symptom
levels.

An event has objective properties, which can be seen as independent of
how the event is experienced by any subject. Events are also experienced
(perceived and evaluated), and these event experiences are in part determined by the person (e.g., attributional style) and in part by the objective
event properties. Finally, the event experience leads to a person-centered
stress response and to changes within the person (including changes in the
level of physical or psychological health). Finally, this process occurs over
time and includes feedback loops whereby event occurrences change the
individual and the ongoing life context. Life event measures focus on
assessing two aspects of this process, the objective stressful environmental

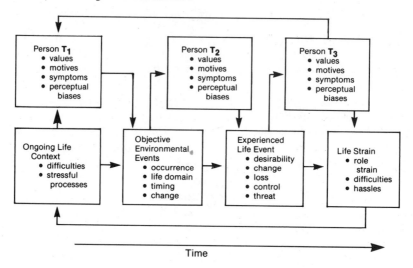

FIGURE 15.1.   Conceptual model of the stress process and life events over time.

stimulation and the perceived stressful stimulation. We will consider life events scales as a measure of each construct. Before doing so, we will briefly consider the ongoing life context in which events occur.

ONGOING LIFE CONTEXT

Events do not simply occur in a vacuum. They occur in the context of an ongoing pattern of transactions and living conditions that characterize the individual's world. These ongoing life processes are normally not considered to be stressful life events, although indeed they may be sources of stress. The concept of ongoing life context is illustrated by two studies that utilized very different approaches. Gersten et al. (1977) studied whether stressful events made an additive contribution to the prediction of psychological disturbance over that made by ongoing life processes. Events were seen as distinct from ongoing processes in that the former represented a change. The subjects were 1034 6- to 18-year-old children who were assessed twice over a 5-year period. Ongoing life processes were assessed via sociodemographic variables (e.g., social class measures, number of children in the family, number of parents in the home), parental variables (e.g., unhappy marriage, parental quarrels, parental physical or mental illness) and parent-child relationship variables (e.g., parents cold, punitive, rejecting). Events were assessed via 34 items representing relatively discrete changes in the environment (e.g., parents divorced, father remarried) over the past 5 years. The investigators used multiple regression to assess the contribution of events to the prediction of child psychological disorder at time 2 after controlling for disorder at time 1 and for ongoing stress processes. They found that both psychological disorder at time 1 and ongoing processes contributed substantially to the prediction of disorder at time 2. Life events, however, did not add to the prediction of disorder after accounting for these variables.

A second study that investigated the stress of the ongoing life context is by Brown and Harris (1978). They identified a concept they called *difficulties*. They defined difficulties as problems that had gone on for at least 4 weeks and assessed them via a structured interview in which they inquired about all areas of the subject's life situation (including housing, money, marriage, children, etc.). They used in-depth probes to obtain descriptive information about each difficulty. As described later in this chapter, events were defined as changes in the subject's life. They found that major ongoing difficulties were related to the onset of depression in their subjects but were *less* important than life events and independent of the effects of life events. Other researchers have proposed that the stress effects of difficulties and life events is additive (Surtees & Ingham, 1981).

LIFE EVENTS AS MEASURES OF THE OBJECTIVE IMPACT OF ENVIRONMENTS

The objective measurement of stress events operationalizes a situation-based definition of stress. It assumes that stress can be assessed as an environmental stimulus, independently of how that stimulus is perceived by the subject. For example, the level of shock, heat, or cold is often used to calibrate the stressfulness of physical stimuli, without assessing how these stimuli are subjectively perceived. It should be noted that the term *objective* is used here to refer to properties of the event that are independent of how the event is experienced. Since life event measures are self-report (either via interview or paper and pencil), how can they be considered measures of the objective environment? One model postulates that the subject is a reporter of the event's objective properties. A variety of qualities of events can be assumed to have a reality independent of how the event is perceived by the subject. For example, whether the event actually occurred, whom the event occurred to, where it occurred, the timing of events, and the degree to which they are a change from the prior life condition might be considered as so-called objective characteristics of events. Each of these characteristics will be discussed in turn.

Events as Objective Occurrences

Do life events scales qualify as valid measures of the objective occurrence of events? Two strategies to assess the validity of event reports as measures of the actual occurrence of events have been (1) to investigate the agreement between the subject and a knowledgeable informant and (2) to assess changes in event reports over the period of recall. Yager et al. (1981) compared the event reports of subjects and a knowledgeable informant. They studied the degree of agreement for psychiatric patients and nonpatients and for different kinds of life event items. Overall they reported low subject-informant agreement for both patients (Kappa = .35) and nonpatients (Kappa = .39). The agreement was somewhat better for more clearly worded items and those that are more likely to be known by the informant. But, even for items that optimize the chances for agreement (clearly worded and knowable), the Kappa only reached .57. These results are quite consistent with other studies in this area (e.g., Horowitz et al., 1977; Hudgens et al., 1970; Neugebauer, 1983; Rahe et al., 1974; Schless & Mendels, 1978).

Several reasons have been proposed to explain the low rate of subject-significant other agreement. Subjects may make errors of memory, in that they may forget that an event occurred or that it occurred in the particular time under consideration. There may also be differences in judgment of whether something that occurred fits the wording of an event (How many arguments constitute a *significant* increase? What qualifies as an *outstanding* personal achievement?) Finally, subjects or informants may be motivated to distort their responses. This may occur either in an attempt to please the interviewer by producing more responses or as a way to explain the subject's current state of mental or physical health. This latter motivated distortion explanation would lead to the prediction that psychiatric patients should be less valid reporters of events than are nonpatients. Grant et al. (1981), however, found only small differences between patients and nonpatients in their subject-significant other agreement, thus casting doubt on the motivated distortion viewpoint.

Neugebauer (1983) made some important methodological points in a study of schizophrenic subject-significant other agreement on reports of life events. One distinction that can be drawn is between agreement on item ratings versus actual agreement about the occurrence of specific events. It is possible for the subject and an informant both to acknowledge the same item, but to do so because of the experience of different events. For example, "death of a relative" may be rated "yes" by the subject because of the death of an uncle, whereas the informant may rate it "yes" because of the death of a second cousin. Similarly, the same actual event may be rated under different items. For example, a job promotion may be rated as either a success at work, an increase in workload, or both. The choice of what to consider an agreement or disagreement hinges on the construct of life events being assessed. If the life event scale is construed as a measure of actual events that occurred, then agreement is not evident in example 1 but is evident in example 2. Neugebauer (1983) took this position and found a mean agreement for the occurrence of events of 22 percent for his sample of schizophrenic-outpatients and knowledgeable informants.

A second approach to investigating the validity of life event reports as measures of the actual occurrence of events is to assess the drop-off in frequency of events reported over time. Since there is no logical reason to expect an actual decrease in the occurrence of events as an individual recalls back over time, such a drop-off can only be attributed to retrospective bias in reporting. Several studies report that progressively fewer events are reported as length of time of recall increases. For example, Jenkins et al. (1979) asked 382 air traffic controllers to rate the occurrence of events on two separate occasions separated by 9 months. On the first occasion, subjects rated events that occurred in the prior 6 months and 7 to 24 months. On the second occasion (9 months later), subjects rated events that occurred in those prior 9 months and the 6 months prior to that. The latter time period corresponded exactly with the immediate 6-month recall rated at time 1, so that their event ratings could be seen as a 6-month delayed retest on the report of events for this period. The authors reported a decline in life stress scores for the 6-month period ranging from 46 to 34 percent depending on the method used to score events. Monroe (1982b) had 69 subjects complete a life event schedule on five occasions. On the first occasion, subjects indicated all events that occurred during the prior 2 years (dating each one for the month of occurrence). Subjects then completed the scale monthly for each of the 4 succeeding months. The data were analyzed by breaking down the 1-year retrospective report into three equal time segments of 4 months each. The four 1-month retrospective reports were combined to constitute a final 4-month interval. Three life event scores were computed for each of the 4-month intervals, using Dohrenwend's designation of events as desirable, undesirable, or neutral ambiguous. For all three event scores, significantly more events were reported in the most recent time period than in each of the three preceding periods. The magnitude of difference was such that the event scores for the 4-month retrospective time periods were only approximately 40 percent as large as the score for the most recent interval assessed via the four 1-month retrospective reports. Furthermore, Monroe reported that desirable events evidenced the largest decline of reporting over time. Other studies report similar decrease in recall of life events with increasing time from the reporting period (Uhlenhuth et al., 1977; Casey et al., 1967).

The evidence about the validity of life events scales as measures of the objective occurrence of specific events is rather discouraging; the scales do not satisfy even lenient criteria of validity (Paykel, 1983). Improvement should be possible by attending to those factors that have been found to relate to concordance between subjects and informants: shorter period of recall, clear wording of events, and dating the time of occurrence of events. These kinds of improvements might be made by the use of structured interviewing in the assessment of events. Recent life event studies show evidence of incorporating such changes (e.g., Monroe, 1982c).

An approach that has successfully used a structured interview format to obtain valid ratings of the objective occurrence of events is the Bedford College life event instrument (Brown & Harris, 1978; 1982). The approach was developed over a series of studies on the relationship between life events and the onset of schizophrenic and depressive disorders (Brown & Harris, 1978). The technique is at variance with traditional checklist procedures in the methods used to (1) solicit information from the subjects (2) measure the occurrence of events, and (3) assess the properties of events. Brown and Harris (1978) propose that these differences solve critical shortcomings in traditional life events methodology. The general technique and its proposed advantages will first be described. Then we will present evidence relevant to the issue of whether this technique yields a valid measure of the objective occurrence of events. In a later section, we will describe how this approach is used to assess the subjective experience of events and the evidence on the construct validity of this strategy.

The procedure was developed to measure life events while avoiding several potential sources of contamination between the measurement of events and disorder, thus enabling causal attributions to be drawn from observed associations between the two (Brown & Harris, 1978). Three sources of potential contamination were carefully described. Direct contamination might occur when the rating of life events is influenced by knowledge of the occurrence of disorder. The reporter's (subject or interviewer) recollection or interpretation of the past is affected by his or her knowledge of the disorder, so that he or she may overreport the occurrence of events in order to explain the disorder. This problem is most acute for retrospective studies. Indirect contamination refers to the possibility that a characteristic of the subject, such as their anxiety level or mood, leads both to an increased report of disorder and an increased report of life events. Finally, some subject characteristic (e.g., anxiety) may influence both the subject's experience of events (i.e., their perception of the events qualities such as stressfulness, threat, etc.) and the occurrence of disorder. In order to avoid these sources of noncausal association between events and disorder, Brown developed special procedures for life event assessment.

The data are collected via an in-depth interview that inquires about the subject's experience of each of 38 types of events. Events were defined as changes in an activity, role, person, health, employment, and so on that usually might be expected to be followed by strong emotion. The definition of what to include as an event is clearly spelled out in advance in an in-depth reference book that clearly prescribes the criteria to be met. The purpose here is to remove ambiguity of event definition that could lead to biases in data scoring. Through interview probes, a trained interviewer obtains the information needed to judge events and precisely dates when the event occurred. The decision as to rating event occurrence is made by trained raters based on the subject's report in the structured interview. The procedure is similar to that which might be used to obtain reliable ratings of any behavior. The behavior sample to be observed is the verbalization of the subjects in response to the structured interview questions. The target behaviors are clearly defined in advance and the raters are trained in their defining characteristics. Thus, it is not surprising that interrater reliability for events is high (correlations between raters of greater than .90). It is also heartening that the agreement between ratings of occurrence of specific events derived from subjects and a close informant is reasonably good (approximately 80 percent) (Brown et al., 1973). Agreement across informants was even better, 91 percent, for those events that are found to be related to the onset of psychiatric disorder (designated as "severe" events, as described later).

The Bedford College life event instrument also fares quite well by the second procedure utilized to assess the validity of life events scales as measures of objectively occurring events. Brown and Harris (1982) report a falloff in the reporting of life events of 3 percent per month over a 1-year period, and Brown and Harris (1978) report a falloff in recall of only 1 percent per month over a 6-month period. Both compare favorably with the 5 percent per month falloff found with self-report life events checklists (Jenkins et al., 1979). Furthermore, Brown and Harris (1982) report no falloff at all in the recall of the etiologically important severe events over a 1-year period. In sum, the Bedford College life event instrument does provide life event data that satisfy the criteria for assessing the occurrence of objective events. The reasons for this are that events are clearly defined and raters are trained to agree in their observations. Not surprisingly, in the absence of such training, the approach is considerably less successful (Brown & Harris, 1982).

Although life events are generally not good measures of the occurrence of specific events, it is possible that they are valid measures of the *total number* of events that occurred. Since life events scales generally aggregate stress across events, validity of the total number of events scores may actually be a more important index than is the validity of any specific events. This issue has received relatively little attention. Moderate levels of test-retest reliability have been reported for total number of events scores. For example, Howowitz et al. (1977) obtained a 6-week test-retest reliability of .84, whereas Sarason et al. (1978) obtained a test-retest reliability of .64 over the same interval. Since new events can be expected to occur during the intervening period, these results are seen as encouraging. Sandler and Lakey (1982) reported a test-retest reliability of .92 over a 2-day period. As Neugebauer (1982) points out, however, assessing the reliability of aggregated scores invokes a very different measurement model than is assumed when we focus on each specific event. The model invoked by aggregate scores is closest to a *domain sampling model* often used in personality assessment. We disagree with Neugebauer's (1981) contention, however, that the domain sampling model necessarily implies that the instrument assesses stress as a subject characteristic rather than as a measure of the number of stressors to which the respondent has been exposed. It is reasonable, in fact, to conceptualize events as a sample of the universe of stressful events that might occur to an individual. Events, for a scale after all, are often generated by sampling those experiences that are nominated by a sample of the population (e.g.,

Dohrenwend et al., 1978). If different subjects had been sampled or different event writers employed, a somewhat different sample of specific events would have been drawn. One modification of the traditional domain sampling model that may be useful is to assume that there is a multiple factorial structure for the domain of life events. That is, family, work environment, leisure pursuits, health, and social life, and so on all may be identifiable domains in which stressors occur. Although we know that events are not simply independent occurrences and do, in fact, intercorrelate (Cleary, 1981), very little theoretical attention has been devoted to understanding these interrelations. Monroe (1982a) has articulated three possible reasons: event redundancy, events causing each other, and a common underlying cause of events. The intercorrelation among events has recently been discussed as a problem for life event scales (Cleary, 1981; Monroe, 1982a). It may be, however, that life event scales should be conceptualized as assessing the amount of stress in different areas of life rather than as discrete independent occurrences, and, therefore, item intercorrelations should be expected. Life event scales, to date, have not been developed based on an articulated domain sampling model, so that this may be an area for future research work.

Although, overall, most life event scales do not satisfy criteria as valid measures of the actual occurrence of specific events, there are some properties of events that can be considered to be "objective." That is, the property which refers to some descriptive characteristic of the event itself, rather than to how the event is experienced. Several characteristics will be considered: how events contrast with the ongoing life context (i.e., change), the timing of events, and the domain of life in which events occur.

Events as Changes

The view that change is a basic defining property of life events is well accepted. As we will discuss later, there is considerable *disagreement* as to whether change is the central *stressful* component of events (Dohrenwend, 1973; Gersten et al., 1974). But even those who do not agree that change is the stressful property of events do include change in their definition of events (e.g., Brown & Harris, 1978). Dohrenwend and Dohrenwend (1981) reviewed the life events literature to arrive at a definition of what is a stressful life event and conlcuded that there was broad agreement on the "idea that stressful life events include those that involve change in the usual activities of most individuals who experience them" (p. 7). In view of this consensus, we will consider two issues: (1) How do life event scales assess change, and (2) should we consider change, as it is usually measured, to be an objective or subjective property of events?

The primary method by which life event scales measure change is via the content of the items. Each event is supposed to represent a change from the normal life pattern of the individual. Despite this claim, a simple reading of most life event scale items reveals that they often do *not* specify change. For example, on the Holmes and Rahe SRRS (Holmes & Rahe, 1967), 18 percent of the items do not specify change (e.g., trouble with boss). Similarly, another popular life event scale, the PERI (Dohrenwend et al., 1978) has 16 percent of its items that are not clearly changes (e.g., had problems in school or training program, had trouble with a boss, had significant success at work, trouble with in-laws). The problem, of course, is that in order to measure change, the investigator must first assess the steady state. Although problems with in-laws may be a change from a steady state of harmony for some people, it may be normal for others.

A second method by which life event scales assess change is by scaling the amount of change involved in each event. Either the subject him- or herself may be asked to make this judgment (Hurst, 1979), or the normative judgment of outside raters can be obtained (Holmes & Rahe, 1967). This judgment often includes the concept of the degree of readjustment required after an event occurs. It is not clear, however, exactly what subjects are rating when they make their judgments. They may be contrasting the event with a hypothetical normal life context and rating its statistical abnormality. They may be judging how much coping an individual would have to do after the event occurs. They may be rating the degree to which the event would be *perceived* as a change. It is clear, however, that their rating is *supposed* to reflect a subjective experience of the person to whom the event occurs; "As defined, social readjustment measures the intensity and length of time necessary to accommodate to a life event . . . " (Holmes & Rahe, 1967, p. 213). We will discuss these ratings further in the section on subjective life event experiences.

Although we are not considering life event change as it usually is assessed—as an objective property of events—it is helpful to discuss briefly what might constitute an objective measure of change. Since change is historically seen as some threat to the state of homeostasis or equilibrium of the organism (Cannon, 1929; Selye, 1956), it is necessary to measure this equilibrium and the disruption caused by the event. Also, since people are constantly changing, we must ask whether the current level of change is different from the normal rate of change? One approach to doing this might be to establish a baseline for the occurrence of events and to treat deviations from this baseline as changes (e.g., this might be done using a time-series design; see Chapter 5, this volume).

Time

Another property of events concerns the length of time since the events occurred. The issue of how the impact of events varies over time has received some (although limited) attention in the life stress literature (Horowitz, et al., 1977; Surtees & Ingham, 1981). The importance of the time concept has long been recognized in the stress literature (e.g., McGrath, 1970). For example, Lazarus and Launier (1978) discuss stress and coping as a continuous dynamic process that occurs over time. Research on specific stressors has consistently pointed out how the effects of these stressors decreases over time. For example, the stressful effects of divorce on children and adults typically peaks at about a year after the divorce and is considerably reduced 2 years after the divorce (Hetherington, et al., 1981). Glick et al. (1974) reported that recovery from the stress of the death of a spouse occurs over time, so that, by 1 year after the death, most widows were beginning to feel more in control of their lives (although not fully recovered).

The variable of time is an important part of life events assessment. For example, life events are reported that occur within a specified time interval. Most frequently this time interval has been 1 year, although there is reason to believe that the 1-year time interval may be overly long. Since the falloff in recall of life events is reported to be about 5 percent per month (Hurst, 1979), a shorter length of retrospective report might yield more valid data. There is also some evidence that the stressful impact of life events is usually manifested within 4 to 6 months (Andrews, 1981; Brown & Harris, 1978).

Time is important for life event measures because these measures summate the stress effects of events that occur within a given period. Although it seems obvious that the effects of stress events dissipate over time, most life event measures do not consider the effects of time as they summate life stress scores. Two approaches to considering the time dimension have been developed (Horowitz et al., 1977; Surtees & Ingham, 1981). We consider the Surtees and Ingham (1981) approach an objective one, since it treats time as a variable without considering how it is experienced by the subject. Although time is treated as an objective variable here, the overall model uses time to summate the subjective stress effect of life events. The model postulates that "the stressful effect of a life event dissipates with time at a constant rate and this rate is the same for all events" (Surtees & Ingham, 1981, p. 25). They further postulate that the stressful effects of life events (and continuous difficulties) summate. Surtees and Ingham utilize the Bedford College life event instrument to obtain ratings of the occurrence, time of occurrence, and initial stressfulness of events. By making the assumption that the stressful effect of the most severe life event completely dissipates over 26 weeks, and by obtaining ratings of the initial stressfulness of all events, the authors are able to calculate the stress value of any event at any given time after it has occurred.

Life Domain of Events

A final group of objective properties of events concerns their descriptive features: who, what, where? Whom did the event happen to (e.g., the subject, a relative, a friend)? What happened (e.g., a change in health, in finances, in interpersonal relations)? Where did it happen (e.g., at work, at home, etc.)? Although these properties of events have not been the focus of much research, they are included in many life event scales. Dohrenwend et al. (1978) organized the 102 events of the PERI scale into 11 topic areas (e.g., school, work, love and marriage, having children, family, residence, crime and legal matters, finances, social activities, miscellaneous, and health). Paykel et al. (1969) identified events that involved an important person leaving the social field (exits) and an important person being added to the social field (entrances). Similarly, many other life event researchers have organized the events in their scales into logically developed content areas (e.g., Block & Zautra, 1981; Chiriboga & Dean, 1978; Horowitz et al., 1977; Hurst, 1979).

Another approach to organizing life events into different domains is by the empirical co-occurrence of events. It might be argued that events that occur in the same area of life should be more likely to co-occur with other changes in that life area. For example, getting a promotion, increased work responsibility, and improving financial status might be expected to co-occur. Rahe et al. (1971) performed a cluster analysis of the life event reports of 2678 navy enlisted men. They obtained four clusters that included 24 of the 42 life events on the SRE. The clusters were labeled personal and social, work, marital, and disciplinary. These clusters were substantially replicated in a study on a second large group of navy personnel (Pugh et al., 1971). Newcomb et al. (1981) identified seven first-order factors from the co-occurrence of 39 life events among adolescents. The seven factors accounted for 44 percent of the covariation among the items and were labeled family/parents, accident/illness, sexuality, autonomy, deviance, relocation, and distress. Although some of the co-occurrence between events might simply reflect item redundancy (e.g., change in social activity, change in recreation) (Cleary, 1981), it is also likely that some event factors contain distinctly different items each of which reflects an aspect of disruption in a life domain. For example, the family/parents factor obtained by Newcomb et al. (1981) included the items, parental divorce, family money problems, parents argued or fought, parent remarried, and parent abused alcohol.

RELATIONSHIP BETWEEN OBJECTIVE EVENT PROPERTIES AND MEASURES OF DISORDER

We have identified three objective properties of events that have been assessed by various life event methodologies: event occurrence, time, and life domain of the event. The question now is whether each of the event properties contributes to the prediction of psychological or physical disorder.

Event Occurrence

Only one instrument satisfies the minimal criterion of interrater reliability to be considered a measure of the occurrence of *specific* events, the Bedford

College life event instrument (Brown & Harris, 1978). How well does the simple occurrence of events relate to measures of disorder? The evidence is quite clear that the relationship between events and disorder (i.e., depression) is due to the meaning of the event to the subject. As we will describe in greater detail later, Brown and Harris (1978) subdivided events on the basis of their probable meaning to the subject, into severe events and nonsevere events. Although severe events were strongly related to depression, nonsevere events were not. Thus, whereas the occurrence of an event is obviously important, the meaning of the event makes it stressful. If we consider the total number of events as our measure of life stress, a similar situation holds. As we will discuss in the later section concerning dimensions of events, it is clear that not all the events currently included in life event scales are related to disorder. Here again the meaning of the event is critical.

Time

The method developed by Surtees and Ingham (1981) allows the time variable to be accounted for in summating the stressful impact of events in an *adversity index*. The adversity index clearly does not itself qualify as an objective property of events (since it also uses inferences about subjective experience of events). The question addressed here is how does the inclusion of the time dimension improve the association with disorder over and above the relationship found for measures based only on the subjective meaning of events. Surtees and Ingham (1981) studied a group of depressed psychiatric patients 7 months after their release from the hospital. They found that, in comparison with a simple measure of the occurrence of a severe event, the adversity index gave higher correlations with a measure of psychological symptoms. In a reanalysis of the community survey data of Brown and Harris (1978), Surtees and Rennie (1983) found further support for the usefulness of their adversity index. They discovered that summating event stress (using their decay function over time) yielded a better ratio for predicting the onset of depression as compared to that obtained when decay over time was not considered. More specifically, fewer false positive predictions of the onset of depression were obtained using the decay function (9.4 percent) as compared to not using the decay function (19.6 percent).

Life Domain of Events

Discussion of the relationship between events from different life domains and measures of disorder needs to include consideration of the issue of *life event-disorder contamination*. The issue essentially is that some events on life event lists are themselves either indicators of physical illness (e.g., unable to get treatment for an illness or injury) or indicators of the level of psychological functioning (e.g., fired from work, increased arguments with spouse).

These contaminated kinds of events are often identified on life event scales [e.g., health events identified by Dohrenwend et al. (1978); deviance events identified by Newcomb et al. (1981)]. Relationships between health events and measures of physical illness, or deviance events and measures of psychological disorder, obviously tell us nothing about the effects of stress. Dohrenwend and Dohrenwend (1978) proposed to deal with this issue by classifying events according to whether they are confounded with psychiatric condition, with physical illness, or not confounded with either one. What happens to the event disorder relationship when confounded events are removed? The evidence on this issue is mixed, being more negative for studies that deal with physical illness and more encouraging for the more numerous studies that deal with psychological disorder.

Two studies on item contamination are particularly relevant to the relationship between life stress events and physical illness. Schroeder and Costa (1984) investigated the relationship between self-reported illness and four different kinds of events; events contaminated by either physical health, neuroticism, or subjective reporting bias, and uncontaminated events. Life event items were selected from the most commonly used life event schedules. Physical health items were those that may either directly (e.g., major personal illness or injury) or indirectly (e.g., change in sleeping habits) reflect physical health status. Neuroticism items were those that could be either a symptom of psychopathology (e.g., major change in eating habits) or the result of neurotic behavior (e.g., divorce or being fired). The authors proposed that since neurotic individuals tend to overreport health complaints, the relationship between neurotic events and illness reports could be due to the association of each with the third variable of neuroticism. Items that were vaguely or ambiguously worded (e.g., major change in financial status) were judged to be susceptible to subjective reporting bias. These items were considered contaminated, because they might easily be influenced by retrospective overreporting as people try to explain their illness. Such items might also be influenced by a simple endorsement response set.

Life event and physical illness 1-year retrospective reports were obtained from 386 adult community residents. Separate event scores were obtained for each of the four types of events. Correlational analysis indicated significant relationships between illness reports and health and neuroticism and subjective events, but *not* for uncontaminated events. Uncontaminated events did not differ from the contaminated events in frequency of occurrence, undesirability, severity, or uncontrollability. Thus, Schroeder and Costa (1984) concluded that measurement contamination probably accounts for the often cited association between life event measures and physical illness.

A similar point is made in a prospective longitudinal study conducted by Thoits (1981). She assessed the occurrence of negative life events over a 16-month period and a self-report of psychophysiological distress at the beginning and end of the 16 months. She subdivided the negative events on her scale into those that are themselves health related and those that are not. Using multiple regression initially to control for time 1 psychophysiological distress and the health-related problems, she reported that nonhealth-related problems did *not* add any significant contributions to the prediction of distress.

Because of the importance of the item contamination issue, we will discuss these findings further by (1) suggesting potential shortcomings of the studies themselves and (2) indicating other life event studies that obtain contradictory results. Schroeder and Costa's work (1984) is a very conservative study in that it considers events contaminated if they simply increase the chance of yielding an association between events and illness but do not themselves indicate illness (e.g., neurotic and subjective events). This may well be overly conservative, resulting in an overly restricted number of life events in the uncontaminated group. Schroeder and Costa (1984) do not report on the frequency of occurrence in their sample of the kind of event that we will later show is the most stable predictor of disorder, negative events. It may be that their study suffered from a restriction of range of this critical variable. Thoits (1981) notes one limitation of her study—the restricted range of socioeconomic sample of her subjects (all were low income). She reported that when the same analyses were done on a broader community sample, nonhealth-related items were associated with higher psychophysiological distress, after controlling for the effects of health-related events.

However, the contamination issue noted in these studies cannot account for the findings of other studies. Cohen and Hoberman (1983), for example, obtained significant relationships between self-reports of physical illness and life events measures that were not confounded with physical illness and beyond the individual's control. Kobasa et al. (1982) found an interactive effect between life events and the personality dimension of hardiness in a prospective study of change in physical illness reports. Life events related more strongly to illness increase for low as compared with high "hardy" individuals. It is difficult to see how the interactive finding can be accounted for by event-illness contamination. Murphy and Brown (1980) discovered that the onset of moderately severe organic disorders (e.g., duodenal ulcer) was significantly associated with a preceding severe event for women between the ages of 18 to 50 (38 percent of the organically ill group experienced a severe event, as compared with 15 percent of a comparison group).

The issue of item contamination with dependent variables has received more research attention in studies on psychological disorder. Numerous studies using both prospective and concurrent research designs have obtained the predicted relationships between events and psychological disorder even for events that do not reflect the level of psychological functioning or physical illness of the subject (e.g., Billings & Moos, 1982; Brown & Harris, 1978; Grant et al., 1981; McFarlane et al., 1980; Mueller et al., 1977; Sandler & Block, 1979).

In addition to addressing the contamination issue, we should ask whether stressors that occur in some particular areas of life are more strongly related to the development of physical or psychological disorder than are stress events in other life areas. Several studies have addressed this issue. Hurst (1979), for example, studied the relationship between life events and the onset of psychological disorder in air traffic controllers, and found that work- and marriage-related events were the only two types that were associated with the development of all four psychological disorder studies. Chiriboga and Dean (1978) reported that different kinds of life events seem to have differential impact as a function of the age and gender of the person who experiences them. Their research involved a prospective study of change in adjustment over time in four groups of adults in transition-situations (high school seniors, newlyweds, middle-aged parents, and retirees). They found that work stress had an important impact on younger and older men, but not on women. For younger women, in contrast, personal and marital stressors were most impactful, whereas, for older women, financial, marital, and habit stressors were most impactful.

ASSESSMENT OF EVENT EXPERIENCE

Two separate components of the rating of subjective event experience need to be discriminated: content of what is assessed and the method of assessment. The content of what is being assessed is the subjective experience of the event. There are obviously multiple dimensions of event experience, but they all share the common characteristic of including some judgment about subjective reaction to the event. Thus, they can be distinguished from properties of events (e.g., timing, life domain) that we have previously described as being "objective," not involving the subjective evaluations of an individual's experience.

Although the content is subjective event experience, the method of assessment can be either subjective or objective. That is, the method may or may not utilize the judgments of the person whose stress level is being assessed. The objective assessment of subjective life event experience is based on the assumption that observers can accurately infer another's experience. For example, Brown & Harris (1978) utilize expert's ratings of the subject's probable experience of the event, based on the expert's knowledge of the circumstances surrounding the event. Another approach (e.g., Henderson et al., 1981) utilized ratings of the event made by a wide range of raters (e.g., general population, others who have experienced the event, mental health professionals). Both approaches have the disadvantage of being indirect measures of subjective experience but have the advantage of avoiding the confoundings that make subjective ratings questionable for some research questions (see discussion that follows).

Other investigators would argue that the assessment of event experience can best be accomplished by obtaining the reports of the people themselves who have experienced the event (Sarason et al., 1978). An event that may be threatening to one person may be perceived as a challenge by another and as irrelevant by a third. We will now discuss methods used to assess event experiences subjectively and objectively.

Subjective Measures of Event Experience

The subjective assessment of event experience is rather straightforward—simply obtain a rating of the experience by the person to whom it occurred. For example, Sarason et al. (1978) developed a response format whereby the subject reports whether an event occurred, whether it was positive or negative, and the magnitude of the impact of the event. Scores can be derived by either obtaining a simple sum of total, positive, or negative events or weighting each item by the magnitude of impact to yield a weighted total, positive, or negative event score.

Rahe (1981) proposed that the subject's own rating of the amount of "force" of his or her life change experiences could capture the effect of the event in light of his or her previous experience, social support, or skills to deal with the events. This scoring method was used in a cross-sectional study of the correlation between life events and physical and mental health symptoms of Vietnamese refugees. The subjective life change scores yielded higher correlations with self-reported physical illness symptoms than did a simple count of events for female but not for male subjects. Rahe (1981) argued that the subjective ratings of event experience lead to better predictions of the stressful effects of events because they include individual factors (e.g., prior history, coping skills), as well as contextual factors (e.g., social support) that influence the stressfulness of events. The disadvantage of including individual factors in these ratings, however, is that the ratings are confounded with measures of the psychological disorder they are often used to predict. Nevertheless, many studies have used subjective ratings of a wide range of event qualities, including positiveness, negativeness, control, attributions of causality, preoccupation with the event, change, and impact (Block & Zautra, 1981; Chiriboga, 1977; Fontana et al., 1979; Grant et al., 1978; Hammen et al., 1981; Hurst, 1979; Kale & Stenmark, 1983; McFarlane et al., 1980; Monroe et al., 1983; Mueller et al., 1977; Vinokur & Selzer, 1975). These qualities will be discussed in more detail later.

Because of their widespread use, it is important to note the criticisms of subjective measures of life events experience (Brown & Harris, 1978; Dohrenwend et al., 1978). Three major criticisms can be identified: confounding of ratings with symptoms, confounding of ratings with individual dispositions, and retrospective distortion of subjective ratings.

The confounding of ratings with symptomatology could occur if symptomatology affected people's ratings of events. Several studies have reported that psychiatric patients give events higher stress ratings than do nonpatient controls (Grant et al., 1976; Lundberg & Theorell, 1976). As

Dohrenwend and Dohrenwend (1978) point out, this confounding between distress ratings and symptomatology creates a circularity of cause and effect that precludes the use of such measures in cross-sectional studies of the impact of events on symptomatology. This criticism, however, is less potent (although not completely eliminated) for some longitudinal designs, where the effects of prior symptomatology are statistically controlled (see Chapter 5 and 6 in this volume).

Subjective measures may reflect a stable personal disposition to perceive events as more stressful. This disposition rather than the event occurrence per se may be related to psychological disorder. Schless et al. (1974), for example, reported that depressed patients rated events as more stressful than did nondepressed controls and that these elevated stress ratings were obtained both at admission (when the patients were symptomatic) and at discharge (when the patients depressed mood was greatly decreased). Similarly, Lundberg & Theorell (1976) found that myocardial infarction (MI) patients rated life events as more upsetting than did a matched control group. They proposed that these differences might be due to preexisting personality characteristics of MI patients. Miller et al. (1982) found that depressed subjects, as compared with normals, manifested a depressive attributional style in their evaluation of stress events that occurred to them. Zimmerman (1983) speculated that the individual's elevated stressfulness ratings of events may be useful to identify people at risk prospectively for psychological disorder (e.g., depression). That is, a subject's ratings of the stressfulness of events might be used to identify that subject's vulnerability to the impact of events.

Finally, the presence of psychiatric or physical disorder may cause subjects to reevaluate their past experience in search for a cause of their problem. Brown & Harris (1978) refer to this reevaluation of the past as "meaning after effect," and propose that it poses a threat to studies of the causal effect of life stress events on disorder. Zimmerman (1983), however, argues that there is little evidence that patients distort their perception of events in this way. He argues that one source of evidence for this distortion would be if psychiatric patients *selectively* magnified the ratings of events that *occurred* to them over those that *did not occur* to them. His review of four out of five studies that investigated patient ratings of events failed to find that experience with the event elevated their stressfulness ratings. A second source of evidence of patient distortion of event meaning could be obtained by comparing patient ratings with the ratings of informed judges. Zimmerman (1983) points out that the two studies that have made this comparison report high levels of agreement. Brown and Harris (1978), for example, found 84 percent agreement (corrected for chance) between the ratings of long-term threat obtained from depressed subjects and trained professional raters using an in-depth interview technique.

These sources of confounding of subjective event reports with symptoms, stable disposition (e.g., anxiety, cognitive set), and motivated retrospective distortion have implications for the use of such measures in life events research. Stone (1982) has noted that the implications of the subjective-objective assessment of life events depends on the research question being investigated and the design being utilized. Two research issues he notes are whether the design is retrospective or prospective and whether the study is intended simply to predict disorder from life events or to address underlying causal connections between events and disorder.

All three sources of subjective event contamination pose serious problems for retrospective studies, particularly where such studies are intended to reveal causal effects of events on psychological disorders. Each source of contamination must be considered as a rival hypothesis to explain the relationship between the event's score and disorder. In a simple correlational study, these rival hypotheses are equally as plausible as the hypothesis that events cause disorder. In a more complex design, however, where the central issue is the differential relationship between events and disorder for separate groups, the problems presented by subjective event measures may work against obtaining the predicted effect. For example, the hypothesis that social support buffers the effects of stress on disorder is often tested by comparing the correlation between the life events measure and disorder for people with high as compared with low social support. It is the difference between these correlations that is of central concern. If the subjective measure of life events is contaminated by disorder (either because it is directly affected by the disorder or because of "effort after meaning", it should equally influence people who receive both high and low support. Thus, it should elevate both correlations and make it more difficult to obtain a significant difference between them.

In a prospective design, where the concern is to identify a causal relationship between events at time 1 and disorder at time 2, subjective events also pose potentially serious problems. If the contamination between events and disorder is due to the fact that subjective judgment is a manifestation of disorder, then the problem can be addressed by partialing out a measure of disorder taken at time 1. If the contamination is due to retrospective bias (effort after meaning), then a prospective design effectively avoids the problem, particularly if the effects of time 1 measure of disorder are partialed out. A more difficult problem, however, is presented if the contamination is due to the effects of a third variable (e.g., anxiety, cognitive set, etc.) on both the measure of events and disorder: (1) Since this variable is assumed to be a stable individual characteristic, it affects measures taken at both time 1 *and* 2. (2) Since the nature of the third variable is often difficult to specify, it may be impossible to measure and control statistically. (3) Since the third variable contamination is often quite plausible, the prospective design does not effectively address the problems posed by the subjective measures of life stress.

Finally, in predictive prospective studies, where there is no special interest in identifying a causal pattern, subjectively weighted events may be a positive advantage. An example of this type of study would be the use of life events to identify groups at high risk for later disorder. This may particularly prove to be the case if the contamination between events and disorder is due to a third, unspecified variable. In that case, since this variable is operative at both times 1 and 2, it should boost the predictive power of the subjective event measure taken at time 1.

Throughout this discussion, it was assumed that because of the contamination issues, subjective reports of event experience correlate more strongly with measures of disorder than do measures that are not influenced by the subject's own report of his or her experience. In fact, however, the evidence on this is surprisingly mixed. Although several studies report that subjective reports yield superior relationships with measures of disorder (Chiriboga, 1977; Hurst, 1979; Lundberg et al., 1975; Rahe, 1981; Vinokur & Selzer, 1975), these differences are usually of minor magnitude and can be attributed to the different event qualities being assessed subjectively. For example, Chiriboga (1977) found that scores based on subjectively rated *negative* events yielded higher correlations with disorder than did scores based on nonsubjective (i.e., normative) ratings of life change or "presumptive stress." In addition, an equal number of studies find that subjective ratings of event experience do not improve the relationship between event scores and disorder over normative ratings (Block & Zautra, 1981; Fontana et al., 1979; Grant et al., 1978; Kale & Stenmark, 1983; McFarlane et al., 1980). Thus, in view of the problems of interpretation and the equivocal prediction advantage, investigators who explore the causal link between stress events and disorder are advised against using subjective measures of event experience.

Objective Measures of Event Experience

An alternative to the use of subjective measures of event experience is to use independent raters to judge how events are likely to be experienced by the individual. Several different procedures have been used to accomplish this and will be reviewed subsequently. These procedures all make the assumption that the experience of events will vary relatively little across people but will vary substantially across events. Thus, given that the investigator has identified the appropriate people and provided them with sufficient information about the event, then their judgment of how the event will be experienced should conform reasonably well with the experience of the typical subject. Another critical issue in assessing event exprience concerns the dimension of event experience for which ratings are obtained. These two issues—what are the appropriate dimensions for rating event experience, and who are the appropriate raters—will be discussed separately.

Dimension of Event Experience.   The choice of what dimensions of event experience are to be assessed often reflects theoretically based hypotheses about the critical stressful characteristic of events. By far the most common dimension to be rated is the *degree of change or readjustment required* by an event (Holmes & Masuda, 1974). This choice is based on a homeostatic model, one that assumes change to be stressful regardless of the desirability of the change. As pointed out later, this concept of change as the essential stress element has often been included (mistakenly, from our perspective) within the definition of what constitutes a stressful life event (Dohrenwend & Dohrenwend, 1981). Over the years of life event research, however, numerous other stressful qualities of events have been identified. The degree to which events possess these qualities has been quantified by a range of different judges. These event qualities include distress (Paykel et al., 1971), exit or loss of a significant other (Finlay-Jones & Brown, 1981; Paykel et al., 1969), entrance or addition of a significant other (Paykel et al., 1969), the degree to which the subject controlled the occurrence or consequence of an event (Dohrenwend & Martin, 1979; Reich & Zautra, 1981; Sandler & Lakey, 1982), long- or short-term threat (Brown & Harris, 1978), danger (Finlay-Jones & Brown, 1981), degree of stress experienced over time (Horowitz et al., 1977), and social desirability or undesirability (Gersten et al., 1974). In each of these cases, the event quality is derived from a conceptual model about what makes an event stressful. For example, the concept of a long-term threat (Brown & Harris, 1978) is based on a model that assumes the stress of an event is derived from its meaning to the person. The effects of control perceptions are based on theory and research on the effects of perceived control as a stress reducer (Dohrenwend & Martin, 1979; Sandler & Lakey, 1982).

A somewhat different, and rarely used, approach to assessing the qualities of events is to *discover* the dimensions along which events are experienced rather than to use theoretically derived properties. Sandler and Ramsay (1980), for example, argued that people may, in fact, utilize many different dimensions to conceptualize the stressful properties of life events and conducted a study to identify these dimensions. They used ratings of event similarity as the basic data in their study. Each event on a 32-item life events scale for children was matched with every other event and subjects (mental health professionals) rated how similar each pair of events would be as experienced by a child. Factor analysis of the transformed similarity ratings yielded seven interpretable dimensions; loss, entrance, family troubles, physical harm, positive events, primary environment change, and sibling problems. Although the study needs replication with a larger sample of raters, the procedure of identifying dimensions of experience has been successfully applied to other social stimuli (e.g., Magnusson, 1971) and appears promising for research on life events.

Redfield and Stone (1979) proposed that three factors contribute to the ratings of life events: individuals, events, and qualitative dimensions of events. They had 85 college students rate 44 life events on each of six qualitative dimensions. Three mode factor analysis (Tucker, 1966) was used to identify individual, event, and dimension quality contributions to the ratings of events. The results indicated three-dimension quality factors— change, desirability, and meaningfulness—three events factors—catastrophe, achievement, and domesticity—and three subject factors—defined by combinations of demographic features. Most significantly, they reported that the ratings of events were often a function of an interaction between individual subject characteristics, event characteristics, and the qualities of event experience being rated. For example, one type of individual might rate all events as being high on change and give domestic type of events as low ratings on desirability and meaningfulness. In contrast, a second type of person might rate all events as low on change, whereas domestic events are high on desirability and meaningfulness. The implication of this finding is that, in view of the complex person × event × dimension interactions that determine event experience, it may not be possible to determine event experience without directly asking the subject. This is a rather extreme position in the life event area that has received relatively little research attention. Instead, the issue of what factors contribute to the rating of events has primarily been treated as a simple univariate problem. The question usually posed has been: Do different kinds of raters give a different magnitude or pattern of ratings across events on a single dimension (with that dimension usually being change)?

Raters of Event Experience.   Several different types of event raters have been utilized: normal subjects, psychiatric patients, subjects who have personally experienced the event, and experts who are particularly knowledgeable about the effects of stressful events.

Dohrenwend and Dohrenwend (1981) have advocated the use of normal subjects as raters of the stressfulness of events. They hypothesize that the stress value of events is learned in a social context and transmitted via social norms. "The impact of life event on an individual will be determined by a learned normative expectancy concerning the stressfulness of that event" (p. 11). They further propose that these normative expectancies may vary from group to group, so that, for example, taking out a mortgage may be a more stressful event in rural North Carolina that in suburban New York, whereas marriage may be relatively less stressful in North Carolina (Miller et al., 1974). Thus, it is important that objective stress ratings be obtained from an appropriate normative group. In view of the multitude of possible groups, identifying the appropriate person for normative ratings is a formidable task. One place to start is to identify those group characteristics that have been found to effect group stressfulness ratings.

Much of the research on life event scaling has focused on demonstrating agreement across groups of raters in the relative scale values of events. These studies use correlational analyses of the mean scale values obtained across events, and they generally demonstrate high intercorrelation. For example, a correlation of .96 was obtained between scale scores of English and American subjects (Paykel et al., 1976), .73 between white, non-Hispanic Americans, and Mexican-Americans, .89 between Mexican-Americans and black Americans, and .79 between black and white Americans (Komaroff et al., 1968). Holmes & Masuda (1974), in reviewing much of this evidence, proposed that it indicated "remarkable consensus" about how events were viewed cross-culturally. Other authors, however, have criticized the conclusion of cross-cultural consistency of event perceptions. Askernasy et al. (1977), for example, noted that the cross-cultural scaling studies had generally been conducted using samples of convenience rather than systematic probability-based derived samples. They suggested that samples of convenience may, in fact, be quite similar in terms of social class, education, and perhaps in their values and interests. They obtained event ratings from a probability sample of raters from New York City. Separate generic mean event scores were derived from the ratings of black, white, and Puerto Rican raters and from raters at four different levels of social class. They then correlated these mean event ratings with published mean ratings from six prior studies. These investigators found that the correlations were generally higher for high as opposed to low social class raters and for white as compared with Puerto Rican raters. They concluded that, contrary to prior reports, there were "sharp differences among groups that differ in social and cultural backgrounds" (p. 430). Similarly, Fairbank and Hough (1981) in their review of the literature on cultural differences in perceptions of life events point out that, despite their emphasis on the cross-cultural similarities, such studies have often identified differences in either the ratings of specific events (e.g., Komaroff et al., 1968; Miller et al., 1974) or the cross-cultural correlation between mean event ratings (Janney et al., 1977). For example, Komaroff et al. (1968) found that Mexican-Americans as compared with Anglo-Americans rated labor and income items as requiring more adjustment. Masuda and Holmes (1967) discovered that Japanese rated violations of the law as more stressful than did Anglo-Americans. Finally, Miller et al. (1974) reported that taking out a mortgage was rated as more stressful by a rural North Carolina sample than by the normative group. Although methodological issues in cross-cultural research prevent drawing firm conclusions about the effects of culture on event perception, it does appear that sufficient evidence of dissimilarity exists to question the assumption that event perceptions are cross-culturally consistent.

Age of the subjects has also been found to effect their ratings of events. Masuda and Holmes (1978), for example, divided raters of life events into three age-based groups; young (under 30), middle-aged (30 to 60), and old (over 60). They found that although intercorrelations of the mean event ratings obtained from the three groups all exceeded .92, the mean ratings of 23 of the 42 events were lower for the older as compared with the two younger groups. Similar findings that younger adults rate life events as more stressful than do older people are also reported by Horowitz et al. (1977) and Jewell (1977) (cited in Masuda & Holmes, 1978). On the other hand, a study by Rosenberg and Dohrenwend (1975) did not obtain rating differences by age. Also, although Paykel et al. (1971) did obtain age differences on 17 of 61 events, they report no interpretable direction to these differences.

Several studies have reported that women rate life events as more stressful than do men. Masuda and Holmes (1978), for example, reported that, although the mean event ratings of men and women correlated .96, females scored 16 of the 42 events as being more stressful. Horowitz et al. (1977) also found that men and women's event scores correlated .96, but that women rated events as being more stressful than did men. Masuda and Holmes (1978) reviewed nine other studies that investigated sex differences in event stress ratings and concluded that, although the results are not unanimous across cultures, there appears to be generally consistent findings of higher event stress ratings by females than by males.

Finally, there has been considerable research on the question of whether having experienced an event affects the scaling of the event's properties. Since the purpose of scaling studies is to provide an objective rating of the probable experience of people to whom events occur, it could be argued that scale scores optimally be obtained from people who have themselves experienced the event. Although this argument is logical, the empirical evidence is mixed on whether experience influences event ratings (Masuda & Holmes, 1978). For example, Rosenberg & Dohrenwend (1975) did not find that experience with an event had a direct effect on college students' ratings of 10 events, even though they did find an ethnicity by experience interaction effect. Horowitz et al. (1977) determined that experience with an event made a small but significant difference in the ratings of two types of events but not for five other types of events. Those who had experienced events classified as minor threats to self-esteem or threats to material well-being rated them as being more stressful than people who had not experienced these events. The main effect of no experience was obtained, however, for events classified as death, separations, major threats to self, arguments with important persons, or changes. Paykel et al. (1971) reported a weak effect (13 of 61 significant differences) for people who have experienced events to rate them as more stressful. Grant et al. (1978) found no differences exceeding chance expectancy between event perceptions of experienced and nonexperienced subjects in two groups—psychiatric patients and controls.

Hurst et al. (1978) investigated the effects of experience on the weights assigned to events by comparing event ratings given by air traffic controllers who had experienced events with normative event weightings. They repeated these analyses for the two most popular life event measures, the SRE (Holmes & Rahe, 1967) and the PUP (Paykel, 1983), and for two of the most common qualities on which events are rated, readjustment and distress. They found that the correlation between the ratings given the events by the two groups were, $r = .85$ for readjustment ratings and $r = .78$ for distress ratings. They also discovered a pattern of differences in the magnitude of the event ratings, such that the experienced subjects gave *higher* readjustment ratings than did the normative group but rated the events as causing *less* distress than did the normative group. These results indicate that different mean event ratings are obtained across groups and rating dimensions. However, since the raters used by Hurst et al. (1978) were both a selective group (air traffic controllers) and people who had experienced the events, the results could be attributed to either the effects of experience with an event or other characteristics of air traffic controllers. Finally, Lundberg and Theorell (1976) found relatively low correlations of event ratings made by subjects who had and those who had not experienced the events (range of correlations across two groups of raters and two scales was .40 to .78). Thus, although the findings from different studies do vary, there is no strong evidence that ratings of events differ consistently as a function of having experienced the event.

The differential results across studies of characteristics of subjects that affect event ratings make it difficult to choose an appropriate reference group for objectively assessing event experience. There simply is no firm empirical grounds to guide the decision as to whether raters need to be of the same sex, age, ethnicity, or experience. Furthermore, there is evidence that the answer often depends on the type of event. One clever approach to solving this dilemma was developed by Dohrenwend et al. (1978). Dohrenwend et al. proposed a general decision model to decide for *each event* on their scale whether the judge's ratings reflect "universal" agreement, differences among persons as a function of their social class or other identified characteristics, or differences among persons unrelated to any identified characteristic" (p. 220). The first was labeled consensus ratings; the second, status dependent ratings; and the third; noisy ratings. Dohrenwend et al. (1978) illustrated the use of this model to develop event ratings for the PERI life event scale. Ratings were made by 89 judges derived from a stratified random community sample in New York City. Subject status differences were assessed on the variables of gender, ethnicity, and social class. An event rating was considered to be status dependent if either a significant and meaningful interaction or main effect was obtained using analysis of variance of the event rating. If no significant status effects were obtained, the issue is to decide whether or not there is consensus on event ratings. If there is a great deal of variability in ratings it is not reasonable to assume that the measure of central tendency of the rating represents the experience of most people to whom the event occurred. Thus, it is more appropriate to identify it as a "noisy" event with unidentified sources of variation accounting for event ratings. Dohrenwend et al. (1978) proposed the coefficient of variation (mean divided by the standard deviation of the rating) as the measure of variability. Applying this general decision model to their community ratings of the stressfulness of the PERI life events, the authors classified 22 percent as status dependent, 19 percent as noisy, and 59 percent as consensually rated events.

A final approach to objectively identifying the stress value of life events is to use the judgment of expert raters. The assumption underlying this approach is that because of their insight into psychological processes, experts can make more valid judgments of the subject's event experience than can the untrained judge. The validity of these assumptions would be difficult to test. Several studies, however, report that the judgments of mental health experts do not correspond very well with those of naive subjects. Yamamoto and Felsenthal (1982), for example, found a correlation of .69 between event stress ratings made by mental health professionals and those made by children (for common childhood stress experiences). Similarly, Wolchik et al. (1983) found a higher correlation between stress ratings (for divorce-related events) given by children and mothers (.87) than for ratings made by mental health professionals and children (.68). This study also reported that mental health professionals tended to rate these events as being more stressful than did children. Horowitz et al. (1977) found a correlation of .76 between stress event ratings of psychiatrists and psychiatric patients and .82 between psychiatrists and nonpatients. Horowitz et al. did not report magnitude differences between the stress ratings given by psychiatrists and non-psychiartists. The limited literature thus indicates general (but not unusually high) agreement in the relative value of stress ratings given by mental health professionals and untrained subjects.

One common, but rather gross, use of professional judgments of life events is to have them categorize events in terms of how they would usually be experienced; as desirable, undesirable, or ambiguous (indeterminate) experiences. Gersten et al. (1974) obtained desirability ratings for 25 child life events from three mental health professionals. Using 80 percent agreement as the criterion, they classified events as being either socially desirable or undesirable and those that did not reach criterion were designated as ambiguous. Sandler & Block (1979) used a similar procedure to identify child life events as being either desirable or undesirable. Dohrenwend et al. (1978) used the consensus of four professional raters to designate items on the PERI as either a gain, loss, or ambiguous. Although this procedure only obtains a limited amount of information about events, it appears that categorization of events for their usual desirability can be readily done.

A different procedure for obtaining expert's judgments about the stressful qualities of event experience is the contextual rating method (Brown & Harris, 1978). As previously described, their procedure for identifying the occurrence of life events involves in-depth description of the event via a structured interview. Procedures were developed to assess the meaning of these to the subjects while avoiding potential contamination of the meaning ratings that might result from basing these judgments on the subject's own ratings. The task, to assess meaning (how the event is experienced) without relying on the subject's own evaluation is, of course, analogous to the normative rating of the properties of stressful life events. The difference is that Brown assumes that meaning of the event can only be understood in the context of a full description of the event itself (e.g., what led up to and followed the event) and of the person's life situation at the time. Thus, an in-depth interview is conducted to attain a full description of the event and what it meant to the person. Trained raters then make 28 ratings about the event (e.g., preparation for the event, immediate feelings, warning, change in routine, short-term threat, long-term threat, etc.). These ratings are made by raters who are not involved in the interview and are based on the "likely meaning of the event for the average person" (Brown & Harris, 1978, p. 90) without knowledge of the subject's reported reaction. Separate ratings are made of the subject's reaction and of the judged meaning of the event, independent of the person's reaction. Although ratings were made on 28 event characteristics, only 1 characteristic was found to play a causal role in the onset of depression: long-term threat. Interrater reliability of ratings of severe or marked long-term threat is reported as 92 percent. On further inspection, losses and disappointments were the central features of most long-term threatening events. It is interesting to note that, although Brown and Harris (1978) emphasize the importance of obtaining ratings of event meaning independently from the subject's own experience, these objective ratings agree highly with those made by the subjects themselves (84 percent agreement for patients, 95 percent agreement for nonpatients).

QUANTIFICATION OF EVENT STRESS AND THE PREDICTION OF PSYCHOLOGICAL DISORDER

One test of the construct validity of different approaches to quantifying the stressful impact of life events is to assess how these methods influence the relationship between life event scores and psychological disorder. It is reasonable to argue that, in the absence of confounding factors, an improved ability to predict psychological disorder is supportive evidence for the construct validity of a life stress measure (Shrout, 1981).

Thus, we will review studies that have investigated how the relationship between life events scores and disorder varies as a function of different methods of quantifying the subjective impact of life events. Because of the different methodological issues involved, we will identify in our discussion those studies that utilize objective methods of quantifying subjective event experience and approaches that use subjective methods.

Change

The most frequently quantified aspect of event experience clearly is the amount of change and readjustment brought about by an event. There has been considerable empirical investigation of whether weighting life events by the amount of change involved increases the relationship between event scores and measures of psychological and physical disorder. Zimmerman

(1983) reviewed 17 studies in which scores based on change weightings were compared with unweighted scores. Of these 17 studies, 14 found no incremental stress disorder relationship for life change weighted events. Two studies are particularly salient examples of this failure to obtain an effect. Ross and Mirowsky (1979) derived 10 different life change-based measures of events. They used both Holmes and Rahe's original normatively derived weights (LCUs) and the modified life change weights developed by Hough et al. (1976). They applied both these change scores to weight the total events, positive events, negative events, ambiguous (no consensual positive or negative event classification), and the desirable minus undesirable event difference score. Using data from a cross-sectional study of a community sample of 720 subjects, they found that neither change weighting made a substantial difference in the event disorder correlation. In fact, for almost all scores the simple unweighted sum of events gave a slightly higher correlation than the weighted score, the highest correlation with disorder being obtained by the simple sum of undesirable events.

One reason life change weights for events do not affect the relationship between event scores and disorder is that weighted scores correlate very highly with unweighted scores. Lei and Skinner (1980), for example, found a correlation of .97 between a simple count of the life events that are reported and a score that weighted these events by the Holmes and Rahe readjustment weights. In fact, the same correlation of .97 was obtained when these weights were assigned *randomly* to events and when events were weighted by randomly generated numbers between 1 and 100.

Zimmerman (1983) found a consistent correlation of about .90 between life change weighted scores and unit weighted life event scores in 17 studies that compared these scores. Both Lei and Skinner (1980) and Shrout (1982) point out that this high intercorrelation between weighted and unweighted scores is consistent with psychometric theory. Lei and Skinner (1980) cite Gulliksen's (1950) formula which indicates that the correlation between a weighted and an unweighted score will decrease as the average intercorrelation between the items decreases, the number of items on the scale decreases, and the ratio of the standard deviation to the mean of the weights increases. These conditions clearly have not been optimized in any of the existing studies of the effects of life change weighting. Thus, two conclusions can be drawn from these studies. There has been an impressive and consistent *failure* to demonstrate that the current methods of life change scaling contributes to the empirical relationship between events and disorder. However, because of the high intercorrelation between the unit and change weighted scores, these studies have not provided a fair test of the validity of the *concept* that life change is a significant stressful element of life events.

Some research has also investigated whether change weights derived from the subject's own report or from an outside rater (e.g., normative group, experts) yield differential relationships with measures of disorder.

These studies do not produce a clear answer. Although some studies find that subjective ratings yield clearly superior relationships with disorder (Hurst, 1979; Lundberg et al., 1975), others find that the advantage of subjective reports is only marginal (Fontana et al., 1979; Vinokur & Selzer, 1975). Still other studies find no advantage for the subjective reports (Grant et al., 1978; McFarlane et al., 1980).

Desirability

A second dimension of life events that has received considerable research attention is the positive versus negative value of the events, or whether they are socially desirable or undesirable experiences. In contrast to the sophisticated scaling studies that have been done to quantify the amount of change required by events, the desirability of events has typically been assessed via a classification of events as being either usually desirable, undesirable, or ambiguous (indeterminate desirability). Although this classification method is unrefined (essentially weighting events as either 0 or 1 on each of the dimensions of desirability), it has the fortunate effect that the resulting scores are only modestly intercorrelated. For example, Block and Zautra (1981) report a correlation of .33 between desirable and undesirable event scores derived from a community sample of 531 subjects. This modest intercorrelation (in contrast to the .90+ correlations between life change weighted scales and unit weighted scales) allows the differential correlates of the desirable and undesirable event scores to emerge. In fact, distinctly different relationships are obtained between desirable and undesirable event scores and measures of psychological disorder.

Zautra and Reich (1983) reviewed 17 studies that assessed the relationship between desirable and undesirable events and measures of psychological distress. A clear pattern of relationships can be seen across studies, indicating that undesirable events relate to higher levels of distress, that this effect is independent of the effects of either desirable or ambiguous events, and that undesirable events account for most of the relationship between the total event score and distress. For example, in the Ross and Mirowsky (1979) comparison of 23 different approaches to scoring life events scales, the best prediction of disorder was obtained from the scores derived from a simple unweighted sum of negative events. As was pointed out earlier, weighting the undesirable event score by readjustment weight did not increase the relationship with disorder. The positive relationship between negative events and psychological distress is the most consistent finding in the life events literature, although the amount of variance in the measure of disorder accounted for by the negative events scores ranges widely. For example, Reich & Zautra (1981) found the negative events score accounted for 39.6 percent of the variance of a measure of general psychiatric symptomatology.

It should also be noted that studies that have used the subject's own rating of event desirability have generally reported the same pattern of results as studies that used normative desirability judgments. Several reports have used both subjective and normative desirability ratings on the same data set and have found only slight differences in the magnitude of relationships obtained with measures of disorder (Block & Zautra, 1981; Fontana et al., 1979; Mueller et al., 1977; Vinokur & Selzer, 1975).

Although the majority of studies on the effects of positive and negative events have utilized retrospective designs, some very interesting prospective longitudinal studies have recently been reported (Billings & Moos, 1982; Cohen et al., in press; Monroe, 1982c; Monroe et al., 1983; Nelson & Cohen, 1983). Monroe et al. (1983), for example, studied the relationship between life events that occurred to college students over the past year and changes in psychological symptomatology over the course of the semester. Measures of life events (for the past year) and general psychological distress were obtained at time 1. At time 2 (approximately 40 days later, during the stress of final examinations), measures of general psychiatric distress, depression, and anxiety were obtained. In completing the life events measure (which was obtained at time 1 only), subjects rated each event on several dimensions including how desirable it was for them and how undesirable, using 7 point rating scales. Monroe et al. (1983) made the interesting point here that each event can have both desirable and undesirable components. Separate scores were derived for desirable events, undesirable events, the difference between undesirable and desirable events, and the total number of events. The initial symptom score and the raw total number of events were entered first in a regression on the time 2 symptom measures. After entering these variables, higher levels of depression were predicted by higher undesirable event scores, higher undesirable minus desirable event scores, and lower levels of desirable events. Further analyses indicated that these three measures accounted for overlapping variance, so that their independent effects could not be ascertained.

Nelson and Cohen (1983) used a slightly different prospective design to test the effects of subjectively rated negative events. Measures of psycho logical disorder and measures of subjectively rated positive and negative life events were administered twice at an interval of two months. After controlling for the effect of time 1 psychological disorder, the number of negative events that occurred in the 2-month interval successfully predicted psychological disorder at time 2. Thus, these two studies clearly indicate that the relationship between subjectively rated negative life events and psychological disorder does not simply reflect the effects of preexisting symptomatology on event occurrence and event ratings and that the undesirability rating does add predictive power over the simple report of event occurrence.

Although a complete review of prospective life events studies is beyond the scope of this review, another important point needs to be made. The relationship between events and symptomatology over time is complex and interactive. For example, Billings and Moos (1982) found that the occurrence of negative events was stable over a 1-year period of time and could not be accounted for by time 1 symptom level or demographic characteristics. Nelson and Cohen (1983) similarly reported that the occurrence of negative events was stable over time, independent of the effects of psychological disorder. There appear to be negative event prone people. Secondly, the course of psychological disorder interacts in a complex way with the occurrence of events over time. Monroe (1982c) reported that the onset of depression in people originally not depressed is related to the occurrence of negative life events. However, Monroe (1982c) also reported a significant event × symptom interaction effect; so that for people who are intially high in symptomatology the occurrence of positive and ambiguous events relates to an *increase* in symptoms.

Although the effects of negative events on disorder is consistently obtained, the effects of positive events on measures of disorder is more controversial. The findings here relate to a fundamental issue in life stress events research—Is change per se stressful? If so, then desirable as well as undesirable events should be related to *higher* levels of distress. Evidence that positive events relate to higher levels of disorder is very weak and inconsistent. Zautra and Reich (1983) reviewed 19 studies that investigated this relationship and reported that, of 63 tests of association, 5 yielded a significant positive relationship and 4 indicated a significant negative relationship. Significant correlations, where they were found, were in the neighborhood of .10. Furthermore, in several cases where positive events related to higher levels of disorder, this relationship was reduced to a nonsignificant level when the effects of negative events were statistically controlled (Block & Zautra, 1981; Reich & Zautra, 1981).

Although positive events have very little direct effect on distress, there is some evidence that they moderate the effects of negative events on distress. Cohen and Hoberman (1983), for example, found a positive event × negative event interaction in the prediction of depressive symptoms and physical health symptoms. The form of the interaction indicated a smaller correlation between negative events and symptoms for people with more as opposed to fewer positive events. Cohen et al. (in press), however, failed to replicate this negative event × positive event interaction in a prospective longitudinal study. Reich and Zautra (1981) experimentally manipulated positive events by having subjects do either 12 or 2 positive events from a preselected list of positive events that are under people's control. They found that people instructed to do 12 positive activities did not show the positive relationship between negative events and distress that was found for the group instructed to do two positive events, and a no-instruction control group.

A somewhat less-studied issue is the effect of desirable and undesirable events on measures of positive affective states and psychological well-being. Zautra and Reich (1983) review much of this literature and find opposite effects of positive and negative events. Positive events relate to higher levels of positive affect and life satisfaction, whereas negative events generally relate to lower levels of these variables (particularly when the effect of positive events is partialed (Block & Zautra, 1981).

One problem with the desirable-undesirable event classification is that it does not capture the more fine-grained dimensions of human experience. On a theoretical level, we can distinguish many ways in which an event may be experienced as undesirable or desirable. For example, Lazarus and Launier (1978) discuss appraisals of events as threatening self-esteem, or physical harm, or as being a challenge. Seligman (1975) discussed uncontrollable experiences as being stressful. Paykel et al. (1969) identified loss as a significant negative aspect of human experience. Much of the most interesting findings in the life events literature concerns the effects of these different life event experiences on psychological distress. In the following sections, we will turn our discussion to studies that have attempted to assess some of these dimensions of event experience.

Control

There is considerable theoretical justification for believing that people's perceptions of control over aversive situations affect the consequent stressful effects of the situations. Although the mechanisms by which the effects are obtained is a matter of debate (e.g., Miller, 1980), there is considerable laboratory (Glass & Singer, 1972; Seligman, 1975; Weiss, 1971) and clinical evidence (Schmale, 1972) that perception of a lack of control (particularly over aversive events) leads to higher levels of stress. Following from this theory and empirical evidence, it is reasonable to predict that perceptions of a lack of control over stressful events leads to higher levels of disorder. Ten studies have attempted to test this hypothesis, using different approaches to assessing perceptions of control over events, yielding different findings. One assessment approach is to consider control perceptions as a cumulative function of the *number* of controllable or uncontrollable events, thus adding events that are so perceived by the subjects. Of the two studies that used this method, one found that low control over negative events gave the highest relationship with psychological disorder (McFarlane et al., 1980), whereas the other failed to obtain this effect (Sandler & Lakey, 1982).

A second approach attempts to obtain a measure of perceived control that is independent of the total number of events that occurred. This is accomplished by either obtaining a mean control rating across events, a proportion score of the number of uncontrollable events divided by the total number of events, or a cumulative uncontrollable score across events but statistically partialing out the effects of the total number of events. Four studies using this approach reported some supportive evidence that perceptions of a lack of control over events predicts higher levels of psychological disorder (Hammen et al., 1981; Husaini & Neff, 1980; Nelson & Cohen, 1983; Monroe et al., 1983).

Nelson and Cohen (1983) present a particularly interesting study in which they separately assessed mean perceptions of control for positive and negative events. Using a prospective design, they found that after controlling for preexisting psychological disorder, negative and positive life events, and locus of control, the interaction between mean negative event control and positive event control scores was a significant predictor of psychological disorder. Perceptions of *external* control on both positive and negative events predicted higher levels of psychological disorder, and this effect was independent of the amount of life stress experienced.

A third methodological distinction in this literature is between studies that assess control separately for positive and negative events and those that combine positive and negative events in a global control scale. Perceptions of control are strongly correlated with perceptions of desirability of events (Nelson & Cohen, 1983; Fontana et al, 1979), so that combining positive and negative events confounds these two concepts. Higher control scores are likely also to reflect more positive events, whereas lower control scores reflect more negative events. Three studies that obtained a significant effect of uncontrollable events indicating higher psychological disorder are subject to this criticism (Grant et al., 1981; Husaini & Neff, 1980; Monroe et al., 1983).

A third issue in the assessment of control is the definition of the critical aspects of the control construct. Different studies have, in fact, utilized substantively different definitions of control. For example, several studies asked about control over the *occurrence* of an event (Husiani & Neff, 1980; Monroe et al., 1983; Sandler & Lakey, 1982), several asked about control over the outcome or impact of an event (Fontana, 1979; McFarlane et al., 1980). Finally, a number of studies also addressed the related issue of attributions about the causalty of an event (Hammen et al., 1981; Monroe et al., 1983). For example, Hammen et al., (1981) only partially supported the model of Abramson et al. (1978) that attributions of internal, stable, and global causes of events lead to higher depression. Using a prospective design, they found that after first entering total life events (weighted for the amount of change), perceptions of uncontrollability and attributions of globality of the cause increased the prediction of depression. No effect was found for the attributions of internality and stability of the cause. Although this work is a useful attempt to utilize attribution theory in the assessment of life event experiences, greater clarity of the issues in defining and operationalizing control perceptions is needed.

Some very interesting work has also been done on the effects of positive events that are perceived as internally caused versus externally caused (Reich & Zautra, 1981; Zautra & Reich, 1980). In several studies, they found that positive events that were beyond people's control (pawn events) tended to be associated with higher levels of psychological distress, whereas this relationship was not found for positive events that people effected (origin event). On the other hand, positive origin events were more strongly related than were positive pawn events to measures of life satisfaction.

Contextual Measures of Threat

Because of the care taken in measuring events and the excellent reliability and validity evidence for their measure, the work of Brown and Harris (1978) is particularly significant. As described previously, the subjective meaning of events is assessed by trained raters, based on a detailed description of the event and the situation surrounding it. One kind of event in particular proved to be an important predictor of psychological disorder, severe events. These events involved some long-term (at least 1 week after the event occurred) threat or unpleasantness and focused on the woman herself or jointly with someone else. Approximately 75 percent of these events involved a loss or disappointment. Brown reported in his survey of women in Camberwell that the rate of occurrence of severe events was over four times as frequent in the time period preceding the onset of depression in a sample of patients (61 percent experienced a severe event), as it was for a comparable time period for a sample of normal community women (20 percent experienced a severe event). Similarly, 68 percent of the women in the community sample who had experienced the onset of clinically significant depression had a severe event precede the onset.

Brown and Harris estimated that 49 percent of the depressed patients had experienced a severe event of causal importance, and 57 percent of the community depressed sample had experienced an event of causal importance. It is further interesting to note that, although there is some evidence that severe events are additive to increase the rate of depression, the major effect is due to the simple occurrence versus nonoccurrence of a severe event.

An important methodological point made in this research concerns the issue of event-symptom contamination. The authors recognized that some events could be brought on by the illness itself rather than being a causal or provoking factor. They, thus, classified events as being either independent (beyond the control of the subject), possible independent, or dependent. Both the independent and possibly independent events were similarly associated with the onset of depression.

The relationship between the occurrence of severe events and the onset of depression found by Brown and Harris (1978) was substantially replicated in a survey conducted in Calgary, Alberta (Costello, 1982). Costello reported that 37 percent of the women who noted a severe event became depressed, whereas only 5 percent with no severe event became depressed ($x^2 = 48.2$, $p < .001$). One of the differences between the findings of the two studies, however, was that the association between severe events and the onset of depression was stronger for possibly independent than for independent events in the Costello (1982) study, whereas it was equally strong for both types of severe events for Brown and Harris (1978).

Tennant et al. (1981) conducted a longitudinal study using the contextual measure of life events. The study is important as a longitudinal replication of the Brown and Harris (1978) findings and because the authors developed a new category of events that relieve distress, the so-called "neutralizing" life event. The design involved two interviews (separated by 1 month) with depressed and nondepressed adult community residents. Eighty-two of the subjects had symptoms sufficient to be categorized as a psychiatric case at time 1, of which 40 were no longer cases at time 2 (remitters), and 42 were still at case levels of symptomatology at time 2. At time 1, 228 were not cases. Threatening events were assessed that were not dependent on subject's psychological disorder. Neutralizing events were identified that were rated as substantially reducing the impact of a prior threatening event. Their analysis of the time 1 data indicated that threatening events occurred more frequently for the cases than for the controls, with 23 percent of the cases attributed to the threatening events in the prior 3 months. Their longitudinal data showed neutralizing life events were significantly more frequent (21 percent) in the remitting than in the nonremitting cases (5 percent) and that 31 percent of all remissions could be attributed to the occurrence of neutralizing events.

Finlay-Jones and Brown (1981) further elaborated on the assessment of severe events to identify the degree of loss and the degree of danger involved. Loss events were defined to include loss of a valued person, physical health, job or possessions, or loss of a cherished idea. Danger events were those that raised the possibility of unpleasant future crises occurring. Interrater reliability for categorization of events as losses and dangers was acceptable (Kappas range from .70 to .92). Data analysis tested whether there were symptom-specific effects of particular kinds of events; loss events being associated with depression but not anxiety, and danger events related to anxiety but not loss. The results confirmed these symptom-specific effects of the loss and danger events.

Other Measures of Subjective Life Event Stress

The presumptive stress score developed by Horowitz et al. (1977) incorporates recency of the occurrence of an event into the objective rater's judgment of how stressful an event would be. Each event is weighted by the presumed level of stress as a function of how recently the event occurred (from 1 week to 3 years in the past). These weightings are derived from the mean ratings given by a group of objective raters. Horowitz et al. (1977) found very small relationships between presumptive stress scores and various measures of psychological disorder. One possible reason for this is that his measure included events that occurred over a lifetime. Kale and Sten mark (1983) obtained more encouraging results using a 2-year time interval for event reporting. They compared the relationship of four frequently used life event scales with a measure of psychiatric symptomatology. The life event measures were the RLCQ (Rahe, 1975), LES (Sarason et al., 1978), PERI (Dohrenwend et al., 1978) and the LEQ (Horowitz et al., 1977). Furthermore, for each of these scales, the score derived using the author's particular weighting procedure was utilized as well as the score derived by simply counting the number of events that occurred (unweighted score). The weighted presumptive stress score from the LEQ correlated only .60 with the unit weighted LEQ score. This relatively low correlation allows the two scores to correlate differentially with a third variable, and, indeed, for females the correlation between the presumptive stress score and psychiatric symptomatology ($r = .60$) was significantly higher ($p < .01$) than was the correlation of the unweighted LEQ score with symptomatology ($r = .47$). This was the only one of the four life events measures used in this study where the weighted score correlated less than .90 with the unweighted score and the weighting improved the correlation with symptomatology.

Chiriboga (1977) compared the effects of seven different event weighting approaches on the relationship between life events scores and indices of psychological and physical health. The weighting approaches included the Horowitz et al. (1977) presumptive stress score, Holmes and Rahe (1967) life change units, the simple sum of events, the sum of the subject's own ratings of positive and negative events, and a weighting of positive and negative events by the degree to which the subjects reported what they still think of the event (preoccupation score). The results indicated that although the weighting by the Horowitz et al. (1977) presumptive stress score and a unit weighted sum score provided generally similar relationships with measures of psychological disorder, the correlation with psychiatric distress was significantly higher for the presumptive stress score ($p < .05$). Overall, however, as in the Kale and Stenmark (1984) paper, the results indicate that scoring events for their negative quality yields the highest relationships with measures of disorder. Similar to other authors, they found that positive events are related to higher positive arousal and unrelated to distress.

The negative preoccupation score introduced in this study and utilized in a second study (Chiriboga & Dean, 1978) is worthy of further comment. The concept of preoccupation seems related to Horowitz's model of stressful events leading to intruding thoughts about the events (Horowitz et al., 1979), although this theoretical connection is not made by the authors. Chiriboga and Dean (1978) broke their scale down to score separately negative preoccupation with events that occurred in nine different life domains (e.g., marital, dating, legal, work, etc.) and derived separate preoccupation scores for each domain. In a 3-year longitudinal study, they used these scores to predict changes in measures of psychological well-being. Two interesting results were obtained. Use of the separate preoccupation scores for dimensions in a stepwise multiple regression yielded substantially higher relationships with measures of change in disorder than did the total preoccupation score. For example, in the prediction of depression, four dimensions entered the regression equation, yielding a multiple R of .60, whereas the zero-order correlation for the total preoccupation score was .30. In and of themselves these differences are not surprising, since the multiple regression optimally weights each score, after acocunting for the effects of other scores, in predicting the criterion. However, within the context of a life span developmental theory the separate dimension scores could inform us about what kinds of experience lead to stress at different stages of life for different sexes. For example, Chiriboga and Dean (1978) found that negative preoccupation with work events related to psychological distress for younger and older men, but were generally poor predictors of distress for women. Of course, these results would need replication in order to be meaningful. A second interesting set of results was that negative preoccupation with events in some life domains (e.g., work and personal changes) were associated with changes in a positive direction for some groups (i.e., men). As the authors suggest, it may be that actively and successfully coping with some stressful experiences leads to positive development (for a contradictory argument, see Zautra & Reich, 1983).

As noted earlier, a different approach to assessing a subject's experience with different kinds of events is illustrated by Sandler and Ramsay (1980). They argued that prior studies had identified the qualitatively different properties of events on the basis of some preconceived theoretical notions rather than by attempting to discover the dimensions people used to think about events. Their analysis of psychologists' similarity ratings of events yielded seven interpretable dimensions labeled loss, entrance, family troubles, positive events, primary environment, sibling problems, and physical harm. The life events reported for young inner-city children were then scored for each of these dimensions. Correlational analyses found that two of the dimensions, family troubles and entrance events, accounted for the associations of the entire scale with measures of child psychological disorder.

Finally, the work of Paykel (1979) is significant for assessing the effects of different subjective experiences of life events. In particular, Paykel and his colleagues have scaled the aversive or unpleasant quality of events as the degree of "upsettingness" and have classified events as exits of important people from the social field and entrances of important new people to the social field. The concept of event distressfulness seems highly related to the concept of negative events, in that both emphasize the aversive quality of events. Not surprisingly, the relationship between psychological disorder and events scaled for distress parallels the findings for undesirable events. Tennant and Andrews (1978), for example, found that the events scored for distress correlated higher with psychological disorder than did the events scored for the degree of change. Furthermore, the relationship between the events scored for distress and the measure of psychological disorder was significant even after the scores reflecting the total number of events or the amount of change were statistically controlled. These findings are similar to the findings for negative event scores.

The concept of loss as an important characteristic of significant life events has considerable theoretical foundation (Bowlby, 1973; Freud, 1971; Klinger,

1975). As mentioned previously, the concept of loss figured prominently in Brown and Harris's classification of severe events, and Finlay-Jones and Brown (1981) found that loss events were related to the onset of depression but not to anxiety disorders. Paykel et al. (1969) were among the earliest life events researchers to identify the relationship between exit events and depression. Paykel (1979), however, notes that exit events are associated with a range of disorders other than depression and that types of events other than exits also relate to depressive symptomatology. It should be noted that Paykel's original concept of exit events as departures of someone from the social field is somewhat more narrow than the concept of loss events as developed by other authors. For example, Finlay-Jones and Brown (1981) included severe events as losses if they involved the loss of a valued person, of physical health, of jobs or possessions, or of a cherished idea.

LIFE STRAINS

How do perceived stressful events lead to psychological or physical disorder? One pathway that has been proposed is that stress events lead to a change in people's ongoing life pattern. This change may be in either their chronic life circumstances or in how they think about their life. One interesting concept that has been proposed here is that of role strain (Pearlin et al., 1981). Role strain was defined as ongoing life difficulties, such as economic, marital, parental, or work problems. For example, loss of a job (a life event) would lead to increased economic strain such as difficulties in acquiring the necessities or luxuries of life. In turn, important ongoing role strains lead to decreased sense of self-esteem and mastery over life which leads to increased levels of depression. Pearlin et al. (1981) tested and found empirical support for this model in a study on the effects of job disruption on depression. Similarly, Billings and Moos (1984) highlight the importance of life strains. They define strains as ongoing life problems (e.g., with children, home environment, spouse, work, etc.). They found that the enduring role strains and negative life events were both related to depression in their subjects and that strains were somewhat more powerful predictors.

An interesting new development in assessment of life stress is relevant here—the concept of small events, or hassles. Although traditionally life events focus on the more major events, there is a recent upsurge of interest in assessing the daily, mundane experience of life (Kanner et al., 1981; Lewinsohn & Amenson, 1978; Monroe, 1983; Reich & Zautra, 1983; Stone & Neale, 1982; Zautra & Dohrenwend, 1984). Kanner et al. (1981), for example, propose that major life events may affect health by leading to an increase in everyday negative events. Small events may be related to life strain in that they may occur more frequently under conditions of strain. In fact, some researchers (Sandler et al., in press) have proposed that the stressful impact of a specific major life event might be due to the specific, smaller experiences that follow. They have developed a life event scale specifically to assess the experiences of children after their parents' divorce.

The initial results of the small events research has been encouraging in that event scores have successfully predicted levels of psychological and somatic symptomatology and have done so at a higher level and independently of the effect of major life events (Delongis et al., 1982; Kanner et al., 1981; Monroe, 1983). This research is in its infancy, however, and many of the methodological problems of major life event scales are evident in the early small event scales (e.g., Kanner et al., 1981). Also, the complex relationships among major life events, small events, and disorder remain to be established.

The astute reader will have noted that we have now come full circle in our description of the stress process. Life strains are, in fact, the same kinds of variables that Brown and Harris (1978) described as difficulties and that Gersten et al. (1977) defined as ongoing life processes. In our schematic diagram of the stress process, we are again in the box labeled "ongoing life context," ready for the next event.

CONCLUSION

The assessment of life stress is as important an endeavor as it is difficult. It is now apparent that the initial attempts were overly simplistic and overly committed to a narrow definition of stress. Although many disputes remain over the most appropriate approach to this issue, some criteria for successful life stress measurement are emerging. Items must be unambiguously worded and not confounded with dependent variables, probes to assure event occurrence and time of occurrence are useful, knowledge of the meaning of the event to the subject is critical, and time is an important variable to account for. The strength of some techniques (i.e., the Bedford College life event instrument) is apparent, although there is reason to believe that with attention to past methodological problems, simpler life event rating scales can achieve satisfactory levels of reliability and validity. Finally, the utility of life event assessment is likely to depend on how well it is integrated with the development of theory about stress processes. There is evidence that this integration is occurring, as studies investigate the complex interrelations among stress events, life strains, small events, coping resources, social support, and physical and psychological health.

References

Abramson, L. Y., Seligman, M. E. P., & Teasdale, J. D. (1978). Learned helplessness in humans: Critique and reformulation. *Journal of Abnormal Psychology, 87,* 49–74.

Andrews, G. A. (1981). A prospective study of life events and psychological symptoms. *Psychological Medicine, 11,* 795–801.

Appley, M. H., & Trumbull, R. (1967). On the concept of psychological stress. In M. H. Appley & R. Trumbull (Eds.),*Psychological stress* (pp. 5−11). New York: Appleton.

Askenasy, A. R., Dohrenwend, B. P., & Dohrenwend, B. S. (1977). Some effects of social class and ethnic group membership on judgements of the magnitude of stressful life events: A research note. *Journal of Health and Social Behavior, 18,* 432−439.

Billings, A. G., & Moos, R. H. (1982). Stressful life events and symptoms: A longitudinal model. *Health Psychology, 1,* 99−117.

Billings, A. G., & Moos, R. H. (1984). Coping, stress, and social support among adults with unipolar depression. *Journal of Personality and Social Psychology, 46,* 877−891.

Block, M., & Zautra, A. (1981). Satisfaction and distress in the community: A test of the effects of life events. *American Journal of Community Psychology, 9,* 165−180.

Bowlby, J. (1973). *Attachment and loss. Vol. II: Separation: Anxiety and Anger.* New York: Basic Books.

Brown, G. W., & Harris, T. (1978). *Social origins of depression.* New York: Free Press.

Brown, G. W., & Harris, T. (1982). Fall-off in the reporting of life events. *Social Psychiatry, 17,* 23−28.

Brown, G. W., Sklair, F., Harris, T. O., & Birley, J. L. T. (1973). Life events and psychiatric disorders. Part I: Some methodological issues. *Psychological Medicine, 3,* 74−87.

Cannon, W. B. (1929). *Bodily changes in pain, hunger, fear and rage.* New York: Appleton.

Casey, R. L., Masuda, M., & Holmes, T. H. (1967). Quantitative study of recall of life events. *Journal of Psychosomatic Research, 11,* 239−247.

Chiriboga, D. A. (1977). Life event weighting systems: A comparative analysis. *Journal of Psychosomatic Research, 21,* 415−422.

Chiriboga, D. A., & Dean, H. (1978). Dimensions of stress: Perspectives from a longitudinal study. *Journal of Psychosomatic Research, 22,* 47−55.

Cleary, P. A. (1981). Problems of internal consistency and scaling in life event schedules. *Journal of Psychomatic Research, 25,* 309−320.

Cohen, L. H., McGowan, J., Fooskar, S., & Rose, S. (In press). Positive life events and social support and the relationship between life stress and psychological disorder. *American Journal of Community Psychology.*

Cohen, S., & Hoberman, H. (1983). Positive events and social supports as buffers of life change stress. *Journal of Applied Social Psychology, 13,* 99−125.

Costello, C. G. (1982). Social factors associated with depression: A retrospective community study. *Psychological Medicine, 12,* 329−339.

De Longis, A., Coyne, J. C., Dakof, G., Folkman, S., & Lazarus, R. S. (1982). Relationship of daily hassles, uplifts, and major life events to health status. *Health Psychology, 1,* 119−136.

Dohrenwend, B. S. (1973). Life event as stressors: A methodological inquiry. *Journal of Health and Social Behavior, 14,* 167−175.

Dohrenwend, B. S., & Dohrenwend, B. P. (1978). Some issues in research on stressful life events. *Journal of Nervous and Mental Disease, 166,* 7−15.

Dohrenwend, B. S., & Dohrenwend, B. P. (1981). What is a stressful life event? In H. Selye (Ed.), *Selye's guide to stress research.* Vol. 1.

Dohrenwend, B. S., Krasnoff, L., Askenasy, A. R., & Dohrenwend, B. P. (1978). Exemplification of a method for scaling life event: the PERI life events scale. *Journal of Health and Social Behavior, 19,* 205−229.

Dohrenwend, B. S., & Martin, J. L. (1979). Personal versus situational determination of anticipation and control of the occurrence of stressful life events. *American Journal of Community Psychology, 7,* 453−468.

Elliot, G. R., & Eisdorfer, C. (Eds.) (1982). *Stress and human health: Analysis and implications for research.* New York: Springer.

Fairbank, D. T., & Hough, R. L. (1981). Cross cultural differences in perceptions of life events. In B. S. Dohrenwend & B. P. Dohrenwend (Eds.), *Stressful life events and their contexts* (pp. 63–85). New York: Prodist.

Finlay-Jones, R., & Brown, G. W. (1981). Types of stressful life event and the onset of anxiety and depressive disorders. *Psychological Medicine, 11*, 803–815.

Fontana, A. F., Hughes, L. A., Marcus, J. L., & Dowds, B. N. (1979). Subjective evaluation of life events. *Journal of Consulting and Clinical Psychology, 47*, 906–911.

Freud, S. (1959). Mourning and melancholia. In E. Jones (Ed.), *Sigmund Freud: Collected papers* (Vol. 4, pp. 152–173). New York: Basic Books (Original work published in 1917).

Freud, S. (1971). Mourning and melancholia. In *Collected papers*. (Vol. 4). London: Hogarth.

Gersten, J. C., Langner, T. S., Eisenberg, J. G., & Orzeck, L. (1974). Child behavior and life events: Undesirable change or change per se? In B. S. Dohrenwend & B. P. Dohrenwend (Eds.), *Stressful life events: Their nature and effects* (pp. 159–171). New York: Wiley.

Gersten, J. C., Langner, T. S., Eisenberg, J. G., & Simcha-Fagan, O. R. (1977). An evaluation of the etiologic role of stressful life changes in psychological disorders. *Journal of Health and Social Behavior, 18*, 228–244.

Glass, D. C. (1977). *Behavior patterns, stress and coronary disease*. Hillsdale, NJ: Erlbaum.

Glass, D. C., & Singer, J. E. (1972). *Urban stress: Experiments on noise and social stressors*. New York: Academic Press.

Glick, I. O., Weiss, R. S., & Parkes, C. M. (1974). *The first year of bereavement*. New York: Wiley.

Grant, I., Gerst, M., & Yager, J. (1976). Scaling of life events by psychiatric patients and normals. *Journal of Psychosomatic Research, 20*, 141–149.

Grant, I., Sweetwood, H. L., Yager, J., & Gerst, M. S. (1981). Quality of life events in relations to psychiatric symptoms. *Archives of General Psychiatry, 38*, 335–339.

Grant, I., Sweetwood, H. J., Gerst, M. S., & Yager, J. (1978). Scaling procedures in life events research. *Journal of Psychosomatic Research, 22*, 525–530.

Gulliksen, H. O. (1950). *Theory of mental tests*. New York: Wiley.

Hammen, C., Krantz, S., & Cochrane, S. (1981). Relationships between depression and causal attributions about stressful life events. *Cognitive Therapy and Research, 5*, 351–358.

Henderson, S., Byrne, D. G., & Duncan-Jones, P. (1981). *Neurosis and the social environment*. New York: Academic Press.

Hetherington, E. M., Cox, M., & Cox, R. (1981). Effects of divorce on parents and children. In M. Lamb (Ed.), *Nontraditional families*. Hillsdale, NJ: Erlbaum.

Holmes, T. H., & Masuda, M. (1974). Life change and illness susceptibility. In B. S. Dohrenwend & B. P. Dohrenwend (Eds.), *Stressful life events: Their nature and effects* (pp. 45–73). New York: Wiley.

Holmes, T. H., & Rahe, R. H. (1967). The Social Readjustment Rating Scale. *Journal of Psychosomatic Research, 11*, 213–218.

Horowitz, M., Schaefer, C., Hiroto, D., Wilner, N., & Levin, B. (1977). Life event questionnaires for measuring presumptive stress. *Psychosomatic Medicine, 39*, 413–431.

Horowitz, M., Wilner, N., & Alvarez, W. (1979). Impact of Event Scale: A measure of subjective stress. *Psychosomatic Medicine, 41*, 209–218.

Hudgens, R., Robins, E., & De Long, W. B. (1970). The reporting of recent stress in the lives of psychiatric patients. *British Journal of Psychiatry, 117*, 635–643.

Hurst, M. W. (1979). Life changes and psychiatric symptom development: Issues of context, scoring and clustering. In J. E. Barrett (Ed.), *Stress and mental disorder* (pp. 17–36). New York: Raven Press.

Hurst, M. W., Jenkins, C. D., & Rose, R. M. (1978). The assessment of life change stress: A comparative and methodological inquiry. *Psychosomatic Medicine, 40*, 126–141.

Husaini, B. A., & Neff, J. A. (1980). Characteristics of life events and psychiatric impairment in rural communities. *Journal of Nervous and Mental Disease, 168,* 159–166.

Jenkins, C. D., Hurst, M. W., & Rose, R. M. (1979). Life changes: Do people really remember? *Archives of General Psychiatry, 36,* 379–384.

Jewell, R. W. (1977). A quantitative study of emotion: The Magnitude of Emotion Rating Scale. Medical thesis, University of Washington, Seattle.

Kale, W. L., & Stenmark, D. E., (1983). A comparison of four life event scales. *American Journal of Community Psychology, 11,* 441–459.

Kanner, A. D., Coyne, J. C., Schaefer, C., & Lazarus, R. S. (1981). Comparison of two modes of stress measurement: Daily hassles and uplifts versus major life events. *Journal of Behavioral Medicine, 4,* 1–20.

Klinger, E. (1975). Consequences of commitment to and disengagement from incentives. *Psychological Review, 82,* 1–25.

Kobasa, S. C., Maddi, S. R., & Kahn, S. (1982). Hardiness and health: A prospective study. *Journal of Personality and Social Psychology, 42,* 168–177.

Komaroff, A. L., Masuda, M., & Holmes, T. H. (1968). The Social Readjustment Rating Scale: A comparative study of Negro, Mexican and White Americans. *Journal of Psychosomatic Research, 12,* 121–128.

Lazarus, R. S., & Launier, R. (1978). Stress related transactions between person and environment. In L. A. Pervin & M. Lewis (Eds.), *Perspectives in interactional psychology* (pp. 287–327). New York: Plenum Press.

Lei, H., & Skinner, H. A. (1980). A psychometric study of life events and social readjustment. *Journal of Psychosomatic Research, 24,* 57–65.

Lewinsohn, P. M., & Amenson, C. S. (1978). Some relations between pleasant and unpleasant mood related events and depression. *Journal of Abnormal Psychology, 87,* 644–654.

Lief, A. (Ed.) (1948). *The commonsense psychiatry of Adolf Meyer.* New York: McGraw-Hill.

Lundberg, V., & Theorell, T. (1976). Scaling of life changes: Differences between three diagnostic groups and between recently experienced and nonexperienced events. *Journal of Human Stress, 2,* 7–17.

Lundberg, V., Theorell, T., & Lind, E. (1975). Life changes and myocardial infarction: Individual differences in life change scaling. *Journal of Psychosomatic Research, 19,* 27–32.

Magnusson, D. (1971). An analysis of situational dimensions. *Perceptual and Motor Skills, 32,* 851–867.

Masuda, M., & Holmes, T. H. (1967). Magnitude estimations of social readjustments. *Journal of Psychosomatic Research, 11,* 219–225.

Masuda, M., & Holmes, T. H. (1978). Life events: Perceptions and frequencies. *Psychosomatic Medicine, 40,* 436–461.

McFarlane, A. H., Norman, G. R., Streiner, D. L., Roy, R., & Scott, D. J. (1980). A longitudinal study of the influence of the psychosocial environment on health status: A preliminary report. *Journal of Health and Social Behavior, 21,* 124–33.

McGrath, J. E. (1970). A conceptual formulation for research on stress. In J. E. McGrath (Ed.), *Social and psychological factors in stress* (pp. 10–21). New York: Holt, Rinehart, and Winston.

Miller, F. T., Bentz, W. K., Aponte, J. F., & Brogan, D. R. (1974). Perceptions of life stress events: A comparative study of rural and urban samples. In B. S. Dohrenwend & B. P. Dohrenwend (Eds.), *Stressful life events: Their nature and effect* (pp. 259–273). New York: Wiley.

Miller, I. W., Klee, S. H., & Norman, W. H. (1982). Depressed and nondepressed inpatients' cognitions of hypothetical events, experimental tasks and stressful life events. *Journal of Abnormal Psychology, 91,* 78–81.

Miller, S. M. (1980). Why having control reduces stress: If I can stop the roller coaster I don't want to get off. In J. Garber & M. E. P. Seligman (Eds.), *Human helplessness: Theory and applications* (pp. 71–97). New York: Academic Press.

Monroe, S. M. (1982a). Life events assessment: Current practices, emerging trends. *Clinical Psychology Review, 2,* 435–453.

Monroe, S. M. (1982b). Assessment of life events. Retrospective vs. concurrent strategies. *Archives of General Psychiatry, 39,* 606–610.

Monroe, S. M. (1982c). Life events and disorder: Event-symptom associations and the course of disorder. *Journal of Abnormal Psychology, 91,* 14–24.

Monroe, S. M. (1983). Major and minor life events as predictors of psychological distress: Further issues and findings. *Journal of Behavioral Medicine, 6,* 189–205.

Monroe, S. M., Imhoff, D. F., Wise, B. D., & Harris, J. E. (1983). Prediction of psychological symptoms under high-risk psychosocial circumstances: Life events, social support, and symptom specificity. *Journal of Abnormal Psychology, 92,* 338–350.

Mueller, D. P., Edwards, D. W., & Yarvis, R. M. (19777). Stressful life events and psychiatric symptomatology: Change or undesirability? *Journal of Health and Social Behavior, 18,* 307–317.

Murphy, E., & Brown, G. W. (1980). Life events, psychiatric disturbance and physical illness. *British Journal of Psychiatry, 136,* 326–338.

Nelson, D. W., & Cohen, L. H. (1983). Locus of control and control perceptions and the relationship between life stress and psychological disorder. *American Journal of Community Psychology, 11,* 705–723.

Neugebauer, R. (1981). The reliability of life event reports. In B. S. Dohrenwend & B. P. Dohrenwend (Eds.), *Stressful life events and their contexts* (pp. 85–107). New York: Prodist.

Neugebauer, R. (1983). Reliability of life-event interview with outpatient schizophrenics. *Archives of General Psychiatry, 40,* 378–383.

Newcomb, M. D., Huba, G. J., & Bentler, P. M. (1981). A multidimensional assessment of stressful life events among adolescents: Derivation and correlates. *Journal of Health and Social Behavior, 22,* 400–415.

Paykel, E. S. (1979). Causal relationships between clinical depression and life events. In J. E. Barrett (Eds.), *Stress and mental disorder* (pp. 71–86). New York: Raven Press.

Paykel, E. S. (1983). Methodological aspects of life events research. *Journal of Psychosomatic Research, 27,* 341–352.

Paykel, E. S., McGuines, B., & Gomez, J. (1976). An Anglo-American comparison of the scaling of life events. *British Journal of Medical Psychology, 49,* 237–247.

Paykel, E. S., Myers, J. K., Dienelt, M. N., Klerman, G. L., Lindenthal, J. J., & Pepper, M. (1969). Life events and depression: a controlled study. *Archives of General Psychiatry, 21,* 753–760.

Paykel, E. S., Prusoff, B. A., & Uhlenhuth, E. (1971). Scaling of life events. *Archives of General Psychiatry, 25,* 340–347.

Pearlin, L. I., Lieberman, M. A., Menaghan, E. G., & Mullan, J. T. (1981). The stress process. *Journal of Health and Social Behavior, 22,* 337–356.

Perkins, D. V. (1982). The assessment of stress using life event scales. In L. Goldberger & S. Breznitz (Eds.), *Handbook of stress: Theoretical and clinical aspects* (pp. 320–332). New York: Free Press.

Pugh, W. M., Erickson, J., Rubin, R. T., Gunderson, E. K. E., & Rahe, R. H. (1971). Cluster analyses of life changes. II. Method and replication in Navy subpopulations. *Archives of General Psychiatry, 25,* 333–339.

Rabkin, J. G., & Struening, E. L. (1976). Life events, stress and illness. *Science, 194,* 1013–1020.

Rahe, R. H. (1975). Epidemiological studies of life change and illness. *International Journal of Psychiatry in Medicine, 6*, 133–146.

Rahe, R. H. (1981). Developments in life change measurement: Subjective life change unit scaling. In B. S. Dohrenwend & B. P. Dohrenwend (Eds.), *Stressful life events and their contexts* (pp. 48–63). New York: Prodist.

Rahe, R. H., Meyer, M., Smith, M., Kjaer, G., & Holmes, T. H. (1964). Social stress and illness onset. *Journal of Psychosomatic Research, 8*, 35–44.

Rahe, R. H., Pugh, W. M., Erickson, J., Gunderson, E. K. E., & Rubin, R. T. (1971). Cluster analyses of life changes. I. Consistency of clusters across large Navy samples. *Archives of General Psychiatry, 25*, 330–332.

Redfield, J., & Stone, A. (1979). Individual viewpoints of stressful life events. *Journal of Consulting and Clinical Psychology, 47*, 147–154.

Reich, J. W., & Zautra, A. (1981). Life events and personal causation: Some relationships with satisfaction and distress. *Journal of Personality and Social Psychology, 41*, 1002–1012.

Reich, J. W., & Zautra, A. (1983). Demands and desires in daily life: Some influences on well-being. *American Journal of Community Psychology, 11*, 41–58.

Ross, C. E., & Mirowsky, J. II. (1979). A comparison of life event weighting schemes: change, undesirability and effect-proportional indices. *Journal of Health and Social Behavior, 20*, 166–177.

Sandler, I. N. (1979). Life stress events and community psychology. In I. G. Sarason & C. D. Spielberger (Eds.), *Stress and anxiety.* (Vol. 6, pp. 213–232). New York: Hemisphere.

Sandler, I. N., & Block, M. (1979). Life stress and maladaptation of children. *American Journal of Community Psychology, 7*, 425–440.

Sandler, I. N., & Lakey, B. (1982). Locus of control as a stress moderator: The role of control perceptions and social support. *American Journal of Community Psychology, 10*, 65–81.

Sandler, I. N., & Ramsay, T. B. (1980). Dimensional analysis of childrens' stressful life events. *American Journal of Community Psychology, 8*, 285–302.

Sandler, I. N., Wolchik, S. A., Braver, S. L., & Fogas, B. S. (In press). Significant events of children of divorce: Toward the assessment of risky situations. In S. M. Auerback & A. L. Stolberg (Eds.), *Crisis intervention with children and families.* New York: Hemisphere.

Sarason, I. G., de Monchaux, C., & Hunt, T. (1975). Methodological issues in the assessment of life stress. In L. Levy (Ed.), *Emotions—their paramaters and measurement* (pp. 399–509). New York: Raven Press.

Sarason, I. G., Johnson, J. G., & Siegel, J. M. (1978). Assessing the impact of life changes: Development of the Life Experiences Survey. *Journal of Consulting and Clinical Psychology, 46*, 932–946.

Schless, A. P., & Mendels, J. (1978). The value of interviewing family and friends in assessing life stressors. *Archives of General Psychiatry, 35*, 565–567.

Schless, A. P., Schwartz, L., Goetz, C., & Mendels, J. (1974). How depressives view the significance of life events. *British Journal of Psychiatry, 125*, 406–410.

Schmale, A. H. (1972). Giving up as a final common pathway to change in health. *Advances in Psychosomatic Medicine, 8*, 20–40.

Schroeder, D. H., & Costa, P. T. Jr., (1984). Influence of life event stress on physical illness: Substantive effects or methodological flaws? *Journal of Personality and Social Psychology, 46*, 853–863.

Selye, H. (1956). *The stress of life.* New York: McGraw-Hill.

Shrout, P. E. (1981). Scaling of stressful life events. In B. S. Dohrenwend & B. P. Dohrenwend (Eds.), *Stressful life events and their contexts* (pp. 29–47). New York: Prodist.

Stone, A. A. (1982). The objectivity and subjectivity of life events. *Journal of Clinical Psychology, 38*, 333–340.

Stone, A. A., & Neale, J. M. (1982). Development of a methodology for assessing daily experiences. In A. Baum & J. E. Singer (Eds.), *Advances in environmental psychology: Environment and health* (Vol. 4, pp. 49–83). New York: Erlbaum.

Surtees, P. G., & Ingham, J. G. (1981). Life stress and depressive outcome. Applications of a dissipation model to life events. *Social Psychiatry, 15*, 21–31.

Surtees, P. G., & Rennie, D. (1983). Adversity and the onset of psychiatric disorder in women. *Social Psychiatry, 18*, 37–44.

Tausig, M. (1982). Measuring life events. *Journal of Health and Social Behavior, 23*, 52–64.

Tennant, C., & Andrews, G. (1978). The pathogenic quality of life event stress in neurotic impairment. *Archives of General Psychiatry, 35*, 859–863.

Tennant, C., Bebbington, P., & Hurry, J. (1981). The short-term outcome of neurotic disorders in the community: The relation of remission, to clinical, factors and to neutralizing life events. *British Journal of Psychiatry, 139*, 213–220.

Thoits, P. A. (1981). Undesirable life events and psychophysiological distress: A problem of operational confounding. *American Sociological Review, 46*, 97–109.

Thoits, P. A. (1983). Dimensions of life events that influence psychological distress. An evaluation and synthesis of the literature. In H. B. Kaplan (Ed.), *Psychosocial stress: Trends in theory and research* (pp. 33–101). New York: Academic Press.

Tucker, L. R. (1966). Some mathematical notes on three-mode factor analysis. *Psychometrika, 31*, 270–311.

Uhlenhuth, E. H., Haberman, S. J., Balter, M. D., & Lipman, R. S. (1977). Remembering life events. In J. S. Strauss, H. M. Babigian, & M. Roff (Eds.), *The origins and course of psychopathology: Methods of longitudinal research* (pp. 117–132). New York: Plenum Press.

Vinokur, A., & Selzer, M. L. (1975). Desirable versus undesirable life events: Their relationship to stress and mental distress. *Journal of Personality and Social Psychology, 32*, 329–337.

Weiss, J. M. (1971). Effects of coping behavior in different warning signal conditions on stress pathology in rats. *Journal of Comparative and Physiological Psychology, 77*, 1–13.

Wolchik, S. W., Sandler, I. N., Braver, S. L., & Fogas, B. S. (1983). The stressfulness of the events of parental divorce from the perspectives of children, parents and clinicians. In D. Pelligrini (Chair.), *Stress: Its mediators in children at risk*. Symposium conducted at the meeting of the American Psychological Association, Anaheim, CA, August.

Yager, J., Grant, J., Sweetwood, H. L., & Gerst, M. (1981). Life event reports by psychiatric patients, non-patients and their partners. *Archives of General Psychiatry, 38*, 343–347.

Yamamoto, K., & Felsenthal, H. M. (1982). Stressful experiences of children: Professional judgments. *Psychological Reports, 50*, 1087–1093.

Zautra, A. J., & Dohrenwend, B. P. (1983). The measurement of small events. In B. P. Dohrenwend (Chair.), *Measurement innovations in the study of life stress processes*. Symposium conducted at the meeting of the American Psychological Association, Anaheim, CA, August.

Zautra, A., & Reich, J. W. (1980). Positive life events and reports of well-being: Some useful distinctions. *American Journal of Community Psychology, 8*, 657–670.

Zautra, A. J., & Reich, J. W. (1983). Positive events and quality of life. *Evaluation and Program Planning, 4*, 355–361.

Zegans, L. S. (1982). Stress and the development of somatic disorder. In L. Goldberger & S. Breznitz (Eds.), *Handbook of stress: Theoretical and clinical aspects* (pp. 134–153). New York: Free Press.

Zimmerman, M. (1983). Methodological issues in the assessment of life events: A review of issues and research. *Clinical Psychology Review, 3*, 339–370.

16

Health Assessment and Public Policy Within a Public Health Framework

CAROL W. RUNYAN

INTRODUCTION

Public health is defined as the "combination of sciences, skills and beliefs that are directed to the maintenance and improvement of the health of all the people" (Last, 1980; p. 3). Implicit within this definition are two essential components: (1) the maintenance and improvement of health or the prevention of illness or disease and (2) attention to the health of "all people" rather than to individuals. McGavran (1958) for example, refers to the "community as the patient" in public health. Because of these emphases on prevention and on the population, interventions at the public policy level are frequently appropriate. Therefore, anyone interested in making improvements in the public's health needs to have an understanding of: (1) the nature of public health as a field and a perspective, (2) the process of policy development and analysis, and (3) how to use public health information to shape policy. A presentation of each of these is the goal of this chapter.

THE PUBLIC HEALTH PERSPECTIVE

The roots of public health typically are traced to the Greeks and the writings of Hippocrates (Rosen, 1958). It was during the Middle Ages, however, that much of the thinking characteristic of modern public health took form. In response to the environmental conditions of the time, efforts to improve sanitation, rodent control, and housing were initiated. The paradigm of miasma, meaning literally "bad air" served as the explanation of disease and hence the foundation for interventions. Although the sanitary improvements suggested by the miasma paradigm were at least somewhat efficacious, they were not based on an understanding of the more modern germ theory of disease causation. This illustrates the principle within public health that intervention planning need not always rely on an understanding of causality. In fact, as Renwick contends, the understanding of causality is sometimes "a longcut to prevention" (Renwick, 1973).

A classical historical example illustrating the basic components of the public health approach is that of John Snow's (1855) work on cholera. In 1855, following extensive mapping of the distribution of cholera cases in London, Snow observed an association between the occurrence of cholera and one particular water source, the Broad Street pump. Although the germ theory had not yet been formulated, Snow's intervention was effective in reducing the spread of disease. He removed the pump handle.

This example demonstrates the important elements that are still central to the public health approach. Through *empirical observation*, Snow identified a health problem and noted its distribution in time and geographic space. Even though he did not have a full understanding of the causal mechanisms of the disease's occurrence, he was able to *take direct action* to protect the population. The specific measure he chose, removing the pump handle, aimed to *prevent* further spread of the disease rather than to treat identified cases. The action was *regulatory* in nature, modifying the environment and, thereby, individual exposure. Although individual freedom in the choice of a water source was restricted by the action, the aim of *population level prevention* could not possibly have been so effectively accomplished had Snow attempted to educate individuals not to use the pump or to treat their water in some way.

Public health continues to embrace many of the elements exemplified in Snow's work. Prevention is the mainstay of public health and is described at three levels: primary, secondary, and tertiary. Primary prevention refers to interventions for avoiding disease or injury (e.g., immunization, preventing the initiation of smoking, preventing unwanted pregnancy). Secondary prevention involves the early identification and treatment of disease or injury with the aim of arresting or reversing the progression of the disease process (e.g., breast self-examination and screening for developmental delays, vision or hearing problems). Tertiary prevention is concerned with remediating the effects of disease or injury (e.g., physical therapy for arthritis or spinal cord trauma; psychotherapy).

Although laboratory-based research and clinical trials are used in public health to examine disease etiology and to test optimal preventive measures, much of epidemiologic research continues to rely on careful observational studies to establish patterns of disease and to identify risk factors. In large part, this is a function of the nature of the questions posed in public health. Rather than being concerned with isolating a biochemical mechanism of disease causation, the goal of public health is to determine complex interactions or risk factors at many levels of analysis (biochemical to environmental) for an entire population of risk (rather than for a single organism), so that interventions can be most efficiently developed.

Furthermore, the planner attempting to generalize from the individual case in planning for a community prevention effort is likely to be unsuccessful and frustrated. The tradition in public health, instead, is to view the community, or population, as more than the sum of the individuals within it. Consequently, preventive efforts need to be geared to protect the *community* as an entity (Forster, 1982). This often raises the issue of designing regulatory interventions since they can protect the community as a whole more efficiently. However, issues of personal freedom are, by no means, clear-cut and pose many difficult dilemmas, as will be discussed in the sections to follow.

The Public Health Model

Maintaining the focus of public health on the protection of the community or population as a unit (i.e., rather than thinkng of the community as a collection of individuals) often requires both several levels of analysis and several levels of intervention. The public health model provides a guide for formulating questions, research designs, and intervention programs. It incorporates a multicausal, interactive, ecologic perspective. That is, events are conceived as the result of the reciprocal (i.e., bidirectional) associations among multiple variables, rather than as a unidirectional cause and effect process. The public health model initially was derived in an infectious disease context (Susser, 1973) but has been applied to many other types of health problems since (e.g., Haddon, 1980; Holmes, 1956; Margolis & Runyan, 1983; Margolis et al., 1983; Runyan et al., 1982).

The public health, or agent-host-environment model incorporates three categories of influence in dynamic interaction. *Host* refers to the individual susceptible to the health problem or concern (e.g., the person at risk of unwanted pregnancy, hepatitis, or suicide). *Agent* refers to the immediate or proximal cause of the health problem. It could be biologic (e.g., bacterium or virus); chemical (e.g., DDT or lead paint); physical (e.g., force of a car crash or bullet); or psychosocial (e.g., stress). The effects of the agent upon the host are variable, depending upon the characteristics of the host. For example, exposure to the same forces in a car crash can be expected to have differing effects upon a 1-year-old, a 25-year-old, and an 80-year-old as a function of the unique resistance of each. Young children and the elderly are more likely to suffer serious consequences, although the mechanism appears to be different for each. For the young child, risks are increased because the child is more likely to be struck in the head during a collision. For the elderly person, recovery from even minor injuries is reduced due to general infirmity and the risk of medical complications associated with restricted activilty and/or hospitalization.

Environment refers to the sociocultural as well as the physical milieu in which the agent and host interaction occurs. But, the concept of environment is not limited to a passive setting in which the disease process takes place. Rather, the environment is an important component that may either be a direct influence in the host and disease process *or* may alter the effect of the agent upon the host. For example, Holmes (1956) described a situation in Seattle in which tuberculosis was observed to be distributed according to neighborhoods, with the poorest neighborhoods having the highest rates of the disease. Although the tubercle bacillus was clearly understood to be the agent, environment appeared to be an important variable. Holmes's observation did not stop there, however. He further examined the distribution of the disease among groups with different host characteristics (e.g., race). What this work revealed was that the association between neighborhood (environment) and tuberculosis varied depending upon race. That is, whereas the highest rate of disease for whites occurred in the poorest neighborhoods, the highest rates for nonwhites were in the affluent areas. Similarly, job mobility of the host was associated with disease occurrence, the more mobile, or marginal persons in their communities experiencing higher rates of disease. In sum, the conclusions reached in the investigation suggested that causation of tuberculosis, although requiring exposure to a bacterial agent, was a function of host and environmental factors as well. In other words, the bacterium was a necessary but not sufficient condition to explain disease occurrence. The complex interactions of agent, host, and environment provide a more accurate perspective from which to view this, and many other, public health problems.

This model is applicable to many kinds of health concerns and is very similar to the ecologic model (Bronfenbrenner, 1979) and the interbehavioral approach (Kantor & Smith, 1975; Pronko, 1980) within psychology.

According to these ecological approaches, persons, objects, and events are conceptualized as mutually causative and changing over time, rather than in a linear cause-effect relationship existing in some static block of time. This emphasis parallels the model of agent-host-environment interaction very closely. Although the public health model is less explicit about longitudinal changes, temporality is discussed in some formulations (Susser, 1973).

Because of their shared concerns, the public health and medical models are frequently confused. However, they are markedly different. The medical model in its extreme form typically refers to a unidirectional, biological, cause-and-effect relationship between agent and host. Such a perspective points to the individually targeted interventions, usually of a curative nature, that are typical of medical practice.

The difference between the medical and public health approaches can be illustrated using the example of child abuse. The medical approach, in its extreme, would focus attention almost entirely upon scrutinizing the characteristics of the victim and determining the most appropriate way to alleviate suffering. Although treatment of the abused child is an undeniably important function of clinical practice, the public health perspective offers a very different view of the situation. In accordance with the public health model, the investigator would consider not only the host characteristics, but would also attempt to understand the interrelationships between parents and among both parents and the child, as well as the environmental context as a contributor to the situation, as Belsky (1980) has discussed. A transaction among the child's crying, the hot, crowded home, and the parental impatience because of job stress or economic pressure cannot be approached through simple interventions directed to the child (host). The public health model calls for a multipronged approach that, in this case, might include individualized behavioral assessment, home modifications (reduced crowding, installation of air conditioning), and reduction of outside stressors (attention to job satisfaction, sources of poverty, etc.).

The implications of taking an ecological or public health perspective are that we focus attention on the multiple factors that contribute to health concerns, as well as on understanding the characteristics of the individual who manifests a problem. Thus, solutions to public health problems often lie outside the traditional biomedical sphere. Instead they may include such diverse domains as housing, transportation, labor relations, welfare, ergonomics, and so on. This approach reduces the tendency to "blame the victim," assuming the individual is solely responsible for the problem, and, therefore, for the solution (Ryan, 1976; Barry, 1975). As Barry points out, the public health approach and its emphasis on community level prevention suggests policy level interventions that frequently require regulatory action to be most effective. For example, a highly effective community level approach to reducing the problem of childhood poisoning is that of requiring the use of childproof caps on medicines and other toxic substances. This is in contrast to an individual, behavior change approach such as teaching mothers to store poisons out of the reach of children (cf. Winett's chapter, in this volume).

Recent emphases within public health have directed attention to individuals' life-styles as contributors to health status. This is, in part, a response to the changing patterns of disease. Chronic, noninfectious diseases (e.g., heart disease, stroke, cancer), and injuries (especially those associated with motor vehicles) have replaced infectious diseases as the major health concerns of today. Thus, developing an understanding of the behavioral aspects of health maintenance and disease prevention recently have gained prominence in public health. There have been increasing attempts to integrate psychological principles into public health practice and research. For example, there has been considerable interest in understanding compliance with preventive measures such as contraception, low cholesterol diets, exercise regimens, seat belt use, reductions in smoking or drinking behavior, and the utilization of health services. Despite the incontrovertible importance of each of these behaviors, they are all aimed at individual rather than population changes; and they, therefore, represent a deviation away from the basic premises that undergird public health.

Although it is occasionally appropriate to protect the population through individual intervention (as in the case with immunization), population-wide protection is not afforded by smoking cessation or weight reduction efforts as it is with vaccines. These individually targeted interventions clearly have their usefulness in alleviating some of the problems of individuals. However, attention *solely* to *host* factors to the exclusion of the *agent* (e.g., modifying nicotine content in cigarettes or salt in packaged food) or the *environment* (e.g., enforcing air pollution standards or providing diet alternatives) is neither consistent with the public health approach nor likely to be the most effective solution for achieving the improved health of the population.

As noted, the preventive and population approach of public health as well as the interactive, multicausal orientation provided by the public health model often require policy level interventions. In the sections to follow, the general issues underlying the development of public health policy will be introduced.

POLICY DEVELOPMENT AND POLICY ANALYSIS

Although policy has been defined in many ways (Gil, 1976), within the context of this discussion, policy will be viewed as the operationalization of social goals. Often, social policies are codified legally, although policies may be derived and "enforced" in less formal ways (e.g., as the standard practices of an institution).

Health policy is frequently viewed as involving only those measures deliberately directed toward improving health or preventing or ameliorating disease; however, the public health approach would suggest that most social policies affecting the social and physical environments should be considered as a health-related policy. For example, economic and employment policies are relevant to public health because employment has been shown to be related to concerns such as fertility (Moore, 1981) and child health (Margolis & Farran, 1981). Thus, within the context of this chapter, any social policy is, by definition, also a health-related policy.

Policies emerge in a variety of ways. Policies may arise from an articulation of social need on the part of a particular constituency. They may also be derived as a response by professionals or policymakers to a problem they have defined.

This policy development process does not always appear to follow the most logical route from the standpoint of optimizing health. Rather, policies occasionally appear to be developed more as a means of satisfying the political needs of decision makers, sometimes in ways that may even be counterproductive to the health and welfare of certain groups. In part, this may be a function of political expediency, but it is also a reflection of the complexity of balancing social goals and values that are often contradictory.

The literature of policy analysis attempts to outline a more rational way to arrive at policies, using the best scientific evidence and explicating the values a person hopes to satisfy and goals he or she aims to achieve. The discussion to follow will summarize the process of policy analysis, as a means for formulating and evaluating social policies.

Policy analysis is a systematic process of evaluating policy options, based on the "application of reason, evidence, and a valuative framework" (MacRae & Haskins, 1981, p. 2). Although there are many variants, policy analysis often is descibed in terms of five general stages: (1) the definition or documentation of a problem, (2) the determination of *pre hoc* criteria by which alternative policies are evaluated, (3) the derivation of alternative policies to address the problem, (4) the delineation of conclusions and recommendations based on the weighing of each policy by the criteria, as well as consideration of the feasibility of policy implementation, and (5) the description of a plan for policy implementation (see Table 16.1).

Different types of information are useful for each portion of the anlysis. Unlike most forms of basic or applied research, policy analysis usually relies on existing, or secondary, data sources (i.e., data that were collected for some other purpose than the task at hand). Hence, it is the role of the analyst to amass and synthesize those data so as to permit the consideration of policies in the most informed manner.

As Fischhoff et al. (1981) point out, "individual scientists create data . . . (but) . . . it is the community of scientists and other interpreters who create facts by integrating data" (p. 44). Throughout this process "values shape facts" *and* "facts shape values" (p. 46). Thus, although the formal process of policy analysis may appear to be objective, it is important to recognize that both facts and values influence policy development throughout the entire process. Value judgments enter into the decisions not only of which topics to define as problems, but also into the determination of which aspects of

TABLE 16.1.   STEPS IN THE POLICY ANALYSIS PROCESS

1. Problem definition—using existing and new data
   Maginitude
   Scope
   Affected groups
   Dimensions of the problem
   Different perspectives
2. Choice of policy analysis criteria
   Definition of each
   Rationale for each
3. Generation of policy alternatives
4. Weighing of each policy by each criterion
5. Consideration of feasibility of enactment and implementation
6. Conclusions and policy recommendations

Source: Adapted from Haskins, R. & Gallagher, J. J. (1981) *Models for analysis of social policy.* Norwood, NJ: Ablex Publishing.

problems to direct attention and by what parameters problems, or their solutions, are measured.

Problem Definition

The definition of a problem warranting policy development may appear on the surface to be an obvious and/or trivial step. It is not. Many considerations underlie the task. First, we must determine that a problem exists, for *whom* it is a problem, and in what *ways* the problem is a problem. Effect upon a large number of people is usually not sufficient justification for defining a problem as deserving of policy attention. Acne, for example, is a problem affecting large numbers of teenagers but would probaly not be considered deserving of policy attention. Severity of the problem itself or its consequences are generally entered into determination of a *policy* problem. Hence, adolescent pregnancy, although less prevalent than acne, is regarded as more deserving of policy attention because ot its more serious consequences.

Determining for whom a given concern is a problem, and in what *way,* (i.e., what outcomes) is frequently a delicate issue in the problem definition stage and also affects the focus of solutions. Adolescent pregnancy is a good example of a problem that may be viewed in a variety of ways. One might express it as a problem for the adolescent parent (i.e., in terms of health or social outcomes for the pregnant mother). Adolescent pregnancy could also be expressed as a health or social problem for the infants born of adolescent mothers. Similarly, we might define the issue in terms of other problems created for society at large, for example, costs for social welfare programs to serve teenage mothers (Runyan, 1982).

Once the dimensions of a problem have been identified, documentation of the magnitude and scope of the problem is critical. Many kinds of public health evidence can be marshaled in this phase. Some of those will be summarized later.

Sources and Types of Data for Problem Definition

There is no one standard way of arriving at a statistical definition of health status. Instead, the task requires careful thought with respect to what information will be most useful and to what ends. It is a creative rather than a rote process. This discussion will focus on four general kinds of information that we might use: (1) vital statistics; (2) medical records; (3) health surveys; and, (4) epidemiologic investigations.

Vital Statistics.   The most basic form of vital statistics are *census* figures, representing an enumeration of the population. Census data are available according to geographic locale, sex, ethnic background, age, marital status, income, education, and occupational categories. Historically, census information has been collected since ancient times. Census taking has been mandated on a systematic basis in the United States since 1790, originally for purposes of determining congressional representation. Three general categories of vital rates are most often used as documentation of health status in the population: (1) fertility rates; (2) mortality rates; (3) morbidity rates. Each will be discussed in turn, with specific types explained. The reader is referred to Table 16-2 for further clarification (and to the chapter by Palinkas and Kaplan, in this volume).

Fertility rates. The crude birthrate is a common fertility rate used in health and population planning. It refers to the number of live births in a given population during a particular period of time (usually 1 year). The bases of fertility rates are birth records, as obtained from birth certificates. Within the United States birth certificates are required to be filed in each state and are tabulated nationally by the National Center for Health Statistics (NCHS).

Mortality rates. The crude death rate is the most basic type of mortalilty rate. It represents the number of deaths occurring in a given population during a particular period of time (usually 1 year). For policy and planning purposes, death rates are usually formulated as: (1) cause-specific, (2) age-specific, and (3) both cause- and age-specific rates. In other words, we might examine the death rate due to cancer in the U.S. population (cause-specific) or the death rate among persons age 24 to 29 in the United States (age-specific) or the death rate due to cancer among persons age 24 to 29 in the United States (cause- and age-specific death rate).

The *infant mortality rate* (IMR) is a particular age-specific death rate referring to the number of deaths among children less than 1 year of age, as a proportion of all live births. The infant mortality rate is frequently used as a marker of health status for comparisons across time or among different populations. For example, the overall IMR for the U.S. population dropped from 47 deaths per 1000 live births in 1940 to 13 deaths per live births in 1979, signaling some improvements in health status during this time period. However, recent reports of the differential between blacks' and whites' infant mortality rates in this country (23.1/1000 live births for blacks and 12.0/1000 for whites) has been used as an indicator of the disparity in health status between the two groups (Select Panel, 1981).

Death certificates are the source of mortality information. As with birth certificates, all states require the recording of deaths and the National Center for Health Statistics compiles and publishes mortality data for the United States overall. At the state level, birth and death records are usually kept by statisticians within the state health agency. These records normally are available for research purposes.

Morbidity rates. Morbidity is defined as "any departure . . . from a state of physiological or psychological well-being" (Last, 1980). Morbidity may be recorded as incidence (new cases) or prevalence (all existing cases) at a point in time (point prevalence) or over a period of time (period prevalence). The implications of using incidence versus prevalence figures are important. The choice depends on the type of health problems being considered and the purposes for which the data are to be used.

Because prevalence figures take into account both the occurrence of new cases (incidence) *and* the duration of those cases, changes in prevalence reflect more than the changing distribution of the disease. Prevalence rates are influenced by recovery from health problems. Over time, as the ability to survive certain conditions (e.g., cancer) improves, the prevalence rate will increase even if there are no increases in the incidence (i.e., new cases). Such changes may be attributable to characteristics of the agent (e.g., lowered virulence of the agent), the host (greater resistance to disease effects), or the environment (improved medical diagnosis or care) at either the secondary or tertiary (treatment) phase. Consequently, prevalence data alone are of limited use in understanding the health of a population. However, together with incidence data, prevalence can be a useful addition for determining policies relevant to secondary and tertiary prevention. For primary prevention purposes, incidence data are probably more helpful because they refer to the initial onset of a disease rather than the disease identification or recovery processes.

Also, the accuracy of morbidity data are variable, depending in large part upon the way in which they were collected and categorized. One problem relates to the determination of what constitutes a "case." This, in turn, is dependent upon the ease with which a given health problem can be both diagnosed and distinguished from other health problems. Some health conditions (e.g., measles, broken hip, or pregnancy) are easier to diagnose, classify, and identify a time of onset for than others (e.g., depression, arthritis, hypertension). In general, acute and/or infectious conditions are easier to identify as cases than those of chronic (often noninfectious) natures. Further difficulty in determining the existence of a health problem stems from their variable durations and remissions, recurrences, or flare-ups (e.g., arthritis, depression, multiple sclerosis).

Reporting practices influence the ease of obtaining and accuracy of morbidity data. For example, a number of infectious diseases are required to be reported by health professionals in all states. Reports filed with the state health authorities are compiled and published nationally by the National Centers for Disease Control in Atlanta, Georgia. In addition, all states mandate reporting of child abuse or neglect so accounting of documented cases is available at the state level. Some states have tumor registries that compile cancer statistics. Unfortunately, even for these few reportable conditions, there are many flaws in the data collection system. Completeness of the data is dependent upon the cooperation of health care providers who typically receive little training or reinforcement for reporting. Similarly, enforcement of reporting requirements is costly and may be pursued with differing vigor in various locales or jurisdictions.

Medical Records.   Hospital records are one source of information about the incidence or prevalence of health problems. In many hospitals basic diagnostic information is computerized and fairly easily obtained, in aggregate form, for research purposes.

The use of medical records as a source of information is not without problems, however. Access to nonaggregated data for research purposes requires obtaining permission from patients. In addition, the accuracy of medical data is dependent upon the recording done by physicians and their adherence to standardized schemas of categorizing problems and designating the primary versus secondary diagnoses. (i.e., the categories used to classify patients' problems). This is subject to substantial variability, depending in part upon the ease of classifying the health problem in question and the individual practitioner's habits. Finally, the use of patient records as a means of estimating population rates of health problems is subject to selection biases in that these data are contingent upon patterns of health care utilization (Sackett, 1979). For example, as of 1976, 24 percent of Americans did not see a physician even once during the year and only 11 percent were hospitalized (Aday et al., 1980). Since there are many factors associated with care-seeking behavior, it is hard to determine how these groups represent the distribution of health problems in the population. Hospital data also typically record only instances of acute illnesses or acute episodes of chronic illness so patterns of occurrence of chronic health problems can only be estimated indirectly.

Health insurance records provide another source of information about health problems that is particularly useful for documenting morbidity. As with hospital data, however, insurance information can only be obtained in aggregate form without patient consent. Furthermore, the data are limited not only to those patients seeking care, but also to that portion having some form of third-party coverage of health care costs. This represents approximately 82 percent of the U.S. population under age 65 as of 1975 (Aday et al., 1980). Also, like medical records, there are problems of missing of inconsistently recorded information.

Records of government assistance. Information about persons receiving assistance is available and can be used to help document health status in a population. *Medicaid*, the federal government's health assistance program, provides coverage for health care expenses for low income families. As of 1976, 7 percent of the U.S. population under age 65 received Medicaid benefits, covering outpatient as well as inpatient health care. Although federally financed, Medicaid is administered at the state level so data are collected by individual states. *Medicare*, a companion to Medicaid, provides coverage for medical expenses to all persons age 65 and over. Consequently, to establish the incidence of health problems for which elderly seek treatment, Medicare records can serve as a useful source of information.

However, there are limitations to using records of government assistance. Levels of poverty allowing eligibility for government assistance are politically determined and change over time. Hence, longitudinal studies using government assistance data, by necessity, are limited to trend, rather than panel designs.

Other health care records. In addition to records from hospitals, government assistance, and private health insurance, records from providers of outpatient health services are sometimes available and useful for obtaining morbidity information. This includes records from private physicians, clinics, or prepaid health plans/health maintenance organizations (HMOs). Increasingly, record keeping by these groups is being computerized, increasing the ease of access to patient information, provided consent can be obtained. However, nonuniformity of patient populations and record keeping across institutions may severely limit the opportunities for making comparisons across groups.

Survey Data. Among the most widely used sources of morbidity information are national surveys of health status. Although there are several such surveys used by health planners (see Table 16.2), the National Health Interview Survey (HIS) is the most comprehensive and most frequently used. Originated in 1957, the HIS is conducted annually by the National Center for Health Statistics. Using a national probability sample, weekly interview data are collected from a total of 40,000 households (116,000 persons) annually. The data include: health status, illness, injuries, disability, utilization of health services, and related social, economic, and demographic information (National Center for Health Services Research, 1979). Data from these surveys have been used to estimate the incidence and prevalence of health conditions and to establish associations between health

TABLE 16.2.   SELECTED NATIONAL HEALTH SURVEYS

National Ambulatory Medical Care Survey
  Annual since 1975
  Sample of patients interviewed from random sample of medical practioners
  Includes principal complaints symptoms of patient and diagnosis, diagnostic
  procedures, and treatment reported by physician
National Health Interview Survey (HIS)
  Since 1957
  40,000 households (110,000 persons) interviewed annually
  Includes demographics, health conditions, and hospital and physician utilization
National Health and Nutrition Examination Survey (NHANES)
  Since 1959 (originally called National Health Examination Survey)
  Approximately 20,000 individuals examined through interviews and laboratory
  tests regarding health status, particularly dietary habits and nutritional condi-
  tions.
National Medical Care Expenditure Survey (NMCES)
  Panel study, 1977–1978
  13,500 households measured as to health status and health care utilization and
  expenditures

For further information consult the National Center for Health Statistics, Hyattsville, MD.

status and a variety of social and economic factors. It must be noted, however, that these are trend and not panel studies. That is, they typically do not provide longitudinal data for individuals, but, rather, successive cross sections of the population. As a result, although conclusions about the population at large can be made, caution must be exercised when making inferences for subgroups of the population and especially for individuals. For policymaking, this drawback is usually not a major one, however, unless policies are targeted to specific groups.

Disability represents a specific form of morbidity. Although defined differently depending on the context, disability usually is quantified in terms of work loss or other disruption of daily functioning. Within the HIS, disability is defined as "any temporary or long-term reduction of a person's activity as a result of illness or injury" (Erhardt & Berlin, 1974, p. 67) for at least 1 day during the 2-week period referred to in the interview. In contrast, "bed disability" refers only to those problems for which the person is confined to bed for more than half the daylight hours.

Thus, measurement of disability is difficult, especially in reference to chronic conditions where the presence, amount, or type of disability may vary considerably over time. As much or more than other forms of morbidity, the determination of disability involves judgment calls on either the part of the interviewer, the respondent, or the health care provider record-ing information in a patient record.

Epidemiologic Studies. The various types of epidemiologic studies have already been described by Palinkas in this volume. Recall, epidemiologic studies generally have one of two purposes. Both types of studies are useful for informing the policy process, although the data yielded by each are quite different. Some studies are done to describe the distribution of given health problems within a population. For example, the preceding sections have discussed various kinds of mortality and morbidity data obtained from descriptive epidemiologic research. Analytic, or explanatory, studies are used to explicate the relationships between health problems and specific risk factors (exposures). They typically result in two kinds of measures of exposure-disease associations: (1) measures of association (e.g., relative risk, odds ratios, incidence density ratios) and (2) measures of potential impact (e.g., attributable risk, attributable benefit). The statistical interpretations of these measures have already been explained in Chapter 2. For further information, refer to Kleinbaum et al. (1982), Lillienfeld and Lillienfeld (1980), Last (1983), and MacMahon and Pugh (1970).

Although extensive discussion of these measures is beyond the scope of this chapter, the distinctions between two types of measures (attributable risk and relative risk) are frequently made by epidemiologists in reference to the uses of data in policymaking and are worth noting. As discussed by Palinkas, relative risk expresses the ratio of disease probabilities under conditions of exposure versus nonexposure to the risk factor in question. Thereby, it serves as an estimate of the degree to which a risk factor (agent) is a cause of a given outcome (disease state). In contrast, attributable risk estimates the proportion of disease in the population that is associated with (attributable to) a given risk factor over and above all other sources of the disease. That is, it is the excess risk. Attributable risk (or benefit) data are, therefore, considered to be more appropriate for policymaking because they suggest the degree to which interventions are likely to be effective in alleviating health problems (Kleinbaum et al., 1982; The Lancet, 1981).

Subjective Assessments for Problem Definition

Although the use of so-called "hard data" is highly recommended as a means of defining health problems for policy attention or program planning, the use of subjective measures should not be ignored. As will be seen in the section to follow, the criterion of satisfying the preferences of the constituents affected by a policy is usually considered important to policymaking. The views of the affected public are not only limited to defining the policy choices, but are also important in defining policy problems. A variety of methods, frequently referred to under the rubric "needs assessment" or "community diagnosis," have been described for soliciting views of community members. These methods may take various forms, including (1) interviews or surveys of "key informants" (e.g., professionals and/or lay community leaders who can identify community needs; (2) open community meetings in which people express their views, often using a variety of group process techniques (e.g., nominal group process, focus groups); (3) the delphi method in which ideas (usually of key informants) are offered individually and, through a sifting process, individuals react to and revise each other's ideas; and (4) community surveys. Although extensive descriptions of these methods is beyond the scope of this chapter, a brief description of each follows. Readers are encouraged to consult Delbecq and Van de Ven (1971), Siegel et al. (1976), and Steadham (1980).

The use of *key informants* is an easy and inexpensive means of obtaining information about perceived needs in a community. The usefulness of this method is dependent on two factors: (1) the choice of informants and (2) the careful, unbiased solicitation of their views. The choice of informants will vary depending upon the health issue and community in question. The primary objective in choosing informants is one of identifying persons who can articulate the views of the groups with whom they are familiar. Unlike the case with population surveys, we are not necessarily striving to obtain a statistically representative sample of respondents, but, rather, composites of what may be diverse minority groups. Consequently, key informants should be quite varied so that the information supplied can tap the range of concerns and perspectives of people in different walks of life. Often it is helpful to think about identifying persons who are in traditional leadership or helping positions (e.g., teachers, ministers, police officers, medical professionals, mental health workers, and neighborhood or organizational leaders). It is also very informative to ask community members whom they seek out for help, and then to interview these lay advisors.

The questions should be as open-ended as possible (e.g., "What concerns do you think people face in this community?"), in order to avoid limiting the viewpoints of the informants to the topics conceived by the investigator/ policy planner to be important. Later in the interview, it would then be appropriate to ask more specific questions such as, "How big a problem is teenage pregnancy?"

What may emerge from this approach is a much broader list of concerns than what the health professional might have anticipated, including issues such as recreation, housing, employment, transportation, economic resources, or pollution. The interviewer must be prepared to deal with these concerns in some way, if only to refer them to another resource and not to ignore them as irrelevant. Narrow-mindedness not only interferes with rapport, but it also may blind the interviewer to important contributors to the total public health picture.

Community meetings can provide a useful forum for obtaining information about people's concerns. It may be helpful to organize such a meeting in collaboration with a community agency or organization, although it is important to choose a sponsor, location, and time that is neutral and will allow maximum participation by community members. For example, some community members may be uncomfortable with a church or school setting and may perceive a fire station, park facility, or library to be more neutral. Although the community meeting format can encourage the voluntary expression of concerns, it may be dominated by the more vocal members of the community and result in less carefully conceived expressions of concern than can other, more individualized methods.

One group process method that can be used to facilitate the expression and prioritization of ideas from all participants is the nominal group process (Delbecq) technique. The process begins with each person thinking individually for a period of time and listing his or her ideas. The leader then asks each member of the group to identify one idea at a time, until all are listed, for all to see, by the group facilitator. Discussion is permitted only after all ideas are listed. At this stage, participants may wish to clarify their points or combine similar ideas. Following discussion, each participant is asked to prioritize the top 5 or 10 ideas by assigning a numerical score to each. This is done privately, with no discussion. Finally, the facilitator tallies the numbers and a consensus is determined.

The advantage of this structured method over open group discussion is that it involves everyone and reduces problems of group dynamics and/or domination by those who are more vocal. The group facilitator must not be too controlling and should allow ample time for discussion and reflection so that participants do not feel manipulated or pressured.

Focus groups, a technique commonly used in marketing research, involve a less-controlled approach. Focus groups are structured so that small clusters of individuals have a free-flowing discussion of a set of open-ended questions posed by the facilitator. Recording the discussion, using either very careful note-taking or an audio recorder, is very important, allowing subsequent sifting of the ideas as expressed in the words of the participants. As with the key informant approach, it is vital that the questions that are posed be as open-ended and neutral as possible so that the investigator does not direct the discussion in a way that reflects his or her own views.

The *delphi procedure* is a multistage process by which a group of individuals is identified, often, but not necessarily, on the basis of their expertise (e.g., as professionals or community leaders). They are surveyed as to their views; the responses are collated, then shared with the entire group along with further questions. This process continues for several rounds, allowing respondents to react to each other's views anonymously. Eventually, the ideas are sifted and consensus is reached. A major advantage of the procedure is its anonymity, reducing peer pressure. Since the procedure relies on mailed responses and does not necessitate assembling the group in one place, it can be especially useful when the informants are geographically spread. Success does depend, however, on the commitments of all respondents to participate in a timely fashion throughout the entire process.

Community surveys can certainly be useful although they usually require substantially more time, effort, and expense than the other methods just described. Self-administered, telephone, and face-to-face data collection methods can provide a wealth of information. If such a procedure is feasible, it may be useful to begin with one of the more open-ended approaches (e.g., focus group, key informants) as a way of generating the questions for the survey. That way, the sample can respond to the issues that have already been identified by subgroups to be relevant. Probability sampling methods afford the greatest opportunity for generalizability but may be more costly than samples of convenience.

In sum, the choice of method should be consistent with the intended purpose of the data collection and with the resources available. Each has advantages as well as drawbacks.

With the possible exception of surveys using a probability sample from the population, it must be recognized that these methods of obtaining information may have major problems of validity. Alone, they usually provide insufficient data for problem definition. However, planning without consideration of such information is unwise. Often information of this type reveals that different groups within a population have quite different perceptions of the dimensions of a given problem. For example, one study demonstrated the disparity between adolescents' views of the teen pregnancy problem and that of their parents and school officials (Family Planning Digest, 1981). Although adults viewed the problem in terms of long-term consequences for the adolescent and her family, the youth cited constriction of social activities and parent-adolescent conflict as the problem. Also, groups approaching a problem from different perspectives often arrive at different, innovative solutions that might not have occurred to professional planners and that may be more acceptable to the community than a professionally derived solution.

Determining Policy Assessment Criteria

After the problem is defined, the second step of the policy analysis process is to delineate those valuative criteria that the investigator wished to optimize with a given policy. Although the specific criteria will vary depending upon the policy issue, several criteria are considered universal by at least some analysts (MacRae & Wilde, 1979; Haskins & Gallagher, 1981). These typically include effectiveness, cost, freedom, preference satisfaction, equity, and stigmatization. The evaluation of any given policy option using the analysis criteria involves determining the importance ascribed to each one relative to the other criteria *and* the extent to which alternative policies exemplify each criterion. The criteria will be defined briefly in the following discussion.

Effectiveness refers to the ability (demonstrated or projected) of a given policy to achieve its stated goals. The effectiveness of current or prior policies can be assessed through a variety of evaluation techniques. The effectiveness of proposed policies is, obviously, much more difficult to estimate but usually relies on extrapolating data from policies concerned with related problems or from similar policies in other locales (i.e., another state or country). For example, the effectiveness of a mandatory seat belt use policy for saving lives in the United States might be projected based on several kinds of data. The effectiveness of seat belts to avert fatalities can be determined from epidemiologic studies comparing fatality rates among seat belt users versus nonusers. It can also be derived from laboratory studies measuring forces upon the body parts (using highly sophisticated test dummies) under various crash conditions. Third, data from countries having seat belt laws can be used to estimate the compliance with such a policy. Finally, an analogous policy, mandated child restraint usage in some states in the United States can be used as a means of estimating compliance with an adult seat belt usage policy in this country.

The *cost* of a given policy refers to the resources expended to implement it. They may be either monetary or nonmonetary, although analysts often translate even nonmonetary costs into financial terms so as to make comparisons (Stokey & Zeckhauser, 1978). As with effectiveness data, information about cost can be obtained directly (though not simply) for existing policies. For proposed policies, cost estimates require extrapolations or interpolations based on other policies, economic theory, and judgment.

Efficiency, a concept often applied in policy analysis, is defined as effectiveness per unit cost. For example, to calculate the efficiency of a mandatory seat belt usage policy, a person would calculate the ratio of the saved lives (and also disabilities averted, medical costs avoided) and the costs of implementing the policy (e.g., publicity and enforcement). Most people would agree that the more efficient a policy is, the better it is. However, the importance ascribed to efficiency in comparison to other policy attributes (e.g., freedom) is often controversial.

Freedom concerns the extent to which individual liberty is affected by a policy. Although many policies limit freedom in some ways, the extent and type of limitation (e.g., mandatory versus coercive versus voluntary) varies considerably among policies. To use the highway safety example again, a policy mandating seat belt usage limits the freedom of motor vehicle occupants. A coercive measure such as health insurance differentials for those who have suffered injuries while wearing versus not wearing seat belts limits freedom in a different way. The current policy by which people have the option to use or not use the seat belts required to be installed in all cars prohibits the choice of cars without seat belts.

Policies also differ on the freedom dimension with respect to *whose* freedom is limited and in what way. Although a mandatory seat belt use policy is directed at individual drivers and passengers, a policy requiring the installation of seat belts or air bags is directed at the producers of motor vehicles and, hence, restricts the freedom of manufacturers.

Within public health, as in many other areas, there is a great deal of controversy surrounding the issue of how much and in what ways the government should have the right or responsibility to limit personal freedom in pursuit of health (Barry, 1975; Beauchamp, 1976; Forster, 1982; Margolis & Runyan, 1983; Wildavsky, 1979). For example, new trends in health promotion are increasingly directing attention to individual responsibility for health practices (e.g., smoking, drinking, occupational safety, overcoming stress). Some would argue that this emphasis is appropriate given that life-style habits (e.g., diet, exercise, smoking) are increasingly recognized as contributors to major contemporary health problems (i.e., heart disease, cancer, emotional disturbance). Others contend that it is inappropriate to "blame the victims" of health problems by implying that they were responsible for their fates (Ryan, 1976; Crawford, 1978; Runyan et al., 1982). Rather, these authors argue from the public health perspective that health problems are the result of multiple causes in interaction with each other and that, consequently, "blame" and responsibility rest with all three portions of the agent-host-environment paradigm. Hence, individual responsibility *and* individual freedom are viewed as secondary to protection of the health of the public at large. This debate is far from resolved among health professionals, let alone among policymakers or the public.

Equity, referring to the fairness or justice of a policy, can be of at least two types: (1) horizontal and (2) vertical (MacRae & Wilde, 1979). Horizontal equity refers to the equal treatment of equally situated persons (e.g., children in every state). The situation in which children in some states are protected by laws requiring that they travel in child car seats whereas in other states no such laws exist, represents an inequity among U.S. children by locale. Even among those states that have car seat laws, some argue that horizontal equity does not exist because of the widespread variability in both the policies themselves and the enforcement of those policies (Margolis & Runyan, 1983).

Vertical equity refers to the unequal treatment of unequals so as to make them more equal. This principle is often used to equalize persons by virtue of socioeconomic status (e.g., subsidized family planning services for poor women or nutritional supplements for low income pregnant women and their children). It may also be applied in the context of equalizing risks or benefits among different groups (e.g., making special safety provisions to protect children or the elderly who, by virtue of their developmental statuses, are at higher risk in motor vehicle crashes, or providing equalized educational opportunities for handicapped youth).

In times of economic crisis, issues of equity come into direct conflict with concerns about cost, efficiency, and freedom. To ensure equity is frequently costly. For example, to provide car seats to poor families would, in one sense, be a costly venture. Some would argue, however, that the cost savings in terms of reductions in injury or death would still render such a program efficient (i.e., by virtue of achieving a high level of effectiveness). The clash of equity and freedom can be illustrated by the example of use of childproof tops on medicines. Whereas children are more equitably protected by this measure (i.e., their risks are equalized with those of adults), adult arthritics are inequitably treated (i.e., the bottles are more difficult to open) and everyone's freedom to purchase products without such tops is restricted (Margolis & Runyan, 1983).

Preference satisfaction is a criterion referring to the extent to which a given policy is consistent with the wishes of the constituency to which it is directed. For example, families' preferences for day care services in large centers or in home settings is an issue to consider in the development of day care policy (Haskins, 1979). It is not uncommon that the issues of preference and freedom overlap, many preferring those options that afford them the most personal freedom. This is not necessarily the case, however. For example, the recent community decision in Morton Grove, Illinois to restrict the possession of handguns within the town is an example of a policy that satisfied the preferences of the majority to protect the community from a known risk, although it limited the freedom of *all* persons to own guns.

The criterion of *stigmatization* is concerned with the issue of whether or not a policy implicitly or explicitly ascribes negative attributes to an individual or group affected or targeted by the policy. For example, requiring that adolescents identify themselves as sexually active before they become eligible for family planning education, counseling, or contraceptive services may stigmatize those youth, either inadvertently or deliberately. Similarly, providing subsidized school lunches only to youth who must document their poverty may single out some children in a way that is stigmatizing. Issues of stigmatization, as with other policy criteria, require difficult judgment calls. Such judgments may put stigmatization in direct conflict with equity, particularly vertical equity. Protecting the interests of disadvantaged persons to achieve vertical equity often necessitates identifying those persons in most need or at greatest risk. By so doing, those individuals or groups are more apt to be stigmatized.

As can be seen from the preceding discussion, issues of values as articulated through policy criteria, necessarily operate in tandem with factual information in shaping policies. Values are hard to define, impossible to quantify, and frequently come into conflict with each other. The extreme difficulty in operationalizing those values in policy decisions cannot be underestimated.

Defining Policy Alternatives

The third part of the policy analysis is the delineation of alternative policies for consideration. This should rely on knowledge, intuition, and imagination. The policies may include both new and existing policies aimed at solving the policy problem and should at least initially be as varied and creative as possible. Ideas for new policies typically come from policy experiences in other places or times or from policies aimed at dealing with similar or related problems. The options of no policy, or no change in policy, are usually considered along with specific new policies. As noted, ideas come from constituents as well as from policymakers and professionals.

Policies may include legislation at the state or national levels [e.g., state child abuse reporting laws or the development of Medicare (national)]; judicial action at any level of the courts (e.g., legalized abortion); or actions by regulatory agencies (e.g., occupational and safety health standards).

Each policy alternative, in order to be evaluated appropriately, must be clearly and completely outlined. It is also important to consider how the policy in question would impinge upon and be affected by existing related policies. Consultation with an attorney may be advisable to ensure the legal status of the proposed policies.

Policy Assessment

The fourth step in the policy analysis process is for the analyst to try to sift out *all* the information associated with *each* policy option and, as clearly as possible, present the advantages and disadvantages of each policy with respect to each criterion and within the context of the policy problem as it has been defined in the analysis. This is, by far, the most difficult portion of the analysis. It requires that the analyst synthesize all the data to document the attributes of each policy. This is easier for existing policies in that at least some data on effectiveness and cost are usually available. Projections associated with proposed new policies can sometimes be made on the basis of experiences with other policies. It may also be possible to document preferences for the alternative policies using information obtained in the community assessment process or through surveys constructed specifically to assess preferences for particular policy options. There are no hard data, however, to document the extent to which freedom is restricted, equity maintained, or stigmatization affected.

The analysis also requires that the information about each policy attribute be used to make recommendations about the policies. These judgments are no simple matter, necessitating the balancing of complex, interrelated, and sometimes conflicting, values.

Once the advantages and disadvantages of each policy are examined in reference to each criterion, the final element of the analysis is usually considered.

This element, *feasibility*, concerns the practicalities of both enacting and implementing a given policy. It takes into account the political climate surrounding the policy problem area and the support or opposition that each policy is likely to receive from powerful individuals or interest groups in getting the measure enacted. In addition, the feasibility of successful policy implementation must be considered. For example, a policy requiring jail sentences for drunk drivers is feasible only if the necessary law enforcement structure exists.

Policy Recommendations

Finally, the analyst's task is to summarize the findings of the analysis and in many instances to formulate a recommendation. Whether or not the analyst recommends a particular policy or what shape that recommendation takes depends in large part upon the analyst's position vis á vis the decision maker (e.g., whether hired as a policy advisor or legislative staff member or functioning in an academic position and/or as an advocate for an interest group). Although hired analysts are often employed with the expressed task of making recommendations, those analysts functioning from an academic position frequently see their role as being limited to informing policymakers or advocates of the pros and cons of the available policy options.

COMMUNICATING WITH POLICYMAKERS: INFORMANTS, ADVISORS, AND ADVOCATES

The appropriate role for scientific researchers vis á vis the policymaking process is ill-defined and the subject of controversy. The debate revolves around the contention that science is (or should strive to be) value-free, whereas policymaking, by its very nature, must rely on value judgments. Applied science is concerned with finding solutions to practical problems. As applied scientists in a field explicitly committed to policy change for the protection of health, public health researchers face difficult dilemmas in determining their roles as informants, advisors, and/or advocates in the policy process. Can we compartmentalize our scientific and policy activities such that we wear our objective, scientific headgear only in the "laboratory" and our value-laden hats only to the legislative hearing room?

The scientific method demands objectivity even though the results are rarely, if ever, unequivocal. Although researchers have learned to contend with uncertainty, policymakers are not prepared to interpret technical jargon or statistics. Understandably, they clamor for testimony by "one-armed scientists" who won't say "on the one hand the evidence is so . . . but on the other hand . . . " (David, 1975). Consequently, scientists frequently become frustrated with the policy process and, as Bazelon (1979) describes, sometimes are tempted to "view the political process with hostility and disdain" and may retreat by "attempting to disguise controversial value decisions in the cloak of scientific objectivity" (p. 278). The tensions between scientists and policymakers have been suggested as a source of skepticism about the use of data in shaping policy (Nelkin & Pollack, 1980).

But, how involved *should* scientists be in policy fray? Should we function only to provide evidence but not interpret the results? Should we advise policymakers by translating our findings into more simple terms and serve as policy analysts by suggesting policy alternatives?

Some might argue that it really does not matter; that decision makers pay little attention to factual evidence anyway. However, there is research evidence to the contrary. Rich (1977) concludes from his interviews with federal administrators that, although mistrust of research does exist, at least policymakers in administrative positions do view research as valuable to their work. Other investigators corroborate that social research is used by certain types of decision makers. Several authors conclude that utilization of social data is most likely when the policy issue is well defined and the data are reported as clear-cut findings (Caplan, 1977; Patton et al., 1977). Caplan's interviews with federal govenment officials further reveal that findings that are (1) objectively believable, (2) consistent with intuition, and (3) point to feasible solutions are those reported as most useful by agency administrators (1977). Weiss and Bucavalas (1977) found that mental health administrators (most of them professionals trained in mental health) use research data for decision making to the extent that those data are perceived to (1) be derived from methodologically sound studies, (2) offer practical solutions, and (3) suggest reforms.

From these studies, the factors that appear to be related to the use of research findings at least by administrative decision makers fall into three categories: (1) clarity of problem definition, (2) the methodological soundness of the study, and (3) the believability and practical utility of the findings.

In addition, an experimental study with proxy policymakers revealed that subjects' decisions about motor vehicle safety policies were significantly influenced by exposure to data about the effectiveness of three policy options (air bags or a seat belt usage law versus the current, voluntary seat belt usage policy) (Runyan, 1983). The results suggest, however, that choices were even more strongly determined by the importance decision makers ascribed to valuative dimensions of the policies (e.g., limitation of freedom) and by their views about other health regulations.

What all these studies suggest is that the *mere* facts contained in data are not considered independently of how they fit with the policymaker's view of the problem and its potential solutions. It is noteworthy that, with the exception of Runyan's (1983) study, all the work reported used either agency officials or program adminstrators as subjects. Such decision makers have more specialized expertise in their areas than the average legislator who is a generalist and must make decisions about a diverse range of issues. Experts tend to make judgments about risk that are more consistent with scientific evidence, whereas lay persons are apt to take other, more subjective factors into account (Slovic et al., 1981). Thus, the prominence of subjective factors in the uses of social science data by administrative personnel might be expected to be magnified by the less technically trained legislator.

How the researcher might approach the task of communicating with policymakers is the subject of a large body of literature on risk assessment and decision-making heuristics. A variety of factors have been demonstrated to be influential in decisions under conditions of uncertainty. These are described in terms of a set of judgmental heuristics that reflect biases in interpreting probablistic data (Tversky & Kahneman, 1981). People tend to overestimate risks that are associated with more memorable events that resemble other phenomena familiar to them. Consequently, their decisions appear to be influenced by the ease with which people can recall similar circumstances or by the salience of the risk to them. Research by Combs and Slovic (1979), for example, revealed that the frequency of violent or catastrophic events both receive proportionately more media attention than less severe events *and* are more memorable to the public.

It also has been suggested that decision makers may respond differently to data expressing negative versus positive outcomes (Tversky & Kahneman, 1981). That is, there appears to be a tendency to select "safer" policy options when data are presented in terms of benefits (e.g., lives saved) rather than of losses (e.g., lives lost).

Testing these hypotheses is still in an embryonic stage and there are no clear-cut findings about the effects of data presentation upon policy decisions. What this means in terms of the role of the public health or other professionals in the policy arena is not simple. It is evident that no matter how cogent the information presented to policymakers, there is no assurance that those data will be interpreted as intended.

By becoming policy advocates, scientists can remove part of the responsibility for interpreting data from policymakers and assume that role themselves. In that position they determine, based on their own understanding of the evidence *and* their own values, what policies to promote. Should public health (or other) scientists attempt to influence policymaking? Although researchers have the edge in terms of understanding results of science, do they have the equivalent expertise in sorting out the valuative dimensions of policy? Some would say "no." Others suggest that the role is acceptable *only* if scientists are explicit that they are functioning as citizens, *not* as scientists *qua* scientists. One argument suggests that applied, public health researchers have the responsibility to endorse health-enhancing policies. Another maintains that scientists can too easily be coopted to choose topics, methods, and conclusions that either oversimplify policy problems or support political positions. It is indeed a dilemma!

CONCLUSION

This chapter has provided an overview of the role of policy in public health and of public health in policymaking. It began with an historical discussion of the conceptual framework of public health as the rationale for the use of policy as a tool for public health intervention. Next, the chapter explained the process of policy analysis, including a discussion of (1) the sources of data for problem definition, (2) valuative criteria as they apply to public health examples, and (3) generation of policy alternatives and recommendations. The final section raised a number of issues about the role of public health professionals and other researchers as advocates for particular policies and highlighted a few of the problems inherent in communicating with policymakers.

ACKNOWLEDGMENTS

Portions of this chapter were inspired by my previous work in collaboration with Robert F. DeVellis, Brenda M. DeVellis, and Godfrey Hochbaum (1982), and with Lewis H. Margolis (1983). I am grateful for the helpful suggestions provided on earlier drafts of this chapter by Robert DeVellis, Brenda DeVellis, Jo Anne Earp, Christopher Ringwalt, Desmond Runyan, and Anna Schenck.

References

Aday, L., Anderson, R., & Fleming, G. (1980). *Health care in the United States: Equitable for whom?* Beverly Hills, CA: Sage.

Barry, P. Z. (1975). Individual versus community orientation in the prevention of injuries. *Preventive Medicine, 4*, 47–56.

Bazelon, D. (1979). Risk and responsibility. *Science, 205*, 277–280.

Beauchamp, D. (1976). Public health as social justice. *Inquiry, 13*, 3–14.

Belsky, J. (1980). Child maltreatment—An ecological integration. *American Psychologist, 35*, 320–335.

Bronfenbrenner, U. (1979). *The ecology of human development.* Cambridge: Harvard University Press.

Caplan, N. (1979). A minimal set of conditions necessary for the utilization of social science knowledge in policy formulation at the national level. In C. Weiss (Ed.), *Using social science research in public policy making.* Lexington, MA: Lexington Books.

Combs, B., & Slovic, P. (1979). Newspaper coverage of causes of death. *Journalism Quarterly, 56*, 837–843.

Crawford, R. (1978). Sickness as sin. *Health PAC Bulletin, 80*, 10–16.

David, E. C. (1975). One armed scientists? *Science, 189*, 891.

Delbecq, A. L., & Vande Ven, A. H. (1971). A group process model for problem identification and program planning. *Journal of Applied Behavioral Science, 7*, 466–492.

Erhardt, C. L., & Berlin, J. E. (Eds.). (1974). *Mortality and morbidity in the United States.* Cambridge, MA: Harvard University Press.

Family Planning Digest. (1981). Teens, parents, officials don't agree on impact of teen motherhood. *Family Planning Perspectives, 13*(2), 81–82.

Fischhoff, B., Lichtenstein, S., Slovic, P., Derby, S. L., & Keeney, R. L. (1981). *Acceptable Risk.* Cambridge: Camgridge University Press.

Forster, J. (1982). A communitarian ethical model for public health interventions: An alternative to individual behavior change strategies. *Journal of Public Health Policy, 3*(2), 150–163.

Gil, D. (1976). *Unravelling social policy.* Cambridge, MA: Schenkman Publishing.

Haddon, W. (1980). Advances in the epidemiology of injuries as a basis for public policy. *Public Health Reports, 95,* 411–421.

Haskins, R. (1979). Day care and public policy. *Urban and Social Change Review, 12,* 3–10.

Haskins, R., & Gallagher, J. J. (Eds.) (1981). *Models for analysis of social policy.* Norwood, NJ: Ablex Publishing.

Holmes, T. H. (1956). Multidiscipline studies of tuberculosis. In P. J. Sparer, (Ed.), *Personality, stress, and tuberculosis.* New York: International Universities Press.

Kantor, J. R., & Smith, N. W. (1975). *The science of psychology—an interbehavioral survey.* Chicago: Principia Press.

Kleinbaum, D. G., Kupper, L. L., & Morgenstern, H. (1982). *Epidemiologic research.* Belmont, CA: Lifetime Learning Publications.

The Lancet. (1981). Editorial: Relative or attributable risk. II (8257), 1211–1212.

Last, J. (1980). Scope and methods of prevention. In Last, J. (Ed.), *Maxcy-Rosenau: Public health and preventive medicine* (11th ed.). New York: Appleton-Century-Crofts.

Last, J. (1983). *A dictionary of epidemiology.* New York: Oxford University Press.

Lillienfeld, A. M., & Lillienfeld, D. E. (1980). *Foundations of epidemiology.* New York: Oxford University Press.

MacMahon, B., & Pugh, T. F. (1970). *Epidemiology—Principles and methods.* Boston: Little, Brown.

MacRae, D., & Haskins, R. (1981). Models for policy analysis. In R. Haskins & J. J. Gallagher (Eds.), *Models for analysis of social policy.* Norwood, NJ: Ablex Publishing.

MacRae, D., & Wilde, J. A. (1979). *Policy analysis for public decisions.* North Scituate, MA: Duxbury Press.

Margolis, L. H., & Farran, D. C. (1981). Unemployment: The health consequences for children. *North Carolina Medical Journal, 12,* 849–850.

Margolis, L. H., McLeroy, K. R., Runyan, C. W., & Kaplan, B. H. (1983). The ecology of type A behavior. *Journal of Behavioral Medicine, 6*(3), 245–258.

Margolis, L. H., & Runyan, C. W. (1983). Accidental policy: An analysis of the problem of unintended injuries of childhood. *American Journal of Orthopsychiatry, 53*(4), 629–644.

McGavran, E. G. (1958). Community as the patient of public health. *Texas State Journal of Medicine, 54,* 719–723.

Moore, K. (1981). Government policies related to teenage family formation and functioning: An inventory. In T. Ooms (Ed.), *Teenage pregnancy in a family context.* Philadelphia: Temple University Press.

National Center for Health Services Research (1979). *Health survey research methods.* Research Proceedings Series. 3rd Biennial Conference. DHHS Publication No. 81–3268. Washington, DC: U.S. Public Health Service.

Nelkin, D., & Pollack, M. (1980). Problems and procedures in the regulation of technological risk. In R. Schwing & W. Albers (Eds.), *Societal risk assessment: How safe is safe enough?* New York: Plenum Press.

Patton, M., Grimes, P., Guthrie, K., Brennan, N., French, B., & Blyth, D. (1977). In search of impact: An analysis of the utilization of federal health evaluation research. In C. Weiss (Ed.), *Using social science research in public policy making.* Lexington, MA: Lexington Books.

Pronko, N. H. (1980). *Psychology from the standpoint of an interbehaviorist.* Monterey, CA: Brooks/Cole.

Renwick, J. H. (1973). Analysis of cause—Longcut to prevention? *Nature, 246,* 114–115.

Rich, R. (1977). Uses of social science information by federal bureaucrats: Knowledge for action versus knowledge for understanding. In C. Weiss (Ed.), *Using social science research in public policy making.* Lexington, MA: Lexington Books.

Rosen, G. (1958). *History of public health*. New York: M. D. Publications.

Runyan, C. W. (1982). Prevention of adolescent childbearing: Comparison and analysis of the 1978 and 1981 federal initiatives. Chapel Hill, NC: Bush Institute for Child and Family Policy. (Unpublished).

Runyan, C. W. (1983). Public health policy making: The role of epidemiologic data in decisions about motor vehicle safety. Dissertation, University of North Carolina, Chapel Hill, NC.

Runyan, C. W., DeVellis, R. F., DeVellis, B. M., & Hochbaum, G. M. (1982). Health psychology and the public health perspective: In search of the pump handle. *Health Psychology, 1*(2), 169–180.

Ryan, W. (1976). *Blaming the victim*. New York: Vintage Books.

Sackett, D. L. (1979). Bias in analytic research. *Journal of Chronic Disease, 32*, 51–63.

Select panel for the promotion of child health (1981). *Better health for our children: A national strategy* (4 vols.). DHHS, Public Health Service Publication No. 79–55071. U.S. Government Printing Office, Washington DC.

Siegel, L. M., Attkinson, C. C., & Carson, L. G. (1976). Need identification and program planning in the community context. In C. C. Attkinson, L. M. Siegel, & L. G. Carson (Eds.), *Evaluation of human service programs*. New York: Academic Press.

Slovic, P., Fischhoff, B., & Lichtenstein, S. (1981). Characterizing perceived risk. In R. W. Kates, & Hohenemser C., (Eds.), *Technological hazard management*. Cambridge, MA: Oelgeschlager, Gunn & Hain.

Snow, J. (1855). *On the mode of communication of cholera*. London: Churchill.

Steadhan, S. (1980). Learning to select a needs assessment strategy. *Training and Development Journal*, January, 1980.

Stokey, E., & Zeckhauser, R. (1978). *A primer for policy analysis*. New York: Norton.

Susser, M. (1973). *Causal thinking in the health sciences—Concepts and strategies of epidemiology*. New York: Oxford University Press.

Tversky, A., & Kahneman, D. (1981). The framing of decisions and the psychology of choice. *Science, 211*, 453–458.

Weiss, C., & Bucavalas, S. (1977). The challenge of social research to decision making. In C. Weiss (Ed.), *Using social science research in public policy making*. Lexington, MA: Lexington Books.

Wildavsky, A. (1979). No risk is the highest risk of all. *American Scientist, 67*, 32–37.

Author Index

Abelson, R. P., 519
Abramson, L. Y., 588
Achenbach, T. M., 239
Adams, H. E., 357
Adams-Webber, J., 309
Adanson, M., 376, 380
Aday, L., 611, 612
Adcock, C. J., 319
Adebimpe, V. B., 73
Adler, A., 375
Adler, C. S., 494
Adler, R., 496
Ager, J. W., 189
Agras, W. S., 5
Ahles, T. A., 9, 528
Aiken, L. H., 197, 201
Akeson, W. H., 498
Aldenderfer, M. S., 393
Aldous, J., 165, 166, 167
Alexander, A. B., 351
Alexander, F., 4, 239, 249, 374
Alexy, W., 448
Alfredsson, L., 445
Algina, J., 223, 225
Alvarez, W., 591
Alwin, D. F., 196
Amenson, C. S., 593
Anderberg, M. R., 382, 383, 385, 388, 393
Anderson, B., 442
Anderson, C. S., 70
Anderson, J. P. 133, 139
Anderson, L. R., 189

Anderson, R., 611, 612
Andrasik, F., 9, 25, 360
Andreasen, N. J. C., 491
Andrew, J. M., 321
Andrews, G., 67, 71, 72, 106, 566, 592
Aneshensel, C. S., 71, 76
Antonovsky, A., 55, 69
Antonucci, T., 446
Aponte, J. F., 577, 578
Appley, M., 67, 557
Arena, J. G., 9
Aristotle, 376, 377
Arguelles, A., 284
Armentrout, D. P., 491
Armitage, P., 93
Arnkoff, D. B., 25
Arthur, R. J., 321
Aronson, E., 187, 195, 199, 200, 203, 206, 288
Ashby, W. R., 484
Ashworth, W., 156
Askenasy, A. R., 564, 565, 566, 569, 572, 578, 580, 581, 590
Atkins, C. J., 139, 142
Atkinson, J. H., 497
Atkinson, J. W., 523
Attkinson, C. C., 615
Auslander, W., 442
Ax, A. F., 282

Baert, A. E., 237, 238
Bahnson, C. B., 248

629

Subject Index